WORLDCOMP'13
July 22-25, 2013
Las Vegas Nevada, USA
www.world-academy-of-science.org

PROCEEDINGS OF THE 2013 INTERNATIONAL CONFERENCE ON SCIENTIFIC COMPUTING

CSC 2013

Editors

Hamid R. Arabnia
George A. Gravvanis
George Jandieri
Ashu M. G. Solo
Fernando G. Tinetti

FIREWALL MEDIA
(An Imprint of Laxmi Publications Pvt. Ltd.)
An ISO 9001:2008 Company
BENGALURU • CHENNAI • COCHIN • GUWAHATI • HYDERABAD
JALANDHAR • KOLKATA • LUCKNOW • MUMBAI • RANCHI • NEW DELHI
BOSTON (USA) • ACCRA (GHANA) • NAIROBI (KENYA)

This volume contains papers presented at The 2013 International Conference on Scientific Computing (CSC'13). Their inclusion in this publication does not necessarily constitute endorsements by editors or by the publisher.

Branches

Bengaluru	080-26 75 69 30	
Chennai	044-24 34 47 26,	24 35 95 07
Cochin	0484-237 70 04,	405 13 03
Guwahati	0361-254 36 69,	251 38 81
Hyderabad	040-27 55 53 83,	27 55 53 93
Jalandhar	0181-222 12 72	
Kolkata	033-22 27 43 84	
Lucknow	0522-220 99 16	
Mumbai	022-24 91 54 15,	24 92 78 69
Ranchi	0651-220 44 64	

PUBLISHED IN INDIA BY

FIREWALL MEDIA
(An Imprint of Laxmi Publications Pvt. Ltd.)

An ISO 9001:2008 Company
113, GOLDEN HOUSE, DARYAGANJ,
NEW DELHI - 110002, INDIA
Telephone : 91-11-4353 2500, 4353 2501
Fax : 91-11-2325 2572, 4353 2528
www.laxmipublications.com info@laxmipublications.com

C—
Printed at Repro Knowledgecast Limited, Thane

Foreword

It gives us great pleasure to introduce this collection of papers to be presented at the 2013 International Conference on Scientific Computing (CSC'13), July 22 through 25, 2013, at The New Tropicana Hotel, Las Vegas, USA.

An important mission of the World Congress in Computer Science, Computer Engineering, and Applied Computing (a federated congress to which this conference is affiliated with) includes *"Providing a unique platform for a diverse community of constituents composed of scholars, researchers, developers, educators, and practitioners. The Congress makes concerted effort to reach out to participants affiliated with diverse entities (such as: universities, institutions, corporations, government agencies, and research centers/labs) from all over the world. The congress also attempts to connect participants from institutions that have **teaching** as their main mission with those who are affiliated with institutions that have **research** as their main mission. The congress uses a quota system to achieve its institution and geography diversity objectives."* By any definition of diversity, this congress is among the most diverse scientific meeting in USA. We are proud to report that this federated congress has authors and participants from 82 different nations representing variety of personal and scientific experiences that arise from differences in culture and values. As can be seen (see below), the program committee of this conference as well as the program committee of all other tracks of the federated congress are as diverse as its authors and participants.

The program committee would like to thank all those who submitted papers for consideration. About 68% of the submissions were from outside the United States. Each submitted paper was peer-reviewed by two experts in the field for originality, significance, clarity, impact, and soundness. In cases of contradictory recommendations, a member of the conference program committee was charged to make the final decision; often, this involved seeking help from additional referees. In addition, papers whose authors included a member of the conference program committee were evaluated using the double-blinded review process. One exception to the above evaluation process was for papers that were submitted directly to chairs/organizers of pre-approved sessions/workshops; in these cases, the chairs/organizers were responsible for the evaluation of such submissions. The overall paper acceptance rate for regular papers was 31%; 4% of the remaining papers were accepted as poster papers (at the time of this writing, we had not yet received the acceptance rate for a few individual tracks.)

We are very grateful to the many colleagues who offered their services in organizing the conference. In particular, we would like to thank the members of the Program Committee of CSC'13, members of the congress Steering Committee, and members of the committees of federated congress tracks that have topics within the scope of CSC. Many individuals listed below, will be requested after the conference to provide their expertise and services for selecting papers for publication (extended versions) in journal special issues as well as for publication in a set of research books (to be prepared for publishers including: Springer, Elsevier, BMC, and others).

- *Dr. Selim Aissi (World Congress Steering Committee); formerly, Chief Strategist - Security, Intel Corp., USA; Senior Business Leader & Head of Global Enterprise Security Architecture, Visa Corporation, USA*
- *Prof. Babak Akhgar (World Congress Steering Committee); Fellow of the British Computer Society, CITP; Professor of Informatics; Co-Director of CENTRIC (Centre of Excellence in Terrorism, Resilience, Intelligence & organised Crime research), Sheffield Hallam University, Sheffield, UK*
- *Prof. Nizar Al-Holou (World Congress Steering Committee); Professor and Chair, ECE Department; Vice Chair, IEEE/SEM-Computer Chapter; University of Detroit Mercy, Detroit, Michigan, USA*
- *Prof. Hamid R. Arabnia (World Congress Steering Committee); Professor, Computer Science; Editor-in-Chief, The Journal of Supercomputing (Springer); Elected Fellow, Int'l Society of Intelligent Biological Medicine (ISIBM); The University of Georgia, Department of Computer Science, USA*
- *Peyman Arebi; Assistant Professor, Department of Computer Engineering, Technical and Vocational University, Bushehr, Iran*
- *Prof. Ezendu Ariwa (Publicity Vice-Chair); Chair, IEEE Consumer Electronics Chapter, UK&RI; Visiting Prof., Gulf University, Bahrain; Visiting Professor, University of Lagos and Kano State Polytechnic, Nigeria*
- *Prof. Juan Jose Martinez Castillo; Director of The Acantelys Research Group and Coordinator of the Computer Engineering Department, Universidad Gran Mariscal de Ayacucho, Venezuela*

- *Dr. Hsi-Ya (Jerry) Chang (PDPTA); Division Chief, National Center for High-Performance Computing, Taiwan; Secretary General of ACCTA; Member, Council of the Taiwan Association of Cloud Computing (TACC); Taiwan, ROC*
- *Prof. Kevin Daimi (World Congress Steering Committee); Director, Computer Science and Software Engineering Programs; Department of Mathematics, Computer Science and Software Engineering; University of Detroit Mercy, Detroit, Michigan, USA*
- *Prof. Leonidas Deligiannidis; Professor, Computer Science, Wentworth Institute of Technology, MA, USA*
- *Prof. George A. Gravvanis (Vice-Chair, CSC); Democritus University of Thrace, Greece*
- *Prof. Houcine Hassan; Universitat Politecnica de Valencia, Spain*
- *Dr. Bing He (PDPTA); Cisco System Inc., San Jose, California, USA*
- *Dr. K. S. S. Iyer; Symbiosis Institute of Telecom Management, Pune, India*
- *Prof. George Jandieri (World Congress Steering Committee); Georgian Technical University, Tbilisi, Georgia; Chief Scientist, The Institute of Cybernetics, Georgian Academy of Science, Georgia; Editorial Board Member: International Journal of Microwaves and Optical Technology; Georgia*
- *Prof. Seifedine Kadry (PDPTA); School of Engineering, American University of the Middle East, Kuwait*
- *Prof. Dong Hwa Kim; Department of Electronic and Control Engineering, Hanbat National University, Korea; Visiting Professor, Budapest University of Technology and Economic, Hungary; International Einstein awardee for Scientific achievement (2010)*
- *Prof. Dattatraya V. Kodavade (World Congress Steering Committee); Head of Computer Science and Engineering, D.K.T.E Society's Textile & Engineering Institute, Ichalkaranji, Maharashtra State, India*
- *Prof. Kun Chang Lee (World Congress Steering Committee); Professor of MIS and WCU Professor of Creativity Science, Business School and Department of Interaction Science, Sungkyunkwan University, Korea*
- *Prof. Zhongyu (Joan) Lu; University of Huddersfield, Huddersfield, UK*
- *Muhammad Naufal Bin Mansor; University Malaysia Perlis, Kangar, Perlis, Malaysia*
- *Prof. George Markowsky (World Congress Steering Committee); Professor and Associate Director, School of Computing and Information Science; Chair International Advisory Board of IEEE IDAACS; Director 2013 Northeast Collegiate Cyber Defense Competition; Cooperating Professor Math & Statistics Department UMaine and School of Policy & International Affairs UMaine; University of Maine, Orono, Maine, USA*
- *Dr. Sara Moein; Editorial Board, International Journal of Science and Technology; Faculty of Engineering, MultiMedia University, Malaysia*
- *Dr. Ali Mostafaeipour; Industrial Engineering Department, Yazd University, Iran*
- *Dr. Saurabh Mukherjee; Banasthali University, Banasthali, Rajasthan, India*
- *Prof. G. N. Pandey (World Congress Steering Committee); Vice-Chancellor, Arunachal University of Studies, Arunachal Pradesh, India; Adjunct Professor, Indian Institute of Information Technology, Allahabad, India*
- *Prof. James J. (Jong Hyuk) Park (World Congress Steering Committee); Professor of Computer Science and Engineering, Seoul National University of Science and Technology (SeoulTech), Korea; President, KITCS; President, FTRA; Editor-in-Chiefs: HCIS, JoC and IJITCC Journals*
- *Prof. R. Ponalagusamy; National Institute of Technology, Tiruchirappalli, India*
- *Prof. Junfeng Qu; Clayton State University, Morrow, Georgia, USA*
- *Prof. Judy Ann Serwatka (EEE); Purdue University, Indiana, USA*
- *Dr. Liang Shi; Senior Researcher, McAfee, USA*
- *Dr. Kok Swee Sim; Faculty of Engineering and Technology, Jalan Ayer Keroh Lama, Melaka, Malaysia*
- *Ashu M. G. Solo, (Publicity Chair); Fellow of British Computer Society, Principal/R&D Engineer, Maverick Technologies America Inc., USA*
- *Dr. Jiao Tao (ICAI); Oracle USA, California, USA*
- *Prof. Fernando G. Tinetti (World Congress Steering Committee); School of Computer Science, Universidad Nacional de La Plata, La Plata, Argentina; Co-editor, Journal of CS and Technology (JCS&T)*
- *Dr. Predrag Tosic (World Congress Steering Committee); Microsoft, Washington, USA*
- *Prof. Ion Tutanescu (ICWN); University of Pitesti, Romania*
- *Prof. Vladimir Volkov (World Congress Steering Committee); The Bonch-Bruevich State University of Telecommunications, Saint-Petersburg, Russia*
- *Prof. Patrick Wang (IPCV + MSV + CGVR); Fellow of IAPR, ISIBM, WASE; Zijiang Chair Professor, ECNU, Shanghai and NTUST, Taipei, Taiwan; Founding President and CEO, Wang Teknowlogy Lab.; MIT Research Consultant; Harvard University, Adj. Faculty, USA; Northeastern University, Boston, MA, USA*
- *Dr. Wei Wei (ICOMP); Xi'an University of Technology, Xi'an, P. R. China*
- *Prof. Dr. Bernd E. Wolfinger (ICOMP); Telecommunications and Computer Networks Division, University of Hamburg, Germany*
- *Prof. Jongwook Woo; California State University, Los Angeles, California, USA*

- *Dr. Qiang Xu; Senior Lecturer, Teesside University, England, UK; UMIST (Institute of Science and Technology), The University of Manchester, England, UK; University of Huddersfield, UK*

As Sponsors-at-large, partners, and/or organizers each of the followings (separated by semicolons) provided help for at least one track of the World Congress: Aldebaran Robotics Inc., USA (http://www.aldebaran-robotics.com); Altera Corporation, USA (http://www.altera.com/); Computer Science Research, Education, and Applications Press (CSREA); Impulse Accelerated Technologies, Inc., USA (http://www.impulseaccelerated.com/); NVIDIA Corporation, USA (http://www.nvidia.com/object/about-nvidia.html); Parallella Community, Supercomputing for Everyone, USA (http://forums.parallella.org/); Pico Computing, Inc., USA (http://picocomputing.com/); SemiWiki.com, The Semiconductor Wiki Project, USA (http://www.semiwiki.com/); Solarflare Communications, Inc., USA (http://www.solarflare.com/); Stream Computing, Performance Engineers, The Netherlands (http://streamcomputing.eu/); Taylor & Francis, UK (http://www.taylorandfrancis.com/); US Chapter of World Academy of Science (http://www.world-academy-of-science.org/) ; and WEBestSOL & Webest Solutions Ltd, UK (http://webestsol.com/). In addition, a number of university faculty members and their staff (names appear on the cover of the set of proceedings), several publishers of computer science and computer engineering books and journals, chapters and/or task forces of computer science associations/organizations from 5 countries, and developers of high-performance machines and systems provided significant help in organizing the conference as well as providing some resources. We are grateful to them all.

We express our gratitude to keynote, invited, and individual conference/tracks and tutorial speakers - the list of speakers appears on the conference web site. We would also like to thank the followings: UCMSS (Universal Conference Management Systems & Support, California, USA) for managing all aspects of the conference; Dr. Tim Field of APC for managing the printing of the proceedings; and the staff of the New Tropicana Hotel in Las Vegas for the professional service they provided. Last but not least, we would like to thank the Co-Editors of CSC'13: Prof. Hamid R. Arabnia, Dr. George A. Gravvanis, Prof. George Jandieri, Ashu M. G. Solo, and Prof. Fernando G. Tinetti.

We present the proceedings of CSC'13.

Steering Committee, 2013
http://www.world-academy-of-science.org/

Contents

SESSION: SIMULATION, MODELING, AND VISUALIZATION METHODS

SESSION: COMPUTATIONAL SCIENCE AND APPLICATIONS

SESSION: WAVE AND DIFFERENTIAL EQUATIONS + TURING MACHINE

SESSION: LATE BREAKING PAPER: DATA PROCESSING + CELLULAR AUTOMATA + SOFT COMPUTING

SESSION

SIMULATION, MODELING, AND VISUALIZATION METHODS

Chair(s)

TBA

Multi-Species Screening in Anti-Ferromagnetic Pair-Annihilation Model Simulations

K.A. Hawick
Computer Science, Massey University, North Shore 102-904, Auckland, New Zealand
email: k.a.hawick@massey.ac.nz
Tel: +64 9 414 0800 Fax: +64 9 441 8181

April 2013

ABSTRACT

Pair-annihilation process models capture the behaviour of important reactions amongst fundamental physical but also chemical systems. We develop a lattice-based pair-annihilation model based on Kawasaki exchange dynamics and with diffusion properties controlled by a lattice-gas temperature. We investigate the effect of multi-species screening in the model when anti-ferromagnetic repulsive coupling forces are used. We find a phase transition manifested by an annihilation induced population collapse around T=0.22 and an additional phase transition in the number of species present around Q=5. We describe a number of quantitative metrics based on graph component labeling and contrast the behaviours of the ferromagnetic and anti-ferromagnetic variants of the model.

KEY WORDS

pair annihilation; simulation; complex systems; phase transition.

1 Introduction

Simulation modelling is still a widely used and indeed necessary tool in developing an understanding of phase transitions and critical phenomena that occur in many physical, chemical and materials systems. Non equilibrium systems that do not have transition rates satisfying a microscopic detailed-balance condition [4] need to be studied on incomplete time-scales where the dynamics forms the basis of the analysis. It is possible however to search for parts of such systems' phases spaces where trajectories are attracted and for which some approximation of the long term behaviour is possible.

There is continued interest in the critical systems literature in models that combine diffusion with multi-species rules and for which processes support or compete. One such model is the pair-annihilation model (PAM) which can be

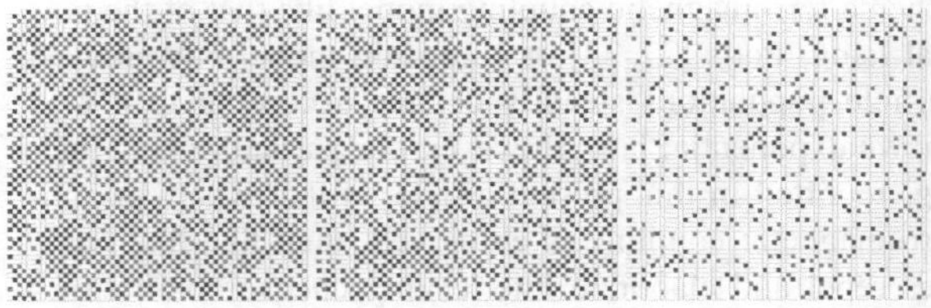

Figure 1: Cold, Warm and Hot Snapshots of the 256^2 system, for Q = 3

used to study processes where two particles meet and mutually annihilate. This is often denoted as $A + A \rightarrow 0$ and is typical of some chemical reaction processes where pairs of molecules combine to leave behind an inert product that plays no further part in the reaction [17, 34]. Annihilation models also play a useful part in understanding more fundamental physical interactions.

The pair-annihilation model [10] has been studied in a number of contexts including: segregation [20]; birth and death combinations [18]; wave pattern formation [1]; asymmetric reactions [3]; and diffusion in various forms [7, 12, 29] and comparisons with other models [2], and with various diffusion mechanisms explored [9]. The PAM has been studied extensively at a theoretical level [31] and with simulations in one dimension [5, 30]. In such cases it models a queue or channel of interacting particles and has relevance for comparisons with theory but is otherwise not particularly representative of any real physical system. A two dimensional system modelling a sheet of interacting particles on a surface is more interesting – but more computationally difficult to simulate.

Many simulation model like the PAM are constructed in terms of lattice simulations with interacting particles at nearest-neighbour interaction ranges [6, 26]. The PAM is usually parameterised in terms of a diffusion rate and particle annihilation and production rates. We find that the Kawasaki site-exchange model [22, 23] is a useful way to formulate the diffusion process in a more realistic way by linking it to a temperature. The Kawasaki model [24] is based on the Ising model [21] but with exchange diffusion dynamics and is effectively a lattice gas model [16] if there are vacancies [8] 2011 present. Details of this are given below in Section 2 but in summary we obtain a model where Q species of lattice cell site diffuse around according to a simple coupling model that is controlled by temperature. Any two particles of the same species that met annihilate one another.

The PAM has been extensively studied with one and two species and some work has explored three states [11]. We are not aware of many higher number of species or states having been explored however – possibly because for normal ferromagnetic coupling systems there does not appear to be any new behaviours for higher Q [19].

When a ferromagnetic coupling model like that of the normal Ising, Potts [27, 33] or Kawasaki model is employed particle populations steadily decline according to a well known exponential law. However, our particular new finding, reported in this present article, is that when an anti-ferromagnetic coupling is employed, then like-like particles repel and elaborate interleaving checkerboard structures form whereby one species of particle effectively shields others from mutual annihilation. We find a phase transition in temperature and another in the number of species of particle present. Particles of different species cannot occupy the same space but otherwise do not couple with one another. We model our system with initial fraction $1/Q$ of each species and we treat one of the species - "state 0" as the vacancies or null reaction products of the pair annihilations [28].

Our Multiple species Pair-Annihilation Model (MPAM) was studied through computer simulations on a 256^2 square lattice model for 2,000 time steps where each site was updated on average once per time step. Some snapshots of the anti-ferromagnetic model are shown in Figure 1 which shows the interleaving shielding checker-board structures forming at cold temperatures, but breaking up at temperatures above the critical temperature which we found to be around $T_c \approx 0.22$. Using graph component labelling [14] and other metrics we investigated the formation of clusters or droplets [13] of non-vacant particles in the system. We also studied different number of species and found an additional transition in $Q \approx 5$ where in our model the vacancies are considered to be one of the Q particles species present.

Our article is structured as follows: In Section 2 we summarise the multi-species pair-annihilation model and the manner in which we implement it on a lattice. We present various screen-shots and quantitative metrics from the simulations in Section 3. In Section 4 we offer a discussion of the implications of the model and results alongwith some conclusions and areas for further work in Section 5.

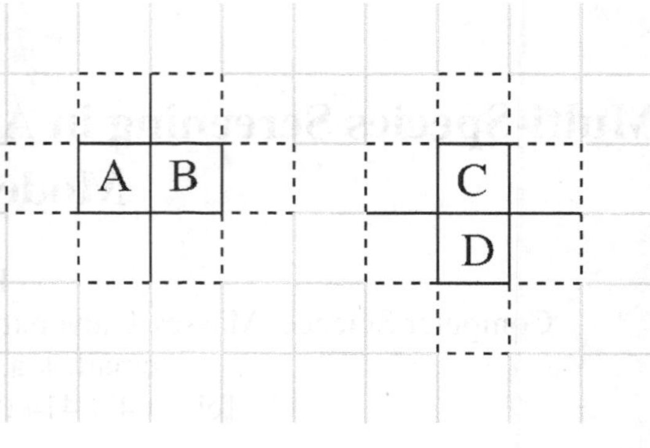

Figure 2: Exchange Mesh showing how A and B exchange, interacting with their nearest neighbours, or C and D do.

2 Multi-Species Pair-Annihilation

Although a number of authors have reported simulation work on the pair annihilation model, no work that we are aware of has studied the effect of anti-ferromagnetic (repulsive) couplings.

The PAM is implemented on a two dimensional lattice with a site exchange diffusion mechanism similar to Kawasaki spin-exchange dynamical model, which itself is based on the Ising model notion of nearest neighbour couplings between sites. Figure 2 shows how two sites arranged horizontally (A-B) or vertically(C-D) interact with their collective six nearest neighbours. At each step of the model the sites are "hit" randomly and the evolutionary process described in Algorithm 1 is followed.

The bonds between sites are supposed to model an interactive coupling between nearest neighbour sites of the form of the Hamiltonian:

$$\mathcal{H} = -\frac{1}{2N} \sum_{<i,j>} J_{i,j}\sigma_i\sigma_j \qquad (1)$$

with the summation over nearest neighbouring sites of which there are four on a two-dimensional square lattice. We take the site variables $\sigma \in \{\pm 1\}$ and the coupling parameter J to be uniform everywhere and a unit of Boltzmann's constant k_B throughout.

Changes in the Hamiltonian $\mathcal{H}$ that result in a lowering of energy (increased bond count) are always accepted and the swap of sites i, j made, but even changes that imply a small increase in energy are accepted stochastically, and this models the effect of thermal fluctuations. The Boltzmann probability condition for testing against a random number is:

$$\mathcal{P} = \exp(-\Delta E / k_B T) \qquad (2)$$

To all intents and purposes have a single parameter model – the temperature T if we measure changes in energy as changes in the number of bonds and use k_B units for J.

Algorithm 1 Like-Pair Annihilation Model.

choose lattice size, shape, eg square 256^2
choose neighbourhood $\mathcal{N}$ eg Nearest
choose number of allowed states Q
for all runs **do**
  initialise N sites randomly
  for all steps, eg 2,000 **do**
    for all sites $i = 1..N$, in random order **do**
      choose neighbouring site $j \in \mathcal{N}$
      if sites i and j are same species **then**
        annihilate i and j, both set to 0
      else
        count changed bonds if i,j swap
        if increased bonds **then**
          swap species at i,j
        else
          with Boltzmann probability
          swap species i,j
        end if
      end if
    end for
    record populations and cluster sizes
  end for
end for
normalise averaged measurements

We implement the model with Q different states, but with one of these used to denote a vacancy site. There are therefore $Q - 1$ non vacant states present in the model and we use the $A + A \rightarrow 0$ like-like pair variation of the pair annihilation model. This is expressed in Algorithm 1 where two sites of the same species annihilate one another completely and with probability one. It is possible to introduce an additional parameter to the model - a probability usually denoted as λ that controls the rate at which such annihilations occur. We use the Kawasaki model's temperature to control the diffusion of species in the spatial lattice. Other authors adopt a simpler non-interaction based approach and introduce a diffusion constant $\mathcal{D}$. A third parameter controlling a production process is also possible. In the work we report here we do not allow new particles to be produced and focus on particle annihilation not production.

In the Ising, Kawasaki and related models the coupling parameter J is taken as a positive number. The upshot is that like particles are attracted to like. This form of system is known as ferromagnetic coupling. However the models also work consistently if we reverse the sign so that like repels like and the species arrange themselves to avoid other members of their own species. In the simple $Q = 2$ case this gives rise to a checkerboard pattern with species completely avoiding any nearest neighbour interactions. More complex inter-plays arise when there are irregularities in the pattern due to prior annihilations.

In the work reported below we experiment with the anti-ferromagnetic coupling version of the Kawasaki dynamics, operated alongside a like-like pair annihilation process.

3 Experimental Simulation Results

Unless otherwise stated, the systems reported are based on a periodic wrap around geometry on a square lattice of size $N = 256^2$ sites and initialised randomly with average initial fraction $f_Q = \frac{N}{Q}$ of each species - including vacancies. The model system is evolved for 2,000 time steps for the data presented, and various snapshots and quantitative metrics are reported.

Figure 1 shows the key result for a small system. The anti-ferromagnetic couplings make the individual species repel one another at nearest neighbour interaction lengths and the surviving particles arrange themselves on checkerboard patterns in which they can maintain themselves for a long time without meeting and annihilating with a particle of the same species. When the temperature is slowly raised however, more thermal fluctuations in the form of particles that have temporarily hopped off the checkerboard and are therefore prone to meeting an annihilation partner particle of the same species. The results are seen at a high temperature, the population of particles starts to drop significantly as particles are no longer screened by the low temperature frozen-in interleaving checkerboard patterns.

This effect is seen manifest in systems at various number of species Q. Figure 3 shows the effect for $Q = 3, 4, 5, 6$. In this illustration we have coloured all non-vacancies a shade of red as this emphasises the long range structure of defects amongst the interleaving checkerboards that have arisen from the anti-ferromagnetic couplings. We have not illustrated the model for ferromagnetic couplings as particles annihilate very rapidly and the long-term (uninteresting) picture is of a very few isolated particles in a sea of vacancies.

There are a number of useful quantitative metrics that we report for both ferromagnetic and anti-ferromagnetic coupled systems however. The simplest to record is a population track of a representative species as the system progresses from its initial random state. Since we treat all non vacant species the same, it is sufficient to track the population of species-1. The population of monomer particles - that is particles with no non-vacant neighbouring particles - is also relatively simple to compute. Using a component labelling algorithm we can also track the number of distinct (non-vacancy) cluster components in the system. These three metrics are shown plotted against time (on a logarithmic scale) for both an anti-ferromagnetic coupling simulation (left) and a ferromagnetic one (right).

Figure 4 shows the dramatic difference between the ferro and anti-ferromagnetic couplings on the PAM. The anti-ferromagnetism essentially creates a screening effect so

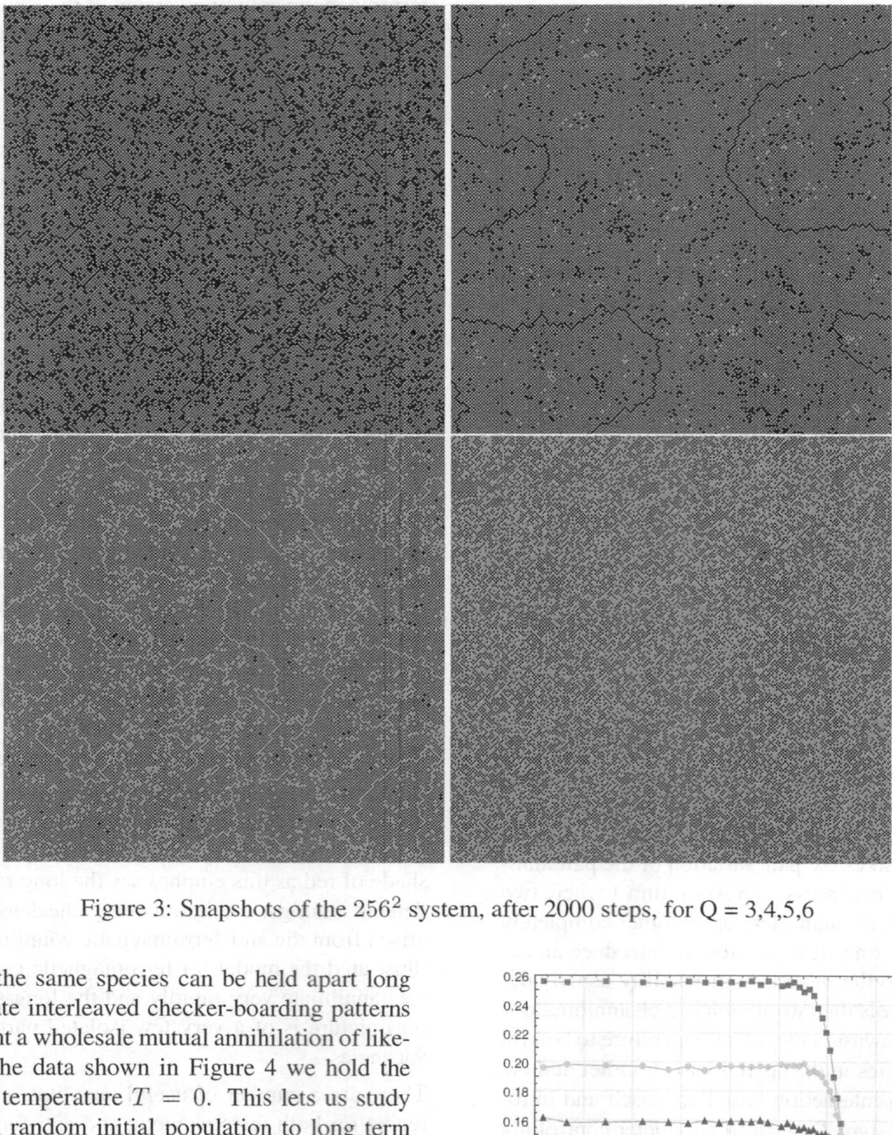

Figure 3: Snapshots of the 256^2 system, after 2000 steps, for Q = 3,4,5,6

that members of the same species can be held apart long enough for intricate interleaved checker-boarding patterns to form and prevent a wholesale mutual annihilation of like-like species. In the data shown in Figure 4 we hold the system cold with temperature $T = 0$. This lets us study the progress from random initial population to long term behaviour.

In the case of the ferromagnetic model, with particle production mutual annihilation progressively removes almost all particles, and those few remaining only survive because of the lowered probability of finding an annihilation partner in the space. The anti ferromagnetic system however allows particles to survive and a steady non zero population fraction, fraction of monomers and number of non-vacancy clusters all result. We can see that at zero temperature, the number of species does not have any obvious complex effect. Increasing Q means the partial volume fraction available to each species is reduced, but also allows species to more effectively "hide from their own" and to survive annihilation for longer based upon the frozen-in long range spatial checker-boarding patterns.

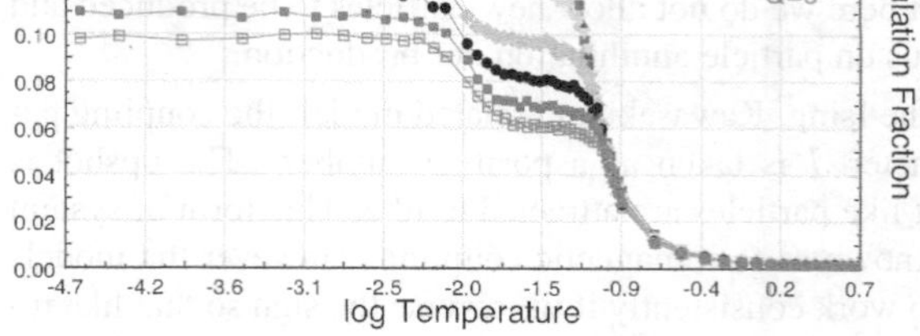

Figure 5: Final population of species vs log of temperature for various numbers Q of species present.

A series of systems were simulated at different temperatures to study the effect of the increasing thermal fluctuations.

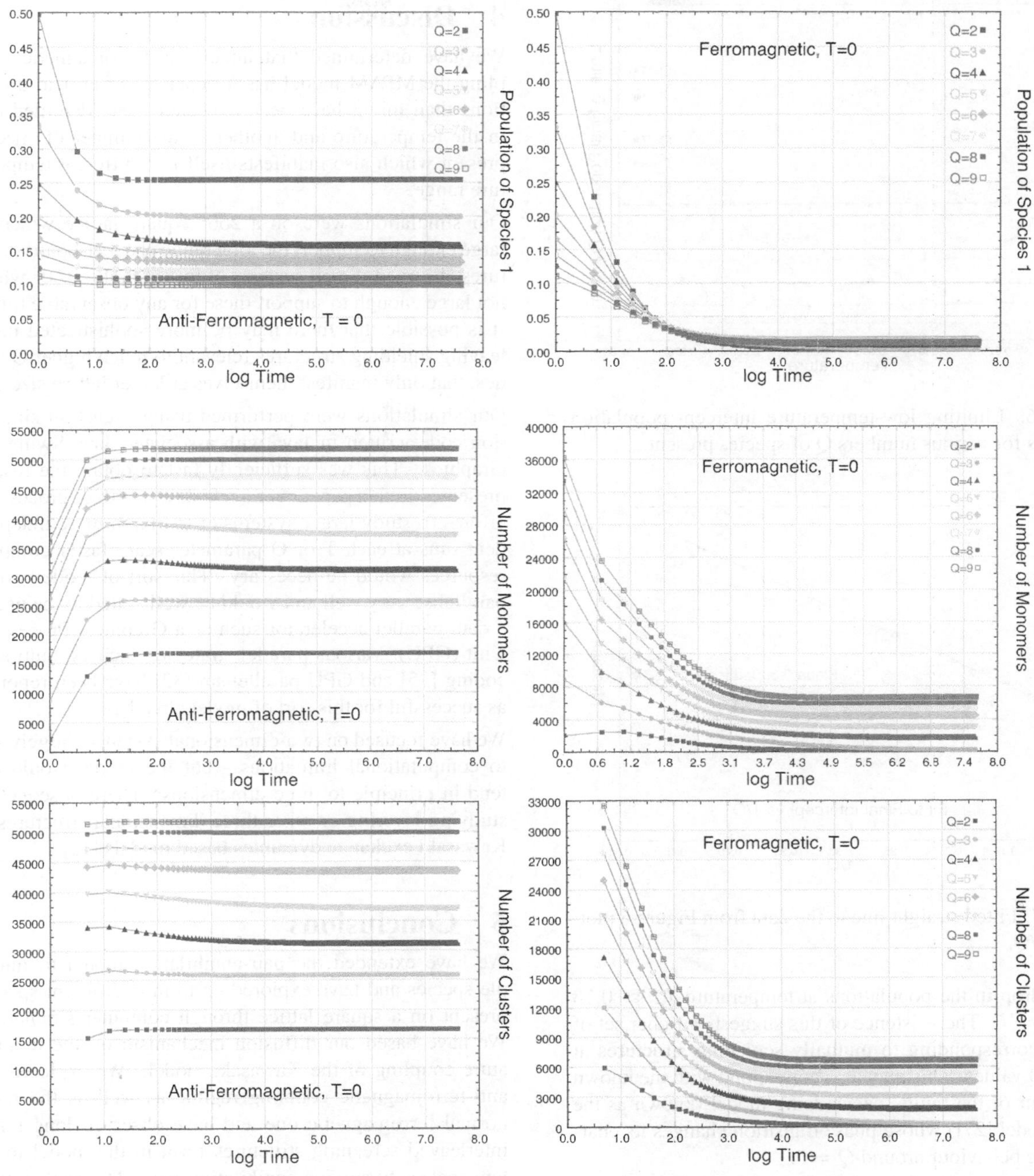

Figure 4: Metrics for the 256^2 system for anti-ferromagnetic coupling (left) and ferromagnetic (right) at Temperature T=0, and for various number of species Q values.

Figure 5 shows a plot of the final value (after 2,000 steps) of the population fraction of representative species number 1, plotted against the diffusion-controlling temperature (on a logarithmic scale) and with different curves for each of the different Q values.

One interesting result is the existence of a marked phase transition for all Q values at temperature $T_c \approx 0.22$. This corresponds to there being sufficient thermal energy for particles to hop out of or across the nearest neighbour checkerboard screening them from their fellows and mutually annihilating. The population drops rapidly above this critical temperature. A more subtle result is that of a second

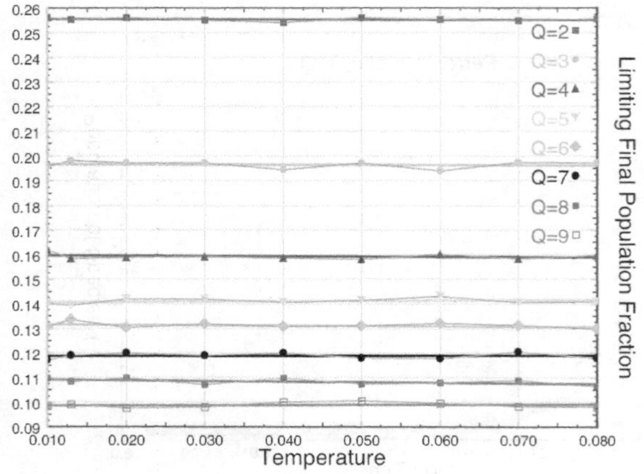

Figure 6: Limiting low-temperature intercept population fractions for various numbers Q of species present.

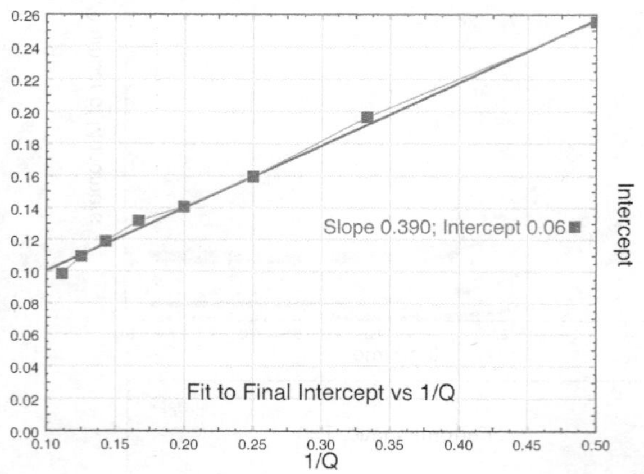

Figure 7: Fitted straight line to the data from Figure 6 plotted vs 1/Q.

partial drop in the populations at temperature $T_c^* \approx 0.13$ for $Q >= 5$. The existence of this suggests a richer set of phases corresponding to mutually screening structures at higher Q values. This may also correspond with the known behaviour of the multi-species Ising model (known as the Potts model [27]) whose phase transition changes its characteristic behaviour around $Q = 5$.

We attempt to investigate how systematic the transition in Q is by plotting the limiting values of the population fractions for each different Q value at low temperatures.

This is shown in Figure 6 where the near horizontal straight line limits suggest they can be characterized by a fitted intercept to each straight line. These intercepts are themselves plotted as a function of $1/Q$ and are shown in Figure 7. There appears to be a straight line relationship with $1/Q$ to within the bounds of experimental error from the experiments reported here.

4 Discussion

We have determined that under anti-ferromagnetic coupling the MPAM model has a richer set of critical transitions than might have been expected. We identified one in the temperature and another in the number of species present which also manifests itself in a different temperature range.

Our simulations were on a 256^2 square lattice which as large enough to support the long range checker-board structures observed. Small systems of for example $< 50^2$ where not large enough to support these for any observable times. It is possible that there may be more sophisticated interleaving shielding structures relevant to much higher Q values, that only manifest themselves at larger lattice sizes.

Our simulations were performed using a custom simulation code written in Java with associated Java Swing 2D Graphics. This was sufficiently fast to obtain the results presented in this paper over a few days worth of processing effort. To study larger systems or to obtain more independent runs at each T or Q parameter scan, faster compute resources would be necessary. This sort of model would parallelise very well and would be well suited to the use of a data parallel accelerator such as a Graphical Processing Unit (GPU). Various parallel strategies such as multi spin coding [25] and GPU parallelism [32] have been reported as successful for this sort of model already.

We have focused on two-dimensional systems - largely due to computational limitations - but the model would extend in principle to three dimensions. There is scope for studying layering or other three dimensional structures in Kawasaki exchange dynamics based models [15].

5 Conclusions

We have extended the pair-annihilation model to multiple species and have explored up to nine different species present on a square lattice through computer simulation. We have based our diffusion mechanism on the temperature coupling of the Kawasaki model. We explored the anti-ferromagnetic coupling regime as well as the more normal ferromagnetic one and have observed long range interleaved screening structures form in the model to allow species to survive annihilation much longer than they would in the ferromagnetic system.

We have found and approximately located the phase transition temperature at which these long range structures are broken up by particles hopping across them as at around $T_c \approx 0.22$. We have also identified a change in behaviour at around $Q \approx 5$ which we believe is linked to a more subtle interaction between the mutual shielding behaviour at high Q. We hypothesis a relationship between the low temperature limit behaviour of the system and the reciprocal of the number of species present Q.

There is scope to investigate these phenomena in more statistical detail and potentially to obtain a full and complete phase diagram of the anti ferromagnetic multiple species pair-annihilation model (MPAM). There is further scope to extend the model to three dimensions where more complex face-centred or body-centred shield structure might form.

References

[1] Alonso, S., John, K., Bar, M.: Complex wave patterns in an effective reaction-diffusion model for chemical reactions in microemulsions. J. Chem. Phys. 134, 094117 (2011)

[2] Amar, J.G., Family, F.: Diffusion annihilation in one dimension and kinetics of the ising model at zero temperature. Phys. Rev. A 41(6), 3258–3262 (March 1990)

[3] Ayyer, A., Mallick, K.: Exact results for an asymmetric annihilation process with open boundaries. J. Phys. A: Math. and Theor. 43(4), 045003–1–18 (2010)

[4] Binder, K. (ed.): Monte Carlo Methods in Statistical Physics. Topics in Current Physics, Springer-Verlag, 2 edn. (1986), number 7

[5] Bramson, M., Lebowitz, J.L.: Asymptotic behavior of densities in diffusion-dominated annihilation reactions. Phys. Rev. Lett. 61(21), 2397–2400 (1988)

[6] Castellano, C., Pastor-Satorras, R.: Irrelevance of information outflow in opinion dynamics models. Phys. Rev. E 83, 016113 (2011)

[7] Catanzaro, M., Boguna, M., Pastor-Satorras, R.: Diffusion-annihilation processes in complex networks. Phys. Rev. E 71, 056104 (2005)

[8] Davydov, S.Y., Lebedev, A.A.: Vacancy model of micropipe annihilation in epotaxial silicon carbide layers. Semiconductors 45(6), 727–730 (2011)

[9] Dickman, A.G., Dickman, R.: Phase diagram and critical behavior of the pair annihilation model. J. Stat. Mech.: Theor. and Expt. May, P05009 (2010)

[10] Dickman, R.: Universality and diffusion in nonequilibrium critical phenomena. Phys. Rev. B 40(10), 7005–7010 (1989)

[11] Dickman, R.: Nonequilibrium critical behavior of the triplet annihilation model. Phys. Rev. A 42(12), 6985–6990 (1990)

[12] Ginzburg, V., Radzihovsky, L., Clark, N.A.: Self-consistent model of an annihilation-diffusion reaction with long-range interactions. Phys. Rev. E 55(1), 395–402 (January 1997)

[13] Hawick, K.A.: Modelling cluster nucleation and growth in alloys. In: Proc. IASTED International Conference on Modelling and Simulation (AfricaMS 2008), Gabarone, Botswana. pp. 73–78. IASTED, Gabarone, Botswana (8-10 September 2008), cSTN-053

[14] Hawick, K.A., Leist, A., Playne, D.P.: Parallel Graph Component Labelling with GPUs and CUDA. Parallel Computing 36(12), 655–678 (December 2010), `www.elsevier.com/locate/parco`

[15] Hawick, K.: Visualising multi-phase lattice gas fluid layering simulations. In: Proc. International Conference on Modeling, Simulation and Visualization Methods (MSV'11). pp. 3–9. CSREA, Las Vegas, USA (18-21 July 2011)

[16] Hawick, K.A.: Domain Growth in Alloys. Ph.D. thesis, Edinburgh University (1991)

[17] Henkel, M., Hinrichsen, H.: Exact solution of a reaction-diffusion process with three-site interactions. J. Phys. A 34, 1561 (2001)

[18] Hernandez-Garcia, E., Lopez, C.: Birth, death and diffusion of interacting particles. J. Phys. Cond. Mat 17, S4263–S4274 (2005)

[19] Hilhorst, H.J., Deloubriere, O., Washenberger, M.J., Tauber, U.C.: Segregation in diffusion-limited multispecies pair annihilation. J. Phys. A: Math. and Theor. 37(28), 7063–7093 (2004)

[20] Hilhorts, H.J., Washenberger, M.J., Tauber, U.C.: Symmetry and species segregation in diffusion-limited pair annihilation. J. Stat. Mech: Theor. and Expt. 10, P10002 (2004)

[21] Ising, E.: Beitrag zur Theorie des Ferromagnetismus. Zeitschrift fuer Physik 31, 253–258 (1925)

[22] Kawasaki, K.: Diffusion constants near the critical point for time dependent Ising model I. Phys. Rev. 145(1), 224–230 (1966)

[23] Kawasaki, K.: Diffusion constants near the critical point for time-dependent ising models. ii. Physical Review 148(1), 375–381 (1966)

[24] Kawasaki, K.: Diffusion constants near the critical point for time-dependent ising models. iii. self-diffusion constant. Physical Review 150(1), 285–290 (1966)

[25] M.Q.Zhang: A fast vectorised multispin coding algorithm for 3d Monte Carlo simulations using Kawasaki spin-exchange dynamics. J.Stat.Phys 56(5), 939–950 (1989)

[26] Postnikov, E.B., Ryabov, A.B., Loskutov, A.: Analysis of patterns formed by two-component diffusion limited aggregation. Phys. Rev. E 82, 051403 (2010)

[27] Potts, R.B.: Some generalised order-disorder transformations. Proc. Roy. Soc pp. 106–109 (1951), received July

[28] Santos, F., Dickman, R., Fulco, U.L.: Pair contact process with diffusion of pairs. J. Stat. Mech.: Theor. and Expet. March, P03012 (2011)

[29] Santos, J.E.: The duality relation between glauber dynamics and the diffusion - annihilation model as a similarity transformation. J. Phys. A 30(9), 3249 (1997)

[30] Santos, J.E., Schut, G.M., Stinchcombe, R.B.: Diffusion-annihilation dynamics in one spatial dimension. J. Chem. Phys. 105, 2399 (1996)

[31] Schute, G.M.: Diffusion-annihilation in the presence of a driving field. J. Phys. A. 28(12), 3405 (1995)

[32] Vigelius, M., Lane, A., Meyer, B.: Accelerating reaction-diffusion simulations with general-purpose graphics units. Bioinformatics Applications Note 27, 288–290 (2011)

[33] Wu, F.Y.: The Potts model. Rev. Mod. Phys. 54(1), 235–268 (Jan 1982)

[34] Zhang, Y., Zhang, Z., Guan, J., Zhou, S.: Diffusion-annihilation processes in weighted scale-free networks with identical degree sequence. J. Stat. Mech.: Theor. and Expt. October, P10001 (2011)

Application of LabVIEW® and SoildWorks®- based Simulation Technique to Hybrid Motion Blending of a 6-axis Articulated Robot

Dong Sun Lee[1]**, Won Jee Chung**[1]**, and Jun Ho Jang**[1]

[1]School of Mechatronics, Chansgwon National University, Changwon-si, Gyeongsangnam-do, South Korea

Abstract - *In general, the movement strategy of industrial robots can be divided into two kinds, PTP (Point to Point) and CP (Continuous Path). In order to cope with high-speed handling of the cooperation of industrial robots with machine tools or other devices, CP should be implemented so as to reduce vibration and noise, as well as decreasing travel time. In this paper, we will realize CP motion (especially hybrid motion) blending in 3-dimensional space for a 6-axis articulated (lab-manufactured) robot (called as "RS2") by using LabVIEW® programming, based on a parametric interpolation. . Another major contribution of this paper is the proposal of motion blending simulation technique based on LabVIEW® and SolidWorks®, in order to figure out whether the hybrid motion blending can be realized before actual implementation. In order to evaluate the performance of hybrid motion blending, simple PTP (i.e., linear-linear) is physically implemented on RS2 as well as hybrid motion (especially joint-linear) blending. The implementation results of hybrid motion blending and PTP will be compared in terms of vibration magnitude and travel time by using the vibration testing equipment of Medallion of Zonic®. It will be confirmed that the hybrid motion blending is with less vibration and shorter travel time when compared to the PTP, by implementing two algorithms on RS2*

Keywords: Hybrid motion blending, LabVIEW® and SoildWorks®- based Simulation Technique, 6-axis articulated robot, LabVIEW® programming, Virtual drivers, Recurdyn® V7

1 Introduction

A 6-axis articulated robot, as one of industrial manipulators, is commonly used for automation lines of welding, assembly and spray painting. For fast and accurate motion of 6-axis articulated robot, more noble motion control strategy is needed. In general, the movement strategy of industrial robots can be divided into two kinds, PTP (Point to Point) and CP (Continuous Path). Early industrial robots in mass production line have been mainly used for simple and iterative jobs in which PTP motion is enough. But recently, industrial robots which should be co-worked with machine tools are increasingly needed for performing various jobs, as well as simple handling or welding. Therefore, in order to cope with high-speed handling of the cooperation of industrial robots with machine tools or other devices, CP should be implemented so as to reduce vibration and noise, as well as decreasing operation time. [1]

More specifically, Fig. 1 shows the comparison of PTP with CP. As shown in Fig. 1, PTP makes a robot move from a starting point to an ending point through a via point, whereas CP makes a robot from a starting point to an ending point without pausing at a via point. Especially CP can result in smooth motion of robot and thereby can shorten travel time of robot.

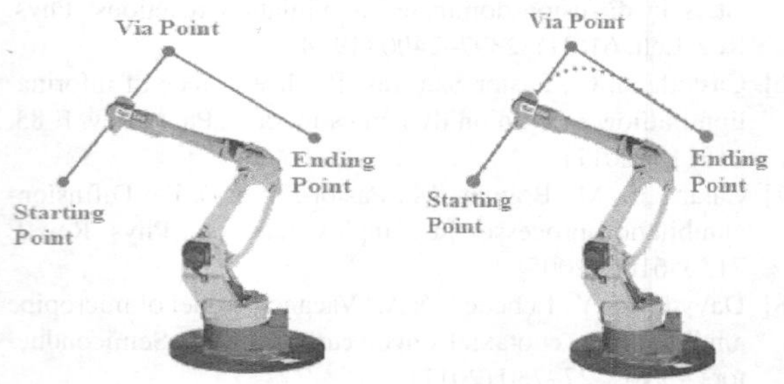

(a) PTP motion (b) CP motion

Fig. 1 PTP motion and CP motion

As shown in Fig. 2, basic operation of CP motion can be achieved by superposing the trapezoidal velocity profiles of two segments (*i.e.*, one segment from a starting point to a *via* point and another segment from a *via* point to an ending point) in the vicinity of a via point. The CP motion can result in reducing both travel time and vibration.

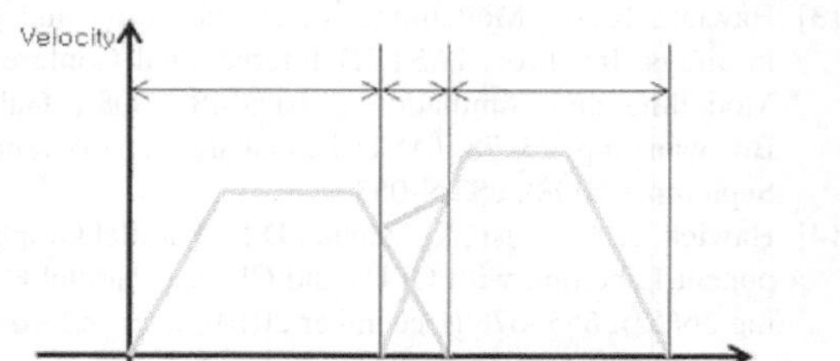

Fig. 2 Superposition of velocity

Reduced travel time due to the CP Implementation and effects of vibration can be obtained. Existing CP method in [2] has proposed a new velocity superposition algorithm in consideration of various velocity cases, as shown in Fig. 3. This algorithm has many equations with difficulties in actual application to a robot. Moreover it can not provide hybrid motion blending such as blending of joint motion with linear motion because it is effective only for homogeneous blending of joint motion with joint motion. As another investigation of velocity superposition, Ju *et al.* [1] has suggested a hybrid motion blending algorithm including velocity superposition by using parametric interpolation. By using a 3-axis (*lab-manufactured*) SCARA robot (called as "RS1") with LabVIEW® controller (see Fig. 4), this simple algorithm was shown to result in less vibration, compared with PTP motion and Kim's algorithm proposed in [2]. However, relatively simple LabVIEW® programming and RS1 have been used for the realization of CP motion blending in *2-dimensional* plane.

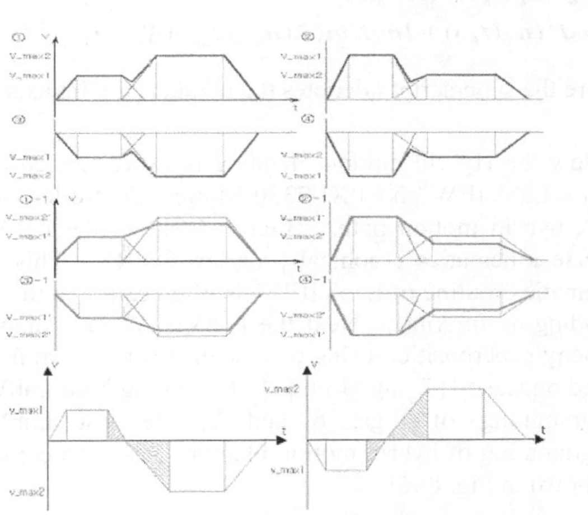

Fig.3 Kim's (velocity superposition) algorithm in [2]

Fig. 4 RS1 (SCARA) and CP motion blending in [1]

In contrast, this paper will realize CP motion (especially Hybrid motion blending) blending in *3-dimensional* space for a *6-axis articulated (lab-manufactured) robot* (called as "RS2") by using LabVIEW® programming, based on the parametric interpolation. Another major contribution of this paper is the proposal of motion blending simulation technique based on LabVIEW® and SolidWorks®, in order to figure out whether the hybrid motion blending can be realized before actual implementation. Moreover, this simulation technique can check any interference between links. In addition, by incorporating the RS2 model of SolidWorks®, Recurdyn® V7 will be used for checking whether the velocity generated by the motion blending algorithm can exceed the maximum of velocity at the end-effector of RS2. Without the simulation technique, the implementation of hybrid motion blending algorithm on RS2 can result in the damage (especially severe twisting of harness nearby a wrist) of robot since it make the joint servo motors of RS2 go over the travel speed ranges of joints. At last, in order to evaluate the performance of hybrid motion blending, simple PTP (*i.e.*, linear-linear) is also physically implemented on RS2 as well as hybrid motion blending. The implementation results of hybrid motion blending and PTP will be compared in terms of vibration magnitude and operation time by using the vibration testing equipment of Medallion of Zonic®. It will be confirmed that the hybrid motion blending is with less vibration and shorter travel time when compared to the PTP, by implementing two algorithms on RS2.

2 Hybrid Motion Blending Algorithm and Its Programming on LabVIEW®

Hybrid motion blending is defined as the blending of different two type's motions such as a blending of joint motion with linear motion and circular motion, in the neighborhood of a *via* point. The types of motion can be classified into 3 categories; joint motion, linear motion, and circular motion. In this paper, joint and linear motions are exclusively selected for explanation, based on [1].

First of all, a parameter $u(t)$ can be introduced as follows:

$$P^i(u(t)) = P^i_e - u(t)(P^i_e - P^i_s), \quad u \in [0,1] \tag{1}$$

where $u(t)$ spans from 0 to 1, having a key role of synchronizing all the joints in acceleration and deceleration time. Here i indicates the number of joint axis; P^i_e denotes the end position of i-th joint, and P^i_s denotes the start position of i-th joint. It can be worth noticing that $u(t)$ is 1 at P^i_s, while $u(t)$ is 0 at P^i_e. Especially the parameter $u(t)$ denotes the ratio of the moved distance l during elapsed time t to the total movement L, which can be defined by

$$u(t) = 1 - l / L \tag{2}$$

Referring to Eq. (1), joint motion segment can be described by

$$J(u(t)) = J_e - u(t)(J_e - J_s), \; u \in [0,1] \tag{3}$$

where $J(u(t))$ denotes a joint position; the subscripts e and s indicates *end* and *start*, respectively. Similarly, a linear motion segment can be given by

$$L(u(t)) = P_e - u(t)(P_e - P_s), \; u \in [0,1] \tag{4}$$

where *L(u(t))* denotes a position of an end-effector in Cartesian coordinates. Especially P_e and P_s indicate the end and start position of the end-effector in Cartesian coordinates. Equations can be re-written in joint coordinates as follows:

$$J(u(t)) = InvKin(L(u(t))) \\ = InvKin(P_e - u(t)(P_e - P_s)),\ u \in [0,1] \tag{5}$$

where $InvKin(\cdot)$ denotes the inverse kinematics routine. Similarly, a circular interpolation can be given by

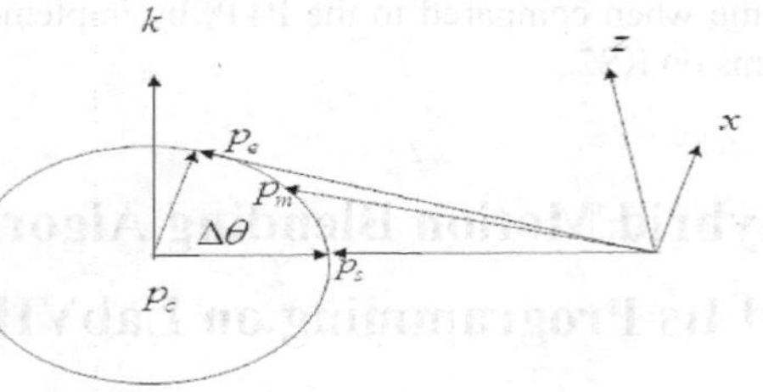

Fig. 5 Element of Circular interpolation

$$C(u(t)) = P_c + (P_s - P_c)\cos((1-u(t))\Delta\theta) \\ + k \times (P_s - P_c)\sin((1-u(t))\Delta\theta) \tag{6}$$

$$J(u(t)) = InvKin(C(u(t))),\ u \in [0,1] \tag{7}$$

where p_c is circle center, p_s is circle starting point, k is normal vector of p_c, $\Delta\theta$ is angle of arc.

The motion blending should be implemented in joint coordinates on the basis of time axis. For example, the (*k* – 1)-th joint motion segment and the *k*-th linear motion segment can be blended in joint coordinates. Thus hybrid motion blending equation using Eqs. (3)-(7) can be defined as 6 equations as follows:

Joint – Linear Blending

$$J_B{}^i(u_k(t_k), u_{k-1}(t_{k-1})) \\ = InvKin(L(u_k(t_k)))^i - u_{k-1}(t_{k-1})(J_{k-1,e}{}^i - J_{k-1,s}{}^i) \tag{8}$$

Joint – Circular Blending

$$J_B{}^i(u_k(t_k), u_{k-1}(t_{k-1})) \\ = InvKin(C(u_k(t_k)))^i + u_{k-1}(t_{k-1})(J_{k-1,e}{}^i - J_{k-1,s}{}^i) \tag{9}$$

Linear – Circular Blending

$$J_B{}^i(u_k(t_k), u_{k-1}(t_{k-1})) \\ = InvKin(C(u_k(t_k)))^i + InvKin(L(u_{k-1}(t_{k-1})))^i - J_{k-1,e}{}^i \tag{10}$$

Circular – Linear Blending

$$J_B{}^i(u_k(t_k), u_{k-1}(t_{k-1})) \\ = InvKin(L(u_k(t_k)))^i + InvKin(C(u_{k-1}(t_{k-1})))^i - J_{k-1,e}{}^i \tag{11}$$

Circular – Joint Blending

$$J_B{}^i(u_k(t_k), u_{k-1}(t_{k-1})) \\ = J^i(u_k(t_k)) + InvKin(C(u_{k-1}(t_{k-1})))^i - J_{k-1,e}{}^i \tag{12}$$

Linear – Joint Blending

$$J_B{}^i(u_k(t_k), u_{k-1}(t_{k-1})) \\ = J^i(u_k(t_k)) + InvKin(L(u_{k-1}(t_{k-1})))^i - J_{k-1,e}{}^i \tag{13}$$

where the superscript *i* denotes the number of joint axis.

Now the Hybrid motion blending is experimented on RS2 with a LabVIEW® NI PXI-7350 Motion Controller, so as to track hybrid motion path. Figure 6 shows the LabVIEW® inverse kinematics graphical program for RS2. This inverse kinematics routine of LabVIEW® is often called in the motion blending as $InvKin(\cdot)$ Next the LabVIEW® programming of velocity superposition using parameter *u(t)* is shown in Fig. 7, based on Case 1, 2, and 3 in [1]. By calling both LabVIEW® programming of Figs. 6 and 7, the last LabVIEW® programming of hybrid motion blending has been constructed as shown in Fig. 8.[6]

Fig. 6 LabVIEW® inverse kinematics graphical program for RS2

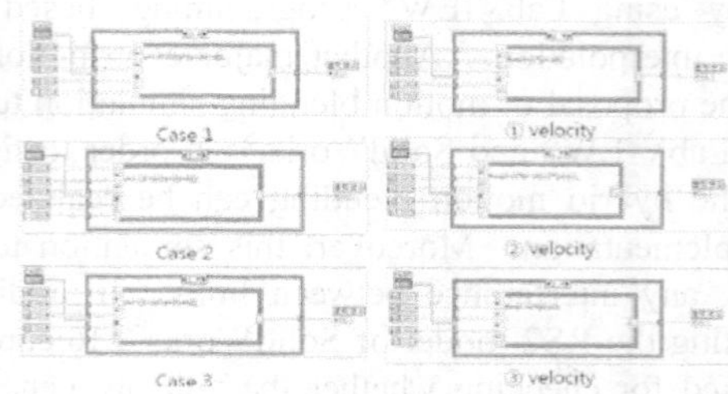

Fig. 7 LabVIEW® programming of velocity superposition using *u(t)*

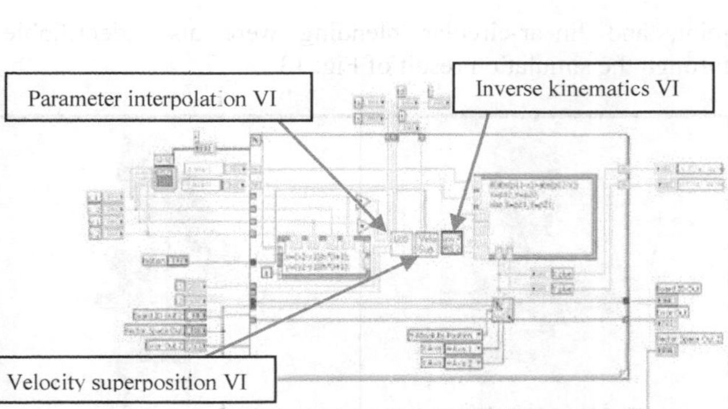

Fig. 8 LabVIEW® programming of hybrid motion blending

In more specific, the hybrid motion blending of LabVIEW® programming be explained as follows. As shown in Fig. 8, 3 VI's are engaged in hybrid motion blending. Here VI means Virtual Instrument of LabVIEW® programming. The 3 VI's are composed of parameter interpolation VI (which is skipped due to simplicity in Eq. (2), velocity superposition VI (see Fig. 7) and inverse kinematics VI (see Fig. 6). Consequently hybrid motion blending VI calls 3 VI's to calculate next points during motion blending.

3 Application of SoildWorks® and LabVIEW® –based Simulation Technique to Hybrid Motion Blending of a 6-axis Articulated Robot

Before applying the hybrid motion blending programs using LabVIEW® to RS2 directly, we would like to check the feasibility of the program in advance to avoid mechanical interference between links or joints. For this purpose, we propose a simulation technique to be applied to hybrid motion blending by by interlocking SolidWorks® and LabVIEW®. In specific, this simulation technique makes it possible to figure put any problem which might occur when the hybrid motion blending program of LabVIEW® is applied to RS2 actually. Especially the technique can make RS2 avoid a severe collision between links or disconnection of harness around a wrist when excessive joint angles can be given by rough motion blending.

For the proposed simulation technique, we first make a 3-dimensional (3-D) modeling of RS2 using SolidWorks® as shown in Fig. 9. In the SolidWorks® 3-D modeling, each joint axis moved by RS2 was set from axis 1 through 6 as shown in Fig. 10. To realize the simulation, the LabVIEW® program used in the previous section of hybrid motion blending was incorporated with SolidWorks®. The 3-D modeling of RS2 in SolidWorks® was loaded into LabVIEW®, instead of the physical robot of RS2. Moreover virtual 6 drivers were generated on the LabVIEW®, making the joint axes of 3-D model coincident with the ones of actual RS2.

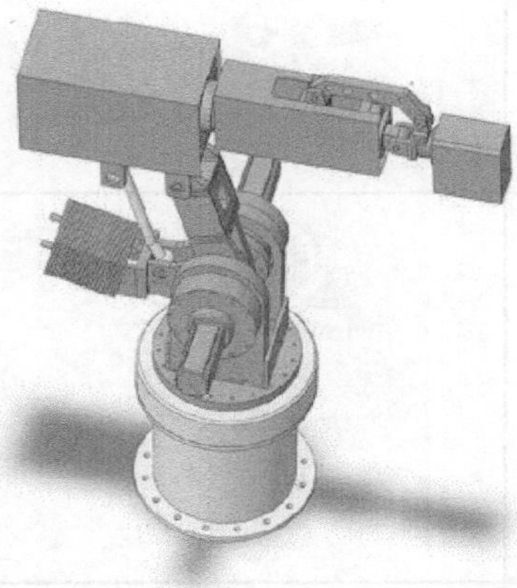

Fig. 9 Using SolidWorks® 3-D modeling of 6-axis articulated robot

In fact, since RS2 has servo drivers taking charge of motor on each axis, and the motor values are set up, it operates as soon as the LabVIEW® program is applied. But, in the case of the RS2 modeling with SolidWorks®, each motor should be set, and the motor value set on the SolidWorks® should be made to be equal to the driver value of LabVIEW®, using the function of generating virtual driver. Figure 10 below shows each joint axis on which a real robot moves in SolidWorks®. Then the LabVIEW® program developed in the previous section was loaded and connected to the virtual drivers. Finally SoildWorks® and LabVIEW®-based simulation is performed as shown in the interlocking program configuration of Fig. 11. [7]

Axis	Setting-up of axes
1	
2	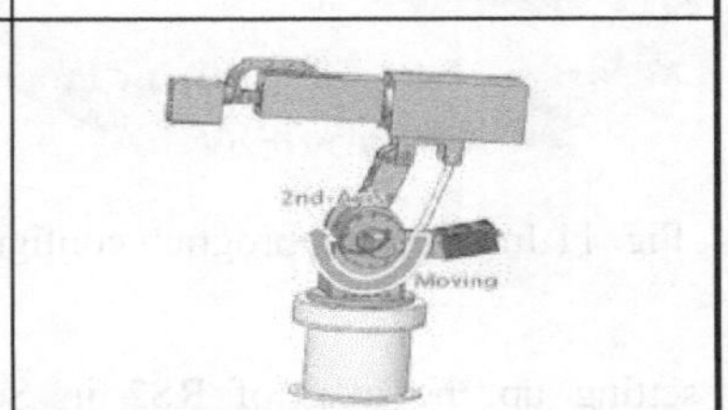

3	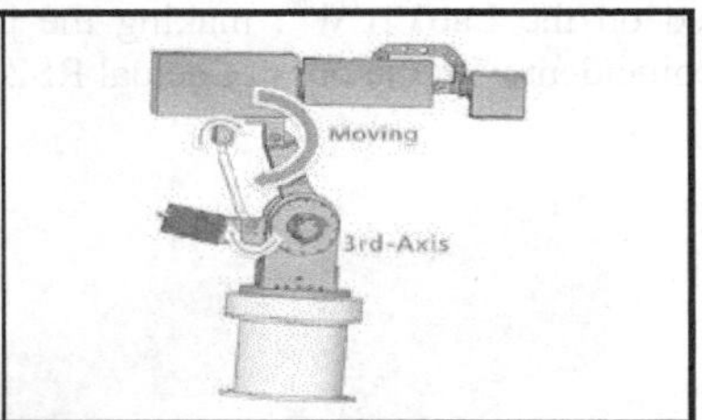
4	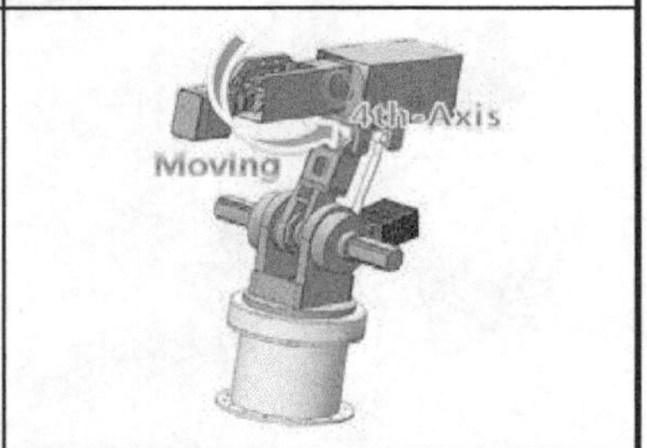
5	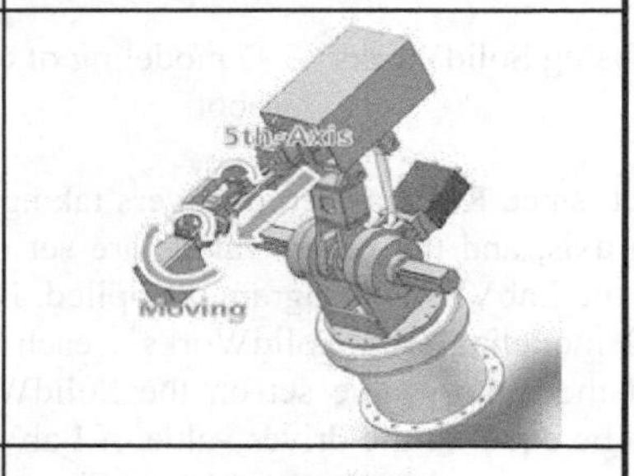
6	

Fig. 10 Setting-up of axes for RS2

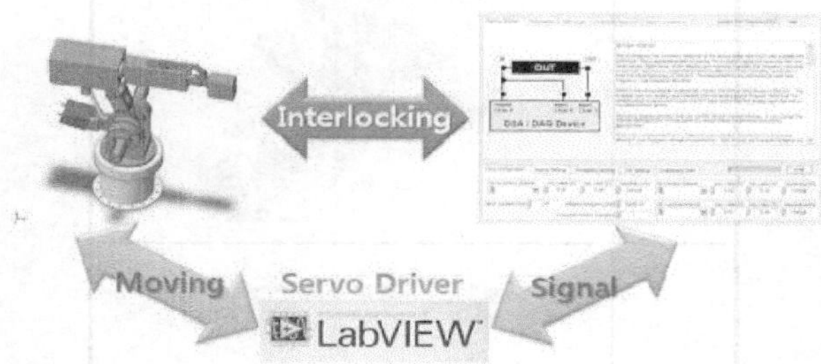

Fig. 11 Interlocking program configuration

After setting up the axes of RS2 in SoildWorks®, the motion-blending program created in LabVIEW® is downloaded into the virtual drivers of SoildWorks® modeling, and then SoildWorks® and LabVIEW® –based simulation is performed. Figure 12 shows the simulation result of PTP motion and joint-linear blending. Trajectories of circular–joint, and linear-circular blending were also identifiable through the simulation result of Fig. 13.

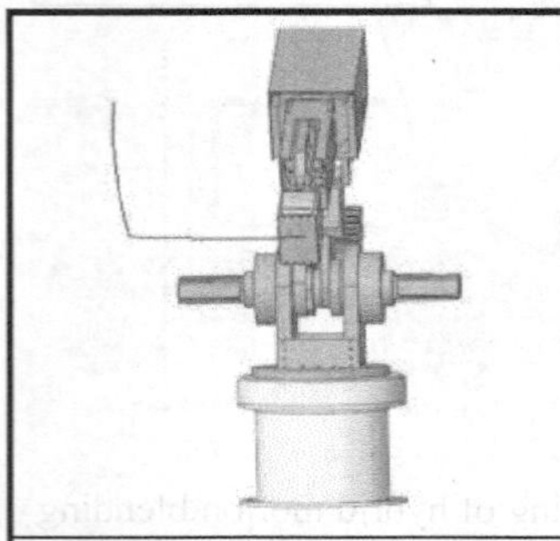	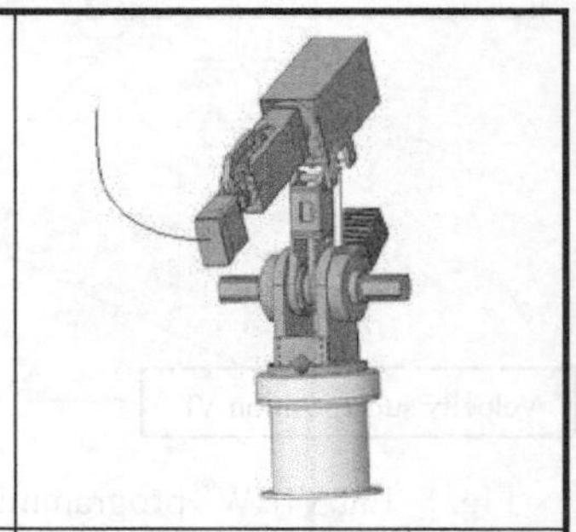
PTP motion	Joint - Linear Blending

Fig. 12 Simulation result of PTP motion and joint-linear blending

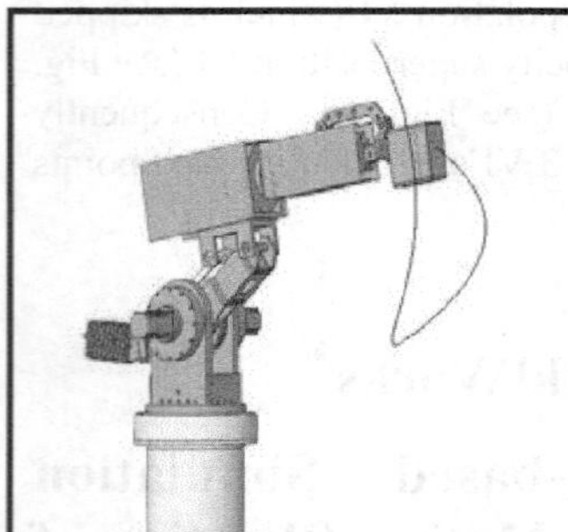	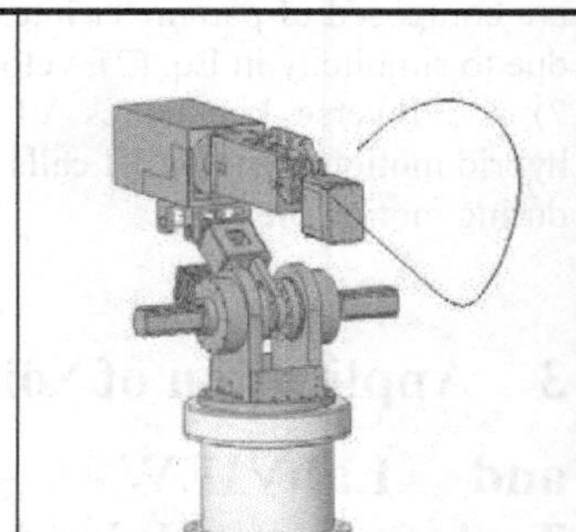
Circular – Joint Blending	Linear - Circular Blending

Fig. 13 Circular– joint and linear–circular blending simulation

Such simulation results make it possible to figure out the problems which can take place when the programs made with LabVIEW® is applied to RS2 in advance, and thereby we can take measures responding to the problems. To be specific, before applying the hybrid motion blending programs using LabVIEW® to RS2 directly, we can check the feasibility of the program in advance to avoid mechanical interference between links or joints. Thus this simulation technique can make RS2 avoid a severe collision between links or disconnection of harness around a wrist when excessive joint angles can be given by rough motion blending.

In addition, by incorporating the RS2 model of SolidWorks®, Recurdyn® V7(multi-body dynamics analysis program tool) will be used for checking whether the velocity generated by the motion blending algorithm can exceed the maximum of velocity at the end-effector of RS2. Without the simulation technique, the implementation of hybrid motion blending algorithm on RS2 can result in the damage (especially severe twisting of harness nearby a wrist) of robot since it make the joint servo motors of RS2 go over the travel speed ranges of joints.

Figure 14 shows the 3-D modeling of RS2 using Solidworks® in Recurdyn® V7, to which hybrid motion blending algorithm given by Eq. (8) is input. The hybrid motion blending simulation can make us check if RS2 could be damaged for excessive joint velocities out of joint velocity limits, which might come from the blending algorithm. The typical example of damage is the entangling of harness nearby the wrist part of RS2. Figure 15-(a) shows an example of joint-linear CP path in terms of Z-position of end-effector. The joint-linear motion blending simulation using Recurdyn® V7 results in the profile of velocity magnitude (or speed) for the end-effector of RS2, as shown in Fig. 15-(b). In this figure, the average end-effector speed was confirmed as about 40 mm/s within the speed limit of 80 mm/s. This means that the hybrid motion blending algorithm can be implemented on RS2 safely for the given joint-linear CP path of Fig. 15-(a). For the CP path (see Fig. 14-(a)) with reliable simulation result of Fig. 15-(b), the motion blending algorithm given by Fig. 8 is now implemented on RS2.

Fig. 14 Recurdyn® V7 simulation

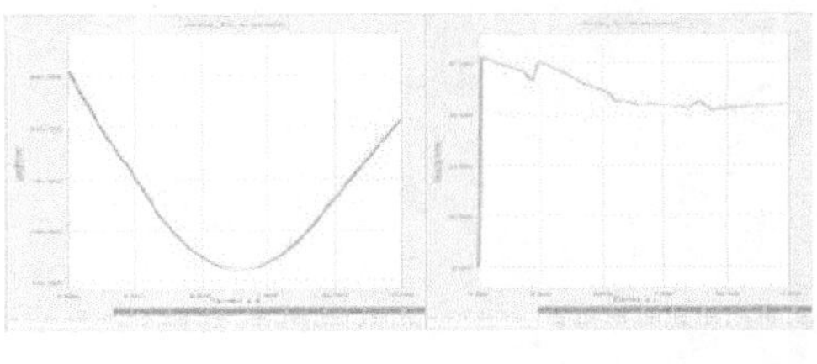

a) Z-Position of End-effector b) Velocity of End-effector

Fig. 15 Velocity profile of end-effector during joint-linear motion blending in Recurdyn® V7 simulation

4 Implementation and Measurement of Hybrid Motion Blending on RS2

In order to evaluate the performance of hybrid motion blending, simple PTP (*i.e.*, linear-linear) is also physically implemented on RS2. The implementation results of hybrid motion blending and PTP are compared in terms of vibration magnitude and travel time by using the vibration testing equipment of Medallion of Zonic®. It can be noticed from Figs. 17 and 18 that, as shown in TABLE I, the vibration peak of joint-linear motion blending has been reduced to 1/10, compared to that of PTP. This comparison is clarified through TABLE I. Besides the travel time of joint-linear motion blending for a given path of Fig. 15-(a) is 3 s while that of PTP is about 5 s. Therefore the joint-linear motion blending is with less vibration and shorter travel time when compared to the PTP, by implementing two algorithms on RS2. For reference, Fig. 19 shows the captured hybrid motion blending pictures of RS2.

Fig. 16 vibration measurement of RS2

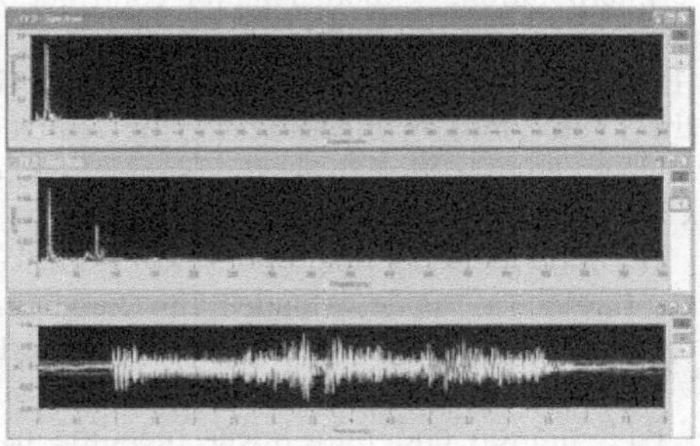

Fig 17 Result of vibration measurement for PTP

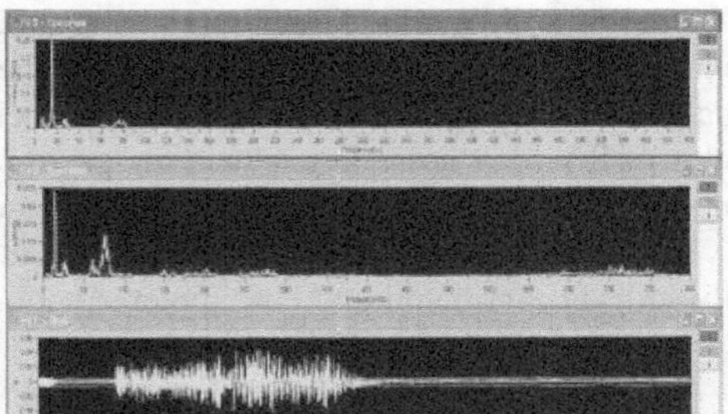

Fig. 18 Result of vibration measurement for joint-linear Blending

Table. 1 Vibration Acceleration of Motion

MOTION TYPE	G[RMS] IN X-COORD.	G[RMS] IN Y-COORD.	G[RMS] IN Z-COORD.	TIME (S)
PTP	0.2596	0.7526	0.02329	5
Hybrid motion blending	0.0025	0.0052	0.0021	3

Fig. 19 Joint-linear motion blending

5 Conclusion

In this paper, the lab-manufactured 6-axis articulated robot (RS2) has been used for investigating motion blending technology in a laboratory. Especially a CP motion blending (hybrid motion blending) in 3-dimensional space for RS2 was realized by using LabVIEW® programming, based on a parametric interpolation. Another major contribution of this paper is the proposal of motion blending simulation technique based on LabVIEW® and SolidWorks®, in order to figure out whether the hybrid motion blending can be realized before actual implementation. Moreover, this simulation technique can check any interference between links. Setting up the axes of RS2 in SoildWorks®, the motion-blending program generated in LabVIEW® is downloaded into the virtual drivers of SoildWorks® modeling, and then SoildWorks® and LabVIEW® –based simulation is performed. The simulation results of PTP motion and joint-linear blending as well as circular–joint and linear-circular blending were also identifiable through simulations. In addition, by incorporating the RS2 model of SolidWorks®, Recurdyn® V7 has been used for checking whether the velocity generated by the motion blending algorithm can exceed the maximum of velocity at the end-effector of RS2. In order to evaluate the performance of hybrid motion blending, simple PTP (*i.e.*, linear-linear) was physically implemented on RS2 as well as hybrid motion (especially joint-linear) blending. The implementation results of hybrid motion blending and PTP was compared in terms of vibration magnitude and travel time by using the vibration testing equipment of Medallion of Zonic®. It has been confirmed that the hybrid motion blending is with less vibration and shorter travel time when compared to the PTP, by implementing two algorithms on RS2.

6 Acknowledgement

This research was supported by Basic Science Research Program through the National Research Foundation of Korea(NRF) funded by the Ministry of Education, Science and Technology (2011-0013902).

7 References

[1] J. H. Ju, W. J. Chung. “A Study on error Analysis and Hybrid Motion Control of LabVIEW® –based 3-axis SCARA Robot”, *School of Mechatronics, Changwon National University, 2008.*

[2] D. Y. Kim, W. J. Chung. “Development of a new weaving Algorithm using a Bezier Spline and A study on the Realization of CP(Continuous Path) Motion with Jerk Continuity”, Master of Engineering treatise, *School of Mechatronics, Changwon National University, 2004*.

[3] Spong, M. and M. Vidyasagar, ”Robot Dynamics and Control”, John Wiley and Sons, 1989, ISBN 047161243X

[4] Y. O. Chung, J. C. Ryu and C. K. Park, "A new method for Solving the Inverse Kinematics for 6 D.O.F. Manipulator," Korean Automatic Control Conference, Vol. 1, No 2, pp.557-562, 1991.

[5] Fu, K. S. Gonzalez, R. C. and Lee, C.S.G, 1987, Robotics, McGraw-Hill, New York, pp. 163-189.

[6] National Instruments Corporation. “Motion control Fundamentals course Manual”, 2002-2004.

[7] C. D. Jung, W. J. Chung, D. S. Lee. “Application of SoildWorks® and LabVIEW®–based Simulation Technuque to Gain Tuning of a 6-axis Articulated Robot” CSC 2012, Vol. 1, pp.132-138, 2012.

Application of Simulation-X® based Simulation Technique to Notch Shape Optimization for a Variable Swash Plate Type Piston Pump

Jun Ho Jang[1], **Won Jee Chung**[1], **Dong Sun Lee**[1] and Young Hwan Yoon[2]
[1] School of Mechatronics, Chansgwon National University, Changwon-si, Gyeongsangnam-do, South Korea
[2]**102-707** Sinbanpo Hanshin Apt., Jamwon-dong, Seocho-gu, Seoul, Korea

Abstract – *This paper focuses on the development of a simulation technique that can calculate the reduction effect of the pressure/flow ripples. First,, the theoretical kinematic analysis according to the variable swash plate angle will be presented to establish the mathematical theory of single piston in order to design single piston pump using the Simulation-X®. Based on this kinematic analysis, the simulation of variable swash plate type axial piston pump will be conducted by changing a notch shape in the valve plate part through modifying the opening area of intake and discharge and thereby figuring out the pressure of outlet. The simulation result according to notch type will show that a V type notch results in smaller pressure pulsation, compared with a circular type notch. Using one-dimensional simulation model of single piston pump, we will connect nine piston pump models by using Simulation-X® for the overall variable swash plate type piston pump, and then proceed with investigation through simulation for searching for the optimal notch design specifications for minimizing pressure and flow ripples. It can be pointed out that the contribution of this paper can be referred to as a the development of Simulation-X® based Simulation Technique to be applied to notch shape optimization for a variable swash plate type piston pump.*

Keywords: Simulation-X® based Simulation Technique, Variable Swash Plate Type Piston Pump, Notch Shape Optimization, Circular Type Notch, V Type Notch, Pressure Pulsation, Flow Ripple.

1 Introduction

Hydraulic systems have been used broadly for construction equipment due to significantly higher power capacity. In addition, most hydraulic parts have a strong durability, which well suits the characteristics of construction equipment in rough work environment. [1] In particular, an excavator's track driving motor or a piston pump needs consideration for the safety of a driver, requiring durability of higher standard. In the case of hydraulic piston pump, mechanic noise from pressure pulsation and flow ripples may heavily affect the safety and convenience of the driver. Moreover, pressure pulsation is generated through the flow ripples generated at the piston pump as well as the mutual interaction of the hydraulic transfer characteristics due to the construction of hydraulic circuits. Such pressure pulsation not only causes the mechanical vibration of system components but also becomes a cause of noise of the hydraulic system. Thus, to develop a simulation technique that can calculate the reduction effect of pressure pulsation / flow ripples becomes a very strong design support in terms of conducting a measure for low-noise of the hydraulic system.[2]

As for the swash plate type hydraulic pump, the power pushing the valve plate gets periodically changed as the pressure inside the cylinder is repetitively changing from low-pressure to high-pressure and also reversely. Such phenomenon generates a negative impact on speed control at a low-speed. Thus, it is necessary to mitigate the pressure variation rate inside the cylinder through optimizing the notch shape of the valve plate appropriately.[3] Currently, it is developed by several dedicated simulations for the swash plate type hydraulic system; however, none of these has a detailed description about the hydraulic model being utilized and there are many ambiguous points in terms of setting the parameters.[4]

This paper deals with pressure pulsation as to the single piston, and then completes the perfect piston shape through connecting nine pistons. This research is supported by kinematic analysis of piston displacement as to the single piston pump. After then, we will conduct investigation as to the pressure variation inside the cylinder, which may become a cause of pressure pulsation, and also carry out a study as to the flow ripples of the nine pistons. Finally we will proceed with investigation simulation for searching for the optimal notch design specifications for minimizing pressure and flow ripples. All simulation process will be performed by using one-dimensional hydraulic analysis software, Simulation-X®.

2 Kinematic Analysis of Piston Displacement for a Single Piston pump

The basic structure of the variable swash plate type axial piston pump is shown in Fig. 1. It is a structure to be pumped by piston motion due to the swash plate, and the control part for the angle of swash plate is composed of a yoke, a spring and a control valve, as depicted in Fig. 1.

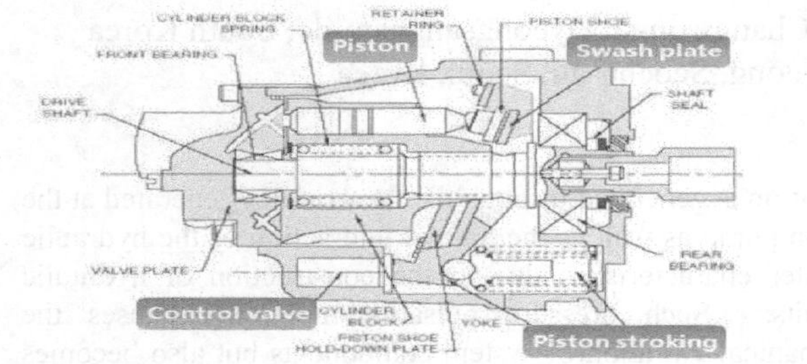

Fig. 1 Basic structure of swash plate type axial piston pump[6]

In this section, we examine the theoretical kinematic concept according to the variable swash plate angle. It aims to interpret in a kinematic term through the mathematical theory of single piston in order to design single piston pump using the Simulation-X®. As shown in Fig. 2, the displacement of piston can be expressed in the consecutive rotations of the drive shaft angle (φ) and the angle of swash plate (α). These rotations are shown in Fig. 3, *i.e.*, the concept diagram of single piston. Thereby a single piston pump has two degrees of freedom. The cylinder block and piston are composed of both the rotatory motion (φ) (which rotates based on the X_0 axis) and the rotary motion (α) of swash plate (which rotates based on the Z_0 axis). Notation of Fixed angle rotation[6] will be utilized as to the displacement of single piston since the single piston rotates by φ based on the fixed X_0 axis and then rotates by α based on the fixed Z_0 .[7] It is possible to calculate the location of the piston number 1 (Point P1) in the system of two degrees of freedom by the number of rotation (φ) of drive shaft and the angle of swash plate (α) as in Fig. 4.

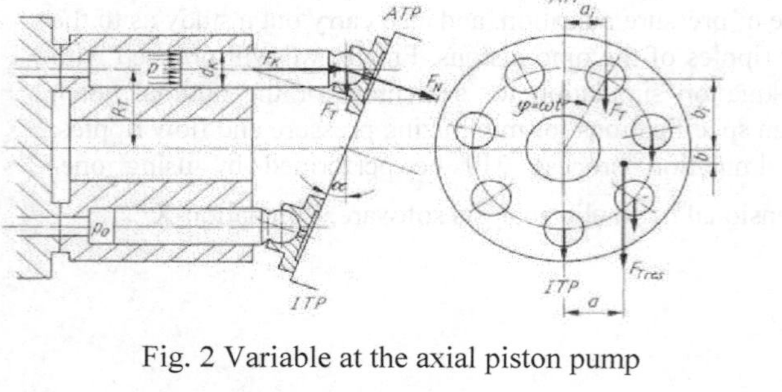

Fig. 2 Variable at the axial piston pump

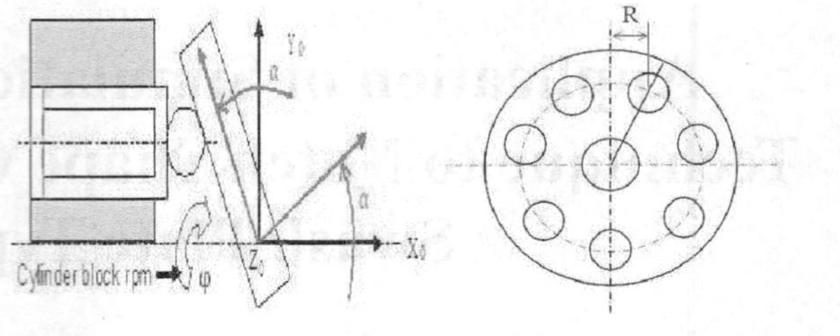

Fig. 3 Coordinate system in piston and swash plate[6]

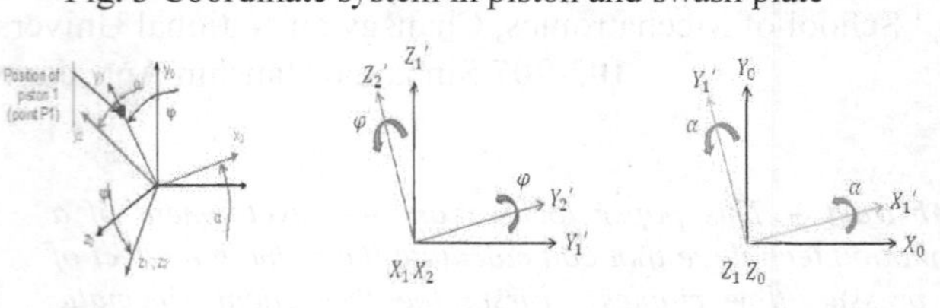

(a)	(b)	(c)
Coordinate system	Cylinder block rotation	Swash plate rotation

Fig. 4 Coordinate system corresponding to the 2-DOF

The rotation of cylinder block about X_0, followed by the rotation of swash plate about Z_0 can be deducted in eq. (1), which is summarized in eq. (2) of fixed angle of rotation.

$$
\begin{aligned}
{}^0_2R &= {}^1_2R \cdot {}^0_1R \\
&= R_Z(\alpha) \cdot R_X(\phi)
\end{aligned} \tag{1}
$$

$$
[X_0\,Y_0\,Z_0] \xrightarrow{R_{X_0}(\varphi)} [X_1\,Y_1\,Z_1] \xrightarrow{R_{Z_0}(\alpha)} [X_2\,Y_2\,Z_2] \tag{2}
$$

As shown in eq. (2), ${}^0_2R$ performs two consecutive rotations based on the fixed angle rotation as shown in Fig. 5. This leads to finding out the location of piston when doing the rotation of coordinate systems about the fixed X_0, followed by the rotation about the fixed Z_0.

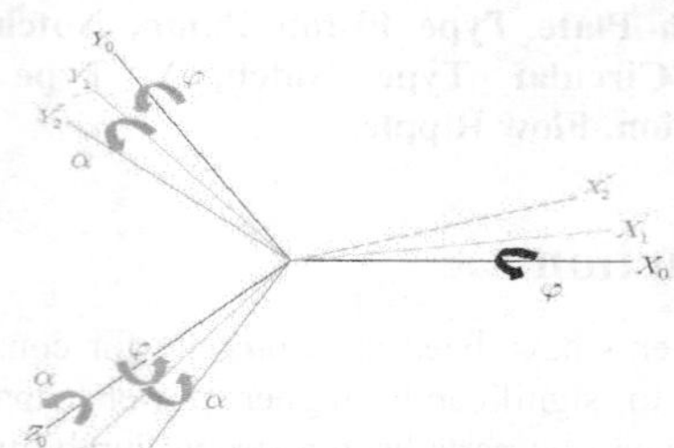

Fig. 5 Two fixed angle rotations

Now ${}^0_2R$ of eq. (1) can be given as follows:

$$
\begin{aligned}
{}^0_2R &= {}^1_2R \cdot {}^0_1R \\
&= R_Z(\alpha) \cdot R_X(\phi) \\
&= \begin{vmatrix} \cos\alpha & -\sin\alpha & 0 \\ \sin\alpha & \cos\alpha & 0 \\ 0 & 0 & 1 \end{vmatrix} \cdot \begin{vmatrix} 1 & 0 & 0 \\ 0 & \cos\phi & -\sin\phi \\ 0 & \sin\phi & \cos\phi \end{vmatrix} \\
&= \begin{vmatrix} \cos\alpha & -\sin\alpha \cdot \cos\phi & \sin\alpha \cdot \sin\phi \\ \sin\alpha & \cos\alpha \cdot \cos\phi & -\cos\alpha \cdot \sin\phi \\ 0 & \sin\phi & \cos\phi \end{vmatrix}
\end{aligned} \tag{3}
$$

Lastly, the equation to find out the displacement of piston can be deducted as follows. In more specific, the location of piston with respect to the base coordinate system, *i.e.,* {0}, can be calculated as follows. As seen in eq. (4) , in the case of ${}^2P_{P1}$, it is the location of piston 1 seen from the coordinate system {2}. Then the consecutive rotation ${}^0_2R$ is performed on ${}^2P_{P1}$. In eq. (4), R denotes the radius of piston cyliner as shown in Fig. 3.

$$
\begin{aligned}
{}^0P_{P1} &= {}^0_2R \cdot {}^2P_{P1} \\
&= \begin{vmatrix} \cos\alpha & -\sin\alpha \cdot \cos\phi & \sin\alpha \cdot \sin\phi \\ \sin\alpha & \cos\alpha \cdot \cos\phi & -\cos\alpha \cdot \sin\phi \\ 0 & \sin\phi & \cos\phi \end{vmatrix} \cdot \begin{vmatrix} 0 \\ R \\ 0 \end{vmatrix} \\
&= \begin{vmatrix} -R \cdot \sin\alpha \cdot \cos\phi \\ R \cdot \cos\alpha \cdot \cos\phi \\ R \cdot \sin\phi \end{vmatrix}
\end{aligned} \tag{4}
$$

$$XO_{P1} = -R \cdot \sin\alpha \cdot \cos\phi \tag{5}$$

$$YO_{P1} = R \cdot \cos\alpha \cdot \cos\phi \tag{6}$$

$$ZO_{P1} = R \cdot \sin\phi \tag{7}$$

The only expression on the piston position in X_0, *i.e.*, eq. (5), is applied to the Simulation-X®-based model for one-dimensional anaylsis, as shown in Fig. 6, even though we have all the expressions of *x, y,* and *z* of the piston position. Especially, In the model of Fig. 6, the back lash element is added to the piston displacement in order to take dynamic effect between a swash plate and a piston cylinder block into consideration for Simulation-X®-based dynamic analysis. Thus, the single piston pump modeling has been completed as shown in Fig. 7 by using Simulation-X®.[8].

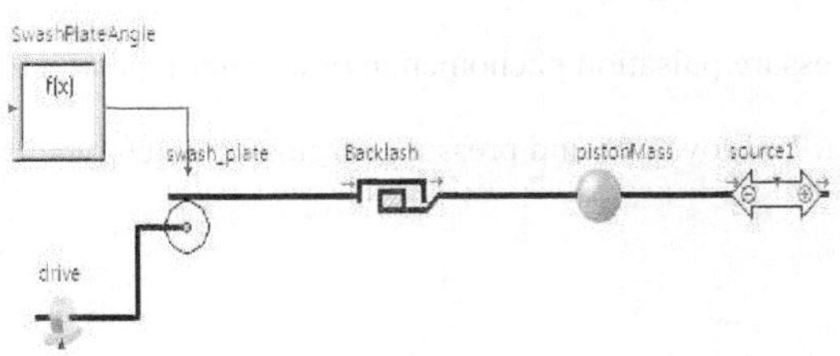

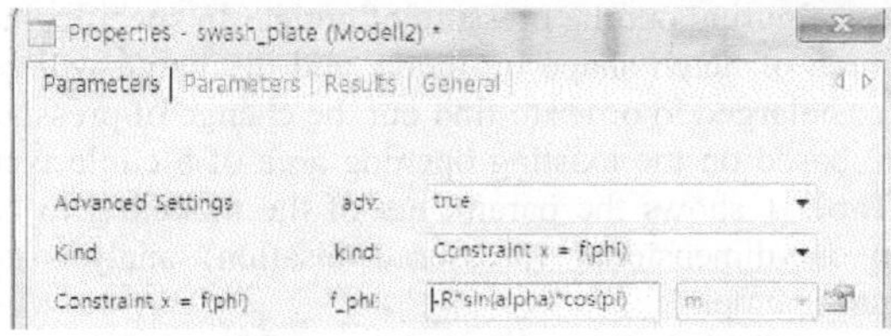

Fig. 6 Simulation-X®-based model of e variable swash plate single piston pump for one-dimensional analysis

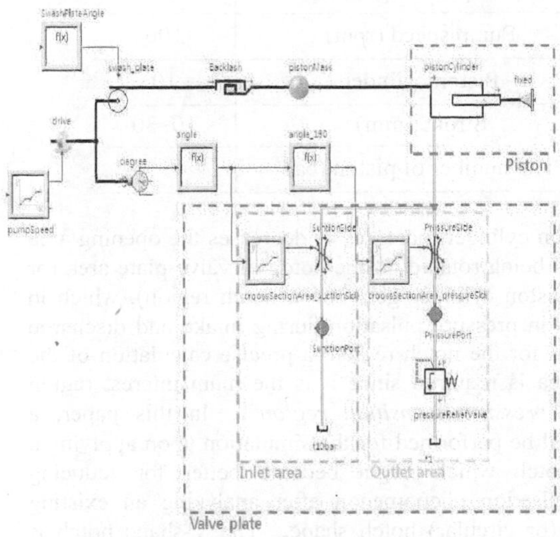

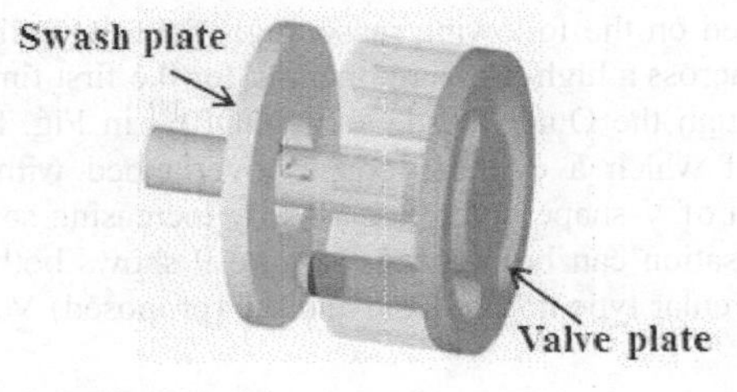

Fig. 7 Single piston model of swash plate type piston pump using the Simulation-X®

3 One-dimensional Simulation of Single Piston Pump

As mentioned in Section 2, Fig. 7 represents the single piston model of variable swash plate type axial piston pump for one-dimensional analysis for which our investigation will be conducted. This model is currently composed of the piston part and the valve plate part (inlet area and outlet area in the upper diagram of Fig. 7). Here hydraulic intake and discharge occur simultaneously in the valve plate part.

As for pressure pulsation, our investigation will be conducted by changing a notch shape in the valve plate part through modifying the opening area of intake and discharge and thereby figuring out the pressure of outlet. In specific, the opening area of notch shape on intake and discharge will be reduced or enlarged in order to find out the change of pressure pulsation, based on the existing opening area of a circle type notch. Table 1 shows the parameters of the modeling to be used for one-dimensional (pressure pulsation) analysis of single piston pump.

Table 1 Parameters of the model

Variable	Value
Swash plate angle (deg)	14
Pump speed (rpm)	100
Piston cylinder	10
Stroke (mm)	10~30
The number of piston (ea)	9

The piston cylinder increases or decreases the opening area of notch by being rotated on the notch of valve plate area (or when the piston cylinder gets into a notch region), which in turn results in pressure pulsation during intake and discharge strokes. As for the notch region, a precise calculation of the opening area is required since it is the main interest region called as "*pressure transition region*". In this paper, a research will be performed for the simulation upon applying a V-shape notch which might become better for reducing pressure pulsation phenomenon after analyzing an existing half-moon (or circular) notch shape. The V-shape notch is selected based on the following reasoning: when the cylinder port comes across a high-pressure opening for the first time as passing through the Outer Dead Point (ODP)[9] in Fig. 8, a flow area of which a cylinder port is overlapped with the opening area of V-shape notch is gradually increasing so that pressure pulsation can be reduced. Figure 9 shows both the (existing) circular type notch shape and the (proposed) V type notch shape.

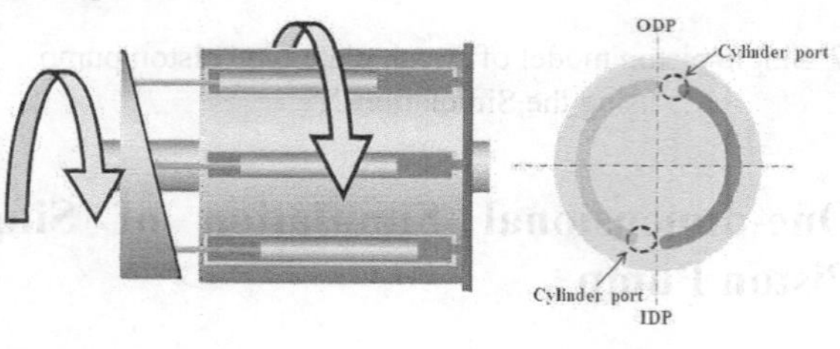

Fig. 8 Internal structure of swash plate type axial piston pump[4]

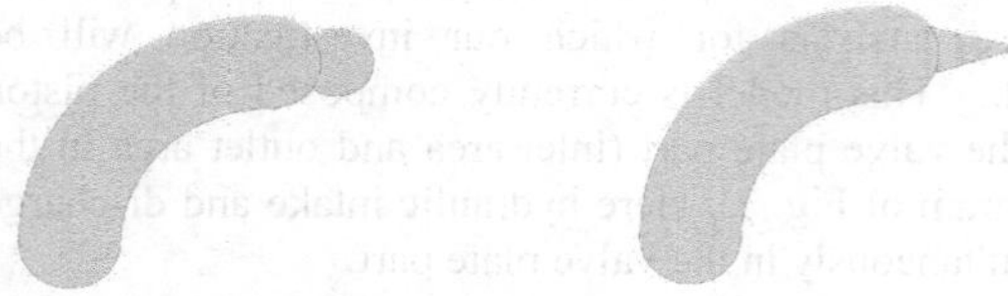

Circular type Notch V type Notch

Fig. 9 Circular type and V type notch shapes

Currently, the area of circular type notch is selected as $80mm^2$. We assume that the entire area of the V-shape notch can be regarded to be almost the same as that of the circular type notch. But the area in which the cylinder port is overlapped with the notch is different depending on both the location of cylinder port on the valve plate and the type of notch shape, when the cylinder rotates on the valve plate. Thus, according to notch type (circular type or V type), an investigation on pulsation is conducted through enlarging and reducing the overlapped area per percentage considering the existing entire circular type notch area as 100%..

The first simulation result according to notch type is illustrated in Fig. 10. Figure 10-(a) shows the overlapped area *vs.* cylinder port location for circular type notch (above) and V type notch (below). In addition, Fig. 10-(b) confirms the pressure pulation phenomenon of circular type notch, which is compared with that of V type notch in Fig. 11. Figure 11 confirms that the V type notch results in smaller pressure pulsation, compared with the circular type notch, since the flow area of which a cylinder port is overlapped with the opening area of V type notch is gradually increasing as shown in Fig. 10-(a).

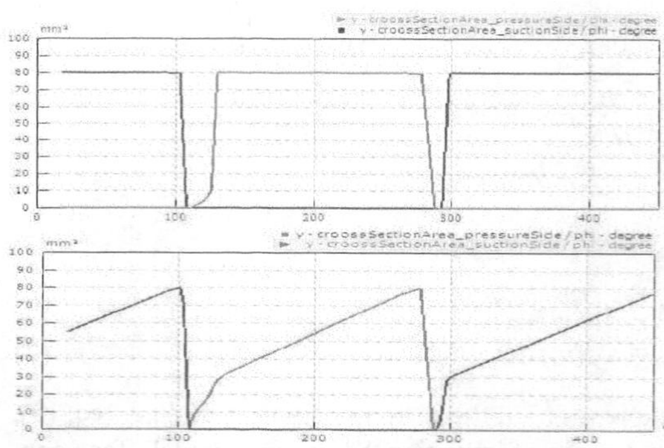

(a) Overlapped area *vs.* cylinder port location for circular type notch (above) and V type notch (below)

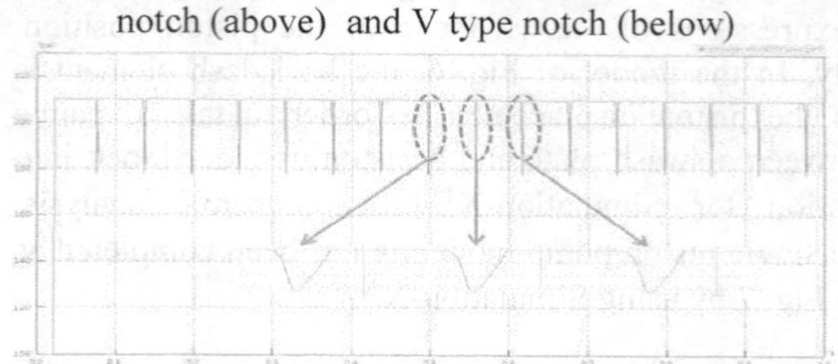

(b) Pressure pulsation phenomenon of circular type notch

Fig. 10 Flow area and pressure surging of notch type

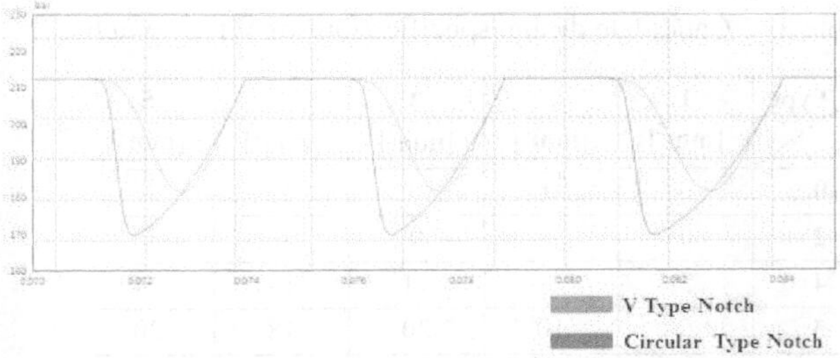

Fig. 11 Pressure pulsation *vs*. Notch type

Now we conduct the second investigation on pressure pulsation of circular type notch and V type notch as enlarging or reducing the area per percentage (80%, 90%, 100%, 110%, 120%) based on the existing entire (circular type notch) area. In Fig. 12, the location of cylinder port on the valve plate is assumed to be same for both the circular type notch and the V type notch. As shown in this figure, the V type notch results in smaller pressure pulsation when compared with the V type notch. This was already pointed out in Fig. 11 that the flow area of which the cylinder port is overlapped with the opening area of V type notch is gradually increasing as shown in Fig. 10-(a). On the other hand, the V-shape notch was not significantly affected by the overlapped area as shown in Fig. 12. Thus it is expected that the V type notch can reduce the impact of pressure pulsation, compared with the circular type notch since the overlapped area increases gradually as the cylinder rotates even though the area gets enlarged.

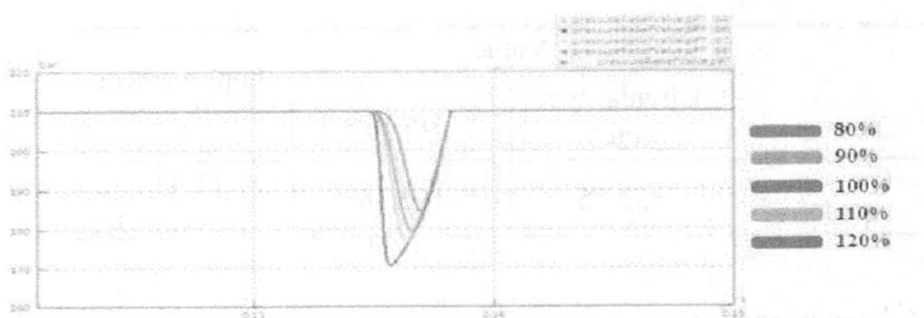

(a) Circular type notch

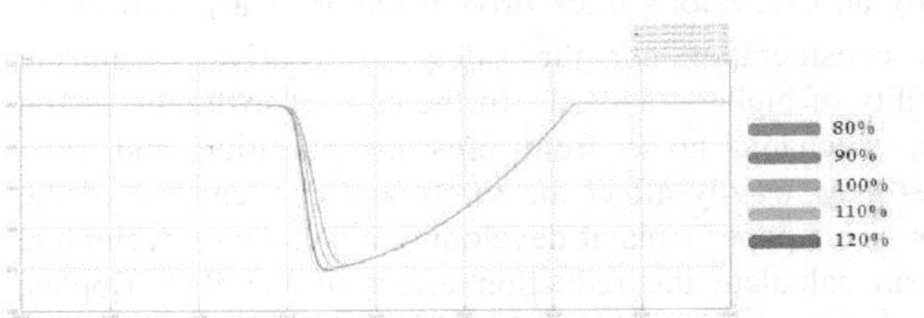

(b) V type notch

Fig. 12 Pressure pulsation of circular and V type notches

4 One-dimensional Simulation of Overall Variable Swash Plate Type Piston Pump Using Simulation-X

Using one-dimensional simulation model of single (variable swash plate type) piston pump (which was described in the previous section), we connect nine piston pump models by using Simulation-X® for the overall variable swash plate type piston pump as shown in Fig. 13. Thus far we have looked into the change of pressure pulsation according to the overlapped area of each notch. Now, we will proceed with investigation through simulation for searching for the optimal notch design specifications for minimizing pressure and flow ripples.

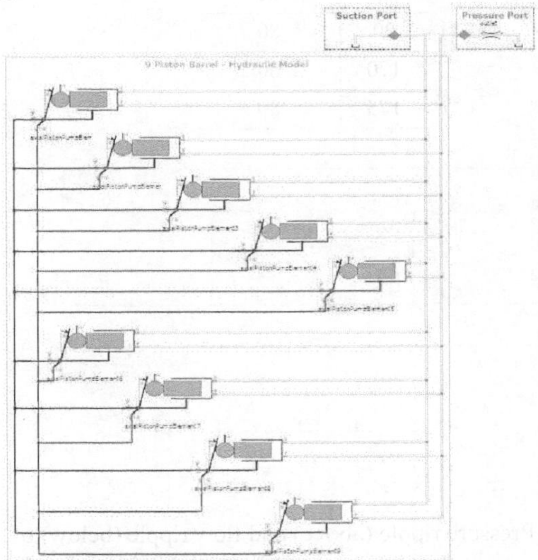

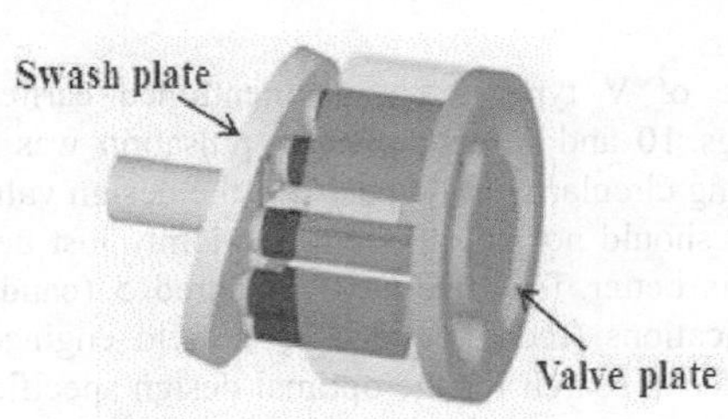

Fig. 13 Overall nine piston pump model using Simulation-X®

For this purpose, we first investigate the effect of circular type notch on pressure and flow ripples as follows. Table 2 shows the overlapped areas which are given by a design specification of circular type notch, according to the rotating angles of a cylinder port. This design specification has been illustrated in Fig. 10-(a). Based on the design specification of Table 2, we noticed that the overlapped area rapidly expands (when moving from 5 to 10 degrees). Figure 14 shows the result of simulation implemented by applying the design values of Table 2. As can be seen in this figure, pressure and flow ripples occur in the section where pressure rises from low to high.

Table 2 Parameters of Circular type notch model

deg	area (mm²)
0	0
2	0
4	0
5	0
8	65
10	80
20	80
170	80
175	80

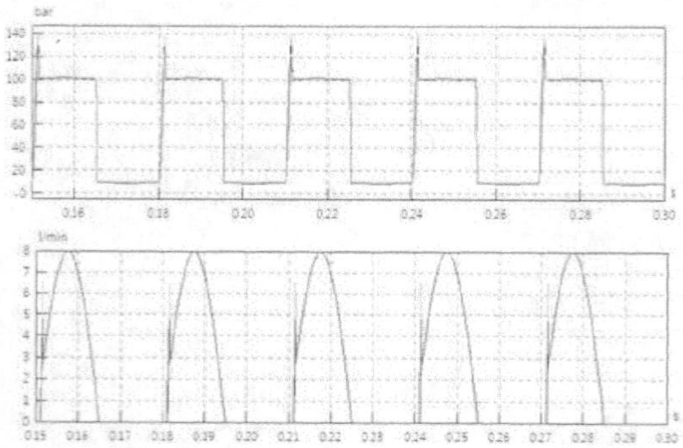

Fig. 14 Pressure ripple (above) and flow ripple (below) of circular type notch

In the case of V type notch, as mentioned earlier, we noticed in Figs. 10 and 11 that pressure pulsation was better than the existing circular notch type. But the design values of V type notch should not be applied randomly just because V type notch is better. Thus we have prepared 5 (candidate) design specifications (recommended by a field engineer) in Table 3 in order to search for the optimal design specification to minimize pressure and flow ripples. By applying each design specification to Simulation-X® -based simulation, we got the results shown in Fig. 15. Based on our examination through above simulations, type 5 (indicated by the green circle) results in no pressure and flow ripples, compared with other 4 design candidates. Also, as seen in Table 4, the best design candidate of type 5 for V type notch has decreased pressure peak by 26.4% (especially without overshoot (see the side figure of Fig. 15) when compared with that of circular type notch. Therefore the best design specification of V type notch can be obtainable by using one-dimensional simulation model of single (variable swash plate type) piston pump and then connecting nine piston pump models, based on Simulation-X®.

Table 3 5 Candidate design specifications of V type notch

deg \ Type	1 [mm²]	2 [mm²]	3 [mm²]	4 [mm²]	5 [mm²]
0	0	0	0	0	0
2	0	0	0	0	0
4	3	8	11	13	14
5	5	10	20	18	20
10	15	20	33	30	35
20	80	80	80	80	80
170	80	80	80	80	80
175	80	80	80	80	80

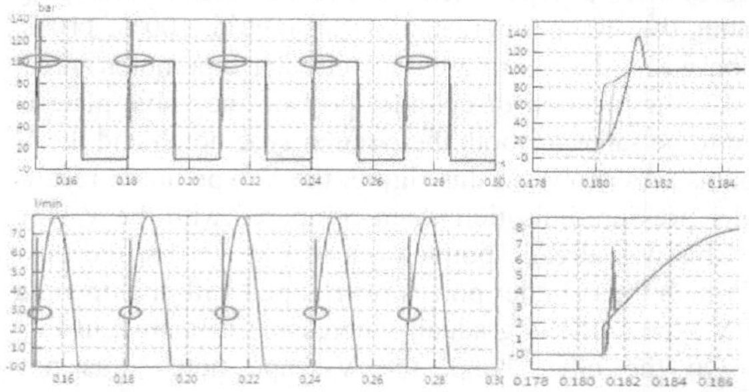

Fig. 15 Pressure Fluctuation and the Flux Pulse after the Alteration

Table 4 Comparion of Intial with Optimal Design

	Value		Improvement Rate
	Circular type notch	V type notch	
Pressure [bar]	139.16	102.36	26.4% (decrease)

5 Conclusion

Usually an excavator's track driving motor or a piston pump needs consideration for the safety of a driver, requiring durability of higher standard. In the case of hydraulic piston pump, mechanic noise from pressure pulsation and flow ripples may heavily affect the safety and convenience of the driver. This paper amis at developing a simulation technique that can calculate the reduction effect of the flow ripples, which becomes a very strong design support in terms of conducting a measure for low-noise of the hydraulic system.

In this paper, the theoretical kinematic analysis according to the variable swash plate angle has been performed to establish the mathematical theory of single piston in order to design single piston pump using the Simulation-X®. Based on this kinematic analysis, a single piston model of variable swash plate type axial piston pump has been conducted by changing a notch shape in the valve plate part through modifying the opening area of intake and discharge and thereby figuring out the pressure of outlet. The first simulation result according to notch type has shown that a V type notch results in smaller pressure pulsation, compared with a circular type notch, since the flow area of which a cylinder port is overlapped with the opening area of V type notch is gradually increasing.

Using one-dimensional simulation model of single (variable swash plate type) piston pump, we have connected nine piston pump models by using Simulation-X® for the overall variable swash plate type piston pump, and then proceeded with investigation through simulation for searching for the optimal notch design specifications for minimizing pressure and flow ripples. Therefor our contribution can be referred to as a the development of Simulation-X® based Simulation Technique to be applied to notch shape optimization for a variable swash plate type piston pump.

6 Acknowledgement

The authors of this paper was also supported by '' Domestic development of a driving device core module for 8~10 ton construction equipment'' of which project was conducted by Korea Industrial ComplеX (KICOX)..

7 References

[1] D. K. Noh, and J. S. Jang, "Shape Design Sensitivity Analysis of the Valves installed in the Hydraulic Driving Motor" Journal of The Korea Society for Fluid Power and Construction Equipments KFSC, 2012

[2] D. H. Jang, S. G. Lee, J. H. Kwon and S. H. Park, "A Study on Pressure, Flow Fluctuation and Noise in the Cylinder of Swash Plate Type Axial Piston Pump"

[3] S. H. Kim, Y. S. Hong, and D. M. Kim, "Influence of valve plate configuration on torque ripple of a bi-directional bent-axis type hydraulic piston pump" The Korea Society for Aeronautical & Space Sciences, Vol. 35, no.3, pp.231~237, 2007

[4] S. L. Choi, "A Basic study on simulation of flow Ripple in Piston Pump", 2011

[5] K. S. Fu, R. C. Gonzalez, and C. S. G. Lee, "ROBOTICS, Contral, Sensing, Vision, and Intelligence"

[6] Y. H. Yoon, J. S. Jang, and Y. B. Lee, "An Analysis of Dynamic Characteristics for Variable Swash Plate Type Axial Piston Pump" Journal of The Korea Society for Fluid Power and Construction Equipments KFSC, 2012

[7] K. J. Park, and J. H. Kim, "Robotics Design & Applications", 2010

[8] Y. H. Yoon, and J. S. Jang, "SimulationX, Multi-domain Simulation and Modeling tool for the Design, Analysis, and Optimization of Complex systems" Journal of The Korea Society for Fluid Power and Construction Equipments KFSC, 2012

[9] Y. Y. Lee "Hydraulic Engineering", 2012

[10] SimulationX user manual and library manual, ITI GmbH, 2011

Parallelization of a Multi-physics Code

William Dai, A.J. Scannapieco, Frederick Cochran, James Painter, Chong Chang
Los Alamos National Laboratory, Los Alamos, New Mexico, United States

Abstract - *Roxane* is a code recently developed at Los Alamos National Laboratory for multi-physics simulations. The physics capabilities include hydrodynamics, material mixing, radiation, magnetohydrodynamics, etc. This document is to present the main physics capability, basic data structures, parallelization, and IO. The focus will be on parallization. The data structures include data layer-out and adaptive mesh refinement. *Roxane* is in the stage of active development, and some of material presented here will possibly be changed in the near future.

Keywords: *numerical simulation, multiphysics, parallel*

1 Introduction

Roxane is a package for multi-physics simulations on Eulerian grids. The physics includes hydrodynamics, advection, three-temperature (3-T) radiation diffusion, ideal and resistive magnetohydrodynamics with circuits, linear solvers, material mixing, and real equations of state. The code is mostly written in Fortran, and a small part in C language.

Simulations are performed through adaptive mesh refinement (AMR). Although there are other kinds of AMR, such as block-based AMR and patch-based AMR, *Roxane* uses cell-based AMR, in which numerical cells are refined cell by cell.

A typical simulation through *Roxane* involves many materials. To effectively use computer memory, material properties in mixing cells are stored as link lists, and only non-zero values of the properties are stored. Isotopes of any material are similarly compressed and stored.

Roxane is a parallel code run on massively parallel computers. The parallel capability was late added after most physics packages and data structures were developed. The design principle of the parallel capability was to minimize the number of communication during each time step and to minimize the modifications in physics packages we had to make for the parallel capability.

The IO capability in parallel environments is for restarting, visualization, connection, and debugging, and it is built on top of MPI IO. Although *Roxane* is able to write arbitrary M files from N processors (N to M) for each dump event, currently N to 1 is the mode for users. The data in a restarting file are of two kinds, one for description of data, called attributes, for which processors have the same values, and the other for arrays that are distributed among processors. For visualization, meshes with AMR, unstructured meshes, and variables defined on the meshes are directly written into files.

To check the correctness of algorithms of physics packages and parallel implementation, a set of regression tests are run daily and weekly. Daily tests are for developers to check any modification of the codes and weekly ones are for more rigorous examinations.

2 Physics capability

In *Roxane*, hydrodynamics is described by the Euler equation. In our applications, physical viscosity may be ignored. Instead, in addition to numerical viscosity, artificial viscosity is typically introduced in calculations. Although the gamma law equation of state is included, *Roxane* uses real EOS tables to close the equations. Each of materials involved in simulations can have many isotopes. These materials are not necessarily in thermal equilibrium. Therefore, the mass density, pressure, energy, and flow velocity in the Euler equation are the collection of these materials.

Roxane accepts Cartesian, cylindrical, and spherical coordinates in one-, two-, and three-dimension. The hydro solver in *Roxane* is not sophisticated, so that various advanced mixing models could be easily incorporated into hydrodynamics. For a given mesh, all the variables are zonal, i.e., defined on volume. *Roxane* uses a dimension split technique to solve two- or three-dimensional hydrodynamics equation in a fixed grid. Therefore, one-dimensional solver is a building block for hydrodynamics. During each one-dimensional pass, momentum is defined on a staggered grid, called "panel".

Each one-dimensional pass may be divided into two steps, flow motion and advection. The flow motion is due to initial flow velocity and acceleration caused by pressure gradient and external force. This step is simple in coding. Following the flow motion is advection, and advection is much more complicated in coding because of the nature of many materials and isotopes.

Before advection takes place, *Roxane* constructs material interface within any mixed cells based on the distribution of mass and volume of each material on each cell. Currently Young's linear interface reconstruct procedure is used to handle materials in mixed cells, and this procedure is expected to be replaced by a modified interface reconstruct algorithm that will result in smoother interfaces between materials. The interface orientation in a mixed cell is determined by the distribution of the material in neighboring cells, and the location of interface is calculated through volume fractions occupied by the materials within the cell.

The advection of materials and their isotopes making the hydrodynamics step a little more complicated. First, each material in each cell is advected through hydrodynamics and the reconstructed material distribution. Each isotope of a material is assumed uniformly distributed within the reconstructed volume of the material.

Magnetohydrodynamics in *Roxane* is mainly to model laboratory experiments that involve the interaction between MHD waves, diffusion of magnetic field in materials, and circuits in experimental devices.

Radiation in *Roxane* could be in the diffusion limit. Temperatures of radiation field, electrons, and ions are coupled and are allowed to be different from each other. Diffusion problems in *Roxane*, such as diffusion of magnetic field in MHD, diffusion of temperatures of radiation fields, electrons, and ions, result in large algebraic systems at each time step. These systems are nonlinear, and material properties involved in the system depend on solutions. The size of time step is such chosen that the material properties will not experience any significant change, and therefore, the material properties of the previous time step are used to calculate the solutions of the current time step.

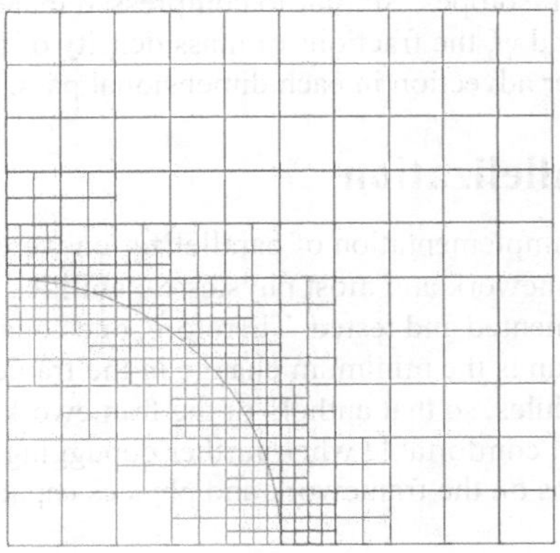

Figure 1. Illustration for a radiation mesh. Different colors represent different materials.

To avoid unknown material properties in mixed cells, mixed cells in an AMR mesh are divided into a set of polygons through material interface reconstruction. Figure 1 shows an example of the "unstructured mesh". In each of these polygons, the material is pure, and its material properties are known. Therefore, the linear solver is for a set of unknowns defined on these polygons, i.e., the diffusions or linear systems are solved on unstructured meshes. Although mixed cells are a small part of cells for many problems, all clean (unmixed) cells are treaded as unstructured cells in the linear solver.

The iterative conjugate gradient method converges slowly, and it is particularly slow for large linear systems. To increase the convergence, multigrid methods are used as preconditioner for the conjugate gradient method. Multigrid methods are particularly efficient because mathematical systems exhibit multiple scales of behavior, for which basic relaxation methods, such as conjugate gradient method, exhibit different rates of convergence for short- and long-wavelength components.

Since the diffusion problems in *Roxane* are described on unstructured meshes, the geometric multigrid is too difficult to implemented, an algebraic multigrid method is used. Unlike geometric multigrid method, algebraic multigrid method automates the coarsening process and interpolation without geometry information. Actually coarsening operators and interpolation can be derived directly from underlying matrices without any references to the grids.

3 Adaptive Mesh Refinement

The use of cell-based mesh refinement technique has quite long history in our institution. Cell-based AMR refines only those cells that are supposed to be refined. In cell-based AMR, cells, including the cells that are not refined, are treated cell by cell. The connectivity of meshes is described by connectivity arrays.

After a mesh of cell-based AMR is generated through the initial setup or refinement and coarsening during simulations, the connectivity between cells must be built before any calculation could precede, such as spatial derivatives of variables. There are several ways to establish the connectivity. Some take advantage of the nature of structured cells, but at the cost of much more memory footprint. Others describe the connectivity in the way for unstructured meshes.

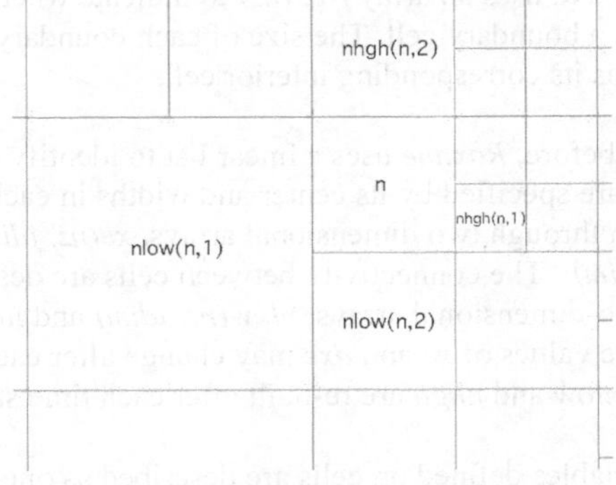

Figure 2. The illustration of the connectivity arrays, nlow and nhgh around cell n.

Roxane takes advantage of the nature of structured cells but with very small memory cost. Two arrays, *nlow(1:nzone,1:dim)* and *nhgh(1:nzone, 1:dim)*, are used for the purpose. Here *nzone* is the number of cells on my processor, including ghost cells (which will be discussed late), and *dim* is the dimensionality of the problem. The value *nlow(nz,i)* gives the cell id of the lower side of the dimension *i*. In the case of one-dimensional problem, this neighboring cell is uniquely determined. In the multi-dimensional case, *nlow(nz,i)* further refers to the cell that is at the lower end of any dimension other than the *ith*. Similarly, *nhgh(nz, i)* gives the neighboring cell of *nz* at the high end of the *ith* dimension, but at the lower end of any dimension other than the *ith*. This is illustrated in Fig.2.

The reason we could effectively use the concept of *nlow* and *nhgh* is that mesh is gradually refined, i.e., an immediate neighboring cell of any cell can only be one level higher or lower. This assumption is also guaranteed across processor interfaces. There are many methods to generate the connectivity arrays. *Roxane* uses a local KD-tree to set up *nlow* and *nhgh*. Each identity in the KD-tree is a rectangular cell. After the array *nlow* and *nhgh* are setup, the tree is not needed anymore until the mesh is changed, typically after one time step. A mixing cell is always refined to the highest level. Furthermore, if any neighboring cell is a mixing or it has different material, this cell will be refined. To resolve shocks, the location of shock fronts is always refined to the highest level.

4 Data structure

Roxane has its own data structures, some are good, and some need to be improved. Some are good for traditional computer platforms, but not good for the (anticipated) future computers.

Roxane currently imposes two kinds of boundary condition, one is the reflection boundary condition, and the other is the continuation boundary condition. For the convenience of the code developers to write the code uniformly for both interior cells and cells on the domain boundaries, *Roxane* introduces one layer of boundary cells attached to each simulation boundary, and uses an array *irdx(nz)* to indicate whether each cell, *nz*, is a boundary cell. The size of each boundary cell is the same as its corresponding interior cell.

As stated before, *Roxane* uses a linear list to identify cells, and each cell are specified by its center and widths in each dimension through two dimensional arrays, *xe(nz, idim)* and *dxe(nz, idim)*. The connectivity between cells are described by two two-dimensional arrays, *nlow(nz, idim)* and *nhgh(nz, idim)*. The values of *xe* and *dxe* may change after each time step, and *nlow* and *nhgh* are re-built after each time step.

Scalar variables defined on cells are described as one-dimensional array, such as *d(nz)*. Flow velocity is defined on panels and described by two two-dimensional arrays *vl(nz, idim)* and *vh(nz,idim)*.

We have to mention two points about the cells in *Roxane*. First, every cell is an active cell, and there are no parent cells. Second, due to historic reason, cells in *Roxane* are sorted according to their levels. As the result of sorting, base cells, whose level is 0, are listed at the beginning in the list of *nzone* cells. After these cells are the cells with level 1, and so on.

To effectively use computer memory, *Roxane* stores only no-zero values of material properties, and these material properties include mass density fraction *df*, volume fraction *vf*, energy fraction *ef*, material strength fraction, such as *txxf*, *tyyf*, magnetic field intensity fraction *hf*, etc.

The integer array in *Roxane*, *ist*, is used first to determine whether each cell is a clean cell (i.e., with one material) or a mixed cell (with more than one material). If *ist(nz)* is bigger than 0, then this cell is a clean cell, and the value is also id of the material. If for a particular cell nz, *ist(nz)* gives a negative integer, this indicates a mixed cell, and the integer, *iax (= -ist(nz))* gives the index which is used in other arrays for the first material in this cell. For example, *df(iax)*, *vf(iax)*, and *ef(iax)* gives the mass, volume, and internal energy fractions of the first material in the cell. For the second material in the cell and its material properties, the value of *nxtf(iax)* gives the index of the second material in the arrays *df*, *vf*, *ef*, etc. This procedure could continue until *nxtf(iax)* gives 0.

Materials in *Roxane* may have different isotopes. The properties of these isotopes have to be stored in memory during calculations. Since it is possible to have many isotopes, but each of them spreads only over a fraction of simulation domain, *Roxane* stores only non-zero values of material properties of isotopes. Similar to compressed material data, such as *df* and *vf*, the fractions of mass density of isotopes changes after advection in each dimensional pass.

5 Parallelization

Design and implementation of parallelization were introduced after the framework and most physics capabilities in *Roxane* were implemented and tested. Therefore, one constraint in parallelization is the minimum change in the framework and physics modules, so that authors of the framework and modules feel comfortable when further debugging or modifications on the framework and physics capabilities are needed.

The parallelization includes partitioning, identifying constructing ghost cells, communication, link from another code project, and comparison between serial and parallel calculations. The design principle of the parallization includes the following three aspects: avoid arrays that has the global size, such as *map_global_to_local(globalid)*, avoid the use of global id, and use less number of communications.

When a simulation runs on more than one processor, mesh and its associated variables are distributed among the processors. The initial mesh used in *Roxane* is generated through Rage, another code project at our insititution. Although Rage and *Roxane* both deal with structured cell-based AMR, they order cells differently. As a result of the different ordering, the part of the initial mesh on each processor may be disconnected in *Roxane*. Therefore, the first task in parallelization was to make the simulations correctly run on this disconnected partition.

At the early stage of development of parallel, for domain partition we intended to depend solely on the open software *Zoltan*, developed by Sandia National Laboratories. But, during the implementation of our parallel strategy, we also developed our own tool for domain partition. There were a couple of reasons for us to do this. First, even if we use *Zoltan*, we have to pack, unpack, implement communications, and reconstruct *Roxane* data structures, which is the majority work of domain partition. Second, a simple partition tool is desired for possible future modification of codes on future computers. There are several common approaches for domain partitions in *Zoltan*, and all the approaches work well for *Roxane*. The home-grown tool uses only bisection, which results in a rectangular domains for each processor.

To avoid additional communications, *Roxane* requires that all the cells generated from a same base cell (i.e., a cell whose level is 0), will be always on the same processors. This constraint eliminated the complexity and many communications. Otherwise, if an interface between processors is along with an interface between refined cells at one instant, the coarsening of the cells will be different from a serial calculation unless more communications are introduced. As expected, this constraint makes load balance imperfect, particularly when the number of base cells on each processor is small. Considering that any load balance in real problem depends on many factors, such as number of material, the number of isotopes of the materials on cells, and the load balance of physics packages imported from other codes, a perfect balance is almost impossible for real problems, unless other parallel strategies, such as task list, are used.

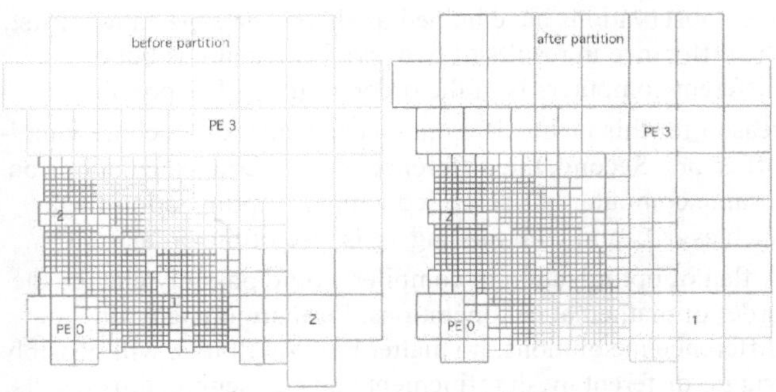

Figure 3. An example of repartition among four.

The input of the domain partition is any given partition. The domain of a processor can be disconnected, and some processors could have zero cells. The partition tool will repartition the simulation domain according to the number of cells and a weighting function *w(nz)* that gives a relative weighting factor of each cell *nz*. Typical weighting functions are based on the number of materials on each cell, *w(nz) = 1 + 0.1 * nmat,* or *w(nz) = w(nmat, physics).* During the repartition, there is no processor own more than its own cells at any instant, and there is no global index in use (this is only true for the home-grown tool). Figure 3 shows an example of repartition among four processors. Each color in the figure shows the domain of one processor. In the input, processor 2 has a disconnected domain.

For domain partition, the following procedure is executed after each time step.

- ∞ Check load balance.
- ∞ If load is balanced, do nothing. Otherwise, do the following.
- ∞ Re-partition to determine the future owner of each cell.
- ∞ Create a set of buffers, pack coordinates, variables, and material data of those cells that will go to other processors, and send each of buffers to a targeting processor.
- ∞ Create another set of buffers to receive data from a set of processors for new cells.
- ∞ Unpack the buffers received from other processors add new cells into the remaining list of cells.
- ∞ Build link lists for material and isotope data for the cells coming from other processors.

Partition or repartition deals with only real cells (contrary to ghost cells). After (re)partition at the initial time or after one time step, ghost cells are to be included in each processor before any physics calculation.

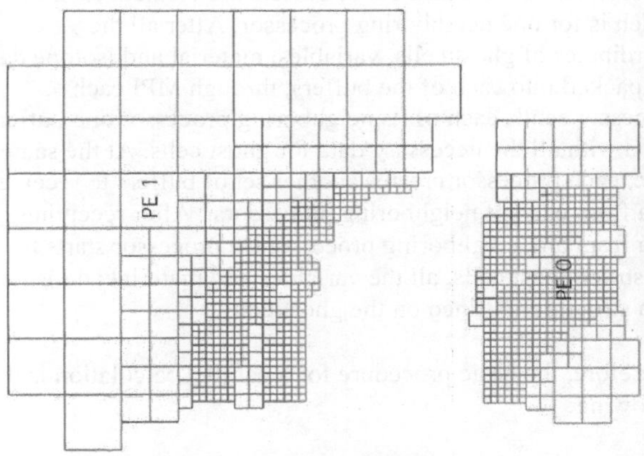

Figure 4. An illustration of two layers of ghost cells.

Several considerations were in the design to build ghost cells. First, we allow any domain partition as an input, rectangular or non-rectangular domains, connected or disconnected domains, base-cell partition or others. Second, each processor communicates only to its neighboring processors. Third, at no instant, one processor owns more cells than those cell on its own domain, and no global arrays and indices are involved. Fourth, for the need of future numerical solvers, the number of layers of ghost cells is a parameter or an input of a subroutine (function) call. Last, to reduce the number of communication, we pack all the variables together before the only communication, including coordinates of ghost cells, the variables with different types (integer, float, etc), compressed material and isotope data, and link lists, etc.

Figure 4 shows an example in which two layers of ghost cells are built. Figure 5 shows the partition among four processors, and the domain of one processor plus the 5 layers of ghost cells.

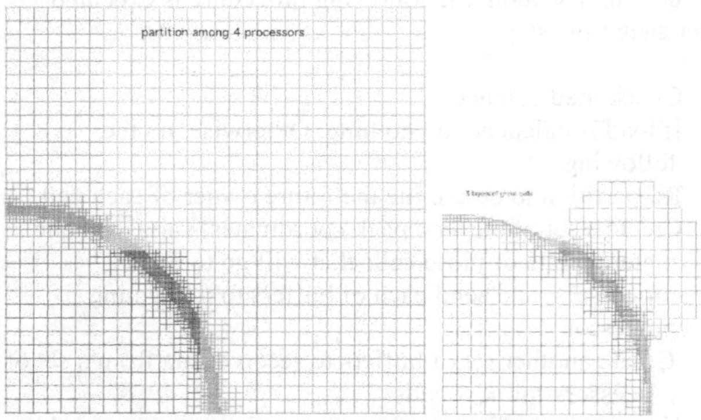

Figure 5. An illustration of 5 layers of ghost cells in a partition of five processors.

After ghost cells are identified, we will prepare for communication. As stated before, we tried to use only one communication to setup ghost cell geometry, variables defined on ghost cells, compressed material and isotope data, and link lists. To do that, we first identifies all the parameters, variables, material data, etc, which has to send to neighboring processors. After that, a set of buffers are created, each of which is for one neighboring processor. After all the coordinates of ghost cells, variables, material and isotope data are packed into each of the buffers, through MPI each processor sends each of its neighboring processor one buffer filled with all the necessary data for ghost cells. At the same time, each processor creates another set of buffers to receive data from each of neighboring processors. After receiving data from any neighboring processors, a processor starts to construct ghost cells, all the variables and material and isotope data structures defined on the ghost cells.

Therefore, the basic procedure for a parallel calculation is the following.

1) Determine the size of time step.
2) Determine neighboring processors
3) Identify cells that are ghost cells of neighboring processors, and identify neighboring processors.
4) Pack coordinates, variables, and material and isotope data into buffers.
5) Send each buffer to an appropriate neighboring processor.
6) Receive one buffer from each of neighboring processors.
7) Construct ghost cells from the buffer received from neighboring processors.
8) Construct data structures on ghost cells from the buffer received from neighboring processors.
9) Construct link lists for material and isotope data.

For AMR in parallel environments, special care must be taken for the constraint of smooth refinement and coarsening near interfaces between processors. In *Roxane*, this constraint is enforced on each refinement level, from the highest to the lowest levels.

For certain problems, *Roxane* has to get initial variables and material data from an output file of another code project. The variables and material data are defined on a set of triangles. Therefore, this capability is often called trilink. The cells in *Roxane* are refined based on material interfaces and shock fronts. Simulation boundaries in trilink are always initially refined because of the consideration of possible reflection boundary conditions, and they will be gradually coarsened during the next few time steps if the boundary condition is of reflecting.

The input file in trilink is often large in size. When it is linked to a parallel calculation, *Roxane* first partitions the simulation domain solely according to area of domains. At that time, *Roxane* has not built the simulation mesh, and has not read variables and material data yet. On the base of this partition, each processor reads a set of triangles and variables defined on the triangles. The area covered by the set of triangles is slightly larger than the domain of the processor, so that valid interpolation could be made for all the cells within the domain.

Correctness of physics models, numerical methods, and implementation of codes is of paramount importance. After we have the confidence on the models, methods, and implementation of serial calculations, the correctness of parallelization becomes important. The errors in parallelization are often subtle and difficult to identify. For the possible differences in simulation results between serial and parallel calculations, what is the expectation we can have?

Two observations have helped us shape our expectation. First, the difference in results of two serial calculations but on different computers is of the order $O(10^{-12})$. The possible reason for this is the different mechanisms for machine round-off errors. Second, the difference of two serial calculations on a same computer but compiled with any optimization flag, such as –O, and with the flag –g is also of the order $O(10^{-12})$. A flag of optimization in compiler would possibly change the order of mathematical operations. Furthermore, any tiny difference in solutions, no matter how small it is, will possibly trigger different mesh refinement and coarsening, thus results in different meshes, and finally gives significantly different results.

Therefore, we have asked for no difference between serial and parallel calculations when the flag –g in compiling is used. Specifically, we have used 10^{-40} as the criterion for the difference. The process to guarantee the difference within 10^{-40} is the one to find subtle bugs in both parallelization and serial code . Almost every difference has led us to find a new bug.

To compare the result between two calculations, for each cell in the parallel run, we have to first find the corresponding cell in the serial run through space coordinates, which is accomplished through KD-tree, and then compare the variables on the two cells. The tool for this comparison is available to users and developers. We find the such a tool is extremely useful to detect any tiny difference.

6 IO

For a long time, *Roxane* didn't have parallel IO capabilities, but had the one for data analysis and visualization tool POP, and had limited restart capabilities for certain problems through the IO module *pio* in *rage*. During the development of *Roxane*, particularly its parallel capabilities of various physics packages, parallel IO capabilities for restart and visualization became necessary and urgent. It seems that it will take a much long time to apply the module *pio* of rage to *Roxane*.

Current IO capabilities in *Roxane* are based on the module *hio*, which consists of two layers, *bio* and *meshio*. The layer of *bio* is a set of functions for writing, querying, and reading, which is based on MPI-IO. On the top of *bio*, there is another layer called *meshio* for AMR mesh, unstructured mesh, possible particles, and their associated variables.

Several users have asked for the structure of the header in a file written through *bio*. Actually, the structure of the header or tail depends on how users use *bio*, and it is designed to hide from users. Instead, querying functions are supplied to get all the data in file without knowing how the file was generated.

As stated before, the module *hio* consists of two layers. The first layer includes bio functions for writing, querying, and reading mata data and arrays. The second layer, *meshio*, is built on the top of bio for writing, querying, reading users' high level data structures, such as AMR meshes, unstructured meshes, particles, scalar and vector variables defined on these meshes and particles, and the relationship between variables and meshes.

Certain capabilities in *bio* and meshio are for possible future use. Currently, *Roxane* uses the mode *N-to-1* in *hio* and *meshio*, in which *N* processors in a parallel run write to *1* file at one dump event, such as restart dump and visualization dump. Another mode is *N-to-M*, through which *N* processors in a parallel run write to *M* files.

The module *bio* also has a buffering mechanism for problem-size arrays. The purpose of this method is to reduce the number of writing into a disk. The buffering IO could improve the IO performance by a factor between 4 and 20, depending on machines and problem sizes. For a typical run on 64 processors, the factor is above 10.

The buffering is the default IO in *Roxane*. To change the default, developers only have to change the parameter, *io_buffering*, from *.true.* to *.false.* All the tools related to *Roxane* could read restart files generated through either buffering or non-buffering IO.

High-level data structures in *Roxane* are directly written into visualization files through the module *meshio*, which is developed on the top of *bio*. The high-level data structures include AMR mesh, unstructured mesh in radiation solvers, triangle meshes in trilink, particles, and the variables defined on the meshes. For cell-based AMR meshes, *meshio* directly write *xe(nzone, dim)* and *dxe(nzone, dim).* The association between variables and meshes is automatically built and stored in files.

The module *meshio* supports a broad range of unstructured meshes, which include meshes with fixed shapes, arbitrary polygons, and arbitrary polyhedrons. Cells with a fixed shape may be triangles, quadrangles, pentagons, tetrahedrons, pyramids, wedges, and pentagon prisms. A cell may be a zone, or face, or edge, i.e., a mesh may be a zone-mesh, face-mesh, edge-mesh, and points. An edge-mesh may be one-, or two-, or three-dimensional, and a face-mesh may be either two- or three-dimensional. Cells of a zone-mesh may be made directly from nodes, or the cells may be made from edges, or the cells may be made from faces and the faces are then made from either edges or nodes.

The module *meshio* also supports ghost mesh elements, boundary faces, boundary edges, boundary nodes, slip faces, slip edges, slip nodes, etc. The variables associated with unstructured meshes may be node-variables, or edge-variables, or face-variables, or zone-variables, and variables may be scalars, or vectors, or tensors.

We should point out that the IO capability in *Roxane* has not gone through any optimization for file systems and hardware.

Roxane writes restart files through *bio* functions listed in the section above. Some data are written the *bio_attr_write* and others through *bio_write*. Although *bio_write* doesn't have to have valid offset and global size of array as inputs, writing one array through *bio_write* will result in one communication. To reduce the number of communications, *Roxane* calculates all the offsets and global sizes through one communication, and then call *bio_write* to write all the arrays.

Roxane writes only necessary but sufficient data for restart, and writes only data on real cells. To restart with the same number of processors, each processor just reads original data back from a file without reconstructing compressed material data. To restart with different number of processors, each processor has to read a part of original data or more than the original data, and thus has to reconstruct compressed material data. We have not implemented this yet. But, to restart with more processors than the original number, some processors read nothing from the file, and then all processors take advantage of repartition to restart the calculation.

Roxane writes its data in the subroutine *Roxane*_write, and reads the data in the routine *Roxane* _read. The restart files of *Roxane* are in the binary format, and could be read on either big-endian or little-endian computers.

An important part of a visualization file is the simulation mesh and its associated variables. The mesh is described by by two-dimensional arrays, *xe(nzone,dim)* and *dxe(nzone,dim)*. *Roxane* could directly write *xe* and *dxe* into the file for the mesh. Currently our main tool for visualization is *EnSight*. Visualization tool developed by Computational Engineering International, Inc. Since *EnSight* doesn't have any capability to directly accept arrays *xe* and *dxe* for visualization, *Roxane* also could convert *xe* and *dxe* to a representation of an unstructured mesh, and then write the unstructured mesh into file.

A reader is developed to visualize *Roxane* visualization files, no matter whether the mesh in the file is of AMR described by *xe* and *dxe* or is unstructured. Currently, the files could be visualized by both *EnSight* and *Visit,* a visualization tool developed in Lawrence Livermore National Laboratory.

Visualization files also could contain some redundant data for convenience in visualization. For example, the working variable, pressure, is never in a restart file, but it may in a visualization file. Also, *Roxane* writes several other meshes. Each of the meshes is actually a part of the simulation mesh occupied by one material. These meshes for materials overlapped with each other because of mixing. *Roxane* also writes all the mixing cells as another mesh so that users could easily view the cells that are mixed. On these meshes for materials and mixed cells there are also all the variables.

To reduce the size of visualization files, variables of floating point are written into files as single precision by default. But, considering that some developers may need variables of double precision for debugging, *Roxane* also could write the variables as double precision. For the size of files, by default, *Roxane* writes only a basic set of variables into files, but more variables could be added into files through commands in input files.

Roxane could write particles and variables associated with the particles into visualization files, and the reader is able to visualize the particles and their variables.

The reader of *Roxane* directly connects the data files to visualization tools, such as *EnSight* and *Visit* without explicit transformation of data files. To meet the requirement of some visualization tools, *Roxane* could also write ghost cells and valid values of variables on ghost cells into visualization files.

7 Regression tests

Roxane goes through its regression tests on main computers daily and weekly. There are three sets of tests. One is for serial calculations to test the correctness of algorithms and modifications of codes, the second set is to test correctness of parallel implementations, and the third is to test those parallel implementations involving third-party software.

For the tests of serial calculations, there is a standard file, called gold file, for each problem. These gold files are actually restart files. We use the same gold file for different computer platforms. Each test will generate a restart file, which will be compared against the gold file of the problem for all the variables. Since there are differences in solutions between different computers, and these differences are typically accumulated with time, the tolerance used in this set of tests may not be as small as it should be for certain test problems. For significant changes in algorithms, we have to re-produce or update those gold files.

For the second set of tests, there are no gold files. Each test on each machine will generate two files, which are restart files too, one from a serial calculation, and the other from parallel calculation. These two files then compare against each other for all the variables. Since numerical results of mathematical operations depend on the order of operations, such as a summation on cells, we are trying to avoid such operations in this set of tests. This is achieved through a command *"use_global_sum = .false."* in input files. Since some global sums in *Roxane* feed back to the dynamics of solutions, such as the refinement/coarsening criteria discussed before, this command actually changes the solutions. But it changes the solutions in both serial and parallel calculations, and in the exactly same way. This command is for parallel regression tests only, and the flag *use_global_sum* should be left as *.true.* (by default) in users' calculations.

In principle, the differences in solutions between serial and parallel calculations should be exactly vanishing for the second set of test problems. But, the executable of *Roxane* in daily regression tests is generated through compiling with optimization flags on. The optimization changes the order of mathematical operation, and changes the order differently on serial and parallel calculations. The optimization results in slightly different results between serial and parallel calculations during each time step. Furthermore, the difference between serial and parallel calculations could be accumulated with time, trigger different refinement and coarsening of meshes, and causes obvious mismatch in final solutions. This is the reason the tolerance is not as small as it should be in some of regression tests.

8 Acknowledgement

Elsie Sandford worked on regression tests, Paul Weber worked on the connection between *Roxane* data files and visualization tools, and Lori Pritchett worked on the integration of the partition tool Zoltan with *Roxane* and performance of calculations. The authors greatly appreciate their effort. LA-UR-12-23138

Global Sensitivity Analysis of Dam Erosion Models

Mitchell L. Neilsen
Dept. of Computing and Information Sciences
Kansas State University
234 Nichols Hall
Manhattan, KS, USA

Abstract

WindowsTM Dam Analysis Modules (WinDAM) is a set of modular software components that can be used to analyze overtopped earthen embankments and internal erosion of embankment dams. These software components are being developed in stages. The initial computational modules address routing of floods through the reservoir with dam overtopping and evaluation of the potential for vegetation or riprap to delay or prevent failure of the embankment. Subsequent modules incorporate dam breach analysis. Current work is underway to include analysis of internal erosion, non-homogeneous, zoned embankments, and the analysis of various other forms of embankment protection. The focus of this paper is on the overall software architecture and its integration with Sandia National Laboratories' DAKOTA software suite to perform global sensitivity analysis on a wide range of input parameters.

Keywords: Erosion, hydraulic modeling, sensitivity analysis, simulation, uncertainty analysis.

1. Introduction

WindowsTM Dam Analysis Modules (WinDAM) is a set of modular software components that can be used to analyze overtopped earthen embankments and internal dam erosion. The development of WinDAM is staged. The initial computational model addresses routing of the flood through the reservoir with dam overtopping and evaluation of the potential for vegetation or riprap to delay or prevent failure of the embankment. The first module, WinDAM A+, also incorporates the auxiliary spillway erosion technology used in SITES. However, unlike SITES, it allows a user to analyze up to three auxiliary spillways and embankment erosion on the dam. The next computational model, WinDAM B, incorporates dam breach analysis; i.e., the breach failure of a homogeneous embankment through overtopping and drainage of stored water in the reservoir. In addition, work is currently underway to include analysis of internal erosion, analysis of non-homogeneous embankments, and analysis of other forms of embankment protection. The two most common causes of earthen embankment and levee failure are overtopping and internal erosion [14].

WinDAM is designed to address the dam safety concerns facing the national legacy infrastructure of over 11,000 small watershed dams constructed with US Federal involvement over a seventy-year period. The US Department of Agriculture -Agricultural Research Service (USDA-ARS), US Department of Agriculture-Natural Resources Conservation Service (USDA-NRCS), and Kansas State University are working jointly to develop and refine this software. Public Law 78-534 – Flood Control Act of 1944 started the small watershed program, and it was followed by Public Law 83-566 – Watershed Protection and Flood Prevention Act of 1954. Starting in 1958, an average of one dam per day was constructed over a period of twenty years.

Figure 1. Internal erosion of USDA-NRCS structure

Most flood routing of dams before the middle 1960's was computed manually. Then, routing software on computers began to replace manual methods. In 1983, the USDA-SCS-ARS Emergency Spillway Flow Study Task Group (ESFSTG) was formed to develop better technology for earth spillway analysis. The ESFSTG collected data on dams that experienced either emergency spillway flow at least three feet deep or significant damage during a storm event. Approximately one hundred sites were selected for more in-depth evaluation and data collection, and data analysis began in 1990 from the field spillway data initially collected. Tests were conducted in the USDA-ARS outdoor Hydraulic Engineering Research Unit (HERU) Laboratory near Stillwater, Oklahoma, during this time to further understand spillway performance processes such as flow concentration, vegetal cover failure, surface detachment, and headcut migration. These findings were incorporated into the DAMS2 software, and then into Stability and Integrity Technology for Earth Spillways (SITES) software in 1994. The bulk length concept was replaced by SITES spillway erosion modeling technology in other USDA-NRCS references. Although SITES may be used to analyze existing dams and spillways, it was developed primarily for design and was developed over a period in which computational capability was much more limited than today. The legacy infrastructure of aging structures also means a transition from design of new structures to analysis of existing structures. For example, existing structures may overtop as a result of watershed changes or sediment deposition within the flood pool leading to inadequate spillway capacity. WinDAM builds on and extends the existing technology in SITES to provide the needed capability for these types of analyses.

Windows™ Dam Analysis Modules (WinDAM) is a collection of modular software components that can be used to design and analyze the performance of earthen dams. The focus of the initial collection of computational modules is to evaluate earth dams subjected to flooding that may result in overtopping of the dam embankment and auxiliary spillway(s) [1]. The reservoir routing model incorporated into the software includes outflow from a principal spillway, up to three auxiliary spillways, and over the top of the dam embankment. For conditions where overtopping of the embankment is predicted, the hydraulic attack on the downstream face can also be evaluated using the initial software modules in WinDAM A+. The downstream face of a dam is typically protected using vegetation or riprap. WinDAM A+ has been extended to include erosion and breach computations for conditions where the hydraulic attack exceeds that which can be withstood by the vegetal or riprap lining, and the resulting modules are in WinDAM B. The next version, WinDAM C, will incorporate analysis of failures caused by internal erosion or piping failures. To evaluate erosion in each auxiliary spillway, the SITES Spillway Erosion Analysis module with Latin Hypercube Sampling (SSEA+LHS) is integrated with WinDAM A+. The Embankment Erosion Module is extended to include a Breach Analysis Module. The current model assumes the dam has a homogeneous embankment. It is most applicable for the analysis or design of embankments constructed from cohesive soil materials. It is anticipated that the model will be expanded to handle zoned embankments in WinDAM D. The breach technology enabling this expansion is currently under development. Inputs to WinDAM include a description of the reservoir inflow hydrograph, reservoir storage capacity, all spillway properties, the dam cross section and profile, properties of the embankment, and input parameters for the breach analysis module. Inflow hydrographs can also be obtained automatically from other reach routing software, such as SITES 2005.1.6, SSEA+LHS [2], HEC-HMS [3], HEC-RAS, or WinTR-20 as shown in Figure 2.

Outputs include a description of the reservoir water surface variation with time, the hydrographs associated with outflow through each of the spillways and over the top of the embankment, and a description of the attack on the dam embankment and downstream embankment face. Output hydrographs can be directed to external reach routing software. Output information is generated in both text and graphical format. The software generates ASCII text and/or XML control files for the model simulator which performs the model calculations. Output from the simulator is written to intermediate XML and/or fixed-format ASCII text files that can be read by a Graphical User Interface (GUI) to display results in both text and graphical format. Due to the well-defined interfaces that automatically convert data to and from different forms, it is easy for software developers to interface the system with existing analysis software and with software under development. Templates that can be used in conjunction with DAKOTA are also automatically generated.

In the DAKOTA system, a strategy is used to create and manage iterators and models [4]. A model contains a set of variables, an interface, and a set of responses, and an iterator operates on the model to map the variables into responses using the interface. The WinDAM system is used to automatically generate DAKOTA input files. For parameter studies, the user indirectly specifies these components through strategy, method, model, variables, interface, and responses keywords. Then, DAKOTA is invoked to iterate on the WinDAM simulation models, or vice versa, as needed to generate output.

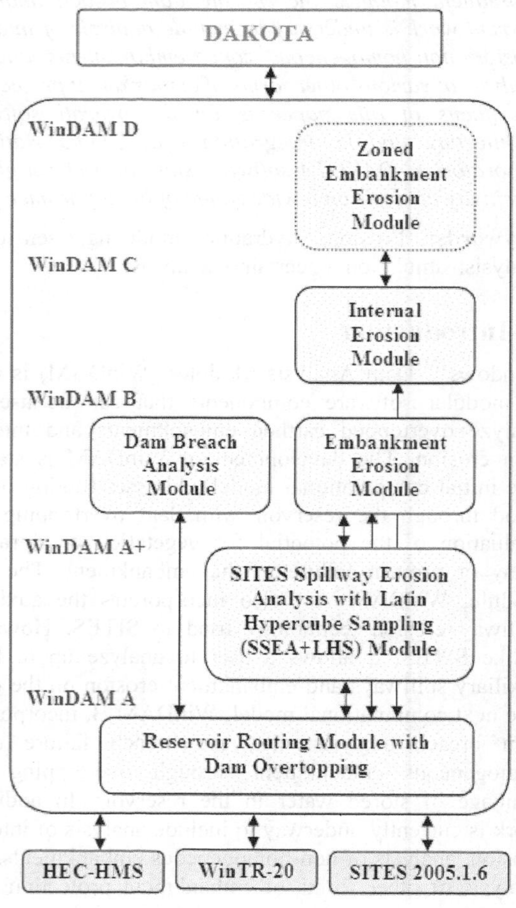

Figure 2. WinDAM software architecture

In what follows, Section 2 covers the WinDAM software which may be used to evaluate dams subjected to flooding that may result in overtopping of the embankment or flow through an existing pathway (conduit) through the embankment – up to WinDAM C.

Then, Section 3 covers integration of WinDAM with DAKOTA to perform simple parameter studies and uncertainty analysis. Finally, Section 4 summarizes the results.

2. Breach and Internal Erosion Analysis

Flow is routed through the reservoir by balancing inflow, outflow, and storage under the assumptions of a level reservoir surface with all outflow being a function of reservoir water surface elevation. Stage-storage properties of the reservoir are entered in tabular format with elevation in feet and the corresponding surface area in acres or storage volume in acre-feet. Reservoir inflow hydrographs are entered into WinDAM as series of time-discharge pairs with time in hours and flow in cubic feet per second (cfs).

Inflow hydrographs are normally computed using other software that is capable of generating a rainfall-runoff hydrograph. The time increment used for entry of the hydrograph is normally used in performing the routing and erosive attack computations.

The computational model incorporated into the WinDAM software assumes stepwise steady-state flow and a level water surface in the reservoir. The mass balance equation governing flow through the reservoir for any given time step may be obtained by averaging conditions over the time step. The inflow to the reservoir is a known function of time only, and is obtained through application of appropriate hydrologic models such as SITES 2005.1.6, HEC-HMS [3], or WinTR-20. The outflow from the reservoir is the sum of the outflow from all spillways and the outflow over the top of the dam. Using the assumptions of a level water surface in the reservoir and stepwise steady flow, each of the individual outflows may be treated as a unique function of the reservoir water surface elevation. Likewise, the storage volume in the reservoir becomes a unique function of the reservoir water surface elevation.

2.1 WinDAM B

The primary purpose of WinDAM B is threefold:

- Hydraulically route one input hydrograph through, around, and over a single earthen dam.
- Estimate auxiliary spillway erosion in up to three earthen or vegetated auxiliary spillways.
- Estimate erosion of the earthen embankment caused by overtopping of the dam embankment.

Since WinDAM B does not include any specific hydrology component, the user must create the input hydrograph using other software. This allows the user the flexibility to choose the hydrologic software most suitable for analysis of site conditions; e.g., HEC-HMS, etc.

WinDAM B assumes the embankment of the dam is a homogenous earthen material. Many USDA-NRCS dams are homogenous earthen fill, so the WinDAM B model applies. Future versions of WinDAM will address zoned embankments where each zone exhibits different erosion resistance from other zones.

Most existing USDA-NRCS dams are built with a single earthen auxiliary spillway. In rehabilitation of old USDA-NRCS-designed dams, it is more common to also utilize additional auxiliary spillways. As a result, WinDAM B allows the user to input up to three auxiliary spillways, each spillway with a zoned embankment and different physical characteristics.

Computation of the discharge through the area of the breach, if any, is unit discharge based on the effective width. If breach is to be evaluated, the associated erosion is assumed to be initiated in an area corresponding to maximum unit discharge over the top of the dam.

Following breach initiation, the unit discharge is computed assuming negligible energy loss from the reservoir to the hydraulic control and critical flow conditions with hydrostatic pressure at the hydraulic control. The processes that determine the erosion during embankment breach are dependent on the breach geometry and the breach area discharge.

The way in which the erosion will progress depends on the local geometry and discharge. Initially, the headcut (local vertical) may not be sufficiently high to generate the plunging action that is associated with typical headcut advance. Likewise, during latter stages of the process, the headcut may become submerged.

The headcut is considered to be submerged for purposes of computing erosion whenever the downstream tailwater elevation is greater than the elevation of the crest of the headcut, or the height of the headcut is less than the critical depth of the flow in the breach area. The latter implies that the minimum depth of water at the base of the headcut is the critical flow depth based on the breach area unit discharge. When the headcut is submerged, the headcut is considered not to advance or deepen from plunging action of the flow over the crest of the headcut. If elevation of the downstream tailwater computed from total flow through the reservoir is below the elevation of the base of the headcut and the base of the headcut is within the embankment, the headcut may continue to deepen as a result of flow on the face of the dam downstream of the headcut. The rate of deepening that is associated with this flow is approximated using a normal flow depth model consistent with that used in evaluating surface protection. The erosion rate resulting in deepening of the headcut is computed by:

$$\varepsilon_r = k_d(\tau_e - \tau_c) \tag{1}$$

where

ε_r = the soil detachment rate in volume per unit area per unit time,

k_d = a detachment rate coefficient that is a property of the embankment material,

τ_e = the erosionally effective stress (in lb/ft^2), and

τ_c = the critical soil stress (in lb/ft^2).

As applied in WinDAM, k_d is expressed in (ft/h)/(lb/ft^2) and is provided as input to the model (see Figure 3). The appropriate value for input may be obtained from soil tests as described by Hanson and Cook [11].

When the tailwater is below the crest of the headcut and the height of the headcut is greater than the critical depth of flow, the flow will tend to plunge over the crest of the headcut. Stresses associated with this plunging flow may govern the rate of downward erosion at the base of the headcut, the rate of headcut advance, or both.

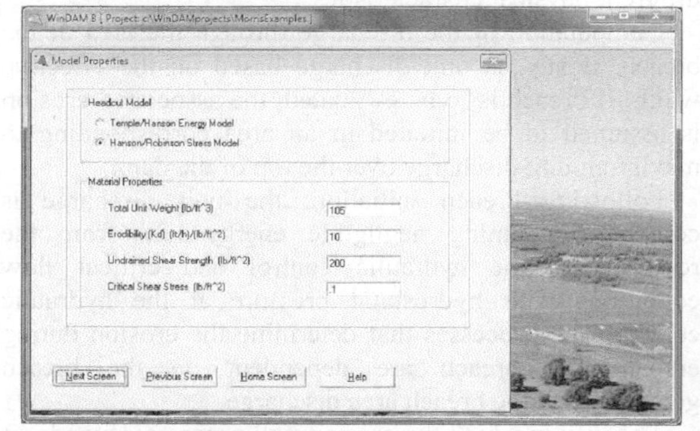

Figure 3. Breach model input

In WinDAM, users may select an energy-based or a stress-based advance rate model. The energy-based model, designated the Temple/Hanson model, is described by Temple et al. [5]. The model is a variation on the semi-empirical model used in the SITES spillway erosion computations [2]. The stress-based model, designated the Hanson/Robinson model, is an adaptation of the model described by Hanson, et al. [10], These advance rate models reflect different degrees of simplification of the complex process and have different input requirements.

2.2 WinDAM C

For WinDAM C, in addition to overtopping breach computations, calculations may alternatively be executed to evaluate breach through internal erosion along an existing flow path through the embankment. Several tests were conducted at the USDA-ARS Hydraulic Engineering Research Unit (HERU) near Stillwater, Oklahoma, to evaluate the impact that different material properties have on the rate of internal erosion, as shown in Figure 4. The internal erosion module assumes a homogeneous embankment with a simple cross section and is most directly applicable to embankments constructed from cohesive soil materials. The initial flow path (conduit) through the embankment is assumed to be horizontal with a rectangular cross section and a constant width and height over its entire length. The initial dimensions and location are specified by the user. The conduit is allowed to expand uniformly vertically and horizontally until a boundary is reached or the upper surface becomes unstable and collapses (as shown in Figure 4 d-e). In addition to expansion of the conduit due to hydraulic stress along the conduit boundary, a headcut is allowed to form at the outlet of the conduit and to progress upstream. Once erosion of the conduit results in removal of the conduit roof, erosion processes and computations are equivalent to overtopping breach computation as in WinDAM B.

Figure 4. Internal erosion analysis at USDA-ARS HERU

Internal erosion calculations represent a simplified approach and are considered a first effort at identifying the dominant processes and incorporating them into an integrated breach model for cohesive embankments. This model will be refined and modified as the overall process is better understood and more validation data becomes available. To that end, it becomes important to perform sensitivity and uncertainty analysis to better understand the model and which parameters are most important.

3. Uncertainty and Sensitivity Analysis

The goal of uncertainty analysis is to obtain a better understanding of the probable range of outputs given that there is a certain amount of uncertainty in the input. In particular, based on uncertain inputs, determine the distribution function (uncertainty) of the outputs and probabilities of failure (reliability metrics); identify the statistical measures (mean, variance, etc.) of the outputs; and identify the inputs whose variance contribute most to variance in the outputs (global sensitivity analysis) [4]. For simplicity, we will focus on the analysis of spillway designs, but the same analysis can be used to evaluate a wide range of properties, including the model inputs as shown in Figure 3 for breach or internal erosion analysis.

Spillway designs are compared by determining both the stability and integrity of the spillway when it is subjected to a given design storm. In a typical design, three types of hydrographs are used: principal spillway hydrographs, stability design hydrographs, and freeboard hydrographs. A *principal spillway hydrograph* is used to size the principal spillway and set the elevation of the crest of the emergency or auxiliary spillway. The principal spillway is typically a conduit through the dam used to pass low flows, whereas the auxiliary spillway is often an open channel capable of passing infrequent large flows. Earth auxiliary spillways are typically wide trapezoidal channels vegetated as appropriate for the local area. A *stability design hydrograph*, when routed through a reservoir, generates the maximum auxiliary spillway outflow that the reservoir will be expected to pass without erosion damage. For the design to be stable, erosion thresholds must bound hydraulic stresses that lead to the initiation of erosion. For flows larger than the stability design hydrograph, spillway erosion may occur, and the spillway may require maintenance (see Figure 1). A *freeboard hydrograph* represents the maximum flow for which the structure is designed. The integrity of the auxiliary spillway, as represented by its resistance to breach, is evaluated for the spillway outflow associated with this hydrograph. Naturally, this is the most important consideration in designing an earth (soil, rock, or both) spillway. Even though extremely large discharges may cause significant erosion, the spillway must not breach during passage of the *freeboard hydrograph*. A spillway is considered breached if the spillway crest is degraded by erosion and floodwater is released through the spillway a fixed depth below the crest elevation.

Breach potential is a function of the spillway system, the characteristics of the spillway outflow hydrograph, the erodibility of the earth materials, the spillway layout, bottom width, and maintenance. Integrity analysis is based on the idea that some erosion is allowable if its occurrence is infrequent, maintenance is provided, and the spillway will not breach during passage of the freeboard hydrograph [7].

The integrated development system for water resource site analysis WinDAM+DAKOTA is designed to fully integrate the simulation models in WinDAM with the uncertainty quantification, sensitivity analysis, and parameter studies capabilities in DAKOTA. This novel, new development environment interactively guides user input, invokes the sampling and simulation models in the background, and parses the results to automatically generate output hydrographs, summary tables, and graphs.

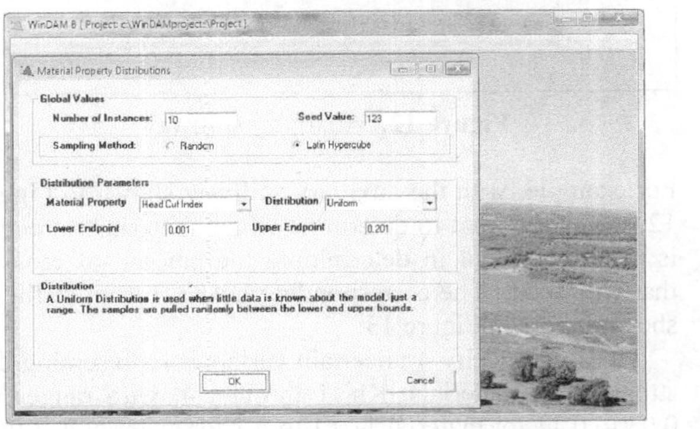

Figure 5. Uniform distribution input

This version of the software also allows a user to conduct parameter studies and specify the inputs to be analyzed based on a list of probability distribution functions. Twenty-five different types of distributions can be specified [2]. For example, a user could specify a Normal Distribution for hydrograph peak discharge with a mean of 50,000 cfs and a standard deviation of 10,000 cfs, or a user could specify a Uniform Distribution for a material property such as headcut index, Kh, for multiple materials or a single material as shown in Figure 5.

Random samples are generated using the Latin Hypercube Sampling (LHS) library routines found in Dakota 5.2. In addition to specifying the types of distributions to be used to generate samples, the user can also specify the number of instances to be generated and the algorithm to be used to generate those samples. In particular, the user can select between Monte Carlo and Latin Hypercube Sampling. With Monte Carlo Sampling, the samples are generated at random. The user can specify a random number seed to generate the same sequence of random samples. With Latin Hypercube Sampling, the samples are more evenly distributed across the search space, resulting in better coverage and fewer samples required [13]. As shown in Figure 5, a user could request 10 instances (samples) to be generated for a given material's headcut index using a Uniform Distribution from 0.001 to 0.201. Then, one sample would be randomly generated for each interval of length 0.02 from 0.001 to 0.201. For this input, the generated samples are shown in Figure 6.

```
@UNCERTAINTY
  @OBSERVATIONS      10
  @VARIABLES       1
    KH(1):
@SAMPLEDATA
 1 1  0.178143860112386
 2 1  0.114162037013804
 3 1  0.153554977141378
 4 1  0.184678807170631      <- min erosion
 5 1  0.140484162236030
 6 1  7.696084019646307E-003 <- max erosion
 7 1  6.790786373412117E-002 <- mean erosion
 8 1  2.112528697716014E-002
 9 1  5.711419140612775E-002
10 1  9.154328306156087E-002
```

Figure 6. Random samples generated

The *Build Interface* is used to generate instances for a given run based on the random variables generated, and then to invoke the simulator for each instance. The Build Interface also parses output to extract summary data.

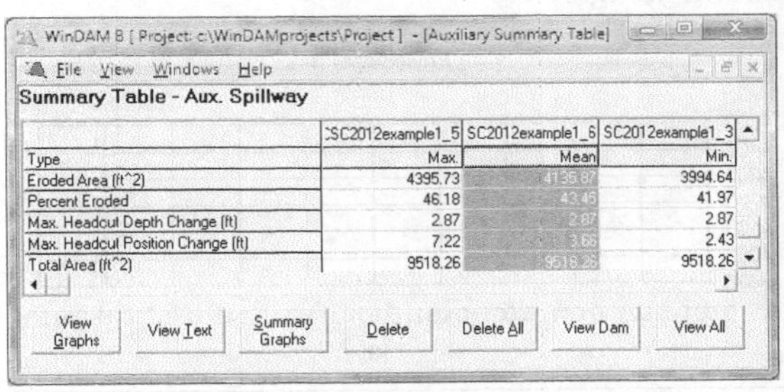

Figure 7. Aux. spillway summary table

The summary data is presented in a two-level table. The top-level table, shown in Figure 7, only displays instances resulting in maximum, mean (actually the run closest to the mean), and minimum erosion, whereas the second-level table, see Figure 8, displays all instances.

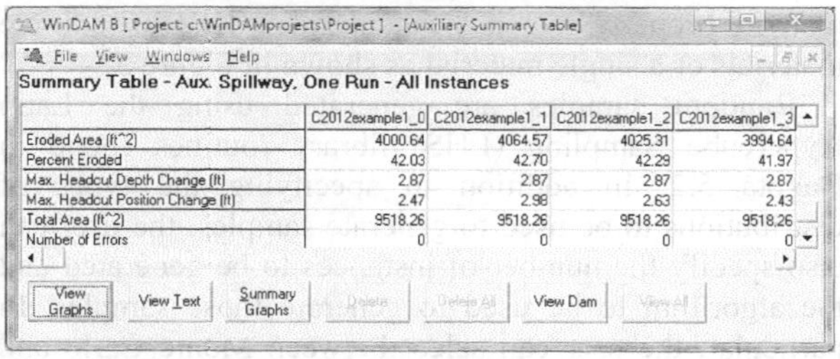

	C2012example1_0	C2012example1_1	C2012example1_2	C2012example1_3
Eroded Area (ft^2)	4000.64	4064.57	4025.31	3994.64
Percent Eroded	42.03	42.70	42.29	41.97
Max. Headcut Depth Change (ft)	2.87	2.87	2.87	2.87
Max. Headcut Position Change (ft)	2.47	2.98	2.63	2.43
Total Area (ft^2)	9518.26	9518.26	9518.26	9518.26
Number of Errors	0	0	0	0

Figure 8. View All runs

After one or more related runs have been processed, they can be analyzed by using the *Output Interface.* The user can quickly compare differences between runs and instances by viewing the Summary Tables and Summary Graphs. By varying these input parameters, a user can quickly determine how changes in each will potentially impact erosion. The output graph for Spillway Erosion includes the option to display the currently selected run with the maximum erosion (shown in orange), the mean erosion (shown in red), and the minimum erosion (shown in green). The erosion for the current run is shown in blue, below in Figure 9.

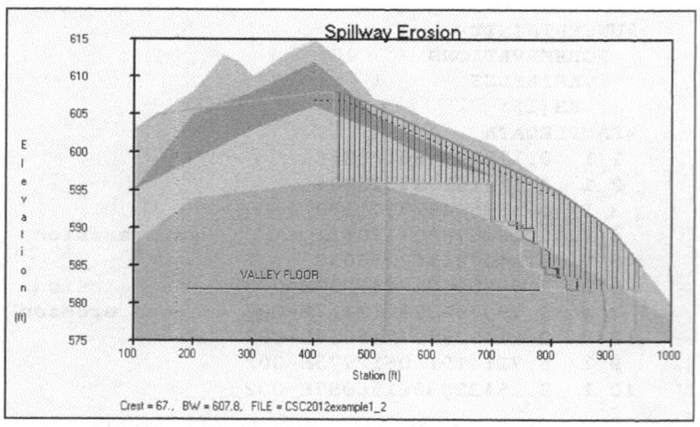

Figure 9. Spillway erosion graph

Finally, the output can be used for a parameter study to determine how changing the value of an input parameter, in our example the headcut index, Kh, will impact the amount of erosion that results. A scatter plot of the results is shown in Figure 10.

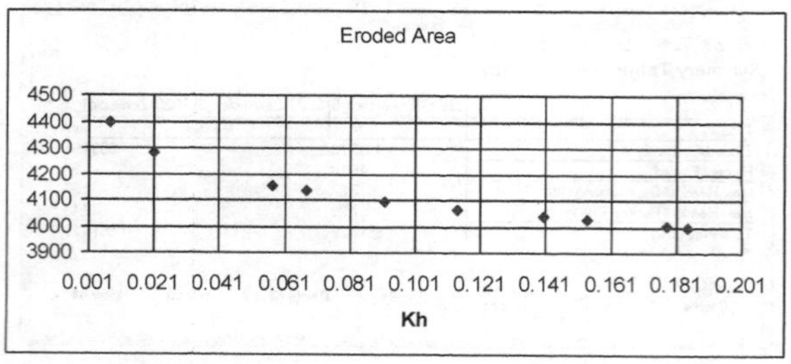

Figure 10. Scatter plot for all runs

As expected, the stronger materials result in less erosion. Note that one sample is selected from each interval due to Latin Hypercube Sampling.

Instead of having WinDAM drive the analysis, we can also allow DAKOTA to be used to drive the analysis in an iterative fashion.

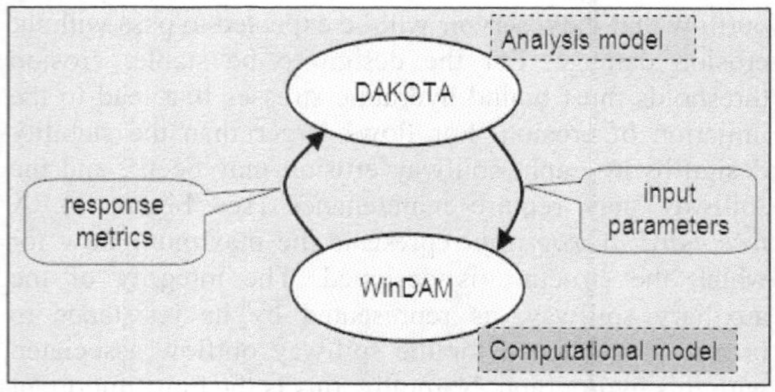

Figure 11. Iterative analysis

Dakota supports several different options for the Design and Analysis of Computer Experiments (DACE):

- *Sensitivity Analysis (SA)* - determine which inputs have the most influence on the output.
- *Uncertainty Analysis (UA)* - compare the relative importance of model input uncertainties on the uncertainty in the model output.
- *Response Surface Approximation (RSA)* - use sample input and output to create an approximation to the simulation output; e.g., neural net, etc.
- *Uncertainty Quantification (UQ)* - take a set of distributions on the inputs and propagate them through the model to obtain distributions on the outputs.

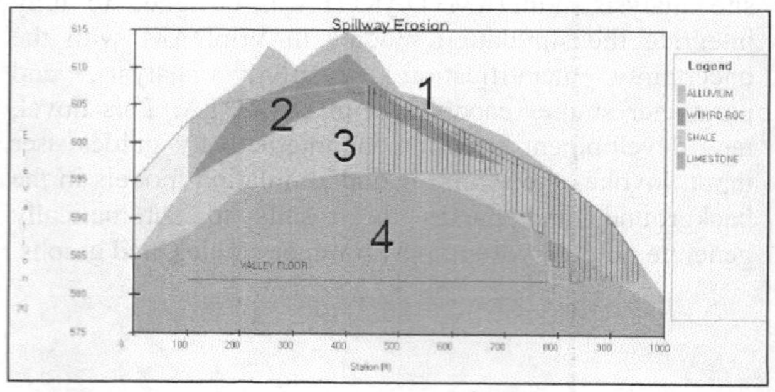

Figure 12. Auxiliary spillway

For example, with the auxiliary spillway shown in Figure 12, we might want to determine which material's strength is most important in determining the amount of erosion that will occur. The corresponding DAKOTA input file is shown below in Figure 13.

Here we specify 4 uncertain variables representing the strengths of materials, Kh, 1 through 4, with ranges of 0.03 to 0.11 for material 1, 0.1 to 0.7 for material 2, 1.0 to 13.0 for material 3, and 100.0 to 300.0 for material 4. Other parameters can be specified in a similar manner, and a user interface, such as Jaguar, can be used to drive the simulation.

```
# DAKOTA INPUT FILE - dakota_sites_uq.in
strategy,
        single_method, graphics,tabular_graphics_data
method,
        dace random
         samples 80,  seed 123
model,
        single
variables,
    interval_uncertain = 4
      num_intervals  = 1 1 1 1
      interval_probs  = 1.0 1.0 1.0 1.0
      interval_bounds = 0.03 0.11 0.1 0.7 1.0 13.0 100.0 300.0
```

Figure 13. DAKOTA input file

The DAKOTA output is shown below in Figure 14.

```
iuv_1 -4.97535e-001  (Kh1),  iuv_2  -6.25741e-001  (Kh2)
iuv_3 -9.10251e-001  (Kh3),  iuv_4  -1.53207e-001  (Kh4)
```

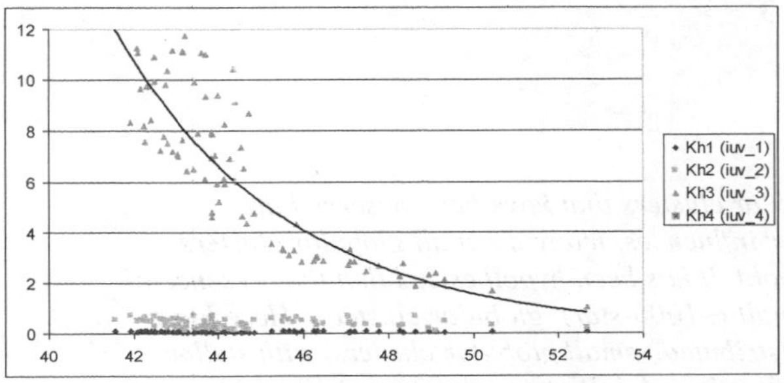

Figure 14. Correlation graph

The output shows that material 3 is the most important with a partial correlation coefficient of -0.91, followed closely by material 2, and then material 1. All are negatively correlated, so as the strength increases, the amount of erosion decreases. Similar types of analyses can be performed by varying any hydrologic or material properties, or erosion model inputs, such as those shown in Figure 3.

4. Conclusions

WinDAM is being developed in stages to evaluate the performance of earth dams. Existing modules with well-defined interfaces enable efficient integration of existing legacy software and future enhancements. The system provides tools that can be used to better understand the structure, function, and dynamics of such structures. This paper describes how uncertainty quantification and sensitivity analysis can be incorporated by linking the WinDAM development environment with DAKOTA. The paper also provides an simple example to show how the system can be used to conduct a parameter study and perform uncertainty analysis.

Acknowledgements

I would like to thank the USDA-ARS and USDA-NRCS for use of the photographic images used in this paper.

References

[1] D.M. Temple, G.J. Hanson, and M.L. Neilsen, "WinDAM -- Analysis of overtopped earth embankment dams", In *Proc. of the ASABE Annual Conference,* Paper Number 062105, 2006.

[2] M.L. Neilsen, D.M. Temple, and J.L. Wibowo, "A distributed hydrologic simulation environment with latin hypercube sampling", In *Proc. of the Intl. Conf. on Env. Modelling and Simulation*, No. 432-032, St. Thomas, USVI, Nov. 22-24, 2004.

[3] United States Army Corps of Engineers, "Hydrologic modeling system HEC-HMS User's Manual", CPD-74A, Ver. 3.5, USACE, HEC, 2010.

[4] B.M. Adams, W.J. Bohnhoff, K.R.Dalbey, J.P. Eddy, M.S. Eldred, D.M. Gay, K. Haskell, P.D. Hough, and L.P. Swiler, "DAKOTA, A Multilevel Parallel Object-Oriented Framework for Design Optimization, Parameter Estimation, Uncertainty Quantification, and Sensitivity Analysis: Version 5.0 User's Manual," Sandia Technical Report SAND2010-2183, Dec. 2009. Updated Dec. 2010 (Ver. 5.1), Feb. 13, 2013 (Ver. 5.3).

[5] D.M. Temple and G. J. Hanson, "Earth dam overtopping and breach outflow", In *Proc. of the World Water and Environmental Resources Congress*, Anchorage, Alaska, ASCE, 8 pp., 2005.

[6] V.T. Chow, "*Open-channel hydraulics*", McGraw Hill Book Company, New York, 680 pgs., 1959.

[7] United States Department of Agriculture, Natural Resources Conservation Service, "Earth spillway erosion model", Ch. 51, Part 628, Dams, *National Engineering Handbook*, 210-VI-NEH, 1997.

[8] D.M. Temple, J. Wibowo, M.L. Neilsen, "Erosion of earth spillways", In *Proc. of 23rd United States Society on Dams (USSD) Annual Meeting and Conference*, pp. 331-339, 2003.

[9] M.L. Neilsen and D.M. Temple, "A concurrent simulation model for analysis of water control structures at the watershed scale", In *Proc. of the Intl. Conf. on Par. and Dist. Proc. Tech. and Apps.*, (PDPTA 2010), pp. 1565-1570, June 26-29, 2000.

[10] G.J. Hanson, K.M. Robinson, and K.R. Cook, "Prediction of headcut migration using a deterministic approach. Trans. ASAE, 44(3): pp. 525-531, 2001.

[11] G.J. Hanson and K.R. Cook, "Apparatus, test procedures, and analytical methods to measure soil erodibility in-situ", in Applied Engineering in Agriculture, ASABE, 20(4):455-462, 2004.

[12] M. D. McKay, W.J. Conover, and R. J. Beckman, "A comparison of three methods for selecting values in the analysis of output from a computer code", *Technometrics*, 21(2):239-245, 1979.

[13] R. Fell, C.F. Wan, J. Cyganiewicz, and M. Foster, "Time for Development of Internal Erosion and Piping in Embankment Dams", in *Journal of Geotechnical and Geoenvironmental Engineering,* ASCE Vol. 129(4):307-314, 2003.

Persistence of Plummer-Distributed Small Globular Clusters as a Function of Primordial-Binary Population Size

Jack K. Horner
P.O. Box 266
Los Alamos NM 87544 USA

CSC 2013

Abstract

Globular stellar clusters are relatively common. All globular clusters that have been observed are relatively large (~10^4 - 10^6 stars). In the absence of other influences, many if not all globular clusters continually lose mass as stars escape their gravitational hold. It has been hypothesized that the presence of primordial binaries helps to increase the persistence of small (~1000-star) globular clusters. Here I use N-body gravitational simulation of isotropic, Plummer-distributed, small globular clusters, with stellar evolution, to assess the persistence of such clusters as a function of initial populations of 100-500 primordial binaries (representing 0.1 - 0.5 of the initial cluster mass). The simulation predicts that in such clusters (a) star-loss is roughly linear in time up to ~300 Myr after t_0, (b) cluster persistence is, more or less, an increasing function of the fraction of primordial binaries at t_0, when such binaries account for 0.1-0.5 of the initial cluster mass.

Keywords: globular cluster, primordial binaries, N-body simulation

1.0 Introduction

1.1 Overview of globular clusters

Globular stellar clusters are roughly spherical, gravitationally bound collections of stars. A large fraction of the total mass of a globular cluster tends to be concentrated in a cluster "core".

All globular clusters observed to date are relatively large (10,000 to 1,000,000 stars). They are relatively common in galactic halos: ~150 have been detected in the Milky Way ([25]); the galaxy M87 may contain ~13,000 ([24]).

1.2 Overview of the *nbody6* simulator

nbody6 ([1],[2]) is a highly parameterized gravitational N-body ([1]) simulator that has been widely used to simulate globular cluster evolution ([26]).

The *nbody6* equations of motion are derived and discussed extensively in [1].

In *nbody6,* single particles and center-of-mass systems are integrated by the neighbor scheme described in [6], using the fourth-order Hermite method ([7]).

Binaries and close two-body encounters are simulated by the Stumpff version of Kustaanheimo–Stiefel ([8]) regularization

([9]), while interactions of compact subsystems are described by the chain regularization method ([10], [11], [12]). Strong interactions in unperturbed triples and quadruples are treated by three-body ([13]) and Heggie ([14]) global regularization ([15]). Hard triples and higher-order systems satisfying a stability criterion ([16],[17]) are reduced to two-body configurations (so-called mergers as opposed to collisions).

Several aspects of synthetic stellar evolution, mass loss, tidal circularization, and collisions are included in the simulator. Binary evolution and collisions ([18]), metallicities ([19]) , Roche lobe overflow, and spin–orbit coupling are also included in the simulator.

Further details of the theory and methods implemented in *nbody6* can be found in [1] and [4].

The *nbody6* software is ~30,000 source lines, distributed over ~300 program units, of a non-standards-conforming variant of Fortran77 ([5]). By modern engineering standards ([23]), the *nbody6* detailed design, testing, and maintenance documentation is meager.

The GRAPE special-purpose supercomputer ([22]) was the principal target platform for *nbody* development. Ports to other platforms have tended to be informal.

2.0 Method

In the absence of external influences, many if not all globular clusters continually lose mass as stars escape their gravitational hold. Small clusters (~1000 stars) may not persist for more than ~500 Myr because their core does not exert a large enough gravitational force to retain stars of average mass and velocity.

It has been conjectured that the persistence of small globular clusters may be enhanced by the presence of primordial binaries. Here, I use *nbody6* to investigate the effect of primordial binaries on the persistence of small globular clusters. N-body simulation of a globular cluster requires a specification of the initial mass distribution of the cluster. I assume an isotropic Plummer density distribution ([20]) at t_0. The isotropic Plummer density distribution is given by

$$\rho_P(r) = \left(\frac{3M}{4\pi a^3}\right)\left(1 + \frac{r^2}{a^2}\right)^{-\frac{5}{2}},$$

where M is the total mass of the cluster, and a is the *Plummer radius*, a scale parameter which sets the size of the cluster core.

Although the Plummer distribution diverges from the distribution of observed globular clusters, it is a mathematically convenient and plausible approximation of the distribution of ~80% of the mass of many observed globular clusters.

nbody6 source code ([2]) was obtained in April 2012 from the URL identified in [2] and ported to the *Vista*/64-bit-*Cygwin* environment ([21]). As distributed [2], the *nbody6* source code contains over 1000 instances of mixed-precision arithmetic. It also contains ~30 Fortran INTRINSIC function calls that violate [5]. Initial testing of executables built from [2] revealed tens of fatal numeric pathologies in the *Cygwin*/gfortran-compiler environment, all resulting from these problems. The source was accordingly re-engineered to eliminate mixed-precision arithmetic and to make the INTRINSIC function calls consistent with [5]. Inaccessible ("dead") code (~300 Fortran statements) was removed.

The makefile distributed at [2] has been maintained primarily support the platform described in [22]. Accordingly, the makefile was modified to be consistent with the *Cygwin*/gfortran compiler environment.

The re-engineered source was rebuilt from the re-engineered makefile.

Selected setup (input file) parameter values (in *nbody6* simulator units unless otherwise noted) for these experiments were (names in caps are input parameter names, as identified in file *define.f* in [2]):

- Total wall clock time limit (TCOMP): 10 minutes
- Initial number of single stars (N): 800, 700, 600, 500
- Set minimum number of particles (NCRIT): 5
- Set maximum number of neighbors (NNBMAX): 95
- Set time step for irregular force polynomial (ETAI): 0.02
- Set time step for regular force polynomial (ETAR): 0.03
- Set initial radius of neighborhood sphere (RS0): 0.3
- Set time interval for parameter adjustment (DTADJ): 2.0
- Set termination time (TCRIT): 500.0 *nbody* time units
- Set energy tolerance (QE): 2.0D-04
- Set virial cluster radius (RBAR): 1.0 pc
- Set mean mass in solar units (ZMBAR): 0.5
- Assume isotropic Plummer distribution at t_0 (KZ5 = 1)
- Use standard tidal field (KZ14 = 1)
- Enable standard treatment of stable triples and quadruples (KZ15 = 1)
- Enable updating of regularization parameters RMIN, DTMIN, and ECLOSE (KZ16 = 1)
- Use Eggleton-Tout-Hurley mass-loss algorithm (KZ19 = 3)
- Use Kroupa initial mass function (KZ20 = 4)
- Enable logging of escaped stars to file ESC (KZ23 = 2)
- Enable slow-down of two-body motion at chain level (KZ26 = 2)
- Enable multiple regularization for all particles (KZ30 = 1)
- Assume no unique density center (KZ39 = 1)
- Time-step criterion for regularization search (DTMIN): 1.0E-05
- Distance criterion for regularization search (RMIN): 1.0D-03
- Set regularized time-step parameter (ETAU): 0.2
- Set binding energy per unit mass for hard binary (ECLOSE): 1.0
- Set relative two-body perturbation for unperturbed motion (GMIN): 1.0E-06
- Set secondary termination parameter for soft KS binaries (GMAX): 0.001
- Set the pre-scaling maximum particle mass (BODY1): 10.0
- Set the pre-scaling minimum particle mass (BODYN): 0.2
- Set number of primordial binary systems (NBIN0): 200, 300, 400, 500
- Set number of primordial hierarchies (NHI0): 0
- Set metal abundance (ZMET): 0.02
- Set evolutionary epoch (EPOCH0): 0
- Set virial ratio (Q): 0.5
- Set maximum time step (SMAX): 1.0
- Set maximum semi-major axis (SEMI): 0.0005
- Set initial eccentricity (ECC): -1.0 (for thermal distribution)
- Mass ratio (RATIO): 0.0
- Set range in SEMI for uniform logarithmic distribution (RANGE): 100.0

Given the above, all other parameters are ignored by *nbody6*, or were set to zero. These setups assume that the cluster does not interact with anything outside the cluster.

Preliminary experiments showed that the simulator typically exceeded the QE maximum-energy-error, then terminated, for simulated times greater than ~500.0 simulator time units (~300 Myr) in the above configurations.

An example of a full setup file is shown in Figure 1.

```
1 10.0 0
800 1 5 45 95 1
0.02 0.03 0.3  2.0 10.0 500.0 2.0D-04 1.0 0.5
0 0 1 0 1 0 6 3 0 0
0 1 0 1 1 1 0 1 3 4
1 0 2 0 0 2 0 0 0 1
0 0 0 0 0 0 0 0 0 1
0 0 0 0 0 0 0 0 0 0
1.0E-05 1.0D-03 0.2 1.0 1.0E-06 0.001
2.3 10.0 0.2 200 0 0.02 0 10.0
0.5 0 0 0 1.0
0.0005 -1.0 0.0 100. 0 0 0
```

Figure 1. An example an *nbody6* setup file used in this study (the setup for 200 primordial binaries is shown).

See [1], [3], [4], and file *define.f* in [2] for a more detailed description of the input file.

The rebuilt *nbody6* was executed on a Dell Inspiron 545 with an Intel Core2 Quad CPU Q8200 clocked at 2.33 GHz, with 8.00 GB RAM, under *Windows Vista Home Premium(SP2)/64-bit-Cygwin* ([21]).

nbody6 produces an "escaped star" log, ESC, one per setup, if parameter KZ23 ≥ 1. The data in the ESC files generated by the method described above were imported as space-delimited text to an Excel spreadsheet and graphed using Excel graphing functions (see Figure 2 in Section 3.0).

3.0 Results

Figure 2 shows stellar escapes vs. time as a function of number of primordial binaries, generated under the conditions described in Section 2.0.

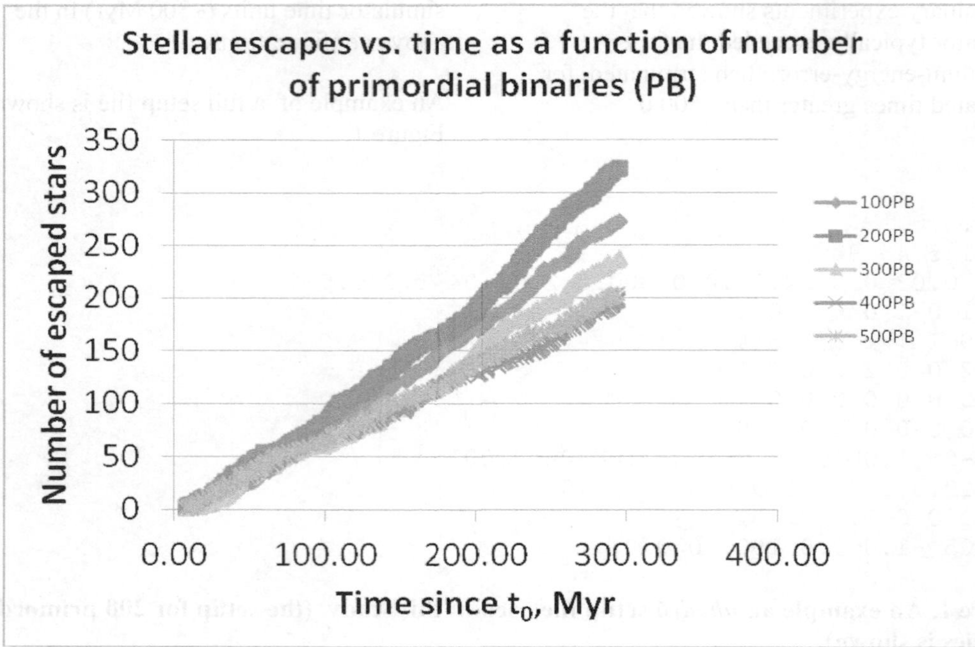

Figure 2. Stellar escapes vs. time as a function of number of primordial binaries in an isotropic, 1000-star, Plummer-distributed globular clusters, generated by the method described in Section 2.0.

Typical CPU utilization per setup on the platform described in Section 2.0 was 25% and typical memory utilization was 1.4 GB. Each setup required 5-9 minutes to complete on that platform.

4.0 Conclusions and discussion

The simulation described in Sections 2.0 and 3.0 predicts that a small globular cluster satisfying the conditions of Section 2.0 (not subject to interaction with anything outside the cluster)

(a) experiences star-loss at a rate that is roughly constant up to ~300 Myr after t_0,

(b) persists approximately as an increasing function of the fraction of primordial binaries at t_0, when such binaries account for 0.1-0.5 of the initial cluster mass.

The mechanism by which primordial binaries enhance the persistence of small globular clusters is not well understood. However, all else being the same, it requires twice as much energy to boost a binary system with mass 2M to escape velocity as it does to boost a single star of mass M to that velocity ([27], esp. Chap. 6).

5.0 Acknowledgements

This work benefited from discussions with Tony Pawlicki and Dave Davin. For any errors that remain, I am solely responsible.

6.0 References

[1] Aarseth SJ. *Gravitational N-Body Simulations: Tools and Algorithms*. Cambridge. 2003. Note: in this document, the description of the *nbody* software distributed at the site identified in [2] have been significantly inconsistent since at least December 2011. [1] remains the best single description of the general physics implemented in *nbody6.*

[2] Aarseth SJ et al. *nbody6.* Circa April 2012. http://www.ast.cam.ac.uk/~sverre/web/pages/nbody.htm. Note: at least as early as December 2011, none of the sample input files distributed at this site would run with the version of *nbody6* distributed at this site. Sample input files that will run with the versions distributed between December 2011 and March 2013 are available from me on request.

[3] Aarseth SJ. *Introduction to Running Simulations with NBODY4 and NBODY6.* July 2006. http://www.ast.cam.ac.uk/~sverre/web/pages/nbody.htm. Note: this document is significantly inconsistent with [2].

[4] Aarseth SJ. *NBODY6 User Manual.* December 2009. http://www.ast.cam.ac.uk/~sverre/web/pages/nbody.htm. Note: this document is significantly inconsistent with [2].

[5] American National Standards Institute. *American National Standard Programming Language Fortran.* ANSI X3.9-1978. 1978.

[6] Ahmad A and Cohen L. A numerical integration scheme for the N-body gravitational problem. *Journal of Computational Physics* 12 (1973), 389–402.

[7] Makino J and Aarseth SJ. On a Hermite integrator with Ahmad–Cohen scheme for gravitational many-body problems. *Publications of the Astronomical Society of Japan* 44 (1992), 141–151.

[8] Kustaanheimo P and Stiefel E. Perturbation theory of Kepler motion based on spinor regularization. *Journal für die reine und angewandte Mathematik* 218 (1965), 204–219.

[9] Mikkola S and Aarseth SJ. An efficient integration method for binaries in N-body simulations. New Astronomy 3 (1998), 309–320.

[10] Mikkola S and Aarseth SJ. A chain regularization method for the few-body problem. *Celestial Mechanics and Dynamical Astronomy* 47 (1990), 375–390.

[11] Mikkola S and Aarseth SJ. An implementation of N-body chain regularization. *Celestial Mechanics and Dynamical Astronomy* 57 (1993), 439–459.

[12] Mikkola S and Aarseth SJ. A slow-down treatment for close binaries. *Celestial Mechanics and Dynamical Astronomy* 64 (1996), 197–208.

[13] Aarseth SJ and Zare K. A regularization of the three-body problem. *Celestial Mechanics* 10 (1974), 185–205.

[14] Heggie DC and Ramamani N. Approximate self-consistent models for tidally truncated star clusters. *Monthly Notices of the Royal Astronomical Society* 272 (1995), 317–322.

[15] Mikkola S. A practical and regular formulation of the N-body equations. *Monthly Notices of the Royal Astronomical Society* 215 (1985), 171–177.

[16] Mardling RA and Aarseth SJ. Dynamics and stability of three-body systems. In *The Dynamics of Small Bodies in the Solar System*, ed. BA Steves and A Roy. Kluwer. 1999. pp. 385–392.

[17] Mardling RA. The three-body problem in astrophysics. In SJ Aarseth, CA Tout, and RA Mardling, eds. *The Cambridge N-Body Lectures.* Springer. 2008. pp. 59-96.

[18] Tout CA, Aarseth SJ, Pols O, and Eggleton P. Rapid binary star evolution for N-body simulations and population synthesis. *Monthly Notices of the Royal Astronomical Society* 291 (1997), 732–748.

[19] Hurley JR, Pols OR, and Tout CA. Comprehensive analytical formulae for stellar evolution as a function of mass and metallicity. *Monthly Notices of the Royal Astronomical Society* 315 (2000), 543–569.

[20] Plummer HC. On the problem of distribution in globular star clusters. *Monthly Notices of the Royal Astronomical Society* 71 (1911), 460-470.

[21] *Cygwin* development team. *Cygwin* CYGWIN_nT-6.0-WOW64 v1.7.15 (0.260/5/3) i686. http://www.cygwin.com/. 2012.

[22] Makino J. Current status of the GRAPE Project. *Proceedings of the International Astronomical Union* 3 (1997), 457-466.

[23] International Standards Organization. *ISO/IEC 12207:2008. Systems and Software Engineering -- Software Life Cycle Processes.* http://www.iso.org/iso/iso_catalogue/catalogue_tc/catalogue_detail.htm?csnumber=43447. 2008.

[24] Kundu A and Whitmore BC. New insights from HST studies of globular cluster systems. I. Colors, distances, and specific frequencies of 28 elliptical galaxies. *The Astronomical Journal* 121 (June 2001), 2950–2973.

[25] Harris WE. *Catalog of Parameters for Milky Way Globular Clusters: The Database*. http://messier.seds.org/xtra/data/mwgc.dat.txt. December 2010.

[26] Aarseth SJ. From NBODY1 to NBODY6: The growth of an industry. *Publications of the Astronomical Society of the Pacific* 111 (November 1999), 1333-1346.

[27] Battin RH. *An Introduction to the Mathematics and Methods of Astrodynamics*. American Institute of Aeronautics and Astronautics. 1987

Scientific Visualization of Occupation Data for Spatial Analysis of Animal Behavior Using OpenGL

ANDREI SANTOS
andreisantoss@hotmail.com
BERNARDO CORREA
bernardocrfp@yahoo.com.br
FELIPE FERREIRA
faguimaraes@sga.pucminas.br
FELIPE VITAL
felipecacique2@hotmail.com
MICHAEL LOPES
michael-lopes02@hotmail.com
RAMON VITOR
ramon00017@hotmail.com
ROSINEI FIGUEIREDO
rosineisfigueiredo@hotmail.com
FLÁVIA FREITAS
flaviamagfreitas@gmail.com
PETR I. EKEL
ekel@pucminas.br

Group for Studies in Images and Signals Processing,
Graduation Program in Electrical Engineering (PPGEE),
Pontifical Catholic University of Minas Gerais (PUC MG)
Belo Horizonte, MG 30535-901, Brazil.
Contact: FLÁVIA FREITAS, flaviamagfreitas@gmail.com.

Abstract —
The overriding goal of this work is to present the implementation of a tool for spatial analysis of georeferenced information as a means of gaining insights into animal behavior from scientific visualization. The spatial occupation data of monkeys from the species *Callicebus nigrifrons*, located in "Santuário do Caraça", in the state of Minas Gerais, Brazil, has been collected by researches of Graduate Program on Vertebrate's Zoology of Pontifical Catholic University of Minas Gerais (PUC Minas). The registers include information regarding gender, age, activity being performed in the moment of the observation and the height occupied in the trees of the forest. The project assumes a multidisciplinary characteristic, with several knowledge areas, such as Geography, Computer Science and engineering, connected together into providing Zoology's scientists with a new comprehension of their problem.

Keywords: Scientific Visualization, Layer's Visualization, Spatial Analysis, OpenGL, Graphics Computation, Graphics Computation, Multidisciplinarity.

I. INTRODUCTION

The Scientific Visualization is an area which evolved from Computer Graphics. It studies algorithms and software to generate images that assist the user interpretation of data. It's also an area that has been growing in recent times due to the increasing computer technology. It's being used not only in Computing, but also in Biology, Geography, Medicine, Electrical Engineering, among others, to meet the need to visualize data sets of high level of complexity and size.

The graphic library chosen to be used for interaction between tool and user was the OpenGL, selected for being easy to implement and offers a wide variety of resources. Its use allowed the application of filters chosen accordingly to the researchers' needs, which were implemented using the concept of geoprocessing layers. From this analysis, it was realized the importance of the information treatment for a better interpretation of the monkeys' spatial occupation raw data collected through the survey conducted by zoology's researchers.

II. OPENGL

The development of high performance graphics applications used to be exclusively of research institutions or companies that owned specialized graphics hardware and skilled programmers. A few years ago, this situation has changed with the appearance of graphic cards for personal computers and the development of graphics libraries which did not require extensive programming knowledge or hardware. One of such libraries widely used is OpenGL [1].

OpenGL can be defined as an open and multiplatform specification of graphics routines and modeling libraries, used for the development of computer graphics applications, such as games and visualization systems. It allows developing interactive applications and generation of 3D images with a high level of realism. Its biggest advantage is the speed, since it incorporates several optimized algorithms, including the graphical primitives draw, texture mapping and other special effects [1].

Its operation is similar to a library of C programming language. However, when is said that a program is OpenGL based, means that it was written in some programming language and uses one or more OpenGL library.

The main OpenGL tools used in this project are:

- Geometrical primitives (points, lines and cubes);
- Geometrical transformations (rotation, translation and scale);
- Texture mapping;
- Rendering;

III. COMPUTER GRAPHICS

Computer Graphics refers to the generation of images which allows the visualization of real and imaginary objects represented in a computer model. It involves the creation, representation, processing, manipulation or evaluation of graphical computer objects, as well as the association of graphical objects with non-graphical data available for access [3]. It's a method applied in many areas, from computers (through the development of graphical interfaces), operational systems and websites, to the development of games and animations.

In the context of data visualization, the Computer Graphics' importance is in developing a human-machine interaction, in order to facilitate data interpretation [4].

Under the area of Computer Graphics, the techniques that allows the generation of images can be divided as:

- Process object modeling.
- The representation, in different forms, of collected data.
- Generation of images with variable degree of realism.

In this research, the following Computer Graphics software were used: Adobe Photoshop, CorelDraw and Blender.

IV. THE VISUALIZATION TOOL

This tool, developed by undergraduation and graduation engineering students, was the result of a research project that consisted initially in the analysis of a great amount of data about the spatial occupation of monkeys from the species *Callicebus nigrifrons*. The research was focused on the search for ways of visualization that would allow the study of animal behavior by Zoology researchers, interested in the observation of several animal groups and in the pattern identification of the male and female behavior.

The programming environment and language used for the development of the visualization tool was the Dev C++ and the C/C++ programming language. The research, which culminated in the tool presentation, was developed by Engineering and Information Systems graduating students. Its process was divided in 2 steps.

1st step:

- Identify, along with the Zoology researchers, the goals to be achieved by their studies, using the visualization tool;
- Identify the spatial occupation raw data available;
- Study the general concepts of Computer Graphics and its applications in the proposed problem;
- Study the OpenGl library and how it could be applied in the image's generation;
- Deepen the knowledge in the C/C++ programming language, chosen to be used in the implementation of this visualization tool;
- Pursue the spatial analysis concept used by Geoprocessing, which consists in the visualization by layers of a raw georeferenced data, searching for patterns identification;
- Implement filters that allows the user to analyze the spatial occupation raw data, by the layering visualization

2nd step:

- Study the ArcView software (part of ArcGis software, which is a Geographic Information System for working with maps and geographic information), whose Analyst 3D tool was used to build the profile of the region's topography, from a topography map;
- Choose 3D models to be used to visualize the spatial occupation data, collected by graduation program in Vertebrate's Zoology researchers of PUC-MG, with the help of OpenGL libraries.
- Apply textures that enrich the viewing, and differentiate the animals by gender;
- Model the studied region's terrain, seeking to carry the Zoology researcher to an environment closest from the real one;

Next we will be describing the tool developing process mentioned in the steps 1 and 2.

IV.1 – THE TOOL'S PRELIMINARY VERSION FOR THE ANALYSIS OF THE ANIMAL SPATIAL OCCUPATION DATA

The research first step culminated with a preliminary version of the software, which made use of simple geometrical primitives (points) to map the spatial coordinates of the data. Besides the "x" and "y" coordinates, the absolute height (measured in relation to the ground) is defined by the "z" axis. At this version, spatial analysis concepts were applied in order to identify behavior patterns.

The tool's initial implementation was based on the reading of the raw data (not yet processed) retrieved from a ".txt" file. From this point forward, the organization of the data was made (name, gender, height in relation to the ground, geographic's coordinates and living group) in specific vectors.

Initially, the monkey's location was represented by points inserted inside a unitary edged cube, which represented the animal's habitat. Following that, assuming the needs of the zoology researchers to study the animal's behavior, the focus became the implementation of selectable layers to filter the displayed data.

Using Computer Graphics resources, we've implemented the first filter, which separated the monkeys between gender (male and female). It was attributed to the males the blue color and the females the red color as seen in Figure 1.

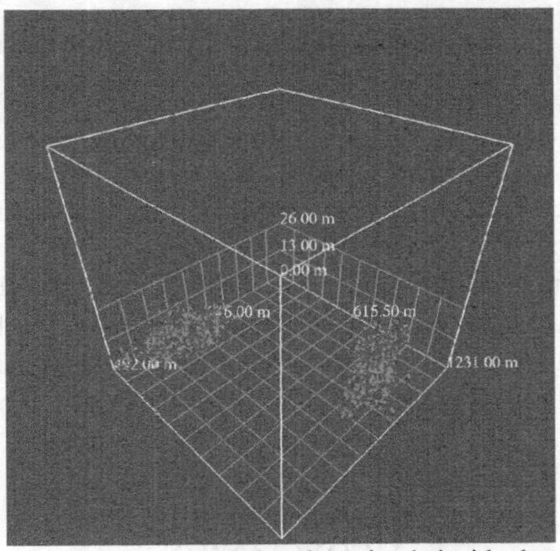

Figure 1 – Points representing the animals inside the cube.

To map the primitives (points) in the cube, the point of smallest coordinate value was determined among the raw data. After that, all the points were translated in the x, y and z axis, using the smallest coordinate value as reference in each axis. This way, the minimal value becames part of the cube's face. Afterwards, a correction was made by dividing the real coordinate of the points by the difference between the maximum and minimal amplitude of the spatial axis in question. This way, the (x,y,z) projection of occupation vectors becomes included between 0 and 1 and, consequently inside the cube.

To better navigate inside the virtual space of the cube, the tool also implemented operations that allows the user to define his degree of proximity to the date in question. Zoom, translations (both using the keyboard) and rotation (using the mouse).

Subsequently, the large data manipulation created the need to implement new filters on data visualization, organizing the content into layers of information [5].

The filters layers provided by the tool, allow to distinguish the monkeys in groups, heights, name and gender, which facilitates the spatial analysis to search for patterns of behavior. As the functions of handling menus with OpenGL are not intuitive, a side menu was created using functions related to the mouse positioning [Fig.2], that allows navigation between layers more practical.

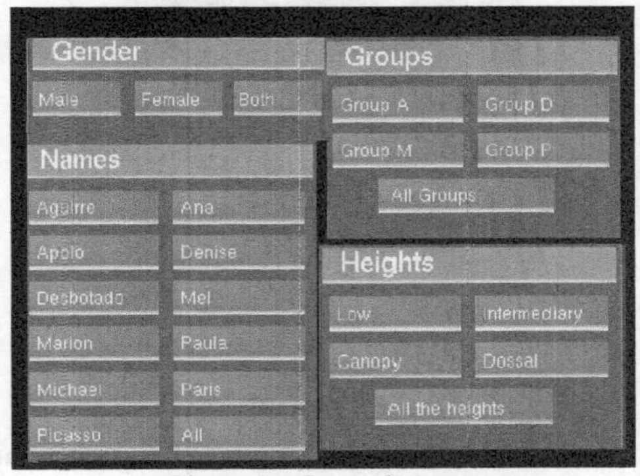

Figure 2 – Layers' menu.

IV.2 – TOOL VERSION WITH IMPROVED VIRTUAL REALITY FOR SPATIAL ANALYSIS OF ANIMAL OCCUPATION DATA

The Virtual Reality can be defined as an interface between user and machine, simulating a real environment and allowing the interaction with it [6].

The second step of the visualization tool development, still undergoing refinement, predicts the implementation of improved Virtual Reality. In this context, the implementation focus became the spatial occupation data refinement, through textures and 3D models. In addition, we performed a graphic mapping of the terrain where the data was collected, using the Analyst 3D tool from ArcGis software. This step was marked by its multidisciplinary characteristic, addressing Geoprocessing and graphics design knowledge.

The texture mapping in OpenGL, consists in loading the texture, defining the vertices in which it will be used and finally applying it.

The 3D modeling is a Computer Graphics' area that acts on the creation of three dimensional entities, which can be statics (rendering) or moving images (animation), with or without interactivity. At this tool developing state, the modeling used has a static characteristic and without interactivity, because of its simplicity in visual data representation. Later studies and implementations will allow the dynamics modeling usage with interactivity, seeking seasonal behavior patterns in an improved Virtual Reality environment closest to the *in loco* animal visualization.

To the modeling, we opted for Blender software, which offers monkeys 3D models. With the model in the 3DS file format, a function was used to load it in the OpenGL environment. With the model inserted, was possible to apply textures and geometrical transformations, in order to suit it in the virtual space formerly occupied by simpler primitives, like points [Fig.3].

Figure 3 – 3D models and applied textures.

For the terrain graphic's mapping was first used the ArcView software to make the geoprocessing of the topographic regions' data. By the vectorization of contour lines, the program creates a Hypsometric map (representation of relieves through colors), which subdivides the relieves in greyscales where the limits are: white, representing the highest point of relief, and black, the lowest [Fig.4].

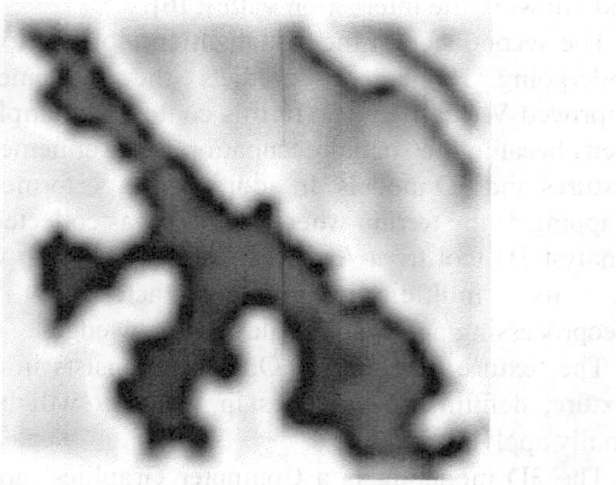

Figure 4 – Heightmap of the worked region.

Afterwards, we used a C/C++ language algorithm (Height Mapping) that performs the reading of a heightmap in ".raw" file format, associating each value of the 256 shades of gray from the file to a corresponding height. The map is then scaled to the dimensions compatible with the cube [Fig. 5].

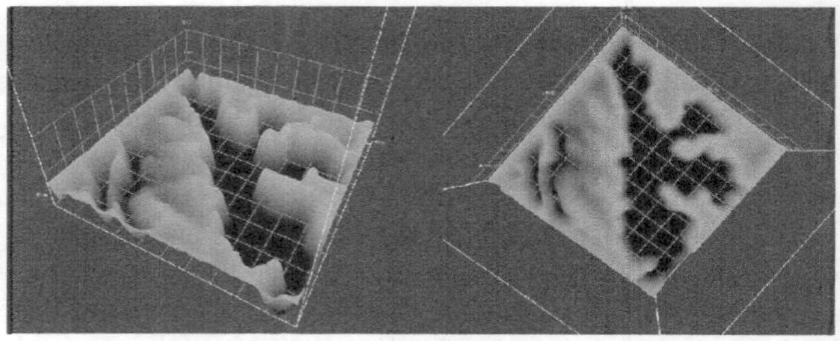

Figure 5 – Terrain rendering.

With the terrain inserted into the cube, the 3D monkey models were loaded in it. The Figure 6 illustrates a scene in which all the monkeys are displayed in different time periods.

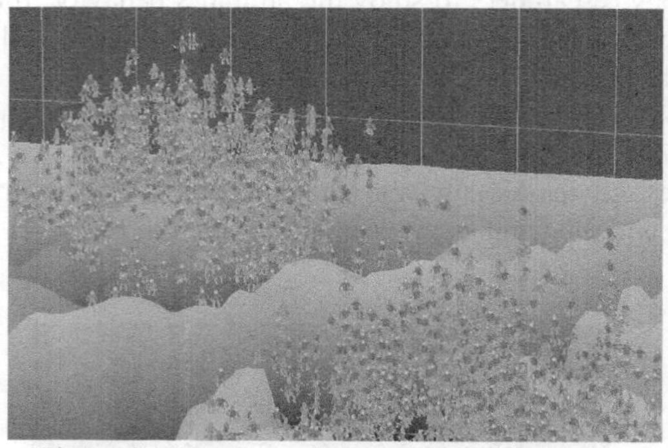

Figure 6 – Terrain rendering with the 3D models.

The current work to improve the tool consists in introducing a dynamic model that allows seasonal visualization of the gross data (including temporal filters), while increasing the Virtual Reality sensation. Furthermore, we will apply texture over the relief, insert 3D models for the trees and also include new models to represent the monkeys' activities, such as: feeding, foraging, getting around, sunbathing, and others.

V.CONCLUSION

To achieve the proposed objectives, it was necessary the use of computational resources such as 3D modeling, geoprocessing, graphical computing and high level programming. Thus was aggregated knowledge from several areas, transforming it into a multidisciplinary work.

As Scientific Visualization serves to assist in the interpretation of large amounts of data, it was necessary to generate images' layers. Thus, we created an interface between data and user, allowing the observation and understanding of factors that might otherwise pass unnoticed by the raw analysis of the data. This fact supports the work of the masters in Vertebrates' Zoology and other researchers in related areas.

The next research goal is to generate images related to spatial occupation density, using parallelism as a way to increase computing performance.

ACKNOWLEDGMENT

We would like to thank the PROBIC (Program of Undergraduate Research at Pontifical University of Minas Gerais - PUC Minas) and the FAPEMIG (Foundation for Supporting Research in the State of Minas Gerais, Brazil). Also, we would like to thank the Department of Geography at PUC Minas, in particular to Professor José Flávio Morais Castro, for his generous contribution in producing this work.

REFERENCES

[1] COHEN, Marcelo and MANSSOUR, Isabel H. OpenGL Uma Abordagem Prática e Objetiva. São Paulo, SP: Novatec Editora, 2006. (In Portuguese).

[2] WRIGHT, Richard S. Jr. SWEET, Michael. OpenGL SuperBible. 2nd ed. Indianapolis, Indiana: Waite Group Press, 2000.

[3] FOLEY, *James David et al.* Computer Graphics: Principles and Practice. 2ª ed. em C. Boston. Addison-Wesley. 1996. 1175p.

[4] JOHNSON, Christopher R. and HANSEN, Charles D. The Visualization Handbook. Saltlake City, Utah: Elsevier Butterworth-Heinemann, 2005.

[5] COSTA, João Vasco E. O. Monitorização e Geovisualização de Pesquisas Web no Portal Sapo. pp. 31-34.

[6] NETO, Antonio V. and MACHADO, Liliane S. and OLIVEIRA, Maria C. F. Realidade Virtual – Definições, Dispositivos e Aplicações. Pp. 5. (In Portuguese).

SESSION

COMPUTATIONAL SCIENCE AND APPLICATIONS

Chair(s)

TBA

Power Spectra of Ionospheric Scintillation

G. V. Jandieri[1], **and A. Ishimaru**[2]
[1]Department of Physics, Georgian Technical University, Tbilisi, Georgia
[2]Department of Electrical Engineering, University of Washington, Seattle, Washington, USA

Abstract *- Peculiarities of the spatial power spectrum (SPS) of scattered radiation in magnetized turbulent anisotropic plasma are investigated by smooth perturbation method taking into account diffraction effects. Second order statistical moments: broadening, wave structure functions, angle-of-arrivals, scintillation index are calculated numerically for both anisotropic and power-law correlation functions of electron density fluctuations using experimental data. New features of the evaluation of a double-humped shape of the SPS for different parameter of anisotropy and angle of inclination of prolate irregularities with respect to the external magnetic field taking into account geometry of the task are revealed for the first time. The gap increases in proportion to the anisotropy factor. The power spectra and scintillation level of scattered ordinary and extraordinary waves have been calculated taking into account movement of ionospheric irregularities.*

Keywords: spatial power spectrum, double-humped effect, scintillation, magnetized plasma.

1 Introduction

Statistical characteristics of scattered electromagnetic waves in randomly statistically isotropic media have been intensively studied [1,2]. However in many cases irregularities are anisotropic and are oriented along a certain direction. In the upper atmosphere ionization becomes significantly anisotropic because electrons can move easily along the magnetic field lines than across them. There is therefore a tendency for all irregularities to become aligned along geomagnetic field [3]. Anisotropic irregularities in the ionosphere lead to the damping and amplification of the amplitude of radio waves, fluctuations of the phase and variations of the angle-of-arrival; ionospheric scintillation is a result of complex action of all these effects. For relatively small irregularities, diffraction effects are important. The features of the SPS of scattered radiation in magnetized anisotropic plasma in the complex geometrical optics approximation using the perturbation method have been investigated in [4-7]. The "Double-humped effect" in turbulent anisotropic magnetized plasma has been discovered recently using the smooth perturbation method taking into account diffraction effects [8]; some peculiarities of statistical characteristics of scattered radiation have been reported in [9,10].

This paper is devoted to the investigation of second order statistical moments of the SPS of scattered electromagnetic waves in turbulent collisionless magnetized plasma with electron density fluctuations. New peculiarities of the "Double-humped effect" are revealed analytically in the SPS of a multiple scattered radiation at oblique illumination of magnetized plasma with prolate irregularities by mono-directed incident radiation using the smooth perturbation method taking into account diffraction effects. Numerical calculations are carried out for both anisotropic Gaussian and power-law correlation functions of electron density fluctuations applying experimental data. It was shown that the SPS has a double-peaked shape for the power-law correlation function, the gap increases in proportion to the anisotropy factor, location of its maximum weakly varies and width substantially broadens with increasing distance travelling by electromagnetic waves in randomly-inhomogeneous magnetized plasma.

2 Formulation of the problem

Consider a plane wave propagating in the z direction and the unit vector $\boldsymbol{\tau}$ of an external magnetic field lies in the YZ coordinate plane ($\mathbf{k_0} \parallel z$, $\mathbf{H_0} \in YZ$ - principle plane), $k_0 = 2\pi/\lambda$, λ is the radio wavelength in free space. Absorption in the layer is negligible for high frequency incident wave and components of second-rank tensor ε_{ij} of the collisionless magnetized plasma are [11]:

$$\varepsilon_{xx} = 1 - \text{v}(1-u)^{-1}, \ \varepsilon_{yy} = 1 - \text{v}(1 - u\sin^2\alpha)(1-u)^{-1},$$

$$\varepsilon_{zz} = 1 - \text{v}(1 - u\cos^2\alpha)(1-u)^{-1},$$

$$\tilde{\varepsilon}_{xy} = -\tilde{\varepsilon}_{yx} = \text{v}\sqrt{u}\cos\alpha\,(1-u)^{-1},$$

$$\tilde{\varepsilon}_{xz} = -\tilde{\varepsilon}_{zx} = -\,\mathrm{v}\sqrt{u}\,\sin\alpha\,(1-u)^{-1};$$

where α is the angle between $\mathbf{k}_0$ and $\mathbf{H}_0$ vectors; $\omega_p(\mathbf{r}) = [4\pi N(\mathbf{r})e^2/m]^{1/2}$ is the plasma frequency, $u(\mathbf{r}) = [eH_0(\mathbf{r})/mc\omega]^2$ and $\mathrm{v}(\mathbf{r}) = \omega_p^2(\mathbf{r})/\omega^2$ are the magneto-ionic parameters, $\Omega_H(\mathbf{r}) = eH_0(\mathbf{r})/mc$ is the electron gyrofrequency. Dielectric permittivity of turbulent magnetized plasma is $\varepsilon_{ij}(\mathbf{r}) = \varepsilon_{ij}^{(0)} + \varepsilon_{ij}^{(1)}(\mathbf{r})$, $|\varepsilon_{ij}^{(1)}(\mathbf{r})| << 1$. The first term is the regular (unperturbed) component of the dielectric permittivity connecting with the ionization distribution in the upper atmosphere at different altitudes above the Earth surface; the second term is a random function of the spatial coordinates caused by electron density fluctuations in the ionosphere; $\mathrm{v}(\mathbf{r}) = \mathrm{v}_0\,[1 + n_1(\mathbf{r})]$.

The electric field $\mathbf{E}$ satisfying wave equation

$$\left(\frac{\partial^2}{\partial x_i\,\partial x_j} - \Delta\delta_{ij} - k_0^2\,\varepsilon_{ij}(\mathbf{r})\right)\mathbf{E}_j(\mathbf{r}) = 0\,, \qquad (1)$$

introduce as $E_j(\mathbf{r}) = E_{0j}\exp(\varphi_0 + \varphi_1 + \varphi_2 + \ldots)$, $\varphi_0 = i k_\perp y + i k_0 z$ ($k_\perp << k_0$); complex phase fluctuations are of the order $\varphi_1 \sim \varepsilon_{ij}^{(1)}$, $\varphi_2 \sim \varepsilon_{ij}^{(1)\,2}$. Wave field Parameter $\mu = k_\perp / k_0$ describing diffraction effects is calculated in zero-order approximation [8]. The irregular plasma structure in the scattering medium imposes a random phase on the transmitted radio wave.

Phase fluctuation in the second order approximation satisfies differential equation

$$\frac{\partial^2\varphi_2}{\partial z\,\partial x} + i\,\mathrm{P}_j\frac{\partial^2\varphi_2}{\partial z\,\partial y} + i k_0\frac{\partial\varphi_2}{\partial x} + (2\Gamma_j k_\perp - \mathrm{P}_j k_0)\frac{\partial\varphi_2}{\partial y}$$

$$-\mathrm{P}_j k_\perp\frac{\partial\varphi_2}{\partial z} - i\Gamma_j\left(\frac{\partial^2\varphi_2}{\partial x^2} + \frac{\partial^2\varphi_2}{\partial y^2}\right) =$$

$$= i\Gamma_j\left[\left(\frac{\partial\varphi_1}{\partial x}\right)^2 + \left(\frac{\partial\varphi_1}{\partial y}\right)^2\right], \qquad (2)$$

where polarization coefficients are [11]:

$$\mathrm{P}_j = \frac{2\sqrt{u_0}\,(1-\mathrm{v}_0)\cos\alpha}{u_0\sin^2\alpha \pm \sqrt{u_0^2\sin^4\alpha + 4u_0(1-\mathrm{v}_0)^2\cos^2\alpha}}\,,$$

$$\Gamma_j = -\frac{\mathrm{v}_0\sqrt{u_0}\,\sin\alpha + \mathrm{P}_j u_0\,\mathrm{v}_0\sin\alpha\cos\alpha}{1 - u_0 - \mathrm{v}_0 + u_0\mathrm{v}_0\cos^2\alpha}\,. \qquad (3)$$

The upper sign (index $j = 1$) corresponds to the extraordinary wave and the lower sign (index $j = 2$) corresponds to the ordinary wave. Ordinary and extraordinary waves in magnetized plasma generally are elliptically polarized.

The knowledge of the solution of two-dimensional spectral component of the phase fluctuation satisfying stochastic differential equation (for $j = z$ component) allows us to calculate variance of the phase fluctuations for arbitrary correlation function of electron density fluctuations:

$$<\varphi_1^2(\mathbf{r})> = 2\pi k_0^4\,L\Omega_5\int_{-\infty}^{\infty}dk_x\int_{-\infty}^{\infty}dk_y\,\frac{1}{G_1}\Big[-k_x^2 + \mathrm{P}_j^2(k_y^2 - k_\perp^2) + 2i\mathrm{P}_j k_x k_y\Big]\,V_n\!\left(k_x,\,k_y,\frac{iG_2 - G_3}{G_1}\right), \qquad (4)$$

where: $\Omega_5 = \dfrac{\mathrm{v}_0^2\,u_0}{(1-u_0)^2}(\sin^2\alpha + 2\mathrm{P}_j\sqrt{u_0}\sin^2\alpha\cos\alpha - 2\Gamma_j\sqrt{u_0}\sin\alpha\cos^2\alpha - 2\mathrm{P}_j\Gamma_j u_0\sin\alpha\cos^3\alpha + \mathrm{P}_j^2 u_0\sin^2\alpha\cos^2\alpha + \Gamma_j^2 u_0\cos^4\alpha)$, k_x, k_y are the spatial wavenumber components in directions X and Y, respectively; L is the physical path through the inhomogeneous plasma, G_i are complicated functions of magnetized plasma parameters.

The knowledge of the correlation function of the phase taking into account that the observation points are spaced apart at a very small distance $\boldsymbol{\rho} = \{\rho_x, \rho_y\}$ perpendicular to the principle plane, allows us to calculate the width of the spatial power spectrum in the XZ and YZ planes respectively:

$$\frac{<\Delta k_x^2>}{k_0^2} = -\left.\frac{\partial^2\tilde{W}_\varphi}{\partial\xi^2}\right|_{\xi=\eta=0},\quad \frac{<\Delta k_y^2>}{k_0^2} = -\left.\frac{\partial^2\tilde{W}_\varphi}{\partial\eta^2}\right|_{\xi=\eta=0} \qquad (5)$$

wave structure functions of the amplitude, phase and mutual correlation functions [1,2]:

$$D_1(\mathbf{r}_1,\mathbf{r}_2) = <\big(\varphi_1(\mathbf{r}_1) - \varphi_1(\mathbf{r}_2)\big)\big(\varphi_1^*(\mathbf{r}_1) - \varphi_1^*(\mathbf{r}_2)\big)>,$$

$$D_2(\mathbf{r}_1,\mathbf{r}_2) = <\big(\varphi_1(\mathbf{r}_1) - \varphi_1(\mathbf{r}_2)\big)^2>,$$

$$D_\chi(\mathbf{r}_1,\mathbf{r}_2) = \frac{1}{2}(D_1 + \mathrm{Re}\,D_2),\quad D_S(\mathbf{r}_1,\mathbf{r}_2) = \frac{1}{2}(D_1 - \mathrm{Re}\,D_2),$$

$$D_{\chi S} = \frac{1}{2}\,\mathrm{Im}\,D_2\,. \qquad (6)$$

where: $\xi = k_0\,\rho_x$, $\eta = k_0\,\rho_y$.

Transverse correlation function of a scattered field $W_{EE^*}(\mathbf{\rho}) = < E(\mathbf{r}) E^*(\mathbf{r}+\mathbf{\rho}) >$ is [8]:

$$W_{EE^*}(\mathbf{\rho}, k_\perp) = E_0^2 \exp\left\{ \mathrm{Re}\left[\frac{1}{2}\left(< \varphi_1^2(\mathbf{r}) > + < \varphi_1^{2*}(\mathbf{r}+\mathbf{\rho}) > \right) \right.\right.$$

$$\left.\left. + < \varphi_1(\mathbf{r})\, \varphi_1^*(\mathbf{r}+\mathbf{\rho}) > + 2 < \varphi_2 > \right] \right\} \exp(-i\rho_y k_\perp), \qquad (7)$$

where E_0^2 is the intensity of incident radiation.

SPS of scattered field in case of incident plane wave $W(k, k_\perp)$ is easily calculated by Fourier transformation from the transversal correlation function of scattered field [2]:

$$W(k, k_\perp) = \int_{-\infty}^{\infty} d\rho_y\, W_{EE^*}(\rho_y, k_\perp) \exp(ik\rho_y). \qquad (8)$$

When the angular spectrum of an incident wave has a finite width and its maximum coincide with z axis, SPS of scattered radiation is given:

$$I(k) = \int_{-\infty}^{\infty} dk_\perp\, W(k, k_\perp) \exp(-k_\perp^2 \beta^2), \qquad (9)$$

where β characterizes the dispersal of an incident radiation (disorder of an incident radiation), k is a transverse component of the wavevector of scattered field [1,2].

Intensity of scintillation is determined by index S_4 characterizing power of a receiving signal. The spatial relationship between the power spectrum of the two-dimensional fluctuating received power $P_S(k_x, k_y, L)$ and the observed power spectrum of the phase fluctuation for a weak scattering medium is given by [12]

$$\tilde{P}_S(k_x, k_y, L) = 4\, \tilde{W}_\varphi(k_x, k_y, L) \sin^2\left(\frac{k_x^2 + k_y^2}{k_f^2} \right), \qquad (10)$$

where $k_f = (4\pi / \lambda L)^{1/2}$ is the Fresnel wavenumber. The sinusoidal term in (10) is responsible for oscillations in the scintillation spectrum. For the scintillation level S_4 (zeroth moment), we have:

$$S_4^2 = \int_{-\infty}^{\infty} dk_x \int_{-\infty}^{\infty} dk_y\, \tilde{P}_S(k_x, k_y, L). \qquad (11)$$

A scintillation spectrum with Fresnel oscillations is interpreted for both Gaussian and power-law wavenumber models. Equations (10) and (11) describe two dimensional diffraction patterns at the ground and also illustrate the strong attenuation of the interference pattern.

If rigid irregularities are moving past the ray path along the Y direction with apparent velocity V_y, the resultant temporal spectrum is given by a strip scan integration along the X axis,

$$P_\varphi(\nu, L) = \frac{2\pi}{V_y} \int_0^\infty dk_x\, \tilde{W}_\varphi\left(k_x, k_y = \frac{2\pi\nu}{V_y}, L \right),$$

$$P_S(\nu, L) = 4\, P_\varphi(\nu, L) \sin^2\left(\frac{\nu}{\nu_f} \right)^2. \qquad (12)$$

The Fresnel frequency $\nu_f = V_y / (\pi \lambda z)^{1/2}$ is directly proportional to the drift velocity V_y transverse to the radio path and inversely proportional to the Fresnel radius $(\lambda z)^{1/2}$, z is the mean distance between the observer and the irregularities. The intensity fluctuations are severely attenuated for irregularities larger than this radius or frequencies less than the Fresnel frequency. The oscillation minimums appear with ratios $1:\sqrt{2}$, $1:\sqrt{3}$, $1:\sqrt{4}$, ... Observable power spectra $P_S(\nu, L)$ allows us to calculate the spectral width (1st and square root 2nd moments) which is a measure of the scintillation rate.

3 Numerical calculations

Numerical calculations are carried out for 40 MHz ($k_0 = 840$ km^{-1}) incident electromagnetic wave; Fresnel radius at the altitude 300 km is equal to 1.5 km. Plasma parameters are: $u_0 = 0.0012$, $v_0 = 0.0133$. We use both Gaussian and power-law spectra. Anisotropic Gaussian correlation function in the principle YZ plane is [5]

$$\tilde{V}_n(k_x, k_y, k_z) = \sigma_n^2 \frac{l_\perp^2 l_\parallel}{8\pi^{3/2}} \cdot$$

$$\cdot \exp\left(-\frac{k_x^2 l_\perp^2}{4} - p_1 \frac{k_y^2 l_\parallel^2}{4} - p_2 \frac{k_z^2 l_\parallel^2}{4} - p_3 k_y k_z l_\parallel^2 \right), \qquad (13)$$

where: $p_1 = (\sin^2\gamma_0 + \chi^2 \cos^2\gamma_0)^{-1} [1 + (1-\chi^2)^2 \cdot$ $\cdot \sin^2\gamma_0 \cos^2\gamma_0 / \chi^2]$, $p_2 = (\sin^2\gamma_0 + \chi^2\cos^2\gamma_0)/\chi^2$, $p_3 = (1-\chi^2) \sin\gamma_0 \cos\gamma_0 / 2\chi^2$, σ_n^2 is variance of electron density fluctuations. This function contains anisotropy factor of irregularities $\chi = l_\parallel / l_\perp$ (ratio of longitudinal and transverse linear scales of plasma irregularities) and inclination angle γ_0 of prolate irregularities with respect to the external magnetic field.

Measurements of satellite's signal parameters passing through ionospheric layer and measurements aboard of satellite show that in *F*-region of the ionosphere irregularities has the power-law spectrum with different spatial scales. We utilize 3D anisotropic power-law spectrum of electron density irregularities. The corresponding spectral function spatial power-law spectrum for $p>3$ has the following form [5]

$$\tilde{V}_n(k_x,k_y,k_z)=\frac{\sigma_N^2}{\pi^{5/2}}\Gamma\left(\frac{p}{2}\right)\Gamma\left(\frac{5-p}{2}\right)\sin\left[\frac{(p-3)\,\pi}{2}\right]\cdot$$

$$\frac{l_{\parallel}^3}{\chi^2\left[1+l_{\perp}^2(k_x^2+k_y^2)+l_{\parallel}^2 k_z^2\right]^{p/2}}, \qquad (14)$$

The value of *p* depends on the specific conditions of development of the turbulence, in particular the instability process involved, the latitude, the altitude, and so on. As observed by measurements with satellite ETS-2, the spectral index is usually between 2 and 4 [13].

Correlation function of the phase fluctuations caused by electron density fluctuations for anisotropic Gaussian correlation function (13) has the following form

$$\tilde{W}_{\varphi}(\xi,\eta,L)=\tilde{\Omega}_5\int_{-\infty}^{\infty}ds\int_{-\infty}^{\infty}dx\,\frac{x^2+\mathrm{P}_j^2(\mu+s)^2}{(\delta_4+x^2)^2}\cdot$$

$$\left\{-T^2\left[\frac{x^2}{4\chi^2}+\frac{p_1 s^2}{4}+p_2\frac{(\delta_3+\delta_2 x^2)^2}{4(\delta_4+x^2)^2}\right.\right.$$

$$\left.\left.+\,2p_3\,s\,\frac{\delta_3+\delta_2 x^2}{\delta_4+x^2}\right]\right\}\exp(-i\,\xi\,x-i\,\eta\,s), \qquad (15)$$

where: $\tilde{\Omega}_5=\frac{1}{\pi}B_0\frac{\Omega_5 T^2}{\chi}$, $B_0=\sigma_n^2\frac{\sqrt{\pi}\,T k_0 L}{4\,\chi}$,

$x=\frac{k_x}{k_0}$, $s=\frac{k_y}{k_0}$, $T=k_0\,l_{\parallel}$, $\delta_2=1-\mathrm{P}_j\Gamma_j\mu-\mathrm{P}_j\Gamma_j s$,

$\delta_3=\mathrm{P}_j s(\mathrm{P}_j\mu-2\Gamma_j\mu^2+\mathrm{P}_j s-3\Gamma_j\mu s-\Gamma_j s^2)$,

$\delta_4=\mathrm{P}_j^2(\mu+s)^2$.

Knowledge of these functions allows us to calculate wave structure function and angle-of-arrival in the *XZ* plane using (6):

$$D_s(\xi,\eta,L)=\frac{2}{\sqrt{\pi}}\tilde{\Omega}_1 T\int_{-\infty}^{\infty}ds\int_{-\infty}^{\infty}dx\,\left[1+\cos(\xi x+\eta s)\right]$$

$$\exp\left[-\frac{T^2}{4}(p_2 m_5^2 x^4+b_6 x^2+b_7)\right] \qquad (16)$$

where: $\Omega_1=\frac{\mathrm{v}_0^2}{(1-u_0)^2}\left[1+u_0-2\sqrt{u_0}\,(\sin\alpha-\cos\alpha+\right.$ $\left.+\sqrt{u_0}\,\sin\alpha\cos\alpha)\right]$, $\tilde{\Omega}_1=\frac{1}{4\sqrt{\pi}}B_0\frac{\Omega_1 T}{\chi}$,

$m_5=\frac{1}{4}[(s+\mu)\mathrm{P}_j+\Gamma_j]\Gamma_j$, $m_6=\frac{1}{2}(s^2+2s\mu)$,

$b_7=\frac{1}{4}p_2 s^4+(p_2\mu+2p_3)s^3+(p_1+p_2\mu^2+4p_3\mu)s^2$,

$b_6=\frac{1}{\chi^2}+2p_2 m_5 m_6+4p_3 m_5 s$.

Figure 1 shows the broadening of the SPS versus anisotropy factor χ (left figure) for prolate electron density irregularities; characteristic longitudinal linear scale $l_{\parallel}=200$ m, electromagnetic wave propagates with respect to the external magnetic field at the angle $\alpha=20^0$. Numerical calculations show that maxima of the SPS are at $\chi=5$ and $\chi=16$ in the *XZ* plane for $\gamma_0=0^0$ and $\gamma_0=30^0$, respectively. Increasing angle $\alpha=40^0$ maximum of the SPS displaced to the right $\chi\approx18$ (for $\gamma_0=30^0$) and not displaced for $\gamma_0=0^0$. The broadening of the SPS of scattered ordinary and extraordinary waves approximately is the same for $L=100$ km. External magnetic field has a substantial influence on the broadening of the SPS and narrows in the principle plane, which is in agreement with [8]. Deformation of the SPS depends on the angle α and the distance travelling by electromagnetic wave in turbulent magnetized plasma; except the case $\gamma_0=0^0$ (prolate irregularities are stretched along the external magnetic field).

Plots of the phase wave structure function D_s of scattered ordinary wave as a function of η for $\gamma_0=0^0\div15^0$ are presented on the right figure in the direction perpendicular to the principle plane. Numerical calculations show that maxima of the D_s function is at $\eta=31$ if $\gamma_0=0^0$; and at $\eta=59$ if $\gamma_0=5^0$; phase wave structure function tends to saturation at $\eta=450$.

Analysis show that the angle-of-arrival in the XZ plane is in the interval $0.5'' \div 2'$.

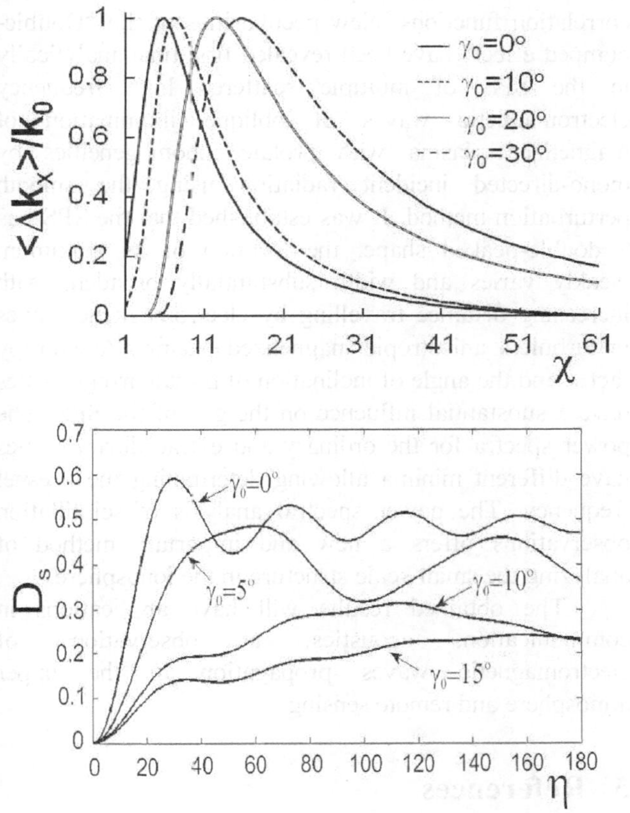

Figure 1. Broadening of the SPS of scattered radiation in the XZ plane as a function of the parameter χ at $\alpha = 20^0$ and different angles of inclination of prolate irregularities with respect to the external magnetic field $\gamma_0 = 0^0 \div 30^0$ (top figure). Phase structure function as a function of the distance between observation points η at $k_\perp = 0.114$, $\chi = 10$, $\alpha = 20^0$ for $P_S(\nu, L)$ (bottom figure).

Scintillation index S_4 for power-law correlation function in the YZ plane is given by

$$S_4^2 = \frac{8\,\tilde{\Omega}_5\,\tilde{Q}}{\pi} \int\limits_{-\infty}^{\infty} dx \int\limits_{-\infty}^{\infty} ds \, \frac{x^2 + \mathrm{P}_j^2\,(\mu + s)^2}{(x^2 + \delta_4)^2} \cdot$$

$$\cdot \left\{ 1 + T^2 \left[\frac{x^2 + s^2}{\chi^2} + \frac{(\delta_2\,x^2 + \delta_3)^2}{(x^2 + \delta_4)^2} \right] \right\}^{-p/2} \cdot$$

$$\sin^2\left[k_0 L\,(x^2 + s^2) \right], \qquad (17)$$

where: $\tilde{Q} = \Gamma\left(\frac{p}{2}\right)\Gamma\left(\frac{5-p}{2}\right)\sin\left[\frac{(p-3)\,\pi}{2}\right]$. Square of the scintillation index is proportional to the thickness of a layer and the root-mean-square deviation of small-scale electron density irregularities σ_n^2 which are responsible for signal fading.

From equations (2), (7) and (14) for the SPS of power-law correlation functions of electron density fluctuations in turbulent non-magnetized plasma we obtain:

$$\frac{W_{EE^*}(\xi, \eta, L)}{E_0^2} = \exp(-i\eta\,\mu)\,\exp\left(\pi^{3/2} \frac{T^2\,\mathrm{v}_0^2\,Q_0}{\chi\,\Gamma\left(\frac{p}{2}\right)}\,k_0\,L \cdot \right.$$

$$\cdot \left\{ -\frac{1}{2}\,\Gamma\left(\frac{p-1}{2}\right) \int\limits_{-\infty}^{\infty} ds \, \frac{1}{(1 + C_1\,s^2)^{p-1}} + \left(\frac{\chi\,\xi}{2\,T}\right)^{(p-1)/2} \cdot \right. \qquad (18)$$

$$\left. \left. \cdot \int\limits_{-\infty}^{\infty} ds \, \frac{\exp(-i\eta\,s)}{\left[1 + \Phi(s)\right]^{(p-1)/2}}\, K_{\frac{p-1}{2}}\left(\frac{\chi\,\xi}{T} \left[1 + \Phi(s)\right] \right) \right\} \right),$$

where: $\Phi(s) = \frac{T^2}{4}\left[s^4 + 4\,\mu\,s^3 + 4\left(\frac{1}{\chi^2} + \mu^2\right) s^2 \right]$,

$Q_0 = \frac{\sigma_n^2}{\pi^{5/2}}\,\tilde{Q}$, $C_1 = \frac{T^2}{\chi^2}(1 + \chi^2\,\mu^2)$, $\Gamma(x)$ is the gamma function, $K_\nu(x)$ is the McDonald function.

Figure 2 illustrates the evaluation of a gap in the SPS of scattered ordinary wave in turbulent anisotropic collisionless non-magnetized plasma with prolate irregularities of electron density fluctuations having characteristic longitudinal linear scale $l_\parallel = 10$ km; spectral index is equal to $p = 3.2$. Numerical calculations show that electromagnetic wave having parameters $\mu = 0.05$, $\alpha = 20^0$, $\beta = 10$ travelling distance 2000 km in the ionosphere broadens on 56% increasing anisotropy factor of prolate irregularities from $\chi = 150$ up to 350. When the scattering is weak, oscillations are observed in the power spectra. These oscillations are attributed to a Fresnel filtering effect. These oscillations are used to calculate the velocity, estimate the irregularity scale size, anisotropy factor and angle of inclination of prolate irregularities with respect to the external magnetic field. The rate of oscillations is dependent on the irregularity velocity. The power spectra

$P_S(\nu, L)$ for the ordinary and extraordinary waves have different minima and allow us to calculate corresponding k_f and ν_f.

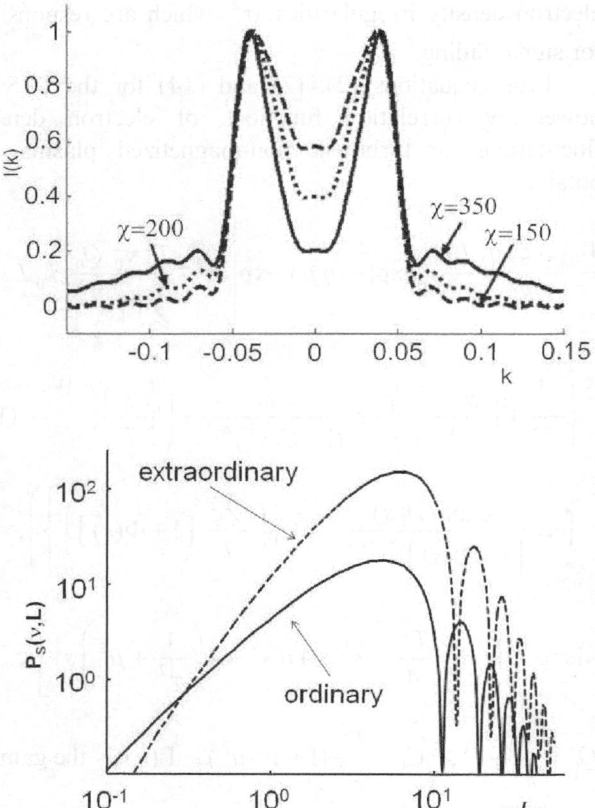

Figure 2 Depicts SPS of scattered ordinary wave versus k for $\mu = 0.05$, $\alpha = 20^0$, $\beta = 10$, at fixed $B_0 = 3300$, plasma parameters: $p = 3.2$, $l_{\parallel} = 10$ km and different anisotropy factor $\chi = 150$, 200, 350 (top figure); The power spectra $P_S(\nu, L)$ for the ordinary and extraordinary waves as a function of non-dimensional frequency parameter ν / ν_f at $\chi = 5$, $T = 250$, $\alpha = 40^0$, $\gamma_0 = 10^0$ are plotted on the bottom figure.

4 Conclusion

Second order statistical moments of scattered radiation: correlation function of the phase fluctuation, broadening of the SPS, angle-of-arrivals and the scintillation index caused by electron density variations are obtained for arbitrary correlation function of electron density fluctuations. Numerical calculations are carried out for both anisotropic Gaussian and power-law correlation functions. New peculiarities of the "Double-humped effect" have been revealed first time analytically in the SPS of multiple scattered high frequency electromagnetic waves at oblique illumination of magnetized plasma with prolate inhomogeneities by mono-directed incident radiation using the smooth perturbation method. It was established that the SPS has a double-peaked shape, the location of its maximum weakly varies and width substantially broadens with increasing distance travelling by electromagnetic waves in turbulent anisotropic magnetized plasma. Anisotropy factor and the angle of inclination of prolate irregularities have a substantial influence on the gap of the SPS. The power spectra for the ordinary and extraordinary waves have different minima allowing determining the Fresnel frequency. The power spectral analysis of scintillation observations offers a new and important method of analyzing the small-scale structure in the ionosphere.

The obtained results will have applications in communication, acoustics, at observations of electromagnetic waves propagation in the upper atmosphere and remote sensing.

5 References

[1] Ishimaru, A. *Wave* Propagation and Scattering in Random Media, Vol. 2, Multiple Scattering, Turbulence, Rough Surfaces and Remote Sensing, IEEE Press, Piscataway, New Jersey, USA, 1997.

[2] Rytov S. M., Yu. A. Kravtsov and V. I. Tatarskii, Principles of Statistical Radiophysics. vol.4. Waves Propagation Through Random Media. Berlin, New York, Springer, 1989.

[3] Gershman, B. N., L. M. Eruxhimov, and Yu. Ya. Iashin, Wavy Phenomena in the Ionosphere and Cosmic Plasma, Moscow, Nauka, 1984 (in Russian).

[4] Jandieri G. V., V. G. Gavrilenko, A. V. Sarokin and V. G. Jandieri, "Some properties of the angular power distribution of electromagnetic waves multiply scattered in a collisional magnetized turbulent plasma," Plasma Physics Report, Vol. 31, 604—615, 2005.

[5] Jandieri G. V., A. Ishimaru, V. G. Jandieri, A. G. Khantadze and Zh. M. Diasamidze, "Model computations of angular power spectra for

anisotropic absorptive turbulent magnetized plasma," Progress In Electromagnetics Research, PIER, Vol. 70, 307—328, 2007.

[6] Jandieri G. V., A. Ishimaru, N. N. Zhukova, T. N. Bzhalava and M. R. Diasamidze, "On the influence of fluctuations of the direction of an external magnetic field an phase and amplitude correlation functions of scattered radiation by magnetized plasma slab," Progress In Electromagnetics Research B, PIER B, Vol. B22, 121—143, 2010.

[7] Jandieri G. V., A. Ishimaru, and V. G. Jandieri, "Depolarization effects of incoherently scattered electromagnetic waves by inhomogeneous magnetized plasma slab," Journal of Electromagnetic Analysis and Application, Vol. 3, 471—478, 2011.

[8] Jandieri G.V., Ishimaru A., Mchedlishvili N.F., Takidze I.G. "Spatial power spectrum of multiple scattered ordinary and extraordinary waves in magnetized plasma with electron density fluctuations," Progress In Electromagnetics Research M (PIER M), Vol. 25, 87—100, 2012.

[9] Jandieri G.V, Zhukova N.N. Diasamidze Zh.M, Diasamidze M.R. „Angular power spectrum of scattered radiation in ionospheric plasma with both electron density and magnetic field fluctuations," WORLDCOMP'12 (The 2012 World Congress in Computer Science, Computer Engineering and Applied Computing), CSC'12 (the 9th International Conference of Scientific Computing): "Numerical methods, Approximation and estimation techniques, Optimization methods", July 16-19, 2012, Las Vegas, Nevada, USA, 39—44, 2012.

[10] Jandieri G.V., Ishimaru A., Mchedlishvili N.F. "Angular power spectrum of scattered electromagnetic waves in randomly inhomogeneous plasma with electron density fluctuations," ISAP2012 (2012 International Symposium on Antennas and Propagation), October 29-November 2, 2012, Nagoya, Japan, 1172—1175, 2012.

[11] Ginzburg V. L., Propagation of Electromagnetic Waves in Plasma. New York: Gordon and Beach, 1961.

[12] Rufenach C.L. "A radio scintillation method of estimating the small-scale structure in the ionosphere," J. Atmosph. Terr. Phys. Vol. 33, 1941—1951, 1975.

[13] Afraimovich E.L., Zherebtsov G.A., Zverzdin V.N., Franke S.J. "Characteristics of small-scale ionospheric irregularities as deduced from scintillation observations of radio signals from satellites ETS-2 and Polar Bear 4 at Irkutsk," Radio Sci., Vol. 29, No 4, 839—885, 1994.

Nonlinear Vibration of Fluid-loaded Double-walled Carbon Nanotubes Subjected To A Moving Load Based on Stochastic FEM

Tai-Ping Chang[1] **and Quey-Jen Yeh**[2]

[1] *Department of Construction Engineering, National Kaohsiung First University of Science and Technology, Kaohsiung, Taiwan*

[2] *Department of Business Administration, National Cheng-Kung University, Tainan, Taiwan*

Abstract - *This paper adopts stochastic FEM to study the statistical dynamic behaviors of nonlinear vibration of the fluid-conveying double-walled carbon nanotubes (DWCNTs) under a moving load by considering the effects of the geometric nonlinearity and the nonlinearity of van der Waals (vdW) force. The Young's modulus of elasticity of the DWCNTs is considered as stochastic with respect to the position to actually characterize the random material properties of the DWCNTs. Besides, the small scale effects of the nonlinear vibration of the DWCNTs are studied by using the theory of nonlocal elasticity. Based on the Hamilton's principle, the nonlinear governing equations of the fluid-conveying double-walled carbon nanotubes under a moving load are formulated. The stochastic finite element method along with the perturbation technique is adopted to study the statistical dynamic response of the DWCNTs. Some statistical dynamic response of the DWCNTs such as the mean values and standard deviations of the non-dimensional dynamic deflections are computed and checked by the Monte Carlo Simulation, meanwhile the effects of the nonlocal parameter and aspect ratio on the statistical dynamic response of the DWCNTs are investigated. It can be concluded that the nonlocal solutions of the dynamic deflections get larger with the increase of the nonlocal parameters due to the small scale effect, and as the aspect ratio increases, the small scale effect has less effect on the maxima non-dimensional dynamic deflections of the DWCNTs.*

Keywords: Nonlinear vibration; Double-walled carbon nanotubes; Stochastic FEM; Perturbation technique; Small scale effect.

1 Introduction

Since the landmark paper published by Iijima [1], carbon nanotubes (CNTs) have attracted worldwide attention due to their potential use in the fields of chemistry, physics, nano-engineering, electrical engineering, materials science, reinforced composite structures and construction engineering. Carbon nanotubes (CNTs) are used for a variety of technological and biomedical applications including nanocontainers for gas storage and nanopipes conveying fluids [2-8]. Some important applications of carbon nanotubes (CNTs) are such as nanotubes conveying fluids [3,7-8], different types of fluid flows like water [9], dynamic flow of methane, ethane and ethylene molecules [10] and the diffusive transport of light gases [11] had been reported, and the effects of these fluids on the mechanical properties of CNTs had been investigated. Natsuki et al. [12] adopted a simplified Flügge shell model to investigate the wave propagation of single- and double-walled CNTs conveying fluid. The single-elastic beam model [13-14] and the multiple-elastic beam model [15-19] were also broadly adopted to study the dynamic behaviors of fluid-conveying single-walled carbon nanotubes (SWCNTs) and multi-walled carbon nanotubes (MWCNTs). The vibration frequencies of the linear system and the system's stability related to the internal moving fluid were investigated. Moreover, the nonlocal elasticity theory was incorporated into the elastic beam model to study the small scale effect on the dynamics of SWCNT conveying fluid [20]. Chang and Liu [21-22] studied small scale effects on the flow-induced instability of double-walled carbon nanotubes (DWCNTs) by using the nonlocal elasticity theory. More recently, Chang [23-24] investigated the thermal-mechanical vibration and instability of fluid-conveying single-walled carbon nanotubes (SWCNTs) based on nonlocal elasticity theory. Generally speaking, the beam models mentioned above are linear; however, the vdW forces in the interlay space of MWCNTs are essentially nonlinear. Furthermore, the slender ratios are normally large if the beam models are adopted, that is, the large deformation will occur. Therefore, it is quite essential to consider two types of nonlinear factors, namely, the geometric nonlinearity and the nonlinearity of vdW force in investigating the dynamic behaviors of fluid-conveying MWCNTs. Kuang et al. [25] investigated the dynamic behaviors of double-walled carbon nanotubes (DWCNTs) conveying fluid by considering two types of nonlinearities mentioned above. Due to the rapid process of nanotechnology, the motion of neutral atoms and nanoparticles in nanotubes has been of remarkable interest [26]. Carbon nanotubes are utilized as molecular channels for the transportation of nanoparticles, such as water and protons [27]. In the process of these applications, carbon nanotubes might be subjected to moving load, and this causes the transverse vibration of carbon nanotubes. Therefore, it is quite necessary to investigate the dynamic behavior of carbon nanotubes under moving loads. So far, most researchers have studied static, buckling or free vibration analysis of nanotubes or nanobeams based on the local or nonlocal elasticity theory, forced vibration of DWCNTs under moving loads is rarely investigated. Until recently, Simsek [28] performed the vibration analysis of a SWCNT under action of a moving harmonic load based on nonlocal elasticity theory. Kiani and Wang [29] adopted nonlocal elasticity theory to investigate the interaction of a single-walled carbon nanotube with a moving nanoparticle.

Salvetat et al. [30] measured the flexural Young's modulus and shear modulus using AFM test on clamped–clamped nanoropes, getting values with 50% of error. Information related to statistical distributions of experimental data is also rare, and the important study from Krishnan et al. [31] provides one of the few examples available of histogram distribution of the flexural Young's modulus derived from 27 CNTs. The Young's modulus was estimated observing free-standing vibrations at room temperature using transmission electro-microscope (TEM), with a mean value of 1.3 TPa - 0.4 TPa/+0.6 TPa. Pronouncedly, in [32], stochastically averaged probability amplitude for the vibration modes is computed to obtain the root-mean-square vibration profile along the length of the tubes. Uncertainty is also associated to the equivalent atomistic-continuum models adopted extensively in particular by the engineering and materials science communities. Hence, to be realistic, the Young's modulus of elasticity of carbon nanotube (CNTs) should be considered as stochastic with respect to the position to actually describe the random property of the CNTs under certain conditions. In the present study, we investigate the statistical dynamic behaviors of nonlinear vibration of the fluid-conveying double-walled carbon nanotubes (DWCNTs) under a moving load by considering the effects of the geometric nonlinearity and the nonlinearity of van der Waals (vdW) force. The Young's modulus of elasticity of the DWCNTs is considered as stochastic with respect to the position to actually characterize the random material properties of the DWCNTs. In addition, the small scale effects on the nonlinear vibration of the DWCNTs are studied by using the theory of nonlocal elasticity. Based on the Hamilton's principle, the nonlinear governing equations of the fluid-conveying double-walled carbon nanotubes under a moving load are formulated. The stochastic finite element method along with the perturbation technique is adopted to study the statistical response of the DWCNTs; in particular, the Newton-Raphson iteration procedure in conjunction with Newmark scheme is utilized to solve the nonlinearity of the dynamic governing equation of the DWCNTs. The effects of the nonlocal parameter and aspect ratio on the statistical dynamic response of the DWCNTs are investigated.

2 Nonlinear beam model for fluid-conveying DWCNTs under a moving load

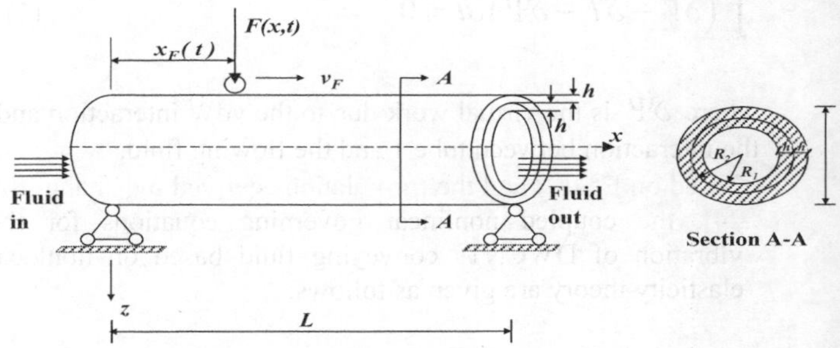

Fig. 1. Fluid-conveying DWCNTs under a moving load

In Fig. 1, the double-walled carbon nanotubes (DWCNTs) is modeled as a double-tube pipe which is composed of the inner tube of radius R_1 and the outer tube of radius R_2. The thickness of each tube is h, the length is L, and Young's modulus of elasticity is E. It is noted that the Young's modulus of elasticity E is assumed as stochastic with respect to the position to actually describe the random material property of the DWCNTs. The internal fluid is assumed to flow steadily through the inner tube with a constant velocity U. Besides, the boundary conditions of the DWCNTs are assumed as simply-supported at both ends. Based on the theory of Euler–Bernoulli beam and a nonlinear strain–displacement relationship of Von Karman type, the displacement field and strain–displacement relation can be written as follows:

$$\begin{aligned} \overline{u}_i(x,z,t) &= u_i(x,t) - z\frac{\partial w_i}{\partial x} \\ \overline{w}_i(x,z,t) &= w_i(x,t) \\ \varepsilon_i &= \frac{\partial \overline{u}_i}{\partial x} + \frac{1}{2}\left(\frac{\partial \overline{w}_i}{\partial x}\right)^2 \end{aligned} \tag{1}$$

where x is the axial coordinate, t is time, $\overline{u}_i$ and $\overline{w}_i$ denote the total displacements of the ith tube along the x coordinate directions, u_i and w_i define the axial and transverse displacements of the ith tube on the neutral axis, ε_i the corresponding total strain, and the subscript $i = 1$ and $i = 2$. Notice that tube 1 is the inner tube while tube 2 is the outer tube.

Based on Eq. (1), the potential energy V stored in a DWCNTs and the virtual kinetic energy T in the DWCNTs as

well as the fluid inside the DWCNTs can be individually determined.
Based on Hamilton's principle, the variational form of the equations of motion for the DWCNTs can be given by

$$\int_{t_0}^{t_1} (\delta V - \delta T - \delta\Psi)\, dt = 0 \tag{2}$$

where $\delta\Psi$ is the virtual work due to the vdW interaction and the interaction between tube 1 and the flowing fluid.

Based on Eq. (2) and the formulations derived by Chang [22, 24], the coupled nonlinear governing equations for the vibration of DWCNTs conveying fluid based on nonlocal elasticity theory are given as follows:

$$\begin{aligned}
&\frac{\partial^2}{\partial x^2}\left\{\left[E(x)I_1-(e_0a)^2 MU^2\right]\frac{\partial^2 w_1}{\partial x^2}\right\}-2(e_oa)^2 MU\frac{\partial^4 w_1}{\partial x^3\partial t}-(e_oa)^2(M+m_1)\frac{\partial^4 w_1}{\partial x^2\partial t^2}\\
&+MU^2\frac{\partial^2 w_1}{\partial x^2}-\int_0^L\left(\frac{\partial w_1}{\partial x}\right)^2\left(\frac{E(x)A_1}{2L}+\frac{MU^2}{2L}\right)dx\frac{\partial^2 w_1}{\partial x^2}+\frac{3MU^2}{2}\left(\frac{\partial w_1}{\partial x}\right)^2\frac{\partial^2 w_1}{\partial x^2}+\\
&(M+m_1)\frac{\partial^2 w_1}{\partial t^2}+2MU\frac{\partial^2 w_1}{\partial x\partial t}-MU\frac{\partial w_1}{\partial t}\frac{\partial w_1}{\partial x}\frac{\partial^2 w_1}{\partial x^2}\\
&=\left(1-(e_0a)^2\frac{\partial^2}{\partial x^2}\right)\left(c_1(w_2-w_1)\right)+c_3\left\{\left[\left(1-(e_0a)^2\frac{\partial^2}{\partial x^2}\right)w_2\right]-\left[\left(1-(e_0a)^2\frac{\partial^2}{\partial x^2}\right)w_1\right]\right\}^3
\end{aligned} \tag{3}$$

$$\begin{aligned}
&\frac{\partial^2}{\partial x^2}\left\{\left[E(x)I_2\right]\frac{\partial^2 w_2}{\partial x^2}\right\}+m_2\frac{\partial^2 w_2}{\partial t^2}-(e_0a)^2 m_2\frac{\partial^4 w_2}{\partial x^2\partial t^2}-\int_0^L\left(\frac{\partial w_2}{\partial x}\right)^2\left(\frac{E(x)A_2}{2L}\right)dx\frac{\partial^2 w_2}{\partial x^2}\\
&=-\left(1-(e_0a)^2\frac{\partial^2}{\partial x^2}\right)\left(c_1(w_2-w_1)\right)-c_3\left\{\left[\left(1-(e_0a)^2\frac{\partial^2}{\partial x^2}\right)w_2\right]-\left[\left(1-(e_0a)^2\frac{\partial^2}{\partial x^2}\right)w_1\right]\right\}^3\\
&+\left(1-(e_0a)^2\frac{\partial^2}{\partial x^2}\right)F_0\delta(x-x_F)
\end{aligned} \tag{4}$$

It is noted that the scale e_0a in the Eq. (3-4) will lead to small scale effect on the response of structures in nano-size. In Eqs. (3-4), it is assumed that the small scale effects on the nonlinear terms due to geometrical nonlinearity are neglected since they are normally small compared with those on the linear terms.

3 Solution by finite element method

In the present study, the finite element method is adopted to determine the solutions to Eqs. (3-4). Using the finite element formulation, we can obtain the governing matrix equation of the structure after assembly as follows:

$$[\mathbf{M}]\ddot{\mathbf{W}}+[\mathbf{C}]\dot{\mathbf{W}}+\mathbf{R}(\mathbf{W})=\mathbf{P} \tag{5}$$

where $[\mathbf{M}]$ is the global consistent mass matrix of the structure, $[\mathbf{C}]$ is the global damping matrix of the structure, $\dot{\mathbf{W}}$ is the global velocity vector of the structure, $\ddot{\mathbf{W}}$ is the global acceleration vector of the structure, $\mathbf{W}$ is the global displacement vector of the structure, $\mathbf{P}$ is the global external force vector of the structure and $\mathbf{R}(\mathbf{W})$ is the global vector of restoring forces of the structure that depends on the displacement field. Based on equation (5), the governing equation of the structure at time $t+\Delta t$ is given by

$$[\mathbf{M}]\ddot{\mathbf{W}}^{t+\Delta t}+[\mathbf{C}]\dot{\mathbf{W}}^{t+\Delta t}+\left[\mathbf{K}_T^t\right]\Delta\mathbf{W}=\mathbf{P}^{t+\Delta t}-\mathbf{R}(\mathbf{W}^t) \tag{6}$$

The above equation can be solved by any direct time integration method even it is nonlinear. In order to improve the solution accuracy, it is necessary to carry out the equilibrium iteration in each time step. In this study, the Newton-Raphson method in conjunction with Newmark scheme is adopted to perform the numerical analysis.

4 Perturbation technique

In this study, only the Young's modulus of elasticity E is assumed to be stochastic in position, the geometric shapes and sizes of the structure and the moving load and the fluid load are assumed to be deterministic. Applying the perturbation technique, the randomly fluctuating Young's modulus of elasticity E can be assumed as:

$$E(x)=E^{(0)}\left[1+\alpha(x)\right]=E^{(0)}+E^{(0)}\alpha(x) \tag{7}$$

where $E^{(0)}$ is the mean value of the Young's modulus of elasticity, $\alpha(x)$ is random variable with zero mean, and $E^{(0)}\alpha(x)$ is homogeneous stochastic field representing the fluctuation of the Young's modulus of elasticity around its mean value. Assuming the random variable α is uniform within the element, then the stochastic nodal displacement vector can be expanded about α by using Taylor series as:

$$\mathbf{W}^{t+\Delta t}=\mathbf{W}^{(0)t+\Delta t}+\sum_{i=1}^{NE}\mathbf{W}_i^{(1)t+\Delta t}\alpha_i+\frac{1}{2}\sum_{i=1}^{NE}\sum_{j=1}^{NE}\mathbf{W}_{ij}^{(2)t+\Delta t}\alpha_i\alpha_j+\ldots \tag{8}$$

$$\Delta\mathbf{W}=\Delta\mathbf{W}^{(0)}+\sum_{i=1}^{NE}\Delta\mathbf{W}_i^{(1)}\alpha_i+\frac{1}{2}\sum_{i=1}^{NE}\sum_{j=1}^{NE}\Delta\mathbf{W}_{ij}^{(2)}\alpha_i\alpha_j+\ldots \tag{9}$$

where the superscript (0) represents the mean value term, both i and j denote the element numbers, NE is the total number of the element and Σ means the merging with respect to element. Similarly, the restoring force vectors and the tangent stiffness matrix can be written in similar fashion. Then applying the perturbation technique to equation (6), the higher order terms are truncated, and comparing equal order terms for the random variable α, the zero, first, and second order equations for the problem are obtained, respectively. The solutions of these equations are achieved successively by using the procedures described in the previous section. The statistical dynamic responses of DWCNTs can be obtained after calculating the zero, first and second order equations. For example, at any fixed time, both expected value of deflection and autocorrelation of the deflection between two different points p and q can be obtained based on the first order approximation by neglecting the third term in equation (8) as follows:

$$E[\mathbf{W}] = \mathbf{W}^{(0)} \tag{10}$$

$$\mathbf{R}_{\mathbf{W}}(x_p, x_q) = E\left[\left(\mathbf{W} - E[\mathbf{W}]\right)\left(\mathbf{W} - E[\mathbf{W}]\right)^T\right] = \sum_{i=1}^{NE}\sum_{j=1}^{NE} \mathbf{W}_{pi}^{(1)}\mathbf{W}_{qj}^{(1)} E\left[\alpha_i \alpha_j\right] \tag{11}$$

$$E\left[\alpha_i \alpha_j\right] = \mathrm{R}_{\alpha}\left(x_i - x_j\right) = \mathrm{R}_{\alpha}\left(\Delta x\right) \tag{12}$$

where $E[\bullet]$ is the expectation and the $R_{\alpha}(\Delta x)$ is the autocorrelation function of random variable α assuming that the Gaussian stochastic process of the Young's modulus of elasticity E is homogeneous with respect to the position, x_p and x_q are the coordinate at the center of the element p and q. Based on equation (11), the stochastic process of deflection is assumed to be homogeneous with respect to position as well, $R_{\mathbf{W}}(x_i, x_j)$ can be replaced by $R_{\mathbf{W}}(\Delta x)$. Therefore, the autocorrelation $R_{\mathbf{W}}(\Delta x)$ can be computed readily provided that the spectra density of the Young's modulus of elasticity is given.

5 Numerical examples and discussion

In the numerical computations, the simply supported boundary condition is considered for the DWCNTs conveying fluid. The inner and the outer tubes are assumed to have the same Young's modulus, the same thickness and the same mass density. The numerical values of the parameters are adopted as follows: Mean value of Young's modulus E=1 Tpa, tube thickness h=0.34 nm, mass density $\rho = 2300 Kg/m^3$, the mass density of water flow is $\rho_f = 1000 Kg/m^3$, the inner radius $R_1 = 0.7nm$ and the outer radius $R_2 = 1.04nm$, the standard deviation of random variable α is assumed as $\sigma_{\alpha} = 0.1$. The length of the DWCNTs is considered as a variable for the different values of the aspect ratio L/d. In the present study, the nonlocal parameter is chosen as $0 \le e_0 a \le 2.0nm$ to investigate the small scale effects on the dynamic responses. For a constant velocity of the moving load, the non-dimensional dynamic deflection is normalized as the ratio between the dynamic deflection and the static deflection, which is $D = F_0 L^3 / 48E^{(0)} I$, of a beam under a point load F_0 at the middle point of the beam. In the following numerical computations, the internal fluid velocity of the DWCNTs is assumed as $U = 400\ m/\sec$, the non-dimensional velocity $\overline{V} = 0.2$ is assumed for the moving load and the aspect ratio $L/d = 10$ is considered, unless they are specified otherwise. In Figs. 2-3, the mean values and standard deviations of the non-dimensional dynamic deflections of the DWCNTs are depicted. Fig. 2 presents the mean value of the non-dimensional dynamic deflections $w_2(L/2, t)/D$ versus the non-dimensional time T for various values of the nonlocal parameter $e_0 a$. As it can be seen from Fig. 2, the numerical results based on the present study are checked by Monte Carlo Simulation, they are in excellent agreements. Fig. 3 presents the standard deviation of the non-dimensional dynamic deflections $w_2(L/2, t)/D$ with respect to the normalized dimensional time T for various values of the nonlocal parameter $e_0 a$. Once again, the numerical results based on the present study are in good agreements with those estimated by Monte Carlo Simulation except that the results from Monte Carlo Simulation are slightly larger than those from the present study. Fig. 4 presents the mean values of the maximum non-dimensional dynamic deflections $w_2(x, t)/D$ versus the aspect ratio L/d for various values of the nonlocal parameter $e_0 a$ at the constant moving load velocity $\overline{V} = 0.2$. As it can be detected from the figure, the maxima non-dimensional dynamic deflections computed by using the nonlocal model are larger than those of the local (classical) model thanks to the small scale effect. Based on the results in Fig. 5, the maxima non-dimensional deflections get larger as the nonlocal parameter increases, and the effect of the nonlocal parameter depends on the aspect ratio.

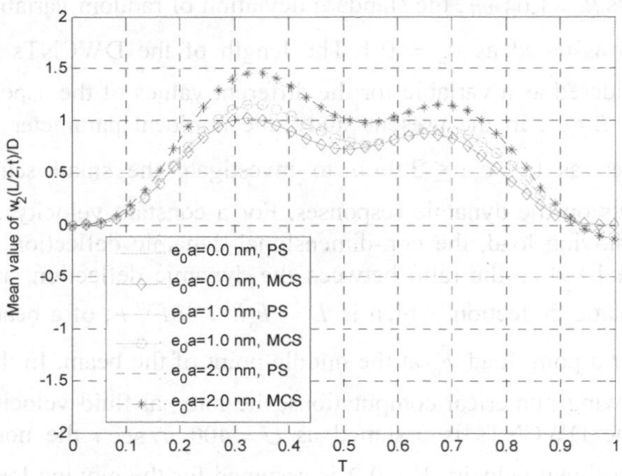

Fig. 2. Mean value of $w_2(L/2,t)/D$ versus dimensionless time T. PS=Present study, MCS=Monte Carlo Simulation.

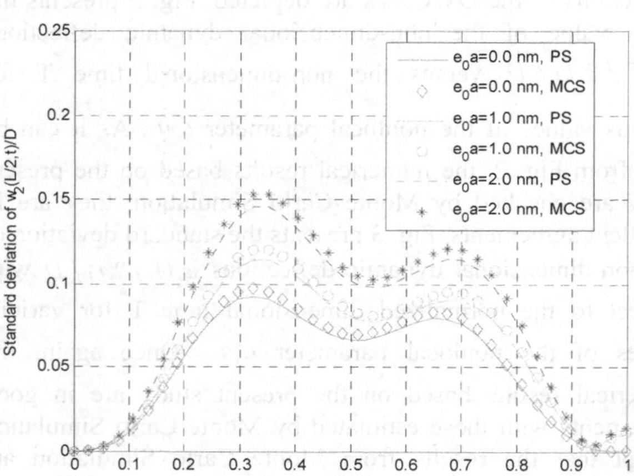

Fig. 3. Standard deviation of $w_2(L/2,t)/D$ versus dimensionless time T. PS=Present study, MCS=Monte Carlo Simulation.

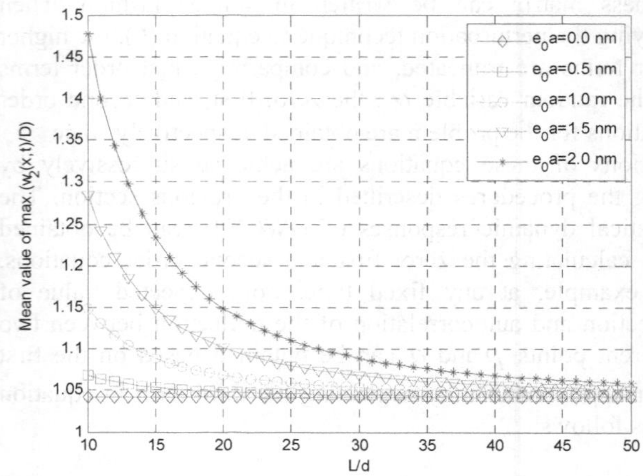

Fig. 4. Mean values of maxima non-dimensional deflections versus the aspect ratio L/d for $\bar{V}=0.2$.

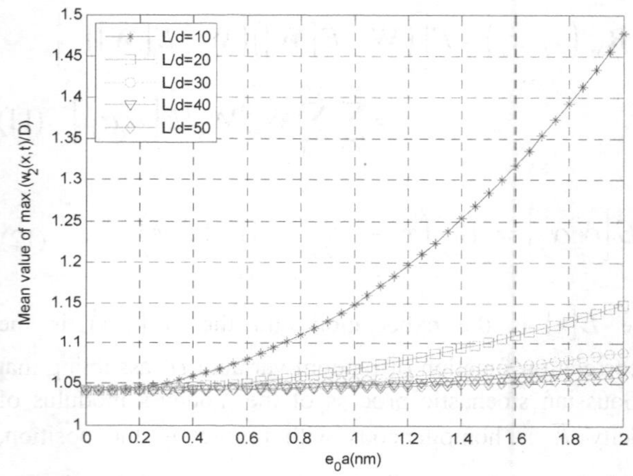

Fig. 5. Mean values of maxima non-dimensional deflections versus the nonlocal parameter e_0a for $\bar{V}=0.2$.

6 Conclusions

This paper investigates the statistical dynamic behaviors of nonlinear vibration of the fluid-conveying double-walled carbon nanotubes (DWCNTs) under a moving load by considering the effects of the geometric nonlinearity and the nonlinearity of van der Waals (vdW) force. The Young's modulus of elasticity of the DWCNTs is considered as stochastic with respect to the position to actually characterize the random material properties of the DWCNTs. In addition, the small scale effects of the nonlinear vibration of the DWCNTs are studied by using the theory of nonlocal elasticity. Based on the Hamilton's principle, the nonlinear governing equations of the fluid-conveying double-walled carbon nanotubes under a moving load are formulated. The stochastic finite element method along with the perturbation technique is adopted to study the statistical esponseof the DWCNTs; in particular, the Newton-Raphson iteration procedure in conjunction with Newmark scheme is utilized to solve the nonlinearity of the dynamic governing equation of the DWCNTs. Some statistical results obtained by the perturbation technique and those from the Monte Carlo simulation approach show good agreements. Some statistical dynamic response of the DWCNTs such as the mean values and standard deviations of the non-dimensional dynamic deflections are calculated, meanwhile the effects of the nonlocal parameter and aspect ratio on the statistical dynamic response of the DWCNTs are investigated. It can be concluded that the nonlocal solutions of the dynamic deflections get larger with the increase of the nonlocal parameters due to the small scale effect. It is noted that the computed stochastic dynamic response plays an important role in evaluating the structural reliability of the DWCNTs.

Acknowledgments This research was partially supported by the National Science Council in Taiwan through Grant NSC-99-2221-E-327-020. The authors are grateful for this support.

7 References

[1] S. Ijjima, Helical microtubules of graphitic carbon, Nature 354 (1991) 56-58.

[2] E. Evans, H. Bowman, A. Leung, D. Needham, D. Tirrell, Biomembrane templates for nanoscale conduits and networks, Science 273 (1996) 933-935.

[3] G.E. Gadd et. al., The World's Smallest Gas Cylinders?, Science 277 (1997) 933-936.

[4] G. Che et. al., Carbon nanotubule membranes for electrochemical energy storage and production, Nature 393 (1998) 346-349.

[5] J. Liu et. al., Fullerene Pipes, Science 280 (1998) 1253-1256.

[6] A. Karlsson et. al., Networks of nanotubes and containers, Nature 409 (2001) 150-152.

[7] Y. Gao,Y. Bando, Carbon nanothermometer containing gallium, Nature 415 (2002) 599.

[8] G. Hummer, J.C. Rasaiah, J.P. Noworyta, Water conduction through the hydrophobic channel of a carbon nanotube, Nature 414 (2001) 188–190.

[9] I. Hanasaki, A. Nakatani, Water flow through carbon nanotube junctions as molecular convergent nozzles, Nanotechnology 17 (2006) 2794–2804.

[10] Z. Mao, S.B. Sinnott, A computational study of molecular diffusion and dynamic flow through carbon nanotubes, J. Phys. Chem. B 104 (2000) 4618–4624.

[11] A. Skoulidas, D.M. Ackerman, K.J. Johnson, D.S. Sholl, Rapid transport of gases in carbon nanotubes, Phys. Rev. Lett. 89 (2002) 185901–185911.

[12] T. Natsuki, Q.Q. Ni, M. Endo, Wave propagation in single- and double- walled carbon nanotubes filled with fluids, J. Appl. Phys. 101 (2007) 034319-034319.

[13] J. Yoon, C.Q. Ru, A. Mioduchowski, Flow-induced flutter instability of cantilever CNTs, Int. J. Solids Struct. 43 (2006) 3337–3349.

[14] L. Wang, Q. Ni, On vibration and instability of carbon nanotubes conveying fluid, Comput. Mater. Sci. 43 (2008) 399–402.

[15] X.Q. He, C.M. Wang, Y. Yan, L.X. Zhang, G.H. Ni, Pressure dependence of the instability of multiwalled carbon nanotubes conveying fluids, Arch. Appl. Mech. 78 (2008) 637–648.

[16] Y. Yan, X.Q. He, L.X. Zhang, C.M. Wang, Dynamic behavior of triple-walled carbon nanotubes conveying fluid, J. Sound Vib. 319 (2009) 1003–1018.

[17] L. Wang, Q. Ni, M. Li, Q. Qian, The thermal effect on vibration and instability of carbon nanotubes converying fluid, Physica E 40 (2008) 3179–3182.

[18] Y. Yan, W.Q. Wang, L.X. Zhang, Dynamical behaviors of fluid-conveyed multi-walled carbon nanotubes, Appl. Math. Modell. 33 (2009) 1430–1440.

[19] L. Wang, Q. Li, M. Li, Buckling instability of double-wall carbon nanotubes conveying fluid, Comput. Mater. Sci. 44 (2008) 821–825.

[20] H. Lee, W. Chang, Comment on Free tr nsverse vibration of the fluid-conveying single-walled carbon nanotube using nonlocal elastic theory, J. Appl. Phys. 103 (2008) 024302-024302.

[21] T.P. Chang, M.F. Liu, Flow-induced instability of double-walled carbon nanotubes based on nonlocal elasticity theory, Physica E 43 (2011) 1419-1426.

[22] T.P. Chang, M.F. Liu, Small scale effect on flow-induced instability of double-walled carbon nanotubes, Eur. J. Mech. A. Solids 30 (2011) 992-998.

[23] T.P. Chang, Thermal-nonlocal vibration and instability of single-walled carbon nanotubes conveying fluid, J. Mech. 27 (2011) 567 -573.

[24] T.P. Chang, Thermal-mechanical vibration and instability of a fluid-conveying single-walled carbon nanotube embedded in an elastic medium based on nonlocal elasticity theory, Appl. Math. Model. 36 (2012) 1964-1973.

[25] Y.D. Kuang et al, Analysis of nonlinear vibrations of double-walled carbon nanotubes conveying fluid, Comput. Mater. Sci. 45 (2009) 875–880.

[26] G.V. Dedkov, A.A. Kyasov, Thermal radiation of nanoparticles occurring at a heated flat surface in vacuum, Tech. Phys. Lett. 33 (2007) 305-308.

[27] G. Hummer, J.C. Rasaiah, J.P. Noworyta, Water conduction through the hydrophobic channel of a carbon nanotube, Nat. 414 (2001) 188-190.

[28] M. Simsek, Vibration analysis of a single-walled carbon nanotubes under action of a moving harmonic load based on nonlocal elasticity theory, Physica E 43 (2010) 182-191.

[29] K. Kiani, Q. Wang, On the interaction of a single-walled carbon nanotube with a moving nanoparticle using nonlocal Rayleigh, Timoshenko, and higher-order beam theories. Eur. J. Mech. A. Solids 31 (2012) 179-202.
[30] J.P. Salvetat, J.A.D. Briggs, J.M. Bonard, R.R. Bacsa, A.J. Kulik, T. Stöckli, N.A. Burnham, L. Forró, Elastic and shear moduli of single-walled carbon nanotube ropes, Phys. Rev. Lett. 82 (5) (1999) 944-947.
[31] A. Krishnan, E. Dujardin, T.W. Ebbesen, P.N. Yianilos, M.M.J. Treacy, Young's modulus of single-walled nanotubes, Phys. Rev. B 58 (20) (1998) 14013-14019.
[32] A. J. Mieszawska, R. Jalilian, G. U. Sumanasekera, F. P. Zamborini, The synthesis and fabrication of one-dimensional and nanoscale heterojunctions, Small 3 (2007) 722-756.

Pulsatile Flow of Hershel- Bulkley Fluid in Tapered Blood Vessels

R. Ponalagusamy
Department of Mathematics
National Institute of Technology
Tiruchirappalli-620 015, Tamil Nadu, India.
rpalagu@nitt.edu

***Abstract*—The present paper sheds some light on investigating the effect of pulsatility on flow through a tapered artery. Blood has been represented by a non- Newtonian fluid obeying Herschel-Bulkley equation. Using the Reynolds number as the perturbation parameter, a perturbation technique is adopted to solve the resulting quasi-steady non-linear coupled implicit system of differential equations. Analytical expressions for velocity, volumetric flow rate, wall shear stress and the mean flow resistance have been obtained. It is observed that the wall shear stress and flow resistance increase for increasing value of taper angle and the axial distance. It is pertinent to point out that the phase lag between the pressure gradient and wall shear stress or flow rate is found to be 2.03 degrees and this phase lag becomes independent of the axial distance and taper angle. The present approach has; in general, validity in comparison with many mathematical models developed by others and may be applied to any mathematical model by taking into account of any type of rheological property of blood. Finally, some biorheological applications of the present model have briefly been discussed.**

Keywords—non-newtonian fluid; pulsatile flow, tapered artery; walls shear stress; resistance to flow

I. INTRODUCTION

It is well known that the investigation on blood flow in tapered arteries and tubes with non-uniform cross-sections could play an important role in the fundamental understanding, diagnosis and treatment of many cardiovascular diseases tubes ([1],[2],[3]). Looking at the immense importance in the fundamental understanding of blood flow, the objective of the present analysis is motivated to provide a generalized model of blood and obtain some information about the flow. Many investigators([4-8] have studied the flow of blood through tapered arteries by treating blood as a Newtonian fluid, Bingham plastic fluid, power-law fluid and Casson fluid and obtained the relationship between the flow rate and pressure drop. Scott Blair et al. [9] have suggested that blood obeys Casson's model only for moderate shear rate flows, and that there is no difference between Casson's and Herschel-Bulkley plots over the range where Casson's plot is valid (for blood). Furthermore, Sacks et al. [10] have experimentally pointed out that blood shows the behavior characteristic of a combination Bingham plastic and Pseudoplastic fluid-Herschel- Bulkley fluid with the fluid behavior index greater than unity. In view of the experimental observation [10] and suggestion made in [9], it is pertinent to consider the behavior of blood as a Herschel- Bulkley fluid. Based on the foregoing views, it is worthwhile to describe a model taking the factors of pulsatility, non-uniform cross-section of a tube and non-Newtonian character into the present analysis and study the flow characteristics.

II. FORMULATION OF THE PROBLEM

Consider a laminar, pulsatile and fully developed flow of blood (Herschel-Bulkley fluid) in the direction through a slightly tapered tube as shown in Fig.1.

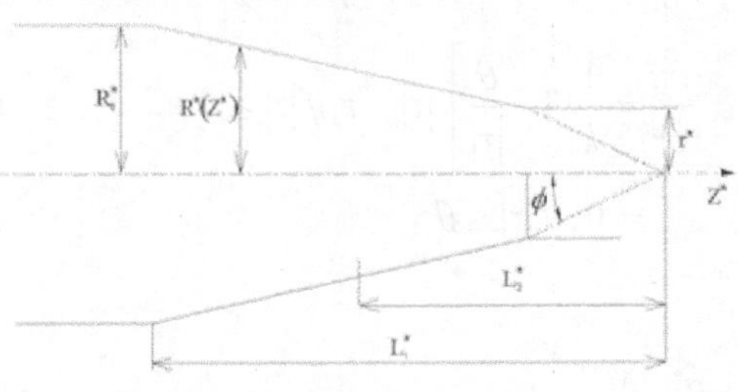

Fig.1. Geometry of Tapered Tube

The wall profile of the flow geometry may mathematically be described as

$$R^*(z^*) = R_0^* - z^* \tan\phi \tag{1}$$

where $R^*(z^*)$ is the radius of tube in the tapered section, R_0^* is the radius of the tube in the normal region, z^* is the axial direction and ϕ is the angle of taper. Further, L_1^* represents the axial distance of the cross section between z^* =0 and the cone apex and L_2^* indicates the axial distance of any cross section at z^* from the apex. We shall take cylindrical coordinate system (r^*, ψ^*, z^*) whose origin is located on the tube axis. (* over a letter denotes the dimensional form of the corresponding quantity).

Let us introduce the following non-dimensional variables:

$$r = \frac{r^*}{R_0^*}, z = \frac{z^*}{R_0^*}, t = \frac{t^*}{T^*}, u = \frac{u^*}{U_0^*},$$

$$\theta = \frac{\tau_y^*}{\left(\mu^* \dfrac{U_0^*}{R_0^*}\right)}, \tau = \frac{\tau^*}{\left(\mu^* \dfrac{U_0^*}{R_0^*}\right)} \quad (2)$$

where T^* is the characteristic time, μ^* the Newtonian viscosity, U_0^* the characteristic velocity which is expressed by the relation $R_0^* = U_0^* T^*$, u^* the axial component of the velocity, t^* the time, r^* the radial direction, τ_y^* the yield stress, τ^* is the shear stress and θ is the dimensionless yield stress

Based on the discussions made by Oka [7], Oka and Murata [8] and Ponalagusamy [11], the radial velocity is negligibly small and can be neglected for a low Reynolds number flow through a tapered tube with an angle of taper up to 2^0. Keeping these in views and using non-dimensional variables, the momentum equations governing the flow are given as

$$\varepsilon \frac{\partial u}{\partial t} = \beta q(z) f(t) + \frac{1}{r}\frac{\partial}{\partial r}[r\tau], \quad (3)$$

$$\frac{\partial u}{\partial r} = \frac{1}{k}\left[1 - \frac{\theta}{|\tau|}\right]^n |\tau|^{n-1}\tau, if|\tau| \geq \theta \quad (4)$$

$$= 0, if|\tau| \leq \theta \quad (5)$$

Where,

$$k = \left(\frac{k^*}{\mu^*}\right)\left(\frac{R_0^*}{U_0^* \mu^*}\right)^{n-1},$$

$$\varepsilon = U_0^* R_0^* \frac{\rho^*}{\mu^*},$$

$$\beta = \frac{q_0^* R_0^{*2}}{\mu^* U_0^*},$$

$$q(z) = \frac{q^*(z^*)}{q_0},$$

$f(t)=1+A \sin(\Omega t)$,

k^* is the consistency index of blood,

n is the power –law index,

$q^*(z^*)$ is the pressure gradient and

q_0^* is the constant pressure gradient in the normal tube region.

Equations (4) and (5) are reduced to that for a Bingham fluid when n=1.0, to that for a Power-law fluid when θ =0.0, and to that for a Newtonian fluid when n=1.0 and θ =0.0. Here $\Omega = \dfrac{\omega^* R_0^*}{U_0^*}$ is the Strouhal number where ω^* is the frequency of the oscillations of the flow. The dimensionless parameter ε is the Reynolds number of the flow.

Taking $\beta = 1$, characteristic velocity U_0^* is expressed as

$$U_0^* = \frac{q_0^* R_0^{*2}}{\mu^*} \quad (6)$$

Consistency then requires that the time scale be chosen as

$$T^* = \frac{\mu^*}{q_0^* R_0^*} \quad (7)$$

The geometry of the tapered tube in dimensionless form is given by

$$R(z) = 1 - z\tan\phi \quad (8)$$

The boundary conditions in dimensionless form are:

(i) τ is finite at r= 0 and (ii) u=0 at r= R(z) (9)

The volumetric flow rate Q(t)is given by:

$$Q(t) = \int_0^{R(z)} ru(r,z,t)dr \quad (10)$$

As mentioned elsewhere in[3], we take

$$R(z) = 1 - z\phi \text{ and } z = L_1 - L_2 \quad (11)$$

III. SOLUTION

The flow variable G is assumed to possess the following form

$$G(r,z,t) = G_0(r,z,t) + \varepsilon G_1(r,z,t) + O(\varepsilon^2) \quad (12)$$

Where $G(r,z,t)$ refers the velocity and shear stress. In what follows, for convenience, we write only function notation deleting its variable(s). It is of interest to note that the Womersley number α is obtained as

$$\alpha = (\varepsilon\,\Omega)^{\frac{1}{2}} = R_0^*\left(\frac{w^*}{\gamma^*}\right)^{\frac{1}{2}}$$

where γ^* is the kinematic viscosity.

Substituting equations (4-5) into equation (3) and integrating twice with the help of the boundary conditions (9), the analytic expression for velocity distribution may be obtained as

$$u = \frac{(qf)^n (1-z\phi)^{n+1}}{k(n+1)2^n}[(1-S)^{n+1} - (r/(1-z\phi) - S)^{n+1} + \{n\varepsilon A\Omega\cos(\Omega t)(1-z\phi)^{n+1}/2kf\}(qf)^{n-1}.$$

$$[(1-S)^n (n+S)\{\frac{(1-S)^{n+1} - (\frac{r}{(1-z\phi)} - S)^{n+1}}{n+1} + (S(1-S)^n - (\frac{r}{(1-z\phi)} - S)^n)/n$$

$$-\frac{n}{(n+1)(n+3)}(1-(\frac{r}{(1-z\phi)})^{2n+2})\} + \frac{S(4n^3+8n^2-6n-6)}{(n+2)(n+3)(2n+1)}(1-(\frac{r}{(1-z\phi)})^{2n+1})$$

$$-2S^2\sum_{j=0}^{2n-1}\frac{(-1)^j (2n) c_j S^j}{(2n-j)}(1-(\frac{r}{(1-z\phi)})^{2n-j})\{\frac{(2n+1)(2n+2)}{(j+1)(j+2)(n+3)} - \frac{(2n+1)^2}{(j+1)(n+2)} + 1\}$$

$$+\frac{6(-1)^{2n}}{(n+2)(n+3)}S^{2n+2}\log(\frac{r}{(1-z\phi)})]] \tag{13}$$

Using equations (10) and (13), after tedious manipulations, the analytic expression for flow rate is obtained as

$$Q(t) = \frac{(qf)^n (1-z\phi)^{3+n}}{2^n k(n+1)(n+2)(n+3)}[(1-S)^{n+1}\{(n+2)(n+1) + 2S(n+1+S)\} + \frac{n\varepsilon A\Omega\cos(\Omega t)k(1-z\phi)^2}{2^{2n-2} f}$$

$$(qf(1-z\phi))^{n-1}[(1-S)^{2n}(n+S)\{(n+2) + 3S + \frac{6S^2}{n(n+1)}(1+S)\} - n(1-S^{2n+4})$$

$$+\frac{S(4n^3+8n^2-6n-6)}{(2n+3)}(1-S^{2n+3}) - 3S^{2n+2}(1-S^2)$$

$$-2S^2\sum_{j=0}^{2n-1}\frac{(-1)^j (2n) c_j S^j}{(2n+2-j)}\{\frac{(2n+1)(2n+2)(n+2)}{(j+1)(j+2)} - \frac{(n+3)(2n+1)^2}{(j+1)} + (n+2)(n+3)(1-S^{2n+2-j})\}]] \tag{14}$$

where $S = 2\theta/\{qf_1(1-z\phi)\}$

The steady flow rate Q_s is expressed as

$$Q_s = \frac{q^n\{(1-z\phi)\}^{3+n}}{2^n k(n+1)(n+2)(n+3)}\left[\{1-\frac{2\theta}{q(1-z\phi)}\}^{n+1}\left\{(n+2)(n+1)+\{\frac{4\theta}{q(1-z\phi)}\}\{n+1+\frac{2\theta}{q(1-z\phi)}\}\right\}\right] \tag{15}$$

The shear stress on the wall τ_w is physiologically important quantity and is given by

$$\tau_w = \frac{qf(1-z\phi)}{2}\left[1+\frac{\varepsilon A\Omega\cos(\Omega t)\{1-z\phi\}^{n+1}\left\{\frac{qf}{2}\right\}^{n-1}}{2^{n+1}(n+1)(n+2)(n+3)f}.\{1-S^n\}\left\{\begin{matrix} n(n+1)(n+2)+ \\ 3n(n+1)S+6nS^2+6S^3\end{matrix}\right\}\right] \tag{16}$$

It is of importance to pin point out here that Chaturani and Ponnalagarsamy [12] have explained the method of calculating the value of steady pressure gradient q (z) for any value of θ using equation (15).

The flow resistance λ is defined as

$$\lambda = \frac{f(t)\Delta p}{Q(t)} \tag{17}$$

where Δp is the pressure drop.

The mean flow resistance over period of the flow cycle is defined as

$$\bar{\lambda} = \frac{1}{2\pi}\int_0^{2\pi}\left(\frac{p_0-p_1}{Q(t)}\right)f(t)dt \tag{18}$$

It is understood that for any value of S, one can numerically compute the values of the flow resistance λ and the mean flow resistance $\bar{\lambda}$ respectively from equations (17) and (18) for different values of the parameters involved in the present work. It is mathematically and physiologically important to obtain an analytic expression for the mean flow resistance.

It is seen from equations (14) and (18) that it is not possible to obtain the analytic expression for the mean flow resistance for any value of S. For small values of S (the fluid having low yield stress value (θ); for example, blood [11])), the analytic expression for the mean flow resistance from equations (14) and (18) may be obtained as

$$\bar{\lambda} = (\frac{n}{3\varphi})(2^n k(n+3))^{\frac{1}{n}}\bar{Q}\left\{\left(\frac{1}{1-z\varphi}\right)^{3/n}-1\right\} + \left\{\frac{2(n+3)\theta Q^*}{\varphi(n+2)}\right\}\log\left(\frac{1}{1-z\varphi}\right) \tag{19}$$

where

$$\bar{Q} = \frac{1}{2\pi}\int_0^{2\pi}\frac{dt}{[Q(t)]^{1-\frac{1}{n}}} \text{ and } Q^* = \frac{1}{2\pi}\int_0^{2\pi}\frac{dt}{Q(t)}$$

The values of $\bar{Q}$ and Q^* have to be numerically computed after computing the value of steady pressure gradient q(z) using equation (15) for different values of the parameter involved in the present work.

The flow resistance λ_s for the steady flow of Herschel-Bulkley fluid through a tapered artery can be obtained from Eq. (19) as

$$\lambda_s = (\frac{n}{3\phi})\left\{\frac{2^n k(n+3)}{Q_s^{n-1}}\right\}^{\frac{1}{n}}\left\{\left(\frac{1}{1-z\phi}\right)^{3/n}-1\right\} + \left\{\frac{2(n+3)\theta}{\phi(n+2)Q_s}\right\}\log\left(\frac{1}{1-z\phi}\right) \tag{20}$$

The steady pressure gradient q (z) and wall shear stress τ_w respectively may be obtained as

$$q(z)=\{2^{n}k(n+3)Q_{s}\}^{\frac{1}{n}}\left(\frac{1}{1-z\phi}\right)^{\frac{n+3}{n}} + \{2(n+3)\theta/(n+2)\}\{\frac{1}{1-z\phi}\} \quad (21)$$

$$\tau_{w}=\{2^{n}k(n+3)Q_{s}\}^{\frac{1}{n}}\{\frac{1}{1-z\phi}\}^{3/n} + \{2(n+3)\theta/(n+2)\} \quad (22)$$

IV. DISCUSSION

A careful observation of the works done by Aroesty and Gross [13-14], Sankar and Hemalatha [15-16] and Desh et al. [17] reveals that they have applied standard perturbation technique and produced an approximate solution in which the flow characteristics are expressed as asymptotic representations in powers of the Womersley number α [18]. Rohlf and Tenti [19] have recently argued that the use of the Womersley number as a perturbation parameter to obtain approximate solutions of the pulsatile flow of non-Newtonian fluid is not appropriate and considering the Reynolds number (ε) as a perturbation parameter, they have made an attempt to validate their results through their perturbation theory in comparison with a numerical integration of the full mathematical model.

It is further noticed that the Womersley number α is not dependent on the flow velocity and thus the same value of α can represent vastly different flow conditions and hence the Womersley number α is not a suitable perturbation parameter. Sankar and Hemalatha [15-16] and Sankar[20] have analyzed the pulsatile flow of Herschel-Bulkley fluid through arteries. It pertinent to point out here that the analytic expressions for flow variables such as velocity, wall shear stress and flow rate obtained by Sankar and Hemalatha [15-16] and Sankar[20] and by the present investigation respectively are entirely different. The reason is attributed to the fact that they have neglected the higher order terms in the binomial expansion of the relationship between the velocity gradient and the shear stress involved the constitutive equation of Herschel-Bulkley fluid. Hence, the results obtained by Sankar and Hemalatha [15-16] and Sankar[20] are not representing the actual behavior of biorheological flow characteristics. Also, they have not derived the analytic expression for flow resistance.

It is of interest to note from Fig.2 that the flow rate decreases with the increase in the axial distance (Z) and taper angle. The percentage of decrease in the flow rate as the value of Z increases is found to be higher for higher value of taper angle.

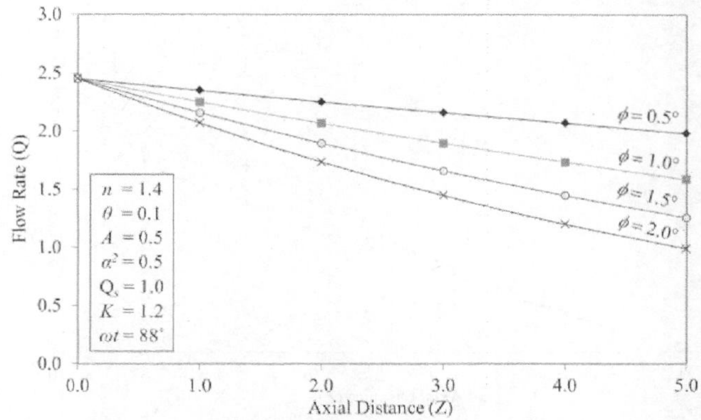

Fig.2. Variation of flow rate with axial distance for different values of taper angle

The variation of wall shear stress with the axial distance and the taper angle has been studied and illustrated in Fig.3. It is clear from Fig.3 that as the taper angle increases, the rate of increase in the wall shear stress with respect to an increase in the axial distance Z is found to be very much significant. Another important result is concerning the variation of mean flow resistance ($\bar{\lambda}$) with respect to the taper for different values of the axial distance (Z) and it is shown in Fig.4. The mean flow resistance increases as the value of the taper angle increases. The main effect of pulsatility on the flow is the phase lag between pressure gradient and flow rate, and wall shear stress. It is noticed from that the phase lag between pressure gradient and flow rate(or wall shear stress) has been found to be 2.03 degrees and its value is unaltered while the increase or decrease in the values of axial distance and taper angle. It may be of importance to note that many standard results regarding steady and uniform tube flow of Power-law, Bingham and Newtonian fluids can be obtained as special cases of the present investigation.

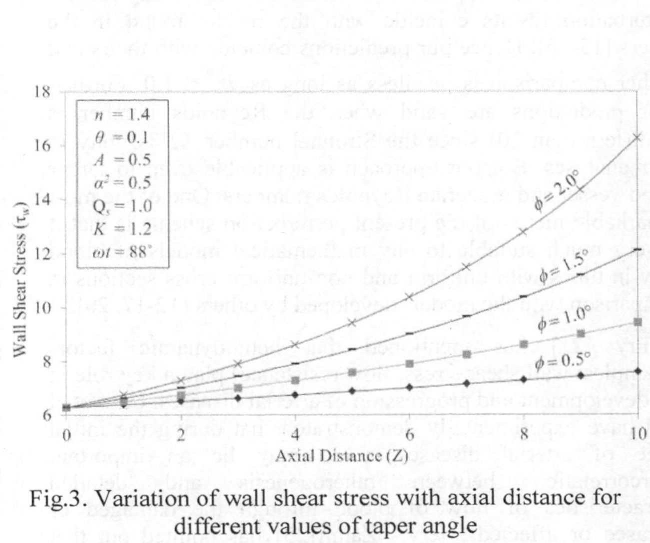

Fig.3. Variation of wall shear stress with axial distance for different values of taper angle

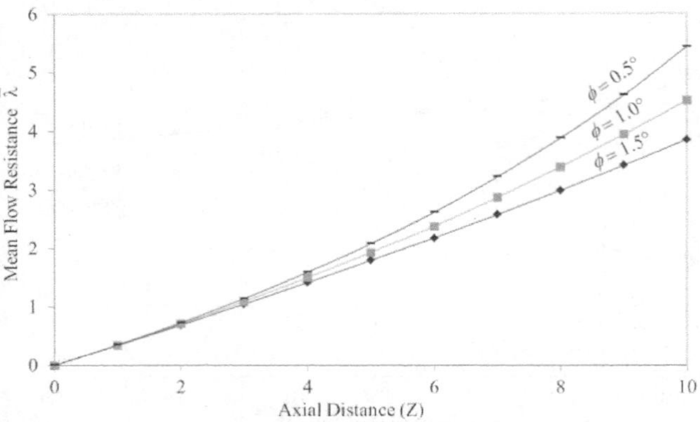

Fig.4. Variation of mean flow resistance with axial distance for different values of taper angle

V. CONCLUSION

The present investigation deals with the problem of pulsatile flow of blood (Herschel-Bulkley fluid) through an artery with mild stenosis. A perturbation technique is adopted to study the flow. The analytical expressions for velocity, flow rate, wall shear stress and mean flow resistance have been obtained. The results have been depicted through graphs. Using the finite volume technique, the quasi-steady non-linear coupled implicit system of differential equations has numerically been solved and the axial velocity is computed. It is verified that the error between the axial velocities obtained by the present perturbation method and the numerical technique becomes less than 1.052% for the values of α^2 lying between 0.0 and 1.0.Further , the error between them becomes more than 9.0% when α^2 takes the value greater than 2.10.

It is pertinent to mention here that when the flow characteristics are expressed in terms of α^2 , the present perturbation results coincide with the results found in the papers [15-16]. Hence our predictions coincide with theirs and further comparison is needless as long as $\alpha^2 < 1.0$. Further, their predictions are valid when the Reynolds number is small(less than 10) since the Strouhal number Ω is unity in their analyses. But our approach is applicable even to larger blood vessel and moderate Reynolds numbers. One of the most remarkable merits of the present perturbation scheme is that it is very much suitable to any mathematical models of blood flow in tubes with uniform and non-uniform cross sections in comparison with the models developed by others [12-17, 20].

Fry [21] has mentioned that hemodynamic factors (examples; wall shear stress, flow resistance) play a key role in the development and progression of arterial diseases. Caro et al [22] have experimentally demonstrated that during the initial stage of arterial diseases, there may be an important intercorrelation between atherogenesis and detailed characteristics of flow of blood through the damaged or diseased or affected artery. Zamir[23] has pointed out that when artery walls are viscoelastic, 10% variations in the artery radius over a cardiac cycle have typically been observed and the wall shear stress is found to be primarily affected by the radial wall motion, as compared to that of rigid artery. Keeping in view of importance of hemodynamic, viscoelastic property of an artery and rheological factors in understanding of blood flow and arteriosclerostic diseases, a modest effort has to be made to investigate the flow of blood through a tapered artery by taking into account of viscoelastic properties of blood and its vessel wall in addition to the non-Newtonian behavior of blood and pulsatile flow effects considered in the present mathematical analysis, which forms the future research work.

REFERENCES

[1] Dwivedi, A.P., Pal, T.S. and Rakesh, L. "Micropolar fluid model for blood flow through a small tapered tube", Indian J. Technology, 20, pp.295-299 (1982).

[2] Chaturani, P. and Pralhad, R. "Blood flow in tapered tubes with biorheological applications, Biorheology, 22, pp.303-314(1985).

[3] Ponnalagarsamy, R. and Kawahara, M. "A finite element analysis of unsteady flows of viscoelastic fluids through channels with non-uniform cross-sections. Int. J. Numerical Methods of Fluids, 9, pp.1487-1501(1989).

[4] Chakravarthy, S. and Mandal, P.K. "Two dimensional blood flow through tapered arteries under stenotic conditions", Int. J. Non-Linear Mech., 35, pp.779-793 (2000).

[5] How, T.V. and Black, R.A. "Pressure losses in non-Newtonian flow through rigid wall tapered tubes, Biorheology, 24, pp.337-351(1987).

[6] Mandal, P.K. "An unsteady analysis of non-Newtonian blod flow through tapered arteries with stenosis", Int. J. Non-Linear Mech., 40, pp.151-164 (2005).

[7] Oka, S. "Pressure development in a non-Newtonian flow through a tapered tube", Biorheology, 10, pp.207-212(1973).

[8] Oka, S. and Murata, T. "Theory of the steady slow motion of non-Newtonian fluids through a tapered tube", Jpn. J. Appl. Phys., 8, pp.5-8 (1969).

[9] Scott Blair, G.W. and Spanner, D.C. "An Introduction to Biorheology", Elsevier Scientific Publishing Company,Amsterdam, Oxford, pp. 1-163 (1974).

[10] Sacks, A.H. Raman, K.R. Burnell, J,A, and Tickner, E.G. "Auscultatory Versus Direct Pressure Measurements for Newtonian Fluids and for Blood in Simulated Arteries",VIDYA Report #119, Dec. 30, (1963).

[11] Ponalagusamy R. Blood Flow Through Stenosed Tube. Ph.D. Thesis, IIT, Bombay, India, 1986.

[12] Chaturani, P. and Ponnalagarsamy, R. "Pulsatile Flow of Casson's Fluid Through Stenosed Arteries with Applications to Blood Flow",Biorheology 23, pp. 499- 511 (1986).

[13] Aroesty,J. and Gross,J.F. "The Mechanics of Pulsatile Flow in Small Vessel-I, Casson Theory", Microvasc. Research 4, pp. 1-12 (1972 a).

[14] Aroesty,J. and Gross,J.F. "Pulsatile Flow in Small Blood Vessels-I, Casson Theory", Biorheology 9, pp. 33-43 (1972 b).

[15] Shankar, D.S. and Hemalatha,K. "Pulsatile flow of Herschel-Bulkley fluid through stenosed arteries - A mathematical model", Int. J. Non Linear Mech. 41, pp 979-990 (2006).

[16] Shankar, D.S. and Hemalatha,K. "Pulsatile flow of Herschel-Bulkley fluid through catheterized arteries- A mathematical model", Applied Mathematical Modelling 31, pp 1497-1517 (2007).

[17] Dash, R.K. Jayaraman, G. and Mehta, K.N. "Flow in a catheterized curved artery with stenosis " , J.Biomechanics 32, pp 49-61 (1999).

[18] Womersley,J.R. "Method for the Calculation of Velocity, Rate of Flow and Viscous Drag in the Arteries When the Pressure Gradient is Known", *J. Physiol.* **127**, pp. 553-562 (1955).

[19] Rollf,K. and Tenti ,G. "The Role of the Womersley Number in Pulsatile Blood Flow: A Theoretical Study of the Casson Model", *J.* Biomechanics **34**, pp. 141-148 (2001).

[20] Sankar, D.S. ‘Two-phase Non-Linear Model for Blood Flow in Asymmetric and Axisymmetric stenosed arteries”, Int. J. Non Linear Mech. 46, pp 296-305 (2011).

[21] Fry, D.L. “Responses of the Arterial Wall to Certain Physical Factors: In Atherogenesis: Initiating Factors”, Ciba Foundation Symp. 12 , pp. 93-125 (1973).

[22] Caro, C.G. Fitzgeralc, J.M. and Schroter, R.C. “Atheroma and Arterial Wall: Observation, Correlation and Proposal of a Shear Dependent Mass Transfer Mechanism of Atherogenesis”, Proc. Roy. Soc. Lond. B 177, pp 109-159 (1971).

[23] Zamir, A. The physics of pulsatile flow, Springer-Verlag, New York, 2000.

Classical Dynamic Ising Model

M. George[1], **C. Turquois**[2], **and F. Yepiz, Jr.**[3]
[1]Department of Physics, Southwestern College, Chula Vista, Ca., U.S.A.
[2]Department of Cognitive Science, University of California San Diego, La Jolla, Ca., U.S.A.
[3]1344 Theresa Way, Chula Vista, Ca., 91911, U.S.A.

Abstract – *We discuss the dynamics of the Ising model as a computational mesoscopic system. The simplicity of the Ising model allows a Hamiltonian dynamics to be developed from renormalization group theory considerations for the model which is not overly complicated and preserves a close connection with thermodynamics. At the same time, the additional structure gives the potential for application to neural networks, as a new fundamental model for networks. This extends the Ising model to a deterministic system, of potential interest for computations.*

Keywords: Ising model, Hamiltonian dynamics, mesoscopic systems, renormalization group theory.

1 Introduction

Interest in developing models for mesoscopic systems has increased in recent times, as technological and scientific developments have led to small macroscopic-scale processes impinging on the microscopic scale, dominated by quantum processes. This interest is seen no more acutely than in biophysics and biochemistry, where organic systems can come very close to scales at which quantum mechanics must be used. We are introducing the dynamic model discussed in this article, in this context, as a model of relevance to mesoscopic systems and to small biosystems. We confine our considerations to classical Ising games, but another paper (George, 2013), will extend this work to quantum systems.

The Ising model has proven to be one of the most useful mathematical models for systems. The principal development of the Ising model ended with the work of Onsager and others in the 1940s (Onsager, 1944), much before the digital age, when it was shown that, as a simple model of a binary alloy or a ferromagnet, it displayed a critical phase transition in the two-dimensional model. The statistical model, while consisting of ensembles of classical spins, and straightforward to describe in "position-space", is actually fairly complicated in "momentum space" (Amit and Martin-Mayor, 2005), and so has proven less tractable to analysis than one might guess from its simplicity. Onsager's demonstration, in fact, is normally regarded as the first time a non-trivial mathematical model succumbed to exact mathematical techniques. The progress in analyzing the three-dimensional model has resulted mainly from numerical work (Rehr et al., 1980; George, 1985; Nickel and Rehr, 1990) and the theoretical framework of the renormalization group theory (Wilson and Kogut, 1974; Amit and Martin-Mayor, 2005). Surveying the early work done on the Ising model does not give a true flavor of the many and varied applications of the model, and the intense work being done on this model even to the present day, and in some areas quite far removed from its origins in theoretical physics. For example, in the area of neural networks, the Hopfield model is based on a version of the Ising model (Hopfield, 1982). The extraordinary utility of the Ising model forces us to consider that there may remain advantages in introducing another dynamic Ising model, despite much progress on the model having been made many years ago.

In biosystems and computer science, the primary application for dynamic Ising models has been to neural networks. The Hopfield model as well as the Boltzmann machine (Hinton and Sejnowski, 1986) are both examples of Ising models with long-range interactions, that have been coupled to a learning network, to produce dynamic models. This demonstrates the versatility of the Ising model in applications, and also indicates a certain potential for addressing the complexity inherent in many biosystems. The new model we propose is based on renormalization group theory, and offers certain advantages, with a simplicity that may make it computationally appealing.

The Ising model is usually studied as a statistical system, under equilibrium conditions. One does not usually think of the Ising model in dynamic terms or in the context of non-equilibrium processes, but it is defined on the basis of a Hamiltonian. Besides the applications that we have mentioned to neural nets, a number of efforts have been made to introduce dynamics in the Ising model. A problem with such a project is that, relative to thermodynamics, one may be taking the description of the model too far from its equilibrium applications in critical phenomena, the area that has resulted in the bulk of knowledge about the Ising model, and the apparatus of equilibrium statistical mechanics (the theory that is ordinarily applied to the Ising model). The other dynamic Ising models we discuss below (the Glauber model and the Monte Carlo simulations of the Ising model) are very closely tied to equilibrium statistical mechanics (Huang, 1987; Reichl, 1998). We shall also see that the new model we propose provides a natural extension of the model's equilibrium behavior. Incursion into non-equilibrium thermodynamics is valuable for modern applications to biosystems and neural networks.

The principal approach to non-equilibrium studies of the Ising model has been through game theory. Game theory allows one to switch from one trajectory to another, so that the Hamiltonian of the system is time-varying. In previous work (George, 2008; George and Ramirez, 2008), we have seen that, relative to Ising games, one would like to develop a dynamics that has some sort of internal structure at the vertices of the model (where the spins are located). This was later noted as well in work on mesoscopic systems (George, 2011). In addition, one would like to alter the "local" nonlinearity at these vertices, so that the alterations in spin, for a classical dynamics, occurs smoothly rather than discontinuously. Such a smooth variation, e.g. with the logistic function, is frequently used for neural nets (Haykin, 2009). In order to preserve a connection with equilibrium thermodynamics, this nonlinear temporal behavior must, in some sense, be kept "small". This is done, for example, with a Boltzmann machine by imposing a stochastic dynamics (Hinton and Sejnowski, 1986). We establish a nonlinear behavior using a linear-like framework, by application of concepts from renormalization group theory in our new model.

The dynamic Ising model, in the picture we are trying to develop, is a simple, nonlinear, and "parallel" mesoscopic, computational system. This contrasts with the brain, which although very analogous to the dynamic Ising model, in operating nonlinearly and as a parallel system, is highly complex. A neural net that simulates the brain would undoubtedly have long-range interactions, while we wish to restrict the model to short-ranges, i.e. low-dimensionality. (The association between system dimension and range of interaction is roughly as follows: Let us suppose the model has interaction range R and density of sites p. Then each site interacts with $(R/p)^d = kN$. Here, N is the number of sites interacting within the interaction range and k is some proportionality constant. It is the case, then, that d varies roughly as the logarithm of N and would be small, if the interaction is short-range and larger for long-range interactions.) It is important to point out that with internal structure, short-range interactions rapidly build to systems of unprecedented complexity, anyway, as if the dimension of the system were high.

We tend to focus on the tremendous information-processing capabilities of biological nervous systems. A dynamic Ising model, albeit very simple, can, too, acquire knowledge from its environment, and store, as well as process information. The stochastic learning machines, such as the Boltzmann model, demonstrate this. The mode of information storage for our model relies on the special features of a renormalization group approach, whereby renormalized parameters can "fix" aspects of the system, while letting other aspects evolve freely. This approach is an extension of simulated annealing (Kirkpatrick et al., 1983).

The basis for a Hamiltonian dynamics for our system arises from an internal structure of currents along edges. The connection with the dynamics of energy flow via currents supplies our model, overall, with the dynamics, but this is not based on stochastic processes. This makes our dynamic Ising model somewhat more complicated than the simple Ising model, and the processes involved more complex than those of Monte Carlo simulations of the Ising model. The physics involved is still that of classical spins, and the classical dynamics does not connect to quantum mechanics. Due to internal structure, the system is inherently mesoscopic, despite lacking a connection to quantum mechanics. The system is fragmented into a large-scale spin regime, a small-scale computational network of currents, and a very-large scale environment from which a system of a games is elaborated in the Ising model and the network. This means there are three different scaling regimes. Thus, this is a slightly more complex environment than usually considered with the renormalization group theory, where the divergence of a single length permits focusing on just one scaling regime. The defining characteristic of mesoscopic systems is not so much that they impinge on the quantum regime as that one must consider several scaling regimes, and boundary limitations or overlap become important.

In the next section, we define the classical Ising model. Following this, we discuss our dynamic Ising model associated with Hamiltonian mechanics, but derived from additional structure beyond spins. Then we give some concluding remarks and a perspective on this system as a biosystem and a mesoscopic system more generally.

2 Classical Ising Model

Now, let us formulate the standard (spin-1/2) Ising model (lacking explicit dynamics). The Ising model has a defining Hamiltonian given by the following expression

$$H\{s_n\} = -J \sum_{<n,m>} s_n s_m \tag{1}$$

Here, we assume that we are concerned with vertices, labeled n and m on a graph (typically some regular lattice). The quantity J represents a coupling constant, and $s_n = \pm 1$ is the spin value for vertex n. The symbol <n,m> means that we are to sum over all nearest neighbor sites n and m. The specific spin configuration is denoted $\{s_n\}$. For a lattice of N sites, there will be 2^N spin configurations.

The thermodynamics of the model is studied by constructing the probability generating function or partition function,

$$Z = \sum_{\{s_n\}} e^{-\beta H(s_n)} \tag{2}$$

This sum is to be taken over all possible spin configurations, in a network of N spins. The quantity β is intended to represent inverse temperature,

$$\beta = 1/k_B T \tag{3}$$

Here, T is absolute temperature and k_B is the Boltzmann constant.

The best-known dynamics for the Ising model was that defined by the Glauber model (Glauber, 1963). This dynamics consists of discrete-time, Markov chains. Because this is defined in terms of relatively simple conditional probabilities, this model is very suitable for Monte Carlo simulations (Metropolis et al., 1953).

We are going to formulate a dynamic Ising model by relating the Hamiltonian to a simple electrical network. Each vertex, n, of the graph will be associated with a spin, s_n, and a potential, v_n. The potential is associated with an internal structure, and we assume that the electrical network to which it relates is just an ordinary network with electronic and microelectronic devices along the edges, which constitute the conducting pathways. In the extended paper (George, 2013), we confine this to a linear, time-independent network, as an idealization,when the spin interactions are removed. This is not critical for the network as a mesoscopic scaling regime, since time-dependence and nonlinearities appear in conjunction with boundary overlap with other scaling regimes.

These circuit elements, between vertices n and m, along an edge, are functions of s'_m and s'_n, where s'_k denotes the sum of products $s_k s_j$, j being a nearest-neighbor site to k. This subjects the energy flow along the edges to the states of the spins in the neighborhood of the edges. We assume that the graph is a directed graph and constitutes a regular lattice. We also assume that the inputs and outputs to the electrical network are at the boundaries of the lattice. The underlying processes in the network are tied to interactions with the spins. We assume that this processing, at fixed spin configuration and in the absence of game moves, is linear. As the spin configurations change, the system shifts from one linear process to another. We incorporate the interactions between these two scaling regimes in a renormalizable Hamiltonian. We are using the game environment, discussed in the extended paper (George, 2013), to represent the broader evolution of the system, both at the microscopic level (quantum Ising games) and the macroscopic level (classical Ising games). This broader game evolution is not accommodated in the renormalizable dynamical model. A game theory approach has the advantage that the necessity of a unified theory for all regimes (which may not be feasible) is avoided, while permitting some treatment of the external environment in the theory of the mesoscopic system. Using games at the periphery is an approach we have previously presented (George, 2011) in which to consider mesoscopic systems. This extension of the renormalization group theory to a two-scale regime can be fairly readily assimilated in this simple model, in terms of renormalized trajectories of a Hamiltonian system. This is akin to real-space renormalization (Kadanoff, 2000).

Each spin is given by

$$s_n = h(v_n) \tag{4}$$

Here, h is a Heaviside-like function which takes the value -1 when v_n is negative and 1 when this value is positive. This is ideal, and must alter under renormalization. Thus, the spin and potential values are inter-dependent. The total energy associated with the lattice of spins is given by the Ising Hamiltonian, Eqn. 1. Because the spin configuration affects the electrical network, and, from (4), the electrical network affects the spins, the resulting system becomes a nonlinear system that switches from one linear process to another as the spin configurations change. Due to the simplicity of the Ising model, the mixing of these two regimes, which for many systems would be extremely complicated with respect to limitations in scaling, can be expressed fairly simply, using renormalization group theory concepts, as a dynamic Ising model which is a Hamiltonian system. We neglect complications in the renormalization procedure, and the resulting approximations rely on empirical fits to data that will either be satisfactory or not, depending on the nature of the fitting procedure. Since many procedures can be formulated, a learning approach can be constructed that turns this dynamic Ising model into a type of neural net.

The next point to consider is that the spins are given functions of potentials, and the currents are determined from network equations, with constants related to spins. Therefore, spins and currents are both presumably determined from these network flows. This in fact, must be the case because to recover the Ising model when the currents are zero, the value of J must be zero. Therefore, to allow for J to have a fixed value, we must introduce scale factors, k_{nm}, and a Hamiltonian :

$$H(\{s_n\}) = \sum_{<n,m>} \left(\frac{k_{nm}}{2\mu_{nm}} (i_{<n,m>})^2 + \frac{J k_{nm}}{2} (s_m - s_n)^2 \right) \tag{5}$$

Although this is a dynamical system, we are using a renormalization group theory approach. The k's and μ's are to be thought of as the results of renormalization from scale changes that involve the two regimes, i.e. the basic Ising model is approximated as a harmonic oscillator system, with respect to dynamics, incorporating another scaling regime (the electrical network). The two regimes are thought of initially as having very large volume to interface ratios, in relationship to one another. There are two types of parameters that scale, k's and μ's. As the system is independently rescaled, these parameters become renormalized to yield a system (when we ignore complications) with a Hamiltonian that still resembles an oscillator system. Then, J can have its constant coupling value associated with the Ising model, and the k's are zero when the currents are zero. In this way, the Hamiltonian arises out of the internal structure of currents and potentials from the network equations. (Along a trajectory, the scaling values k and the mass values μ will normally be correlated in order to maintain a constant H.) The dual rescaling, related to this simple dynamics, neglects many complications, and, in particular, some of the complications that arise as the boundary or interface becomes significant. Therefore, we must think of the k's and μ's as empirically determined. This is discussed in a longer version of this paper (George, 2013).

Our model is suited to Ising games (George, 2008 ; George and Ramirez, 2008) and to neural nets. We have made an effort to create a dynamics where the system displays an internal structure. This structure allows us to think in terms of mesoscopic systems, with a number of scaling regimes. We associated the dynamical Ising model with weights for edges in the network, and scaling factors that signified sampling rates (these are the k's). The two types of parameters (k's and μ's) are suited to an empirical approach to the renormalization group theory, in this more complex situation. We note that as these sampling rates tend toward zero, the usual Ising model is recovered. By virtue of the sampling, we can treat the system as discrete. At a given time t, there is both a spin configuration $\{s_n\}$ and a current configuration $\{i_{nm}\}$. However, the Hamiltonian model implies that we can determine the thermodynamics of the system from the spin configuration, alone. An initial ensemble of systems evolves as a time series, and the partition function is a function of time. In a game environment, the system can be artificially switched from one trajectory to another. Therefore, the partition function for an ensemble changes from move to move of the game. This third type of scaling regime, from a large-scale environment, was not accommodated by our renormalization group theory approach. This means that, in the long-run, the game moves lead to shifts from trajectory to trajectory of the Hamiltonian model, and that the system cannot be dealt with theoretically in an equilibrium context.

3 Thermodynamics

The thermodynamics of the dynamic Ising model, as we have presented it, arises out of the evolution of the initial ensemble of models. The partition function, Z(N), is, typically, not describing an equilibrium system. The temperature parameter β becomes absorbed in the sampling rate k, as the combination βk_{nm}, for each edge.

This means that in the thermodynamics of this model, temperature and sampling rate become intertwined. The combination leads to a spread of temperature effects, differing for each edge, and these edge effects change with time as the k's change. Thus, although the renormalization group theory helps us to partially formulate the theory of this mesoscopic system in an equilibrium context, the effective temperature, as measured by k values, in different parts of the lattice, will not be the same.

There is a potential for a variety of local thermal conditions to prevail throughout such a model. In an ensemble, this means that some areas of the model's graph, at a specific time, are equilibrating slowly, while others can do so rapidly. If a game is progressing in each member of the ensemble, decisions made in moves in certain regions of the lattice will be randomized much more rapidly than in other regions, as a result of differing k values. The game moves can occur at the level of the underlying electrical network, altering parameters such as capacitances and resistances. Interactions with spins then result in switching from one linear network to another. Where the moves are not rapidly randomized, significant differences will persist in the network, as if frozen into the network system. In other regions, randomization will lead to local equilibrium. By carefully setting k values, one can impose specific conditions in various regions. Thus, not only can network parameters be seen as subject to game moves, but also k values. If the networks are being used as neural nets, this leads to high variability from model to model in the ensemble, where changes are frozen, and to little change in ensemble characterisitcs in other regions. This diverse thermal behavior can be seen as a type of simulated annealing. However, it arises from a game milieu, with players intruding in the spontaneous dynamics of each system. By this strategem, the game players can seek to evolve the ensemble so that some members of the ensemble achieve the goal state of the game. This approach, especially in a training phase of a neural net, could be advantageous.

4 Concluding Remarks

We have supplied a dynamics for the Ising model, based on Hamiltonian mechanics, but we have also related it to the stochastic aspects of the Ising model and to thermodynamics. A major consideration, with respect to this, consisted in outlining the model, discussing salient features we wish to address, and potential applications, especially to Ising games and neural nets. Other dynamics, for example the Glauber model and Monte Carlo simulations of the Ising model, are probabilistic. The progenitors of the model we consider here are not only these two models (referring to Monte Carlo simulations loosely as stochastic models), but the Boltzmann machine and the Hopfield model in neural nets. This is a new type of model that extends the previous stochastic models to mesoscopic systems.

Spin differences turn out to correspond to canonical coordinates, and currents are the canonical momenta. These choices are explained in depth in another paper (George, 2013). The spin influences current by virtue of allowing parameters defining the electrical network to be affected by spin values, and the current affects spin values by defining the spin value at a vertex by virtue of the potential values at the vertex. These relationships result in setting the scaling parameters in the Hamiltonian, and allow us to apply an empirical version of the renormalization group theory to this system.

We have succeeded in introducing a new dynamic Ising model. An extended discussion will be published elsewhere (George, 2013), elaborating considerably on what has been discussed here. This model may be of interest because it is not a probabilistic model, like the others we have examined, but is still closely reflective of the thermodynamics of the Ising model, and extends previous work. This extension to mesoscopic systems, also represents a new type of extension of the renormalization group theory to non-equilibrium systems. It may prove to be tractable in numerical applications, due to the fact that, although slightly more complex than the original Ising model, it is, to a large extent a linear model.

5 References

[1] Amit, D. J. and Martin-Mayor, V. (2005). *Field Theory, the Renormalization Group and Critical Phenomena* (third edition). World Scientific.

[2] George, M. J. (1985). *Series Analysis in Statistical Mechanics*. Ph.D. thesis. University of Washington.

[3] George, M. J. (2008). Classical and quantum Ising games. International Journal of Pure and Applied Mathematics, 42, pp. 529 – 534.

[4] George, M. J. (2011). Computation as a mesoscopic phenomenon. Proceedings of the 2011 International Conference on Scientific Computing, pp. 43 – 47.

[5] George, M. J. (2013). Dynamic Ising Model. To be submitted for publication.

[6] George, M. J. and Ramirez, A. (2008). Ising games. Proceedings of the 2008 International Conference on Scientific Computing.

[7] Glauber, R. J. (1963). Time-dependent statistics of the Ising model. Journal of Mathematical Physics, 4, pp. 294 – 307.

[8] Haykin, S. (2009). *Neural Networks and Learning Machines* (third edition). Prentice Hall.

[9] Hinton, G. E. and Sejnowski, T. J. (1986). D. E. Rumelhart, J. L. McClelland, and the PDP Research Group, ed. Learning and relearning in Boltzmann machines. *Parallel Distributed Processing : Explorations in the Microstructure of Cognition . Volume 1 : Foundations.* Cambridge : MIT Press, pp. 282 – 317.

[10] Hopfield, J. J. (1982). Neural networks and physical systems with emergent collective computational abilities. Proceedings of the National Academy of Sciences of the United States of America, 79, pp. 2554 – 2558.

[11] Huang, K. (1987). *Statistical Mechanics* (second edition). Wiley.

[12] Kirkpatrick, S. ; Gelatt, C. D. ; and Vecchi, M. P. (1983). Optimization by simulated annealing. Science, 220, pp. 671 – 680.

[13] Metropolis, N. ; Rosenbluth, A. W. ; Rosenbluth, M. N. ; Teller, A. H. ; and Teller, E. (1953). Equations of state calculations by fast computing machine. Journal of Chemical Physics, 21, pp. 1087 – 1092.

[14] Nickel, B. G. and Rehr, J. J. (1990). High-temperature series for scalar-field lattice models : generation and analysis. Journal of Statistical Physics, 61, pp. 1 – 50.

[15] Onsager, L. (1944). Crystal Statistics. I. A two-dimensional model with an order-disorder transition. Physical Review, 65, pp. 117 – 149.

[16] Rehr, J. J. ; Joyce, G. S. ; and Guttmann, A. J. (1980). A recurrence technique for confluent singularity analysis of power series. Journal of Physics A, 13, pp. 1587 – 1602.

[17] Reichl, L. E. (1998). *A Modern Course in Statistical Physics* (second edition). Wiley Interscience.

[18] Wilson, K. G. and Kogut, J. (1974). The renormalization group and the ϵ expansion. Physics Reports, 12, pp. 75 – 200.

FLOW OF A MICROPOLAR FLUID THROUGH A STENOSED ARTERY WITH RADIALLY VARIABLE VISCOSITY

A.K. Banerjee, R. Ponalagusamy and R. Tamil Selvi
Department of Mathematics, National Institute of Technology
Tiruchirappalli – 620 015, INDIA

Abstract

A study of the steady flow of blood through a horizontally symmetric artery with mild stenosis is presented by considering blood as a micropolar fluid. The viscosity of blood is considered as radial coordinate dependent. The non-linear pressure equations governing the flow are solved numerically using finite difference technique. The effects of micropolar fluid parameters and hematocrit on axial velocity, microrotation velocity, wall shear stress, wall couple stress and the volumetric flow rate in the stenotic region and at the maximum height of the stenosis (stenosis throat) have been discussed. The results have been compared with the corresponding flow for a Newtonian fluid.

1. Introduction

The flow of fluids in pipes or channels is important in many biological and biomedical systems, particularly in the human cardiovascular systems. Researches related to many biological phenomena were undertaken from a fluid dynamical point of view. Some of them include the blood flow in an artery with stenosis (i.e. abnormal and unnatural growth in the lumen of the artery). The presence of constriction (stenosis) in the lumen of an artery disturbs the normal blood flow and causes arterial diseases. Several attempts [1-5] have been made to understand the flow characteristics of blood through arteries by assuming blood as Newtonian. The assumption of Newtonian behavior of blood is acceptable for high shear rate flow that is the case of flow through larger arteries. It has been pointed out that under diseased conditions, blood exhibits non-Newtonian fluid properties.

Young [4], Macdonald [5], Deshpande et al [6], Sankar and Hemalatha [7] etc. have analyzed the flow of blood through an arterial stenosis. Lee and Fung [8] have obtained the numerical results for the streamlines and distribution of velocity, pressure, vorticity and shear stress for different Reynolds number in blood flow through locally constricted tubes. In the above models, the flow of blood is represented as one-layered.

Bugliarello and Hayden [9] and Bugliarello and Sevilla [10] have experimentally observed that when blood flows through narrow tubes, there exists a cell-free plasma layer near the wall. In view of their experiments, instead of a one-layered model, a two-layered model was considered by Shukla et al [11-12] in which the peripheral plasma layer and the core are both Newtonian in character.

Ponalagusamy [13], Ikbal et al [14], Chaturani and Kaloni [15], Chaturani and Ponalagusamy [16] etc. have analyzed the flow characteristics of blood by considering the blood as a two- layered model. The micropolar fluid model for blood flow through stenosed artery has been considered by many investigators [17-21]. In all these studies mentioned above, whether it is one-layered model or two-layered model, the viscosity of blood is treated as constant.

The unsteady flow of blood through artery with mild stenosis has been studied by Venkateswarulu and Rao [22] assuming blood to be suspension of red cells in plasma and the fluid to be Newtonian with variable viscosity. The effect of magnetic field in the transverse direction of blood flow in a stenotic artery was investigated by Bali and Awasthi [23] considering viscosity of blood to be radial coordinate dependent and the fluid to be non-Newtonian.

Blood is a suspension of red cells, white cells and platelets in plasma. The main advantage of using micropolar fluid to study the blood flow in comparison with other classes of non-Newtonian fluids is that it takes care of the rotation of the fluid particles by means of an independent kinematic vector called microrotation vector. With this view in mind, in the present study an one-layer model is considered for blood flow through stenosed artery, wherein the flowing blood is represented by Eringen's micropolar fluid[24] considering the viscosity of blood as radial coordinate dependent and the microelements are rigid cells suspended in plasma.

2. Formulation of the problem

The stenosed artery is considered as a narrow cylindrical tube of length L. The blood is represented by an incompressible micropolar fluid of density ρ with radially variable viscosity $\mu(r)$. Let (r, θ, z) be the coordinate of a material point in the cylindrical polar coordinate system. The origin is located on the vessel (stenosed artery) axis, z-axis is taken along the axis of the artery while r and θ are along the radial and circumferential directions respectively.

Based on the discussions made by Young [1], Ponalagusamy [26] and Philip and Chandra [(27] the radial velocity is negligibly small and can be neglected for low Reynolds number flow through an artery with mild stenosis. Keeping these in view, the governing equations of motion and viscosity are given by

$$\frac{\partial p}{\partial r} = 0 \tag{1}$$

$$\frac{\partial p}{\partial z} + k\frac{\partial^2 w}{\partial r^2} + \frac{k}{r}\frac{\partial w}{\partial r} + \frac{k}{r}\frac{\partial}{\partial r}(rv_\theta) + \frac{1}{r}\frac{\partial}{\partial r}\left[r\mu(r)\frac{\partial w}{\partial r}\right] = 0 \tag{2}$$

and $$-2k\,v_\theta - k\frac{\partial w}{\partial r} + \gamma\frac{\partial}{\partial r}\left[\frac{1}{r}\frac{\partial}{\partial r}(rv_\theta)\right] = 0 \tag{3}$$

where $\mu(r) = \mu_0\left[1 + \beta_1 h_m\left(1 - \frac{r}{R_0}\right)^{m_2}\right]$.

Here w is the axial velocity component, v_θ is the microrotation component in the rz-plane, p is the pressure, $\mu(r)$ is the viscosity of blood, μ_0 is the viscosity near the wall, k is the rotational viscosity, γ is the gyro viscosity, h_m is the maximum hematocrit at the centre of the tube, β_1 is a constant, m_2 is the power law index involved in viscosity profile and R_0 is the radius of the normal tube. Since the flow is axisymmetric, all the variables are independent of θ.

The shear stress and the couple stress are respectively defined as $\tau_{rz} = (\mu + k)\frac{\partial w}{\partial r} + kv_\theta$ and

$$M_{r\theta} = \gamma\frac{\partial v_\theta}{\partial r}.$$

The boundary conditions for the equations (1) to (3) are of the form

$$w = v_\theta = 0 \text{ at } r = R(z)\,; \quad \frac{\partial w}{\partial r} = 0 \text{ at } r = 0;$$

w and v_θ are finite at $r = 0$. (4)

Using the following non-dimensional parameters,

$$R^* = \frac{R}{R_0},\ r^* = \frac{r}{R_0},\ z^* = \frac{z}{R_0},\ p^* = \frac{pR_0}{w_0\mu_0},$$

$w^* = \frac{w}{w_0}$ and $v_\theta^* = \frac{v_\theta R_0}{w_0}$ and dropping stars, equations (1) to (3) reduce to

$$\frac{\partial p}{\partial r} = 0 \tag{5}$$

$$\frac{\partial p}{\partial z} = \frac{1}{1-N}\left[\frac{\partial^2 w}{\partial r^2} + \frac{1}{r}\frac{\partial w}{\partial r} + \frac{N}{r}\frac{\partial}{\partial r}(rv_\theta)\right] + \beta_1 h_m\left[1 - (1+m_2)\left(\frac{r}{R}\right)^{m_2}\right]\frac{1}{r}\frac{\partial w}{\partial r} + \beta_1 h_m\left[1 - \left(\frac{r}{R}\right)^{m_2}\right]\frac{\partial^2 w}{\partial r^2} \tag{6}$$

$$\frac{\partial w}{\partial r} + 2v_\theta = \frac{2-N}{m^2}\left[\frac{\partial}{\partial r}\left\{\frac{1}{r}\frac{\partial}{\partial r}(rv_\theta)\right\}\right] \tag{7}$$

Here w_0 is the velocity averaged over the section of the tube of radius R_0, $N = \frac{k}{\mu + k}$ is the coupling number and $m^2 = \frac{R_0^2\mu_0}{\gamma}$ is the micropolar fluid parameter. The parameters N and m^2 determine the concentration and size of the microelements. For a Newtonian fluid $N = m^2 = 0$.

The boundary conditions (4) in dimensionless form become

$$w = v_\theta = 0 \text{ at } r = R(z)\,; \quad \frac{\partial w}{\partial r} = 0 \text{ at } r = 0;$$

w and v_θ are finite at $r = 0$. (8)

The geometry of the stenosis is shown in Fig.1 and can be described as [25, 26]

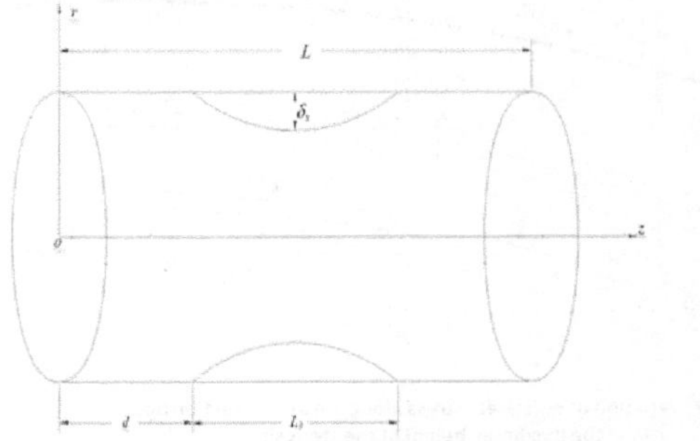

Fig.1. Geometry of the stenosed artery

$$R(z) = 1 - \beta_1\left[L_0^{m_1-1}(z-d) - (z-d)^{m_1}\right] \; d \le z \le d + L_0$$

$= 1$, otherwise

where $R(z)$ is the radius of the stenosed artery, L_0 is the length of the stenosis, d denotes its location and $\beta_1 = \dfrac{\delta_s}{R_0 L_0^{m_1}} \dfrac{m_1^{m_1/(m_1-1)}}{m_1 - 1}$, δ_s is the maximum height of the stenosis at $z = d + \dfrac{L_0}{m_1^{1/(m_1-1)}}$ such that $\delta_s / R_0 << 1.0$. When $m_1 = 2$, the geometry of the stenosis becomes symmetric at $z = d + \dfrac{L_0}{2}$.

3. Solution of the problem

Applying finite difference scheme, the equations (6) and (7) are solved using the boundary conditions (8). To prove convergence of finite difference scheme, the computation is carried out for lower values of step size. No significant change was observed in the value of w and v_θ.

The volumetric flow rate of the fluid in the stenotic region is given by $Q = \int_0^{R(z)} w(r) r dr$.

The skin friction coefficient τ_w at the surface of the stenosis is given by

$$R_e \tau_w = \left[\left\{1 + \beta_1 h_m \left(1 - \frac{r}{R_0}\right)^{m_2} + \frac{N}{1-N}\right\} \frac{\partial w}{\partial r}\right]_{r=R(z)},$$ where

R_e is the Reynolds number of the fluid.

The couple stress coefficient M_w at the surface of the stenosis is given by $R_e M_w = \dfrac{1}{m^2}\left(\dfrac{\partial v_\theta}{\partial r}\right)_{r=R(z)}$.

4. Discussion and Conclusions

Axial velocity, microrotation rate component, volumetric flow rate, the wall shear stress and the wall couple stress are computed at the stenotic region for various values of the micropolar fluid parameters N and m^2, and the maximum hematocrit value h_m.

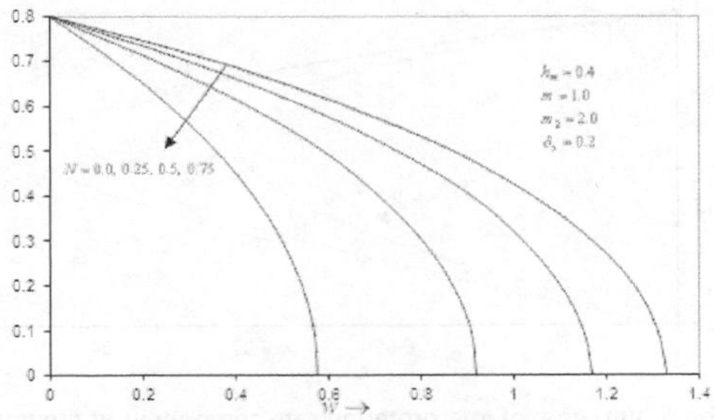

Fig.2. Variation of axial velocity at the mid-point of the stenotic region

The axial velocity profile w has been plotted for different values of N in Fig.2 for a fixed value of h_m and for different values of h_m in Fig.3 for a fixed value of N. The effect of h_m on the axial velocity for Newtonian fluid is shown separately in Fig.4.

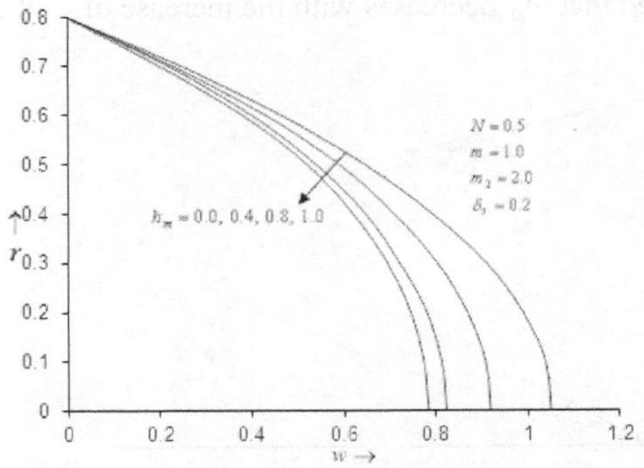

Fig.3. Variation of axial velocity at the mid-point of the stenotic region

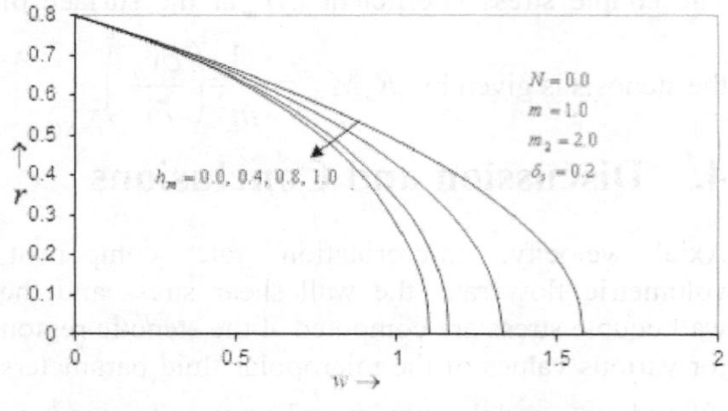

Fig.4. Variation of axial velocity at the mid-point of the stenotic reg

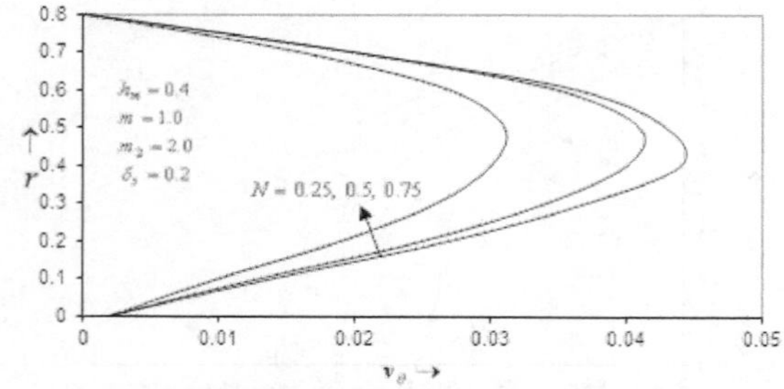

Fig.5. Variation of microrotation rate component at the mid-point of stenotic region

We observe that an increase in h_m or N decreases the axial velocity w. The same effect of h_m on Newtonian fluid velocity field was also observed. The microrotation rate component v_θ has been plotted in Fig.5 for different values of N and for a fixed value of h_m, and vice versa in Fig.6. It is observed that v_θ decreases with the increase of N.

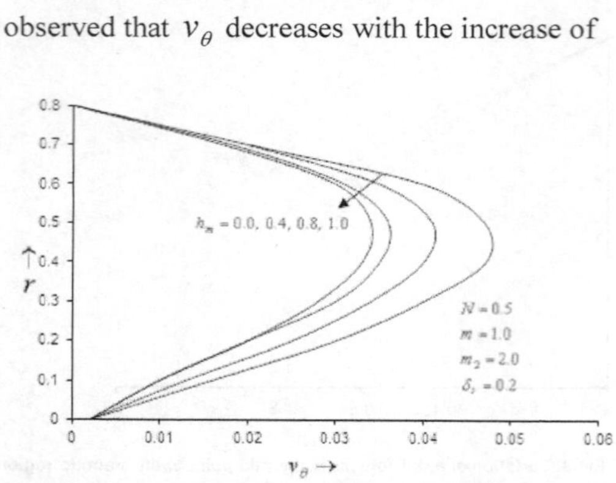

Fig.6. Variation of microrotation rate component at the mid-point of the stenotic region

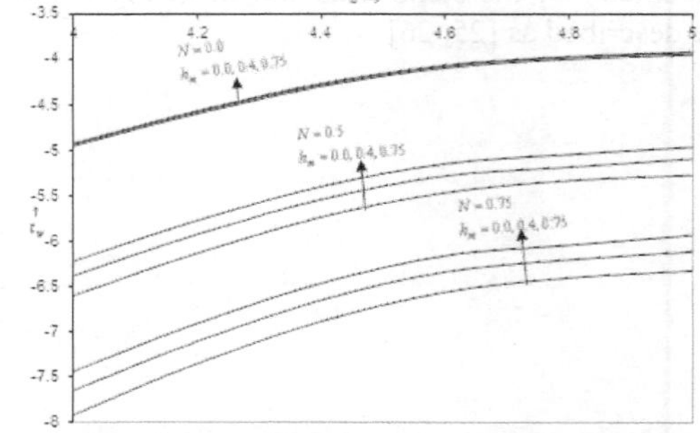

Fig.7. Variation of wall shear stress along the axial direction upto the maximum height of the stenosis

The wall shear stress τ_w and the wall couple stress M_w at the stenotic wall are plotted respectively in Figs. 7 and 8. It is observed that the wall shear stress increases with the increase of h_m but decreases with N, whereas the wall couple stress increases with the increase of h_m. The same type of behavior of h_m on the wall shear stress for a Newtonian fluid was noticed. The variation of flow rate Q with respect to the parameters h_m and N is tabulated in Table-1. It is observed that with the increase in values of h_m and N the flow rate decreases.

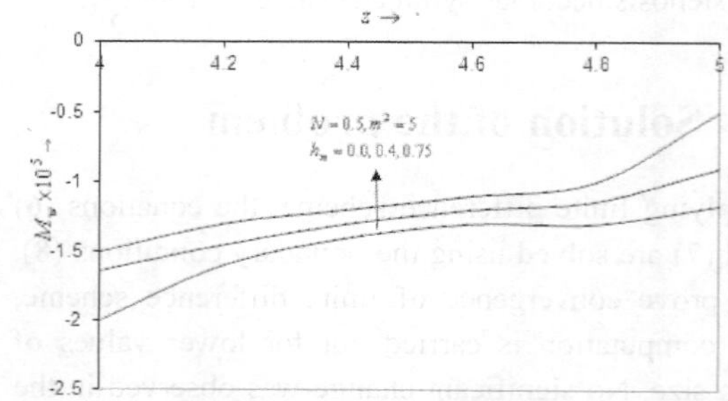

Fig.8. Variation of couple stress along the axial direction upto the maximum height of the stenosis

Table-1. Variation of volumetric flow rate (Q) at the mid-point of the stenotic region

h_m	Flow rate (Q)			
	N			
	0.0	0.25	0.5	0.75
0.0	0.2538	0.2335	0.1692	0.1015
0.4	0.2255	0.1949	0.1531	0.9442
0.8	0.2049	0.1830	0.1404	0.8867

References

[1] Young, D.F. Effect of time dependent stenosis on Flow through a tube. J. Eng. Ind. 90, 248-254 (1968).

[2] Forrester, J.H. and Young, D.F. Flow through a converging-diverging tube and its implications in occlusive vascular disease – I and II, J. Biomech. 3, 297-316 (1970).

[3] Young, D.F. and Tsai, F.Y. Flow characteristics in models of artificial stenosis – II, unsteady flow, J. Biomech. 6, 547 – 561 (1973).

[4] Young, D. F. Fluid Mechanics of arterial stenosis, J. Biomech. Eng. – T ASME, 101, 157-175 (1979).

[5] Macdonald, D. A. On steady flow through modeled vascular stenosis, J. Biomech. 12, 13-20 (1979).

[6] Deshpande, M. D., Giddens, D.P. and Mabon, R.F. Steady laminar flow through modeled vascular stenosis, J. Biomech. 9, 165-174 (1976).

[7] Sankar, D. S. and Hemalatha, K. Pulsatile flow of Herschel-Bulkley fluid through stenosed arteries- A mathematical model , Int. J. Nonlin. Mech. 4, 979-990 (2006).

[8] Lee, J. S. and Fung, Y. C. Flow in locally constricted tubes at low Reynolds number, J. Appl. Mech. Tran. ASME, 37, 9-16 (1970).

[9] Bugliarello, G. and Hayden J.W. Detailed characteristics of the flow of blood in vitro, Trans. Soc. Rheol. 7, 209-230 (1963).

[10] Bugliarello, G. and Sevilla, J. Velocity distribution and other characteristics of steady and pulsatile blood flow in fine glass tubes, Biorheology, 7, 85-107 (1970).

[11] Shukla, J.B., Parihar, R.S. and Rao, B.R.P. Effect of peripheral layer viscosity on blood flow through the artery with mild stenosis, B. Math. Biol. 42, 797-805 1980).

[12] Shukla, J. B., Parihar, R.S. and Rao, B.R.P. Biorheological aspects of blood flow through artery with mild stenosis; Effects of peripheral layer, Biorheology, 17, 403-410 (1980).

[13] Ponalagusamy, R. Blood flow through an artery with mild stenosis: A two-layered model, different shapes of stenosis and slip velocity at the wall, J. Appl. Sci. 7, 1071-1077 (2007).

[14] Ikbal, Md. A., Chakravarty, S. Wong, K.K.L., Mazumdar, J. and Mandal, P.K. Unsteady response of non-Newtonian blood flow through a stenosed artery in magnetic field, J. Comput. Appl. Math. 230, 243-259 (2009).

[15] Chaturani, P. and Kaloni, P. N. Two-layered Poiseuille flow model for blood flow through arteries of small diameter and arterioles, Biorheology, 13, 243-250 (1976).

[16] Chaturani, P. and Ponalagusamy, R. A two layered model for blood flow through stenosed arteries, Proc. of 11th National Conf. on Fluid Mechanics and Fluid power. BHEL (R & D) Hyderabad, India, 6-22 (1982).

[17] Devanathan, R. and Parvathamma, S. Flow of micropolar fluid through a tube with stenosis, Medical and Biological Engineering and Computing 21, 438-445 (1983).

[18] Mekheimer, Kh. S. and El Kot, M.A. The micropolar fluid model for blood flow through a tapered artery with a stenosis, Acta Mech. Sin 24, 637-644 (2008).

[19] Muthu, P., Rathish Kumar, B.V. and Peeyush Chandra, A study of micropolar fluid in an annular tube with application to blood flow, Journal of Mechanics in Medicine and Biology 8, 561-576 (2008).

[20] Ikbal, Md. A., Chakravarty, S. and Mandal, P.K. Two layered micropolar fluid flow through stenosed artery: Effect of peripheral layer thickness, Computers and Mathematics with Applications 58, 1328-1339 (2009).

[21] Pandey, S.K. and Chaube, M.K. Peristaltic flow of a micropolar fluid through a porous medium in the presence of an external magnetic field, Commun. Nonlinear Sci. Numer. Simulat. 16, 3591-3601(2011).

[22] Venkateswarulu, K. and Rao, J. Anand, Numerical solution of unsteady blood flow through an indented tube with atherosclerosis, Indian Journal of Biochemistry and Biophysics 41, 241-245 (2004).

[23] Rekha Bali and Usha Awasthi, Effect of a magnetic field on the resistance to blood flow through stenotic artery, Applied Mathematics and Computation 188, 1635-1641 (2007).

[24] Eringen A.C. Theory of micropolar fluid, J. Math. & Mech. 16,1-18 (1966).

[25] Haldar, K. Effects of the shape of the stenosis on the resistance to blood flow through an artery, Bull. Math. Biol. 47, 545-550 (1985).

[26] Ponalagusamy, R. Blood flow through stenosed tube, Ph. D. Thesis IIT Bombay, India (1986).

[27] Philip, D. and Peeyush Chandra, Flow of Eringen Fluid (Simple microfluid) through an artery with mild stenosis, Int. J. Eng. Sci. 34, 87-99 (1996).

SESSION

SCIENTIFIC COMPUTING + DATA MANAGEMENT + CRYPTOGRAPHY

Chair(s)

TBA

A framework for scientific data management in the cloud

Verena Kantere
Institute of Services Science, University of Geneva
1227 Carouge, Switzerland

Abstract - *The efficient management of scientific data has been an increasing challenge until now, because of the complexity, diversity and size of the data, query sets and user groups. Cloud computing gives possibilities for offering adaptive large-scale services for the management of scientific data that promise to tackle this challenge. The goal is therefore to create cloud data management systems that will serve scientific data. Such systems need to be able to handle unstructured data, i.e. data that are stored originally and primarily in files, as is the vast majority of scientific data. We describe the design of an ongoing research project that aims to coalesce the existing research and business technologies into the provision of an all-inclusive solution for the management of scientific data in the cloud. The project includes a framework and an economy for a cloud data management system, as well as a novel query mechanism that implements a novel query language.*

Keywords: Scientific data and queries, heterogeneous scientific data, big data management, cloud data management, file management, unstructured data

1 Introduction

Public archiving of large persistent scientific datasets from various disciplines, such as geophysical, environmental, biological, astronomical data etc, gains more and more credence. Data is massively collected and queried by large groups of scientists. Cloud computing, the new trend for service infrastructures in the IT domain that allows heavy user multi-tenancy as well as efficient data processing, seems to be the perfect management infrastructure for such data. Already, big scientific institutes, like CERN [1], maintain enormous distributed datacenters that serve the research needs of thousands of scientists. Such a cloud necessitates various technological capabilities. Most importantly, it is required that cloud data services run with minimal capital expenditure, but, nonetheless, can support efficiently multi-user tenancy.

The efficient management of scientific data has been an increasing challenge until now. Moreover, the need for in-depth analysis on huge amounts of data has increased the demand for additional computational support. Unfortunately, current commercial data management tools are incapable to support the unprecedented scale, rate, and complexity of scientific data collection and processing.

A cloud of databases that archives data supports cloud caching, meaning common unrestricted caching for all cloud data. Users are customers of the cloud that consume its resources as a utility service. Specifically, the users can query the cloud data, paying the price for what they use. User payment is employed for coverage of short and long-term cost. Short-term cost refers to the respective query execution, and long-term cost to the self-preservation of the cloud infrastructure and improvement of the cloud services.

In order to exploit the capabilities offered by the cloud paradigm for the benefit of the management of scientific data, we need cloud data management systems that are able to handle unstructured data, i.e. data that are stored originally and primarily in files. The vast majority of scientific data is stored in files and is manipulated through a file system, meaning that all the processing, from search to computation is performed in the content of the files. Existing persistent scientific data in files is huge and, therefore, will not be moved to databases, even if the latter obtain the desired capabilities to satisfy scientific experimentation. Moreover, the tradition in applications that manipulate scientific data files is long and the overhead of implementing the same functionality such that it is plug-able on database systems is tremendous. These two facts lead to the necessity of a full-fledged querying mechanism for files in the cloud, similar to that of a database system.

In this paper we describe the design of an ongoing research project that aims to coalesce the existing research and business technologies into the provision of an all-inclusive solution for the management of scientific data in the cloud. The project includes the development of a framework and an economy for a cloud data management system. Our focus is on the management of scientific data, since their variety, volume and extreme data management requirements makes them the best candidates to use as guidelines for research and experimentation. Our overall solution, however, is intended to be generic and applicable to any kind of unstructured data that may need cloud management.

The framework and economy that will result from this research is the adaptation and the extension of our already published work on a cloud economy for the management of structured data, i.e. data that reside in databases [2][3][4]. The framework that handles unstructured data includes a novel query mechanism for data in files. The mechanism is designed to implement a novel query language as well as a novel respective execution model. The query engine is complemented with an associative storage manager that fits the results of queries on unstructured data in a structured format and stores them in backend databases. The storage manager is accompanied by data pre-fetching techniques. Storing interesting unstructured data in databases leads eventually to querying mostly data in databases and not in files. The latter allows for broad and efficient multi-query optimization as well as for optimized storage design.

In the cloud and on top of the database and file management system we create a middleware that can route queries appropriately. The middleware comprises a query planner that enables the service of sets or sequences of queries on both structured and unstructured data. The cloud economy that we already have is extended in order to handle such query combinations. In this way, the cloud framework is able to serve in an optimal manner even demanding analysis tasks on data (which is very common for scientific data). We intend to extensively study and experiment on the proposed cloud framework with real and synthetic datasets.

2 State of research

This research aims to contribute in two major research fields in computer science, cloud computing and scientific data management. The progress of these fields is essential to the rising era of pervasive computing and data sharing of enormous variety and volume.

Cloud computing. Cloud computing is a brand new area of research. Although scientific data have been long collected and shared in large datacenters [1][8], and IT business in cloud computing [5][6][7] have emerged, research has been left behind.

Research on cloud computing currently considers an infrastructure that comprises a set of independent edge caches that cooperate in order to deliver web content. Content sharing among caches [9][10][11] involves (i) content retrieval from sibling caches instead from the server, (ii) routing and sharing of content updates, and (iii) sharing cache resources, in order to achieve efficient collaborative data placement/replacement/update/lookups etc. Being more compliant with the business domain, the described research project focuses on self-tuned cloud caches that share resources, rather that self-organization of independent caches. Concerning the management of scientific data, existing research solutions [12], consider network bandwidth to be the only important resource, and, therefore, the sole basis for cost computation. However, cloud businesses usually prorate cost to more types of resources. For instance, GoGrid [5] gives network bandwidth for free. A self-tuned cache [13] reduces query execution costs adaptively to the workload. As a step further towards commercial applications, we propose an economy that takes into consideration the overall cost of the infrastructure beyond network bandwidth: disk I/O, storage and CPU.

Cloud computing is the natural dilation of grid computing [14], as it enables an integrated collaborative use of high-end computing owned and managed by multiple organizations. Grid databases [15] are federated database servers over a grid, which are viewed as a virtual database system through a service federation middleware [16]. Querying the grid data guaranteeing high performance is one of the key issues for distributed queries across large datasets. This issue is inherited in cloud computing, and becomes more complicated, since it is augmented with the issue of providing an accounting service that supports a payment scheme for cloud usage. Our response to this challenge is the proposal of a data-aware cloud economy that fills the essential gap of tuning the provision of data management services for remuneration.

Related to this research project on a cloud economy is the research on auctioning and accounting systems. Accounting in wide-area networks that offer distributed services have long been the target of research in computing. Mariposa [17] discusses an economic model for querying and storage in a distributed database system. In Mariposa clients and servers have an account in a network bank and users allocate a budget to each of their queries. The processing mechanism aims to service the query in the allotted budget by executing portions of it on various sites. The latter place bids for the execution of query parts, and the bids are accumulated in query brokers. The decision of selecting the most appropriate bids is delegated to the user. In contrast, our cloud proposal recommends to the user an efficient but also profitable for the cloud query plan. In the spirit of Mariposa, a series of other works have proposed solutions for similar frameworks [18][19][20][21][22]. These focus on job scheduling and bid negotiation, which are orthogonal issues to those that will be tackled by the ongoing research.

Scientific data management. The efficient management of scientific data has been a challenge until now. The need for in-depth analysis on huge amounts of data has increased the demand for additional computational support. Unfortunately, current commercial data management tools are incapable of supporting the unprecedented scale, rate, and complexity of scientific data collection and processing. Independently of the categories that scientific data belong to, their management is essentially divided into the following coarse phases: workflow deployment, management of metadata, data integration, data archiving and finally data processing [23]. All these phases suffer from tremendous data management problems that concern automation, online processing, data and process integration and file management [24]. This research contributes to the issues of process integration and file management.

Currently, scientists need to tightly collaborate with computer engineers in order to develop custom solutions that efficiently support data storage and analysis for each different experiment [25][26]. Beyond the fact that constant collaboration of multidisciplinary scientists and engineers is hard, time and effort consuming, the experience gained by such collaboration is not inherited widely to the scientific community, so that next generation experimental setups can benefit from it. It is absolutely necessary to develop generic solutions for storage and analysis of scientific data that can easily be extended and customized. Developing generic solutions is feasible, since there are low-level commonalities in the way that experimental data are represented or analyzed [23][26]. Therefore, frequently, scientific data processing encompasses generic procedures. Current research, however, has not proposed any solution for the support of such processes.

In this research we study a variety of analysis cases of scientific data in order to extract common low-level procedures. Based on this study we develop templates for stored procedures that can be customized in a declarative manner and can suit the specific needs of each scientific experimental analysis. This solution enables the leverage of process scheduling (parallel and pipelined processing) from the scientists to the cloud data management system. For this purpose we develop a cloud middleware that performs overall planning and execution of the analysis procedures.

Scientific data (more than any other kind of data) are represented both in structured (i.e. stored in databases) and unstructured (i.e. stored in files) forms. The challenge resides into providing a management solution for both representations. Specifically, experimental metadata are usually stored in databases and raw data - the vast majority of scientific data - are stored in files. Therefore raw data are manipulated through a file system, meaning that all the processing, from search to computation is performed in the content of the files. Existing persistent scientific data in files is huge and, therefore, will not be moved to databases, even if the latter obtain the desired capabilities to satisfy scientific experimentation. Moreover, the tradition in applications that manipulate scientific data files is long and the overhead of implementing the same functionality such that it is plug-able on database systems is tremendous. These two facts lead to the necessity of a full-fledged querying mechanism for files, similar to that of a database system.

Current commercial products, such as Oracle 11g [27] have been extended to support only semi-structured data (e.g. XML and RDF representations). Moreover, research in querying and, generally, management of unstructured data is nascent. Some efforts exist to integrate the scientific files into DBMSs, (Netlobs [28] on Oracle, Barrodale [29] on Postgres), but they are not generic enough to be extensible to other file formats such as ROOT [31], the data analysis format of CERN. Also, they do not provide complete support of DBMS features on these files. Recent proposals on querying unstructured data focus on storage issues [32] or assume keyword searching and storage of keywords in databases [33]. Therefore, the necessity for a language that can express complex queries on purely unstructured data and can extract structured information in a straightforward manner is still missing.

In our research we work towards the proposal of such a query language for data in files and we create the respective query engine. In order to support query planning and optimization, we also propose caching methods and index structures for unstructured data. The advantage of this stand-alone file-querying mechanism is that it includes only procedures that are targeted to querying, avoiding any implications caused by the complicated database mechanisms that serve transactions.

The middleware that we develop in our research enables transparent management on top of a database and a file system that manages structured and unstructured data. The middleware accepts as input the analysis procedures as sets or sequences of queries and routes them appropriately to the database or the file system. The middleware will provide uniform high-level query optimization possibilities and, therefore, overall query execution efficiency. Upcoming grid middleware promise to support this kind of integration [34], but are still nascent.

3 Management of unstructured data

As mentioned, the vast majority of scientific data is unstructured, stored in files and manipulated through a file system, meaning that all the processing, from search to computation is performed in the content of the files. In order to manage data residing in files, it is necessary to perform the following steps in the presented order:

1. <u>Develop a file query mechanism</u>: We are designing a querying mechanism that can serve queries on unstructured data. There are two possible ways to do this: (i) Extend an open-source DBMS kernel (e.g. PostgreSQL [41]) in order to query files, or (ii) create the file query mechanism from scratch. We choose to create the mechanism from scratch: In this way, we avoid time-consuming extensions to the DBMS that are unnecessary for querying data in files, such as extensions on transaction management modules. Moreover, creating the mechanism from scratch makes it easier to adhere to the special needs and characteristics of data in files, without being limited by the rationale of structured data representation. Nevertheless, based on our experience on the functionality of DBMSs, we will be able to copy the query functionality from a DBMS that can be adjusted for files, rather than reinventing it.

2. <u>Develop a storage technique for query results</u>: It is essential that the results from queries on files are stored in backend databases. In this way, we achieve two goals. From the big volume of data in files, the part that is actually interesting is extracted and stored in a structured way so that (i) it is easily accessed, since we can perform standard query optimization techniques available in commercial DBMSs, and (ii) it is transparently queried with the original content of the

backend databases, so that multi-query optimization is more efficient.

3. Extend the cloud economy for queries on files: The economy proposed in our recent work [2][3][4] will be extended for the provision of data services on files.

In the following we describe the above research steps.

3.1 Query mechanism for data in files

Our effort to create a query mechanism for data that reside in files is based on their real querying needs, focusing on the needs of scientific data. Currently, we are studying the common characteristics and querying needs of scientific data. The outcome of this study can be the guideline for the definition of a query language and respective execution model for data in files.

Study of file data processing. Our study is based on real processes performed on real unstructured datasets focusing on scientific data files, such as data from CERN [30], the animal house Institut Clinique de la Souris [37] and the BlueBrain project [39]. The study comprises three steps.

First, the recognition of the most fundamental operations performed on unstructured data, as well as the identification of the common characteristics of the respective operators. Such observations are paired with the respective file structure (for example, ASCII, binary, tabular, following a specific schema such as HDF [41]). A preliminary study that we have already completed indicates that the most common operations are file scanning, attribute value matching and selections.

Second, the extraction of common low-level procedures on unstructured data. Our intention is to recognize the most common combinations of basic operations on unstructured data, as well as identify the common characteristics of the data that feed these procedures.

Third, the extraction of common processing strategies on unstructured data and the identification of common algorithmic processing for the major tasks of data analysis: mining, provenance, cleaning and integration. We acquire this information by observing the scientific query workloads at our disposal, but also by meeting with selected scientific groups and recording their testimonials about scientific data processing.

Definition of the query language. We create a declarative language for querying unstructured data. This language is based on the SQL3 standard, in order to exploit the vast experience accumulated in the most popular database query language. Guided by the study on unstructured data processing, we include in the declaration of the new language the following:

1. Basic data types based on the operands of basic operations identified in the study. We estimate that common data types are the numerical and string type, as well as a type that refers to file linkage.

2. Basic operators respective to the basic operations identified in the above study. Basic operators in the SQL3 standard, such as AND, OR, JOIN are necessary in the new language. Furthermore, operators that perform sorting and set operations are necessary, too.

3. Basic templates for stored procedures, based on the common processing algorithms identified in the study. The new query language includes the parameterization of these templates in its declaration syntax in order to allow the customization of the involved procedures by the users.

The declaration of the new query language is followed by the definition of an execution model. The latter concerns the default query execution planning.

3.2 Storage of unstructured query results in a database

The query engine described above enables systematic querying on unstructured data. The query results are also unstructured data, but it is beneficial in the long-term to express these data in a structured format and store them in the databases. There are two major problems for which we design techniques: (i) the selection of the most appropriate storage format, and (ii) the planning of the timing and extension of data pre-fetching.

Storage format. The results of queries on data in files have to be stored in a database. We assume that the database is row-store and relational, as this is the case for most of the existing commercial and research databases. The schema of the database has to be decided beforehand in a semi-automatic way. The structure of the schema plays an important role in the efficiency of query execution. Depending on the schema, a query execution may need different number of joins among tables. Conceptually, the query results can be divided into three categories: (i) values of complex entities, (ii) values of single attributes, or (iii) values of groups of attributes. Therefore, we intend to propose three respective schema templates:

Storage of objects. If the query results constitute values of complex conceptual entities that are characterized by hierarchical conceptual inter-relationships, then these results should be stored such that access to all properties of an entity is efficient. Therefore, the appropriate schema template follows object-relational storage techniques [42][43]. The characterization of query results as complex entities is possible if based on knowledge of the file format.

Storage of columns. If the query results are values of single attributes, then the best way to store them is in two column tables (attribute id and value). This kind of storage allows for very fast processing on single tables and achieves excellent exploitation of storage space, since there are no null values. Moreover, it offers possibilities for compression and querying techniques recently proposed for column-store databases [44].

Storage of views. If the query results are values of groups of attributes that are not related conceptually in a complex way that indicates hierarchically organized entities, then the best way to store them is in multicolumn tables as materialized views. Depending on the overlap of different query results, view maintenance may require view merging or division. For this we develop a methodology to use and combine existing view maintenance techniques [45].

Data pre-fetching. While storing query results appropriately is the first step towards ensuring efficient execution of future queries on these data, the second step is to predict to some extent what will be the query results on data in files in the future and pre-fetch them. Employing data pre-fetching, situations in which related unstructured data are gradually queried and therefore gradually stored in databases can be avoided. Instead, pre-fetching and storing in databases all related data gives a global view of their conceptual and access relationships and, therefore, allows for optimized storage decisions. Data pre-fetching can be performed towards two dimensions:

Vertical pre-fetching. We can pre-fetch values for data attributes that are not comprised in the query results. This kind of pre-fetching is beneficial particularly for data that are conceptually complex entities.

Horizontal pre-fetching. We can pre-fetch values for attributes comprised in the query results. This kind of pre-fetching is beneficial particularly for data that conceptually constitute flat groups of attributes or single attributes. Pre-fetching values assists in query execution efficiency in a straightforward manner, as no index or compression updates are necessary.

3.3 Cloud economy for data in files

In order to offer unified cloud services for both structured and unstructured data, the cloud economy that we have already proposed in [2][3][4] has to be extended. Very briefly, the proposed economy constitutes a complex module that comprises the following: (i) a cost model that estimates as accurately as possible the cost of every query service, (ii) a regret scheme that accumulates and quantifies data management experience in order to assist the cloud into taking decisions for building data structures for future query execution, (iii) a prediction model for the amortization of the cost of building data structures on prospective queries, (iv) service pricing scheme that assigns prices to query services and allows for cloud profit, and (v) an estimation metric for query service correlations.

The economy extension for handling unstructured data refers mainly to the extension of the cost model in order to estimate the cost of the new data operations for unstructured data. We intend to extend the cost model in order to estimate the cost of (i) executing queries on files in the file query mechanism, and (ii) storing unstructured query results in databases. Moreover, the pricing scheme, the prediction model and the correlation measure will be revised and calibrated to fit peculiarities of queries on data in files.

4 A middleware for querying structured and unstructured data

The utmost goal of this research is to propose a cloud economy for the unified management of structured and

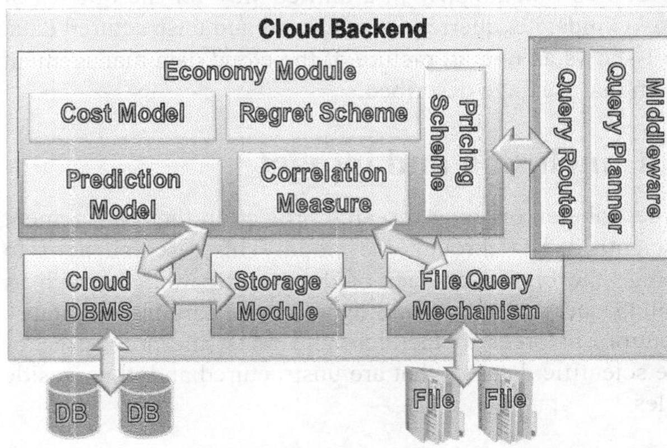

Fig. 1. Design of the cloud database management system

unstructured data. This economy should be applicable to the most demanding cloud computing environments, such as scientific datacenters. As mentioned, fine-grained scientific data may be unstructured and reside in files, whereas the respective meta-data are structured and reside in databases. Analysis of scientific data usually involves both collected data and metadata in various combinations and querying sequences. The unification of the two ends of cloud data management will be achieved through the development of a middleware.

The development of the middleware includes the definition of its basic functionality that ensures transparent querying of databases and files, as well as the design of a query planner that enables efficient scheduling of these queries.

Middleware basic functionality. We define the functionality of the middleware that takes as input a set of queries for structured or unstructured data and routes these queries into the cloud appropriately. More specifically, the user may input a workflow of queries, i.e. a set of parallel and sequential combinations of queries that she wants to execute on both structured and unstructured data. Such a query workflow may represent an experimental analysis on scientific data and may be accompanied by data computing that has to be performed between queries. The middleware architecture enables the realization of such analysis workflows by providing interaction of queries. The challenge in designing the middleware is to achieve a functionality that resembles that of a declarative programming language. The analysis workflow should be received by the middleware as a program by a interpreter. The comprised queries correspond to the parameterized functions of the program that have to be executed in a specific (partial) order.

Middleware query planner. The middleware functionality is extended with an overall query planner that schedules the queries involved in a workflow (or even more in many workflows). The planner enables parallel processing of independent queries. For this task we employ experience in job scheduling and query optimization. It is imperative to provide this functionality in a unified way for the queries of the two kinds, i.e. queries on structured and unstructured data. Fig. 1 shows an overall picture of the cloud data management system that we have described.

5 Conclusion and impact

We describe an ongoing research project on the management of scientific data through the cloud. This research aims to leverage the big advantages of the cloud paradigm, such as enabling query servicing and dynamically parallelizing query execution, in order to facilitate and boost the processing of large scientific datasets that are unstructured and, thus, reside in files.

This research focuses on cloud computing, which gives the opportunity for the maximization of the potential of data management, as a result of its tremendous capabilities in storage and caching, distribution and parallelization of tasks. Therefore we believe that cloud data management will be able to cope with the unprecedented scale and rate of scientific data collection and processing, and will boost their performance. Moreover, this research aims at systematizing the way that scientific experimentation is currently performed worldwide and interdisciplinary. It proposes a solution of scientific data management that abstracts the data analysis and supports generic customizable procedures. In this way this research contributes significantly towards the obliteration of the requirement of custom-based solutions for scientific experimental analysis. Finally, our solution addresses the management of both structured and unstructured data. Therefore, it is applicable in real scientific environments, in which data are hold in both forms.

Research in many science disciplines (astronomy, physics, environmental, sociological) depends on the observation and study of large amounts of data. Independent scientists, group of scientists or even scientific centers lack the possession of all the data needed for them to perform proper research. The proposed cloud data management economy contributes to overcome this obstacle of scientific isolation. It enables scientists to have access to diverse data collections from all over the world. Definitely, such a scale of data sharing will boost scientific research. Furthermore, our management solution contributes to the utmost social requirement for unconstrained information sharing of any kind. Beyond pure scientific data centers, our solution benefits any other organizations, as well as individuals or companies that may desire to share their data through the Internet.

Beyond data sharing, the proposed solution will have a positive impact to the domain of business. Preliminary industry attempts to offer data management services in the web are already a fact. Yet, this new computer business trend needs to be supported by a systematic scientific study on the maximization of its potential. Our solution contributes to the maximization of the performance of such web services, while maintaining predictable behavior and guaranteeing appropriate adaptation to environmental and system changes, such as hardware failures and changes in workload.

Cloud computing is a new research field in computer science. Yet, as mentioned, the industry as well as scientific centers are already exploring and offering cloud data management solutions. It is important that research catches up with practice, so that applied solutions are supported by research results. Our solution aims to fill the gap between existing research and business technologies and maximize the potential of cloud data management.

6 References

[1] http://www.cern.ch

[2] Dash Debabrata, Verena Kantere, Anastasia Ailamaki. An Economic Model for Self-Tuned Cloud Caching. In Proc. of the 25th International Conference on Data Engineering – ICDE, p. 1687-1693, March 2009.

[3] Verena Kantere, Debabrata Dash, Georgios Gratsias, Anastasia Ailamaki. Predicting cost amortization for query services. In ACM International Conference of Special Interest Group on Management Of Data (SIGMOD), 2011.

[4] Verena Kantere, Debabrata Dash, Gregory Francois, Sofia Kyriakopoulou, Anastasia Ailamaki. Optimal Pricing for a Cloud Cache. In the IEEE Transactions on Knowledge and Data Engineering Journal, Special Issue on Cloud Data Management, Vol. 23 No. 6, Pages 1345 – 1358, 2011

[5] http://aws.amazon.com/ec2

[6] http://www.gogrid.com

[7] http://code.google.com/appengine

[8] http://www.sdss.org

[9] L. Ramaswamy, L. Liu, and A. Iyengar, "Cache clouds: Cooperative caching of dynamic documents in edge networks," in Proceedings of the 25 the International Conference on Distributed Computing Systems (ICDCS-2005, 2005, pp. 229–238.

[10] L. Ramaswamy, L. Liu, and A. Iyengar, "Scalable delivery of dynamic content using a cooperative edge cache grid," IEEE Trans. Knowl. Data Eng., vol. 19, no. 5, pp. 614–630, 2007.

[11] S. Bhattacharjee, K. L. Calvert, and E. W. Zegura, "Self-organizing wide-area network caches," in IEEE

Infocom'98, 1998. model and initial results," in ICN, 2008, pp. 752–757.
[12] T. Malik, R. C. Burns, and A. Chaudhary, "Bypass caching: Making scientific databases good network citizens," in ICDE, 2005, pp. 94–105.
[13] X. Wang, R. C. Burns, A. Terzis, and A. Deshpande, "Network-aware join processing in global-scale database federations," 2008.
[14] I. Foster, "What is the grid? a three point checklist. http://www-fp.mcs.anl.gov/ foster/articles/whatisthegrid.pdf," 2002.
[15] M. A. Nieto-Santisteban, J. Gray, A. S. Szalay, J. Annis, A. R. Thakar, and W. J. Omullane, "When database systems meet the grid," in CIDR, 2005, pp. 154–161.
[16] P. Watson, "Databases and the grid," Grid Computing: Making The Global Infrastructure a Reality, Tech. Rep., 2001.
[17] M. Stonebraker, P. M. Aoki, W. Litwin, A. Pfeffer, A. Sah, J. Sidell, C. Staelin, and A. Yu, "Mariposa: A wide-area distributed database system," VLDB J., vol. 5, no. 1, pp. 48–63, 1996.
[18] M. P. Wellman, W. E. Walsh, P. R. Wurman, and J. K. Mackie-mason, "Auction protocols for decentralized scheduling," Games and Economic Behavior, vol. 35, p. 2001, 1998.
[19] C. Ernemann, V. Hamscher, and R. Yahyapour, "Economic scheduling in grid computing," in Scheduling Strategies for Paral lel Processing. Springer, 2002, pp. 128–152.
[20] R. A. Moreno, "A.B.: Job scheduling and resource management techniques in economic grid environments," in Across Grids 2003. Volume 2970 of LNCS. Springer, 2004, pp. 25–32.
[21] M. Kradolfer and D. Tombros, "Market-based workflow management," International Journal of Cooperative Information Systems, World Scientific Publishing Co, vol. 7, 1998.
[22] C. Chen, M. Maheswaran, and M. Toulouse, "Supporting co-allocation in an auctioning-based resource allocator for grid systems," in IPDPS, 2002, pp. 89–96.
[23] The Office of Science Data-Management Challenge. Report from the DOE Office of Science Data-Management Workshops March–May 2004
[24] Ailamaki, V. Kantere and D. Dash. Managing Scientific Data. In the Communications of the ACM (CACM), 53 (6): 68-78, 10.1145/1743546.1743568, 2010.
[25] Jim Gray, Alexander S. Szalay, Ani Thakar, Christopher Stoughton, Jan vandenBerg: Online Scientific Data Curation, Publication, and Archiving. CoRR cs.DL/0208012 (2002)
[26] Jim Gray, David T. Liu, María A. Nieto-Santisteban, Alexander S. Szalay, David J. DeWitt, Gerd Heber: Scientific Data Management in the Coming Decade. CoRR abs/cs/0502008 (2005)
[27] www.oracle.com
[28] Netlobs. A netcdf catridge for oracle. http://datafedwiki.wustl.edu/images/f/ff/Dews_poster_2006.ppt.
[29] BCS. Barrodale computing services, ltd. http://www.barrodale.com/
[30] Series of meetings of the EPFL-IC-IIF-DIAS lab with CERN employees in data management, started on the December 9th 2008.
[31] http://root.cern.ch
[32] Aravindan Raghuveer, Meera Jindal, Mohamed F. Mokbel, Biplob K. Debnath, David Hung-Chang Du: Towards efficient search on unstructured data: an intelligent-storage approach. CIKM 2007: 951-954
[33] Eric Chu, Akanksha Baid, Ting Chen, AnHai Doan, Jeffrey F. Naughton: A Relational Approach to Incrementally Extracting and Querying Structure in Unstructured Data. VLDB 2007: 1045-1056
[34] Antonioletti, M., Atkinson, M., Baxter, R., Borley, A., Hong, N. P. C., Collins, B., Hardman, N., Hume, A. C., Knox, A., Jackson, M., Krause, A., Laws, S., Magowan, J., Paton, N. W., Pearson, D., Sugden, T., Watson, P., and Westhead, M. 2005. The design and implementation of grid database services in OGSA-DAI. Concurrency and Computation: Practice and Experience 17.
[35] D. Dash, v. Kantere and A. Ailamaki. An economic model for self-tuning cloud caching. To appear in proc. of the International workshop on Self Managing Database Systems (SMDB) 2009.
[36] Joel Israel. Critical analysis of softwares and databases used in mouse research. MSc thesis EPFL 2009.
[37] www-mci.u-strasbg.fr
[38] www.merck.com/mrl
[39] http://bluebrain.epfl.ch
[40] T. N. Minh and L. Wolters. Modeling parallel system workloads with temporal locality. In Workshop on Job Scheduling Strategies for Parallel Processing, 2009.
[41] http://www.hdfgroup.org
[42] http://www.postgresql.org
[43] http://www.agiledata.org/essays/mappingObjects.html
[44] http://monetdb.cwi.nl
[45] Gupta, Inderpal Singh Mumick. Maintenance of Materialized Views: Problems, Techniques, and Applications. In IEEE Data Engineering Bulletin, 1995.

An Effective Method for Managing Voluminous Data: Reducing Data to Significant Size for Efficient Results

Haydar Teymourlouei
Department of Computer Science
Bowie State University,
Bowie, MD, USA

Abstract— *The emergence of large, complex datasets has made effective data processing a challenging task for existing methods. In spite of this, organizing large datasets is a difficult task regardless of the technologies. However, this research proposes effective methods that can be utilized for managing, analyzing, and extracting useful information from large, diverse data. We propose an efficient way to catalogue and retrieve data by creating a directory file. More specifically, an improved method that would allow file retrieval based on its time and date. We also offer an efficient data reduction method that effectively condenses the amount of data. Moreover, the algorithm enable users to store the desired amount of data in a file and decrease the time in which observations are retrieved for processing. This is achieved by using a reduced standard deviation range to minimize the original data to a significant size.*

Keywords: Big data, data reduction, data retrieval, directory file

1 Introduction

The rapid acceleration in the expanding volume of complex and diverse types of data results in the emergence of a fast paced algorithm. Big data refer to voluminous data beyond the capabilities of the current database technology. The sheer amount of data generated that must be ingested, analyzed, and managed is of relevant importance and must be considered when attempting to propose useful tools. The speed with which data must be received and processed must also be considered. The rise of information coming from new sources has taken a toll on IT and, therefore, data management is a much more difficult task using only the traditional methodologies.

Typically, data obtained from satellites, for example, can be confusing. In spite of several attempts at standardization by most of the agencies around the world, there is still some confusion and lack of consensus. Some clarification is necessary in order to have a meaningful discussion about such data [2]. Most remotely sensed data require steps of basic pre-processing before it can be used. Agencies use a common set of "levels" to describe the types of data processing. After the data is processed, data becomes ready to be passed on to scientists for utilization. The descriptions explained in Table 1 show that the processing levels are hierarchical; Level 2 data starts with the processing included in Level 1 and adds more features [2]. This processing is recursively applied to successive data levels. Table 1 shows the Committee on Data Management and Computation (CODMAC) data level numbering system. Details for each instrument are described below.

Table 1: Data Processing Levels (Earth Science Reference Handbook [5])

NASA	COMAC	Description
Packet Data	Raw-level 1	Telemetry data stream as received at ground station, with science and engineering data embedded.
Level 0	Edited-Level 2	Instrument science data (e.g., raw voltages, counts) at full resolution, time ordered, with duplicates and transmission errors removed.
Level 1-A	Calibrated-Level 3	Level 0 data that have been located in space and may have been transformed (e.g., calibrated, rearranged) in a reversible manner and packaged with needed ancillary and auxiliary data (e.g., radiances with the calibration equations applied).
Level 1-B	Resampled - Level 4	Irreversibly transformed (e.g., resampled, remapped, calibrated) values of the instrument measurements (e.g., radiances, magnetic field strength).
Level 2	Derived - Level 5	Geophysical parameters, generally derived from Level 1 data, and located in space and time commensurate with instrument location, pointing, and sampling.
Level 3	Derived - Level 5	Geophysical parameters mapped onto uniform space-time grids.

Level 1 data processing proceeds by operating on the raw data (which comes from the sensors attached to the instrument). In other words, level 1 data processing converts raw data from the sensor outputs to scientific units, calculating any additional oceanographic parameters of interest and reducing the data set to a tractable size [8]. Given this process, it is always best to archive raw data because once it has been processed, it cannot be reversed. On the other hand, level 2 data conversion "starts with the raw data (i.e., .dat or .hex) file. It takes the information contained in the configuration (.con or .xmlcon) file and converts it to scientific units" [9]. Data has to be translated in a way that the information makes sense to the client. Data processing levels allows data to be translated in understandable quantities.

2 Data acquisition techniques

Clarification is the critical process of making sense of the data. Data has to be processed effectively in order to convert raw data into meaningful information. See Figure 1 for details.

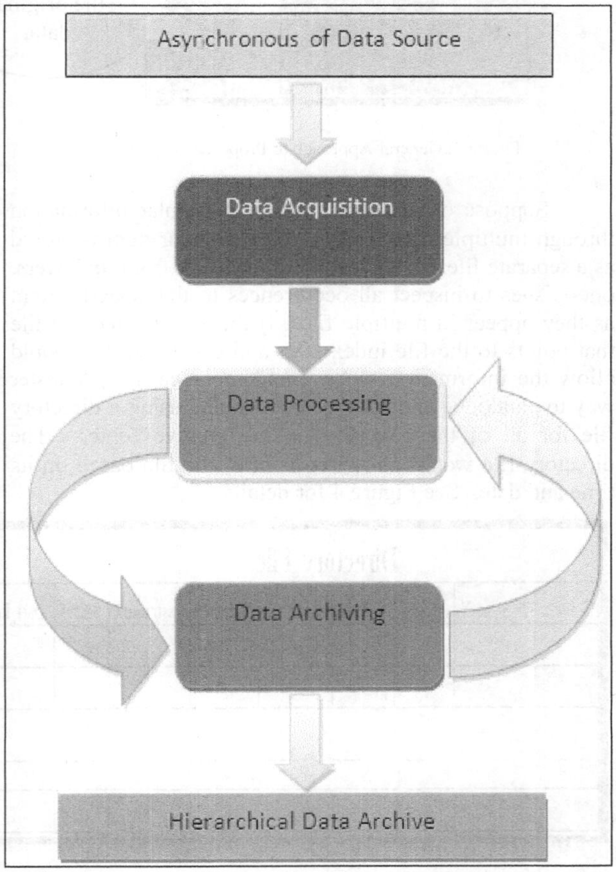

Figure 1: Data Management

Converting raw data into an easily usable form involves a great deal of data processing [6]. Computers conduct data processing, which accepts the raw data as input and then provides information as output. Figure 2 shows how data is being collected, processed, and separated by the instrument from spacecraft.

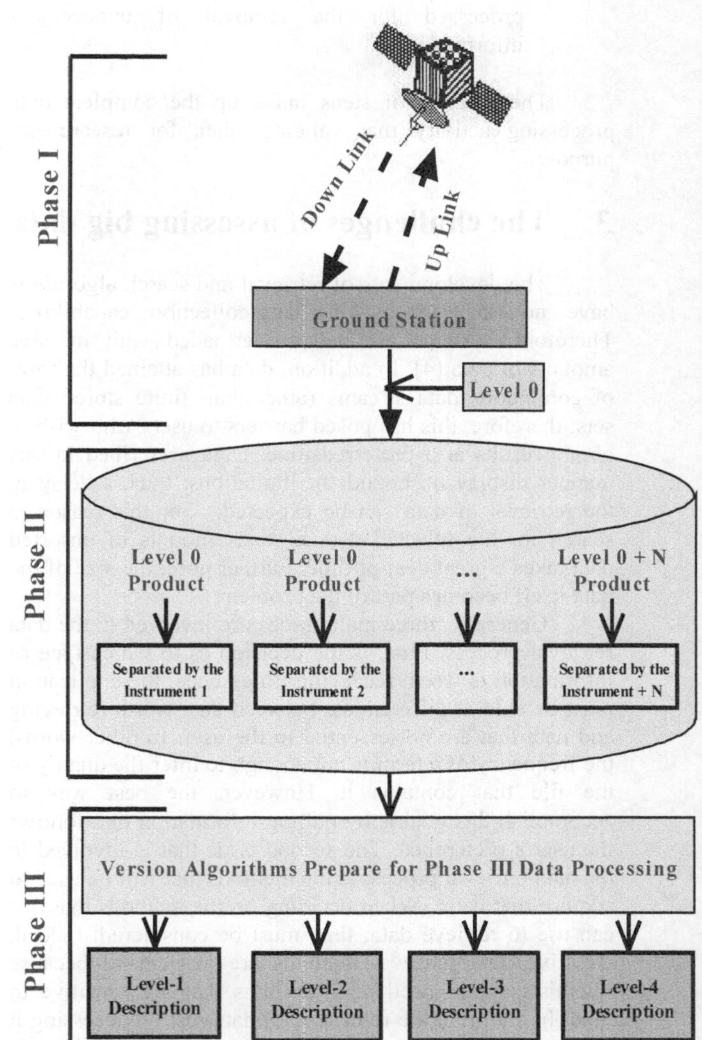

Figure 2: Data Generation and Processing

Once data has been generated, processed, and stored, it can then be made available in a more useful form for scientists' research.

- Phase I: Access data is removed from data directly received from the spacecraft through the spacecraft's zero level processor (this is the command processor that the spacecraft relies on when the main processor is offline).
- Phase II: Data is separated according to instrument and header information. When data is uploaded from the instrument, the header for internally recorded data is written. Header tells the program how many bytes of data should be read for each variable, which is defined in the header information (e.g., float, double, integer, etc.).
- Phase III: A different level of data processing is applied to the data file before the data is analyzed. This data processing allows the files to be

processed for the removal of unnecessary information.

These series of steps make up the complete data processing activity that validates data for researchers' purpose.

3 The challenges of assessing big data

The developments of retrieval and search algorithms have not kept pace with data-collection capabilities. Therefore, systems are being overloaded with massive amounts of data [4]. In addition, data has attained the form of continuous data streams rather than finite stored data sets; therefore, this has posed barriers to users who wish to obtain results at a preferred time. Data prescribed in this manner display no bounds or limitations; thus, a delay in the retrieval of data can be expected. For this reason, a search for the selected data in vast amounts of unsorted data takes a great deal of time. Furthermore, the size of the data itself becomes part of the problem.

Generally, three main issues are involved in the data retrieval process. First, is the decision as to which type of information is worth retrieving. In essence, the application must be able to differentiate between data worth retrieving and data that are not essential to the user. In other words, the frequency of a term is not enough to infer the quality of the file that contains it. However, the best way to accomplish this goal is by pulling information that follows the user's preference. The second issue that is involved in the data retrieval process is the methods that will be used to acquire that data. When deciding on the methods that one can use to retrieve data, time must be considered. Indeed, effective data retrieval methods are in demand because scientists are in need of algorithms that are sensitive to time. In addition, the relevance of data rest on accessing it on time. The third issue that must be accounted for lies in the methods that will be used to analyze the data. Data must be analyzed fairly quickly in order to provide users with the ability to pull data in a reasonable amount of time.

4 Methodology and experiment

This study proposes a novel approach to using file header information that is entity specific (e.g. to spacecraft, instrument, or experiment) to improve the efficiency in the processing in large spacecraft data, which could be used to significantly reduce the burden on the current search and retrieval systems. The solution encompasses the use of file headers that contain only essential and instrument-specific information. This would allow a search through files to be done quicker. Also, it would provide scientists with the ability to evaluate files for matches to the searched query without searching the entire file itself by having data that is already stripped down to bare essentials to generate useful search results. This would involve summarizing the relevant data in the header, reducing it so that it is more accessible and searchable. See Figure 3 for a general approach. The objective is to obtain only relevant information from large datasets. Figure 3 shows data in its original state and the portion of data that has been extracted.

Figure 3: General Approach to Proposed Algorithm

Suppose one is searching for particular information through multiple files where each particular item is stored as a separate file. After receiving feedback from reviewers, one wishes to inspect all occurrences of that specific item as they appear in multiple files. If there is a directory file that points to the file index start and end time, this would allow the information to be found more easily. A faster way to catalogue and retrieve data entails using a directory file for all of the data files in the archive center. The directory file would allow retrieval of the file based on its time and date. See Figure 4 for details.

Directory File

F_Index	F_Name_N	S_Time	E_Time	Chap_N	Satellites	Instrument	Sensor	Data_Level
—	—	—	—	—	—	—	—	—

Figure 4: Directory File Format

Figure 4 shows the proper format of directory files. Each data file consists of a start time and an end time for each data block in the current file. This illustration indicates that the next file's start time will be the previous file's end time. Also, the end position of the previous file will have the current file's start position.

Ultimately, the algorithm known as *Direct* will generate the directory file, add header information, and place the header at the beginning of each data file. The header for internally recorded data is written when the data is uploaded from the instrument. The steps below present the procedures that the program will perform.

Steps to assessing data:

- editing: discards the inappropriate data and retains relevant data;
- coding: arranges data in a comprehendible format;
- data entry: after the data has been properly arranged and coded, it is entered into the software that performs the eventual cross tabulation;
- validation: data validation refers to the process of thoroughly checking the collected data to ensure optimal quality levels;
- Tabulation: arranges data in a systematic format so that it can be further analyzed.

These series of steps form a complete data processing activity ensuring data access. Searches through files are done more quickly and effectively. This will provide scientists with an improved capability to find and access data in the file.

How to effectively develop a directory file that catalogues data:

- Step 1: Read data file to locate start and end time of the file. Then, count the chapter number of each file.
- Step 2: Increment file index and chapter number, and write the start and end time.
- Step 3: Continue this process for all the selected data files.

Table 2: Structure of a Directory File

Directory File								
F_Index	F_Name_N	S_Time	E_Time	Chap_N	Satellites	Instrument	Sensor	Data_Level
Index 1	Filename 1	00:00:00	10:59:00	0	Aura	Ozone	22	4
Index 2	Filename 2	10:59:00	15:59:00	T_Num + 1	AEM	Aerosol	PRI(1)	3
Index 3	Filename 3	15:59:00	23:59:00	T_Num + 1	Terra	MISR	12	2
....	....	....	....	....	....	....	....	....
Index + N	Filename + N	00:00:00	00:00:00	T_Num + 1	Satellites + N	Instrument + N	Sensor + N	D_Level + N

Table 2 shows how the directory file is structured.

More specifically, this study suggests establishing an algorithm that generates a directory file that encompasses the following information:

- File index;
- File name;
- Start and end time for every file;
- Start address and end address (position of the file).
- Start and end chapter number
- Satellites name
- Instrument
- Sensor
- Data Level

```
Algorithm: Search and retrieve file time and file index
Get_Select_Record (pointer to array, size of array and input selected time)
    In: Array of files, array size, selected time
    Out: File index, record
    Set LowTime, HighTime, Range, HighIndex, LowIndex, Midpoint
    Set Diff_Index, Diff_selected_time, Diff_KeyTime, Diff_Time
    WHILE array (HighTime) >= && selected time > array (LowTime)
    MidPoint ← HighIndex + LowIndex / 2
    If selected time > array (MidPoint) then
    LowIndex ← MidPoint
    else
    HighIndex ← MidPoint
    end
    Diff_KeyTime ← selected time – LowTime [LowIndex]
    Diff_Time ← HighTime [HighIndex] – LowTime [LowIndex]
    Diff_Index ← HighIndex – LowIndex
    Range ← Diff_selected_time / Diff_Time * Diff_Index + LowIndex
    If selected time > array (Range) then
    LowIndex ← Range + 1
    else if selected time > array (Range) then
    HighIndex ← Range + 1
    else if selected time == array (Range) then
    LowIndex ← Range
    end
    end
```

This will provide a tool for rapidly accessing data within these parameters. A Pseudocode for searching and retrieving file time and file index is provided below for clarification of the proposed algorithm:

We proceed by strategizing how to effectively compress vast amounts of data to a relatively significant size. In many instances, researchers require only a portion of data; however, data is delivered in voluminous amounts. This leaves scientists to combat an even bigger disadvantage, which is the cost it takes for these data to be transferred. It is very expensive to transfer just one bit of data down from a spacecraft; therefore, the proposed solution is effective in condensing data to desired amounts so that scientists do not disburse on any unwanted data. This goal is achieved by using an effective reduced standard deviation range. The algorithm is provided below:

```
Algorithm: Data Reduction Assuming Valid Columns are Known

Get_Data (Pointer to list data files, Data header info, Input percent Stdev)

        In: Pointer to the date files, Percentage of standard deviation, Header Info
        Out: ValidColumn

1. Set ValidFile ⟶ FALSE
2. Set ValidColumn ⟶ Zero
3. Set NextFile ⟶ Zero
4. Set Avg_Data, Stddeviation, Stdev_percent ⟶ Zero
5. For loop (Open File 1 ⟶ File N)
6.    If ValidFile ⟶ Continue
7.    Else Stop
8. For loop (Column ⟶ Zero; Column < Get_HeaderColSize ( ); Column++)
9.    Set Data Pointer ⟶ Verse & Column        // Store data into the class
10. End for loop
11. For loop (Verse ⟶ Zero; Verse < Get_HeaderVerseSize ( );
12.      For loop (Column ⟶ Zero; Column < Get_HeaderColSize ( ); Column++)
13.         Sum ⟵ Data [Verse & Column]
14.      End for Loop
15. End for Loop
16. Avg_Data ⟵ Compute Mean
17. Stddeviation ⟵ Compute Standard Deviation
18. Stdev_percent ⟵ (Stdev/100) + Stddeviation
19. For loop (Verse ⟶ Zero; Verse < Get_HeaderVerseSize ( );
20.    For loop (Column ⟶ Zero; Column < Get_HeaderColSize ( ); Column++)
21.       If ((Data [Verse & Column] - Avg_Data) > Stdev_percent)
22.          ValidColumn ⟵ TRUE
23.       Else
24.          ValidColumn ⟵ FALSE
25.    End for Loop
26. End for Loop
```

This algorithm effectively reduces data density. The unique feature of this algorithm that differs from the ordinary existing data reduction tools is that it reduces data in reference to the researcher's desired percentage. Conversely, many of the existing data reduction methods are comprised of lossy of lossless data; however, this algorithm is not to be categorized as a lossy or lossless data. This algorithm presents data in a desired percentage. In other words, this algorithm obtains only the portion of data that a scientist wishes to inspect.

5 Results

The practical value of the proposed algorithm is presented through empirical results. Figure 5 shows the results of the proposed algorithm.

```
-------------------------------------------------------------------------------
--Selected Time Not found and Nearest Neighbor Search located closest Time---
-------------------------------------------------------------------------------
                         Search time
                    ********************
                    *   1249977195     *
                    ********************

FileIndex File Names    Start Time   End Time      S_ChapterNum E_ChapterNum
------- , ----------- , ---------- , ----------- , ---------- , ------------
25       , FileName.1st , 1249995572 , 1249997439 , 108600      , 110224
```

Figure 5: Results of Proposed Algorithm

This algorithm located the selected file from large datasets. Essentially, keying the desired time will provide the user with the file index and its corresponding start and end time as shown in Figure 5.

As a matter of fact, the relevancy of data lies with the researcher's ability to access such results in a timely manner. Therefore, the proposed algorithm is quite suitable for such a case. This algorithm has made a significant advancement from existing algorithms. See Table 3 for additional details.

Table 3: Proposed Algorithm Iterative Computation

```
-----------------------------------------------------------
---------------------------Binary Search Alg---------------
-----------------------------------------------------------
low          high           mid           iteration
-------      ----------     ----------    ---------
1513         3024           1512          1
2269         3024           2268          2
2647         3024           2646          3
2836         3024           2835          4
2931         3024           2930          5
2978         3024           2977          6
2978         3000           3001          7
2990         3000           2989          8
2996         3000           2995          9
2999         3000           2998          10
***********Record found***************
The record is found  : 5042858
**************************************

-----------------------------------------------------------
---------------------------:Advanced Search Alg------------
-----------------------------------------------------------
low_diff   range_diff   count_diff   range      iteration
-------    ----------   ----------   -------    ---------
4941442    4979067      3024         3001       1
4941442    4942947      3000         2999       2
***********Record found***************
The record is found  : 5042858
**************************************
```

Table 3 reveals that the proposed algorithm is sensitive to time and, therefore, suitable for researchers' purpose. The binary search is the most common approach used to efficiently sort and search data. Based on research, the binary search is the most important and efficient means to date [3] [10]. However, it is not best suited for researchers. Table 3 shows that the proposed algorithm effectively reduces the number of iterations, therefore, achieving efficient results. The binary search algorithm took six (6) iterations to arrive at the selected data whereas the proposed algorithm took only three (3) iterations to arrive at the desired data. This reveals that the proposed method is effective in reducing the time it takes to locate the file.

Furthermore, data can be reduced using standard deviation. For instance, we minimized the original plotted data to a relative size by using a reduced standard deviation range. Figure 6 shows the results of reduced data through the use of standard deviation.

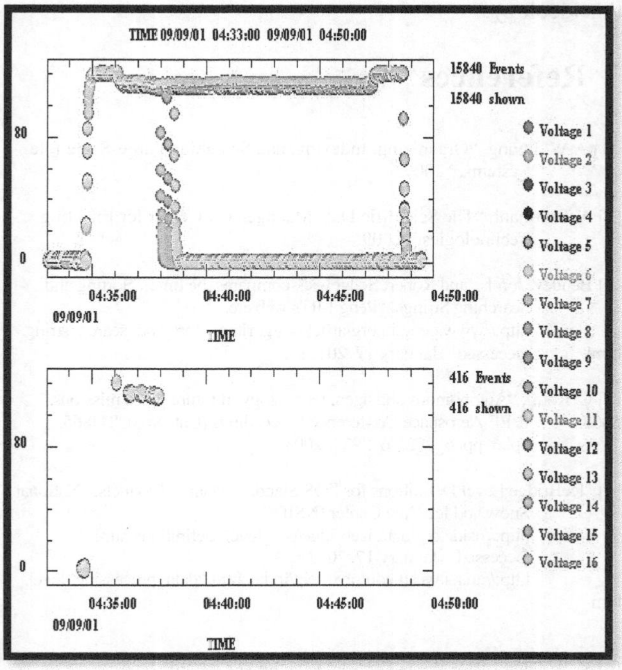

Figure 6: Data Reduction

The use of a reduced standard deviation range effectively condensed the amount of data as seen in Figure 6.

The algorithm enables users to reduce data by percentage. The program instructs the user to input the following:

- Maximum and minimum voltage.
- The desired percentage that such data should be reduced.

Table 4 presents a sample of a typical dataset.

Table 4: Data File Sample

1	Time	Voltage1	Voltage2	Voltage3	Voltage4	Voltage5	Voltage6
2	9/8/2012 21:44	95.2175	95.1491	95.2859	95.0124	94.8757	94.739
3	9/8/2012 21:44	102.464	101.848	102.053	102.19	102.259	101.917
4	9/8/2012 21:44	107.454	107.044	107.18	106.907	107.454	106.975
5	9/8/2012 21:44	110.94	110.735	110.325	110.462	110.94	110.872
6	9/8/2012 21:44	113.469	113.264	112.923	112.991	113.469	113.333
7	9/8/2012 21:44	115.178	115.11	114.768	114.973	115.178	115.11
8	9/8/2012 21:44	116.341	116.204	116.341	115.93	116.272	116.546
9	9/8/2012 21:44	117.298	117.161	117.298	117.093	117.366	117.503
10	9/8/2012 21:44	118.05	117.571	117.981	117.571	117.913	118.186
11	9/8/2012 21:44	118.528	118.118	118.391	117.913	118.118	118.323
12	9/8/2012 21:44	118.87	118.46	118.733	118.118	118.255	118.733
13	9/8/2012 21:44	118.938	118.733	118.938	118.595	118.391	118.801
14	9/8/2012 21:44	119.348	119.075	119.075	118.665	118.528	118.801
15	9/8/2012 21:44	119.485	119.212	119.417	118.87	118.87	119.212
16	9/8/2012 21:44	119.553	119.007	119.28	118.938	118.733	119.212
17	9/8/2012 21:44	119.69	118.733	118.938	119.075	118.801	118.938
18	9/8/2012 21:44	119.69	119.007	118.938	119.417	119.143	119.075
19	9/8/2012 21:44	119.622	119.075	119.007	119.417	119.417	119.143
20	9/8/2012 21:44	119.622	118.528	118.801	119.28	119.485	119.212
21	9/8/2012 21:44	119.417	118.938	118.733	119.417	119.348	119.28
22	9/8/2012 21:44	119.28	118.938	119.007	119.759	119.143	119.007
23	9/8/2012 21:45	119.622	118.87	118.733	119.417	119.075	118.87
24	9/8/2012 21:45	119.759	119.007	119.212	119.28	119.485	119.143
25	9/8/2012 21:45	119.553	119.007	119.007	119.28	119.622	119.485

The data displayed in Table 5 shows the results of using the recommended method. This dataset is reduced by 700% and can be reduced at any percentage desired. Note that this table is the same sample of the previous file shown in Table 4; however, it has been compressed using the proposed method. Notice the difference between Table 4 and 5. This indicates that the algorithm was able to successfully condesne the amount of data to a desirable volume.

Table 5: Results of the Compressed Data

1	Time	Voltage1	Voltage2	Voltage3	Voltage4	Voltage5	Voltage6
2	9/8/2012 21:44	-1	-1	-1	-1	-1	-1
3	9/8/2012 21:44	102.464	-1	-1	-1	-1	-1
4	9/8/2012 21:44	107.454	-1	-1	-1	107.454	-1
5	9/8/2012 21:44	-1	-1	-1	-1	-1	-1
6	9/8/2012 21:44	-1	-1	-1	-1	-1	-1
7	9/8/2012 21:44	-1	-1	-1	-1	-1	-1
8	9/8/2012 21:44	-1	-1	-1	-1	-1	116.546
9	9/8/2012 21:44	-1	-1	-1	-1	-1	117.503
10	9/8/2012 21:44	-1	-1	-1	-1	-1	118.186
11	9/8/2012 21:44	-1	-1	-1	-1	-1	-1
12	9/8/2012 21:44	118.87	-1	-1	-1	-1	-1
13	9/8/2012 21:44	-1	-1	-1	-1	-1	-1
14	9/8/2012 21:44	119.348	-1	-1	-1	-1	-1
15	9/8/2012 21:44	119.485	-1	119.417	-1	-1	-1
16	9/8/2012 21:44	119.553	-1	-1	-1	-1	-1
17	9/8/2012 21:44	119.69	-1	-1	-1	-1	-1
18	9/8/2012 21:44	119.69	-1	-1	-1	-1	-1
19	9/8/2012 21:44	-1	-1	-1	-1	-1	-1
20	9/8/2012 21:44	-1	-1	-1	-1	-1	-1
21	9/8/2012 21:44	-1	-1	-1	-1	-1	-1
22	9/8/2012 21:44	-1	-1	-1	119.759	-1	-1
23	9/8/2012 21:45	119.622	-1	-1	-1	-1	-1
24	9/8/2012 21:45	119.759	-1	-1	-1	-1	-1
25	9/8/2012 21:45	-1	-1	-1	-1	-1	-1

The negative numbers illustrated in Table 5 instructs the program to ignore those numbers. Therefore, in that particular illustration, there are now only a few data that are of significance based on the percentage that the program was instructed to perform. This critical reduction makes data easily retrievable and accessible. In addition, it provides researchers with the amount of data that they wish to inspect.

6 Conclusion

The recent expansion of the media industry and the transformation of every aspect of life controlled by modern technology resulted in the establishment of huge data of mostly unstructured data. However, through better analysis of the large volumes of data, there is a potential of making faster advances and improving the profitability and success of many enterprises. Therefore, the proposed method is anticipated to decrease the complications involved in searching through massive datasets. This algorithm can obtain the selected files from large amount of data, and it is done in less iteration as opposed to the existing algorithms. It sorts through a range of elements, searching for an element that is equivalent to a specified time file index. Essentially, the algorithm is able to condense large amounts of data to desirable amounts to avoid combating vast amounts of unwanted data by simply using a reduced standard deviation range. This method is also time-sensitive and best suited for researchers' usage in the field of computing. The methods and results presented confirm this ideology.

7 References

[1] A.W. Leung, "Organizing, Indexing, and Searching Large-Scale File Systems," 2009.

[2] A. Shoshani, "The Scientific Data Management Center for Enabling Technologies," 2009.

[3] Bentley, Jon L., and Robert Sedgewick compares the time. "Sorting and Searching Strings. "Peng LIU's website. http://www.pengliu.org/articles/algorithm_sort_and_search_string.html (accessed January 17, 2013).

[4] C. Rouff, "Autonomous and agent technology in future space missions," 2003 IEEE Aerospace Conference Proceedings (Cat. No.03TH8652), vol.6, pp. 6_2925-6_2935, 2003.

[5] "IceBridge Level Definitions for EOS Standard Data Products. "National Snow and Ice Data Center (NSIDC). http://nsidc.org/data/icebridge/eos_level_definitions.html (accessed January 17, 2013). http://an.rsl.wustl.edu/phx/help/index.html?data_processing_level.htm

[6] K. A. Facts, "Key Aqua Facts," Delta, pp. 73-93, 2002.

[7] G. Shen and A. Ortega, "Transform-based distributed data gathering," Signal Processing, IEEE Transactions on, vol. 58, no. 7, pp. 3802–3815, 2010.

[8]"Processing steps and data levels: Aviso. "Home: Aviso.http://www.aviso.oceanobs.com/en/data/product-information/processing-steps-and-data-levels/print.html (accessed January 17, 2013).

[9] S. Johnston, "Encouraging collaboration through a new data management approach," 2006.

[10]"Sorting and Searching Algorithms." The Object Oriented ProgrammingWeb. http://oopweb.com/Algorithms/Documents/Sman/Volume/BinarySearchTrees.html (accessed January 17, 2013).

Reverse Factorization and Comparison of Factorization Algorithms in attack to RSA

Sadi Evren SEKER
Dept. of Business Administration,
Istanbul Medeniyet University
academic@sadievrenseker.com

Cihan MERT
Electrical Engineering Dept.
The University of Texas at Dallas
Cihan.Mert@utdallas.edu

ABSTRACT

Factorization algorithms have a major role in the computer security and cryptography. Most of the widely used cryptographic algorithms, like RSA, are built on the mathematical difficulty of factorization for big prime numbers. This research, proposes a new approach to the factorization by using two new enhancements. The new approach is also compared with six different factorization algorithms and evaluated the performance on a big data environment. The algorithms covered are elliptic curve method, quadratic sieve, Fermat's method, trial division and Pollard rho methods. Success rates are compared over a million of integer numbers with different difficulties. We have implemented our own algorithm for random number generation, which is also explained in the paper. We also empirically show that the new approach has an advantage on the factorization attack to RSA.

Keywords

Factorization, Cryptography, Benchmarking

Acknowledgement

Work of Sadi Evren SEKER is supported by Istanbul University, research projects department under project number YADOP-27254

1. INTRODUCTION

This study can be viewed as three major steps. In the first layer, we have generated big integers with a new approach on the generation. After the generation, the factorization algorithms including the new approach are executed. Finally, on the last step the performance of the algorithms are evaluated.

In this paper, the problem will be defined and an overview of the problem will be demonstrated in the problem statement section. The related work section will cover a brief literature review about the contemporary studies on the factorization algorithms. The background chapter will briefly describe the details of the factorization algorithms we have implemented in this study. The experiments section will go into the details of the big number of integers their properties after generation and evaluation of the algorithms.

2. PROBLEM STATEMENT

A stepwise approach to the study can be viewed as in the Figure 1.

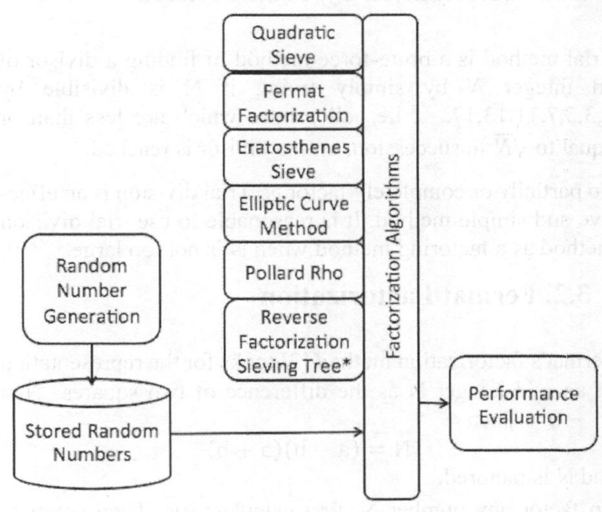

Figure 1. Overview of Study

In order to simulate the RSA prime number factorization problem, we have only concentrated on the semi-prime numbers. The random generator is designed to generate the semi-prime numbers. In order to make the time performance more explicit we have generated huge number of semi-prime numbers and stored them in a database. After storing, the factorization algorithms are executed on those numbers. Finally each algorithm is evaluated in the time performance.

3. BACKGROUND

From the early times, the factorization of composite numbers has been an interesting area of studying and there are some algorithms carried on like Sieve of Eratosthenes (276 – 194 BC).

Also the by the spreading usage of modern cryptographic systems which some are built on the difficulty of factoring, like RSA[1], the factorization problem has been a studying area.

Initially factoring started with dividing a number by larger and larger primes until you had the factorization. This trial division was not improved until Fermat's method in which the factorization of the difference of two squares is used. While Fermat's method is much faster than trial division, when it comes to the real world of factoring, for example for factoring several hundred digits long RSA modulus, the purely iterative Fermat's method is too slow. This led the development of several other methods, such as a pair of probabilistic methods by Pollard in the mid 70's, the $p - 1$ method and the ρ method, the Elliptic Curve Method discovered by H. Lenstra in 1987 . However, the fastest algorithms such as the Number Field Sieve (and its variants), the Quadratic Sieve (and it variants), and Continued Fraction Method utilize the same trick as Fermat. The remainder of this paper will briefly discuss some of the above methods and focus on reverse factorization method, a new approach.

3.1. Factorization by Trial Division

Trial method is a brute-force method of finding a divisor of an integer N by simply trying if N is divisible by 2,3,5,7,11,13,17,..., i.e., all primes which are less than or equal to $\sqrt{N}$ in succession, until a divisor is reached.

To partially or completely factor N, Trial division is an effective and simple method. It is reasonable to use trial division method as a factoring method when N is not too large.

3.2. Fermat Factorization

Fermat's factorization method [2] looks for the representation of an odd integer N as the difference of two squares $N = a^2 - b^2$. Then

$$N = (a - b)(a + b)$$

and N is factored.

To factor any number N, first calculate $\sqrt{N}$. Then compute $a^2 - N$ starting with a, the first integer greater than $\sqrt{N}$ and continue until reaching a square b^2. Since $a^2 - N = b^2$, $N = a^2 - b^2$. So N is factorized into $N = (a - b)(a + b)$ .If the only factors found are N and 1, then N is a prime number. If N is not prime, use the same algorithm for each factor.

Fermat's method works well when the number is factorized into two terms of approximately equal size. It works poorly when the factors are of very different sizes.

3.3. Quadratic Sieve

To factorize a number n, quadratic sieve method [3] attempts to find two numbers x and y such that $x \not\equiv \pm y \ (mod\ n)$ and $x^2 \equiv y^2 (mod\ n)$. If two such numbers are found, this implies that $(x - y)(x + y) \equiv 0 \ (mod\ n)$. Then, $x - y$ must have non-trivial factors in common with n. To achieve this, a common strategy for finding such x and y is the following. Choose a smoothness bound B. The number $\pi(B)$,which denotes the number of prime numbers less than B, will control both the number of vectors needed and the length of the vectors. Then use sieving to locate $\pi(B) + 1$ numbers x_i such that $y_i \equiv (x_i^2\ mod\ n)$ is B-smooth. Factor the y_i and generate exponent vectors mod 2 for each one. Find a subset of these vectors which add to the zero vector. Multiply the corresponding x_i together naming the result *mod n*: *x* and the y_i together which yields a B-smooth square y^2. Next, obtained equality $x^2 \equiv y^2 (mod\ n)$ gives two square roots of $(x^2\ mod\ n)$, one by taking the square root in the integers of y^2 namely y, and the other the a computed in previous step. Having desired identity$(x - y)(x + y) \equiv 0(mod\ n)$, compute the $GCD(x - y, n)$. This gives a factor. If the factor is trivial, try again with a different a or linear dependency.

3.4. Pollard Rho

Pollard's rho method [4] is based on a combination of two ideas on Floyd's cycle-finding algorithm and birthday paradox that are also useful for various other factoring methods.

Let N be a number that is neither a perfect power nor a prime and p the smallest prime factor of N.

Generate sequence of numbers $x_0, x_1, x_2, ...$ from Z_N uniformly, independently at random then after at most $p + 1$ such pickings for the first time, there are two numbers x_i and x_s with $i < s$ such that $x_i \equiv x_s \ (mod\ p)$. Since N is not a perfect power, there is another prime factor $q > p$ of N. Since the numbers x_i and x_s are randomly chosen from Z_N, by the Chinese remaindering theorem, $x_i \not\equiv x_s \ (mod\ q)$ with probability $1 - 1/q$ even under the condition that $x_i \equiv x_s \ (mod\ p)$. Therefore, $gcd(x_i - x_s, N)$ is a nontrivial factor of N with probability at least $1 - 1/q$.

Since the $x_i\ mod\ p$ behave more or less as random integers in $0,1, ..., p - 1$, by computing $gcd(x_i - x_j, N)$, for $i \neq j$, the factorization of N after about $c\sqrt{p}$ elements of the sequence can be computed, for some small constant c.

This suggests that approximately $(c\sqrt{p})^2/2$ pairs x_i , x_j have to be considered. However, this can easily be avoided by only computing $gcd(x_i - x_{2i}, N)$ for $i = 0,1, ...$, i.e., by generating two copies of the sequence, one at the regular speed and one at the double speed. This can be expected to result in a factorization of N after approximately $2\sqrt{p}$ gcd computations. If this GCD ever comes to N, then the algorithm terminates with failure, since this means $x_i = x_{2i}$ and therefore, by Floyd's cycle-finding algorithm, the sequence has cycled and continuing any further would only be repeating previous work.

4. Semi-prime Factorization in RSA

This study focus on the fast and efficient factorization for the semi-prime numbers. The semi-prime numbers are considered as the multiplication of two prime numbers, say p and q. In some sources the semi-prime numbers are also named as pq numbers for this reason.

The advantage of factorizing the semi-prime numbers in RSA crypto system is the two prime factors of semi-prime numbers should be in equal digists or almost in equal digits. The reason is, if the number of digits of one prime of the semi-prime number is smaller than the other, the system woul have a weakness.

The weakness can be explained like this. The RSA system is built on the time complexity of factorizing the semi-prime number into two factors. The time complexity increases by the number of digits. For example the time required to factorize a 20 digit number is muh more higher than the time required for factorizing 19 digit number. But if one of the factors of the high digit number is so small. Let's give an example of extreme case with one digit prime like 2,3,5 or 7. Than factorizing the number would be much more easier. And finding any factor of the number would make it even easier to find the second factor. So, in most of the cases, RSA uses the two prime numbers with equal digits to generate a semi-prime number.

The novel approach proposed in this study, considers this as a vulnerability and and proofs that, using the same digit primes to generate a semi-prime is also makes easier to get factorization with the novel method explained in this paper.

5. A Novel Approach to Semi-prime Factorization

In the new approach, we see the problem as a search problem, where the factors *p and q* of a semi-prime number *sp* are smaller than the $p, q < \sqrt[2]{sp}$ we propose to implement a sieving approach, which increaes the speed of searching by eliminating some of the possibilities in each check. On the other hande, we propose to keep a factor tree for fast elimination of the alternatives.

The sieving approaches like, Erotathene's Sieve[6] or Sieve of Atkin or Rational Sieve [7] are eliminating alternatives, strating from the smallest prime number and the number searched increases in each step.

This iterative approach from small to bigger prime numbers has a certain advantage while finding the prime factors of a composite number. But in the case of factoring for the semi-prime numbers which are specially generated for the RSA crypto system, starting from small prime numbers has a disadvantage since we are aware that the searched prime number is much mor close to the square root of semi-prime number ($\sqrt[2]{sp}$).

Our approach is as in Algorithm 1. By the definition, any composite number *cn* can be rewritten as in equation (1).

$$\mathrm{cn} = \mathrm{p} \prod_{i=1}^{m} \mathrm{c_i} \qquad (1)$$

Where the number of prime factors of *cn* is consierede as *m+1*.

For the given cn, the equation (2) can be concluded.

$$(n \in N \wedge n|f_i) \Leftrightarrow n_i|\left\{\mathbb{Z}_{|n} = \left(\bigcap_{i=1}^{m} \mathbb{Z}_{|f_i}\right)\right\} \qquad (2)$$

Where N is the domain set of search for the prime numbers, which are the numbers from 2 to $\sqrt[2]{cn}$.

If, any number $n \in N$ is also a composite number with m factors, than testing the situation of $cn \mid n$ means, for all the m factors of n are already tested. Depending on the situation, since we are running a search algorithm, if the searched factor is found, than the search finishes. If, n is not the factor of cn, than the search, can be reduced by also eliminating the factors of cn from the search space.

5.1. Sample Run

In order to present the new approach, we are also demonstrating a sample run over over the semi-prime number 47 x 53 = 2491.

The search space is the numbers from 1 to 49, since the $\sqrt[2]{2491} = 49$. The search algorithm starts by a sieve and tests the first alternative number 49 from the end of the sieve. Since 2491|49 = false, we can remove all the factors of composite number 49 from the search space.

Table 1.Removing first factors of composite number 49 after the first iteration

1	2	3	4	5	6	7
8	9	10	11	12	13	14
15	16	17	18	19	20	21
22	23	24	25	26	27	28
29	30	31	32	33	34	35
36	37	38	39	40	41	42
43	44	45	46	47	48	49

In the second iteration, the second number from the end of the search space is considered, which is 48. Since the 2491|48 is false, all the factors of composite number 48, can be removed from the search space. The factors of 48 are 2 and 3 and the composite numbers can be generated from those factors are eliminated as shown on the Table 2.

Table 2. After eliminating the factors and composite numbers from thos factors of 48 in second iteration

1	2	3	4	5	6	7
8	9	10	11	12	13	14
15	16	17	18	19	20	21
22	23	24	25	26	27	28
29	30	31	32	33	34	35
36	37	38	39	40	41	42
43	44	45	46	47	48	49

From the sieve in table 2, the next number in the search space is 47. Testing the 2491 | 47 is true, so we are finished with searching the numbers.

If the results of 2491 | 47 would be false, than searching whould have conitnue and since all the numbers until 43 are eliminated, the next number in the search iteration would be 43. In table 2, the number of numbers in search space is reduced to 14 possibilities only, from the initial 49 numbers.

From the sample run, we have found the factor in 3 steps. Any sieving approach would find the factor after trying all the prime numbers until 47. This brings up a performance obviously.

During the elimination of factors of any composite number a factor tree can be implemented.

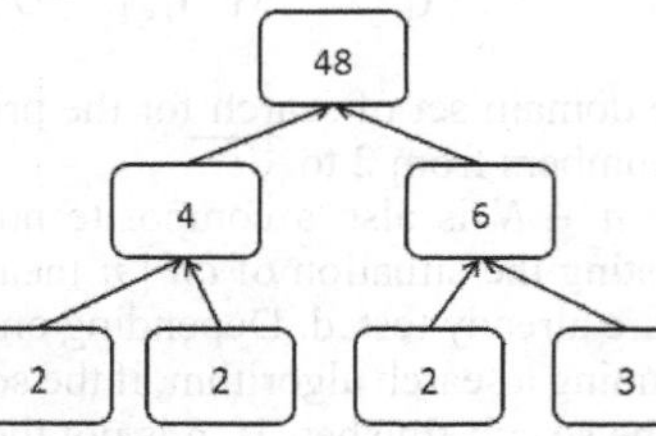

Figure 2. Factorization tree for composite number 48

In figure 2, the factor tree holding the factors of 48 are demonstrated. Also the tree is ambigious since the same tree can be redrawn as in figure 2.

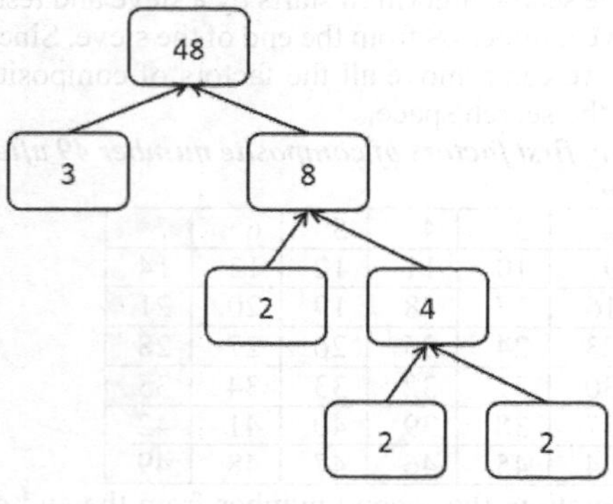

Figure 3. Ambigious alternative factorization tree for composite number 48

Any drawing of the tree can be useful in the elimination of the search space. The deepest tree for any composite number can have maximum of numbers as given in equation (3).

$$Max\ depth\ of\ factor\ tree = \log_2 n/_2 - 1 \qquad (3)$$

Please remember the smallest prime number is 2 and the maximum internal node count can be 1 minus half of the total numbers of the nodes in a binary tree.

Algorithm 1: A Novel Factorization for RSA Semi-Prime

Let SP be a semi-prime with high factors,
Let C be Closings of Stockmarket,
for i ← $\sqrt[2]{SP}$ *down to 2 begin*
if SP | i return i as factor
else begin
create a factor tree of i;
eliminate all factors in sieve;
decrease i;
end else;
end for;

Above algorithm demonstrates the execution of novel approach. The iterator value i starts from $\sqrt[2]{sp}$ and iterates until the smallest prime number. In fact, we are aware that, one of the factors of semi-prime of RSA can never be 2 because of the vulnerability, but algorithm is designed in this manner for the worst case analysis.

6. EVALUATION

The results of executions of various algorithms are demonstrated on the Table 3.

Table 1. Execution Performance of the Factorization Algorithms

Method	Average Execution
Pollard Rho	398 mins
ECM	3443 mins
Fermat	30 mins
Quadratic Sieve	326 mins
Erathostene	*1267052 mins*
Trial Division	*5510739 mins*
New Approach	5 mins

In the table 3, the results are gathered from execution of thousands of random numbers with 8 digits.

Also, in order to visualize the increase of time spent of algorithms, the execution times of algorithms for 6 of the methods are plotted in figure 4.

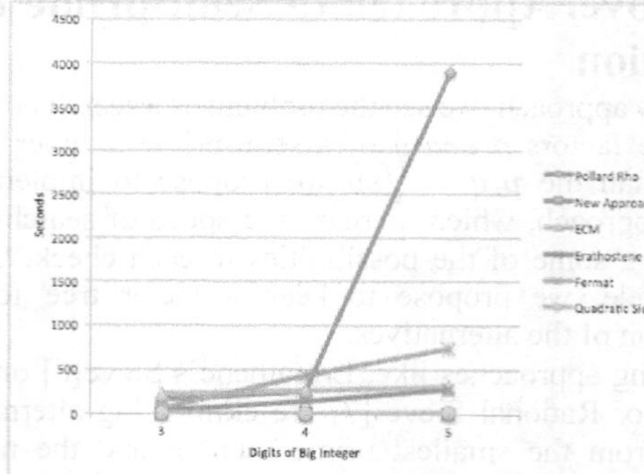

Figure 4. Performance evaluation of methods while the number of digits are increasing.

The digits are quite low in Figure 4 and plotting is stopped for 5 digits, where the algorithms are still close to each other. After the number of digits are increased, some of the algorithms consumes higher time than the rest.

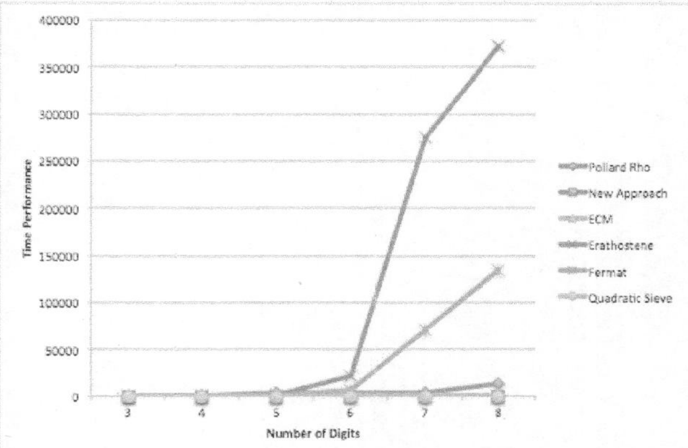

Figure 5. Performance evaluation of methods while the number of digits are further more increasing.

Depending on the setup time and difficulty of the numbers, some algorithms yield worse results than the rest.

From the analytical perspective, it is known that the time complexity of the algorithms are as in Table 4.

Table 4. Time Complexity of the Methods

Method	Time Complexity	
Pollard Rho	O(B × log B × $\log_2$n)	Where B is the bound and n is the composite number.
ECM	O(L(p)M(log n))	Where M(log n) is the complexity of multiplication mod n, and $L(p) = e^{c(\log p)^{\alpha}(loglogp)^{1-\alpha}}$
Fermat	O(d)	Where d is the distance between the two factors of the composite number.
Quadratic Sieve	O(log B loglog B)	Where B is the bound.
Erathostene	$O(\sqrt{n} + p)$	Where p is the number of primes below $\sqrt{n}$
Trial Division	$O(\sqrt{n})$	
New Approach	O(dp)	Where dp is the number of primes within the two factors of composite number.

7. CONCLUSION

This study, brings up a new approach to the semi-prime number factorization very similar to the Fermat's factorizatino algorithm. The biggest impact of semi-prime number factorization is the attack against crypto systems like RSA. During the study, we have evaluated the new approach and compare the success against most significant factorization algorithms. The success rate of the new approach seems quite convincing besides the encouraging analytical performance of the algorithm. We would also like to test the success of the new approach in bigger integer numbers like 50+ digits and also parallelization would be a challanging future work.

REFERENCES

[1] Rivest, R.; A. Shamir; L. Adleman (1978). "A Method for Obtaining Digital Signatures and Public-Key Cryptosystems". Communications of the ACM 21 (2): 120–126. doi:10.1145/359340.359342.

[2] McKee, J. Speeding Fermat's Factoring Method, Math. Comput. 68, 1729–1738,1999.

[3] Pollard, J. M. A Monte Carlo method for factorization, BIT, Vol. 15 (1975) pp. 331–334

[4] Lenstra, H. W. Jr. "Factoring Integers with Elliptic Curves." Ann. Math. 126, 649-673, 1987..

[5] Gerver, J. Factoring Large Numbers with a Quadratic Sieve, *Math. Comput.* 41, 287-294, 1983.

[6] Horsley, Rev. Samuel, F. R. S., "Κόσκινον Ερατοσθένους or, The Sieve of Eratosthenes. Being an account of his method of finding all the Prime Numbers," Philosophical Transactions (1683–1775), Vol. 62. (1772), pp. 327–347.

[7] A.O.L. Atkin, D.J. Bernstein, Prime sieves using binary quadratic forms, Math. Comp. 73 (2004), 1023-1030

SESSION

NOVEL SCIENTIFIC AND ENGINEERING ALGORITHMS AND APPLICATIONS + COMPLEX SYSTEMS + MEDICAL SCIENCE

Chair(s)

TBA

A Random Number Based Method for Monte Carlo Integration

J. Wang and G. Harrell
Department Math and CS, Valdosta State University, Valdosta, Georgia, USA

Abstract - *A new method is proposed for Monte Carlo integration. This method is more efficient with wider coverage, including improper integrals, while the classical Monte Carlo integration can only handle bounded domain integrals. To implement this method in computer programming, you only need a random number generator. Unlike the deterministic numerical integration methods, the expected error of this method is independent of the integral dimensionality. This method is powerful and dominates other numerical integral methods for the higher-dimensional integrals.*

Keywords: Monte Carlo integration; Output analysis; Trapezoid rule; Simpson rule; Error analysis; Improper integral

1 Introduction

In single variable calculus ([8]), the general way to evaluate a definite integral $\int_a^b f(x)\,dx$ is to find a formula $F(x)$ for one of the antiderivatives of $f(x)$ such that

$$\int_a^b f(x)\,dx = F(b) - F(a).$$

However some antiderivatives are not easy to find, and others, like $\frac{\sin x}{x}$ and $\sqrt{1+x^4}$ have been proved that no such closed-form $F(x)$ formulas exist [8]. There is a need to evaluate the definite integral of such functions. Two different types of numerical methods are involved in approximating $\int_a^b f(x)\,dx$. The first numerical method is called the deterministic integration, such as the trapezoidal rule and the Simpson rule. The second numerical method is called the Monte Carlo integration.

In Section 2, we introduce the Monte Carlo integration in a general d-dimensional integral setting. Selecting a probability density function, having the same domain as the integral domain, is an important part in the Monte Carlo integration. The efficiency of the Monte Carlo integration depends on the degree of difficulty for generating the random sample according to the selected density function. The most popular method in practice is the simple Monte Carlo integration. This method only works for bounded integral domain. It does not work for any improper integrals with unbounded domains.

In Section 3, we propose a new method for Monte Carlo integration. It is simple and efficient. It can be used to approximate integrals with unbounded domains for any dimensional integrals. The key idea is to convert the original integral domain to a new integral domain – a unit hyper-cube. The implementation of this new method is much easier. A random number generator is the only thing you need.

In Section 4, we conduct the variance analysis. It helps us to decide when the Monte Carlo simulation run should stop, and what the random sample size should be. For the new proposed method, the expected value of error is $O\left(\frac{1}{\sqrt{n}}\right)$, which is independent of the integral dimensionality. Comparing the new method with Trapezoid rule and the Simpson Rule, the new method is getting better and better when the integral dimension number is large than 8. It is particularly attractive and powerful for higher dimensional integrals.

2 Monte Carlo Integration

Monte Carlo ([2], [4]) integration is a simple and powerful method for approximating complicated integrals. In general, we are interested in evaluating the integral of a function g over a domain D,

$$\theta = \int_D g(\vec{x})\,d\vec{x} \tag{1}$$

Here we use vector notation to indicate that g is a d-dimensional function. In fact, Monte Carlo techniques are more attractive for estimating higher-dimensional integrals.

We assume that there is a probability density function (pdf) f defined on the same domain D. Therefore (1) equals to,

$$\theta = \int_D \left[\frac{g(\vec{x})}{f(\vec{x})}\right] f(\vec{x})\,d\vec{x} \tag{2}$$

The integral (2) is equivalent to the expectation of $\frac{g}{f}$ with respect to a random variable distributed following to the cdf f,

$$\theta = E\left[\frac{g(\vec{x})}{f(\vec{x})}\right]. \tag{3}$$

According to the cdf f, we generate n independent random samples $\{\vec{x}_i, i = 1, \ldots, n\}$. The Monte Carlo integration estimator is defined as following,

$$\hat{\theta}_n = \frac{1}{n}\sum_{i=1}^{n}\frac{g(\vec{x}_i)}{f(\vec{x}_i)}. \tag{4}$$

Based on the Strong Law of Large Numbers ([1]), we have, with probability 1,

$$\lim_{n\to\infty} \frac{1}{n}\sum_{i=1}^{n} \frac{g(\vec{x}_i)}{f(\vec{x}_i)} = E\left[\frac{g(\vec{x})}{f(\vec{x})}\right].$$

This means, with probability 1,

$$\lim_{n\to\infty} \hat{\theta}_n = \theta.$$

The Monte Carlo approximation $\hat{\theta}_n$ is a consistent estimator of θ.

The efficiency of this method depends on how to generate the random samples. The important sampling technique ([2], [7]) can be used here to reduce the Monte Carlo integration error (the sample variance). How to pick a cdf f defined on D is a major concern in using important sampling techniques.

Another important efficient factor is how to generate the random sample. Sometime it may be very expensive depending on the selected cdf f. In practice, the most commonly used method is called the simple Monte Carlo simulation. We define the volume of the integration domain in (1),

$$V = \int_D d\vec{x}$$

The cdf selected for the simple Monte Carlo integration is,

$$f(\vec{x}) = \begin{cases} \frac{1}{V}, & if\ \vec{x} \in D \\ 0, & othewise. \end{cases}$$

In the implementation of simple Monte Carlo integration, we only need to generate random samples uniformly over the integral domain D. The efficiency is depending on the shape of integral domain D.

3 Using Random Numbers to Approximate Integrals

As we discussed in the previous section, the shape of the integral domain D is an issue here for the simple Monte Carlo integration. It is only feasible when the shape of D is a hyper-rectangle. For an improper integral with unbounded domain D, the simple Monte Carlo technique does not work. It is impossible to generate random samples uniformly over an unbounded integral region D.

For the general Monte Carlo integration technique, the issue here is how to select a cdf f. The necessary condition for f is having the same domain D. Can we generate random samples from this density function f efficiently and how?

In order to solve these issues discussed above, we propose a new random number base method for the Monte Carlo integration. The key idea is that we use the change variable (substitution) method to transfer the original integral domain D (including unbounded case) into the new domain: a unit hyper-cube. Therefore, we can easily generate random samples uniformly over a unite hyper-cube.

We introduce the new method for one-dimensional integration first. This method can be easily generalized into multiple d-dimensional situations.

What is a random number? By definition, a random number X is a continuous random variable following a uniform distribution over the interval [0,1]. Its pdf is given by,

$$f(x) = \begin{cases} 1 & if\ 0 < x < 1 \\ 0 & otherwise. \end{cases} \tag{5}$$

The cumulative distribution function (cdf) is given by

$$F(x) = P\{X \le x\} = \begin{cases} 0 & x \le 0 \\ x & 0 < x < 1 \\ 1 & x \ge 1. \end{cases} \tag{6}$$

In connecting the random numbers, we begin with a special case. Let $g(x)$ be a one-dimension function and we want to approximate the integral value of $g(x)$ on [0,1].

$$\theta = \int_0^1 g(x)\, dx. \tag{7}$$

If U is a random number having cdf (5), then the expectation of $g(U)$ is given by

$$E[g(U)] = \int_0^1 g(x) f(x)\, dx = \int_0^1 g(x) * 1\, dx.$$

Therefore

$$\theta = E[g(U)].$$

If $U_1, U_2, \dots, U_n$ are independent random numbers, we have that $g(U_1), g(U_2), \dots, g(U_n)$ are independent and identically distributed random variables with a mean $E[g(U)]$, which is equivalent to θ. Therefore, by the Strong Law of Large Numbers, we have, with probability 1,

$$\lim_{n\to\infty} \frac{1}{n}\sum_{i=1}^{n} g(U_i) = \theta.$$

We can use a large number of random numbers to approximate the definite integral (7). The natural approximation of θ based on random numbers $U_1, U_2, \dots, U_n$ is defined by,

$$\hat{\theta}_n = \frac{1}{n}\sum_{i=1}^{n} g(U_i). \tag{8}$$

We define this approximation technique as a random number based method for Monte Carlo integration.

In general, we want to approximate integral,

$$\theta = \int_a^b g(x)\, dx. \tag{9}$$

Here the integral lower and upper bounds a and b can be any real numbers, or positive and negative infinities. For any arbitrary combination of a, b, and $g(x)$ in (9), we will provide detailed steps to convert (9) as a basic integral (7) over the interval [0.1]. The key idea is to find a suitable variable substitution. That is, we substitute variable x in terms of t. This substitution will transfer the original integral interval $[a,b]$ into the new integral interval $[0,1]$. The transformation process can be described as following,

$$\theta = \int_a^b g(x)\,dx = \int_0^1 g^*(t)\,dt. \quad (10)$$

where the new integrand,

$$g^*(t) = g(x^{-1}(t)) * J(t).$$

here $J(t)$ is the Jacobian of the t variable substitution.

If the transformation (10) exists, we can use the method (8) to approximate θ in (9),

$$\hat{\theta}_n = \frac{1}{n}\sum_{i=1}^{n} g^*(U_i). \quad (11)$$

Here $\hat{\theta}_n$ will converge to the true integral value θ in (9) with probability 1.

Let's classify all possible combinations of the integral lower and upper bounds a and b in (9) into different cases, and then we discuss each individual one.

Case A: For

$$\theta = \int_a^b g(x)\,dx,$$

here a and b are both finite real numbers and $a \neq b$, we define the following substitution,

$$t = \frac{x-a}{b-a}.$$

Then we have,

$x = a$, implies $t = 0$, and

$x = b$, implies $t = 1$.

The inverse function of x is,

$$x^{-1}(t) = a + (b-a)\,t.$$

The Jacobian of the t substitution,

$$J(t) = \frac{d}{dt}[x^{-1}(t)] = b - a.$$

Therefore, we have

$$g^*(t) = g(x^{-1}(t)) * J(t)$$
$$= g(a + (b-a)t) * (b-a).$$

We have done the transformation,

$$\theta = \int_a^b g(x)\,dx = \int_0^1 g^*(t)\,dt.$$

Case B: For

$$\theta = \int_a^\infty g(x)\,dx,$$

here a is a finite real number, we define a nonlinear transformation,

$$t = \frac{1}{x-a+1}.$$

Then we have,

$x = a$, implies $t = 1$, and

$x \to \infty$, implies $t = \lim_{x\to\infty} \frac{1}{x-a+1} = 0.$

The inverse function of x is,

$$x^{-1}(t) = \frac{1}{t} - 1 + a.$$

The Jacobian of the t substitution,

$$J(t) = \frac{d}{dt}[x^{-1}(t)] = -\frac{1}{t^2}.$$

Therefore, we have

$$g(x^{-1}(t)) * J(t) = g\left(\frac{1}{t} - 1 + a\right) * \left(-\frac{1}{t^2}\right).$$

Using the negative sign to switch the integral lower and upper bounds, we have,

$$g^*(t) = g\left(\frac{1}{t} - 1 + a\right) * \frac{1}{t^2}.$$

This implies,

$$\theta = \int_a^\infty g(x)\,dx = \int_0^1 g^*(t)\,dt.$$

Here $g^*(t)$ may be unbounded when $t = 0$. However this improper integral is convergent if θ is finite. There is no problem when we perform the Monte Carlo simulation, since all pseudo random numbers are from open interval (0,1) and can't be zero.

Case C: For

$$\theta = \int_{-\infty}^b g(x)\,dx,$$

here b is a finite real number, we define a nonlinear transformation,

$$t = \frac{1}{1+b-x}.$$

Then we have,

$x \to -\infty$, implies $t = \lim_{x\to-\infty} \frac{1}{1+b-x} = 0,$

and

$x = b$, implies $t = 1$.

The inverse function of x is,

$$x^{-1}(t) = 1 + b - \frac{1}{t}.$$

The Jacobian of the t substitution,

$$J(t) = \frac{d}{dt}[x^{-1}(t)] = \frac{1}{t^2}.$$

Therefore, we have

$$g^*(t) = g(x^{-1}(t)) * J(t)$$
$$= g\left(1 + b - \frac{1}{t}\right) * \frac{1}{t^2}.$$

This implies,

$$\theta = \int_{-\infty}^b g(x)\,dx = \int_0^1 g^*(t)\,dt.$$

A typical application of Case C is the Normal cdf,

$$F(x_0) = \int_{-\infty}^{x_0} \frac{1}{\sqrt{2\pi}\,\sigma} e^{-\frac{(x-\mu)^2}{2\sigma^2}}\,dx.$$

For this special integral, the closed-form of its antiderivative does not exist.

Case D: For

$$\theta = \int_{-\infty}^{\infty} g(x)\, dx,$$

we rewrite this integral into a sum of two integrals,

$$\theta = \int_{-\infty}^{\infty} g(x)\, dx = \int_{-\infty}^{0} g(x) + \int_{0}^{\infty} g(x).$$

We apply Case C method to the first integral and Case B method to the second integral, where $b = 0$, and $a = 0$ respectively. Therefore, we have,

$$g^*(t) = g\left(1 - \frac{1}{t}\right) * \frac{1}{t^2} + g\left(\frac{-t}{t-1}\right) * \frac{1}{(1-t)^2}$$

Then we have,

$$\theta = \int_{-\infty}^{\infty} g(x)\, dx = \int_{0}^{1} g^*(t)\, dt.$$

We have discussed all possible situations of the integral (9) so far. In other words, we can use the random number based method to approximate the integral (9) for any arbitrary lower and upper bounds.

This idea can be generalized to approximate the multiple integrals. For a general d-dimensional integral,

$$\theta = \int_{a_1}^{b_1} \int_{a_2}^{b_2} \dots \int_{a_d}^{b_d} g(x_1, x_2, \dots, x_d) dx_1 dx_2, \dots, dx_d, \quad (12)$$

we may transfer (12) into the following integral,

$$\theta = \int_{0}^{1} \int_{0}^{1} \dots \int_{0}^{1} g^*(t_1, t_2, \dots, t_d) dt_1 dt_2, \dots, dt_d. \quad (13)$$

Integral (13) has a unit hyper-cube domain and is equivalent to,

$$\theta = E[g^*(U_1, U_2, \dots, U_d)],$$

where $U_1, U_2, \dots, U_d$ are independent random numbers. To approximate the θ value of the d-dimensional integral (13), we only need to generate $n * d$ independent random numbers over the unit hyper-cube $[0,1]^d$:

$$U_j^i, i = 1, \dots, n;\ j = 1, \dots, d.$$

Therefore, we can estimate the integral value of θ by,

$$\hat{\theta}_n = \frac{1}{n} \sum_{i=1}^{n} g^*(U_1^i,\ U_2^i, \dots, U_d^i). \quad (14)$$

By the Strong Law of Large Numbers, with probability 1,

$$\lim_{n\to\infty} \hat{\theta}_n = \lim_{n\to\infty} \frac{1}{n} \sum_{i=1}^{n} g^*(U_1^i,\ U_2^i, \dots, U_d^i) = \theta.$$

We only need a random number generator ([5], [6]) to implement our method in computer programming.

4 Error Analysis

The implementation the Monte Carlo integration is a computer simulation. The Monte Carlo integration estimate convergences to the true integral value with probability 1. In practice, we need to consider when to stop the Monte Carlo simulation, which essentially is deciding the appropriate sample size n. The quality of the Monte Carlo integration estimator is depending on this sample size. Typical error analysis in Monte Carlo simulation is called the output analysis – using sample variance to evaluate the quality of Monte Carlo estimator ([2], [7]). In this section, we are assuming that the variance is finite so that the Central Limit Theory can be applied.

The mean value of $\hat{\theta}_n$ in (14) is,

$$E[\hat{\theta}_n] = \theta.$$

This implies that $\hat{\theta}_n$ is an unbiased estimator. The variance of $\hat{\theta}_n$ is given by,

$$Var(\hat{\theta}_n) = \frac{\sigma^2(g^*)}{n}.$$

where, $\sigma^2(g^*)$ is the variance $g^*(\vec{U})$ and $\vec{U}$ is the unit uniform random vector over the hyper-cube $[0,1]^d$ ([2], [7]). In practice, we use the following sample variance to estimate the about true variance.

$$S^2 = \frac{\sum_{i=1}^{n} \left(g^*(U_1^i, U_2^i, \dots, U_d^i) - \hat{\theta}_n\right)^2}{n-1}.$$

This variance decreases asymptotically to zero as $\frac{1}{n}$. The expected value of the error is proportional to the standard deviation, which is $O\left(\frac{1}{\sqrt{n}}\right)$. From the Central Limit Theory, within one-σ error, the confidence level is about 68%. Within two-σ error, the confidence level is about 95%. Within three-σ error, the confidence level is about 99.7%. We can decide the sample size n based on the desired confidence level. The swing digit ideal in ([9]) is a good method for reporting simulation outputs. To increase accuracy in one more digit, you need to increase the sample size 100 times.

The expected value of the error for this new method is always $O\left(\frac{1}{\sqrt{n}}\right)$, which does not depend on the integral dimensionality. However, for the deterministic numerical integration, it does depend on the integral dimensionality. For a d-dimensional integral, the Trapezoid rule provides an error of $O\left(\frac{1}{n^{\frac{2}{d}}}\right)$, and the Simpson rule provides an error of $O\left(\frac{1}{n^{\frac{4}{d}}}\right)$ ([3]).

In comparing error orders, for lower dimension integrals, the Trapezoid rule and Simpson rule are better than the Monte Carlo integration. As the dimensionality increases, for $d > 4$, the Monte Carlo integration is better than the Trapezoid rule, and for $d > 8$, the Monte Carlo integration is better than the Simpson Rule. Particularly, the Monte Carlo method is powerful for high dimension integrals. When the dimensional number d is higher than 20, the only working numerical method is the Monte Carlo integration in many existing software packages.

5 Conclusions

In reality, an analytical form for a given integral is sometimes difficult to find. We turn this situation into numerical integration. The popular deterministic numerical methods are the Trapezoid rule and the Simpson rule. The statistical numerical method is the Monte Carlo integration. In general, you need to select a probability density function, which has the same domain as the given integral domain. Generating a sample according to the selected density function is sometimes very expensive or inefficient. For the most popular method - simple Monte Carlo integration, the integral domain has to be a bounded hyper-rectangle. This method does not work for any integral with an unbounded integral domain.

The new proposed method in this paper is more efficient and easier to implement in computer programming. We have covered all possible integral situations, including improper integrals. Detailed steps are provided for converting the given integral domain into a new domain – a unit hyper-cube. You only need to generate random samples uniformly over a unit hype-cube.

When the integral dimensional number is lower, there is no significant in errors for different numerical integration methods. When the integral dimensional number is higher, say larger than 8, the new proposed method for Monte Carlo integration dominates all other numerical integration methods.

6 References

[1] Billingsley, P. "Convergence of Probability Measures". Wiley, 2nd Edition, New York, NY, 1999.

[2] Bratley, P., Fox, B. L., and Schrage, L. E. "A Guide to Simulation". Springer-Verlag, New York, NY, 1987.

[3] Burden, R. L., Faires, J. D., and Reynolds, A. C. "Numerical Analysis". PWS Publishers, 2nd Edition, Boston, MA, 1979.

[4] Hammersley, J. M. and Handscomb, D. C. 1964. "Monte Carlo Methods", Methuen, London, 1964.

[5] D. H. Lehmer, D. H. "Mathematical Methods in Large-Scale Computing Units. Annals of the Computation", Laboratory of Harvard University, 26, 141–146, 1951.

[6] L'Ecuyer, P. "Uniform Random Number Generation", Annals of Operations Research, 53, 77–120, 1994.

[7] Ross, S. M. "A Course in Simulation". MacMillan, New York, NY, 1990.

[8] Thomas Jr., G. B., Weir, M. D., Hass, J. R., and Giordano, F. R. 'Thomas' Calculus Early Transcendentals". Addison Wesley, 10th Edition, New York, NY, 2001.

[9] A. L. Wang, A. L. and Kicey, C. J. "On the Accuracy of Buffon's Needle: A Simulation Output Analysis. Proceedings of the 49th Annual ACM SE Conference, ACM Press, New York, NY, 233–236, 2011

Design of an Efficient Object-Oriented Software for an FPGA-based Scan Probe Microscope Controller

Adam Kollin[1], Steffen Porthun[2], Darrin Hanna[3], Charles Otlowski[3], Aarin Covyeau[3], Katherine LaBelle[3], Michael Lohrer[3], and Jason Gorski[1]
[1]RHK Technology, Inc., Troy, MI, USA
[2]Schaefer Technologie GmbH, Langen, Germany
[3]Department of Electrical and Computer Engineering, Oakland University, Rochester, MI, USA

Abstract - *Modern advancements in computing hardware, namely FPGAs, have allowed greater flexibility in system design. However, deciding how to make use of this flexibility can be a challenge. A control system for a scanning probe microscope usually requires multiple devices, which has several downsides. A single, generic device can both allow greater flexibility and better results, and coupled with generic software can allow easy reconfiguration to accommodate any user's needs.*

Keywords: software controller design SPM

1 Introduction

Frequently hardware systems such as controllers have software systems that enable users to set parameters, initiate procedures, and communicate with the hardware. In any of these systems, the hardware is only as easy to use as the supporting software. In addition to user-friendliness, engineers must balance the hardware/software co-design issue correctly by determining which functions should occur in hardware and which can occur in software; a controller that computes heavily on the software side may be slow if the supporting hardware does not provide enough resources. For many years, systems have made use of microcontrollers or application-specific integrated circuits (ASICs). With the more recent increase in density and lowering costs of field-programmable gate arrays (FPGAs), engineers are incorporating them into next-generation designs. These FPGA-based designs provide a great deal of flexibility in the hardware, and create many more options for users and procedures, since FPGAs allow programmers to configure hardware components on a single chip rather than using several chips that are hard-coded for specific purposes.

Even though FPGAs introduce a great deal of flexibility and options, the software often falls short of placing this flexibility into the hands of the user. Typically, companies extend legacy software to include more parameters and pull-down menus to access and configure this new flexibility and it is more complex and anything but user-friendly for users. Unfortunately, the net result of this is a system that does more but seems worse than previous version, while the hardware is much more advanced and capable than its predecessor.

An example of a system in which FPGAs have added significant flexibility and presents these software challenges is a scanning probe microscope (SPM) controller. The hardware can become extremely complex going from one component to another. Often, external cables connecting the hardware introduce a significant amount of noise in extremely sensitive data. Therefore, packaging the system into a single unit offers many benefits, including a significant noise reduction. Section 3 of this paper presents several important benefits to a single-box SPM system.

The software interface must be designed to take full advantage of this flexibility. Too much flexibility makes the system difficult to use, while a simpler software interface may limit the user's configuration options. The High-Performance Embedded Systems lab at Oakland University has had the opportunity to work with RHK Technologies to create such a software system from scratch for their next generation SPM controller that uses a high-density FPGA, for the first time. Using FPGAs, they have created an architecture that allows scientists to create their own experiments with magnitudes more flexibility than ever. Instead of extending their legacy software that has evolved and accompanied their controllers for the past twenty five years, RHK concluded that a completely new software architecture was in order. The software uses the FPGAs in the system to create hardware components specific to the experiments developed by the scientists using it. The interface uses a drag-and-drop design in order to make the program as intuitive as possible, while simultaneously providing a large amount of control over the hardware parameters. To develop this new architecture, RHK, external consultants, and members from the lab engaged in a lengthy but valuable process of engineering the software efficiently.

This paper discusses the outcomes of the design and implementation work, including the efficient software interface for an object-oriented design of the system. Section 2 covers some background information about SPMs in order to have a better understanding of the system requirements and the challenges they impose. In the third section, the benefits of creating a system in a single unit are discussed. The following section goes into detail about the general challenges of hardware/software co-design and developing a software interface for a controller containing an FPGA with great flexibility. Next, section 5 explains the design of RHK's R9 system to overcome these problems. Finally, a brief explanation of the software is presented, as well as the debugging tools that are critical in development, its architectural layers, and the benefits of making the tools object-oriented and multithreaded.

2 Background of Scanning Probe Microscopy

The development of scanning probe microscopes (SPMs) has provided scientists the opportunity to both obtain an image of a sample at a very high resolution and interact with the atoms in the sample. The field of scan-probe microscopy incorporates several different types of microscopy measurement techniques, such as scanning tunneling microscopy (STM), scanning tunneling spectroscopy (STS), contact mode atomic force microscopy (AFM), non-contact mode AFM, and more. The choice of measurement depends upon the scanning environment, the type of sample being analyzed, and the data to be obtained.

In general, an SPM consists of a probe that scans the surface, a sensor to detect the vertical position of the tip, and a feedback system to control the probe's position. In a typical mode, the probe can interact with the sample in which the measured signal is used as the input of a feedback loop to maintain a constant distance above the surface. There is now a wide range of scanning probe microscopes designed to measure samples in a variety of environments, such as in liquids, air, and vacuums, and at a variety of temperatures ranging from a few millikelvin to over 1000 kelvin.

Clearly, there are several configuration parameters for scientists to set in a SPM controller. Many of these parameters not only involve a linear sequence of events in the experiment but also require different hardware components. FPGAs provide the flexible configuration of hardware components, but most SPM controllers still involve a lot of external equipment that introduces new problems. These issues and a possible solution are discussed in the following section.

3 Benefits of a Single-Box System

Previous commercially available SPM control systems required multiple hardware devices in order to measure data. A power supply, PLL, lock-in amplifier, high-voltage piezo driver, and possibly more items all required separate boxes and needed to be manually wired together. The external wiring introduced more noise in the system, in addition to the inaccuracy produced from multiple digitization steps. Moreover, external wiring involves a careful and sometimes extensive setup that is difficult to replicate unless careful documentation is kept. It is especially inconvenient for cases in which the person who initially set up the wiring configuration leaves, and a new employee may not fully understand it.

RHK has released an SPM control system called R9. In this system, everything is in one box with hardware capable of performing all of the required tasks. The power supply, PLL, lock-ins, high voltage driver, and even more components are all available. The system uses data acquired in a single digitization step, which requires few to no external wires other than the microscope control wires. All of the internal signals are digital and cannot pick up noise. The configuration occurs internally in the hardware and is set up with a software system. The software setup can be saved and loaded again later, with generic configurations available pre-setup. If additional hardware modules are required, scientists can add them into the experiment without adding additional hardware components. A huge benefit of a single-unit system is reproducibility in production; in essence, one box behaves like the other. If loose cables make the external connections, this would not be possible.

Although the physical hardware design is greatly improved by a single-unit system, problems still arise in partitioning the system into hardware and software components.

4 Co-design and Software Interfacing

In general, the development of an SPM controller involves a long list of requirements. It has to lock onto a frequency and piezoelectric drives, change the tunneling current, change parameters, collect data, convert the data into pixels, and more. For this project, the hardware uses FPGAs and a SHARC processor that runs FORTH, while the software interacts with the system through an Ethernet cable connecting to a PC. The interaction between the hardware and software has proved to be a formidable challenge.

As discussed in previous sections, a highly configurable single-box SPM controller demands the hardware flexibility that FPGAs offer. To this end, RHK has designed a single-unit SPM controller using high-density FPGAs. The FPGAs are connected to A/D converters, D/A converters, counters, network interfaces, and other peripherals. This allows the system to run the required signal processing tasks massively parallel, thereby outperforming any single processor design.

On top of this FPGA runs a FORTH system in an embedded SHARC processor. This system has access to all FPGA functions by means of registers and contains an interpreter that makes it especially useful for debugging. The FORTH language has some unique features that make it particularly well-suited for this purpose. Any FPGA feature can immediately be accessed by the FORTH console. In addition, FORTH contains a simple yet powerful compiler to build code both at boot-up and on the fly, which an important ability. In summary, the problems listed above need to be designed in either software or hardware.

We have found that the partitioning of tasks between FPGA code and FORTH code is efficiently achieved according to these rules: (1) physical hardware items are reflected by FPGA code items, and (2) software procedures are implemented in FORTH code. The FPGA routing facilities are used to implement all the options of the hardware space of the controller. The big challenge in this design lies in building the interfacing logic that translates the IHDL (software) procedures into FORTH instructions. IHDL procedures and hardware space are discussed in further detail in the next section.

The current R9 system evolved out of the PLLPro2 NCAFM controller. One piece of legacy hardware is the

SHARC DSP processor that runs the FORTH system. Before R9 development began, large amounts of code/libraries were already written for this FORTH system. For this reason, we kept the SHARC DSP processor. It will soon be replaced by a soft core FORTH processor.

The PLLPro2 had a separate board with two 20 bit A/D converters and nine 18 bit D/A converters. This board was not connected to the main FPGA chip and could only be accessed from the SHARC DSP processor. As a result, the SHARC was heavily loaded with a DAC and A/D interfacing interrupt service routine. We removed this board from the design. DACs and ADCs are now directly interfaced by the FPGA chip, allowing us to fully implement the IHDL hardware space representation inside the FPGA.

The hardware of the R9 system is designed to maximize the flexibility that FPGAs offer. In order to take advantage of the benefits of this hardware controller, the software interface must be similarly flexible. R9's software (R9S) allows the user to select the hardware components for an experiment as well as developing the steps to collect data. R9S was designed from scratch to ensure that the code runs as efficiently as possible while providing an interface that is both easy to use and to configure.

5 Software Architecture

The main concern in designing a system for any purpose is determining the degree of flexibility. If the system is too rigid, it limits the hardware that can be used with the system as well as the actual tasks that can be accomplished. If the system is too flexible, then it has many possible configurations but no clear built-in purpose or configuration that the user can easily apply. The purpose for the R9S software architecture is to allow scientists to design experiments on hardware that supports different microscopes, vendors, and versions. In order to achieve this objective, FPGAs were included to support multiple hardware configurations. Another goal is to prevent the use of pull-down menus containing hundreds of configuration options, which causes RHK employees to reconfigure the system constantly. In order to achieve this functionality, the system should give advanced users the ability to connect the hardware components themselves in a simple and efficient manner.

The approach to achieving these requirements involves creating a space for hardware components (Figure 2), a software procedure space (Figure 3), and also a scan area window for scan-specific functions (Figure 1). Different iterations of this design were made to make it more flexible. Originally, there was no scan area window and the system was designed very generically. Since the main purpose is to use this hardware as a scanner, the third domain for scanning was created. With two generic domains and one specific domain, the system is flexible with a built-in purpose that is obvious to its users. The procedure space can literally be used for anything, and was made very basic (stop, start, etc.) to control the hardware dynamically, whereas the hardware space can be used to represent specific hardware configurations.

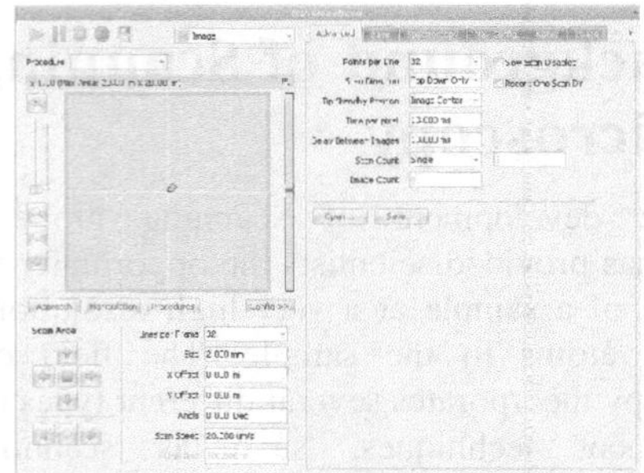

Figure 1. Scan Window

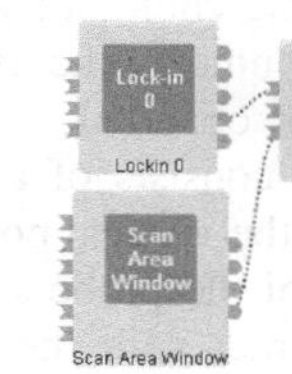

Figure 2. Hardware Space

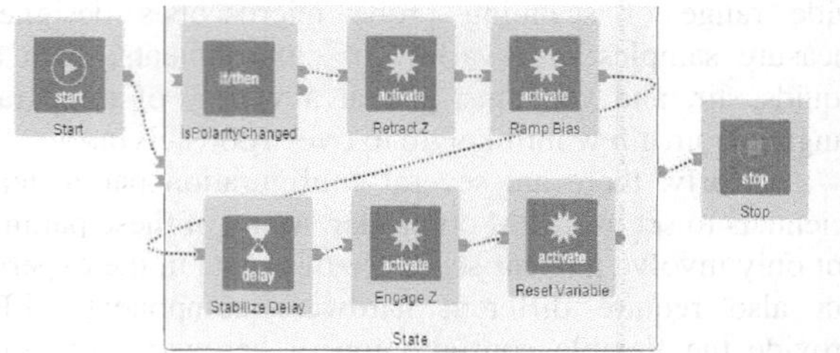

Figure 3. A fairly simple procedure space setup

After much consideration regarding flexibility versus usability, the software was designed to send down configurations to the FPGAs, which would then use a multiplexer to select certain hardware configurations. Hardware and procedure space are represented as visual interconnected blocks called IHDL.

5.1 Introduction to IHDL

The backbone of the R9 software is called IHDL (Iconic Hardware Description Language). IHDL is a visual programming language that allows users to create programs by manipulating them graphically, rather than with text. A visual programming language provides flexibility in the software and takes advantage of the flexibility of the FPGAs. Some parts of hardware could be implemented in the FPGAs, while certain portions of hardware could be implemented in the software, and vice versa. In order for the software to take full advantage of the FPGAs, the software needs to use parallelism. IHDL is inherently parallel and is easier to debug than an imperative programming language. The usage of IHDL in the R9 software provides a very easy and understandable method of connecting hardware, creating procedures, and designing experiments.

IHDL solves several of the issues that have been found in SPM software programs. One such issue is a complex user interface that requires several clicks to accomplish routine changes in the configuration. Other problems may include a lack of integration with the hardware or a lack of extensible design.

In the R9 controller, IHDL is used to represent the available hardware items for use in experiments. In order to replace dials, knobs, and other external configurations, these IHDL hardware items provide simple graphics (text boxes, drop down menus, etc.) in order to provide input to the hardware. A user simply drags the item from the palette and drops it onto the workspace. Altogether, these items represent a fixed digital file which can be saved and reused.

If the user wishes to repeat experiments, procedure items offer this feature. The IHDL workspace has many groups of hardware items, but the procedure workspace has exactly nine (Figure 4). The low number of procedure items makes it easy to create control systems for the IHDL items while keeping procedures from becoming overcomplicated. The procedure items connect to one another in the same manner as IHDL workspace items.

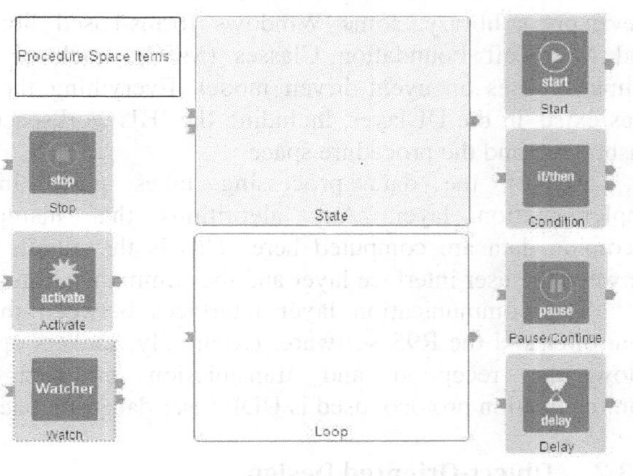

Figure 4. R9S procedure space items

The software that controls the R9 system was designed to be both simplistic and flexible. It contains several powerful tools, such as a debugger for experiments that alerts the users if components are incorrectly connected. It consists of three main layers: the graphical user interface, the implementation of the GUI, and the communication between the code and the hardware. Each layer is run on a separate thread to ensure that the GUI is responsive. Finally, the code takes advantage of object-oriented design to create an intuitive drag-and-drop display.

The R9 software has the advantage of being built on top of the hardware, rather than being built separately. Since R9S is visual and includes no language-based syntax, the user is free to learn the system as if he/she were building and connecting up the hardware. This process will be logical to those individuals familiar with hooking up the hardware components.

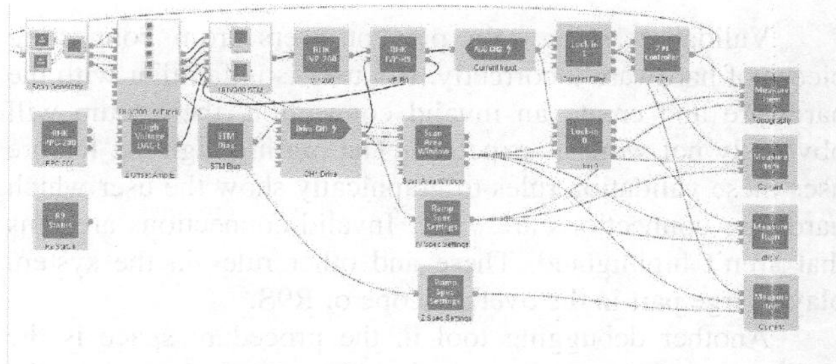

Figure 5. IHDL hardware setup in the R9S workspace

The IHDL items (shown in Figure 5) are represented as blocks in their respective workspaces of R9S. Many of the blocks contain multiple input and output pins. The pins and their connections provide the user with a more efficient and stable version of the hardware, instead of manually connecting cables. With this design, users have a neat and organized toolbox of components with which they design experiments.

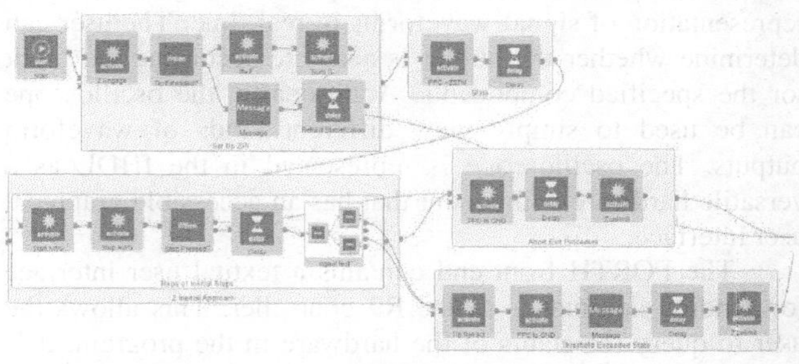

Figure 6. Part of a complex experiment in the R9S procedure space

Procedure items (Figures 4, 6) are used for activation and deactivation of hardware, states, loops, if/else conditions, etc. Since IHDL simplifies the process of creating an experiment, low-cost custom experiments are possible.

For the changes to properties of the procedures and workspace items to take effect, the configuration information must be sent down to the FPGAs/hardware. This is accomplished through the press of a button, called initialization. Once initialization begins, the hardware is configured. In order to run the experiment, the start button must be pressed to run the procedure on the board. A customer that wants to be able to run a general type of spectroscopy experiment with a push of a couple of buttons now has that ability.

5.2 Debugging Tools

The R9S system contains many in-software debugging and bug-prevention tools to ensure a user-friendly experience. For example, when trying to connect one item to another, the available pins are highlighted when making the connection. There is also a method to trigger graphical messages during a procedure. Moreover, a software-based oscilloscope is available to check signals, as well as a FORTH front end that allows users to directly check the state of the R9 controller while the software runs.

Validation rules help prevent users from connecting pieces of hardware incorrectly. If a user is unfamiliar with the hardware and create an invalid connection, their setup will obviously not work as expected. The pin highlighting feature uses these validation rules to graphically show the user which hardware connections are valid. Invalid connections are pins that aren't highlighted. These and other rules in the system play a large part in the overall scope of R9S.

Another debugging tool in the procedure space is the ability to add message blocks. The user designing the experiment can receive custom pop-up messages to provide whatever information that the user sees necessary. This method is analogous to software debugging, in which a user prints out a message to the console at certain points in order to help trace the flow of the program. In this case, the user adds pop-up messages to help trace the flow of the procedure itself, therefore granting the user a real-time view of the currently running experiment.

The software-based oscilloscope in R9S gives a visual representation of signal waveforms in real time. The user can determine whether the output is accurate according the input for the specified components. Additionally, the oscilloscope can be used to simply view different kinds of waveform outputs. The oscilloscope is represented in the IHDL as a versatile hardware component that has an accessible graphical user interface.

The FORTH front end contains a textual user interface for sending commands to the R9 controller. This allows the user to query the status of the hardware in the program. It is mostly useful for RHK technicians in diagnosing any errors that may occur while the software is running. The FORTH front end, combined with the previously mentioned debugging tools, serves to ensure that the user has a smooth, productive experience with the R9S software.

5.3 Organization

5.3.1 Layers

In order to keep the R9 software organized, a three layer model was used: the user interface (UI), implementation, and communication. The UI layer contains all of the graphical components and the functions that allow the user to interact with the software. The implementation layer holds the code that models the software's required behavior. Finally, the communication layer provides the communication from the software to the hardware (or to any other external actor). Figure 7 shows the layers together as a model.

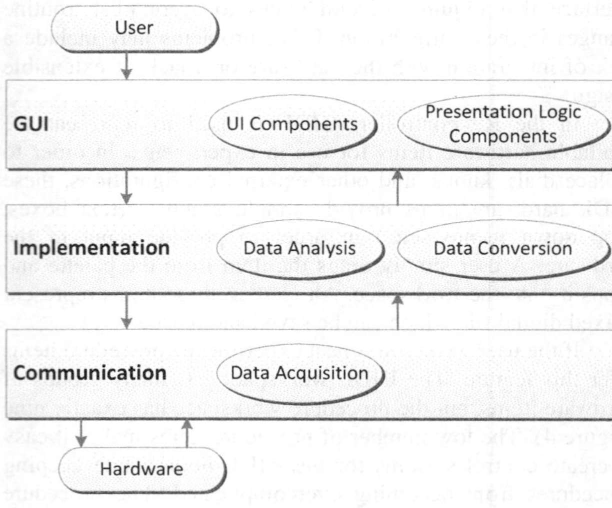

Figure 7. R9S Software Layer Model

The user interface layer contains code written using the DevExpress library, some Windows forms-based libraries, and Microsoft Foundation Classes (MFC). Each of these primarily uses an event-driven model. Everything the user sees exists in the UI layer, including the IHL workspace, the dashboard, and the procedure space.

All of the data processing takes place in the implementation layer. Any algorithms that manipulate incoming data are computed here. This is the middle layer between the user interface layer and the communication layer.

The communication layer interfaces between the R9 controller and the R9S software. Essentially, sockets open to allow the reception and transmission of data. The communication protocol used is UDP (user datagram packet).

5.3.2 Object-Oriented Design

In an effort to make R9S easy to understand, the software is completely object-oriented. Hardware items are considered to be objects and have a base class. Furthermore, another class extends the base class that contains more detailed information. This polymorphic design allows for better versatility and re-usability of code.

An object-oriented design models real-world items such that they can be accurately represented in software. This is especially applicable in the creation of Iconic Hardware Description Language (IHDL). Connections between the items are represented through pins and wires. Pins are objects and wires are pointers between the two pins.

5.3.3 Threading

In order to ensure that the interface has a quick response time, each of the three layers exists on its own thread. R9S uses several other threads, but these are the main ones. Communication between threads is often difficult when sharing data between them.

Shared data introduces the problem of race conditions. If all threads have the ability to read and write simultaneously, the data may be inconsistent between threads. To prevent these conditions from occurring, semaphores are used to define critical sections where only one thread can read and/or write the data at a given time. In addition to the use of semaphores, function pointers are stored between threads to allow data to be passed from thread to thread.

Often, the implementation layer contains newly processed data that has not been updated in the GUI yet. In order to update the GUI, the implementation layer refers to a callback function that passes the data to the GUI. [4]

5.4 Architecture Summary

The R9S software implements an interface that focuses on data configuration and achieves it through visual programming. It provides the ability to control SPM experiments and the parameters through software procedures. This powerful, user-friendly system is what has ultimately led to the success of R9S. Users no longer need to manually set up components with cables that can easily hinder the advancement of SPM. RHK's one-box solution with its flexible software package has remedied the problems that have continuously plagued the industry. Since R9S stores its hardware connections in savable files, they are always available to the user. The user is in full control with R9S and the software continues to provide an easy yet extremely powerful way for its customers to work with SPM.

6 System Benefits

The development of IHDL allows RHK to present the user with a highly flexible and versatile control system without the drawback of being too complex to configure and operate. The IHDL allows the integration of a large number of real components, such as ADCs and DACs with an even larger number of virtual components, such as feedback loops, lock in amplifiers, signal multiplexers, into a wide variety of experimental configurations in an intuitive manner that graphically resembles the connection of separate instruments with electronic cables.

Another advantage of the IHDL is that the hardware-firmware configuration, which is normally set once for a specific type of experiment, is separated from the actual measurements that are made using that hardware configuration, which are changed frequently. The user can switch between topographic and spectroscopic measurements, atomic manipulations and other types of surface modifications without requiring any change to the hardware configuration. Other types of software configuration languages such as Labview intertwine the hardware configurations and the operations performed on those configurations. This makes changes to existing experiments much more time-consuming and requires a much longer learning curve. Users can start to make modifications to their IHDL setups within a day or when just starting to use the system.

The integration of multiple feedback loops, lock-in amplifiers, and phase-locked loops inside of a single large-scale FPGA has also enabled the ability to detect, measure, and receive feedback off of any harmonic or sideband of the mixture of different input signals over a wide frequency range. This capability is greatly reduced in systems composed of separate components connected through analog cables as precise frequency and phase information is compromised due to the multiple analog to digital conversions that are utilized.

As powerful as the existing R9 system is currently, the system's capabilities continue to grow as more firmware components are added to the existing FPGAs. As customers push the limits to what can be done with the existing firmware implementations, RHK has been responding by adding the capabilities to keep pushing the experimental envelope. The initial firmware release provided for a single feedback loop (for Z feedback) and a single lock-in amplifier to demodulate one signal. The current firmware now contains three feedback loops (Z feedback, KFM, interferometer), one lock-in amplifier and one PLL. The next firmware release will add additional feedback loops, one more PLL and two more lock-in amplifiers. New capabilities enabled by these firmware components include multi-frequency excitation and simultaneous demodulation of multiple harmonics. None of these enhancements require any changes to the existing hardware. All existing R9 customers can upgrade to the latest capabilities via a simple software upgrade.

7 Results

RHK's previous SPM control system, the SPM1000, had been the used for a generation by research scientists. However, as a mostly analog system, it was eventually eclipsed by other control systems that allowed digital control of most parameters. These control systems, while more flexible than an analog system, are limited by their reliance on data acquisition systems developed by other companies and not optimized specifically for SPM operation. Utilizing circuitry developed completely in-house specifically for SPM use has provided the R9 system with a unique combination of high speed operation with low noise precision. The addition of the IHDL interface is already positioning the R9 to be the system of choice for the top tier of research scientists across the globe. Over 50 of them have been delivered and are in use worldwide.

8 Conclusions and Future Work

In conclusion, the problems of hardware/software co-design and the creation of a software interface are common to numerous applications. Several solutions have been presented: combining the system into a single box to reduce noise and complexity, using the flexibility of FPGAs to design hardware components, and finally designing an object-oriented, multi-threaded software controller with a drag-and-drop interface. Using these approaches, RHK has successfully a powerful SPM controller to efficiently scan and measure data while making it easy for scientists to use. Furthermore, by having the ability to endlessly reconfigure the lab in a single box and save previous configurations, scientists have been able to experiment more and will be able to revert to configuration from the past in years to come, even after graduate students and post-docs who once setup the systems and configurations have gone.

Currently, a soft-core FORTH processor has been developed and is undergoing testing. This project will eliminate the SHARC processor, which is legacy hardware from the PLL Pro 2. Eliminating the SHARC processor by replacing it with a soft core in the FPGA will offer even more flexibility and speed. Future improvements are endless, but the approaches described in this paper provide a solid foundation.

9 References

[1] K. Asawaree and E. A. Lee, "A Hardware-Software Codesign Methodology for DSP Applications," *IEEE Design & Test of Computers,* vol. 10, no. 3, pp. 16-28, 1993.

[2] D. U. Meyer-Baese, Digital Signal Processing with Field Programmable Gate Arrays, Tallahassee: Springer-Verlag Berlin Heidelberg, 2007.

[3] R. Howland and L. Benatar, A Pratical Guide To Scanning Probe Microscopy, Park scientific instruments, 1996.

[4] "Multithreaded Programming Guide," Sun Microsystems, Inc., 1994.

The development and validation of the creep damage constitutive equations for P91 Alloy

Xin Yang[1]**, Qiang Xu**[1]**, Zhongyu Lu**[2]
[1]School of Science and Engineering, Teesside University, Middlesbrough, TS1 3BA, UK
[2]School of Computing and Engineering, University of Huddersfield, Huddersfield, HD1 3DA, UK

Abstract - *This paper presents research on the validation of a set of creep damage constitutive equations for P91 alloy under multi-axial states of stress, and its applicability under lower stress level. Creep damage is one of the serious problems for the high temperature industries and computational creep damage has been developed and used, complementary to the experimental approach, to assist safe operation. In creep damage mechanics, a set of constitutive equations needs to be developed and validated. Recently, a mechanism-based approach for the developing creep damage constitutive equation for this type of high Cr alloy has merged and several versions of creep damage constitutive equations have been proposed. However, so far, they are limited to uni-axial case under medium to high stress level. In fact, multi-axial states of stress and lower stress level are more pertinent to the real industrial applications. That is the objective of this research. This paper contributes to the methodology and specific knowledge.*

Keywords: P91, Creep mechanism, CDM Model

1. Introduction

Scientists estimate that the world power requirement will increase by up to 50% in the next 20 years. Hence, it is essential to develop the advanced energy resources which must be cost effective, sustainable and environmental friendly [1]. The Cr-Mo steels have been the material of choice for using in the power generation plants [2]. During 1960s, the Ferritic-martensitic steels with 9-12 wt% Cr were developed for fossil-fuel-fired power plants [3], and used for boiler tube in the advanced gas-cooled reactors [4, 5] later on. P91 (9Cr-1Mo-V-Nb) steel is mostly used in thermal power plants because of its high strength at high temperatures and it has already about ten years for its practical application. Because of concerns about the age-degradtion in the mechanical properties at elevated temperatures of structural components manufactured, more and more research have been conducted to predict the creep life and residual life of base metal of P91 steel [6].

Recently, continuum damage mechanisms modeling were applied to simulate the creep behavior of modified 9Cr-1Mo steel. Firstly, the Orowan Equation was employed to relate the density of mobile dislocations and their glide velocity. Blum et al. (2002) said that the evolution of dislocations was estimated based on a model proposed [7]. Secondly, Orowan's equation was modified by adding the contributions of influences of various creep damage mechanisms such as solid solution depletion, precipitate coarsening, and cavitation. Creep cavitation (nucleation, growth, and coalesces) is another mechanism which affects creep strain, creep damage and rupture. Yin and Faulkner (2006) [8] advanced the approach of continuum creep damage mechanics modelling of McLean and Dyson (2000) [9] by introducing a specific formula to count for the creep cavity damage for 9Cr alloy. Recently, Yunxiang and Ke Yang (2011) [10] have developed a set of creep damage constitutive equations for P91 alloy under the medium and high stress level, following the similar approach, and they have included strain hardness, solute depletion, and particle coarsening, ignoring the multiplication of mobile dislocations.

In this paper, the objectives are respectively divided into below three aspects:

1. To understand the creep damage, continuum creep damage mechanisms, effectively use the numerical method of Euler integration by software of Excel.

2. To validate a set 3D creep damage constitutive equations generalized from Chen Yunxiang and Ke Yang (CK formulation) for P91 at 600°C under high stress.

3. To extend the uniaxial creep damage constituteve equations of Chen Yunxiang and Ke Yang for P91 at 600°C under plane stress condition and plane strain condition and apply the uniaxial model from high stress for middle and low stress.

2. Continuum creep damage mechanics modeling

The theory of continuum mechanics is the establishment of the basis of the hypothesis of presented continuous research on realizable on law of motion. The theory of continuum mechanics has a great advantage on the mathematical modeling. Therefore, there are many existing with some microscopic defects inside of materials, such as dislocation, inclusions, cavitation at el. In order to describe the effects of the microscopic defects, Kachanov provided the concept of continuous damaged mechanics. The development and evolution of the continuum damage modeling is based on the concept later on. The main microstructural changes of P91 (high Cr) alloy is summarized below:

2.1. Solid solution depletion (Ds)

The alloying elements are added to enhance the resistance for dislocation motion, which increase the creep resistance of the material. The experimental data on 9Cr-1Mo have shown the creep resistance of precipitation is decreasing during Fe2Mo laves phase. During the conditions of long term high temperature and stress exposure, the Mo depletion in the subgrain matrix produced the decreasing of creep resistance. The element of Mo is added to the material in order to increase the mechanism of solid solution strengthening. There is no helping for the dislocations motion decreasing by the large size of the Laves phase of Fe2Mo and the low volume fraction [1]. The large size Laves phases at grain boundaries are the most likely source of cavity nucleation and the intergranular fracture. This mechanism is described the damage evolution of void nucleation and crack formation. According to Y.F. Yin (2006) [8], the damage owing of the solute depletion (Ds) is defined:

$$\text{Ds} = 1-\frac{\overline{Ct}}{Co} \qquad (1)$$

where Co is the initial concentration of solid solution in the matrix, and $\overline{\text{Ct}}$ is their average concentration at time t. In addition, the rate of change of Ds by Dyson's approach follow by Wert-Zener equation [11] is

$$\dot{\text{D}}_s = \text{KsDs}^{1/3}(1-D_s) \qquad (2)$$

where the parameter of constant Ks is defined as:

$$\text{Ks} = [48\pi^2(\text{C}_0-\frac{Ce}{C\beta})^{1/3}\text{n}^{2/3}\text{D}] \qquad (3)$$

where D is the diffusion coefficient of Mo in matrix, the n is the number of precipitate particles and C_β is the concentration of solid solution in the precipitate of Laves. The values of Co and Ce using Thermo-Calc and found Co = 0.56 mol% and Ce= 0.33 mol% [1].

2.2. Precipitate particle coarsening (Dp)

In Dyson's approach, creep damage is owing to particle coarsening which is because of the interparticle spacing of the hardening particles [12]. The modifying of the precipitate coarsening of 9Cr-1Mo steel plays an important role in the creep resistance of this material that Nakajima et al. (2003) studied the coarsening of $M_{23}C_6$ and MX precipitates in T91 steel during creep processes. The stress, which required for dislocations to climb over precipitates, is decreased by the increased interparticle spacing. Following the damage because of the coarsening of $M_{23}C_6$ precipitate particles following Dyson's approach [12], Dp is defined as

$$\text{D}_p = 1-\frac{Po}{Pt} \qquad (4)$$

where Po is the initial particle diameter and Pt is the particle size at any time t. It is a supposed that the coarsening of the particles obeys Livshitz-Wagner equation:

$$r^3-ro^3 = Kt \qquad (5)$$

where the K is a constant determined by diffusivity, interfacial energy, equilibrium solute concentration. The above equation just only could apply to intragranular spherical particles such as MX, but could not for $M_{23}C_6$.

The rate of precipitate particle coarsening is described by

$$\dot{\text{D}}_p = \frac{Kp}{3}(1-Dp)^4 \qquad (6)$$

Where Kp is the rate constant normalized by K and the third power of the initial particle size. As a result, 0< Dp <1.Using a constant Kp and an activation energy parameter Qp, the below equation is shown the relationship of Kp and temperature T.

$$\text{Kp} = \text{K}'_p \exp(-\frac{Q_p}{RT}) \qquad (7)$$

Where the R is the universal gas constant, the T is the temperature; the Qp is an activation energy parameter.

2.3. Void nucleation and crack formation (Dn)

Creep damage of 9Cr-1Mo steel is dependent on different mechanisms such as void nucleation and cavity formation [1]. The damage parameter (Dn), which is for cavity nucleation and growth, is defined as the fraction of grain boundary facets cavitation [8]. The below equation shows the evolution of Dn:

$$\dot{D}_n = \frac{K_n}{\varepsilon_{fu}}\dot{\varepsilon} \qquad (8)$$

Where the ε_{fu} is the uniaxial strain at fracture and the k_n is a limit value blew 1/3. It is mean the damage of cavitation in proportion to strain rate.

Yin and Faulkner [8] proposed the rate of evolution of D_n for P91 alloy as:

$$\dot{D}_n = A' \dot{\varepsilon} \varepsilon^{B'} \quad (9)$$

where the material constant of A and B are a function of temperature and stress. Where A' (A'=AB) and B' (B'=B-1) are large strains and high strain rates, Dn may be equal to or larger than one. This will cause a divergence in the computation at high stress and strain; so, the magnitude of Dn should not reach one, thus 0< Dn <1.

2.4. Dimensionless parameter of strain harding (H)

The model of primary creep [13] is a modification of that suggested by Ion et al. [14]. The dimensionless parameter H is defined as

$$H = \frac{\sigma_i}{\sigma} \quad (10)$$

Where σ is the stress and σi is an internal back stress generated during stress redistribution within strain Harding as inelastic strain accumulates. The H is as follows

$$\dot{H} = \frac{h'}{\sigma}[1 - \frac{H}{H^*}]\dot{\varepsilon} \quad (11)$$

The value of H is ranging from zero to a microstructure dependent maximum of H* (H*<1). The constant h' = EΦ, where E is the Young's modulus and Φ is the volume fraction.

3. Creep damage constitutive equations

3.1. Kachanov and Robotnov's equations

In order to descript the influence of the micro defect for mechanical properties of materials, Kachanov [15] originally put forward the fundamental theory of continuous damaged mechanics, and Rabotnov [16] lead damage fraction (D) to macroscopic constitutive equation in order to represent the damage state of materials characterized by distributed cavities in terms of appropriate mechanical variables (internal state variables), and then to establish mechanical behaviour of damaged materials.

$$\dot{\varepsilon} = \dot{\varepsilon}_0 \left[\frac{\sigma}{\sigma 0(1-D)}\right]^{n} \quad (12)$$

$$\dot{D} = \dot{D}_0 \left[\frac{\sigma}{\sigma 0(1-D)}\right]^{v} \quad (13)$$

where the $\dot{\varepsilon}$ is the creep rate during the process of creep; σ is the applied stress for materials during the process of creep. The symbol with the mark of zero is the initial state; n is the constant of materials and normally named stress exponent. Where $\dot{D}$and $\dot{D}_0$ are respectively meaning the change of creep rate in the materials during the creep processes and the creep rate at the beginning of the creep; the v is the material constant.

3.2. Ion's equations

During the secondary creep, it will occur strain hardening and recovery. Ion et.al [14] leads in the dimensionless parameter of H to the creep constitutive equations in order to present the influence of the working hardening. The creep constitutive equations of Robotnov will be changed and shown in below:

$$\dot{\varepsilon} = \dot{\varepsilon}_0 \left[\frac{\sigma(1-H)}{1-D}\right]^{n} \quad (14)$$

where $\dot{\varepsilon}$ is the creep rate during the process of creep; σ is the applied stress for materials during the process of creep. The symbol with the mark of zero is the initial state; n is the constant of materials and normally named stress exponent; H is the dimensionless parameter.

$$\dot{D} = \dot{D}_0 \left[\frac{\sigma(1-H)}{\sigma 0(1-D)}\right]^{v} \quad (15)$$

where $\dot{D}$and $\dot{D}_0$ are respectively meaning the change of creep rate in the materials during the creep processes and the creep rate at the beginning of the creep; the v is the material constant; H is the dimensionless parameter.

3.3. Dyson's equations

The creep constitutive equation of Robotnov is based on the phenomenological theory. Using the D to indicate many microdefects such as solid solution depletion, precipitate coarsening, void nucleation and crack formation et.al, it is too simple to show the influence of multiple microdefects for the process of creep. Dyson modified the CDM model, and summarized the effects of creep rate including particle coarsening (Dp), solute depletion (Ds), cavity nucleation and growth (Dn) and dislocations (Dd) et.al creep damage mechanisms [2]. The physically based CMD model of Dyson shows below:

$$\dot{\varepsilon} = \dot{\varepsilon}_0 \frac{1}{(1-Ds)(1-Dd)} \times \sinh\left[\frac{\sigma(1-H)}{\sigma 0(1-Dp)(1-Dn)(1-Dcor)(1-Dox)}\right],$$
$$\dot{H} = \frac{h'}{\sigma}(1-\frac{H}{H*})\dot{\varepsilon},$$
$$\dot{D}_s = K_s D_s^{1/3}(1-D_s),$$
$$\dot{D}_p = \frac{Kp}{3}(1-Dp)^4,$$
$$\dot{D}_n = A' \dot{\varepsilon} \varepsilon^{B'}. \quad (16)$$

3.4. Chen Yunxiang and Yang Ke's equations

$$\dot{\varepsilon} = \dot{\varepsilon}_0 \frac{1}{(1-Ds)} \left[\frac{\sigma(1-H)}{\sigma 0(1-Dp)(1-Dn)}\right]^{n},$$
$$\dot{H} = \frac{h'}{\sigma}(1-\frac{H}{H*})\dot{\varepsilon},$$
$$\dot{D}_s = K_s D_s^{1/3}(1-D_s),$$
$$\dot{D}_p = \frac{Kp}{3}(1-Dp)^4,$$
$$\dot{D}_n = A' \dot{\varepsilon} \varepsilon^{B'} \quad (17)$$

where the σ is engineering stress, the $\dot{\varepsilon}$ is creep rate.

4. Methodalogy

Firstly, to collect all the parameters used in the creep modeling for P91 at 600℃ with stress above 130MPa from the paper of Chen Yunxiang and Ke Yang [10]. The software of Excel is mainly computation tool for analysis the creep damage constitutive equations of Chen Yunxiang and Ke Yang for P91 at 600°C under middle and high stress.

Secondly, to develop, validate, and use the Excel software. The computational software for uniaxial case was developed and validated against the published creep strain rate against time under 130 MPa [10]. Further detailed the damage evolutions and their contributions have been obtained.

Thirdly, to generalize 3D version of the creep damage constitutive equations and validate it. The generalization is based on the classical assumption in plasticity/creep theory that the relationship between effective creep strain and effective stress is the same as that of creep strain and stress under uni-axial case. The validation is limited to plane stress and plain strain cases due to the limited experimental data.

Finally, to assess the applicability of the model of Chen Yunxiang and Ke Yang's creep damage constitutive equations for P91 under lower stress level.

5. Development and validation

5.1. Development and validation of the Excel Software for uni-axial Case

The creep constitutive damage equations for P91 steel proposed by Chen Yunxiang and Ke Yang, the uniaxial creep constitutive damage equations is in third part of three. Creep damage constitutive equations.

$\dot{\varepsilon}_0$, H*, h', n, Kp, Ks, A and B are the material constants which are calculated by the experiment date and collected together in Chen yunxiang and Ke Yang's paper from different papers and literatures [10]. The table below is the values and units of those material constants.

Table1. Materials constants

Term	Value	Unit
H*	0.269	
h'	10000	Mpa
Kp	1.5×10^-7	s^{-1}
Ks	5× 10^-8	s^{-1}
A	1.5	
B	2	
A'	2.9	
B'	0.95	
n	10.186	
σ_0	200	Mpa
$\dot{\varepsilon}_0$	5.7×10^-6	s^{-1}

The model of creep damage constitutive equations for P91 at 600°C under uniaxial stress is calculated by the Euler integration method using the science tool of Excel. For example, the parameter H for describing primary creep is solved numerically at each time interval as follows [8]:

$$\Delta H=\frac{h'}{\sigma}\left(1-\frac{H_{i-1}}{H^*}\right)\Delta\varepsilon_{i-1} \quad (18)$$

$$H_i=H_{i-1}+\Delta H \quad (19)$$

The subscript i and i-1 indicate the current and the previous time step respectively. The e uations of H ,$\dot{D}s$, $\dot{D}p$ and $\dot{D}n$ are calculated once by incremental time . hour, the new results of those will be inset into the e uation of ε , it gets the current creep rate and the current strain, and then can be calculate according the below equation:

$$\varepsilon_i=\varepsilon_{i-1}+\dot{\varepsilon}\Delta t \quad (20)$$

Based on the data produced by the software of Excel, the graphs of strain against time and stress against time under different middle and high stress could be drawn out and shown in below:

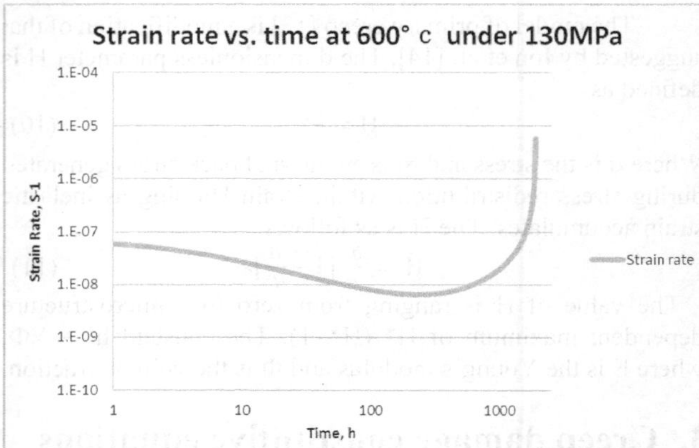

Figure1. The curve of strain rate vs. time at 600°C under 130MPa

From the comparison of the results obtained from the current Excel Software, shown by Figs 1 to 3, with that published in [10], it is concluded that the Excel software has been developed correctly. Furthermore, detailed evolution and damages and their contributions to the creep strain rate and creep strain have been obtained. Due to the limit of space, they will not be reported here.

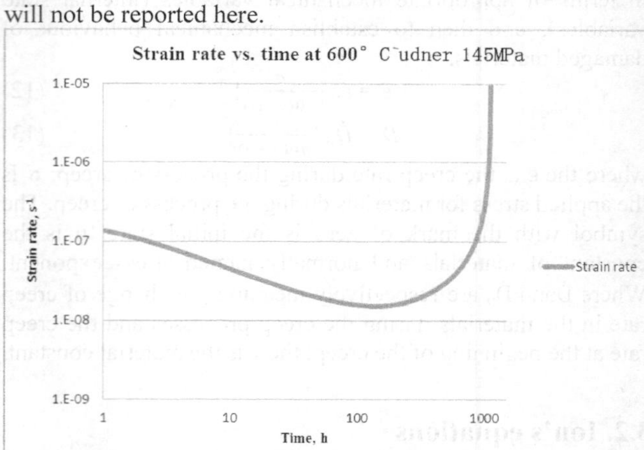

Figure2. The curve of strain vs. time at 600°C under 145MPa

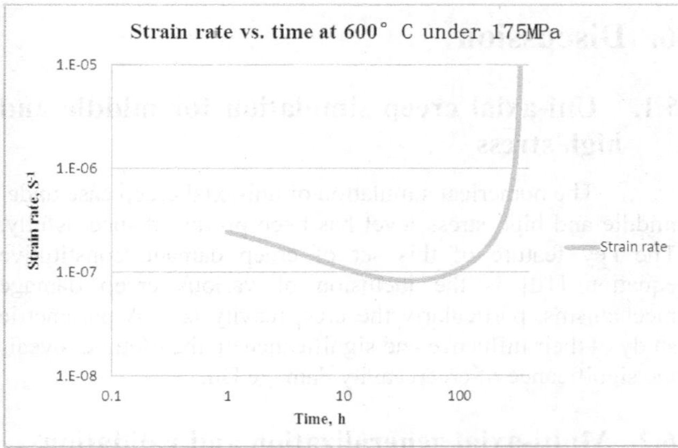

Figure3. The curve of strain vs. time at 600°C under 175MPa

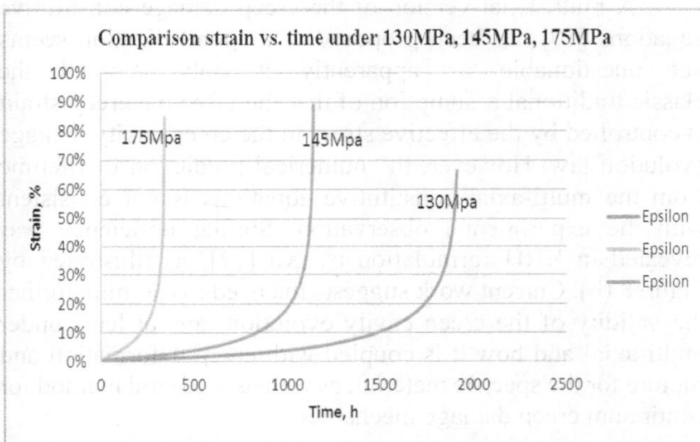

Figure4. The comparison of the curve of strain vs. time at 600°C under different middle and high stress

5.2. 3D generalization and validation

The multi-axial creep damage constitutive equations are based on the uniaxial creep damage constitutive equations of Chen Yunxiang and Ke Yang, the uniaxial stress is replaced by the effective stress (equivalent stress). The multi-axial creep damage constitutive equations are shown below:

$$\dot{\varepsilon} e = \dot{\varepsilon}_0 \frac{1}{(1-Ds)} \left[\frac{\sigma e(1-H)}{\sigma 0(1-Dp)(1-Dn)}\right]^n,$$

$$\dot{H} = \frac{h'}{\sigma e}\left(1-\frac{H}{H*}\right) \dot{\varepsilon}_e,$$

$$\dot{D}_s = KsDs^{1/3}(1-D_s),$$

$$\dot{D}_p = \frac{Kp}{3}(1-Dp)^4,$$

$$\dot{D}_n = A' \dot{\varepsilon} \varepsilon^{B'} \quad (21)$$

For practical validation under plane stress and plain strain conditions, the von Mises stress has been derived explicitly and given bellow.

$$\sigma_e = 1/\sqrt{2}\,[(\sigma_1-\sigma_2)^2+(\sigma_2-\sigma_3)^2+(\sigma_3-\sigma_1)^2]^{1/2} \quad (22)$$

1. To calculate the biaxial stress σ_1 and σ_2 under plane stress, the relationship between σ1 and σ2 is tangent function, and the value of σ_3 is zero.

$$\tan\alpha = \frac{\sigma 1}{\sigma 2};\ \sigma_3 = 0 \quad (23)$$

Submitting the two equations into the equation of the effective stress will get:

$$\sigma_e = \sigma_1 \sqrt{1 + (tan\alpha)^2 - tan\alpha} \quad (24)$$

2. To calculate the biaxial stress σ_1 and σ_2 under plane strain, the relationship between σ1 and σ2 is tangent function, and the value of σ_3 is shown in below equation:

$$\sigma_3 = \frac{\sigma 1+\sigma 2}{2},\ \tan\alpha = \frac{\sigma 1}{\sigma 2} \quad (25)$$

Submitting the two equations into the equation of the effective stress will get:

$$\sigma_e = \sigma_1 \sqrt{3\left(\frac{1}{4} + \frac{K^2}{4} - \frac{K}{2}\right)} \quad (26)$$

The model of multi-axial creep damage constitutive equations is repeatedly operating at interval of every 5°C with the first principle stress calibrated to yield the same failure time with uniaxial model. After the above steps, the result is the isochronous rupture locus shown in below graph; a boundary representation of the stress at any angle that produces the creep failure of the material in the same time period.

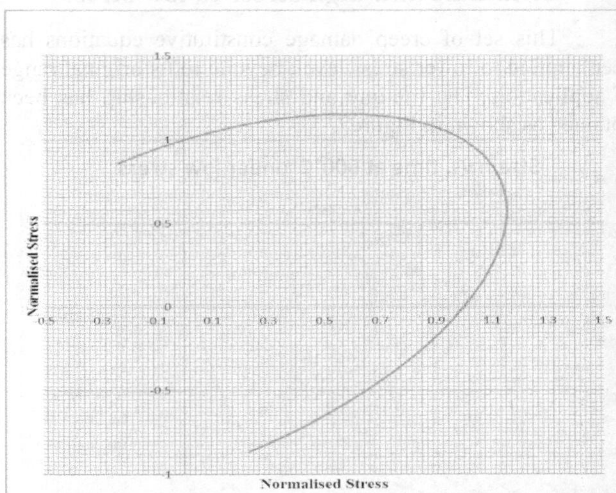

Figure5. Isochronous rupture loci for multi-axial formulation under plane stress condition for P91 at 600°C

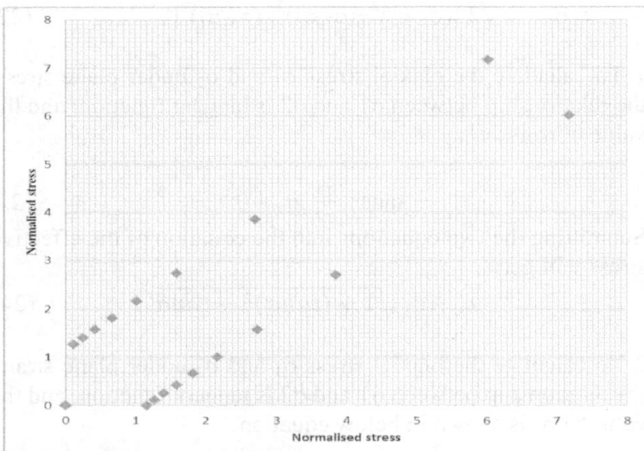

Figure6. Isochronous rupture loci for multi-axial formulation under plane strain condition for P91 at 600℃

Figure6 shows that under high (not even pure) hydrostatic pressure, the creep strength is extremely high, which is not true: the hydrostatic pressure does promote the creep cavity and rupture.

This problem is rooted by the adoption of the classic/traditional assumption that the plastic/creep strain rate is controlled by the effective stress, and the creep damage evolution is controlled by the creep strain.

5.3. Application of the equations of Chen Yunxiang and Ke Yang for P91 at 600℃ for middle and high stress to low stress

This set of creep damage constitutive equations has been applied to lower stress level, beyond to its original range of application. The lifetime and stress relationship has been obtained as shown in Figure7.

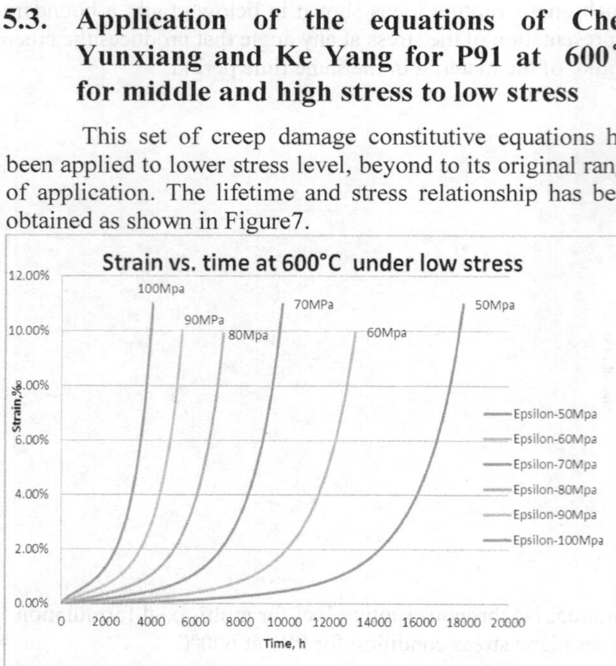

Figure7. The graph of strain against time under low stress

6. Discussion

6.1. Uni-axial creep simulation for middle and high stress

The numerical simulation of uni-axial creep case under middle and high stress level has been produced successfully. The key feature of this set of creep damage constitutive equation [10] is the inclusion of various creep damage mechanisms, particularly the creep cavity law. A parametric study of their influence and significance on the lifetime reveals the significance of creep cavity damage Dn.

6.2. Multi-axial generalization and validation

A multi-axial version of the creep damage constitutive equations [10] has been proposed. This generalization seems not questionable as apparently it only adopted the classic/traditional assumption of that the effective creep strain is controlled by the effective stress in the creep cavity damage evolution law. However, the numerical prediction of lifetime from the multi-axial constitutive equations is not consistent with the experimental observation. Similar deficiency was revealed in KRH formulation by Xu [17], as illustrated by Figure8 (b). Current work suggests the need to examine further the validity of the creep cavity evolution law, at least under multi-axial and how it is coupled with creep deformation and rupture for the specific material, as well as a general method for continuum creep damage mechanics.

6.3. Extension to lower stress level

Due to the apparent success of this type of creep damage constitutive equations (uni-axial version only) under middle and high stress level [9, 8, 10], it is nature to hope that it will work under the lower stress level. This research has examined this. The authors are not ignorant about the breakdown concept and phenomena, generally and specifically to this alloy.

It seems that the shape of the creep curve under lower stress is not the right type as the leading to rupture is not sharp enough to be observed as brittle type.

The detailed results on the predicted individual creep damage evolutions provide the basis for future improvement. Research work on this aspect is ongoing and will be reported in future.

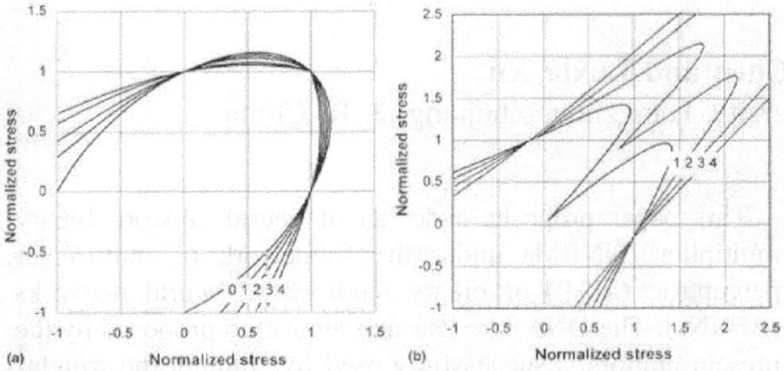

Figure8. (a) Isochronous rupture loci under plane stress conditions, (b) Isochronous rupture loci under plane strain conditions (Q. Xu, 2001) [17]

7. Conclusion

Significant progress has been noted in the developing creep damage constitutive equations, in terms of generic methodology of mechanism-based approach from Dyson's work, or its specific applications to P91 alloy [8, 9, and 10]. One of the key ingredients for the success is the creep cavity damage evolution law. However, the progress is limited to medium and high stress level and uni-axial case.

This research has proposed a multi-axial version creep damage constitutive equations based on the classic/traditional plasticity/creep theory that the creep strain is controlled by the effective stress and bears the same relationship of creep strain and stress under uni-axial case, in the creep cavity damage evolution law. The validation exercise conducted in this research revealed that this approach was not successful. It shows that further research on the precise nature of creep cavity evolution, hope to leading rupture, and the coupling between creep damage and creep deformation.

A simple extension exercise has confirmed that further dedicated research is needed for the developing of creep damage constitutive equation for lower stress level; it cannot be achieved as a byproduct for high stress level.

8. References

[1] M. Basirata, T. Shresthab, G.P. Potirnichea, I. Charitb, K. Rinka, "A study of the creep behavior of modified 9Cr–1Mo steel using continuum-damage modeling", International Journal of Plasticity Volume 37, Pages 95–107, October 2012.

[2] Triratna Shresthaa, Mehdi Basiratb, Indrajit Charita, Gabriel P. Potirnicheb, Karl K. Rinkb, "Creep rupture behavior of Grade 91 steel", Materials Science and Engineering: A, Volume 565, Pages 382–391, 10 March 2013.

[3] I. Charit, K.L. Murty J. Mater., 62, pp. 67–74, 2010.

[4] E. Barker Mater. Sci. Eng., 84, pp. 49–64, 1986.

[5] R.L. Klueh Int. Mater. Rev., 50, pp. 287–310,2005.

[6] T. Watanabe, M. Tabuchi, M. Yamazaki, H. Hongo, and T. Tanabe, International Journal of Pressure Vessels and Piping Volume 83, Issue 1, Pages 63–71, January 2006.

[7] W. Blum, P. Eisenlohr, and F. Breutinger, Understanding creep – a review. Metallurgical and Materials Transactions A33, 291-303, 2002.

[8] Yin Y F, Faulkner R G. Mater Sci Technol, 22: 929; 2006.

[9] McLean M., Dyson B.F., "Modeling the effects of damage and microstructural evolution on the creep behavior of engineering alloys.",Journal of Engineering Materials and Technology, 122, pp. 73–278, 2000.

[10] Chen Yunxiang, Yan Wei, Hu Ping, Shan Yiyin, Yang Ke, "CDM MODELING OF CREEP BEHAVIOR OF T/P91 STEEL UNDER HIGH STRESS", ACTA METALLURGICA, Vol.47, No.11, pp.1372-1377, Nov. 2011.

[11] Wert, C., and Zener, C., J. Appl. Phys., 21, p. 5, 1950.

[12] B. F. Dyson, "Using of CDM in materials modeling and component creep life prediction", J. Pressure Vessel Technol., 122, pp. 281-296, 2000.

[13] B. F. Dyson, "in Creep Behavior of Advanced Materials for the 21st Century", Mishra, R.S., Mukherjee, A. K., and Murty, K.L., eds., TMS Warrendate, PA, 3-12, 1999.

[14] Ion, J. C., Barbosa, A.,Ashby, M. F., Dyson, B.F., and McLean, M., NPL Report DMA (A115), 1986.

[15] Kachanov L. M; "Time of rupture process under deep conditions", Izv. Akad. Nauk. SSSR, 8, pp. 26, 19 8.

[16] Rabotnov, Y. M., 1969, Creep Problems in Structural Members (English translation ed. F.A. Leckie), Ch. 6, Amsterdam: North Holland

[17] Q. Xu, "Creep damage constitutive e uations for multi-axial states of stress for 0.5Cr0.5Mo0.25V ferritic steel at 9 °C", Theoretical and Applied Fracture Mechanics, Volume 36, Issue 2, Pages 99–107, September–October 2001.

Neural Network Binary Multiplier

Han Huang, Fangyue Chen and Luxia Xu
School of Science, Hangzhou Dianzi University, Hangzhou, Zhejiang, P. R. China

Abstract—*Almost all signal processing applications demand a considerable number of multiplications. As addition, multiplication is also the speed-limiting element in the core of arithmetic logic unit (ALU) in a microprocessor. In this paper, the perceptron of artificial neural network (ANN) is used to build a binary multiplier, named neural network binary multiplier(NNBM). It is shown that many advantages of ANN such as synchronous, parallel and fast speed on processing information are taken by the multiplier.*

Keywords: Arithmetic logic unit, multiplication, Perceptron, neural network binary multiplier

1. Introduction

As addition, multiplication is also an essential arithmetic operation for common DSP applications [1–4]. Almost all signal processing applications demand a considerable number of multiplications, and every microprocessor design company always wants a fast multiplier design that will allow their processor to be the fastest on the market. The only problem with this is the fact that the faster the multiplier, the smaller the chip area becomes for other important parts of the microprocessors [5,6].

Usually, a binary multiplier is an electronic circuit used in digital electronics to multiply two binary numbers, for example, a circuit logic diagram of a 2-bit by 2-bit binary multiplier is shown in **Fig. 1**.

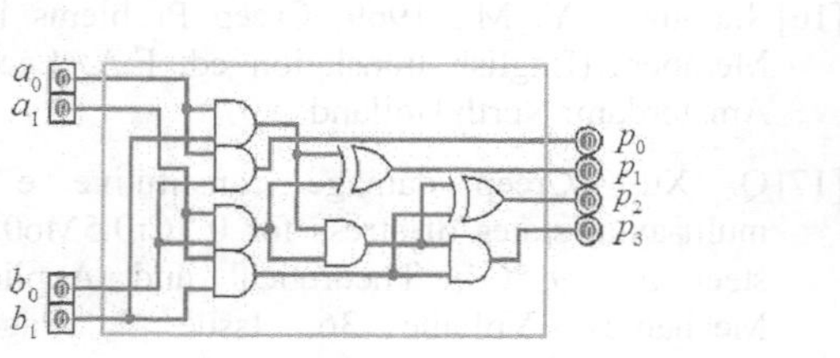

Fig. 1: Logic diagram of a 2-bit by 2-bit binary multiplier.

In order to allow for a faster design that takes up less space, one must find an innovative way to design the circuitry. Fortunately, perceptron of feedforward neural networks, which was inspired by the threshold logic unit neuron model of McCulloch and Pitts, can be used to design a binary multiplier [7,8]. However, it can be very difficult for a designer to find the best design when the number of inputs of the perceptron is a large number [5,6].

This paper proposes a design of neural network binary multiplier (NNBM) under the framework of multi-layer perceptron (MLP) of binary feedforward neural networks (BFNNs). The DNA-like learning algorithm proposed by the present authors is successfully used for training the weight-threshold values of NNBM [9-11].

2. Design of NNBM

2.1 Partial products of multiplication

For two integers n and m ($n \geq m$), let n-bit unsigned binary number $A = (a_{n-1}, a_{n-2}, \cdots, a_0)$ is multiplicand, and m-bit unsigned binary number $B = (b_{m-1}, b_{m-2}, \cdots, b_0)$ is multiplier, then $P = A \cdot B = (p_{n+m-1}, p_{n+m-2}, \cdots, p_0)$ is the $(n+m)$-bit binary product, where

$$\begin{cases} p_i = \mathrm{mod}(\sum_{j+k=i} a_j b_k + c_i, 2) \\ c_{i+1} = [\sum_{j+k=i} a_j b_k / 2] \\ \quad (i = 0, 1, \cdots, m+n-2; \\ \quad j = 0, 1, \cdots, n-1; \\ \quad k = 0, 1, \cdots, m-1) \\ p_{m+n-1} = c_{m+n-1} \end{cases} \tag{1}$$

where $c_0 = 0$ is the initial carry, and $[x]$ represents the first integer larger than x. The multiplication process is shown in **Fig. 2**.

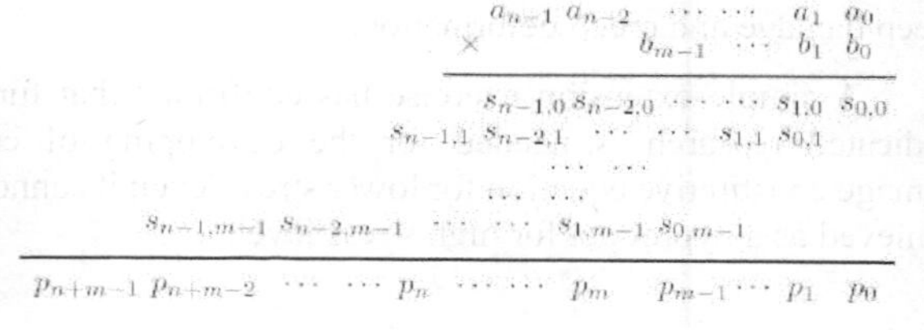

Fig. 2: Multiplication process

Here, $s_{j,k} = a_j b_k (j = 0, 1, \cdots, n-1;\ k = 0, 1, \cdots, m-1)$ are mn partial products in the multiplication process. In fact, in order to obtain the products, each row of the process should be extended into $(m+n)$-bit binary number, and the supplementary numbers are zero. For example, the k-th ($k = 0, 1, \cdots, m-1$) row of the partial products is,

$$s_{j,k} = \begin{cases} a_j b_k & \text{if } 0 \leq j \leq n-1, \\ 0 & \text{if } -k \leq j \leq -1 \\ & \text{and } n \leq j \leq m+n-k-1 \end{cases} \tag{2}$$

A network with inputs $A = (a_{n-1}, a_{n-2}, \cdots, a_0)$ and $B = (b_{m-1}, b_{m-2}, \cdots, b_0)$, and produces outputs $P = A \cdot B = (p_{n+m-1}, p_{n+m-2}, \cdots, p_0)$ is named binary multiplier. If the network is the neural network, then the corresponding multiplier ia called neural network binary multiplier (NNBM).

2.2 Truth table of NNBM

Based on the multiplication process and the partial products of the binary multiplication, the array representation of the truth table of NNBM can be easily obtained as shown in Table 1.

Table 1: Truth table of NNBM

$(a_{n-1}, \cdots, a_0)$	$(b_{m-1}, \cdots, b_0)$	$(p_{n+m-1}, \cdots, p_0)$
$A^{(0)}$	B	$P^{(0)}$
$A^{(1)}$	B	$P^{(1)}$
$\vdots$	$\vdots$	$\vdots$
$A^{(2^n-2)}$	B	$P^{(2^n-2)}$
$A^{(2^n-1)}$	B	$P^{(2^n-1)}$

In Table 1, B is a $(2^m \times m)$-order array:

$$B = \begin{pmatrix} 0\,0 & \cdots & 0\,0 \\ 0\,0 & \cdots & 0\,1 \\ \vdots\,\vdots & \cdots & \vdots\,\vdots \\ 1\,1 & \cdots & 1\,0 \\ 1\,1 & \cdots & 1\,1 \end{pmatrix},$$

the decimal code of the i-th row ($b_{i,0}$, $b_{i,1}$, $\cdots$, $b_{i,m-1}$) of B, $\sum_{j=0}^{m-1} b_{i,j} \cdot 2^{m-1-j}$, is $i(i = 0, 1, \cdots, 2^m - 1)$. $A^{(0)}$ is a ($2^m \times n$)-order zero array, and $A^{(i)}$ is the array with all identical rows, and the decimal code of every row is i ($i = 1, 2, \cdots, 2^n - 1$). At the same time, $P^{(0)}$ is a $(2^m \times (n+m))$-order zero array, and

$$P^{(i+1)} = P^{(i)} + D. \tag{3}$$

Where D is a $2^m \times (n + m)$-order array:

$$D = \begin{pmatrix} 0 & \cdots & 0 & 0\,0 & \cdots & 0\,0\,0 \\ 0 & \cdots & 0 & 0\,0 & \cdots & 0\,0\,1 \\ 0 & \cdots & 0 & 0\,0 & \cdots & 0\,1\,0 \\ \vdots & \vdots & \vdots & \vdots\,\vdots & \vdots & \vdots\,\vdots\,\vdots \\ 0 & \cdots & 0 & 1\,1 & \cdots & 1\,1\,0 \\ 0 & \cdots & 0 & 1\,1 & \cdots & 1\,1\,1 \end{pmatrix}.$$

In D, its first column to the n-th column is $A^{(0)}$, the $(n+1)$ -th column to the last column is B, and the i-th row of $P^{(i)}$ adds to the i-th row of D is the i-th row of $P^{(i+1)}$, the "+" is binary addition. So $P^{(i)}(i = 1, 2, \cdots, 2^n - 1)$ can be obtained by the recursion formula (3). For example,$P^{(1)} = D$, $P^{(2)} = P^{(1)} - D = D + D$, i,e

$$P^{(2)} = \begin{pmatrix} 0\cdots 0 & 00\cdots 000 \\ 0\cdots 0 & 00\cdots 001 \\ 0\cdots 0 & 00\cdots 010 \\ \vdots\;\vdots\;\vdots & \vdots\;\vdots\;\vdots\;\vdots\;\vdots \\ 0\cdots 0 & 11\cdots 110 \\ 0\cdots 0 & 11\cdots 111 \end{pmatrix} + \begin{pmatrix} 0\cdots 0 & 00\cdots 000 \\ 0\cdots 0 & 00\cdots 001 \\ 0\cdots 0 & 00\cdots 010 \\ \vdots\;\vdots\;\vdots & \vdots\;\vdots\;\vdots\;\vdots\;\vdots \\ 0\cdots 0 & 11\cdots 110 \\ 0\cdots 0 & 11\cdots 111 \end{pmatrix}$$

$$= \begin{pmatrix} 0\cdots 0 & 00\cdots 000 \\ 0\cdots 0 & 00\cdots 010 \\ 0\cdots 0 & 00\cdots 100 \\ \vdots\;\vdots\;\vdots & \vdots\;\vdots\;\vdots\;\vdots\;\vdots \\ 0\cdots 1 & 11\cdots 100 \\ 0\cdots 1 & 11\cdots 110 \end{pmatrix}$$

Furthermore, the $2^{(m+n)}$-bit binary outputs of the $n+m$ Boolean functions implementing the $(n+m)$-bit multiplier, say $p_{n+m-1}, p_{n+m-2}, \cdots, p_2, p_1, p_0$ respectively are the last $n + m$ columns in Table 1. For example, the $2^{(m+n)}$-bit binary outputs of p_0 is: $p_0 = (p^{(0)}, p^{(1)}, \cdots, p^{(2^n-1)})$, where $p^{(0)} = (0, 0, \cdots, 0), p^{(1)} = (0, 1, 0, 1, \cdots, 0, 1)$, and if i is an even number, $p^{(i)} = p^{(0)}$, if i is an odd number, $p^{(i)} = p^{(1)}(i = 0, 1, \cdots, 2^n - 1)$. Since $p^{(i+1)}$ can be obtained from $p^{(i)}$ by the recursive formula (3), therefore $p_{n+m-1}, p_{n+m-2}, \cdots, p_2, p_1, p_0$ are called multiplier Boolean functions (MBFs).

2.3 Truth table and Boolean functions of 3-bit by 2-bit NNBM

For the specific input number of a NNBM, its truth table and Boolean functions are easily determined. The truth table of the 3-bit by 2-bit NNBM is shown in Table 2.

It generates five Boolean functions p_0, p_1, p_2, p_3 and p_4, each holds 2^5 binary output symbols.

$$\begin{aligned} p_0 &= 0000\ 0101\ 0000\ 0101\ 0000\ 0101\ 0000\ 0101, \\ p_1 &= 0000\ 0011\ 0101\ 0110\ 0000\ 0011\ 0101\ 0110, \\ p_2 &= 0000\ 0000\ 0011\ 0010\ 0101\ 0101\ 0110\ 0111, \\ p_3 &= 0000\ 0000\ 0000\ 0001\ 0011\ 0011\ 0010\ 0010, \\ p_4 &= 0000\ 0000\ 0000\ 0000\ 0000\ 0000\ 0001\ 0001. \end{aligned}$$

3. Decomposition of MBF and Perceptron Implementing NNBM

It was known that all Boolean functions can be divided into two classes: linearly separable Boolean function (LSBF) and non-linearly separable Boolean function (non-LSBF). Based on the criterion for LSBF [9-11], the MBF p_0 and p_4 are linearly separable, and the MBF p_1, p_2 and p_3 are non-linearly separable. Furthermore, any non-LSBF can be decomposed as the logic $\oplus$ (XOR) operation of a sequence of LSBFs. By using the DNA-like algorithm in [9,10], it is easily to know that p_1, p_2 and p_3 can be decomposed as:

Table 2: Truth table of 3-bit by 2-bit NNBM

a_2, a_1, a_0	b_1, b_0	p_4, p_3, p_2, p_1, p_0
0 0 0	0 0	0 0 0 0 0
0 0 0	0 1	0 0 0 0 0
0 0 0	1 0	0 0 0 0 0
0 0 0	1 1	0 0 0 0 0
0 0 1	0 0	0 0 0 0 0
0 0 1	0 1	0 0 0 0 1
0 0 1	1 0	0 0 0 1 0
0 0 1	1 1	0 0 0 1 1
0 1 0	0 0	0 0 0 0 0
0 1 0	0 1	0 0 0 1 0
0 1 0	1 0	0 0 1 0 0
0 1 0	1 1	0 0 1 1 0
0 1 1	0 0	0 0 0 0 0
0 1 1	0 1	0 0 0 1 1
0 1 1	1 0	0 0 1 1 0
0 1 1	1 1	0 1 0 0 1
1 0 0	0 0	0 0 0 0 0
1 0 0	0 1	0 0 1 0 0
1 0 0	1 0	0 1 0 0 0
1 0 0	1 1	0 1 1 0 0
1 0 1	0 0	0 0 0 0 0
1 0 1	0 1	0 0 1 0 1
1 0 1	1 0	0 1 0 1 0
1 0 1	1 1	0 1 1 1 1
1 1 0	0 0	0 0 0 0 0
1 1 0	0 1	0 0 1 1 0
1 1 0	1 0	0 1 1 0 0
1 1 0	1 1	1 0 0 1 0
1 1 1	0 0	0 0 0 0 0
1 1 1	0 1	0 0 1 1 1
1 1 1	1 0	0 1 1 1 0
1 1 1	1 1	1 0 1 0 1

$$\begin{aligned}
P_1 &= 00000011010101100000001101010110 \\
&= 00111111011111110011111101111111 \\
&\oplus 00111111001111110011111100111111 \\
&\oplus 00000011000101110000001100010111 \\
&\oplus 00000000000000010000000000000001, \\
P_2 &= 00000000011001001010101010100111 \\
&= 00000000011001101110111111111111 \\
&\oplus 00000000000100010011001111111111 \\
&\oplus 00000000000100000001000101110111 \\
&\oplus 00000000000000000000000000010000, \\
P_3 &= 00000000000000010011001100100010 \\
&= 00000000000000010011001100110011 \\
&\oplus 00000000000000000000000000010001.
\end{aligned}$$

Perceptron, inspired by the threshold logic unit neuron model of McCulloch and Pitts, introduced by Rosenblatt, is one of the most important and significant aspects of ANN [7,8].

It was also known that LSBF can be realized by an single-layer perceptron (SLP), and non-LSBF needs MLP to realize it. Furthermore, let $(u_1, u_2, u_3, u_4, u_5) = (a_2, a_1, a_0, b_1, b_0)$ and by using the DNA-like learning algorithm [9-11], the weights-threshold values of a perceptron is easy to be determined. Thus, all SLP and MLP implementing p_0, p_4, p_1, p_2 and p_3 can be obtained as follows.

The SLP implementing p_0 is

$$y = f(2u_3 + 2u_5 - 3) \tag{4}$$

The SLP implementing p_4 is

$$y = f(2u_1 + 2u_2 + 2u_4 + 2u_5 - 7) \tag{5}$$

The MLP implementing p_1 is

$$\begin{cases} y_1^{(1)} = f(2u_2 + 4u_3 + 4u_4 + 2u_5 - 3) \\ y_2^{(1)} = f(2u_3 + 2u_4 - 1) \\ y_3^{(1)} = f(2u_2 + 4u_3 + 4u_4 + 2u_5 - 7) \\ y_4^{(1)} = f(2u_2 + 2u_3 + 2u_4 + 2u_5 - 7) \\ \quad y = f(2y_1^{(1)} - 2y_2^{(1)} + 2y_3^{(1)} - 2y_4^{(1)} - 1) \end{cases} \tag{6}$$

The MLP implementing p_2 is

$$\begin{cases} y_1^{(2)} = f(6u_1 + 4u_2 + 4u_4 + 2u_5 - 7) \\ y_2^{(2)} = f(6u_1 + 4u_2 + 4u_4 + 2u_5 - 9) \\ y_3^{(2)} = f(6u_1 + 4u_2 - 2u_3 + 4u_4 + 4u_5 - 11) \\ y_4^{(2)} = f(2u_1 + 2u_2 - 2u_3 + 2u_4 + 2u_5 - 7) \\ \quad y = f(2y_1^{(2)} - 2y_2^{(2)} + 2y_3^{(2)} - 2y_4^{(2)} - 1) \end{cases} \tag{7}$$

The MLP implementing p_3 is

$$\begin{cases} y_1^{(3)} = f(6u_1 + 2u_2 + 2u_3 + 8u_4 + 2u_5 - 13) \\ y_2^{(3)} = f(2u_1 + 2u_2 + 2u_4 + 2u_5 - 7) \\ \quad y = f(2y_1^{(2)} - 2y_2^{(2)} - 1) \end{cases} \tag{8}$$

Where f is the first-order jump function defined by

$$f(x) = sign(x) = \begin{cases} 1 & \text{if } x > 0, \\ 0 & \text{if } x \leq 0 \end{cases} \tag{9}$$

Summarizing (4) to (8), the networks of 3-bit by 2-bit NNBM is obtained **Fig. 3**.

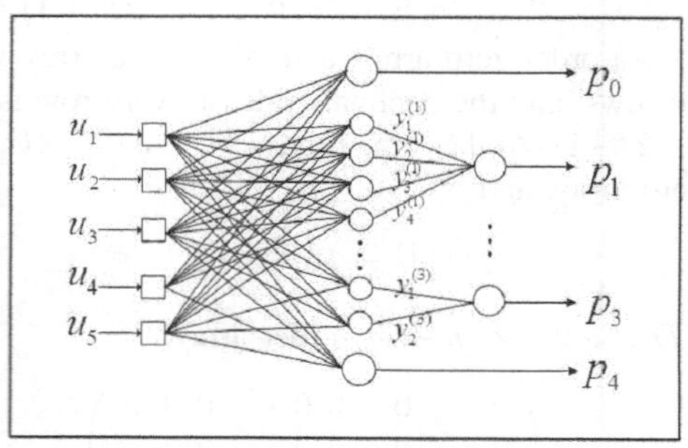

Fig. 3: MLPs implementing NNRM

4. Remarks and Conclusions

As stated in the previous section, an NNBM with n-bit by m-bit inputs will receives $n + m$ inputs and generates $n + m$ MBFs as outputs, and the serial MBFs is called to have implemented the $(n + m)$-bit multiplier.

The efficiency of NNBM and digital multiplier can be evaluated by comparing the number of hidden neurons of the MLPs with the number of product terms required to implement the MBFs [12].

According to formula (1), it is easy to know that $p_i = mod(\sum_{j+k=i} a_j b_k + c_i, 2)$, and $c_{i+1} = [\sum_{j+k=i} a_j b_k/2]$ $(i = 0,1,2,3;\ j = 0,1,2;\ k = 0,1)$, then the number of product terms of 3-bit by 2-bit digital multiplier is $2 \times 3 \times 2 \times 4 = 48$. However, the number of hidden layer neurons of the MLPs is only 10.

The successful design of computational systems is often predicated on the realization of fast multiplication in digital or analog hardware. A key design issue is the tradeoff between speed, complexity, and chip area. With this in mind and some advantages of ANN such as synchronous, parallel and fast speed, an innovative fast neural network multiplier has been designed in this paper. Similarly, in the future, other combinational logic circuits such as selector, code translator, and so on, can be considered by using ANN. They will be able to perform various real-world applications in the microprocessor technology.

Acknowledgment

This research was jointly supported by NSFC (Grants 11171084 and 60872093) and the Hong Kong Research Grants Council (Grant No. CityU117/10).

References

[1] R. Guanasekaran, "A Fast Serial-Parallel Binary Multiplier," *IEEE Trans. Computers*, vol. 34, pp. 741–744, 1985.

[2] H. M. A. Andree, G. T. Barkema, W. Lourens, and A. Taal, "A Comparison Study of Binary Feedforward Neural Networks and Digital Circuits", *Neural Network*, vol. 6, pp. 785–790, 1993.

[3] M. C. Wen, S. J. Wang, Y. N. Lin, "Low-power Parallel Multiplier with Column Bypassing", *Electronics Letters*, vol. 41, pp. 581–583, 2005.

[4] J. D. Moni, A. K. Priyadharsini, *Design of Low-Power and High Performance Radix-4 Multiplier*, New York, U.S.A.: IEEE Press, 2012.

[5] D. C. Biederman, E. Ososanya, "Capacity of Several Neural Networks with Respect to Digital Adder and Multiplier", in *Proc. Southeastern Symposium on System Theory'27*, 1995, p. 305–308.

[6] D. C. Biederman, E. Ososanya, "Design of a Neural Network-based Digital Multiplier", in *Proc. Southeastern Symposium on System Theory'29*, 1997, p. 320–326.

[7] W. S. McCulloch, W. Pitts, "A Logical Calculus of the Ideas Immanent in Nervous Activity". *Bulletin of Math, Biophysics*, vol. 5, pp. 115–133, 1943.

[8] F. Rosenblatt, "The Perceptron: a Probabilistic Model for Information Storage and Organization in the Brain", *Cornell Aeronautical Laboratory, Psychological Review*, vol. 65, pp. 386–408, 1958.

[9] F. Y. Chen, G. R. Chen, G. L. He, X. B. Xu and Q. B. He, "Universal Perceptron and DNA-like Learning Algorithm of Binary Neural Networks: LSBF and PBF Implementation", *IEEE Trans. Neural Netw.*, vol. 20, pp. 1645–1658, 2009.

[10] F. Y. Chen, G. R. Chen, Q. B. He, G. L. He, and X. B. Xu, "Universal Perceptron and DNA-like Learning Algorithm of Binary Neural Networks: Non-LSBF Implementation", *IEEE Trans. Neural Netw.*, vol. 20, pp. 1293–1301, 2009.

[11] F. Y. Chen, G. L. He, G. R. Chen, "Realization of Boolean Functions via CNN: Mathematical Theory, LSBF and Template Design", *IEEE Trans. Circ. Syst. I*, vol. 53, pp. 2203–2213, 2006.

[12] H. M. A. Andree, G. T. Barkema, W. Lourens, and A. Taal, "A Comparison Study of Binary Feedforward Neural Networks and Digital Circuits", *IEEE Trans, Neural Netw.*, vol. 6, pp. 785–790, 1993.

The development of finite element analysis software for creep damage analysis

D. Liu[1], Q. Xu[1], Z. Lu[2], D. Xu[1], F. Tan[1]
[1]School of Science and Engineering, Teesside University, Middlesbrough, TS1 3BA, UK
[2]School of Computing and Engineering, University of Huddersfield, Huddersfield, HD1 3DA, UK

Abstract - *The development and application of computational creep damage is very active among research community and high temperature industry. This paper presents a development and preliminary validation of in-house finite element analysis software for creep damage analysis. The Fortran 90 and existing finite element library were adopted and used in the software development. The validation case study was conducted and reported, using uni-axial creep case.*

Keywords: Computational Creep Damage Mechanics; FE Algorithm; Non-linear Material; Validation

1 Introduction

This paper reports a development and preliminary validation of in-house finite element software for creep damage analysis. Creep damage mechanics has been developed and applied for the analysis of creep deformation and the simulation for the creep damage evolution and rupture of high temperature components [1]. The computational capability relies on the availability of a computational tool and a set of creep damage constitutive equations which can accurately depicts the complex phenomena. This paper addresses the former.

The need of such computational capability and the justification for developing in-house software was conducted and reported in the early stage of this research [2, 3]. Essentially, the creep damage problem is of time dependent, non-linear material behavior, and multi-material zones. The standard software does not provide the computational capability to simulate the tertiary creep stage readily without the development of complicated material user subroutine. The computational capability can only be obtained by either the development and use of special subroutine in junction with standard commercial software such as ABAQUS and ANSYS or the development and use of dedicated in-house software, each has its own advantages and disadvantages [2]. Hyde [4] and Hayhurst [5] have reported the development and the use of their in-house software for creep damage analysis; furthermore, Ling has presented a detailed discussion and use of Runge-Kutta type integration algorithm [6]. On the other hand, it is noted that Xu revealed the deficiency of KRH formulation and proposed a new formulation for the multi-axial generalization in the development of creep damage constitutive equations [7]. The new creep damage constitutive equations for low Cr-Mo steel and for high Cr-Mo steel are under developing by colleagues in this research group [8, 9].

The purpose of this paper is to present the finite element method based on CDM to design FE software for creep damage mechanics. More specifically, it reports the structure of the new FE software and the existing FE library applied in obtaining such computational tool via an approach for stress and field variable updating, and preliminary validation of current version of such software via a uni-axial tension model. The contribution of this paper is to provide a new version of in-house software to solve the whole process of all the three stages of creep deformation and damage problem.

2 The finite element method based on CDM

2.1 The Continuum Damage Mechanics (CDM)

The continuum damage mechanics (CDM) used the concept of creep damage as internal variable [10, 11, 12]. One of the features of CDM is phenomenological and the damage parameter can in this context represent creep damage. In creep damage mechanics, the material gets damaged does not essential has to be understood in detail and the damage should be considered in analysis [13].

The creep deformation is typically divided into primary, secondary and tertiary stages. Initially, the characteristics of the primary-secondary (steady state) creep deformation behavior are observed by simple experiments, but later the mathematical description of tertiary creep through the use of CDM.

The finite element technique combined with continuum damage mechanics has been testified to be an efficient tool in assessing the performance of the structural components [14-16]. In many commercial finite element packages, the user-routines can be written for implemented taking into account one or more damage mechanisms [17].

Rupture processes can also be investigated by use of CDM approach [18]. Some investigations of creep crack initiation and growth in notched specimens have been performed with promising results [19, 20].

2.2 The general structure of the finite element software

The structure of developing in-house finite element software for creep damage analysis is listed in Figure 1.

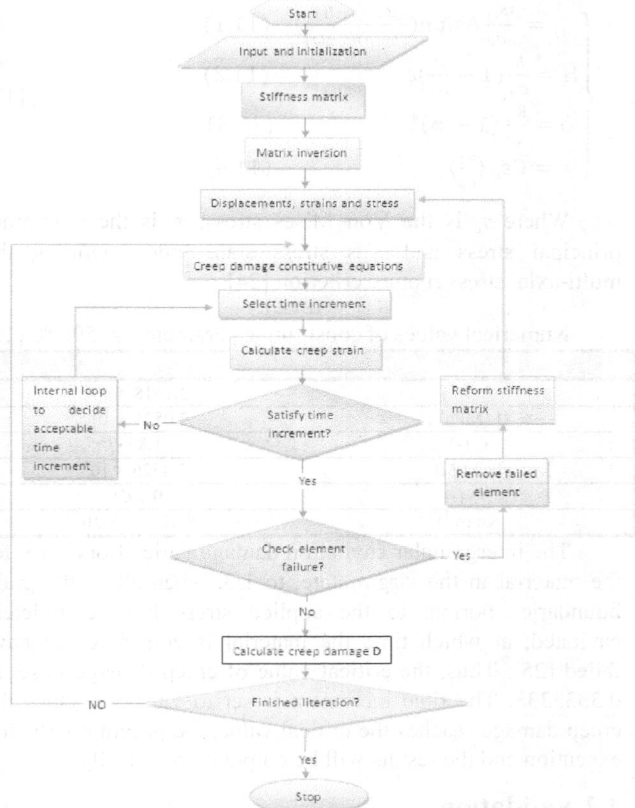

Fig. 1. The flow diagram of the structure of the new finite element software

The steps for the development of finite element software can be summarized in:

1. Input the definition of a specific FE model including nodes, element, material property, boundary condition, as well as the computational control parameters
2. Calculate the initial elastic stress and strain
3. Integrate the constitutive equation and update the field variables such as creep strain, damage, stress; the time step is controlled
4. Remove the failed element [21] and update the stiffness matrix
5. Stop execution and output results

2.3 The integration of creep damage constitutive equation

The FEA solution critically depends on the selection of the size of time steps associated with an appropriate integration method. Some integration method has been reviewed in previous work [3]. In the current version, Euler forward integration subroutine, developed by colleague [22], was adopted here for simplicity. More sophisticated Runge-Kutta type integration scheme will be adopted and explored in future.

2.4 The finite element algorithm for updating stress

The Absolute Method [23] has been given for the solution of the structural creep damage problems. The principle of virtual work applied to the boundary value problem is given:

$$\mathbf{P_{load}} = [\mathbf{K_v}] * \mathbf{TOTD} - \mathbf{P_c} \tag{1}$$

Where $\mathbf{P_{load}}$ is applied force vector, and $[\mathbf{K_v}]$ is the global stiffness matrix, which is assembled by the element stiffness matrices $[\mathbf{K_m}]$; **TOTD** is the global vector of the nodal displacements and $\mathbf{P_c}$ is the global creep force vector.

$$[\mathbf{K_m}] = \iint [\mathbf{B}]^T [\mathbf{D}] [\mathbf{B}] \, d_x d_y \tag{2}$$

The **[B]** and **[D]** represent the strain-displacement and the stress-strain matrices respectively.

$$\mathbf{TOTD} = [\mathbf{K_v}]^{-1} * (\mathbf{P_{load}} + \mathbf{P_c}) \tag{3}$$

The initial $\mathbf{P_c}$ is zero and the Choleski Method [14] is used for the inverse of the global stiffness matrix $[\mathbf{K_v}]$. By giving the $\mathbf{P_{load}}$, the elastic strain $\boldsymbol{\varepsilon_{ek}}$ and the elastic stress $\boldsymbol{\sigma_{ek}}$ for each element can be obtained:

$$\boldsymbol{\varepsilon_{ek}} = [\mathbf{B}] * \mathbf{ELD} \tag{4}$$

$$\boldsymbol{\sigma_{ek}} = [\mathbf{D}] * \boldsymbol{\varepsilon_{ek}} \tag{5}$$

The element node displacement **ELD** can be found from the global displacement vector and the creep strain rate $\boldsymbol{\varepsilon_{ckrate}}$ for each element can be obtained by substituting the element elastic stress into the creep damage constitutive equations. The creep strain can be calculated:

$$\varepsilon_{ck(t+\Delta t)} = \varepsilon_{cK(t)} + \varepsilon_{cKrate} * \Delta t \tag{6}$$

The node creep force vectors for each element are given by:

$$\mathbf{P_{ck}} = [\mathbf{B}]^T [\mathbf{D}] * \boldsymbol{\varepsilon_{cK}} \tag{7}$$

The node creep force vector $\mathbf{P_{ck}}$ can be assembled into the global creep force vector $\mathbf{P_c}$ and the $\mathbf{P_c}$ is used to up-date equation (1). Thus, the elastic strain can be updated:

$$\boldsymbol{\varepsilon_{totk}} = [\mathbf{B}] * \mathbf{ELD} = \boldsymbol{\varepsilon_{ek}} + \boldsymbol{\varepsilon_{ck}} \tag{8}$$

$$\boldsymbol{\varepsilon_{ek}} = [\mathbf{B}] * \mathbf{ELD} - \boldsymbol{\varepsilon_{ck}} \tag{9}$$

Where the $\boldsymbol{\varepsilon_{totk}}$ and $\boldsymbol{\varepsilon_{ck}}$ are represent the total strain and creep strain for each element respectively; and the elastic strain $\boldsymbol{\varepsilon_{ek}}$ is used to up-date the equation (5).

3 The application of existing finite element library

In the development of this software, the existing FE library and subroutines such as [23] was used in programming. The subroutines can perform the tasks of finite element meshing, computing and integrating the element matrices, assembling element matrices into system matrices and carrying out appropriate equilibrium, eigenvalue or propagation calculations.

3.1 The finite element meshing

The existing subroutines [23] are available in performing the mesh of element for the triangles, quadrilaterals and hexahedra "bricks". For example, the subroutine geometry_3tx (iel, nxe, aa, bb, coord, num) can form the coordinates and node vector for a rectangular mesh of uniform 3-node triangles. More specifically, it is counting in the x-direction and local numbering clockwise. For the quadrilateral elements and the hexahedra "bricks" elements, the subroutine geometry_4qx and the subroutine geometry_8bxz are also available in [23].

3.2 The element stiffness matrix assembly

The special purpose subroutines such as subroutine formnf, subroutine formkb, subroutine formku, and subroutine fsparv can assembly the individual element matrices to form the global matrices. The selection of element stiffness matrix subroutine is according with the definition of the geometrical details, especially in the nodal coordinates of each element and the element's place in overall node numbering scheme. More details see [23].

3.3 The solution of equilibrium equation for creep problem

Direct solution methods and iterative solution methods have been used in solving the creep problem [13]. In direct solution method, the subroutine sparin and subroutine spabac based on Cholesky direct solution method are used to solve the sets of linear algebraic equations [23]. In iterative solution method, the subroutine cholin and subroutine chobac based on Jacobi iterative solution methods can be used in programming.

4 Validation of finite element software and FE model

4.1 The creep constitutive equation

Creep damage constitutive equations are proposed to depict the behaviors of material during creep damage (deformation and rupture) process, especially for predicting the lifetime of materials, within the CDM-based numerical computational tool. Kachanov-Rabatnov-Hayhurst (KRH) constitutive equations [24] are introduced as followed in details and used in current program.

– Uni-axial form

$$\begin{cases} \dot{\varepsilon} = A\sinh\left(\frac{B\sigma(1-H)}{(1-\varphi)(1-\omega)}\right) & (10.1)\\ \dot{H} = \frac{h}{\sigma}\left(1-\frac{H}{H^*}\right)\dot{\varepsilon} & (10.2)\\ \dot{\varphi} = \frac{K_C}{3}(1-\varphi)^4 & (10.3)\\ \dot{\omega} = C\dot{\varepsilon}^* & (10.4) \end{cases} \quad (10)$$

Where A, B C, h, H* and Kc are material parameters. H (0<H< H*) indicates strain hardening during primary creep, φ (0< φ < 1) describe the evolution of spacing of the carbide precipitates [24].

– Multi-axial form

$$\begin{cases} \dot{\varepsilon_{ij}} = \frac{3S_{ij}}{2\sigma_e}\mathrm{Asinh}\left(\frac{B\sigma_e(1-H)}{(1-\varphi)(1-\omega)}\right) & (11.1)\\ \dot{H} = \frac{h}{\sigma_e}\left(1-\frac{H}{H^*}\right)\dot{\varepsilon} & (11.2)\\ \dot{\varphi} = \frac{K_C}{3}(1-\varphi)^4 & (11.3)\\ \dot{} = C\dot{\varepsilon_e}\left\langle\frac{\sigma_1}{\sigma_e}\right\rangle & (11.4) \end{cases} \quad (11)$$

Where σ_e is the Von Mises stress, σ_1 is the maximum principal stress and is stress state index defining the multi-axial stress rupture criterion [24].

TABLE I.
Numerical values of constitutive parameters at 590 °C [25]

Coefficient	Value
A (h^{-1})	2.1618×10^{-9}
B (MPa^{-1})	2.0524×10^{-1}
C (-)	1.8537
h(MPa)	2.4326×10^{5}
H* (-)	0.5929
Kc (h^{-1})	9.2273×10^{5}

The intergranular cavitation damage varies from zero, for the material in the virgin state, to 1/3, when all of the grain boundaries normal to the applied stress have completely cavitated, at which time the material is considered to have failed [25]. Thus, the critical value of creep damage is set to 0.3333333. The time increment is set to 1.0 hour. Once the creep damage reaches the critical value, the program will stop execution and the results will be output automatically.

4.2 Validation

Preliminary validation of such software was performed and it was conducted via a two- dimensional uni-axial tension model given bellow.

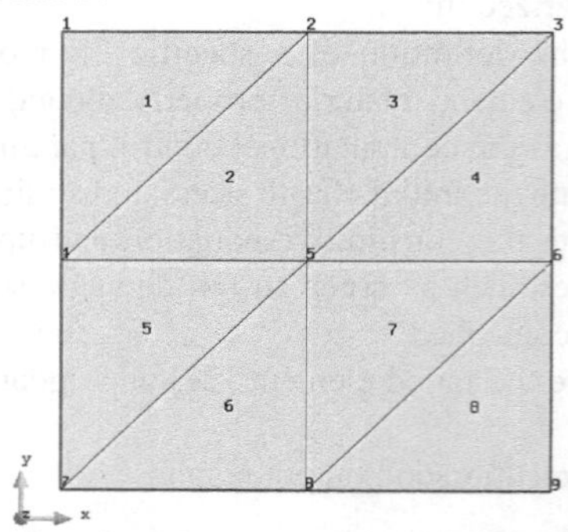

Fig. 2. The uni-axial tension model and boundary conditions

The length of a side is set to 1 meter.

The Young's modulus and Poisson's ratio are set to 1000000 KN/m^2 and 0.3 respectively.

A uniformly distributed load 40KN/m was applied on the top line of this uni-axial tension model. The boundary constraint conditions are given in Table II.

TABLE II.
The Numerical boundary constraint

Node number	Constraint in x direction	Constraint in y direction	Load in x direction	Load in y direction
Node No.1	shut	open	0 KN/m^2	10 KN/m^2
Node No.2	open	open	0 KN/m^2	20 KN/m^2
Node No.3	open	open	0 KN/m^2	10 KN/m^2

Node No.4	shut	open	0 KN/m^2	0 KN/m^2
Node No.5	open	open	0 KN/m^2	0 KN/m^2
Node No.6	open	open	0 KN/m^2	0 KN/m^2
Node No.7	shut	shut	0 KN/m^2	0 KN/m^2
Node No.8	open	shut	0 KN/m^2	0 KN/m^2
Node No.9	open	shut	0 KN/m^2	0 KN/m^2

The theoretical stress in Y direction can be found as:

$$\sigma = \frac{P}{A} = \frac{40}{1.0} = 40\ KN/m^2$$

The stress in X direction should be zero.

These stress values should remain the same throughout the creep test up to failure.

Using the theoretical stress value into uni-axial version of creep constitutive equations, the theoretical rupture time, creep strain rate, creep strain and damage can be obtained by a excel program [26] and some of them are shown in Table III.

TABLE III.

The theoretical rupture time, creep strain rate, creep strain and damage obtained by excel program

Rupture time	Creep strain rate	Creep strain	Creep damage
104062	0.000065438	0.179934333	0.33333335

5 FE results and discussion

TABLE IV.

The initial elastic stress obtained from FE software

Element number	Stress in x-direction	Stress in y-direction
Element No.1	-0.3388E-06	0.4000E+02
Element No.2	-0.3388E-06	0.4000E+02
Element No.3	-0.3388E-06	0.4000E+02
Element No.4	-0.3388E-06	0.4000E+02
Element No.5	-0.3388E-06	0.4000E+02
Element No.6	-0.3388E-06	0.4000E+02
Element No.7	-0.3388E-06	0.4000E+02
Element No.8	-0.3388E-06	0.4000E+02

The initial elastic stress and the stress involving creep deformation and stress updating are shown in Table IV and Table V, respectively. Both confirmed the uniform distribution of stresses, and the values of stress in Y direction obtained from FE software are correct, and the stress in X direction is negligible.

TABLE V.

The stress obtained from FE software with the stress update program

Element number	Stress in x-direction	Stress in y-direction
Element No.1	-0.3388E-06	0.4000E+02
Element No.2	-0.3388E-06	0.4000E+02
Element No.3	-0.3388E-06	0.4000E+02
Element No.4	-0.3388E-06	0.4000E+02
Element No.5	-0.3388E-06	0.4000E+02
Element No.6	-0.3388E-06	0.4000E+02
Element No.7	-0.3388E-06	0.4000E+02
Element No.8	-0.3388E-06	0.4000E+02

TABLE VI.

Rupture time, creep strain rate, creep strain and damage obtained from FE software at failure

Element number	Rupture time	Strain rate	Creep strain	Creep damage
Element No.1	0.1040E+06	0.6540E-04	0.1798E+00	0.3334E+00
Element No.2	0.1040E+06	0.6540E-04	0.1798E+00	0.3334E+00
Element No.3	0.1040E+06	0.6540E-04	0.1798E+00	0.3334E+00
Element No.4	0.1040E+06	0.6540E-04	0.1798E+00	0.3334E+00
Element No.5	0.1040E+06	0.6540E-04	0.1798E+00	0.3334E+00
Element No.6	0.1040E+06	0.6540E-04	0.1798E+00	0.3334E+00
Element No.7	0.1040E+06	0.6540E-04	0.1798E+00	0.3334E+00
Element No.8	0.1040E+06	0.6540E-04	0.1798E+00	0.3334E+00

TABLE VII.

The percentage error

$Rupture\ time\ percentage\ error = \lvert\frac{104000-104062}{104062}\rvert \times 100 = 0.0596\%$
$Strain\ rate\ percentage\ error = \lvert\frac{0.0000654-0.000065438}{0.000065438}\rvert \times 100 = 0.0581\%$
$Creep\ strain\ percentage\ error = \lvert\frac{0.1798-0.179934333}{0.179934333}\rvert \times 100 = 0.0747\%$
$Damage\ percentage\ error = \lvert\frac{0.3334-0.33333335}{0.33333335}\rvert \times 100 = 0.02\%$

Other results are shown in Tables VI to VII. They show the results obtained from the FE software do agree with the expected theoretical values and the percentage errors are negligible.

In the current version, Euler forward integration subroutine, developed by colleague [22] was adopted here. Rupture time, strain rate, creep strain and damage obtained from FE software have been revealed that have a good agreement with the theoretical values obtained from the excel program. Work is ongoing in this area and will be reported in future

6 Conclusion

This paper reports the finite element method based on CDM to design FE software for creep damage mechanics. It presents the structure of the new FE software and the use of existing FE library in obtaining such computational tool via an approach for stress and field variable updating. It further investigates preliminary validation of current version of such software via a uni-axial tension model.

The immediate future development work includes: 1) multi-materials; 2) implementing R-K integration scheme; 3) intelligent and practical control of time step; 4) removal of failed element and update stiffness matrix; and 5) further validation.

7 Reference

[1] J. Lemaitre and J. L. Chaboche, "Mechanics of Solid Materials", Cambridge University Press, 1st ed. Cambridge, 1994.

[2] D. Liu, Q. Xu and Z. Lu, "The review of computational FE software for creep damage mechanics," Advanced Materials Research, vol. 510, pp. 495-499, 2012.

[3] D. Liu, Q. Xu and Z. Lu, "Research in the development of computational FE software for creep damage mechanics," 18th International Conference on Automation and Computing (ICAC), Loughborough University, Leicestershire, 8th September 2012.

[4] *FE-DAMAGE User's Manual*, 1st ed., University of Nottingham, Nottingham, UK, 1994.

[5] D. R., Hayhurst and A. J., Krzeczkowski, "Numerical solution of creep problems", *Compute. Methods App. Mech. Eng.*, vol. 20, pp.151-171 (1979).

[6] X. Ling, S. T. Tu and J. M. Gong, "Application of Runge-Kutta-Merson algorithm for creep damage analysis", *International Journal of Pressure Vessels and Piping*, vol. 77, pp. 243-248, 2000.

[7] Q. Xu, "Creep damage constitutive equations for multi-axial states of stress for 0.5Cr0.5Mo0.25V ferritic steel at 590°C", *Theoretical and Applied Fracture Mechanics*, vol. 36, pp. 99-107, 2001.

[8] Q. H. Xu, Q. Xu, Y.X. Pan and M. Short, "Current state of developing creep damage constitutive equation for 0.5Cr0.5Mo0.25V ferritic steel", *Advanced Materials Research*, vol. 510, pp. 812-816, 2012.

[9] L. An, Q. Xu, D. Xu and Z. Lu, "Review on the Current State of Developing of Advanced Creep Damage Constitutive Equations for High Chromium Alloy", *Advanced Materials Research*, vol. 510, pp. 776-780, 2012.

[10] L.M. Kachanov, "On the rupture time under the condition of creep", *Izv. Akad. Nauk SSSR, Otd. Tekh. Nauk*, Vol. 8, pp. 26-31, 1958.

[11] Y.N. Rabotnov, "Creep problems in structural members", *North-Holland*, 1969.

[12] S. Murakami, "Notion of continuum damage mechanics and its application to anisotropic creep damage theory", *ASME J. Eng. Mater. Technol.*, Vol. 105, pp. 99-105, 1983.

[13] E. J. Barbero, P. Lonetti and K. Sikkil, "Finite Element Continuum Damage Modeling of Plain Weave Reinforced Composites", *Composites part B*, vol. 37, pp. 137-147, 2006.

[14] F.R. Hall and D.R. Hayhurst, "Continuum damage mechanics modeling of high temperature deformation and failure in a pipe weldment", *Proc. R. Soc. Lond. A*, Vol. 433, pp. 383-403, 1994.

[15] D.R. Hayhurst, "High-temperature design and life assessment of structures using continuum damage mechanics", *Sixth Int. Conf. on Creep and Fatigue*, London: IMechE Conference Transaction, pp. 103-121, 1996.

[16] T.H. Hyde, W. Sun and A. A. Becker, "Creep crack growth in welds: a damage mechanics approach to predicting initiation and growth of circumferential cracks", *International Journal of Pressure Vessels and Piping*, Vol. 78(11-12), pp. 765-771, 2000.

[17] H.T. Yao, F.Z. Xuan, Z.D. Wang and S.T. Tu, "A review of creep analysis and design under multi-axial stress states", *Nuclear Engineering and Design*, Vol. 237(18), pp. 1969-1986, 2007.

[18] S. Peter, "Numerical simulation of weldment creep response", PhD Thesis, Department of Materials Science and Engineering, Royal Institute of Technology (KTH), Sweden, 2002.

[19] H. Riedel, "Creep crack growth under small-scale creep conditions", *Int. J. of Fracture*, Vol. 42, pp. 173-188, 1990.

[20] S. Murakami and Y. Liu, "Mesh-dependence in local approach to creep fracture", *Int. J. Damage Mechanics*, Vol. 4, pp. 230-250, 1995.

[21] M.T. Wong, "Three-Dimensional Finite Element Analysis of Creep Continuum Damage Growth and Failure in Weldments", PHD thesis, University of Manchester, UK, 1999.

[22] F. Tan, Q. Xu, Z. Lu and D. Xu, "The preliminary development of computational software system for creep damage analysis in weldment", Proceedings of the 18th International Conference on Automation & Computing, Loughborough University, Leicestershire, UK, 8 September 2012.

[23] I.M. Smith and D.V. Griffiths, "Programming the Finite Element Method", *John Wiley & Sons Ltd.*, 4th ed. Sussex, 2004.

[24] D. R., Hayhurst, P. R. Dimmer and G. J. Morrison, "Development of continuum damage in the creep rupture of notched bars", *Trans R Soc London A*, vol. 311, pp. 103–129, 1984

[25] I.J. Perrin and D.R. Hayhurst, "Creep constitutive equations for a 0.5Cr–0.5Mo–0.25V ferritic steel in the temperature range 600–675 °C", *J. Strain Anal. Eng*, Vol. 31, 299–314.1996.

[26] Q. Xu, M. Wright and Q. H., Xu, "The development and validation of multi-axial creep damage constitutive equations for P91", ICAC'11: The 17th international conference on automation and computing, Huddersfield, September 10, 2011.

Implementing Universal CNN Neuron

Luxia Xu, Fangyue Chen, and Han Huang
School of Science, Hangzhou Dianzi University, Hangzhou, Zhejiang, P. R. China

Abstract— *The universal CNN neuron can realize arbitrary Boolean functions including both linearly separable Boolean functions (LSBF) and linearly not separable Boolean functions (non-LSBF). However, determining the optimal (or near-optimal) orientation vector and the parameters in the multi-nested discriminant function contained within a universal CNN neuron is still a difficult task. By the aid of the DNA-like learning algorithm proposed a few years ago on the feedforward binary neural networks, the bottleneck problem can be solved if the number of input variables is not large.*

Keywords: Universal CNN neuron, Boolean function, multi-nested discriminant function, DNA-like learning algorithm

1. Introduction

A cellular neural network(CNN) [1,2] is a biologically inspired system where computation emerges from a collection of simple nonlinear locally coupled cells. An uncoupled CNN cell (or neuron) is a standard CNN cell described by the following equations [3]:

$$\sigma = \sum_{k,l\in\{i-1,i\,i+1\}\times\{j-1,j,j+1\}} b_{k,l}u_{k,l} = \sum_{i=1}^{9} b_i u_i \quad (1)$$

$$\dot{x}_{i,j} = -x_{i,j} + a_{i,j}f(x_{i,j}) + \sigma + z \quad (2)$$

$$y_{i,j} = f(x_{i,j}) = \frac{1}{2}(|x_{i,j}+1| - |x_{i,j}-1|), \quad (3)$$

where $\{i,j\}$ are two integer labels indicating the position of the CNN cell $C_{i,j}$ within a two-dimensional grid, $\{k,l\}$ are similar indices indicating the position of the neighboring cells, $u_{k,l}$ represents the "9" inputs coming from the cell itself, and from its eight neighbors, $x_{i,j}$ is the scalar state variable associated with the CNN cell and $y_{i,j}$ is the associated output. The scalar variable σ is called an excitation, and in the case of the standard CNN cell, it is computed as a linear correlation between the feed-forward (controlling) template vector $\boldsymbol{b} = (b_1,\cdots,b_n)$, which is a repacked version of the $\boldsymbol{B}$ template [1], and its associated input vector $U = (u_1,u_2,\cdots,u_n)$, as defined in (1) (here $n = 9$). The second notation, with the index "j" replacing the pair of indices $\{k,l\}$ is more general and can be applied to arbitrary choices of CNN architectures and spheres of influence. From this perspective, n represents the number of cell inputs and $\boldsymbol{R}^n$ is the cell input space.

It was proved in [4] that when the central feedback coefficient $a_{i,i} > 1$, and $a_{i,j} = 0, i \neq j$, the cell dynamics starting from $x_{i,j}(0) = 0$ converges towards a stable steady state for which $y_{i,j}(\infty) = sgn(\sigma+z)$. The "infinity" symbol here denotes the time for the dynamics to reach a steady state output, and represents a small transient period which depends on the implementation technology. It follows that an uncoupled CNN cell maps a continuous input space $\boldsymbol{R}^n$ into a binary (Boolean) output space. In the special case where the inputs are binary, the cell can realize various Boolean functions.

The standard CNN cell (1) to (3) can be generalized to the following universal CNN neuron (or universal CNN cell) [5-7].

$$\sigma = \sum_{i=1}^{n} b_i u_i \quad (4)$$

$$\dot{x} = -x + af(x) + \omega(\sigma) \quad (5)$$

$$y = f(x) = \frac{1}{2}(|x+1| - |x-1|), \quad (6)$$

where the discriminant $\omega(\sigma)$ is a multi-nested piecewise-linear function

$$\omega(\sigma) = s(z_m + |z_{m-1} + |\cdots + |z_1 + |z_0+\sigma||\cdots||), \quad (7)$$

and $\{s, z_0,\cdots,z_m\}$ is an additional set of $m+2$ parameters, $s = 1$ or -1. This model includes the standard CNN cell as a special case $w(\sigma) = s(\sigma + z)$ (there is no absolute value sign in formula (7)), and has the advantages of simplicity and tractability due to its piecewise-linear nature.

It follows from (5) and (6) that the steady state CNN output equation is

$$y(\infty) = sgn(\omega(\sigma)) = \begin{cases} 1 & if \quad \omega > 0 \\ -1 & if \quad \omega \leq 0 \end{cases} \quad (8)$$

Model (4) to (6) is said an universal CNN neuron (UCNNN) means that every 2^{2^n} Boolean functions of n input variables $(u_1,u_2,\cdots,u_n)$ can be realized by finding an optimal (or near-optimal) orientation vector $\boldsymbol{b} = (b_1,\cdots,b_n)$ and a set of appropriate parameters $\{s, z_0,\cdots,z_m\}$.

Since Boolean functions always play a key role in information processing and computer science, large-scale effective realization of Boolean functions is very important but also extremely difficult [3,8]. For example, how to "learn" the suitable template values of a CNN to perform a given task is a "bottleneck" [9]. All $2^{2^3} = 256$ Boolean functions of 3 input variables were realized via UCNNN in [6]. However, for $n = 4$, the problem is so complex that not only computing the orientation vector but also the additional set of parameters in UCNNN for a non-LSBF takes a lot of computation time [7].

By the aid of DNA-like algorithm of the feedforward binary neural networks [10,11], the issues will be easier to be solved. This paper focuses on implementing UCNNN, an effective method to determine the optimal (or near-optimal) orientation vector and the set of parameters in the multi-nested piecewise-linear function in UCNNN for 4 inputs Boolean functions is obtained.

2. Realization of Boolean Functions via UCNNN

2.1 Orientation vector and excitation

According to the convention used in the CNN literature, a "0" (or false) logic level is coded with -1, while a "1" (or true) logic level is still coded with 1.

A Boolean function of n variables is defined as the following binary map from $\{-1,1\}^n$ to $\{-1,1\}$: $F(U)=v$, where $U=(u_1,u_2,\cdots,u_n)$ is the input window and v is the output corresponding to U of the map. Let $k=\sum_{i=1}^{n}\bar{u}_i 2^{n-i}$, where $\bar{u}_i=1$ if $u_i=1$ or else 0, i.e., k is the decimal code of the input window U. There are 2^n different input windows denoted by $U^{(k)}$ $(k=0,1,\cdots,2^n-1)$. Thus, the map F can be rewritten as $F(U^{(k)})=v_k$ $(k=0,1,\cdots,2^n-1)$. Obviously, such a map can generate an output symbol tape $[v_0,v_1,\cdots,v_{2^n-1}]$ consisting of 2^n symbols "-1" and "1". Conversely, a symbol tape $[v_0,v_1,\cdots,v_{2^n-1}]$ completely determines a Boolean function.

An n inputs Boolean function $[v_0,v_1,\cdots,v_{2^n-1}]$ can be coded by a decimal integer $N=\sum_{i=0}^{2^n-1}\bar{v}_i 2^{(2^n-1-i)}$, where $\bar{v}_i=1$ if $v_i=1$ or else 0. For example, the decimal code of $[1,-1,1,-1,1,-1,1,-1,-1,-1,1,-1,1,1,1,1]$ is 43567.

A Boolean function $[v_0,v_1,\cdots,v_{2^n-1}]$ is realized by a UCNNN is equivalent to determining a vector $\boldsymbol{b}=(b_1,b_2,\cdots,b_n)$ and a set of parameters $\{s,z_0,\cdots,z_m\}$ such that $sgn(\omega(\sigma_k))=v_k$ in the UCNNN (4) to (6), where $\sigma_k=\sum_{i=1}^{n}b_i u_i^{(k)}=\boldsymbol{b}\cdot U^{(k)^T}$ $(k=0,1,\cdots,2^n-1)$.

The vector $\boldsymbol{b}=(b_1,b_2,\cdots,b_n)$ in (4) is called the orientation vector of UCNNN [5,7], 2^n excitations $\sigma_k=\boldsymbol{b}\cdot U^{(k)^T}$ $(k=0,1,\cdots,2^n-1)$ is a projection from n input windows $U^{(k)}$ $(k=0,1,\cdots,2^n-1)$ to a scalar one-dimensional projection axis. These excitations $\{\sigma_k\}_0^{2^n-1}$ form a projection tape on the projection axis, and is a sequence which possesses many interesting properties such as symmetry, self-reproduction and self-similarity [10,12,13]. Furthermore, $\{\sigma_k\}_0^{2^n-1}$ is a DNA-like sequence in which only n values $\{\sigma_0,\sigma_1,\sigma_2,\sigma_{2^2}\cdots,\sigma_{2^{n-3}},\sigma_{2^{n-2}}\}$ are independent, and $\{\sigma_k\}_0^{2^n-1}$ can be obtained by coping the n excitation values [11,14]. There is a relationship between $\boldsymbol{b}=(b_1,b_2,\cdots,b_n)$ and $\{\sigma_0,\sigma_1,\sigma_2,\sigma_{2^2}\cdots,\sigma_{2^{n-3}},\sigma_{2^{n-2}}\}$ in the sequence $\{\sigma_k\}_0^{2^n-1}$ [10,13]:

$$\begin{pmatrix} b_1\\ b_2\\ b_3\\ \vdots\\ b_{n-1}\\ b_n \end{pmatrix}=\begin{pmatrix} ((n-3)\sigma_0-\sum_{i=0}^{n-2}\sigma_{2^i})/2\\ (\sigma_{2^{(n-2)}}-\sigma_0)/2\\ (\sigma_{2^{(n-3)}}-\sigma_0)/2\\ \vdots\\ (\sigma_2-\sigma_0)/2\\ (\sigma_1-\sigma_0)/2 \end{pmatrix} \tag{9}$$

2.2 Minimum number of transitions of Boolean function and DNA-like learning algorithm

Formula (9) shows that training orientation vector $\boldsymbol{b}=(b_1,b_2,\cdots,b_n)$ of a CNN is equivalent to training its n excitation values $\{\sigma_0,\sigma_1,\sigma_2,\sigma_{2^2}\cdots,\sigma_{2^{n-3}},\sigma_{2^{n-2}}\}$.

For a given orientation vector $\boldsymbol{b}=(b_1,b_2,\cdots,b_n)$, the corresponding excitation sequence $\{\sigma_k\}_0^{2^n-1}$ certainly has an order relationship: $\sigma_{i_0}\le\sigma_{i_1}\le\sigma_{i_2}\le\cdots\le\sigma_{i_{2^n-1}}$, where $\{i_0,i_1,\cdots,i_{2^n-1}\}$ is a replacement of $\{0,1,2,\cdots,2^n-1\}$. A Boolean function $[v_0,v_1,\cdots,v_{2^n-1}]$, if it satisfies $v_i=v_j$ when $\sigma_i=\sigma_j$ $(i\neq j)$, then say it conforms to the orientation vector $\boldsymbol{b}$, or the vector $\boldsymbol{b}$ conforms the Boolean function. Furthermore, if $v_{i_{k_0}}\neq v_{i_{k_0+1}}$ when $\sigma_{i_{k_0}}<\sigma_{i_{k_0+1}}$, where $i_{k_0},i_{k_0+1}\in\{i_0,i_1,\cdots,i_{2^n-1}\}$, then say the Boolean function has a transition with respect to the vector $\boldsymbol{b}=(b_1,b_2,\cdots,b_n)$, denoted by $T|_{(\sigma_{i_{k_0}},\sigma_{i_{k_0+1}})}$. It is clear that $N|_{Tr}$, the number of transitions of a Boolean function, depends on the orientation vector $\boldsymbol{b}$, i.e., a Boolean function may have different numbers of transitions for different orientation vectors. Therefore, the orientation vector which guarantees the number of transitions of a given Boolean function is minimum certainly is an optimal or near-optimal orientation vector.

Example 1: For 4 inputs Boolean function: $[v_0,v_1,\cdots,v_{15}]=[-1,1,1,1,1,1,1,-1,1,1,1,1,1,-1,-1,-1]$, its decimal code is $\sum_{i=0}^{15}\bar{v}_i 2^{15-i}=32504$, where $\bar{v}_i=1$ if $v_i=1$ or else 0. If take the orientation vector $\boldsymbol{b}=(1,3,1,1)$, then one has $\sigma_0=-6$, $\sigma_1=\sigma_2=\sigma_8=-4$, $\sigma_3=\sigma_9=\sigma_{10}=-2$, $\sigma_4=\sigma_{11}=0$, $\sigma_5=\sigma_6=\sigma_{12}=2$, $\sigma_7=\sigma_{13}=\sigma_{14}=4$, $\sigma_{15}=6$. Thus, the order relationship of the excitations $\{\sigma_k\}_{k=0}^{15}$ is $\sigma_0<\sigma_1=\sigma_2=\sigma_8<\sigma_3=\sigma_9=\sigma_{10}<\sigma_4=\sigma_{11}<\sigma_5=\sigma_6=\sigma_{12}<\sigma_7=\sigma_{13}=\sigma_{14}<\sigma_{15}$. It is easy to prove that the orientation vector $\boldsymbol{b}=(1,3,1,1)$ conforms to the Boolean function. Since $v_0\neq v_1$ $(\sigma_0<\sigma_1)$, $v_{12}\neq v_7$ $(\sigma_{12}<\sigma_7)$. Thus, the Boolean function has two transitions, i.e., $N|_{Tr}=2$ for the orientation vector $\boldsymbol{b}$.

If take another orientation vector $\boldsymbol{b}=(7,3,2,1)$ which also conforms to the Boolean function, then one has $\sigma_0=-13$, $\sigma_1=-11$, $\sigma_2=-9$, $\sigma_3=\sigma_4=-7$, $\sigma_5=-5$, $\sigma_6=-3$, $\sigma_7=-1$, $\sigma_8=1$, $\sigma_9=3$, $\sigma_{10}=5$, $\sigma_{11}=\sigma_{12}=7$, $\sigma_{13}=9$, $\sigma_{14}=11$, $\sigma_{15}=13$. Thus, their order relationship is $\sigma_0<\sigma_1<\sigma_2<\sigma_3=\sigma_4<\sigma_5<\sigma_6<\sigma_7<\sigma_8<\sigma_9<\sigma_{10}<\sigma_{11}=\sigma_{12}<\sigma_{13}<\sigma_{14}<\sigma_{15}$.

It follows that $v_0 \neq v_1$ $(\sigma_0 < \sigma_1)$, $v_6 \neq v_7$ $(\sigma_6 < \sigma_7)$, $v_7 \neq v_8$ $(\sigma_7 < \sigma_8)$, $v_{12} \neq v_{13}$ $(\sigma_{12} < \sigma_{13})$. Thus, it has four transitions, i.e., $N|_{Tr} = 4$ for the orientation vector $\boldsymbol{b} = (7, 3, 2, 1)$.

The DNA-like learning algorithm is an effective algorithm to train the excitation sequence $\{\sigma_k\}_0^{2^n-1}$ and compute the minimum number of transitions for a Boolean function [11,14]. In fact, the minimum number $Min\{N|_{Tr}\}$ of transitions for all 4 inputs Boolean functions can be calculated by using the DNA-like algorithm, the detail is shown in Table 1. From the table, one can find that 4 inputs Boolean function have no more than 5 transitions. Obviously, the Boolean function which only has one transition is linearly separable. It was known that there were 1882 LSBFs in the set of 4 inputs Boolean functions [10,11,13], the result is consistent with the conclusion in Table 1.

Table 1: Minimum number of transitions of 4 inputs Boolean functions

	65536 Boolean functions with 4 inputs				
$Min\{N\|_{Tr}\}$	1	2	3	4	5
Amount of BFs	1882	14244	30216	19002	192
Percentage(%)	2.87	21.73	46.11	28.99	0.29

2.3 Designing optimal multi-nested discriminant function

The m-nested discriminant function

$$\omega(\sigma) = s(z_m + |z_{m-1} + |\cdots + |z_1 + |z_0 + \sigma||\cdots||)$$

is a piecewise-linear function on variable σ, its number of roots is 2^m, and the number doubles on m [7]. Thus, for a suitable set of parameters $\{s, z_0, z_1, , \cdots, z_m\}$, the σ axis can be divided into $2^m + 1$ parts by the curve of the discriminant function.

In general, realizing a given n inputs Boolean function via a UCNNN by designing an optimal multi-nested discriminant function should perform the following steps:
(1) determine the orientation vector $\boldsymbol{b} = (b_0, b_1, \cdots, b_n)$ which conforms to the function and the corresponding excitations sequence $\{\sigma_k\}_0^{2^n-1}$ by using DNA-like learning algorithm;
(2) calculate all transitions of the function with respect to the vector $\boldsymbol{b}$;
(3) determine the number m based on the minimum number of transitions and the distribution of these transitions;
(4) calculate parameters $\{z_0, z_1, \cdots, z_m\}$ and s based on the roots of the multi-nested discriminant function.

Example 2: For 4 inputs Boolean function $[v_0, v_1, \cdots, v_{15}] = [1, -1, 1, -1, 1, -1, 1, -1, -1, -1, 1, -1, 1, 1, 1, 1]$, its decimal code is 43567.
(1) by using DNA-like algorithm, one can obtain the orientation vector $\boldsymbol{b} = (-8, -10, -2, 4)$, and the excitations $\sigma_0 = 16$, $\sigma_1 = 24$, $\sigma_2 = 12$, $\sigma_3 = 20$, $\sigma_4 = \sigma_{10} = -4$, $\sigma_5 = \sigma_{11} = 4$, $\sigma_6 = -8$, $\sigma_7 = \sigma_8 = 0$, $\sigma_9 = 8$, $\sigma_{12} = -20$, $\sigma_{13} = -12$, $\sigma_{14} = -24$, $\sigma_{15} = -16$;
(2) there are 3 transitions respectively $T|_{(\sigma_4,\sigma_7)}$, $T|_{(\sigma_9,\sigma_2)}$ and $T|_{(\sigma_0,\sigma_3)}$, and the minimum number of transitions is 3;
(3) based on the distribution of these transitions, take $m = 2$, i.e., $\omega(\sigma) = s(z_2 + |z_1 + |z_0 + \sigma||)$;
(4) let $\omega(\sigma) = 0$, its 4 roots are respectively $\bar{\sigma}_1^{(2)} = -z_0+z_1+z_2$, $\bar{\sigma}_2^{(2)} = -z_0+z_1-z_2$, $\bar{\sigma}_3^{(2)} = -z_0-z_1+z_2$ and $\bar{\sigma}_4^{(2)} = -z_0-z_1-z_2$, and z_1, z_2 must be negative. It follows that $\bar{\sigma}_1^{(2)} < \bar{\sigma}_2^{(2)} < \bar{\sigma}_3^{(2)} < \bar{\sigma}_4^{(2)}$. Take the middle value of two excitations that appear in a transition as a root of $\omega(\sigma)$, then has $-z_0 + z_1 + z_2 = (\sigma_4 + \sigma_7)/2$, $-z_0 + z_1 - z_2 = (\sigma_9 + \sigma_2)/2$ and $-z_0 - z_1 - z_2 = (\sigma_0 + \sigma_3)/2$. Thus, one finally obtains $z_0 = -14$, $z_1 = -10$ and $z_2 = -6$.

Thus, the 2-nested discriminant function which can be used to implement the UCNNN realizing the given Boolean function is

$$\omega(\sigma) = -6 + |-10 + |-14 + \sigma||,$$

where take $s = 1$ because here $sgn(\omega(\sigma_k)) = v_k$ $(k = 0, 1, \cdots, 15)$.

Note: In literature [7], for the Boolean function in Example 2, it was said that "any attempt to find a realization with $m = 2$ failed", in that paper, by using Alopex algorithm, the final orientation vector and 3-nested discriminant function were respectively $\boldsymbol{b} = (7, -11, -6, 4)$ and $\omega(\sigma) = -(-3 + |-6 + |-12 + |10 + \sigma|||)$. Obviously, the result in this paper is better than previous one.

Example 3: For the 4 inputs Boolean function $[v_0, v_1, \cdots, v_{15}] = [-1, 1, 1, 1, 1, 1, 1, -1, 1, 1, 1, 1, 1, -1, -1, -1]$ whose decimal code is 32504 in Example 1, there are two transitions $T|_{(\sigma_0,\sigma_1)}$ and $T|_{(\sigma_{12},\sigma_{13})}$, one can take 1-nested discriminant function $\omega(\sigma) = s(z_1 + |\sigma + z_0|)$. let $\omega(\sigma) = 0$, then its 2 roots are respectively $\bar{\sigma}_1^{(1)} = -z_0 + z_1$ and $\bar{\sigma}_2^{(1)} = -z_0 - z_1$. Take each of them as the middle value of two excitations that appear in the corresponding transition, i.e., $-z_0 + z_1 = (\sigma_0 + \sigma_1)/2$ and $-z_0 - z_1 = (\sigma_{12} + \sigma_{13})/2$. Finally one obtains $z_0 = 1$, $z_1 = -4$ and $s = -1$, i.e., $\omega(\sigma) = 4 - |1 + \sigma|$.

The two m-nested discriminant functions in Example 1 and 2 are shown in **Fig. 1** and **2**.

3. Conclusion

In literature [3], the founders, Prof. Chua and Roska of CNN and CNN-UM, once pointed "presently no theory exists which allows one to determine whether an arbitrary Boolean function is realizable by a CNN". Indeed, the UCNNN (or universal CNN cell, UCNNC) is a good model to treat the difficult problem, which only needs a single neuron (cell). In this paper, the UCNNN realizing a given Boolean function can effectively be implemented by using DNA-like algorithm if the number of the input variables is

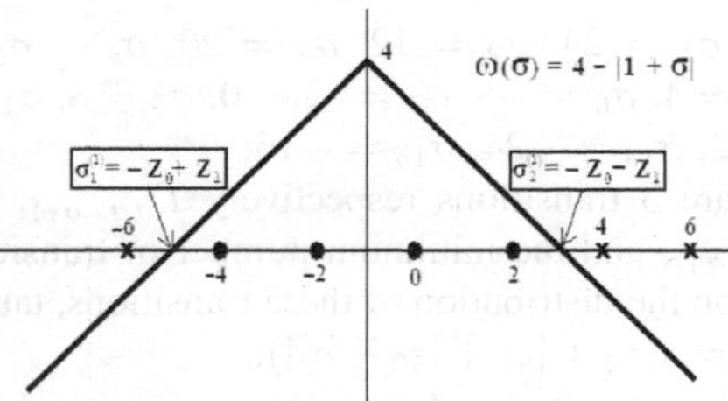

Fig. 1: Multi-nested discriminant function $\omega(\sigma) = 4 - |1+\sigma|$ for 4 inputs Boolean function $[v_0, v_1, \cdots, v_{15}] = [-1,1,1,1,1,1,1,-1,1,1,1,1,1,-1,-1,-1]$ in Example 1, the orientation vector is $\boldsymbol{b} = (1,3,1,1)$.

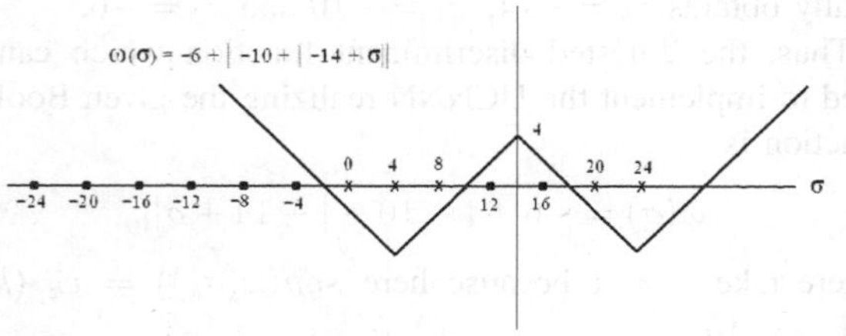

Fig. 2: Multi-nested discriminant function $\omega(\sigma) = -6 + |-10 + |-14+\sigma||$ for 4 inputs Boolean function $[v_0, v_1, \cdots, v_{15}] = [1,-1,1,-1,1,-1,1,1,1,-1,-1,1,-1,1,1,1,1]$ in Example 2, the orientation vector is $\boldsymbol{b} = (-8,-10,-2,4)$.

not large. In future, further researches are needed such as on how to perform the Boolean function of bigger number of input variables via UCNNN, increase the computing speed, reduce the store space in a computer and so on.

Acknowledgment

This research was supported by NSFC (Grants 11171084 and 60872093).

References

[1] L. O. Chua, L. Yang, "Cellular Neural Networks: Theory," *IEEE Trans. Circuit Syst. I Reg. Papers*, vol. 35, pp. 1257–1272, 1988.

[2] L. O. Chua, L. Yang, "Cellular Neural Networks: Application," *IEEE Trans. Circuit Syst. I Reg. Papers*, vol. 35, pp. 1273–1290, 1988.

[3] L. O. Chua, T. Roska, *Cellular Neural Networks and Visual Computing, Foundations and Applications*, Cambridge, U.K.: Cambridge University Press, 2002.

[4] L. O. Chua, *CNN: A Paradigm for Complexity*, Singapore: World Scientific, 1998.

[5] L. O. Chua, V. I. Sbitnev, S. Yoon, "A Nonlinear Dynamical Perspective of Wolfram's New Kind of Science. Part II: Universal Neuron," *Int. J. Bifurcat. Chaos*, vol. 13, pp. 2377–2491, 2003.

[6] R. Dogaru, L. O. Chua, "CNN Genes for One-dimensional Cellular Automata: A Multi-nested Piecewise-linear Approach," *Int. J. Bifurcation. Chaos*, vol. 8, pp. 1987–2001, 1998.

[7] R. Dogaru, L. O. Chua, "Universal CNN cells," *Int. J. Bifurcat. Chaos*, vol. 9, pp. 1–48, 1999.

[8] I. Wegener, *The Complexity of Boolean Functions*, New York, America: Wiley, 1987.

[9] L. Fortuna, P. Arena, D. Balya, A. Zarandy, "Cellular Neural Networks: A Paradigm for Nonlinear Spatio-temporal Processing," *IEEE Mag. Circuit Syst.*, vol. 1, pp. 6–21, 2001.

[10] F. Y. Chen, G. L. He, G. Chen, "Realization of Boolean Functions via CNN with von Neumann Neighborhoods," *Int. J. Bifurcat. Chaos*, vol. 16, pp. 1389–1403, 2006.

[11] F. Y. Chen, G. Chen, Q. B. He, G. L. He, X. B. Xu, "Universal Perceptron and DNA-like Learning Algorithm of Binary Neural Networks: Non-LSBF Implementation," *IEEE Trans. Neural Netw.*, vol. 20, pp. 1293–1301, 2009.

[12] F. Y. Chen, G. Chen, "Realization and Bifurcation of Boolean Functions via Cellular Neural Networks," *Int. J. Bifurcation. Chaos*, vol. 15, pp. 2109–2129, 2005.

[13] F. Y. Chen, G. L. He, G. Chen, "Realization of Boolean functions via CNN: Mathematical theory, LSBF and template design," *IEEE Trans. Circuit Syst. I Reg. Papers*, vol. 53, pp. 2203–2213, 2006.

[14] F. Y. Chen, G. Chen, G. L. He, X. B. Xu, Q. B. He, "Universal Perceptron and DNA-like Learning Algorithm of Binary Neural Networks: LSBF and PBF Implementation," *IEEE Trans. Neural Netw.*, vol. 20, pp. 1645–1658, 2009.

Practical guidance on the application of R-K integration method in finite element analysis of creep damage problem

F. Tan[1], Q. Xu[1], Z. Lu[2], D. Xu[1], and D. Liu[1]
[1]School of Science and Engineering, Teesside University, Middlesbrough, TS1 3BA, UK
[2]School of Computing and Engineering, University of Huddersfield, Huddersfield, HD1 3DA, UK

Abstract - *A practical user guidance of Runge-Kutta (R-K) integration method with the context of non-linear time dependent finite element analysis (FEA) was proposed in this paper. Following the literature review of different integration method within the finite element analysis framework, detailed numerical experiments were conducted to find out the right balance between computing accuracy and efficiency. It contributes to knowledge to the numerical analysis software development in general and specific to computational creep damage mechanics.*

Keywords: integration method, creep damage, finite element analysis

1 Introduction

In general finite element analysis software, the complete processing progress can be divided into three stages. The first stage is pre-processing where topology of a FEA model, boundary condition, and type of problem (where the solution method needs to be specified) is defined. The second stage is a numerical problem solving, for example, the stress and strain will be calculated and other field variables will be updated. The third stage is post-processing where the numerical results obtained in second stage will be presented and analyzed by users, typically with interaction with graphic presentation. There is readily available commercial software for the pre- and post- processing now, such as FEMSYS or GID [1, 2].

Creep damage problem is complicated and dynamically developing, and there is not readily available analysis capability in most of the commercial analysis software. There is still a need, to certain degree, to develop and then use in-house software in research community. Tan et al. [3] reviewed the current situation of computational tools in 2012 and reported, for example, 1) DAMAGE XX [4] is an early creep damage analysis solver, for 2D problem, developed at and used by the researchers at UMIST, and DAMAGE XXX [5] is a new advanced version for 3D problem; 2) FE-DAMAGE is another in-house code developed at University of Nottingham; 3) HTΣ is a Chinese package used for creep damage analysis which proposed by Tu [6]; 4) A Japanese in-house code was mentioned by Haigihara [7].

The nature of creep damage analysis is of time dependent and the field variables such as stress, strain, and creep damage variables need to be updated where an integration scheme needs to be implemented. Liu et al. [8] proposed some detailed algorithms to build an in-house FE package.

From literature review [6, 9], it seems that the fourth-order R-K method is a good choice due to its computing efficiency and accuracy. This paper reports an investigation about the balance between accuracy and efficiency in its use to integrate creep damage constitutive equations. It contributes to knowledge to the numerical analysis software development in general and specific to computational creep damage mechanics.

2 Integration method

2.1 Euler's method

The Euler method is a first-order numerical procedure for solving ordinary differential equations with a given initial value [10]. The Euler method required extremely small time steps to ensure the convergence of iterations and accuracy of calculations in creep fracture problem [11]. The method has advantages of brevity and simplicity in concept and programming. Unfortunately, this scheme is only conditionally stable and the stability condition is rather stringent. In creep fracture problem, high concentration of creep strain exists near the crack tip; the use of Euler method for creep damage simulation is quite uneconomic.

It can be found from literature that this method was adopted by an in-house code was developed by Tsing Hua University [11]. It is understood that DAMAGE XX has incorporated it as one of the integration methods while the user has to make decision on which one to use.

2.2 Runge-Kutta method

Actually, in order to improve the efficiency of Euler's method, a new numerical method was suggested. A standard way to determine whether the Runge–Kutta values are sufficiently accurate is to re-compute the value at the end of each interval with the step size cut in half. The method is also called “step doubling” [5]. If this makes a change of negligible magnitude, the results are accepted; if not, the step is halved again until the results are satisfactory.

It is generally understood that R-K method is more accurate and efficient in comparison with forward Euler method, and thus its application has been reported. For instance, DAMAGE XX [6] incorporated fourth order R-K integration method. HT∑ is a Chinese package used for creep damage analysis. The core of this code is an advanced integration method subroutine within Runge-Kutta-Merson algorithm which developed by Ling et al. [6]. As an in-house code, the accuracy and efficiency of this program had been proved by the solution of a thick cylinder problem.

3 The overall equilibrium equations

The creep deformation and damage can be calculated from creep damage constitutive equations; however, in FE area, constitutive equation cannot be used immediately [6]. It is not only a mathematical problem but also a boundary balance need to be considered in FE simulation. In order to achieve this goal, assumed total strain increment as:

$$\Delta_{\varepsilon} = \Delta_{\varepsilon^e} + \Delta_{\varepsilon^c} \qquad (3.1)$$

Where Δ_{ε}, Δ_{ε^e}, Δ_{ε^c} total strains, elastic strain, and creep are strain respectively; Then ensure the relation between stress increment and total strain increment:

$$\Delta_{\sigma} = D \times (\Delta_{\varepsilon} - \Delta_{\varepsilon^c}) \qquad (3.2)$$

Where D is elastic modulus, Δ_{σ} is stress increment; to relate to the displacement vector, equation (3.2) will be expressed:

$$\Delta_{\sigma} = D \times (B \times \Delta_{\mu} - \Delta_{\varepsilon^c}) \qquad (3.3)$$

Where B is strain matrix, Δ_{μ} is displacement vector; the equilibrium equation can be addressed as:

$$\int_v B^T \times \Delta_{\sigma} \times dV = \Delta_R \qquad (3.4)$$

Where Δ_R is nodal mechanical load increment, V is element volume; Combine equations (3.3) and (3.4):

$$\int_v B^T \times D \times (B \times \Delta_{\mu} - \Delta_{\varepsilon^c}) \times dV = \Delta_R \qquad (3.5)$$

The integration of creep damage constitutive equations occurs on the determination of Δ_{ε^c}. Such constitutive equations also need to be normalized because they are stiff in nature [9]. The normalization of variables is based on the selection of an appropriate normalizing stress. This is in order to remain the values of stress close to unity during the computation because the constitutive equations raise stresses to a power, which may be quite large for some materials. If absolute values of stress are used, very large or very small values are obtained; the algebraic manipulation of these numbers leads to numerical rounding errors.

4 Specific constitutive equations

The KRH uni-axial constitutive equations [12] were used in the test:

$$\dot{\varepsilon} = A\sinh\left(\frac{B\sigma(1-H)}{(1-\varphi)(1-\omega)}\right) \qquad (4.1)$$

$$\dot{H} = \frac{h}{\sigma}\left(1 - \frac{H}{H^*}\right)\dot{\varepsilon} \qquad (4.2)$$

$$\dot{\varphi} = \frac{K_c}{3}(1-\varphi)^4 \qquad (4.3)$$

$$\dot{\omega} = C\dot{\varepsilon}^* \qquad (4.4)$$

The KRH multi-axial constitutive equations can be expressed:

$$\dot{\varepsilon}_{ij} = \frac{3S_{ij}}{2\sigma_e} A\sinh\left(\frac{B\sigma_e(1-H)}{(1-\varphi)(1-\omega)}\right) \qquad (4.5)$$

$$\dot{H} = \frac{h}{\sigma_e}\left(1 - \frac{H}{H^*}\right)\dot{\varepsilon}_e \qquad (4.6)$$

$$\dot{\varphi} = \frac{K_c}{3}(1-\varphi)^4 \qquad (4.7)$$

$$\dot{\omega} = C\dot{\varepsilon}^*\left(\frac{\sigma_1}{\sigma_e}\right)^{\nu} \qquad (4.8)$$

Where $A=2.1618\times10^{-9}MPah^{-1}$, $B=0.20524MPa^{-1}$, $C=1.8537$, $h=2.4326\times105MPa$, $H^*=0.5929$, $Kc=9.2273\times10^{-5}MPa^{-3}h^{-1}$, $v=2.8$.

5 NAG routine

D02BHF (NAG) [13] integrates a system of first-order ordinary differential equations solution using Runge-Kutta-Merson method. This subroutine can be adopted in the FEA software of creep damage analysis development, and a detailed instruction on how to use it was published by the company [13]. Basically, this routine can be written as:

```
SUBROUTINE D02BHF (X, XEND, N, Y, TOL, IRELAB,
HMAX, FCN, G, W, IFAIL)

INTEGER   N, IRELAB, IFAIL

REAL   X, XEND, Y (N), TOL, HMAX, G, W (N, 7)

EXTEERNAL     FCN, G
```

D02BHF aims to solve ordinary differential equation using Runge-Kutta-Merson method, until a user-specified function of the solution is zero; therefore, it cannot be adopted completely. The variables which mentioned above should be re-identified in creep damage analysis application area.

1. X – real

The X means the start moment t1

2. XEND – real

The XEND means the finish moment t2

3. N – integer

The N means the number of constitutive equations

4. Y (N) - real array

The Y (N) means the arrays which store the data of strain, damage, hardness respectively

5. TOL – real

The TOL means the tolerance for controlling the time steps

6. IRELAB – integer

The IRELAB means the type of error control, in here, normally set as 1.

7. HMAX – real

HMAX means the original user-defined time step

8. FCN – subroutine

The FCN means the constitutive equations statement

9. G – real function

The G was originally developed for terminate this program when the specific function equal to zero. This function would not be used in creep damage analysis because all constitutive equations should not be expected to appear a solution equal to zero. The G was suggested to set as the default G=Y (1).

10. W (N, 7) – real array

11. IFAIL – integer

IFAIL means the routine error feedback, and must be set to 0, -1 or 1.

6 Numerical experiment

This case is uni-axial creep under stress of 40MPa. The component is deemed failed if the damage parameter reaches 0.33 which is the criterion used here. To solve this set of constitutive equations within NAG routine, the terminated time should be predicted for prepared this numerical experiment because this routine was suggested from one specific time to another specific time

6.1 Result based on Euler's method

In order to make sense the most exactly lifetime, a simple Euler's method program had been coded. And the code was tested using different time increment such as 1, 0.1, 0.01, 0.001, 0.0001 hour respectively.

Three Tables were listed to show the detail of the results. The Table I shows the terminated time and omega depending on the size of time interval. The time interval 0.0001 is the most accurate between the five different intervals. Table II and Table III displayed the specific creep strain value, H which is the primary creep state variable (strain hardening), and φ which is the precipitate coarsening state variable.

Even from mathematic aspect, the interval 0.0001 is the best selection; however, from the physics aspect, 0.0001 hours equal to 0.36 second, and this is a too short time interval. Therefore, the author selects the time interval 0.01 hour as the master accuracy control parameter. Following that, the lifetime value can be observed from table 1 is 104032.27 hours.

TABLE I

Time interval (s)	Terminated time (h)	ω
1	104034.0000	0.333435236633273
0.1	104032.4000	0.333339889351067
0.01	104032.2700	0.333333868058920
0.001	104032.2580	0.333333386466599
0.0001	104032.2577	0.333333316847831

TABLE II

Time interval (s)	ε_f
1	0.179875512020971
0.1	0.179824075821904
0.01	0.179820827565906
0.001	0.179820567765346
0.0001	0.179820530208621

TABLE III

Time interval (s)	H	φ
1	0.592900000000000	0.544764812531457
0.1	0.592899999999999	0.544760827698831
0.01	0.592899999999992	0.544760468843807
0.001	0.592899999999917	0.544760434279127
0.0001	0.592899999999174	0.544760430559092

6.2 Result based on Runge-Kutta method

Because of the nature of NAG subroutine, the variable TOL was designed as the accuracy control parameter. Give the duration from t=0 to t=104032.27 to NAG routine, and record the results of seven different TOL value ranging from 0.1E-01 to 0.1E-07 as shown in the following Table IV.

Tables IV and V show the detailed results. And a comparison will be processed with previous results which based on Euler's method to looking for the most accurate value of TOL, strain and damage value.

TABLE IV

TOL	ε_f	ω
0.1E-01	0.136548062074	0.253119148370
0.1E-02	0.178172199475	0.330277813609
0.1E-03	0.179803968745	0.333302624373
0.1E-04	0.179819797001	0.333331965213
0.1E-05	0.179820066343	0.333332464492
0.1E-06	0.179820072754	0.333332476375
0.1E-07	0.179820072807	0.333332476473

TABLE V

TOL	H	φ
0.1E-01	0.597028574423	0.544760420284
0.1E-02	0.593389925900	0.544760420697
0.1E-03	0.592883124271	0.544760420959
0.1E-04	0.592873878039	0.544760421042
0.1E-05	0.592899874301	0.544760421049
0.1E-06	0.592900018328	0.544760421049
0.1E-07	0.592899978356	0.544760421050

6.3 Accuracy Analysis

The accuracy analysis conducted bellow is essentially based on uni-axial displacement controlled relaxation: e.g. the inaccuracy of creep strain will be converted into the elastic strain, then the stress. The worst case of inaccurate creep strain, strain at failure is used.

The elastic strain under 40MPa is $\varepsilon = \frac{\sigma}{E} = \frac{40MPa}{200GPa} = 2 \times 10^{-4}$, and an error in the calculated creep strain will eventually affect the stress updating. The master curve (assuming accurate enough) creep strain at failure is 0.179820827565906 obtained with Euler's method at interval 0.01h;

When TOL=0.1x10-3, strain at failure is 0.179803968745

The error in creep strain at is

$$Error = |0.179303968745 - 0.179820827565906| = 1.68588820906 \times 10^{-5}$$

$$error\ rate = \frac{1.68588820906 \times 10^{-5}}{2 \times 10^{-4}} = 8.42\%$$

When TOL=0.1×10^{-7}, strain at failure is 0.179820072807

The error in creep strain at failure is

$$Error - |0.179320072307 - 0.179820827565906| - 7.54758906 \times 10^{-7}$$

$$error\ rate = \frac{7.54758906 \times 10^{-7}}{2 \times 10^{-4}} = 0.37\%$$

Similarly, the error rate in creep strain was calculated and all the results were shown in Table VI.

From this table, the TOL=0.1×10^{-7} is obviously satisfied the accuracy requirement, and the TOL=0.1×10^{-3} is too big than the expected value, say 1%, due to the high exponential or power law relationship between stress level and creep strain rate. It can be seen that when TOL value is 0.1E-05 is a very good choice.

TABLE VI

TOL	Percentage errors of strain at failure
0.1E-01	21636%
0.1E-02	824%
0.1E-03	8.43%
0.1E-04	0.51%
0.1E-05	0.38%
0.1E-06	0.37%
0.1E-07	0.37%

6.4 Efficiency Analysis

This constitutive equations subroutine offered the solutions of strain and damage value in each given durations. Once the subroutine running, an integration point would be solved in the finite element analysis processing. Basic that, a complete finite element analysis will call this subroutine over all the integration points and time iterations, typically in the order of thousands times thousands.

A problem occurred here is running this subroutine once, and the running time cannot be present by computer because the value is too small. In order to test the efficiency of this subroutine, 10,000 times calling was supposed, and the total calculation times following different TOL value were recorded and used for comparison.

The Euler's method was also tested for efficiency following the same experimental setting. The results are shown in Table VII and Table VIII.

It can be seen that, from Table VII, when TOL = 0.1×10^{-5}, the program running time is 16.1149s. From Table VIII, when time interval is 0.001h, the program running time is 17.6593132s. It can be defined a speed percentage like:

$$percentage = \frac{17.6593132 - 16.1149}{16.1149} = 9.58\%$$

As mentioned before, the accuracy of Euler's method at interval 0.001h can be derived as 0.13%; however, the absolute error is similar with R-K method at TOL of 0.1E-05.

From the above discussion, it is clear that, based on the balance of accuracy and efficiency, the Euler method should not be used and the TOL of 0.1E--04 or 0.1E-05 is a good choice for R-K method on the balance of accuracy and computing efficiency. It is also further noted that further reducing the value of TOL does increase the accuracy significantly, nor costs that much more time.

TABLE VII

Runge-Kutta Method Test

TOL	Programme Running Time (s)
0.1	NONE
0.1×10^{-1}	10.2649
0.1×10^{-2}	15.2569
0.1×10^{-3}	15.7717
0.1×10^{-4}	15.8653
0.1×10^{-5}	16.1149
0.1×10^{-6}	16.4113
0.1×10^{-7}	17.0665
0.1×10^{-8} (Over Load)	1.56×10^{-2}

TABLE VIII

Euler's method test

Time interval	Programme running time (s)
1	1.5600100E-02
0.1	0.1716011
0.01	1.7628113
0.001	17.6593132
0.0001	175.64153

7 Conclusions

This paper reviewed the position which the creep constitutive equations in the finite element analysis method. An advance numerical method, Runge-Kutta method was suggested by Hyhurst, and a Chinese scholar also follows this approach. The more efficient NAG routine was adopted in this research to help the creep FE software development. A specific computational experiment was written detailed, and highlight the way to find a satisfied TOL value.

8 References

[1] J .Manie, A. Wolthers, "Fem GV User's Manual: pre- and post-processing", (2008).

[2] "GID user manual".

[3] F. Tan, Q. Xu, Z. Lu, D. Xu, "Literature review on the development of computational software system for creep damage analysis for weldment", Advanced Materials Research Vol. 510, 2012, pp 490-494

[4] F.V. Tahami, D.R. Hayhurst, M.T. Wong. "Hightemperature creep rupture of low alloy ferritic steel buttwelded pipes subjected to combined internal pressure and end loadings", Philosophical Transactions of the Royal Society A. 363 (2005) 2629-2611.

[5] Wong, M.T. Three-dimensional finite element analysis of creep continuum damage growth and failure in weldment. PhD edn., 1999, UMIST: Manchester.

[6] X. Ling, S. Tu, J. Gong., "Application of Runge-Kutta-Merson algorithm for creep damage analysis," Int.J.Pressure Vessels Piping. 77, 2000, P. 243-248.

[7] Hagihara, S. and Miyazaki, N. "Finite element analysis for creep failure of coolant pipe in light water reactor due to local heating under severe accident condition", Nuclear Engineering and Design, 238(1), 2008, pp. 33-40.

[8] D. Liu, Q. Xu, Z. Lu, D. Xu, "Research in the development of computational FE software for creep damage mechanics", 18th International Conference on Automation & Computing, Loughborough University, Leicestershire, UK, 2012, pp113-118

[9] D. Hayhurst, P. Dimmer, C. Morrison, "development of continuum damage in the creep rupture of notched bars", Phil. Trans. R. Soc. Lond. A 311, 1984, pp103-129

[10] A. F. Bastani and M. Tahmasebi, "Strong convergence of split-step backward Euler method for stochastic differential equations with non-smooth drift," Journal of Computational and Applied Mathematics, vol. 236, Issue 7, 2012, pp. 1903-1918.

[11] X.N. Wang, X.C. Wang, Finite element analysis on creep damage, Comput.Struct. 60, 1996, pp. 781-786.

[12] I.J. Perrin, D.R. Hayhurst. "Continuum damage mechanics analyses of type IV creep failure in ferritic steel crossweld specimens", Int.J.Pressure Vessels Piping. 76, 1999, 599-617.

[13] "The NAG Fortran Library", Mark 23, The Numerical Algorithms Group Ltd, Oxford, UK.

On the exact explicit solutions of a generalized (2+1)-dimensional Zakharov-Kuznetsov-Benjamin-Bona-Mahony equation

Khadijo Rashid Adem Chaudry Masood Khalique
International Institute for Symmetry Analysis and
Mathematical Modelling, Department of Mathematical Sciences, North-West University, Mafikeng Campus,
Private Bag X 2046, Mmabatho 2735,
Republic of South Africa
Email: Khadijo.R.Adem@gmail.com Masood.Khalique@nwu.ac.za

Abstract— *This paper obtains the solutions of the generalized two-dimensional nonlinear Zakharov-Kuznetsov-Benjamin-Bona-Mahony (ZK-BBM) equation. The Lie group analysis is used to carry out the integration of this equation. Furthermore, we employ the simplest equation method to obtain more exact solutions. The solutions obtained are solitary waves.*

1. Introduction

Many physical phenomena in the fields such as physics, chemistry, biology, fluid dynamics, etc., can be in general described by nonlinear evolution equations (NLEEs) . Thus, it is important to investigate the exact explicit solutions of NLEEs. Unfortunately, it is almost impossible to find all the solutions of a nonlinear evolution equation. Nevertheless, various methods, inverse scattering transform method [1], Darboux transformation [2], Hirota's bilinear method [3], Bäcklund transformation [4], multiple exp-function method [5], the (G'/G)-expansion method [6], the sine-cosine method [7], the F-expansion method [8], the exp-function expansion method [9] and the Lie symmetry method [10]–[14] have been developed by researchers to find explicit solutions for the NLEEs.

The purpose of this paper is to study one such NLEE, namely the generalized (2+1)-dimensional nonlinear Zakharov-Kuznetsov-Benjamin-Bona-Mahony (ZK-BBM) equation [15] that is given by

$$u_t + u_x + a(u^n)_x + b(u_{xt} + u_{yy})_x = 0. \quad (1.1)$$

Here, in (1.1) a, b and $n > 1$ are real valued constants.

The solutions of (1.1) have been studied in various aspects. See for example the recent papers [15]–[20]. Wazwaz [15], [16] used the sine-cosine method, the tanh method and the extended tanh method for finding solitary solutions of this equation. Abdou [17], [18] used the extended F-expansion method and the extended mapping method with symbolic computation to obtain some exact solutions. Mahmoudi [19] used the Exp-Function method to obtain some solitary solutions and periodic solutions. Song [20] used bifurcation method to obtain exact solitary wave solutions and kink wave solutions.

In this paper Lie group analysis [10]–[14] in conjunction with the simplest equation method [21] is employed to obtain some exact solutions of (1.1).

2. Symmetry analysis

In this section we first calculate the Lie point symmetries of (1.1) and latter use them to construct exact solutions.

2.1 Lie point symmetries

The symmetries of ZK-BBM equation (1.1) will be generated by the vector field of the form

$$X = \xi^1 \frac{\partial}{\partial x} + \xi^2 \frac{\partial}{\partial y} + \xi^3 \frac{\partial}{\partial t} + \eta \frac{\partial}{\partial u}, \quad (2.2)$$

where ξ^i, $i = 1, 2, 3$ and η depend on x, y, t and u. Applying the third prolongation $\mathrm{pr}^{(3)}X$ to (1.1) we obtain an overdetermined system of linear partial differential equations. Solving resultant system of linear overdetermined partial differential equations one obtains the following three translation symmetries:

$$X_1 = \partial_x, \quad X_2 = \partial_y, \quad X_3 = \partial_t.$$

2.2 Exact solutions

First of all we utilize the symmetry $X = X_1 + \nu X_2 + X_3$ and reduce the ZK-BBM equation (1.1) to a PDE in two independent variables. It can be seen that the symmetry X yields the following three invariants:

$$f = y - \nu t, \quad g = t - x, \quad \theta = u. \quad (2.3)$$

Now treating θ as the new dependent variable and f and g as new independent variables, the KP-BBM equation (1.1) transforms to

$$-\nu\theta_f - an\theta^{n-1}\theta_g - \nu b\theta_{fgg} + b\theta_{ggg} - b\theta_{ffg} = 0, \quad (2.4)$$

which is a nonlinear PDE in two independent variables. We now use the Lie point symmetries of (2.4) and transform it to an ordinary differential equation (ODE). The equation (2.4) has the two translational symmetries, viz.,

$$\Gamma_1 = \frac{\partial}{\partial f}, \quad \Gamma_2 = \frac{\partial}{\partial g}.$$

The combination $\Gamma_1 + \Gamma_2$, of the two symmetries Γ_1 and Γ_2 yields the two invariants

$$r = f - g, \quad \psi = \theta,$$

which gives rise to a group invariant solution $\psi = \psi(r)$. Consequently using these invariants, (2.4) is transformed into the third-order nonlinear ODE

$$-\nu\psi' + an\psi^{n-1}\psi' - \nu b\psi''' = 0. \tag{2.5}$$

Integrating the above equation once and taking the constants of integration to be zero we obtain a second-order ODE

$$-\nu\psi + a\psi^{n} - \nu b\psi'' = 0. \tag{2.6}$$

Multiplying equation (2.6) by ψ', integrating once and taking the constant of integration to be zero, we obtain the first-order ODE

$$-\frac{1}{2}\nu\psi^2 + \frac{a}{n+1}\psi^{n+1} - \frac{1}{2}\nu b\psi'^2 = 0. \tag{2.7}$$

One can integrate the above equation by separating the variables. After integrating and reverting back to the original variables, we obtain the following group-invariant solutions of the ZK-BBM equation (1.1) for arbitrary values of n in the form:

$$u(x,y,t) = \left(\frac{\nu(n+1)}{2a}\right)^{\frac{1}{n-1}} \operatorname{sech}^{\frac{2}{n-1}}[Q], \tag{2.8}$$

$$\begin{aligned} Q &= \gamma\left(\sqrt{\frac{2}{b\nu}}r - C\right), \\ \gamma &= \sqrt{-\frac{\nu}{8}}(1-n), \\ r &= (x + y - (\nu+1)t). \end{aligned}$$

For $n = 1$,

$$u(x,y,t) = \exp\left[\mp\frac{C_1\sqrt{-\nu+a}}{\sqrt{2}} \pm \frac{\sqrt{\nu-a}}{\sqrt{-\nu b}}r\right], \tag{2.9}$$

$r = (x + y - (\nu+1)t)$,
for $n = 2$,

$$u(x,y,t) = -\frac{3}{\nu}\operatorname{sech}^2\left[\frac{1}{2}\left(\pm C_2\sqrt{-\frac{\nu}{2}} \mp \sqrt{\frac{-1}{b}}r\right)\right]. \tag{2.10}$$

$r = (x + y - (\nu+1)t)$ By taking $n = 2$, $a = -1$, $b = 1$, $\nu = 6$, $t = 0$ and $C = 1$ in (2.8), the profile of the solution is given in Figure 1.

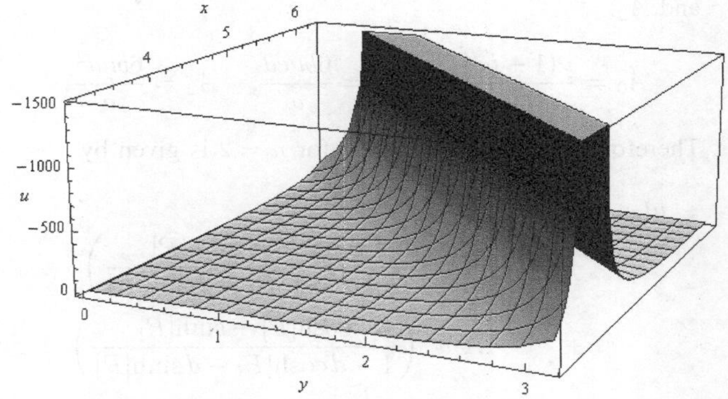

Fig. 1: Profile of solution (2.8)

3. Simplest equation method

In this section we use the simplest equation method [21] to solve the third-order ODE (2.5) for $n = 2, 3$. The simplest equations that will be used are the Bernoulli and Ricatti equations. Their solutions can be written in terms of elementary functions. See for example [14].

Let us consider the solution of (2.5) in the form

$$\psi(r) = \sum_{i=0}^{M} A_i (H(r))^i, \tag{3.11}$$

where $H(r)$ satisfies the Bernoulli and Ricatti equations, M is a positive integer that can be determined by balancing procedure and $A_0, \cdots, A_M$ are parameters to be determined.

3.1 Solutions of (2.5) using the equation of Bernoulli as the simplest equation

3.1.1 $n = 2$

The balancing procedure yields $M = 2$ so the solutions of (3.11) are of the form

$$\psi(r) = A_0 + A_1 H + A_2 H^2. \tag{3.12}$$

Substituting (3.12) into (2.5) and making use of the Bernoulli equation [14] and then equating all coefficients of the functions H^i to zero, we obtain an algebraic system of equations in terms of A_0, A_1 and A_2. These algebraic equations are

$$\begin{aligned} &4aA_2^2 d - 24bA_2 d^3\nu = 0, \\ &2aA_0A_1c - bA_1c^3\nu - A_1c\nu = 0, \\ &6aA_1A_2d - 54bA_2cd^2\nu - 6bA_1d^3\nu + 4aA_2^2c = 0, \\ &-12bA_1cd^2\nu - 38bA_2c^2d\nu + 6aA_1A_2c \\ &+2aA_1^2d - 2A_2d\nu + 4aA_0A_2d = 0, \\ &-7bA_1c^2d\nu + 4aA_0A_2c - 2A_2c\nu + 2aA_1^2c \\ &+2aA_0A_1d - A_1d\nu - 8bA_2c^3\nu = 0. \end{aligned}$$

Solving the above system of algebraic equations with the aid of Mathematica, we obtain the following values of A_0, A_1

and A_2:

$$A_0 = \frac{\nu(1+bc^2)}{2a}, \quad A_1 = \frac{6b\nu cd}{a}, \quad A_2 = \frac{6b\nu d^2}{a}.$$

Therefore the solution of (1.1), for $n = 2$ is given by

$$\begin{aligned} u(x,y,t) &= A_0 \\ &+ A_1 a\left(\frac{\cosh[P]+\sinh[P]}{1-d\cosh[P]-d\sinh[P]}\right) \\ &+ A_2 a^2\left(\frac{\cosh[P]+\sinh[P]}{1-d\cosh[P]-d\sinh[P]}\right)^2, \end{aligned}$$

where $P = c(r+C)$ and $r = x+y-(\nu+1)t$ and C is a constant of integration.

3.1.2 $n = 3$

The balancing procedure yields $M = 1$ so the solutions of (3.11) are of the form

$$\psi(r) = A_0 + A_1 H. \quad (3.13)$$

As before, substituting (3.13) into (2.5), we obtain the algebraic system of equations

$$\begin{aligned} 3aA_1^3 d - 6bA_1 d^3\nu &= 0, \\ -A_1 c\nu - bA_1 c^3\nu + 3aA_1 A_0^2 c &= 0, \\ 6aA_1^2 A_0 d + 3aA_1^3 c - 12bA_1 cd^2\nu &= 0, \\ 3aA_1 A_0^2 d - A_1 d\nu + 6aA_1^2 A_0 c - 7bA_1 c^2 d\nu &= 0, \end{aligned}$$

which on solving yields

$$A_0 = \sqrt{\frac{2bd^2\nu}{a}}, \quad A_1 = c\sqrt{\frac{b\nu}{2a}}.$$

Therefore the solution of (1.1), for $n = 3$ is given by

$$\begin{aligned} u(x,y,t) &= A_0 \\ &+ A_1 a\left(\frac{\cosh[P]+\sinh[P]}{1-d\cosh[P]-d\sinh[P]}\right), \end{aligned} \quad (3.14)$$

where $r = x+y-(\nu+1)t$ and C is a constant of integration.

3.2 Solutions of (2.5) using Riccati equation as the simplest equation

3.2.1 $n = 2$

The balancing procedure yields $M = 2$ so the solutions of (3.11) are of the form

$$\psi(r) = A_0 + A_1 H + A_2 H^2. \quad (3.15)$$

Substituting (3.15) into (2.5) and making use of the Riccati equation [14], we obtain algebraic equations in terms of A_0, A_1, A_2 by equating all coefficients of the functions H^i to zero. The corresponding algebraic equations are

$$\begin{aligned} &4aA_2^2 c - 24bA_2 c^3\nu = 0, \\ &6aA_1 A_2 c - 6bA_1 c^3\nu + 4aA_2^2 d - 54bA_2 c^2 d\nu = 0, \\ &-2bA_1 ce^2\nu + 2aA_0 A_1 e - 6bA_2 de^2\nu - bA_1 d^2 e\nu \\ &-A_1 e\nu = 0, \\ &4aA_0 A_2 c - 38bA_2 cd^2\nu + 6aA_1 A_2 d - 2A_2 c\nu \\ &-12bA_1 c^2 d\nu + 2aA_1^2 c + 4aA_2^2 e - 40bA_2 c^2 e\nu = 0, \\ &-14bA_2 d^2 e\nu + 4aA_0 A_2 e - A_1 d\nu - bA_1 d^3\nu - 2A_2 e\nu \\ &+2aA_1^2 e + 2aA_0 A_1 d - 8bA_1 cde\nu - 16bA_2 ce^2\nu = 0, \\ &-7bA_1 cd^2\nu + 6aA_1 A_2 e - A_1 c\nu + 2aA_0 A_1 c \\ &-52bA_2 cde\nu + 4aA_0 A_2 d - 8bA_1 c^2 e\nu - 8bA_2 d^3\nu \\ &-2A_2 d\nu + 2aA_1^2 d = 0. \end{aligned}$$

Solving the above equations yield

$$A_0 = \frac{1}{2a}(\nu bd^2 + 8\nu bce + \nu), \quad A_1 = \frac{6\nu bcd}{a}, \quad A_2 = \frac{6\nu bc^2}{a}$$

and hence the solutions of (1.1) for $n = 2$ are

$$\begin{aligned} u(x,y,t) &= A_0 + A_1\left(-\frac{d}{2c} - \frac{\theta}{2c}\tanh\left[\frac{1}{2}\theta(r+C)\right]\right) \\ &+A_2(-\frac{d}{2c} \\ &- \frac{\theta}{2c}\tanh\left[\frac{1}{2}\theta(r+C)\right])^2 \end{aligned} \quad (3.16)$$

and

$$\begin{aligned} u(x,y,t) &= A_0 + A_1(-\frac{d}{2c} - \frac{\theta}{2c}\tanh\left(\frac{1}{2}\theta r\right) \\ &+ \frac{\operatorname{sech}\left(\frac{\theta r}{2}\right)}{C\cosh\left(\frac{\theta r}{2}\right) - \frac{2c}{\theta}\sinh\left(\frac{\theta r}{2}\right)}) \\ &+A_2(-\frac{d}{2c} - \frac{\theta}{2c}\tanh\left(\frac{1}{2}\theta r\right) \\ &+ \frac{\operatorname{sech}\left(\frac{\theta r}{2}\right)}{C\cosh\left(\frac{\theta r}{2}\right) - \frac{2c}{\theta}\sinh\left(\frac{\theta r}{2}\right)})^2 \end{aligned}$$

where $r = x+y-(\nu+1)t$ and C is a constant of integration.

3.2.2 $n = 3$

The balancing procedure yields $M = 1$ so the solutions of (3.11) are of the form

$$\psi(r) = A_0 + A_1 H. \quad (3.17)$$

Substituting (3.17) into (2.5), we obtain the following algebraic system of equations:

$$
\begin{aligned}
&-6bA_1c^3\nu + 3aA_1^3c = 0,\\
&6aA_1^2A_0c + 3aA_1^3d - 12bA_1c^2d\nu = 0,\\
&3aA_1A_0^2e - 2bA_1ce^2\nu - A_1e\nu - bA_1d^2e\nu = 0,\\
&-8bA_1cde\nu - A_1d\nu + 6aA_1^2A_0e - bA_1d^3\nu\\
&+3aA_1A_0^2d = 0,\\
&-A_1c\nu + 3aA_1^3e - 7bA_1cd^2\nu + 3aA_1A_0^2c\\
&+6aA_1^2A_0d - 8bA_1c^2e\nu = 0.
\end{aligned}
$$

Solving the algebraic equations one obtain

$$
\begin{aligned}
c &= \frac{-2 + bd^2}{4be},\\
A_0 &= 2bd\sqrt{\frac{\nu}{8abe^2}},\\
A_1 &= \sqrt{\frac{\nu(-2 + bd^2)^2}{8abe^2}}.
\end{aligned}
$$

Hence we have the following solutions of (1.1) for $n = 3$:

$$
\begin{aligned}
u(x,y,t) &= A_0\\
&+A_1\left(-\frac{d}{2c} - \frac{\theta}{2c}\tanh\left[\frac{1}{2}\theta(r + C)\right]\right) \qquad (3.18)
\end{aligned}
$$

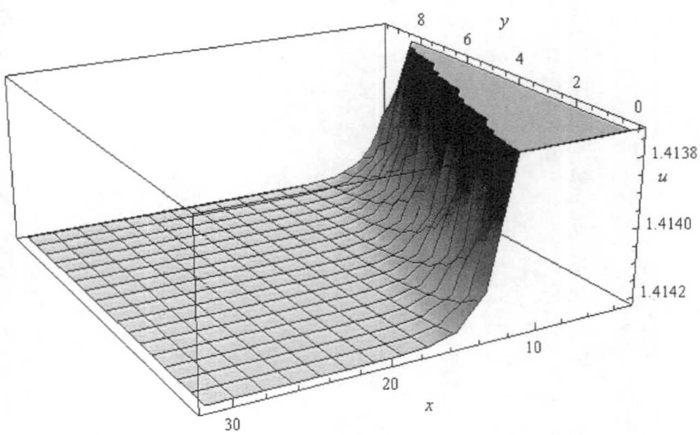

Fig. 2: Profile of solution (3.18)

and

$$
u(x,y,t) = A_0 + A_1(-\frac{d}{2c} - \frac{\theta}{2c}\tanh\left(\frac{1}{2}\theta r\right)
$$

$$
+\frac{\text{sech}(\frac{\theta r}{2})}{C\cosh(\frac{\theta r}{2}) - \frac{2c}{\theta}\sinh(\frac{\theta r}{2})}), \qquad (3.19)
$$

where $r = x + y - (\nu + 1)t$ and C is a constant of integration.

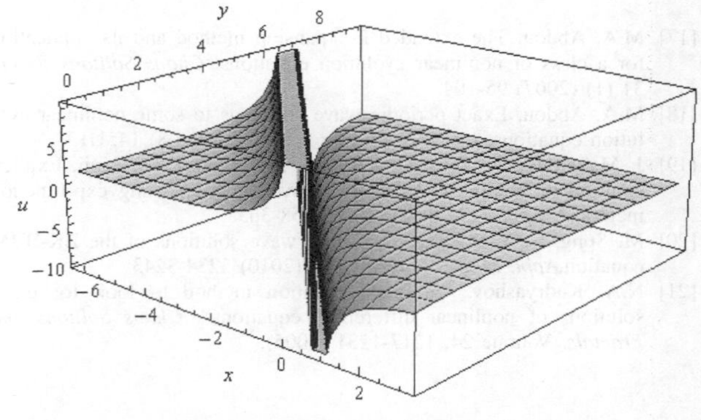

Fig. 3: Profile of solution (3.19)

4. Concluding remarks

In this paper we obtained the solutions of the generalized (2+1)-dimensional nonlinear Zakharov-Kuznetsov-Benjamin-Bona-Mahony equation by employing the Lie group analysis and the simplest equation method. The solutions obtained are solitary waves and non-topological solitons.

References

[1] M.J. Ablowitz, P. A. Clarkson, Soliton, Nonlinear Evolution Equations and Inverse Scattering, Cambridge University Press, Cambridge, 1991.

[2] V.B. Matveev, M. A. Salle, Darboux Transformation and Soliton, Springer, Berlin, 1991.

[3] R. Hirota, The Direct Method in Soliton Theory, Cambridge University Press, Cambridge, 2004.

[4] C.H. Gu, Soliton Theory and Its Application, Zhejiang Science and Technology Press, Zhejiang, 1990.

[5] W.X. Ma, T. Huang, Y. Zhang, A multiple exp-function method for nonlinear differential equations and its applications, Phys. Scr. 82 (2010) 065003

[6] M. Wang, L.X. Xiangzheng, Z.J. Jinliang, The (G'/G)-expansion method and travelling wave solutions of nonlinear evolution equations in mathematical physics, Physics Letters A 372 (2008) 417-423.

[7] M. Wazwaz, The Tanh and Sine-Cosine Method for Compact and Noncompact Solutions of Nonlinear Klein Gordon Equation, Appl. Math. Comput. 167 (2005) 1179-1195.

[8] M. Wang, X. Li, Extended F-Expansion and Periodic Wave Solutions for the Generalized Zakharov Equations, Phys. Lett. A. 343 (2005) 48- 54.

[9] J.H. He, X. H. Wu, Exp-Function Method for Nonlinear Wave Equations, Chaos Soliton Fract. 30 (2006) 70.

[10] G.W. Bluman, S. Kumei, Symmetries and Differential Equations, Applied Mathematical Sciences, 81, Springer-Verlag, New York, 1989.

[11] P.J. Olver, Applications of Lie Groups to Differential Equations, Graduate Texts in Mathematics, 107, 2nd edition, Springer-Verlag, Berlin, 1993.

[12] N.H. Ibragimov, CRC Handbook of Lie Group Analysis of Differential Equations, Vol 1-3, CRC Press, Boca Raton, Florida, 1994-1996.

[13] L.V. Ovsiannikov, Group Analysis of Differential Equations, Academic Press, New York, (English translation by W.F. Ames) 1982.

[14] K.R. Adem, C.M. Khalique, Exact solutions and conservation laws of Zakharov-Kuznetsov modified equal width equation with power law nonlinearity, Nonlinear Analysis:Real World Applications. 13 (2012) 1692-1707.

[15] A.M. Wazwaz,Compact and noncompact physical structures for the ZK-BBM equation, *Appl. Math. Comput.* 169 (1) (2005) 713-725.

[16] A.M. Wazwaz, The extended tanh method for new compact and noncompact solutions for the KP-BBM and the ZK-BBM equations, *Chaos Solitons Fract.*, 38 (5) (2008) 1505-1516.

[17] M.A. Abdou, The extended F-expansion method and its application for a class of nonlinear evolution equations, *Chaos Solitons Fract.*, 31 (1) (2007) 95-104.
[18] M.A. Abdou, Exact periodic wave solutions to some nonlinear evolution equations, *Int. J. Nonlinear Sci.*, 6 (2) (2008) 145Ű153.
[19] J. Mahmoudi, N. Tolou, I. Khatami, A. Barari, D.D. Ganji, Explicit solution of nonlinear ZKŰBBM wave equation using exp-function method,*J. Appl. Sci.*, 8 (2) (2008) 358-363.
[20] M. Song, C. Yang, Exact traveling wave solutions of the ZK-BBM equation,*Appl. Math. Comput.*, 216 (2010) 3234-3243
[21] N.A. Kudryashov, "Simplest equation method to look for exact solutions of nonlinear differential equations". *Chaos Solitons and Fractals*. Volume 24, 1217-1231 (2005).

Emergent properties, identical elements in a recursive loop and systems with unobservable energy

Author Guido Massa Finoli
IT Advisor, Rome, Italy
guidomassafinoli@virgilio.it

Abstract *– Our goal is to demonstrate how, with a self-generating operator, can be achieved emergent properties and how the measurements of a physical system can be expressed by a recursive bi-cyclic, in the S/T. We pushed this to determine level jumps and identical entities, and how the two are related to each other. In addition, by analogy with the numerical model, we try to prove the existence of a change in energy between aggregate system and single(or unique) system. Conceptualize the possibility that a system, with identical entities, has a form of unobservable energy.*

Keywords: *emergent properties, recursive loop, identical entities, tearing space and time, the numerical model, unobservable energy.*

1 Systems, emerging Properties and Self-generating Operator

. One of the crucial points, in the study of complex systems, is to determine the difference between holistic system (or Single, Unique) and aggregate system. A holistic system is, typically, defined as a system of elements, that has properties do not found in the individual elements that make it up. The combination of these elements together, under certain conditions, reveals new properties. [1]

1.1 Definition of emerging Properties

In general terms, an emergent property is a property not present in the constituents of the system, but present in the system as a whole. They occur after exceeding a critical level, a crucial point, emerges as a real jump in level. Our first step is to define this jump in level, in terms of measure, and the reference system. In my paper of 2006, I called the measure, of an emergent property, in the following way:

If we measure the constituents of a system $e_1, e_2, \ldots, e_k$, with respect to a reference system μ, their aggregation with $\sum_k e_k$, and E_α the measurement of the single system, with respect to a reference system U. Therefore, an emergent property, can be measured if between the measures $\sum_k e_k$ and the summed measure E_α, there is a factor of incommensurability Θ. But this definition is valid only for systems that have the points of incommensurability in a change or bifurcation point. For example, if we take 4 components, measured in μ, (1, 2, 3, 4) and two systems resulting, measured in U, that are A, if $\sum_k e_k < 10$, and B, if $\sum_k e_k \geq 10$. We set a rule, that you can add only 3 and more elements without repetition, and that any measurement of an element can bring with it a factor θ, from 0 to 0.5. Then we have: 1 + 2 + 3 = 6 ÷ 7, and the result will always be A, the same is true for 1 + 3 + 4. With 1 + 2+ 3 + 4 = 10 ÷ 11, the result will always be B. If we have 2 + 3 + 4 the result will fluctuate as a bifurcation point 9÷ 10, so we will have some cases with A and other with B.[2] As can be seen, the incommensurability factor, present to the measure, becomes a decisive factor only if it helps to determine the transition from one branch or the other, at the point of bifurcation. But there is another way in which the factor θ can interfere with the determination of the properties of a single system (or holistic), and is in the determination of entities measured as identical, and which together form the system. We will try to demonstrate how precisely their presence can generate new emergent properties, that are manifested by changes in energy and real level jumps between constituents and systems.

1.2 Generation of a measured system through the Operator Γ

In the essay "Lineamenti per un nuovo modello per i sistemi complessi" called a self-generating operator Γ, can occur as a rule and as a symbol, and then be able to act on itself by determining the space of possibilities of the system. The mathematical operator, that is closest to this idea, is the recursive loop, and we explained how the measure of Γ, Msr (Γ), is precisely the space defined by a recursive loop, which we call space ω.[3]

We consider $\Gamma^k(\Gamma)$, how the action of Γ on Γ generating a space of possibilities, yet to be determined since it is not measured. Now call a reference system capable of measuring as coexisting, these states of the system, i.e. $\Gamma^3(\Gamma) = \Gamma + \Gamma + \Gamma$. We have seen how, in terms of the operator Γ, this means having a system with ordinality 3, or Γ3, and a system with cardinality 3, or 3Γ. The different position of the measurement allows us to switch from one to another reference, in fact:

With the measure $Msr(\Gamma^3(\Gamma))$, we have one of the states of the system and with $\Gamma^3(Msr(\Gamma))$, we have the determination of 3 different measures. But if we consider the system with respect to a time interval Δt, it can be seen its components coexisting to the condition that they are all differentiable. [4] So we have:

$$Msr(\Gamma^3(\Gamma)) = Msr(\Gamma_1 + \Gamma_2 + \Gamma_3) \text{ and} \quad (1)$$

$$\Gamma^3(Msr(\Gamma)) = Msr(\Gamma_1) + Msr(\Gamma_2) + Msr(\Gamma_3) \quad (2)$$

In the first case, we have the measure of the system as a single system, in the second case as an aggregate of elements. But what exactly is the Msr (Γ) with respect to a reference system μ? We have defined a measure as a certain algorithm that expresses the result in a specified value (finite) space-time. [5]

$$\Gamma_1 = Msr(\Gamma_1) + \theta_1 = s_1\mu + \theta_1 \quad (3)$$

Where s_1 is the measured value with respect to the unit of measure of the μ, and θ is the factor of incommensurability of measurement. Now if we consider these 3 measurements as 3 components of a system, their sum give the system as an aggregate of elements:

$$Msr(\Gamma_1) + Msr(\Gamma_2) + Msr(\Gamma_3) = (s_1 + s_2 + s_3)\mu \quad (4)$$

If we consider the measure of the system as a whole, as a single system, then we will make an overall measure of it with respect to a U. That is:

$$Msr(\Gamma^3(\Gamma)) = Msr(\Gamma_1 + \Gamma_2 + \Gamma_3) = SU \quad (5)$$

But even here we have:

$$\Gamma^3(\Gamma) = Msr(\Gamma_1 + \Gamma_2 + \Gamma_3) + \Theta = SU + \Theta \quad (6)$$

Where Θ is the factor of incommensurability, we have:

$$Msr(Msr(\Gamma_1) + \theta_1 + Msr(\Gamma_2) + \theta_2 + Msr(\Gamma_3) + \theta_3) \quad (7)$$

$$Msr(s_1 + s_2 + s_3) + Msr(\theta_1 + \theta_2 + \theta_3) \quad (8)$$

Since the two measurement systems μ and U are always commensurate with each other, and will be $Msr(s_1 + s_2 + s_3)$, as a factor U. The question is whether we can measure with U, the sum of the factors of incommensurability components $Msr(\theta_1 + \theta_2 + \theta_3)$, or if this is not possible. If we can, then we have:

$$Msr(\theta_1 + \theta_2 + \theta_3) = S_b U \text{ e } Msr(s_1 + s_2 + s_3) = S_a U \quad (9)$$

and the total size of the system $(S_a + S_b)U$ and so, with U, will be measuring something different from the sum of the measures μ. If it is not possible then, $Msr(\theta_1 + \theta_2 + \theta_3) = \Theta$ and this means that $Msr(s_1 + s_2 + s_3) = SU$, the aggregate of elements corresponds to the measurement system as a whole. We can also have the intermediate case where only a part of the factor of incommensurability is measured. The example we have done previously is part of this formalization. These considerations have a value of example; they are unlikely to be encountered in real cases. Our goal is to assume the existence of an energy corresponding to this factor of incommensurability and it can be linked to the presence of identical entities in a system, so we can have a proof of this factor of incommensurability. But first we need to define how we can get the same measures.

2 Recursive Cyclic and measures of a system

What I want to say here, is that we can represent the space of measures of a system, through a recursive loop, as a result of the action of the operator Γ. We will call the space thus obtained, Space ω; and see how, the measure of identical entities in this space, is able to generate level jumps and especially a differentiation between classical systems and quantum systems.

2.1 Why the space ω can represent the space of the measures of a system

Our idea [6] is that the measure is the result of an invariant and it is given by the relationship between the Instrument of Measure and the Object Measured. The result of a measurement is a number, this number has particular characteristics, and one of them is that it is not isolated. A measure makes sense if in relation to other measures, performed by the same instrument, at the same object, in the same way. A further aspect of the measure is that the process associated with it must always end in a finite time, limited. We can not imagine a measure that gives us its result in an infinite time. Therefore, the measurement process is similar to that of an algorithm (a Turing machine) that gives us the result in a given time, finite. The consequence of this is that the numerical values of the measures are finite numbers. So, when we show that the measure is a determination, will highlight its aspect, discreet and limited in space / time. An important consequence of this is that the set of measures is always a countable set.

Now we extend a hypothesis of quantum physics, which is a measure of an object causes a change. The act of measurement changes the measuring instrument, but according to our model, it forms, with the measured object, an invariant. This means that there must be also equal change in the object, and then the measure, as a value obtained, speaks of this variation from the side of the instrument, but there is also a corresponding from the object side. The measurement obtained is the measurement from the side of the instrument of the action of the invariant Γ. It contains, in itself, the result of this interaction, which becomes a measurement of the variations of the object when the same instrument performs multiple measurements over time. So there is one aspect that speaks to us of the correlation between the side of the instrument and the object side, correlation is bound to the value of the invariant. But the side of the object can be varied only in a virtual way, because the actual measurement is, and remains always, the one given to us by the instrument. The use of complex numbers might represent this aspect, the imaginary component is the one given by virtual variation of the measured object, while the real component is the measure produced by the instrument.

The measure that we obtain, understood as a component of the instrument and a component of the object, and expressed by a complex number, represent the value obtained by the relation invariant. And then follows that the next action of the invariant, i.e. the next measurement, applies precisely the object of the previous measurement result; that, from the point of view of the invariant, is the result obtained from its previous action. The action of the invariant is applied on the object, but also on the measuring instrument (changed) and therefore on the number that contains this double variation. This means that the result of its action is a complex number and that its next action is applied to this value. The invariant Γ behaves in all respects as a recursive function, which is always the combination of the variation from the object side and on the side of the instrument. Its next action has, therefore, in turn, as components these two aspects that become the object of its action and so on. In the case of systems that do not have variations from the object side, the action of the invariant coincides with the only real numbers and then with the measures given by the instrument. In this context, the value of the norm has a particular meaning, that of explaining the invariant as a measure.

2.2 Cyclical Recursive and Space ω of measures of a System

A recursive function is a function that has, as arguments-values, the previous results of the same function; starting from a series of initial values that are called, origin of the recursive (or trigger). The recursive can have one or more variables (in $\mathbb{R}$ or $\mathbb{C}$), the result of the function is always unique. In the most trivial, we have:

$$\Re(x_0) = x_1$$

$$\Re(x_1) = \Re(\Re(x_0)) = \Re^2(x_0) = x_2 \qquad (10)$$

$$\Re(x_2) = \Re(\Re(\Re(x_0))) = \Re^3(x_0) = x_3$$

....

Generalizing, we have a k-topple of argument values, also some properties are defined: the set of values resulting form an infinite set U. There may be singular points of the function and there is always an order of the values, obtained from the number of times that the same is applied with respect to an initial value, the order will be isomorphic to $\mathbb{N}$.

We define the space ω as an infinite and countable, described by the action of recursive $\Re$.

1) There are the origin points of the space ω, represented by the values of trigger.
2) The space ω is ordered and countable.
3) The space ω is limited.
4) Given 2 points of ω, $P_i; P_k$ it will always have that $P_i \neq P_k$.

Another fundamental characteristic of the recursive $\Re$, generating such a space, is to be cyclic, i.e.: $\exists k$ t.c. $\Re^k = I$ and then k is the modulus for the n values of cyclic. As we shall see if k is a prime number from which n = m * k + p, the cyclic is not decomposable, otherwise it is. Then a recursive loop creates k congruence classes $U_1, U_2, ..., U_k$, where you distribute points ω, so we have: $\bigcup_k U_k = \omega$.

But the recursive cyclical that generates ω, has an additional feature, the infinity points in each of the sets $U_1, U_2, ..., U_k$ will have a function F(t). So the space ω will be limited by the space described by all of the functions:

$$\{F_1(x), F_2(x), ..., F_k(x)\} = \Omega \qquad (11)$$

Ultimately the space Ω, unlike space ω, is a continuous space. The recursive cyclic gives rise to a space ω therefore has the characteristic of being contained in a finite set of continuous functions, whose number coincides with the modulus of recursive and denoted as space Ω. The trigger conditions change only the phase and the height of the function, and leave modulus unchanged. Also the space Ω is a limited space, the functions described therein are limited and therefore are continuous. [7]

2.3 Bi-cyclic Operator as result of a Recursive. Symmetry

If the space of measures ω is covered by the space generated by the functions $\{F_1(t'), F_2(t'), ..., F_k(t')\}$ and whether they are limited in the range of (n, M), it follows that between 2 measurements, of a certain function F(t), there will always be one, then ω is a dense set and isomorphic to $\mathbb{Z}$ [8]. In addition, the functions F(t) are cyclic in the range Δt, this means that we will have an infinite number of sets

$$\sigma_1 = \sigma(\Delta t'_a) \subset \omega$$

$$\sigma_2 = \sigma(\Delta t'_b) \subset \omega \qquad (12)$$

....

$$\sigma_n = \sigma(\Delta t'_n) \subset \omega$$

and $\sigma_1 \neq \sigma_2 \neq ... \neq \sigma_n$, being the interval Δt constant, it follows there exists an operator P that can translate in time, from the initial set $\sigma_2 = \mathrm{P}(\sigma_1)$. So we have $\sigma_k = \mathrm{P}^k(\sigma_1)$, then:

$$\omega = \bigcup_{i=1}^{\infty} \sigma_i \quad \text{and} \quad \omega = \bigcup_{i=1}^{\infty} \mathrm{P}^i(\sigma_1) \qquad (13)$$

But, we have seen, $\bigcup_k U_k = \omega$ and the functions F(t) are generated by the same operator, then we have a functor such that $F_2 = \Phi(F_1); F_3 = \Phi^2(F_1)$ and this can be applied to a subset U_1 of the range Δt. So we have:

$$\sigma_1 = \bigcup_k \Phi^k(U_1(\Delta t)) \quad \text{and} \quad \omega = \bigcup_{i=1}^{\infty} \mathrm{P}^i(\bigcup_k \Phi^k(U_1(\Delta t_1))) \qquad (14)$$

Leads us to conclude as the space of measures ω may be expressed by a recursive bicyclical, result of a shift in space and time of operators.

If we define Ω as the continuous space where there are emergent properties of the measures, how can we move from a countable dense set ω to a continuous set Ω.? The answer is that in every measure, there is a factor that determines an incommensurability around the same measure. This means that for each point ω will exist a neighbourhood of points $\bar{\omega}$ of Ω that converge at the same point. Then the values calculated, in that neighbourhood, converge to the same measure with a certain margin of error. It can be represented as a Hilbert's space of convergent sequences, to the limit values ω. These sequences are an infinite number but countable, their limits are the real measures ω. And for every limit, there will be N possible sequences that converge to the same limit, the resulting set of points N^N, will be a continuous infinity of points Ω. Formally we can say $\omega \supset \Omega$ e $\bar{\omega} = \Omega$. This means that if there will be an operator $\Re$ that generates the space of measures ω, then there will also operators P and Φ that define a bicyclic S/T translation. If we can measure a symmetry in $\bar{\omega}$, called emergent symmetry, it will look like the symmetry of neighbourhood measures. But if there is a symmetry in the S/T of $\bar{\omega}$, then we should have a bicyclic given by P and Φ, and therefore $\Re$.

3 Symmetry and emerging jumps Level

An emergent symmetry allows us to seize regularity that the measurements carried, do not seem to have. Many times the measures analyzed seem to have a chaotic distribution, but if we consider the factors of incommensurability, which we indicate as a factor in the neighbourhood of the measure, then their sum leads us to discover shapes and symmetries unpredictable.[9]

3.1 Example of emergent symmetry

We have many examples of such symmetry in fractals, in recursive cyclic mesomorphic; here we want to use the function defined by Hofstadter which we will call RH [10].

$Q(n) = Q(n - Q(n-1)) + Q(n - Q(n-2))$ (15)

and $Q(1) = Q(2) = 1$ Where n is the index of the sequence and Q is resulting value.

If we consider the distances given by P (n) = Q (n +1) - Q (n), we see that it is clearly a symmetry similar to a homothety, and it is only evident if we consider the area of neighbourhood of points.

Fig. 1

This means that will exists an operator that will transform an area of $A(P_j)$ points in an area of $A(P_k)$ points. What we find, in this symmetry, is that at some point in the sequence, there is a jump, what we want to demonstrate is how an operator self-generating, on the type of Γ, will generate a structure of this type. And as the presence of these jumps is a consequence of the presence of identical entities, in the cycle of the recursive.

3.2 Self-generating Operator, identical elements and level jumps

If we analyze the formula RH, we see that it looks like a Fibonacci's function, except that the values of the two preceding elements become indices that tell us how far the current values we take the new values, and add them together. Thus, the value becomes the index and index tells us on its value. When we defined the operator Γ, a characteristic was that, the action of Γ on Γ defined an order of execution. For example $\Gamma^2(\Gamma) = \Gamma 2$, but also that it defined the cardinality of Γ with, $\Gamma^2(\Gamma) = 2\Gamma$. By measuring, this double aspect of Γ was made explicit and separated, with:

$$Msr(\Gamma^n(\Gamma)) \text{ e } \Gamma^n(Msr(\Gamma)) \quad (16)$$

Thus the action of Γ on Γ can be an ordinal action or an action that defines a cardinality, the resulting value can be interpreted either in one direction or another, and this is exactly what happens in RH. Obviously in RH, the action has on two previous elements, and then in the same way we have:

$$\Gamma(\Gamma^k(\Gamma) + \Gamma^{k+1}(\Gamma)) = \Gamma^{k+2}(\Gamma) \quad (17)$$

Now $\Gamma^k(\Gamma)$ and $\Gamma^{k+1}(\Gamma)$ represent two cardinal values, if they are equal to the ordinal values, we have $k\Gamma = \Gamma k$ and $(k+1)\Gamma = \Gamma(k+1)$. But if they are different, they will be $k'\Gamma \neq \Gamma k$ and $(k+1)'\Gamma \neq \Gamma(k+1)$, if we consider the corresponding ordinal of cardinal values, we have $k'\Gamma = \Gamma q$ and $(k+1)'\Gamma = \Gamma p$, the function will come back in the index q and p, and will take the corresponding cardinal values. [11] The cardinal value, of the corresponding index values, will be added together to get the value of cardinal $\Gamma^{k+2}(\Gamma)$. Now it is quite easy to prove as if the first two ordinal items have the same cardinality, $\Gamma^1(\Gamma) = 1\Gamma$ and $\Gamma^2(\Gamma) = 1\Gamma$ or $\Gamma^3(\Gamma) = 3\Gamma$ and $\Gamma^4(\Gamma) = 3\Gamma$, the system will assume the structure jumps. This happens when, with a different ordinality, we have two identical items with the same cardinality. If we try to force the cardinality making them different, the resulting structure would no longer jumps. So, despite the ordinality cycle is always increased, this does not happen for the cardinality; we can say that, ordinality acts as a factor of incommensurability, present but not measured, however intervening in the determination of the measure. The point is then, that a jumping structure is generated when an operator has self-generating elements identical, and one of the reasons is the fact, that having same cardinality means take the same value of an index, and then this doubling the values, and this factor is propagated in the recursive and proceeds forward. .

4 Identical Elements as a tear in the symmetry S/T. Interpretation of a Numerical Model with energy levels

We start from the consideration that the identical elements are measured as identical, in a relativistic reference system, where is the uncertainty principle of Heisenberg. If the space of the measurements, of a physical system, can be represented by a recursive, then the use of the transform Λ allows us to verify if and when, you have on it the same measures.

4.1 The Bi-cyclic recursive embedded in S/T

The identity of measures is seen as a singularity in the S/T, it is the result of an asymmetry which looks like a real tear in space/time. We can represent a physical system immersed in the S/T relativistic, as a recursive bicyclic that moves in space and time, in the following manner: (18)

$$\begin{array}{llll} z_3 = \varphi_2\varphi_1(z_1) & z_6 = \varphi_2\varphi_1\Theta_1(z_1) & z_9 = \varphi_2\varphi_1\Theta_2\Theta_1(z_1) & z_{12} = \varphi_2\varphi_1\Theta_3\Theta_2\Theta_1(z_1) \\ z_2 = \varphi_1(z_1) & z_5 = \varphi_1\Theta_1(z_1) & z_8 = \varphi_1\Theta_2\Theta_1(z_1) & z_{11} = \varphi_1\Theta_3\Theta_2\Theta_1(z_1) \\ z_1 & z_4 = \varphi_3\varphi_2\varphi_1(z_1) & z_7 = \Theta_2\Theta_1(z_1) & z_{10} = \Theta_3\Theta_2\Theta_1(z_1) \end{array}$$

Where: $z_2 = \varphi_1(z_1); z_3 = \varphi_2(z_1); z_4 = \varphi_3(z_1);...$

The first cycle z_1, z_2, z_3 , are all different states observed at the same time, and thus the cycle z_4, z_5, z_6 , it also consists of 3 different states measured at the same time, and that will be placed at a distance from the first time, δt. We can imagine an operator $\mathfrak{R}$ that translates the states of the first cycle z_1, z_2, z_3 in time:

$$\begin{array}{llll} z_3 & z_6 = \mathfrak{R}''(z_3) & z_9 = \mathfrak{R}_1''(z_6) & z_{12} = \mathfrak{R}_2''(z_9) \\ z_2 & z_5 = \mathfrak{R}'(z_2) & z_8 = \mathfrak{R}_1'(z_5) & z_{11} = \mathfrak{R}_2'(z_8) \\ z_1 & z_4 = \mathfrak{R}(z_1) & z_7 = \mathfrak{R}_1(z_4) & z_{10} = \mathfrak{R}_2(z_7) \end{array} \quad (19)$$

as well as an operator Φ, that moves the states spatially, for which we have: (20)

$$\begin{array}{llll} z_3 = \Phi^2(z_1) & z_6 = \mathfrak{R}''(\Phi^2(z_1)) & z_9 = \mathfrak{R}_1''(\Phi^2(z_1)) & z_{13} = \mathfrak{R}_2''(\Phi^2(z_9)) \\ z_2 = \Phi(z_1) & z_5 = \mathfrak{R}'(\Phi(z_1)) & z_8 = \mathfrak{R}_1'(\Phi(z_1)) & z_{12} = \mathfrak{R}_2'(\Phi(z_8)) \\ z_1 & z_4 = \mathfrak{R}(z_1) & z_7 = \mathfrak{R}_1(z_4) & z_{11} = \mathfrak{R}_2(z_7) \end{array}$$

If we set: $\mathfrak{R} = \varphi_3\varphi_2\varphi_1 = \Theta_{32}\varphi_1$ and $\mathfrak{R}' = \varphi_1\varphi_3\varphi_2 = \varphi_1\Theta_{32}$ then the transformation Λ, applied to each cycle z_1, z_2, z_3, z_4, z_5, z_6 , is commutant, in the S/T, only if they remain distinct. In fact, in the case $\Lambda_S^T = \Lambda_T^S$, if $z_1 \neq z_2$ and $z_4 \neq z_5$, then $\Theta_{32}\varphi_1 = \varphi_1\Theta_{32}$. If two cycle states become identical, for example $z_4 = z_5$, then the transformed Λ will be such that $\Lambda_S^T \neq \Lambda_T^S$. The system is not commutant, it is not isomorphic to the S/T, in fact being $z_1 \neq z_2$, to have $z_4 = z_5$ then $\Theta_{32}\varphi_1 \neq \varphi_1\Theta_{32}$. We can also say that if $z_1 \neq z_2$, for $z_4 = z_5$, will be $\mathfrak{R}(z_1) = \mathfrak{R}'(\Phi(z_1))$, or $\mathfrak{R}' = \mathfrak{R}(\Phi^{-1})$ (21). [12]

4.2 The measure of identical entities through transformed Λ

In Appendix of work [13], we explain in brief the operation of the transform Λ. It is nothing other than the measure of the states of the cyclic, respect to a relativistic reference system and in which applies the uncertainty principle of Heisenberg. If we measure a state as in the figure:

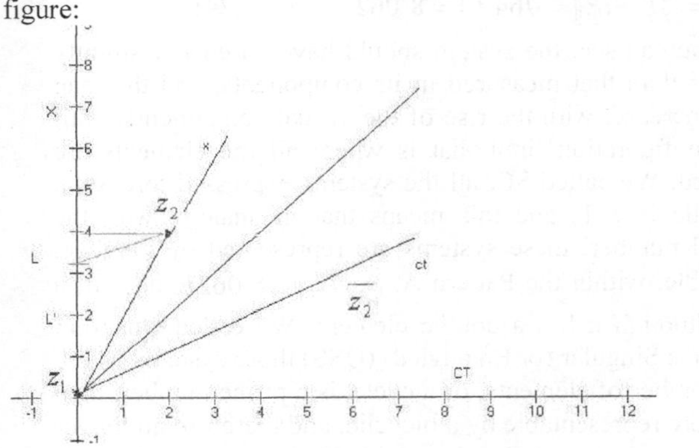

Fig.2

We take two states of bicyclic recursive (18) and embedded in this relativistic system reference. We have from z_1 to measure the distance z_2, now if z_2 is located in the upper part of the dial (a <45), separated from the straight line of light, the two states are different and synchronic, the measured distance is given by the equation Lorentz:

$$L' = \gamma L = \sqrt{1 - \frac{v^2}{c^2}} L \quad (22)$$

If, instead, is located at the bottom (a > 45), will be measured $\overline{z_2}$ as identical to z_1 , but for the exclusion principle, will be diachronic to z_1. So this is what we have to use the transformed Λ, and have the measures of bicyclic operator. We measure, through Λ, state by state, and we are able to determine whether the next state is above or below the line of light. In the first case, states will be differentiated; in the second case will be measured as identical. But we can also say that $\overline{z_2}$, is a virtual value of a hypothetical value, corresponding real, i.e. iL. Is it possible that this virtual value is the factor of incommensurability for the identical elements? This, in terms of the measure of the element, has no value, but it can make sense in the composition of the system as a single system. As aggregate of system, we have identical elements, but when measuring a system as a single system, is it possible to show that this factor of incommensurability emerges and contributes to the formation of the measurement of the single system?

4.3 Analogy of recursive bicyclic with the numerical model

The analogy between the recursive bicyclic and numerical model, leads us to define a model of systems where, if we consider the elements in the range Δt as the end of the cycle time, they will determine the aggregate of elements forming the system. We can represent an aggregate system as a translation operator Φ in Space and as a translation operator $\mathfrak{R}$ in Time. If the elements remain distinct, then the two operators themselves can switch with one another, from which: $\mathfrak{R}^4(\Phi^3) = \Phi^3(\mathfrak{R}^4)$, but this is in turn equivalent to $\mathfrak{R}^3(\Phi^4)$. With the analogy of the numerical model, we have systems of the type (Pattern A):

$$\begin{array}{llll} \mathfrak{R}^2(\Phi^2) & \mathfrak{R}^2(\Phi^3) & \mathfrak{R}^2(\Phi^4) & \mathfrak{R}^2(\Phi^5) \\ \mathfrak{R}^3(\Phi^2) & \mathfrak{R}^3(\Phi^3) & \mathfrak{R}^3(\Phi^4) & \mathfrak{R}^3(\Phi^5) \\ \mathfrak{R}^4(\Phi^2) & \mathfrak{R}^4(\Phi^3) & \mathfrak{R}^4(\Phi^4) & \mathfrak{R}^4(\Phi^5) \\ \mathfrak{R}^5(\Phi^2) & \mathfrak{R}^5(\Phi^3) & \mathfrak{R}^5(\Phi^4) & \mathfrak{R}^5(\Phi^5) \end{array}$$

Fig.3

In terms of measure, in the S/T, this means that we have n distinct measures, in the previous 12. Arranged as shown:

$$\begin{array}{|llll} z_3 & z_6 & z_9 & z_{12} \\ z_2 & z_5 & z_8 & z_{11} \\ z_1 & z_4 & z_7 & z_{10} \\ \hline \end{array}$$

Fig.4

It should be noted that the measurement of 12 elements is possible only when they are all different in the S/T or reconstructed on orbits distinct, they are not more so, when the system is in superposition and their orbits can not be distinguished.

These elements, separated by an interval Δt, form the cycle of the system, and it can be regarded as an aggregate system of elements. Now if, in such a system, 2 elements become identical, then the possible states will be no longer 12 but 11, and 11, being a prime number, can not be represented through a recursive bicyclic. The system will no longer be seen as a system in space/time, no longer belong to the Pattern A, becomes a quantum singularity. [14]

4.4 Example of identity elements and energy variation in the Model

In general, we can say that an element is differentiated when it is locatable in space and time. A quantum superposition occurs when two or more elements are located at the same instant S/T, this determines the increase of frequency of a certain state compared to other measurable. Also means that identical items, of the same state, can be measured only in chronological order, i.e. they are diachronic. As we have seen, if we measure $\overline{z_2}$ as z_1, we could say that there will still be a factor of incommensurability, which presents itself as an imaginary. The problem we have is: This factor can not be measured as part of the system, as element. Can it become part of the measurement system, as a single system?
To answer this question we need to define an energy interpretation of the numerical model. Consider a system consisting of 9 items by a recursive bicyclic in the S/T. 9 elements are all distinguishable even if in the first cycle are synchronous, this may happen because the functions of which they lie are distinguishable. Now we want to define the elements of such a system from the point of view of energy; give, each element, an energy value and see what happens in the case of elements which are identical. We construct a system of reference energy in the following way: [15] Rotate the axis S / T of 45 degrees, so you have on the Y axis the change in energy ΔE, and on the X-axis, temporal variation ΔT. As shown below:

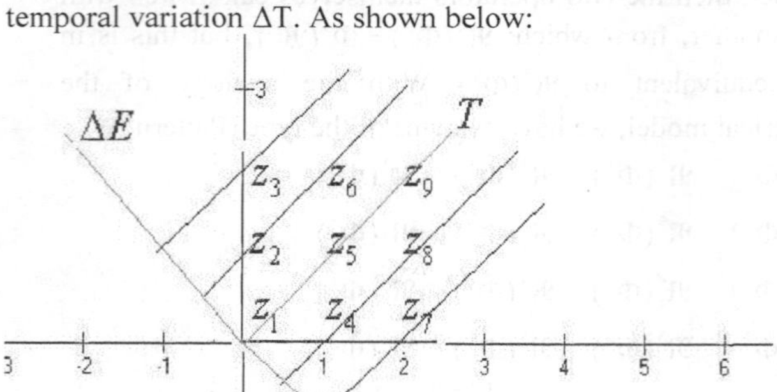

Fig.5

In a classic system (SC) all values will be distinguishable as ΔT, to make the idea of this, we must consider the values $z_1; z_2; z_3$ are not perfectly aligned with those of $z_4; z_5; z_6$; in such a way that the measure z_2 and z_4 is carried out on different points of T. Furthermore, if we assume $(z_1; z_5; z_9)$, that have the energy level E, then $(z_2; z_6)$ they will have the energy level E+ΔE, and so level $(z_4; z_8)$, E-ΔE. The result will be that systems SC, will have elements (and orbits) differentiated, the whole energy level will be $E_{tot} = 9E$. But what happens if we have two measured elements as identical? As in the previous case of $z_2 = z_1$? To explain this, let's see what happens if the elements of such a system are all aligned (as shown). In this case, the instant T_2 we will measure or an element with energy level E + ΔE or with value E - ΔE. This means that states distinguishable are no longer 9 but 5. What happens to the other possible states? Will be part of the system as a single system?
In fact, it is as if these states are not in a real way, but in a virtual way. In our model we measure a system with total energy $E_{tot} = 5E$ with a delta of +ΔE and –ΔE. That is $E_{tot} = 5E \pm 4\Delta E$, but this is the energy of the system into its components, the single system is the measure of the system as a whole and not only the real part, but also of the imaginary. And the imaginary part is represented by its elements, can not be measured as elements, or i4E. [16]
Then:

$$E_U = \|E_{OB} + iE_{NOB}\| \quad (23)$$

Where E_U is the energy of the system, as a single system, E_{OB} is the energy observed in the component and E_{NOB} the energy is not observable. It is present only virtually in the system but is realized when the system becomes one. In the previous model, which will measure the energy in the single system is not 5E, but $\sqrt{41} = 6,403$..
The case examined, is different entities measured at the same time, but the same thing happens for the same entity at the same time. In the instant T we will measure only one element of the possible ones. The other elements are still present in the system, but in a virtual way. If the instants are the same, the presence may only be virtual, so if we have 1 double element and the others distinguishable, the energy level of the single system will be:

$$E_{U2} = \|8E + iE\| = \sqrt{64+1} = 8,062 \quad (24)$$

As you can see, the system should have an energy slightly higher than that measured in its components, and this gap will increase, with the rise of the virtual components, until the configuration limit that is where all the elements are aligned. We called SC, all the systems expressed through a bicyclic in S/T, and this means that in analogy with the model number, these systems are represented by numbers divisible, within the Pattern A. So $E_{U2} = 8,062E$ it's still a SC although it has a double element. We called Quantum Systems Singular (or Entangled) (QSS) those systems where the number of elements, of a cycle, is a prime number, then no more representable by a bicyclic, and therefore no longer present in Pattern A. Systems with 5E, then, no longer have a measurable structure in the S/T, they are singular systems in S/T, the energy value is assigned to a reference standard, which we call q. Therefore the systems that have, as components values of the whole, a prime number, must have a singularity which we call q, but it is not said that this singularity is also present in the single system, in fact in the former case we have:

$$E_{U5} = \|5E + i4E\| = \sqrt{41} = 6,403 \qquad (25)$$

This means that aggregate system is therefore a QSS, while the single system is a QSC and is observable in the S/T relativistic.

Let us summarize the key aspects of our model:

1) Identical elements of a recursive bicyclic generate a superposition of states. The factor of incommensurability that follows, presents itself, in terms of energy, as Energy unobservable.

2) The bicyclic systems in S/T have analogy with the numbers divisible, by a numerical model. The resulting systems can be called SC-symmetric, in S/T.

3) Systems in the asymmetric S/T are singularities, tears in the fabric S/T, have analogy with prime numbers and we call them, Quantum Systems Singularities.

4) An aggregate system, representable by two cycles of a recursive in the S/T, in analogy with the numerical model, can be measured with respect to a reference system ΔE/T. The elements in it distinguishable form the energy observable, and the elements indistinguishable form the energy not observable, expressed as a value imaginary.

5) The measurement of a single system will be given by the norm of the complex number, obtained by the observable energy and the unobservable energy.

6) If the resulting energy represents a number divisible, it will be expressed by a bicyclic recursive in the S/T, if it is a prime number, the system will be seen as a singularity in the S/T, as an event entangled.

If such a model corresponds to reality, then we have a way to explain the existence of the hidden energy. There must be a way to generate power from a system, making observable, energy that is not observable and must, therefore, exist an efficient way to decide whether a number is prime or not.

5. References

[1] G. Massa Finoli. "Un modello logico filosofico per i sistemi complessi", 2006. Pg. 9-17. The conditions of aggregation are as important as the aggregation itself, an example for all are the properties of materials at very low temperatures.

[2] G. Massa Finoli. Ibidem, 2006, Pg.25-28;46-50;147-162 .

[3] G. Massa Finoli, "Lineamenti per un nuovo modello interpretativo dei sistemi complessi",2012, pg.73-97.

[4] G. Massa Finoli. Ibidem, 2012, Pg.226-232. The idea is that in every cycle, we have one and only one measure, but if the states are on different orbits and remain on them, then you can define, in a given time, the position of co-existing measures.

[5] G. Massa Finoli. Ibidem, 2012, Pg.50-56.

[6] G. Massa Finoli. Ibidem, 2012, Pg.31-42.

[7] G. Massa Finoli. Ibidem, 2012, Pg.105-130.

[8] G. Massa Finoli. Ibidem, 2012, Pg.131-136;250-261.

[9] G. Massa Finoli. Ibidem, 2012, Pg.65-73. Another way to define an emergent symmetry is the External Measure, defined as a limit to infinity of successive measures. An External Measure is a measure NOT in the reference system which makes the measurements. For example π is a MisEst of actual measurements of π .

[10] Hofstadter D.R. and Dennet D.C., Goedel, Escher and Bach, 1979.

[11] Or that will be positioned on the index-values $\Gamma(k)-\Gamma q$ and $\Gamma(k+1)-\Gamma p$.

[12] G. Massa Finoli. Ibidem, 2012, Pg.181-194.

[13] G. Massa Finoli. "Self-generating operator, symmetry in a model of Primes and proof of a link in S/T Tears", FCS 2013

[14] G. Massa Finoli. Ibidem, 2012, Pg.295 e seg.

[15] We note that such a system is a simple conceptual model developed with the aim to uncover possible hidden aspects of physics realty. It should be noted that the energy of the elements is purely indicative and symbolic, and so the calculation resulting.

[16] The idea is that the measure of a single system is given by the norm of the real measurements of elements and the factors of incommensurability present as imaginary values. Ultimately the real part of a measurement is the measurement instrument side, the imaginary part, side object, contributes to form the measure of the system as a single system through the determination of the norm. The norm should be the measure of the system as a single, or unique, system with his emergent aspects.

Intuitionistic Fuzzy Bi-Ideal of a Ring

P.K. Sharma[1], **Aradhna Duggal**[2]
[1]P.G.Department of Mathematics, D.A.V. College, Jalandhar City, Punjab, India
[2]Department of Mathematics, S.G.G.S. Khalsa College, Mahil Pur, Punjab, India

Abstract - *In this paper, the notion of intuitionistic fuzzy bi-ideal of a ring are defined and discussed. Some of their properties are studied.*

Keywords: Intuitionistic fuzzy set (IFS), Intuitionistic fuzzy subring (IFSR), Intuitionistic fuzzy ideal (IFI), Intuitionistic fuzzy bi-ideal (IFBI)

1 Introduction

The notion of bi-ideals in associative ring was introduced by S. Lajos, F. Szasz in [12]. Chelvam and Ganesan in [4] define bi-ideals in near rings. Later Kuroki [11] introduced the notion of fuzzy bi-ideals in semi-groups and Liu [19] studied them in rings. A detail work about bi-ideals and fuzzy bi-ideals in a ring can be found in [5]. Later Datta [5 -7] introduced the notion of anti fuzzy bi-ideal in a ring and characterize them in terms of lower level cut subsets.

The notion of intuitionistic fuzzy set (IFS) was introduced by Atanassov [1] as a generalization of Zadeh's fuzzy sets. Hur, Kang and Song [8-9] define and study the notion of intuitionistic fuzzy subring. Basnet [3] study the (α, β)-cut of intuitionistic fuzzy ideals of a ring. Sharma [16-17] study the translation of intuitionistic fuzzy subring and ideal. Here in this paper, we introduce the notion of intuitionistic fuzzy bi-ideal in a ring and study some of their properties.

2 Preliminaries

Throughout this paper, let R denote a ring unless other specified.

Definition (2.1)[3, 13] Let R be a ring. An IFS A = { < x, $\mu_A(x)$, $\nu_A(x)$ >: x ∈R} of R is said to be *intuitionistic fuzzy subring* of R (IFSR) of R if

(i) $\mu_A(x-y) \geq \text{Min}\{\mu_A(x), \mu_A(y)\}$

(ii) $\mu_A(xy) \geq \text{Min}\{\mu_A(x), \mu_A(y)\}$

(iii) $\nu_A(x-y) \leq \text{Max}\{\nu_A(x), \nu_A(y)\}$

(iv) $\nu_A(xy) \leq \text{Max}\{\nu_A(x), \nu_A(y)\}$, for all x , y∈R

Definition(2.2)[13] An IFS A ={< x, $\mu_A(x)$, $\nu_A(x)$>: x∈R} of a ring R said to be

(a) *intuitionistic fuzzy left ideal* of R (IFLI) of R if

(i) $\mu_A(x-y) \geq \text{Min}\{\mu_A(x), \mu_A(y)\}$

(ii) $\mu_A(xy) \geq \mu_A(y)$

(iii) $\nu_A(x-y) \leq \text{Max}\{\nu_A(x), \nu_A(y)\}$

(iv) $\nu_A(xy) \leq \nu_A(y)$, for all x , y ∈R

(b) *intuitionistic fuzzy right ideal* of R (IFRI) of R if

(i) $\mu_A(x-y) \geq \text{Min}\{\mu_A(x), \mu_A(y)\}$

(ii) $\mu_A(xy) \geq \mu_A(x)$

(iii) $\nu_A(x-y) \leq \text{Max}\{\nu_A(x), \nu_A(y)\}$

(iv) $\nu_A(xy) \leq \nu_A(x)$, for all x , y ∈R

(c) *intuitionistic fuzzy ideal* of R (IFI) of R if

(i) $\mu_A(x-y) \geq \text{Min}\{\mu_A(x), \mu_A(y)\}$

(ii) $\mu_A(xy) \geq \text{Max}\{\mu_A(x), \mu_A(y)\}$

(iii) $\nu_A(x-y) \leq \text{Max}\{\nu_A(x), \nu_A(y)\}$

(iv) $\nu_A(xy) \leq \text{Min}\{\nu_A(x), \nu_A(y)\}$, for all x , y ∈R

Theorem (2.3)[13] If A = {< x , $\mu_A(x)$, $\nu_A(x)$ > : x ∈R} be IFSR of ring R , then

(i) $\mu_A(0) \geq \mu_A(x)$ and $\nu_A(0) \leq \nu_A(x)$

(ii) $\mu_A(-x) = \mu_A(x)$ and $\nu_A(-x) = \nu_A(x)$, for all x , y ∈ R

(iii) If R is ring with unity 1, then $\mu_A(1) \leq \mu_A(x)$ and $\nu_A(1) \geq \nu_A(x)$, for all x∈ R

Definition (2.4)[3] Let A be Intuitionistic fuzzy set of a ring R. Then (α , β)-cut of A is a crisp subset $C_{\alpha,\beta}(A)$ of the IFS A is given by $C_{\alpha,\beta}(A) = \{ x \in R : \mu_A(x) \geq \alpha , \nu_A(x) \leq \beta \}$, where $\alpha , \beta \in [0,1]$ with $\alpha + \beta \leq 1$

Theorem(2.5)[3] Let A be a IFS of a ring R. Then A is IFSR (IFI) of R if and only if $C_{\alpha,\beta}(A)$ is subring (ideal) of R, for all $\alpha , \beta \in [0,1]$ with $\alpha + \beta \leq 1$.

Definition(2.6) ([12]) A subring S of a ring R is called a bi-ideal of R if $SRS \subseteq S$ holds, where SRS is the additive subgroup of R generated by the set of all elements of the form srs, $s \in S$ and $r \in R$.

Definition (2.7) ([5]) A non-empty fuzzy subset μ of a ring R (i.e. $\mu(x) \neq 0$ for some $x \in R$) is called an *fuzzy bi-ideal* of R if

(i) $\mu(x-y) \geq \text{Min}\{\mu(x), \mu(y)\}$,

(ii) $\mu(xy) \geq \text{Min}\{\mu(x), \mu(y)\}$, and

(iii) $\mu(xyz) \geq \text{Min}\{\mu(x), \mu(z)\}$ for all $x, y, z \in R$.

Definition (2.8) ([6]) A non-empty fuzzy subset μ of a ring R (i.e. $\mu(x) \neq 0$ for some $x \in R$) is called *anti fuzzy bi-ideal* of R if

(i) $\mu(x-y) \leq \text{Max}\{\mu(x), \mu(y)\}$,

(ii) $\mu(xy) \leq \text{Max}\{\mu(x), \mu(y)\}$, and

(iii) $\mu(xyz) \leq \text{Max}\{\mu(x), \mu(z)\}$ for all $x, y, z \in R$

3 Intuitionistic fuzzy bi-ideal of a ring

Definition(3.1) An IFS $A = \{< x, \mu_A(x), \nu_A(x) > : x \in R\}$ of a ring R is said to be *intuitionistic fuzzy bi-ideal* of R (IFBI) of R if

(i) $\mu_A(x-y) \geq \text{Min}\{\mu_A(x), \mu_A(y)\}$

(ii) $\nu_A(x-y) \leq \text{Max}\{\nu_A(x), \nu_A(y)\}\ \forall\, x, y \in R$

(iii) $\mu_A(xy) \geq \text{Min}\{\mu_A(x), \mu_A(y)\}$

(iv) $\nu_A(xy) \leq \text{Max}\{\nu_A(x), \nu_A(y)\}$, for all $x, y \in R$

(v) $\mu_A(xry) \geq \text{Min}\{\mu_A(x), \mu_A(y)\}$

(vi) $\nu_A(xry) \leq \text{Max}\{\nu_A(x), \nu_A(y)\}$, $\forall\, r, x, y \in R$

Example1. Let R be the ring of all 2×2 matrices over the ring of integers with respect to the matrix addition and multiplication. Let $A = \{< x, \mu_A(x), \nu_A(x) > : x \in R\}$ be a intuitionistic fuzzy subset of R defined as follows:

$$\mu_A\left(\begin{pmatrix} a & b \\ c & d \end{pmatrix}\right) = \begin{cases} 1 & , \text{ if } a = b = c = d = 0 \\ \frac{1}{2}, & \text{if } a \neq 0, \text{ even and } b = c = d = 0 \\ \frac{1}{3}, & \text{if } a \neq 0, \text{ odd and } b = c = d = 0 \\ 0, & \text{in all other cases} \end{cases}$$

and

$$\nu_A\left(\begin{pmatrix} a & b \\ c & d \end{pmatrix}\right) = \begin{cases} 0 & , \text{ if } a = b = c = d = 0 \\ \frac{1}{3}, & \text{if } a \neq 0, \text{ even and } b = c = d = 0 \\ \frac{1}{2}, & \text{if } a \neq 0, \text{ odd and } b = c = d = 0 \\ 1, & \text{in all other cases} \end{cases}$$

Then A is a intuitionistic fuzzy bi-ideal of R.

Theorem(3.2) Every IFLI (IFRI) of a ring R is IFBI of R

Proof. In view of (3.1), we need only to prove the condition (v) and (vi) Let A be IFLI of the ring R and $x, y \in R$ and $a \in A$

$\mu_A(x\,a\,y) \geq \mu_A((x\,a)y) \geq \mu_A(y) \geq \text{Min}\{\mu_A(x), \mu_A(y)\}$ and

$\nu_A(x\,a\,y) \leq \nu_A((x\,a)y) \leq \nu_A(y) \leq \text{Max}\{\nu_A(x), \nu_A(y)\}$

Hence A is IFBI of R. The right case is proved in an analogous way.

Next, we give an example of a IFBI of the ring, which is neither IFLI nor IFRI

Example2. Consider the ring R of real numbers under usual addition and multiplication operations. Define the IFS $A = (\mu_A, \nu_A)$ of R by

$$\mu_A(x) = \begin{cases} 0.8 & , \textit{if } x \text{ is rational} \\ 0.4 & , \textit{if } x \text{ is irrational} \end{cases}$$

and

$$\nu_A(x) = \begin{cases} 0.1 & , \textit{if } x \text{ is rational} \\ 0.5 & , \textit{if } x \text{ is irrational} \end{cases}$$

It is easy to check that A is neither a IFLI nor a IFRI of R. But A is a IFBI of R.

Theorem(3.3) Let $A = (\mu_A, \nu_A)$ be IFBI of a field F. Then A is of the form

$$\mu_A(x)=\begin{cases}\mu_A(1) & , \text{ if } x\neq 0\\ \mu_A(0) & , \text{ if } x=0\end{cases} \quad \text{and}$$

$$\nu_A(x)=\begin{cases}\nu_A(1) & , \text{ if } x\neq 0\\ \nu_A(0) & , \text{ if } x=0\end{cases}$$

where $\mu_A(1) \le \mu_A(0)$ and $\nu_A(1) \ge \nu_A(0)$.

Proof. Let $A = \{< x, \mu_A(x), \nu_A(x) > : x \in F\}$ be an IFBI of a field F. Let $0 \neq x \in F$ be any element. Then

$\mu_A(x) = \mu_A(1.x.1) \ge \text{Min}\{ \mu_A(1), \mu_A(1)\} = \mu_A(1) = \mu_A(1.1) = \mu_A\{(xx^{-1})(x^{-1}x)\} = \mu_A\{x(x^{-1}x^{-1})x\} \ge \text{Min}\{\mu_A(x), \mu_A(x)\} = \mu_A(x)$

i.e. $\mu_A(x) = \mu_A(1)$ and

$\nu_A(x) = \nu_A(1.x.1) \le \text{Max}\{ \nu_A(1), \nu_A(1)\} = \nu_A(1) = \nu_A(1.1) = \nu_A\{(xx^{-1})(x^{-1}x)\} = \nu_A\{x(x^{-1}x^{-1})x\} \le \text{Max}\{\nu_A(x), \nu_A(x)\} = \nu_A(x)$

i.e. $\nu_A(x) = \nu_A(1)$

Corollary (3.4) If A is IFBI of a field F such that $\mu_A(0) = \mu_A(1)$ and $\nu_A(0) = \nu_A(1)$, then A is constant.

Theorem (3.5) If A and B be two IFBI's of a ring R, then $A \cap B$ is IFBI of ring R.

Proof. Let $A = (\mu_A, \nu_A)$ and $B = (\mu_B, \nu_B)$ be two IFBI's of a ring R. Let $x, y \in A \cap B$ be any element. Then

$\mu_{A\cap B}(x-y) = \text{Min}\{ \mu_A(x-y), \mu_B(x-y)\}$

$\ge \text{Min}\{\text{Min}\{\mu_A(x), \mu_A(y)\}, \text{Min}\{\mu_B(x), \mu_B(y)\}\}$

$= \text{Min}\{\text{Min}\{\mu_A(x), \mu_B(x)\}, \text{Min}\{\mu_A(y), \mu_B(y)\}\}$

$= \text{Min}\{\mu_{A\cap B}(x), \mu_{A\cap B}(y)\}$

Thus $\mu_{A\cap B}(x-y) \ge \text{Min}\{\mu_{A\cap B}(x), \mu_{A\cap B}(y)\}$

Similarly, we can show that

$\nu_{A\cap B}(x-y) \le \text{Max}\{\nu_{A\cap B}(x), \nu_{A\cap B}(y)\}$

Also, $\mu_{A\cap B}(xy) = \text{Min}\{ \mu_A(xy), \mu_B(xy)\}$

$\ge \text{Min}\{\text{Min}\{\mu_A(x), \mu_A(y)\}, \text{Min}\{\mu_B(x), \mu_B(y)\}\}$

$= \text{Min}\{\text{Min}\{\mu_A(x), \mu_B(x)\}, \text{Min}\{\mu_A(y), \mu_B(y)\}\}$

$= \text{Min}\{\mu_{A\cap B}(x), \mu_{A\cap B}(y)\}$

Thus $\mu_{A\cap B}(xy) \ge \text{Min}\{\mu_{A\cap B}(x), \mu_{A\cap B}(y)\}$

Next, let $x, y \in A \cap B$ and $r \in R$ be any element, then

$\mu_{A\cap B}(xry) = \text{Min}\{ \mu_A(xry), \mu_B(xry)\}$

$\ge \text{Min}\{ \text{Min}\{\mu_A(x), \mu_A(y)\}, \text{Min}\{\mu_B(x), \mu_B(y)\}\}$

$= \text{Min}\{ \text{Min}\{\mu_A(x), \mu_B(x)\}, \text{Min}\{\mu_A(y), \mu_B(y)\}\}$

$= \text{Min}\{ \mu_{A\cap B}(x), \mu_{A\cap B}(y)\}$

Thus $\mu_{A\cap B}(xry) \ge \text{Min}\{ \mu_{A\cap B}(x), \mu_{A\cap B}(y)\}$

Similarly, we can show that

$\nu_{A\cap B}(xry) \le \text{Max}\{\nu_{A\cap B}(x), \nu_{A\cap B}(y)\}$

Hence $A \cap B$ is IFBI of ring R.

Corollary (3.6) Intersection of an arbitrary family of IFBI's of a ring R is again a IFBI of R.

Theorem (3.7) Let A be IFLI and B be IFRI of a ring R, then $A \cap B$ is IFBI of ring R.

Proof. Let $A = (\mu_A, \nu_A)$ and $B = (\mu_B, \nu_B)$ be two IFBI's of a ring R. Let $x, y \in A \cap B$ be any element. Then

$\mu_{A\cap B}(x-y) = \text{Min}\{ \mu_A(x-y), \mu_B(x-y)\}$

$\ge \text{Min}\{\text{Min}\{\mu_A(x), \mu_A(y)\}, \text{Min}\{\mu_B(x), \mu_B(y)\}\}$

$= \text{Min}\{\text{Min}\{\mu_A(x), \mu_B(x)\}, \text{Min}\{\mu_A(y), \mu_B(y)\}\}$

$= \text{Min}\{\mu_{A\cap B}(x), \mu_{A\cap B}(y)\}$

Thus $\mu_{A\cap B}(x-y) \ge \text{Min}\{\mu_{A\cap B}(x), \mu_{A\cap B}(y)\}$

Similarly, we can show that

$\nu_{A\cap B}(x-y) \le \text{Max}\{\nu_{A\cap B}(x), \nu_{A\cap B}(y)\}$

Also, $\mu_{A\cap B}(xy) = \text{Min}\{ \mu_A(xy), \mu_B(xy)\}$ ....(1)

Since A is IFLI and B is IFRI of the ring R. Therefore, we have $\mu_A(xy) \ge \mu_A(y)$ and $\mu_B(xy) \ge \mu_B(x) \Rightarrow$

$\text{Min}\{\mu_A(xy), \mu_B(xy)\} \ge \text{Min}\{\mu_A(x), \mu_B(y)\}$................(2)

As $A \cap B \subseteq A$ and $A \cap B \subseteq B$. So $\mu_{A\cap B}(x) \le \mu_A(x)$ and $\mu_{A\cap B}(y) \le \mu_B(y)$

$\Rightarrow \text{Min}\{\mu_A(x), \mu_B(y)\} \ge \text{Min}\{\mu_{A\cap B}(x), \mu_{A\cap B}(y)\}$..........(3)

Therefore from (1), (2) and (3), we have

$\mu_{A\cap B}(xy) = \text{Min}\{ \mu_A(xy), \mu_B(xy)\}$

$\ge \text{Min}\{\mu_A(x), \mu_B(y)\}$

$\ge \text{Min}\{\mu_{A\cap B}(x), \mu_{A\cap B}(y)\}$

Thus, we have $\mu_{A\cap B}(xy) \ge \text{Min}\{\mu_{A\cap B}(x), \mu_{A\cap B}(y)\}$

Similarly, we can show that

$\nu_{A\cap B}(xy) \le \text{Max}\{\nu_{A\cap B}(x), \nu_{A\cap B}(y)\}$

Further, let $x, y \in A \cap B$ and $r \in R$, then

$\mu_{A\cap B}(xry) = \text{Min}\{\mu_A(xry), \mu_B(xry)\}$ ....(4)

But $\mu_A(xry) \ge \mu_A((xr)y) \ge \mu_A(y)$ and $\mu_B(xry) \ge \mu_B(x(ry)) \ge \mu_B(x)$ implies that

$\text{Min}\{\mu_A(xry), \mu_B(xry)\} \geq \text{Min}\{\mu_A(y), \mu_B(x)\}$ ....(5)

As $A \cap B \subseteq A$ and $A \cap B \subseteq B$. So $\mu_{A\cap B}(y) \leq \mu_A(y)$ and $\mu_{A\cap B}(x) \leq \mu_B(x)$

$\Rightarrow \text{Min}\{\mu_A(y), \mu_B(x)\} \geq \text{Min}\{\mu_{A\cap B}(y), \mu_{A\cap B}(x)\}$ ....(6)

From (4), (5) and (6), we get
$\mu_{A\cap B}(xry) \geq \text{Min}\{\mu_{A\cap B}(y), \mu_{A\cap B}(x)\}$

Similarly, we can show that
$\nu_{A\cap B}(xry) \leq \text{Max}\{\nu_{A\cap B}(y), \nu_{A\cap B}(x)\}$

Hence $A \cap B$ is IFBI of ring R.

Theorem(3.8) Let A be IFS of a ring R, then A is IFBI of R if and only if $C_{\alpha,\beta}(A)$ is bi-ideal of R, for all $\alpha, \beta \in [0,1]$ with $\alpha + \beta \leq 1$, where $\mu_A(0) \geq \alpha$ and $\nu_A(0) \leq \beta$

Proof. Firstly, let A be IFBI of a ring R. Then by definition of (α, β) –cut of A, we have

$C_{\alpha,\beta}(A) = \{ x \in R : \mu_A(x) \geq \alpha, \nu_A(x) \leq \beta \}$

Since $\mu_A(0) \geq \alpha$, $\nu_A(0) \leq \beta \Rightarrow C_{\alpha,\beta}(A) \neq \varnothing$.

Let $x, y \in C_{\alpha,\beta}(A)$ be any elements, then

$\mu_A(x) \geq \alpha$, $\mu_A(y) \geq \alpha$, $\nu_A(x) \leq \beta$., $\nu_A(y) \leq \beta$

$\Rightarrow \text{Min}\{\mu_A(x), \mu_A(y)\} \geq \alpha$ and $\text{Max}\{\nu_A(x), \nu_A(y)\} \leq \beta$

Now $\mu_A(x-y) \geq \text{Min}\{\mu_A(x), \mu_A(y)\} \geq \alpha$ and
$\nu_A(x-y) \leq \text{Max}\{\nu_A(x), \nu_A(y)\} \leq \beta$

Also, $\mu_A(xy) \geq \text{Min}\{\mu_A(x), \mu_A(y)\} \geq \alpha$ and
$\nu_A(xy) \leq \text{Max}\{\nu_A(x), \nu_A(y)\} \leq \beta$

$\Rightarrow x - y \in C_{\alpha,\beta}(A)$ and $xy \in C_{\alpha,\beta}(A)$. Thus $C_{\alpha,\beta}(A)$ is a subring of R.

Next, let $x, y \in C_{\alpha,\beta}(A)$ and $r \in R$ be any element. Then

$\mu_A(xry) \geq \text{Min}\{\mu_A(x), \mu_A(y)\} \geq \alpha$ and $\nu_A(xry) \geq \text{Max}\{\mu_A(x), \mu_A(y)\} \leq \beta$

$\Rightarrow xry \in C_{\alpha,\beta}(A)$. Thus $C_{\alpha,\beta}(A)RC_{\alpha,\beta}(A) \subseteq C_{\alpha,\beta}(A)$

Hence $C_{\alpha,\beta}(A)$ is bi-ideal of R.

Conversely, let $C_{\alpha,\beta}(A)$ be bi-ideal of R, for all $\alpha, \beta \in [0,1]$ with $\alpha + \beta \leq 1$, where $\mu_A(0) \geq \alpha$ and $\nu_A(0) \leq \beta$. Then $C_{\alpha,\beta}(A)$ is a subring of R and $C_{\alpha,\beta}(A)RC_{\alpha,\beta}(A) \subseteq C_{\alpha,\beta}(A)$.

This implies that A is intuitionistic fuzzy subring of R (by Theorem (2.5))

Let $x, y, r \in R$ and such that $\mu_A(xry) < \text{Min}\{\mu_A(x), \mu_A(y)\}$

Choose $\alpha \in [0,1]$ such that $\mu_A(xry) < \alpha < \text{Min}\{\mu_A(x), \mu_A(y)\}$, this implies that $\mu_A(x) \geq \alpha$, $\mu_A(y) \geq \alpha \Rightarrow \nu_A(x) \leq 1 - \mu_A(x) \leq 1-\alpha$ and $\nu_A(x) \leq 1 - \mu_A(x) \leq 1-\alpha$.

Thus, $x, y \in C_{\alpha,1-\alpha}(A)$ and so $xry \in C_{\alpha,1-\alpha}(A)$. i.e. $\mu_A(xry) \geq \alpha$, a contradiction.

So, $\mu_A(xry) \geq \text{Min}\{\mu_A(x), \mu_A(y)\}$. Similarly, we have
$\nu_A(xry) \leq \text{Max}\{\nu_A(x), \nu_A(y)\}$

Hence A is IFBI of the ring R.

Theorem (3.9) If every bi-ideal of a ring R is a ideal of R, then every IFBI of R is IFI of R.

Proof. Let A be IFBI of R. Then by theorem (3.8), $C_{\alpha,\beta}(A)$ be bi-ideal of R, for all $\alpha, \beta \in [0,1]$ with $\alpha + \beta \leq 1$, which implies that $C_{\alpha,\beta}(A)$ be ideal of R, for all $\alpha, \beta \in [0,1]$ with $\alpha + \beta \leq 1$ and so by theorem (2.5), A is IFI of R.

4. Intuitionistic fuzzy magnified translation of bi-ideal of a ring

The notion of intuitionistic fuzzy magnified translation(IFMT) of intuitionistic fuzzy set has been defined and discussed by the first author in [16]. Here, in this section, we discuss the IFMT of IFBI of a ring and its homomorphic image.

Definition(4.1)[16] Let $A = (\mu_A, \nu_A)$ be an intuitionistic fuzzy subset of X and $\beta \in [0,1]$ and $\alpha \in [0, 1 - \text{Sup}\{\mu_A(x) + \nu_A(x) : x \in X, 0 < \mu_A(x) + \nu_A(x) < 1\}]$. Then the intuitionistic fuzzy magnified translation (IFMT) T of A is an object of the form :

$T = \{<(x, \mu^A_{(\beta,\alpha)}(x), \nu^A_{(\beta,\alpha)}(x)>: x \in X\}$ or briefly as $\{<(x, \mu_T(x), \nu_T(x)> : x \in X\}$, Where the functions $\mu^A_{(\beta,\alpha)} = \mu_T : X \rightarrow [0,1]$ and $\nu^A_{(\beta,\alpha)} = \nu_T : X \rightarrow [0,1]$ are defined as :

$\mu_T(x) = \mu^A_{(\beta,\alpha)}(x) = \beta\mu_A(x) + \alpha$, $\nu_T(x) = \nu^A_{(\beta,\alpha)}(x) = \beta\nu_A(x) + \alpha$, for all $x \in X$.

Example(4.2): Let $X = \{1, \omega, \omega^2\}$. Let $A = \{< 1, 0.3, 0.4 >, < \omega, 0.1, 0.25 >, < \omega^2, 0.5, 0.3 >\}$ be an IFS of X. Then $[0, 1 - \text{Sup}\{\mu_A(x) + \nu_A(x): x \in X, 0 < \mu_A(x) + \nu_A(x) < 1\}] = [0, 0.2]$. Take $\alpha = 0.1$ and $\beta = 0.2$. Then IFMT of the IFS A is given by $T = \{< 1, 0.16, 0.18 >, < \omega, 0.12, 0.15 >, < \omega^2, 0.2, 0.16 >\}$

Theorem(4.3) : Let T is an IFMT of an IFBI A of a ring R, then T is also an IFBI of R.

Proof: Assume that T is an IFMT of an IFBI A of a ring R. Let x, y, z∈R , we have

$$\begin{aligned}\mu_T(x - y) &= \beta\mu_A(x - y) + \alpha \\ &\geq \beta.\text{Min}\{\mu_A(x), \mu_A(y)\} + \alpha \\ &= \text{Min}\{\beta\mu_A(x) + \alpha, \beta\mu_A(y) + \alpha\} \\ &= \text{Min}\{\mu_T(x), \mu_T(y)\}\end{aligned}$$

also

$$\begin{aligned}\mu_T(xy) &= \beta\mu_A(xy) + \alpha \\ &\geq \beta.\text{Min}\{\mu_A(x), \mu_A(y)\} + \alpha \\ &= \text{Min}\{\beta\mu_A(x) + \alpha, \beta\mu_A(y) + \alpha\} \\ &= \text{Min}\{\mu_T(x), \mu_T(y)\}\end{aligned}$$

also
$$\begin{aligned}\nu_T(x - y) &= \beta\nu_A(x - y) + \alpha \\ &\leq \beta.\text{Max}\{\nu_A(x), \nu_A(y)\} + \alpha \\ &= \text{Max}\{\beta\nu_A(x) + \alpha, \beta\nu_A(y) + \alpha\} \\ &= \text{Max}\{\nu_T(x), \nu_T(y)\}\end{aligned}$$

And
$$\begin{aligned}\nu_T(xy) &= \beta\nu_A(xy) + \alpha \\ &\leq \beta\,\text{Max}\{\nu_A(x), \nu_A(y)\} + \alpha \\ &= \text{Max}\{\beta\nu_A(x) + \alpha, \beta\nu_A(y) + \alpha\} \\ &= \text{Max}\{\nu_T(x), \nu_T(y)\}\end{aligned}$$

$$\begin{aligned}\mu_T(xyz) &= \beta.\mu_A(xyz) + \alpha \\ &\geq \beta.\text{Min}\{\mu_A(x), \mu_A(z)\} + \alpha \\ &= \text{Min}\{\beta\mu_A(x) + \alpha, \beta\mu_A(z) + \alpha\} \\ &= \text{Min}\{\mu_T(x), \mu_T(z)\}\end{aligned}$$

And
$$\begin{aligned}\nu_T(xyz) &= \beta\nu_A(xyz) + \alpha \\ &\leq \beta\,\text{Max}\{\nu_A(x), \nu_A(z)\} + \alpha \\ &= \text{Max}\{\beta\nu_A(x) + \alpha, \beta\nu_A(z) + \alpha\} \\ &= \text{Max}\{\nu_T(x), \nu_T(z)\}\end{aligned}$$

Hence T is also an intuitionistic fuzzy bi-ideal of R.

Example (4.4): Let T is an IFMT of an IFBI A of a ring R, then $H = \{x \in R : \mu_T(x) = \mu_T(0) \text{ and } \nu_T(x) = \nu_T(0)\}$ is bi- ideal of R.

Proof: Easy exercise

Example (4.5): Let T is an IFMT of an IFBI A of a ring R, then $H = \{< x, \mu_T(x) > : \mu_T(x) = \mu_T(0) \text{ and } \nu_T(x) = \nu_T(0)\}$ is a fuzzy bi- ideal of R.

Proof: Easy exercise

Example (4.6): Let T is an IFMT of an IFBI A of a ring R, then $H = \{< x, \nu_T(x) > : \mu_T(x) = \mu_T(0) \text{ and } \nu_T(x) = \nu_T(0)\}$ is an anti-fuzzy bi- ideal of R .

Proof: Easy exercise.

Proposition (4.7): Let R and R^I be any two rings. Then the homomorphic image of an IFMT of an IFBI of R is an IFBI of R^I.

Proof: Let R and R^I be any two rings and $f: R \rightarrow R^I$ be a ring homomorphism.

Therefore $f(x + y) = f(x) + f(y)$ and

$f(x y) = f(x) f(y)$ for all x and y∈R.

Let $V = f(T)$, where T is an IFMT of an IFBI A of R. We show that V is also an IFBI of R^I.

Now, for f(x) and f(y) in R^I, we have

$$\begin{aligned}\mu_V[f(x) - f(y))] &= \mu_V[f(x - y)] \\ &\geq \mu_T(x - y) \\ &= \beta\mu_A(x - y) + \alpha \\ &\geq \beta\,\text{Min}\{\mu_A(x), \mu_A(y)\} + \alpha \\ &= \text{Min}\{\beta\mu_A(x) + \alpha, \beta\mu_A(y) + \alpha\} \\ &= \text{Min}\{\mu_V(f(x)), \mu_V(f(y))\}\end{aligned}$$

Thus $\mu_V[f(x) - f(y))] \geq \text{Min}\{\mu_V(f(x)), \mu_V(f(y))\}$

And

$$\begin{aligned}\mu_V[f(x) f(y)] &= \mu_V[f(xy)] \\ &\geq \mu_T(x\,y) \\ &= \beta\mu_A(x\,y) + \alpha\end{aligned}$$

$\geq \beta\, Min\{ \mu_A(x), \mu_A(y) \} + \alpha$

$= Min\{ \beta\mu_A(x) + \alpha ,\ \beta\mu_A(y) + \alpha \}$

$= Min\{ \mu_V(f(x)), \mu_V(f(y)\}$

Thus $\mu_V[f(x) f(y)] \geq Min \{\mu_V(f(x)), \mu_V(f(y)\}$ also

$\nu_V[f(x) - f(y)] = \nu_V[f(x - y)]$

$\leq \nu_T(x - y)$

$= \beta\nu_A(x - y) + \alpha$

$\leq \beta.\ Max\{ \nu_A(x), \nu_A(y \} + \alpha$

$= Max\{ \beta\nu_A(x) + \alpha ,\ \beta\nu_A(y) + \alpha\}$

$= Max\{ \nu_V(f(x), \nu_V(f(y)\}$

Thus $\nu_V[f(x) - f(y)] \leq \nu_V(f(x)) \vee \nu_V(f(y))$.

also

$\nu_V[f(x) f(y)] = \nu_V[f(xy)]$

$\leq \nu_T(x y)$

$= \beta\nu_A(x y) + \alpha$

$\leq \beta.\ Max\{ \nu_A(x), \nu_A(y) \} + \alpha$

$= Max\{ \beta\nu_A(x) + \alpha, \beta\nu_A(y) + \alpha\}$

$= Max\{ \nu_V(f(x), \nu_V(f(y)\}$

Thus $\nu_V[f(x)(f(y)] \leq Max\{ \nu_V(f(x), \nu_V(f(y))\}$

And

$\mu_V[f(x) f(y) f(z)] = \mu_V[f(xy^z)]$

$\geq \mu_T(xyz)$

$= \beta\mu_A(x yz) + \alpha$

$\geq \beta\, Min\{ \mu_A(x), \mu_A(z) \} + \alpha$

$= Min\{ \beta\mu_A(x) + \alpha ,\ \beta\mu_A(z) + \alpha \}$

$= Min\{ \mu_V(f(x)), \mu_V(f(z))\}$

Thus $\mu_V[f(x) f(y) f(z)] \geq Min \{\mu_V(f(x)), \mu_V(f(z)\}$ also

$\nu_V[f(x) f(y) f(z)] = \nu_V[f(xyz)]$

$\leq \nu_T(x yz)$

$= \beta\nu_A(x yz) + \alpha$

$\leq \beta.\ Max\{ \nu_A(x), \nu_A(z) \} + \alpha$

$= Max\{ \beta\nu_A(x) + \alpha, \beta\nu_A(z) + \alpha\}$

$= Max\{ \nu_V(f(x)), \nu_V(f(z))\}$

Thus $\nu_V[f(x)(f(y) f(z)] \leq Max\{ \nu_V(f(x)), \nu_V(f(z))\}$

Therefore, V is an IFBI of a ring R^l.Hence the homomorphic image of an IFMT of an IFI A of R is an IFBI of R^l.

4 References

[1] K.T. Atanassov, "Intutionistic fuzzy sets," Fuzzy Sets and Systems, vol. 20, no. 1, pp. 87–96, 1986.

[2] K. T. Atanassov, "New operations defined over the intuitionistic fuzzy sets," Fuzzy Sets and Systems, vol. 61, no. 2, pp. 137–142, 1994.

[3] D.K. Basnet, "(α, β)-Cut of Intuitionistic Fuzzy Ideals", International Journal of Algebra, Vol. 4, 2010, no. 27, 1329 – 1334

[4] T.T. Chelvam and N. Ganesan , "On Bi-Ideals of near rings, Indian J. pure and appl. Math., 18 (1987), 1002-1005

[5] S.K. Datta, "On Bi-Ideals and Fuzzy Bi-Ideals of Rings", M.Phil. Thesis, under the guidance of Professor Tapan Datta, Department of Pure Mathematics, University of Calcutta (1997).

[6] S.K. Datta, "On anti fuzzy bi-ideals in rings", International Journal of Pure and Applied Mathematics, Volume 51 No. 3, 2009, 375-382

[7] S.K. Datta, "On the lower level sets of anti fuzzy bi-ideals in rings", International Journal of Pure and

Applied Mathematics, Volume 51 No. 3, 2009, 359-362

[8] K. Hur, H. W. Kang and H.K. Song, "Intuitionistic fuzzy subgroups and subrings", Honam Math J. 25(1) , 2003 , 19-41

[9] K. Hur, S. Y. Jang, and H. W. Kang, "Intuitionistic fuzzy ideals of a ring," Journal of the Korea Society of Mathematical Education. Series B, vol. 12, no. 3, pp. 193–209, 2005.

[10] K.H. Kim, "Intuitionistic fuzzy ideals of semi-groups", Indian J. pure appl. Math. 33(4), 2002, pp. 443-449.

[11] N. Kuroki, "On fuzzy ideals and fuzzy bi-ideals in semi-groups", Fuzzy Sets and Systems, 5(1981), 203-215

[12] S. Lajos, F. Szasz, "Bi-ideals in associative rings", Acta Sci. Math., 32 (1971), 185-193.

[13] K. Meena and K.V. Thomas, "Intuitionistic L-fuzzy Subrings", International Mathematical Forum ,Vol. 6, 2011 , no. 52 , 2561-2572

[14] A. Rosenfeld, "Fuzzy groups", J. Math. Anal. Appl., 35 (1971), 512-517.

[15] P.K.Sharma, "Intuitionistic Fuzzy Ideals of Near Rings", International Mathematical Forum, Vol. 7, 2012, no. 16, 769 - 776

[16] P.K. Sharma ,"On Intuitionistic fuzzy magnified translation in Rings", International Journal of Algebra ,Vol. 5, 2011 , no. 30 , 1451-1458

[17] P.K.Sharma, "Translates of Intuitionistic fuzzy subring", International Review of Fuzzy Mathematics, Vol. 6, No. 2, 2011, 77-84

[18] M. Shabir, Y. B. Jun and M. Bano, "On prime fuzzy bi-ideals of semi- groups", Iranian Journal of Fuzzy Systems Vol. 7, No. 3, (2010) 115-128

[19] Wang-Jin Liu, Fuzzy invariant subgroups and fuzzy ideals, Fuzzy Sets and Systems, 8 (1982), 133-139.

[20] L.A. Zadeh, "Fuzzy sets", Information and Control, 8 (1965), 338-353.

A review of creep deformation and rupture mechanisms of low Cr-Mo alloy for the development of creep damage constitutive equations under lower stress

Q.H. Xu[1], Q. Xu[1], Z. Lu[2], Y. Pang[1], M. Short[1]
[1]School of Science and Engineering, Teesside University, Middleborough, TS1 3BA, UK
[2]School of Computing and Engineering, University of Huddersfield, Huddersfield, HD1 3DA, UK

Abstract— *This paper presents a review of creep deformation and rupture mechanisms of low Cr-Mo alloy for the development of its creep damage constitutive equations under lower stress level. The existing phenomenological type of creep damage constitutive equations, proposed and developed by Hayhurst, do suffer the deficiency of inaccuracy in predicting the creep strain under multi-axial situation. Furthermore, it was not developed specifically for low stress. The paper reports a critical review on the cavity nucleation and the cavity growth, the deformation mechanisms and the creep damage evolution characteristics of the low Cr-Mo alloy at the temperature ranging from 723K to 923K (450 ℃ ~650 ℃), particularly under low stress level (0.2~0.4 σ_Y), to form the physical base for the development of creep damage constitutive equation. It covers the influence of the stress level, states of stress, and the failure criterion.*

Keywords: cavitation, creep damage, ductility, low Cr-Mo alloy, stress level, stress state

1 Introduction

Low Cr-Mo alloy steel is widely used for steam pipeworks in the power generation industry, particularly in fossil fuel plants and nuclear reactors at elevated temperatures of 723K-823K (450°C-550°C) and varying stress levels of 40MPa-200MPa. This steel is selected since it offers the necessary creep strength at optimal cost. A number of service experiments were reported at the temperature range of 723K-923K (450°C-650°C) and at varying stress levels of 30MPa-350MPa [1]. The lower stress level is associated with the expected long life of power generation installation.

Clearly evidences from the industry and institutions show that a new set of creep damage constitutive equations is required to be developed to depict the mechanical damage behavior and rupture lifetime [2-4].

The most popular Kachanov-Robatnov-Hayhurst (KRH) formulation was not developed for low stress and cannot depict the creep strain accurately under multi-axial state of stress due to its three-dimensional generation method used [4-6]; moreover, its disadvantages have been reported in detail by Xu and his fellows [4- 6]. In 2004, the European Creep Collaborative Committee (ECCC) [2] established a new project to develop a new set of constitutive equations for low alloy steel because the previous creep model cannot present accurate results for the high temperature industry. Likewise, the same requirement raised by ECCC was raised by the Nuclear Research Index (UK) [3] to ensure the inspection of operated components. In 2012, the simulation results presented in Hosseini *et al.*'s work from the Swiss Federal Laboratories (SFL) shows by using the five predicting creep damage constitutive models the lifetime for lower stress is overestimated; moreover, these creep models cannot depict the tertiary stage which is closely related with lifetime fracture [7]. Therefore, it is important to conduct a critical review on the creep deformation process and rupture mechanisms to firmly establish the foundation for the development of a set of creep damage constitutive equations. At this current stage, the authors believe that for low alloy Cr-Mo steel there is a lack of clarity of the damage processes at low, intermediate, high stress levels and stress states, and also there is a lack of understanding of the microstructure changes during creep services.

In this paper, a critical analysis of creep deformation and rupture under creep stress levels and states at varying constant temperature on the low Cr-Mo alloy, such as 2.25Cr-1Mo (T/P22) steel is reported. It shows that the different stress levels and the stress states have a significant influence on the creep evolution, creep rupture and rupture ductility. Also the physical base for constitutive modeling of creep deformation and damage is given.

2 Effect of stress level under uni-axial creep

The data of the specimens to analyze the creep deformation and rupture processes were extracted from published literatures and research institutions' (universities, companies and high temperature industries) laboratories [1, 8-11].

2.1 Effect of the stress level on creep lifetime

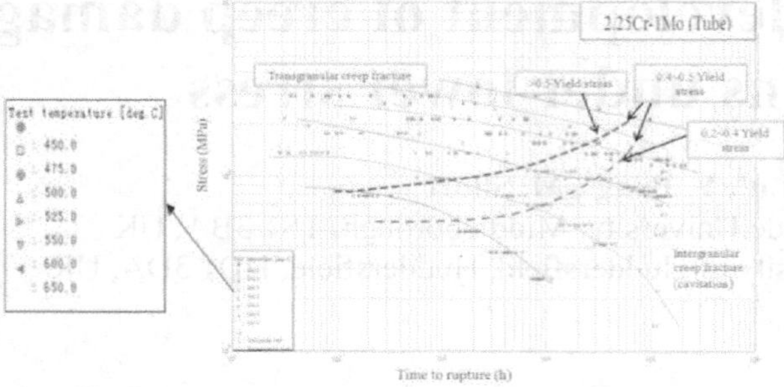

Fig. 1. Stress versus time to rupture at 450,475, 500,525, 550, 600 and 650°C for P22 steel Tubes, adapted from [1]

Figure.1 shows the long-term performance of the transition from higher stresses (> 0.5 σ_Y) to lower stresses (0.2~0.4 σ_Y) for 2.25Cr-1Mo steel depends on the creep rupture time. This figure reflects that at higher stress levels the damage mechanism differs from the low stress levels; this observation indicates that the former constitutive equation modeling based on the analysis of short-term data extrapolation from high stress to low stress is not reliable.

Based on the experimental data of the stress versus time to the rupture, the mechanical relationship could be assumed as:

$$T_f \propto \frac{1}{\sigma - \sigma_0} \quad (1)$$

Where T_f is fracture time, σ_0 is the initial elastic creep stress.

2.2 Effect of the stress level on strain at failure

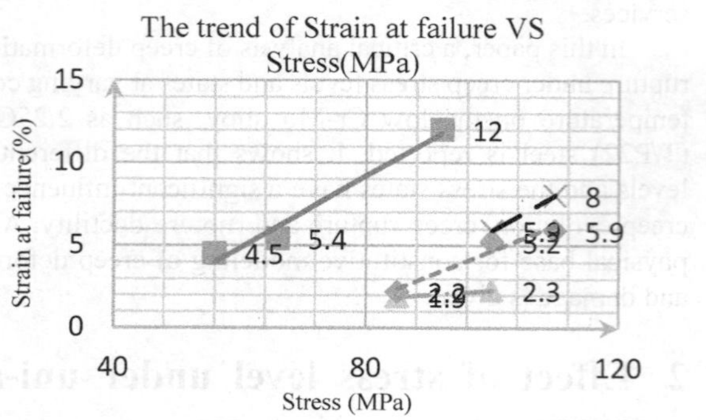

Fig. 2. Experimental data summarized from [11] at the temperature of 640°C (Dash line) and 620°C (Solid line), data collected from ERA report

Figure. 2. shows the strain at failure is increasing as the stress level increases.

Based on the experimental data of strain at failure versus stress, the mechanical relationship could be assumed as:

$$\varepsilon_f \propto A(\sigma - \sigma_0)^n \quad (2)$$

Where, ε_f is fracture strain and σ is external stress, σ_0 is the initial elastic creep stress.

2.3 Effect of the stress level on creep rate

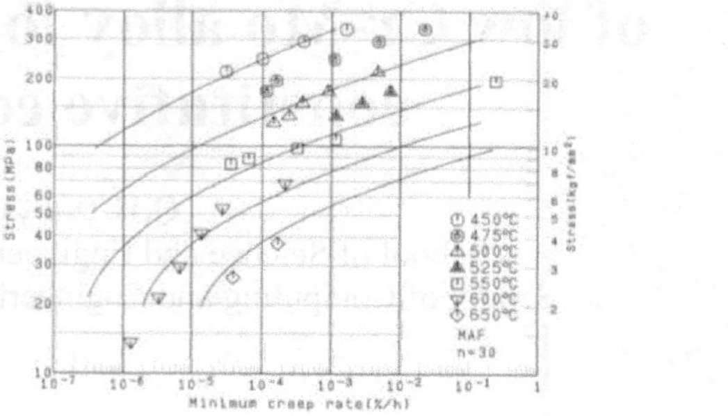

Fig. 3. Stress versus minimum creep rate for P22 steel tubes [10]

Figure. 3 shows the creep behavior of the alloy 2.25Cr-1Mo at 450°C-650°C (minimum creep rate against stress). The above observation indicates that the stress level does influence the creep behavior of the alloy, having a larger effect on the minimum creep rate. A careful analysis was carried out with the creep data only to check the variation of the minimum creep rate with stress and verify the possibility of expressing the data according to this relation.

Based on the experimental data for stress versus minimum creep rate, the mechanistic relationship could be assumed as:

$$\dot{\varepsilon}_{min} \propto e^{\frac{\sigma - n}{m}} \quad (3)$$

Where, $\dot{\varepsilon}_m$ is minimum creep rate, σ is external stress, n, m are materials parameter.

2.4 Effect of the stress level on ductility

An investigation from experimental aspects shows that at different regime of rupture ductility varies with externally applied stresses [12, 13]. The various ductility regimes are associated with distinct rupture mechanisms which affect the accuracy in investigating the constitutive equation [12-14].

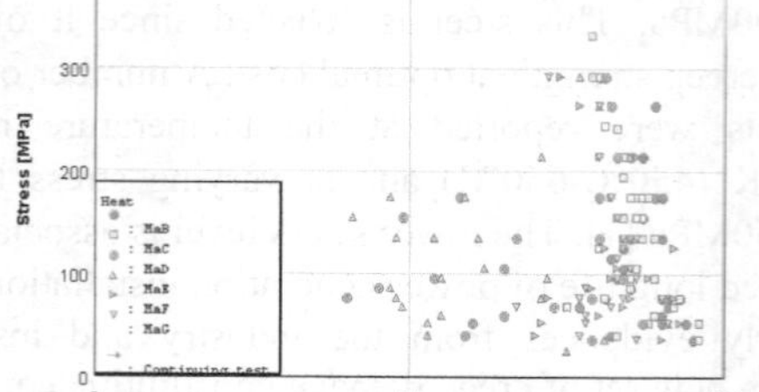

Fig. 4. The stress depends on reduction of area for 2.25Cr-1Mo steel (P22) [1]

Figure. 4 exhibited the ductile failure results of the sample under higher stresses; also, it exhibited low ductility results of the samples under lower stresses level.

ECCC proposed a general trend of elongation versus the

log rupture time to depict the effect on ductility [14]. However, this analysis of the effect of the stress level on ductility has been carried out with the reduction of the specimen area, which is due to the effect on the estimate of the true stress based on elongation (likely to be inaccurate as regards the behavior of the region with ultimately failure; such as, necking behavior).

TABLE. I

The summerised ductility equation for dominate mechanism under low stress, intermediate stress and high stress has been slected from ECCC [2]

	Stress level	Dominate mechanism	Model Developer	Ductility Model
Multi-axial rupture ductility model	Under High stress level $> 0.5\sigma_Y$	Grain boundary cavity growth	Marlof [15]	$\frac{\bar{\varepsilon}_f}{\varepsilon_{fu}} = \frac{1}{3}\frac{\sigma_{vm}}{\sigma_m} = \frac{\left(\frac{3}{2}\frac{\sigma_1-\sigma_m}{\sigma_{vm}}\right)}{\left(3\frac{\sigma_m}{\sigma_{vm}}\right)} = \frac{1}{2}\frac{(\sigma_1-\sigma_m)}{\sigma_m}$ (4)
			Ewald [16]	$\frac{\bar{\varepsilon}_f}{\varepsilon_{fu}} = \frac{3}{2}\frac{\sigma_1-\sigma_m}{\sigma_1}$ (5)
			Sheng [17]	$\frac{\bar{\varepsilon}_f}{\varepsilon_{fu}} = \frac{3}{2}\frac{(\sigma_1-\sigma_m)}{\sigma_{vm}}\left(\frac{\sigma_{vm}}{\sigma_1}\right)^m$ (6)
	Between high and low stress $0.4\sigma_Y \sim 0.5\sigma_Y$	Diffusion controlled cavity growth	Hales [18]	$\frac{\bar{\varepsilon}_f}{\varepsilon_{fu}} = \frac{2}{3}\frac{\sigma_1}{S_1}\left(\frac{\sigma_{vm}}{\sigma_1}\right)^{m+1}$ (7)
	Under Low stress $0.2\sigma_Y \sim 0.4\sigma_Y$	Constrained cavity growth	Spindler [19]	$\frac{\bar{\varepsilon}_f}{\varepsilon_{fu}} = \exp\left[p\left(1-\frac{\sigma_1}{\sigma_{vm}}\right) + q\left(\frac{1}{2} - \frac{3\sigma_m}{2\sigma_{vm}}\right)\right]$ (8)

2.5 Effect on the characteristic and mechanism under high stress range

At high stress ($0.4\sigma_Y$) the plasticity-controlled cavity growth mechanism is predominant, and there is an increasing rupture strain with the increasing creep strain rate [20, 21]. Under this stress level, the creep rupture occurs based on the wedge-type micro-crack which forms at a triple grain junction and the growth cracks will lead to local grain-boundary separation [20, 21]. Furthermore, failure occurs relatively quicker and is accompanied by elongation deformation at this stress level [20, 21]. The speed of the plastic strain increases rapidly after the external loading is applied. In this condition, the fracture is based on the transgranular cavities [20-22]. Further study shows the creep failure is associated with ductility because the reduction area of the specimens presented is around ¾ of the cross section under high strength condition [20-22].

2.6 Effect on the characteristic and mechanism under moderate stress range

Mohyla and Foldyna [23] report that at 873K (600°C) and at 110MPa ($0.4\text{-}0.5\sigma_Y$), the microstructure of the experimental specimens has seen the elliptical creep cavities, wedge type creep cavities and grain boundary cavities. These results indicate that the creep deformation and rupture behavior is a mixture under the stress level of ($0.4\text{-}0.5\sigma_Y$).

2.7 Effect on the characteristic and mechanism under low stress range

At low stress ($0.2\sim0.4\sigma_Y$); Parker and Parsons claimed that the nucleation controlled constrained cavity growth is the predominant mechanism [20, 21]; and the fracture is due to the intergranular cavities behavior.

The experimental data which has been plotted as the typical creep curve (creep strain versus lifetime) for low Cr-Mo alloy shows the primary creep stage often occupied approximately 10% of the total specimens' lifetime; however, the tertiary creep stage takes the largest portion of about 80% of the total lifetime [20-22].

In 2004 Dobrazanski classified the creep evolution of low-alloy Cr-Mo steel as the development of cavities, the formation of microcracks and macrocracks which lead to eventual rupture [24, 25]. His research reflects that under low stress level, the 1Cr-0.5Mo steel and T/P23 steel start to nuclei at $0.4\sim0.6T_R$; the report from EPRI shows similar result that T/P22 steel starts to nuclei at $0.25T_R$[4]; these results seem to contradict the earlier assumption about instant nucleation cited and then used by Dyson [26]. Consequently, this leads to the question of the need to examine the applicability of Dyson's creep damage constitutive equation under low stress.

3 Effect of multi-axial stress state

3.1 Effect of the stress state on notched bar (Tri-axial stress state)

Comparing with the specimens' lifetime under the tensile stress and notched bar (which provide the tri-axial stress state) condition, the life under the tri-axial stress state has been extended due to the reduction of von Mises stress occurred when hydrostatic stress is imposed on uni-axial tension [27].

Needham [28], by comparing smooth and notched specimens (under higher stresses), examined the effect of the stress state on the nucleation rate in two Cr-Mo steels. He found that it is the maximum principal stress, σ_1 which controls the nucleation; likewise, von-Mises equivalent rate is usually less important at high stresses. Currently, the experiment of the creep deformation performance on the notched bar of 2.25Cr-1Mo steel under higher stresses is been conducted [29], the results illustrate that the cavity size around the crack tip increases dramatically, but the cavity number only increases slightly [29].

3.2 Effect of the stress state on ductility

As has been reported by Longsdale and Flewitt [30] and Chuman *et al.* [31] the hydrostatic stress has great influence on the multi-axial stress; Also they [30, 31] have indicated that the domination multi-axial stress is hydrostatic stress which leads to final creep fracture under lower stresses [31], and the equivalent stress is dominant to evaluate the creep fracture under higher stresses [32]. Therefore, further work will focus on the experimental results which could show the dominate stress that could reflect the multi-axial state influence; If this has been carried out, a hypothesis will be made to derive uni-axial equations set to multi-axial equations set; this has been discussed in section III.

4 Creep rupture criterion

4.1 Summary of the existing creep rupture criterion

TABLE. II

Fuilure criterion been used for low alloy creep damage constitutive equaitons

Types of constitutive equation used for low Cr-Mo alloy	Originated from Year	Failure Criterion
Kachanov [33]	1958	Critical damage D=1
Kachanov Robatnov(KR) [34]	1969	Critical damage ω_c
Lemaitre [35]	1985	Critical damage D_c
Piques [36]	1989	f=porosity
Kachanov –Robatnov-Hayhurst (KRH) [37]	1995	Critical damage ω_c
Dyson and McLean [38]	2000	Critical strain at failure $\varepsilon_f = 5\%$
Qiang Xu's [4]	2000	Critical damage ω_c
Michel [39]	2004	limit load $\|\vec{P}_L(\sigma_0)\|$
Lmaitre and Desmorat [40]	2004	Critical damage D_c
Whittaker, Wilshire [41]	2012	Limited activity energy: Q_c^*

Table II summarized the different creep rupture criterion which has been applied in creep damage constitutive equations for low alloy; nevertheless, these creep rupture criteria do not necessarily have clear physical meanings associated with the creep rupture behavior and rupture mechanism [32].

The statistic creep rupture criterion do not have physical meanings and are not able to predict the accurate creep curve and creep deformation behavior [3-5]; therefore, a new consideration of the rupture criterion should be conducted.

4.2 Effect of the low stress level on the cavity nucleation rate and cavity growth rate

Longsdale and Flewitt reported that under lower stresses (55.6, 60.6 and 70.6 MPa, at 873K (600°C)) for 2.25Cr-1Mo steel, the cavity rate of accumulation increases monotonically with time and at a given time. It was greatest for the largest applied stress [30]; the density of the cavity observed on the grain surfaces increased continuously throughout the creep life; its cavity growth rate is slightly increased with the accumulation of time [30] From the experimental observations on the cavity nucleation and cavity growth, Needham [28] found that the functional relationship for cavity nucleation rate, cavity growth rate, and the rupture lifetime for 2.25Cr-1Mo steel and 1Cr-0.5Mo steel are inversely related to maximum principal stress,σ_0, by a power law, under lower stresses; the power law index number is presented in Table. III for these two Grades.

TABLE. III

Summary of stress index for power law behaviour under the low stress [28]

Under low stresses (0.2~0.4 yield stress) MPa			
depends on maximum principal stress	Cavity nucleation rate	cavity growth rate	rupture lifetime
power law stress index	5~7	3.5~4.5	4.8

4.3 Effect of the high stress level on the cavity nucleation rate and cavity growth rate

Kawashima and *et al.* reported that for 2.25Cr-1Mo steel the creep ruptures lifetime depends on the cavity nucleation rate and cavity growth size [42].

TABLE. IV

The cavity growth rate versus stress in low Cr-Mo alloy, under the high stress [42]

cavity growth rate(m/s)	stress (MPa)
3.16228E-14	117.5
5.62341E-14	127.5
7.49894E-14	145
1.77828E-13	160
3.16228E-13	170
1.77828E+12	190
3.16228E-12	225

Table. IV shows the growth rate increases with the increase of the applied stresses under higher stresses [30]. These results indicate that the cavity growth behavior is associated with the creep rupture behavior and mechanism.

TABLE. V

Summary of stress index for power law behaviour under the low stress [28]

Under intermediate and high stresses (>0.4 yield stress) MPa			
depends on maximum principal stress and equivalent stress	Cavity nucleation rate	cavity growth rate	rupture lifetime
power law stress index	3.5~5	3.5~5	3.5~5

As the cavity nucleation rate is strongly dependent upon the maximum principal stress (under low stress conditions), and dependent upon both of the maximum principal stress and the equivalent stress (under intermediate and high stresses), the rupture lifetime could be predicted from knowledge of the nucleation rate determined under a uniaxial tensile [28]. Therefore, further work will focus on the critical value of the void nucleation rate and the growth rate depending on the creep lives. If this has been carried out, a hypothesis of a new creep rupture criterion will be developed to conduct the physical–based creep rupture behavior and mechanism.

5 Multi-axial stress rupture criterion

The multi-axial stress rupture criterion of low Cr-Mo alloy has been determined from analyses of hollow cylindrical, notched bar and hollow cruciform specimens [27, 30, 42].

From the analyses of the previous experimental data, the results show the maximum principal stress, σ_1, Mises stress σ_{Mises} and hydrostatic σ_H are associated with creep damage process which leading to the rupture [31]. Moreover, the results indicate that the dominated stress system which leading to the intergranular fracture seems to be the hydrostatic stress, and the rupture behavior has a strong dependence on maximum principal stressσ_1; therefore, the equation of the multi-axial stress rupture criterion [30] could be expressed as:

$$\sigma_{eq} = \alpha\sigma_1 + \beta\sigma_{Mises} + \gamma\sigma_H \quad (9)$$

$$\gamma > \alpha > \beta$$

6 Result and discussion

Based on the review of experimental data and the microstructure observation under varying stress ranges and stress states, the new set of creep damage constitutive equation to be developed should satisfy the following requirements which should be able to:

1) represent the transition between lower-shelf intergranular rupture and upper-shelf ductile-transgruanlar rupture as a function of temperature, strain rate, stress and material pedigree;
2) express the mechanistic relationship between applied stress versus time to rupture:

$$T_f \propto \frac{1}{\sigma - \sigma_0} \quad (1)$$

3) reflect the mechanistic relationship between the strain at failure versus stress:

$$\varepsilon_f \propto A(\sigma - \sigma_0)^n \quad (2)$$

4) show the mechanistic relationship between between minimum stress rate and applied stress:

$$\dot{\varepsilon}_{\min} \propto e^{\frac{\sigma - n}{m}} \quad (3)$$

5) depict the dominated constrained cavity growth deformation mechanism under low stress level, $0.2\sigma_Y \sim 0.4\sigma_Y$;
6) depict the dominated plastic hole growth deformation mechanism under high stress, $> 0.5\sigma_Y$;
7) depict the diffusion deformation mechanism stress in between $0.4\sigma_Y$ and $0.5\sigma_Y$;
8) show the effect of the stress states on creep ductility, under multi-axial conditions;
9) show, under lower stresses, the rupture criterion is amalgamated with the cavity density;
10) show, under higher stresses, the rupture criterion is amalgamated with the cavity size;
11) express the multi-axial stress rupture criterion:

$$\sigma_{eq} = \alpha\sigma_1 + \beta\sigma_{Mises} + \gamma\sigma_H \quad (9)$$

$$\gamma > \alpha > \beta$$

7 Conclusion

This paper provides a critical analysis of the obtained experimental observation on the creep deformation and the creep damage evolution mechanisms. The requirements of the creep damage constitutive equation in terms of lifetime and strain at failure under a range of stress states and stress levels have been investigated. Further work will focus on the development of the creep damage constitutive equations for low Cr-Mo alloy which could be used in engineering design, or with the finite element continuum damage mechanics methods.

8 References

[1] NIMS, creep data sheet. *National Institute for Materials Sciences*. No. 3B, 1986. [online] available: http://smds.nims.go.jp/cgi-bin/MSDS/factOpen/directv8_en.cgi?key=52 (Accessed on 20/3/2013)

[2] S.R. Holdsworth, G. Merckling, 'Developments in the Assessment of Creep-Rupture Properties' [online].ECCC (2012).http://www.ommi.co.uk/etd/eccc/advancedcreep/SRHGMpap1.pdf (Accessed on 25/3/2012)

[3] Nuclear Research (2010), Nuclear Research Index Section A, Structural Integrity, http://www.hse.gov.uk/nuclear/nri-topics/2012/section-a.pdf. (Accessed on 25/3/2012)

[4] Q. Xu. (2000) Development of constitutive equations for creep damage behaviour under multi-axial states of stress. *Advances in Mechanical Behaviour, Plasticity and Damage*. pp. 1375-1382

[5] Q. Xu., M. Wright. And Q.H. Xu. (2011) The development and validation of multi-axial creep damage constitutive equations for P91. *ICAC 11: The 17th international conference on automation and computing*. Huddersfield, UK. September 10. 2011

[6] Q.H. Xu., Q. Xu., Y.X. Pang, and M. Short (2012). Current state of developing creep damage constitutive equation for 0.5Cr0.5Mo0.25V ferritic steel, The 2nd International Conference on Machinery, *Materials Science and Engineering Applications (MMSE 2012)* 16th-17th, June 2012. Wuhan, China.

[7] E. Hosseini., S.R. Holdsworth and E. Mazza. (2012). Creep constitutive model considerations for high-temperature finite element numerical simulations. *The Journal of Strain Analysis for Engineering Design*. *47*. pp. 341-349

[8] NRIM creep data sheet. *National Research Institutive for Metals*. No 11B, 1997

[9] NIMS creep data sheet. *National Institute for Materials Sciences*. No. 36B, 2003

[10] NIMS, creep data sheet. *National Institute for Materials Sciences*. No. 3B, 1986

[11] R.J. Hayhurst, R. Mustata, and D.R. Hayhurst, (2005) Creep constitutive equations for parent, Type IV, R-HAZ, CG-HAZ and weld material in the range 565–640 °C for Cr–Mo–V weldments. *International Journal of Pressure Vessels and Piping*. 82. pp.137–144

[12] R. Hales. (1994) the role of cavity growth mechanisms in determining creep rupture under multi-axial stresses. *Fatigue fracture Engieering Material*. *17*. pp. 579-591

[13] R. Hales. and R.A. Ainsworth. (1995) multiaxial creep-fatigue rules. *Nuclear Engineering and Design, 153(2-3)*. pp.257-264

[14] S.R. Holdsworth, and R.B. Davies. (1999) A recent advance in the assessment of creep rupture data. *Nuclear Engineering and design*. pp. 287-296

[15] R. H. Marloff. M. Leven and G.O. Sankey. (1981) creep of rotors under tri-axial tension, proc. *Int. Cof. Om Measurements in Hostile Environments*, *Brit. Soc. For Strain Measurement*. Newcaslte-upon-Tyne

[16] J. Ewald, (1991) Verminderung des Verformungsvermogen bei mehrachsigen Spanungszustanden im plastichen Zustand und bei Kriechbeanspruchung, *Mat.-wiss. U. Werkstoffech*. *22*.pp. 359-369

[17] S. Seng. (1992) Anwendung von Festigkeishypothesen im Kriechbereich bei mehrachsigen Spannungs-Formanderungszustanden, Dissertation, Universittat Stuttgart

[18] R. Hales. (1994) the role of cavity growth mechanisms in determing creep-rupture under muti-axial stresses. *Fatigue Fract*. Engng. Struct. *17*. pp.279-291

[19] M.W. Spindler. (2004) the multi-axial creep ductility of austenitic stainless steel. *Fatigue. Fract. Engng. Struct. 17*. pp. 279-291

[20] J.D. Parker. and A.W.J. Parsons. (1995), High temperature deformation and fracture processes in 2.25Cr1Mo-0.5Cr0.5Mo0.25V weldments, *International Journals of Pressure Vessels and Piping. 63*, pp.45-54

[21] J.D. Parker. (1995) Creep behaviour of low alloy steel weldments, *International Journals of Pressure Vessels and Piping*, *63*. pp. 55-62

[22] J.D. Parker. and A.W. Parsons. (1994) The tempering performance of low-alloy steel weldments. *International Journals of Pressure Vessels and Piping, 57*. pp.345-352

[23] P. Mohyla. and V. Foldyna (2009). Improvement of reliability and creep resistance in advanced low-alloy steels, *Materials Science and Engineering: A*, *510–511. (15)*. pp. 234-237

[24] J. Dobrzański. (2004) Internal damage processes in low alloy chromium–molybdenum steels during high-temperature creep service, *Journal of Materials Processing Technology*. *157–158*. pp. 297-303

[25] J. Dobrzański, A. Zieliński, M. Sroka, Microstructure. (2009) properties investigations and methodology of the state evaluation of T23 (2.25Cr-0.3Mo-1.6W-V-Nb) steel in boilers application, *32*. pp. 142-153

[26] B. Dyson. (2000) Use of CDM in materials modeling and component creep life prediction, *American Society of Mechanical Engineers. 122(3)* pp. 281-296

[27] M. Fujimoto. M. Sakane. S. Date and H. Yoshia. (2005) Multi-axial creep rupture and damage evalution for 2.25Cr-1Mo Froged Steel, *Soc. Mat. Sci. 54*. pp. 149-154.In Japanese

[28] N. G. Needham. (1983) Cavitation and Fracture in Creep Resisting Steels: Final Report. Commission of the European Communities.

[29] T. Yokobori. A. Jr. (1999) difference in the creep and creep crack growth behavior between creep ductile and brittle materials, *Engineering fracture mechanics*. pp. 61-78

[30] D. Longdale. and P.E.J. Flewitt. (1981) The effect of hydrostatic pressure on the uniaxial creep life of a $2\frac{1}{4}$%Cr1%Mo steel. *Proc. R. Soc.Lond. A 373*. pp. 491-509

[31] Y. Chuman. M. Yamauchi. and T. Hiroe. (2000), Study of evolution procedure of multi-axial creep strength of low alloy steel. *171-174*. pp. 305-312

[32] R.N. Hore and Ghosh. (2011) Computer simulation of the high temperature creep behaviour of Cr–Mo steels, *Materials Science and Engineering: A. 528. Issues 19–20*, pp. 6095-6102

[33] L.M. Kachanov. (1985) Time of the rupture process under creep conditions, *TVZ Akad Nauk SSR Otd Tech*. Nauk 8

[34] Y.N. Rabotnov. (1969) Creep Problems in Structural Members Amsterdam. *North-Holland*

[35] Lemaitre, J. and Chaboche, J.L. (1985). Mécanique des matériaux solides, Dunod, Paris. *Mechanics of Solid Materials*, Springer Verlag, Berlin.

[36] R. Piques. E. Molinie. A. Pineau. (1991) Comparison between two assessment methods for defects in the creep range. *Fatigue and fracture of engineering materials and structures. 14(9).* pp871-885

[37] R.J. Hayhurst, F. Vakili-Tahami, D.R. Hayhurst (2005), Verification of 3-D parallel CDM software for the analysis of creep failure in the HAZ region of Cr–Mo–V crosswelds, International Journal of Pressure Vessels and Piping. 86(8). pp. 475-485

[38] B.F. Dyson, and M. McLean (1990). Modeling the effects of damage and microstructural evolution on the creep behavior of engineering alloys. *ISIJ Int., 30* pp. 802–811

[39] B. Michel. (2004) Formulation of a new intergranular creep damage model for austenitic stainless steels, *Nuclear Engineering and Design. 227(2)*. January, Pages 161-174

[40] J. Lemaitre. R. Desmorat. (2005) Engineering damage mechanics: ductile. Creep. *Fatigue and brittle failures. Springer.* Amsterdam. 2005

[41] M. T. Whittaker. and B. Wilshire. (2013) Advanced procedures for long-term creep data prediction for 2.25 chromium steels. *Metallurgical and materials transactions. 44(1).* Pp. 136-153

[42] F. Kawashima, T. IGRI, T. Tokiyoshi, A. Shiibashi and N. Tada (2004), Micro-macro combined simulation of the damage progress in low-alloy steel welds subject to Type IV creep failure. *47*, pp. 410-418

A combined algorithm for analyzing structural controllability and observability of complex networks

Luis Úbeda[1,2], **Carlos Herrera**[1,2,3], **Iker Barriales**[1,2], **Pedro J. Zufiria**[1,2], **and Mariluz Congosto**[4]
[1]Depto. Matemática Aplicada a las Tecnologías de la Información, ETSI Telecomunicación, Universidad Politécnica de Madrid (UPM), Spain
[2]Cátedra Orange. ETSI Telecomunicación, Universidad Politécnica de Madrid (UPM), Spain
[3]Dept. Civil and Environmental Engineering. Massachusetts Institute of Technology, USA
[4]Departamento de Telemática. Universidad Carlos III de Madrid, Spain
E-mail: *lubeme23@gmail.com, chyague@gmail.com, ibarriales@ono.com, pedro.zufiria@upm.es, mariluz.congosto@gmail.com*

Abstract—*In this paper a combined algorithm for analyzing structural controllability and observability of complex networks is presented. The algorithm addresses the two fundamental properties to guarantee structural controllability of a system: the absence of dilations and the accessibility of all nodes. The first problem is reformulated as a Maximum Matching search and it is addressed via the Hopcroft-Karp algorithm; the second problem is solved via a new wiring algorithm. Both algorithms can be combined to efficiently determine the number of required controllers and observers as well as the new required connections in order to guarantee controllability and observability in real complex networks. An application to a Twitter social network with over 100,000 nodes illustrates the proposed algorithms.*

Keywords: Complex networks, controllability, observability, maximum matching, Twitter

1. Introduction

Classical dynamical system theory is based on the characterization of systems via time-evolution models (e.g. difference or differential equations) [18], [24]. Such characterization can be employed to perform two fundamental and dual tasks in dynamical system theory: on the one hand, the estimation of system's internal state from the measurement of accessible system outputs, defining the so-called observation problem; on the other hand, the modification of system's internal state via the injection of appropriate system inputs, defining the so-called control problem [6]. These problems have been thoroughly studied in the literature so that observability and controllability conditions are well defined, specially for linear systems [3], [8].

The study of complex systems composed by many interconnected elements can be addressed by analyzing the underlying network (or graph) which characterizes these interconnections [1]. Such network gathers some fundamental structural system properties which in general do not depend on the specific system parameter values. In general, both node dynamics and their connectivity are relevant in complex systems control [4], [5], [22]; here in this paper we focus on structural aspects to provide a fundamental reference information for a detailed controllability analysis.

Along this line, structural controllability theory has been developed [14], [15], [20], [21] in order to characterize the implications of system internal connectivity in its state space controllability. The existing results can be formalized via either matrix algebraic structural properties or graph theoretical properties. Parallel results have also been obtained for the dual structural observability problem [16], [23]. Supported by this duality, the exposition of results in this paper will mainly refer to the controllability problem.

System structural controllability becomes determined by both its internal connection structure and the set of inputs defined in such system. Given the network underlying the system connectivity structure and a set of inputs, a system is structurally controllable if and only if all nodes (or vertices) are accessible from the inputs and the network does not have dilations [14].

The first part of this paper addresses the problem of guaranteeing system structural controllability by making use of a minimum number of input controllers. Graph theoretical tools are mainly employed to find such minimum number of control inputs for avoiding dilations, where the concept of Matching becomes crucial [15], [21]. In addition, the concept of wiring is developed to guarantee accessibility of all nodes preserving such minimum number of control inputs.

The second part of the paper illustrates the application of the proposed algorithms to both the controllability and the (dual) observability problems.

In the following section we summarize some of the basic results concerning system structural controllability.

Corresponding author: Pedro J. Zufiria. Depto. Matemática Aplicada a las Tecnologías de la Información, ETSI Telecomunicación, Universidad Politécnica de Madrid (UPM), Ciudad Universitaria s/n, E-28040 Madrid, Spain.

2. Structural controllability fundamental results

As stated in Section 1, a network is structurally controllable if and only if all nodes are accessible from the inputs and the network has no dilation [15]. We start addressing the analysis of dilations.

2.1 Dilation and Matching

A graph (or network) is defined by $G := (V, E)$, a pair of sets where V is the set of vertices (or nodes) and E the set of edges (or links). Every edge belonging to E is defined as a pair of vertices $(v_i, v_j) \in E$ where $v_i, v_j \in V$. For directed graphs, the pair defining an edge is ordered.

A network has a dilation if we can find a subset $S \subset V$ of the vertices of the graph that verifies:

$$|S| > |T(S)| \quad (1)$$

where $T(S)$ represents the set of vertices that point to any vertex $v_i \in S$.

On the other hand, a bipartite graph is defined as $G_b := (X, Y, E_b)$ where X and Y are two (potentially) different sets, and E_b is the set of edges linking one element of X with an element of Y, i.e $E_b = \{(v_i^X, v_j^Y) : v_i^X \in X, v_j^Y \in Y\}$. Given a set of nodes $S \subseteq Y$, we define $T(S) \subseteq X$ such that $T(S) = \{v_i^X \in X : \exists (v_i^X, v_j^Y) \text{ with } v_j^Y \in S\}$.

Graph Theory provides the following result:

Theorem 1 (Hall): A bipartite graph $G_b := (X, Y, E_b)$ has a matching which covers every vertex in X if and only if

$$|T(S)| \geq |S| \ , \ \forall S \subseteq Y \quad (2)$$

Hall's theorem provides a criterion for bipartite graphs to have a perfect matching, as long as they also verify:

$$|X| = |Y| \quad (3)$$

This condition on the existence of a perfect matching is condensed in the following corollary:

Corollary 1.1: A bipartite graph $G_b := (X, Y, E_b)$ has a *perfect matching* if and only if it verifies both (2) and (3).

Given a graph $G := (V, E)$ one can define its associated bipartite graph $G_b := (V^+, V^-, E_b)$ where $V^+ = V^- = V$ and E_b is constructed as follows

$$E_b = \{(v_i^+, v_j^-) : \exists (v_i, v_j) \in E\}$$

Defined this way, $G_b : (V^+, V^-, E_b)$ will obviously verify (3). Therefore, a network has no dilation if and only if it has a perfect matching.

Alternatively, based on the pioneering work of [14], the Maximum Matching (MM) Algorithm is proposed in [15] as a good tool to determine the minimum number of inputs required to guarantee that there are no dilations in a network. Precisely, the number of required inputs would correspond with the number of vertices not matched by an edge in the maximum matching of the network.

2.2 Accessibility and wiring

However, as stated earlier, the matching criterion verifies the condition of no dilation in the network, but not the accessibility condition. The network might present some internal structures that being matched by edges of the maximum matching might not be accessible from the inputs. This happens with matching solutions containing cycles. In these cases, it is necessary to add new connection edges from the calculated inputs to the non-accessible structures; we call this process *wiring*. Note that this process keeps the number of control inputs unchanged.

In the following Section, a version of the MM Algorithm is proposed and analyzed. In addition, a new wiring algorithm is developed, in order to find the structures matched by the MM that are not accessible from the inputs, and to create the required external edges from the inputs to a node of such structures.

3. The combined MM and wiring algorithm

3.1 The Hopcroft-Karp algorithm

Complex networks are usually formed by a very large amount of nodes (or vertices) and links (or edges). Hence, the time efficiency of the Maximum Matching (MM) detection algorithm is very important when dealing with this type of huge networks. For this purpose, the Hopcroft-Karp algorithm has been selected which runs in $O(\sqrt{V}E)$ time [11].

The Hopcroft-Karp algorithm directly deals with non-directed bipartite graphs; nevertheless it can also be applied to general non-bipartite directed graphs, provided an appropriate transformation is previously performed. As mentioned earlier, given the original graph $G := (V, E)$ one can define its associated bipartite graph $G_b := (V^+, V^-, E_b)$ where $V^+ = V^- = V$. Note that the edges in the bipartite graph adjacent to any $v_i^+ \in V^+$ represent the out-links of $v_i \in V$ and the edges adjacent to $v_i^- \in V^-$ represent the in-links of v_i.

Given a matching M_b of G_b, if $(v_i^+, v_j^-) \in M_b$, then $(v_i, v_j) \in M$ where M is the corresponding matching of G. $(v_i^+, v_j^-) \in M_b$ makes nodes v_i^+, v_j^- to be matched on the non-directed bipartite graph G_b while $(v_i, v_j) \in M$ makes v_j to be matched on the directed graph G. Therefore, once we compute the Hopcroft-Karp algorithm over G_b and obtain a maximum matching M_b^* (where $*$ stands for maximum), the unmatched nodes of the set V^- will be the unmatched nodes of the matching M^* in G.

Following the minimum inputs theorem [15] the unmatched nodes given a maximum matching will be the driver nodes of the network, so a controller node must be linked to each one of these driver nodes.

3.2 The accessibility and wiring algorithms

As stated in section 2.2 it is not enough to obtain the maximum matching M^* of the graph G to find the nodes that need to be controlled. Placing the controllers on the unmatched nodes only guarantees the absence of dilations on the graph; hence, it is necessary to additionally perform a search for the inaccessible nodes from the controllers of the network. From section 2.2 it follows that these inaccessible nodes will be placed in the loops of the considered maximum matching M^* of G. The method proposed here consists then on looking for loops on M^* in order to determine those which are not accessible from any controller node. As we are dealing with a directed network, looking for loops in the network given by the matching is equivalent to looking for its strongly connected components [19]; thus, it is possible to perform this search by applying the Tarjan algorithm which runs in $O(|V| + |E|)$ time [13]. Since we are only interested in the strongly connected components of the sub-graph given by M^* (in which $|E| = |M^*|$ and $|V| = |M^*| - 1$ or $|V| = |M^*|$ in the case of a perfect matching, where $|M^*|$ stands for the number of links in the maximum matching), Tarjan's algorithm will run in $O(|M^*|)$. Since the computational cost of this search is much lower than the Hopcroft-Karp maximum matching search over the whole graph, the running time of the Tarjan algorithm is almost negligible.

Once the loops of M^* have been found, an accessibility analysis from the controller nodes must be done. A possible strategy to accomplish this purpose is making a BFS (Breath-First Search [13] for every found loop. Nevertheless, the BFS algorithm must be modified in order to allow the root and the goal of the search to be sets of nodes instead of single nodes, the root set being the nodes of the loop under analysis and the goal set being the unmatched nodes of the network. In addition, an early termination mechanism has also been implemented since once a controller node is found, accessibility is guaranteed and therefore the search can be finished. Based on these modifications, the original BFS algorithm running time of $O(|V| + |E|)$ for each loop can be significantly reduced. Note also that this modified BFS algorithm will deal with short depth paths when dealing with complex networks. The small world [25] property of the network guarantees that if the loop is accessible it will likely be at a short distance from a controller node. Furthermore, it has also been proved that in this kind of networks a giant component arises that contains most of the nodes in the network; hence, if the loop is not accessible from any controller node it will probably belong to a small component, resulting also in a very short depth search.

Finally, a wiring process for the discovered inaccessible loops is performed, adding links between a node of each of these loops and a controller node. Putting all the steps together, the search of the nodes that need to be controlled on a graph G can be summarized in the following four steps:

1) Find the maximum matching M^* of G and link a new different controller node to each unmatched node.
2) Find the loops in M^*.
3) Find those loops of M^* that are not accessible from the controller nodes obtained at step 1.
4) For each found inaccessible loop select a node belonging to it and wire it up to a controller node.

4. Controllability and observability on a real complex network

During the latest years the study of social networks using digital communication records as a proxy for human interactions has enormously grown. Phone calls, texts, or online communications allow researchers to analyze human interaction in unprecedented scales. In order to provide a real world example of controllability in complex networks we have considered the interaction between users in the social site Twitter. First, the data collection process is described and some basic characteristics of the social network are provided. Finally, a controllabillity (and observability) analysis using the techniques explained in previous sections is performed.

4.1 Data description and network characteristics

Our data-set consists of over 11 million tweets containing interactions between users in the Madrid urban area during February 2012. Interactions can be either mentions (user A mentions B in a message) or re-tweets (user A broadcasts to its followers a message from B). In both cases, the interaction is modeled as a directed link from B to A. This interaction network has been referred previously in the literature as the *dynamic* network as opposed to the *static* network where links represent a declared follower-followee relationship. Data have been gathered using Twitter's Streaming API, which allows for geographic filtering; users need to have authored at least one tweet in the data-set to be considered as a node in the resulting network (i.e., re-tweets not authored in Madrid were discarded).

The resulting network consists of 119,217 nodes, whose degrees distributions are presented in figure 1. Average degree in the network is $\langle k_{in} \rangle = \langle k_{out} \rangle = 7.83$. Although both distributions present a certain long tail, this tail is longer for the out degree one. Precisely the maximum out degree is 10,150 while the maximum in degree is 663. The explanation for this difference lies on the limited cognitive capacity of human beings: a person may influence millions of people, but an individual cannot be influenced by the behaviors of millions of people. This reasoning is supported by empirical evidence in primates [7] and more recently in Twitter itself [10]. Apart from an heterogeneous degree, the network exhibits small-world behavior [25]: it presents a high number of triangles (clustering coefficient 0.015, two orders of magnitude more than the equivalent random graph) and short diameter (estimated $\langle l \rangle = 4.14 \pm 0.23$ using 100 random different origins to traverse the graph). Additionally, 21.01% of the relationships are mutual and 96.63% of the nodes belong to a giant connected component. Overall, this network presents general characteristics which are similar to the ones observed in other complex networks [17].

4.2 Analysis of results

Applying the algorithms described on section 3 to the dynamic Twitter network we obtained a total of $N_D = 27.129$ required controller nodes. This set of nodes is sufficient to avoid dilations on the network; however in order to guarantee full structural controllability all nodes must be accessible; thus a search for inaccessible nodes is performed according to the wiring algorithm described in Section 2.2. An average of 800 wired nodes (with a standard deviation two orders of magnitude smaller) are required for the network to satisfy the accessibility condition, and therefore to be controllable. From the above analysis one can see that this network needs almost 25% of the nodes to be directly influenced by a driver node; this means that it cannot be easily controlled.

Since the maximum matching of a network is not unique, a Montecarlo analysis was performed in order to quantify the importance of every node on the different control configurations of the network. The algorithm described on section 3 may provide a different set of controlled nodes for each iteration; since we are interested in estimating the frequency each node shows up in the controlled nodes set, such algorithm has been run up to 40,000 times to guarantee a low estimation variance. Gathering nodes with the same frequency, Figure 2 is obtained. It can be seen that almost all the nodes have a well defined role on the control configuration, since they are either always ($p = 0$) or never ($p = 1$) present in the controlled nodes set. An interesting fact can also be observed: the histogram shows high peaks for values of $p = \frac{1}{4}$, $p = \frac{1}{3}$, $p = \frac{1}{2}$, $p = \frac{2}{3}$, $p = \frac{3}{4}$, $p = \frac{4}{5}$... This phenomenon was explained in [23] to be a consequence of the effect of some repetitive micro-structures (motifs) that commonly appear on these networks.

A parallel study was made regarding the observability of the network [23], obtaining similar results to the above commented for controllability. However a significantly bigger amount of nodes was required on the wiring stage to satisfy the accessibility condition. This difference comes from the asymmetry between the in-degree and out-degree distributions of the network.

In order to assess the information obtained by the controllability and observability analysis, a cross-correlation analysis of both indices with some usual metrics used in complex networks was performed. Such selected metrics are the PageRank [2], betweeness centrality[1], out/in-degree, and a physics based influence index proposed in [9]. Figure 3 displays the results of this analysis, where one can observe that both controllability and observability are almost totally uncorrelated with all the considered metrics; this means that the information provided by this analysis can complementarily shed some new light in the node characterization of complex networks.

5. Concluding remarks

An algorithm for analyzing structural controllability and observability of complex networks has been presented. The algorithm combines a Maximum Matching search and a new *wiring* algorithm to efficiently determine the number of required controllers and observers as well as the new required connections in the network. The application to a Twitter social network with over 100,000 nodes has illustrated the applicability of the algorithm on a real complex network. The results suggest that these measures (number of required controllers and observers) provide new metrics to characterize the network structural properties.

Acknowledgments

The authors want to acknowledge the financial support of Orange (Spain and France), in the framework of Cátedra Orange at the ETSI Telecomunicación in the Universidad Politécnica de Madrid (UPM), Spain. The work has been also partially supported by projects MTM2010-15102 of Ministerio de Ciencia e Innovación, and Q10 0930-144 of UPM, Spain.

References

[1] A. L. Barabási and R. Albert, "*Emergence of scaling in random networks*" Science, 286 , pp. 509-512, 1999.

[2] Brin, S. and Page, L., "*The anatomy of a large-scale hypertextual Web search engine*", Computer networks and ISDN systems, 30, 107-117, 1998.

[3] T.-C. Chen, "*Linear System Theory: the state space approach*", Oxford University Press, 1999.

[4] S. P. Cornelius, W. L. Kath and A. E. Motter, "*Controlling Complex Networks with Compensatory Perturbations*", arXiv.1105.3726, 2011.

[5] N. J. Cowan, E. J. Chastain, D. A. Vilhena, J. S. Freudenberg and C. T. Bergson, "*Nodal dynamics, not degree distributions, determine the structural controllability of complex networks*", arXiv.1106.2573, 2011.

[6] R. C. Dorf and R. H. Bishop, "*Modern Control Systems*", Pearson, 2011.

[7] Dunbar, R. I. "*Neocortex size as a constraint on group size in primates*". Journal of Human Evolution, 22(6), 469-493, 1992.

[8] B. Friedland, "*Control System Design: An introduction to state-space methods*", Dover, 1986.

[1] Betweeness centrality is a common topological measure in complex networks, defined as the fraction of shortest paths in the network which cross a certain node: classic example is the Anchorage airport in Alaska, which is not a *hub* (does not have many connections to others), but it is indeed a crucial node in the air traffic network since allows refuel for many America-Asia connections.

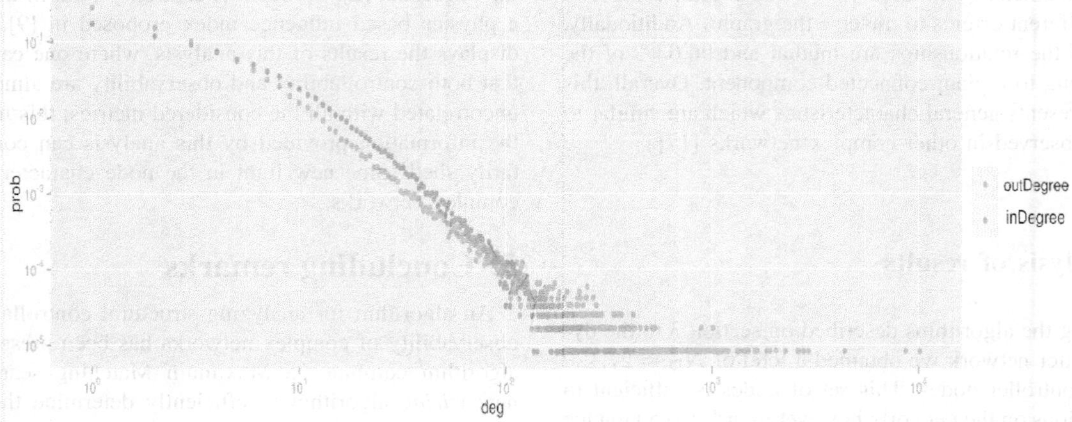

Fig. 1: In-degree and out-degree distributions of the network.

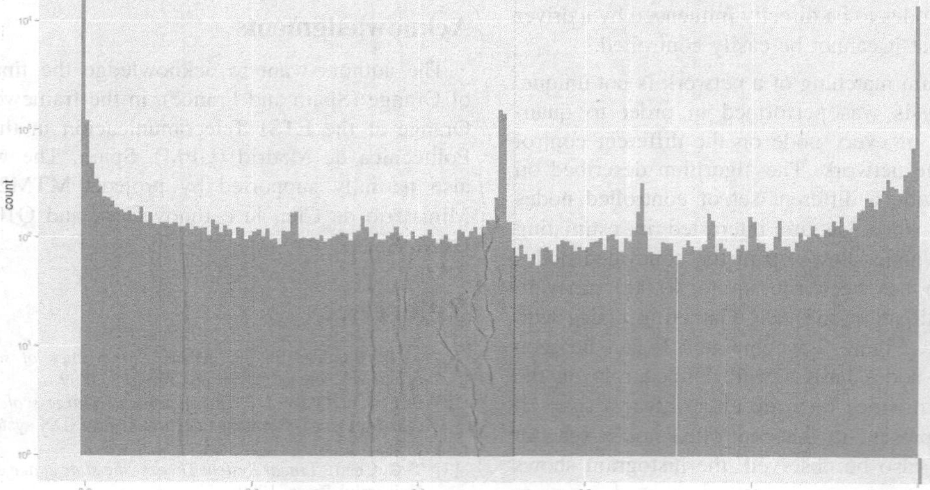

Fig. 2: Frequency of appearance of the nodes on the controller nodes set.

[9] D. Gayo-Avello, D. J. Brenes, D. Fernández-Fernández, M. E. Fernández-Menéndez and R. García-Suárez, " *De retibus socialibus et legibus momenti*" (On social networks and the laws of influence, EPL (Europhysics Letters), (94) 38001, doi: 10.1209/0295-5075/94/38001.

[10] Goncalves, B., Perra, N., and Vespignani, A."*Validation of Dunbar's number in Twitter conversations*". arXiv preprint arXiv:1105.5170.,2011.

[11] J. E. Hopcroft and R. M. Karp, "*An $n^{5/2}$ algorithm for maximum matchings in bipartite graphs*", SIAM J. Comput. 2, 225 (1973).

[12] R. E. Kalman, J. Soc. Indus. and Appl. Math. Ser. A 1, 152, 1963.

[13] Knuth, Donald E., "The Art Of Computer Programming Vol 1. 3rd ed.", Boston: Addison-Wesley, ISBN 0-201-89683-4, 1997.

[14] Ching-Tai Lin, "*Structural Controllability*", IEEE Trans. AC-19(3) 201-208, 1974.

[15] Y. Liu, J. Slotine and A. L. Barabási, "*Controllability of Complex Networks*", Nature 473, 168, 2011.

[16] Y. Liu, J. Slotine and A. L. Barabási, "*Observability of Complex Networks*", PNAS (DOI: 10.1073/1215508110), 2013.

[17] Newman, M. E. J., "*The structure and function of complex networks*", SIAM review, 45 (2) 167-256 , 2003.

[18] B. Friedland, "*Introduction to Dynamic Systems: Theory, Models and Applications*", John Wiley & Sons, 1979.

[19] Sedgewick, R., "*Graph algorithms*", Algorithms, Addison-Wesley, ISBN 0-201-06672-6, 1983.

[20] R. W. Shields and J. B. Pearson, "*Structural Controllability of Multi-Input Linear Systems*", IEEE Transactions on Automatic Control,

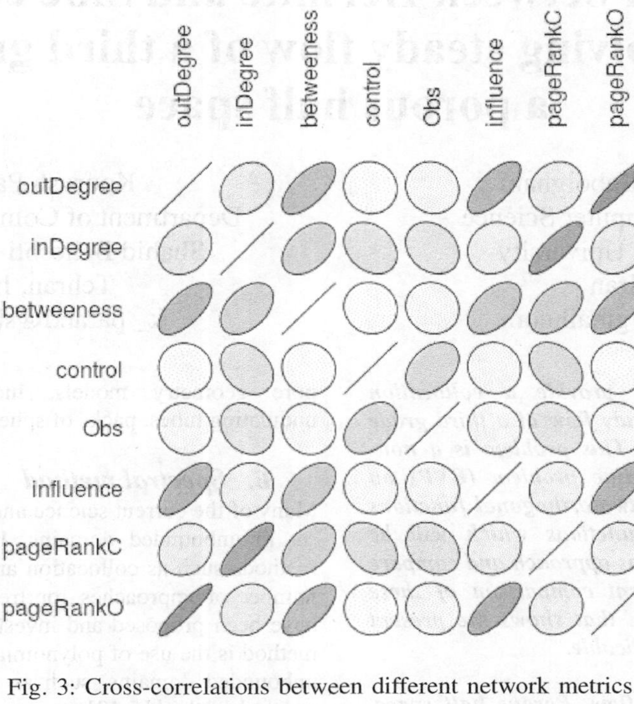

Fig. 3: Cross-correlations between different network metrics.

VOL. AC-21, NO. 2, APRIL 1976.

[21] R. W. Shields and J. B. Pearson, *"Author's Reply to Corrections to Structural Coatrollability of Multi-Input Linear Systems"*, IEEE Transactions on Automatic Control, VOL. AC-23, NO. 3, JUNE 1978.

[22] J. Sun, S. P. Cornelius, W. L. Kath and A. E. Motter *"Comment on "Controllability of Complex Networks with Nonlinear Dynamics""*, arXiv.1108.5739, 2011.

[23] L. A. Úbeda Medina, *"Controlabilidad y observabilidad en redes complejas"*, Proyecto Fin de Carrera, ETSI Telecomunicación, Universidad Politécnica de Madrid, Octubre 2012.

[24] M. Vidyasagar, *"Nonlinear Systems Analysis"*, SIAM, 2002.

[25] Watts, D. J. and Strogatz, S. H, *"Collective dynamics of small-world networks"*, Nature, 393, 6684, 440-442, 1998.

Comparison between Hermite and Sinc collocation methods for solving steady flow of a third grade fluid in a porous half space

Fattaneh Bayat Babolghani
Department of Computer Science
Shahid Beheshti University
Tehran, Iran
fattaneh.bayat@gmail.com

Kourosh Parand
Department of Computer Science
Shahid Beheshti University
Tehran, Iran
k_ parand@sbu.ac.ir

Abstract—***In this paper, we provide a collocation method for the problem of steady flow of a third grade fluid in a porous half space. This problem is a non-linear, two-point boundary value problem (BVP) on semi-infinite interval. We use two orthogonal functions namely Hermite and Sinc functions which will be defined as basis functions in this approach and compare them together. We also present comparison of these works with numerical solution that shows the present solutions are accurate and applicable.***

Keywords-component: Steady flow, Porous half space, Hermite function, Sinc function, Spectral methods, Semi-infinite.

I. Introduction

A. Introduction of the problem

The flow of non-Newtonian fluids has several technical applications, especially in the paper and textile industries. Out of many models which have been used to describe the non-Newtonian behavior exhibited by certain fluids. The fluids of the differential type have received special attention. Fluids of the second and the third grade have been studied in various types of flow situations which form a subclass of the fluids of the differential type. Boundary layer theories for fluid similar to a second grade fluid have been formulated by Rajeswari and Rathna, Bhatnagar, Beard and Waiters, and Frater. Rajagopal et al. developed a boundary layer approximation for a second grade fluid [1].

The third grade fluid models even for steady flow exhibits such characteristics. The present study deals with the problem of non-Newtonian fluid of third grade in a porous half space. Due to the widespread applications, flow through porous media received substantial attention. The attempts to include porous media in the flows of the complex fluids need some new physical parameters besides non-Newtonian fluid parameters. Thus, Darcys equations or some generalization of it depending on pressure field, not neglecting porosity, are appropriate to study this type of flows thorough the porous media which is rigid or nearly rigid solid. Also the modeling of polymeric flow in porous space has essential focus on the numerical simulation of viscoelastic flows in a specific pore geometry models, including: capillary tubes, undulating tubes, packs of spheres or cylinders [2, 3].

B. Spectral method

Many of the current science and engineering problems are set in unbounded domains. In the context of spectral methods such as collocation and Galerkin methods [4], a number of approaches for treating unbounded domains have been proposed and investigated. The most common method is the use of polynomials that are orthogonal over unbounded domains, such as the Hermite and Laguerre spectral method [5-12].

Guo [13-16] proposed a method that proceeds by mapping the original problem in an unbounded domain to a problem in a bounded domain, and then using suitable Jacobi polynomials such as Gegenbauer polynomials to approximate the resulting problems. The Jacobi polynomials are a class of classical orthogonal polynomials and the Gegenbauer polynomials, and thus also the Legendre and Chebyshev polynomials, are special cases of these polynomials which have been used in sevral literatures for solving some problems [17, 18].

On more approach is replacing infinite domain with $[-L, L]$ and semi-infinite interval with $[0, L]$ by choosing L, sufficiently large. This method is named domain truncation [19].

There is another effective direct approach for solving such problems which is based on rational approximations. Christov [20] and Boyd [21, 22] developed some spectral methods on unbounded intervals by using mutually orthogonal systems of rational functions. Boyd [21] defined a new spectral basis, named rational Chebyshev functions on the semi-infinite interval, by mapping to the Chebyshev polynomials. Guo et al. [23] introduced a new set of rational Legendre functions which are mutually orthogonal in $L^2(0,\infty)$. They applied a spectral scheme using the rational Legendre functions for solving the Korteweg-de Vries equation on the half-line. Boyd et al. [24] applied pseudospectral methods on a semi-infinite interval and compared rational Chebyshev, Laguerre and mapped Fourier sine methods.

Parand et al. [25-30], applied spectral method to solve nonlinear ordinary differential equations on semi-infinite intervals. Their approach was based on rational tau and collocation methods.

In this paper, we are going to solve the model Eq. (1) numerically by using two orthogonal functions, namely Hermit function and Sinc function in collocation method and compare our result together. we also have a comparison with solutions of [31].
Sections *III* and *V* review the desirable properties of Hermit function and Sinc function with solution of the problem with collocation method by these functions, respectively. In Section *VII* we describe our results via tables and figures. Finally, concluding remarks will be presented in Section *VIII*.

II. Mathematical formulation

In this section we focus on Hayat et al. [2] who have discussed the flow of a third grade fluid in a porous half space. For unidirectional flow, they have generalized the relation [2]

$$(\nabla p)_x = -\frac{\mu\varphi}{k}(1+\frac{\alpha_1}{\mu}\frac{\partial}{\partial t})u,$$

for a second grade fluid to the following modified Darcy's Law for a third grade fluid

$$(\nabla p)_x = -\frac{\varphi}{k}[\mu u + \alpha_1\frac{\partial u}{\partial t} + 2\beta_3(\frac{\partial u}{\partial y})^2 u],$$

where μ is the dynamic viscosity, u is the denote the fluid velocity and p is the pressure, k and φ, respectively represent the permeability and porosity of the porous half space which occupies the region $y>0$ and α_1, β_3 are material constants. Defining non dimensional fluid velocity f and the coordinate z

$$z = \frac{V_0}{\nu}y, \quad f(z) = \frac{u}{V_0},$$
$$V_0 = u(0), \quad \nu = \frac{\mu}{\rho},$$

where ν and V_0 represent the kinematic viscosity, the boundary value problem modeling the steady state flow of a third grade fluid in a porous half space becomes [2]

$$f''(z) + b_1 f'^2(z) f''(z) - b_2 f(z) f'^2(z) - b_3 f(z) = 0,$$
$$f(0) = 1, \quad f(\infty) = 0. \qquad (1)$$

Where b_1, b_2 and b_3 are defined as:

$$b_1 = \frac{6\beta_3 V_0^4}{\mu\nu^2},$$
$$b_2 = \frac{2\beta_3\varphi V_0^2}{k\mu},$$
$$b_3 = \frac{\varphi\nu^2}{kV_0^2}.$$

Note that the parameters are not independent, since

$$b_2 = \frac{b_1 b_3}{3}.$$

The homotopy analysis method for solution of Eq. (1) found in [2]. Later Ahmad gave the asymptotic form of the solution and utilize this information to develop a series solution [31].

III. Hermite function

This section are devoted to elaborate the properties of Hermite functions. First of all, we should mention Hermite polynomials are generally not suitable in practice due to their wild asymptotic behavior at infinities [32]; therefore, we shall consider the Hermite function. The normalized Hermite functions of degree n is defined by [33]

$$\tilde{H}_n = \frac{1}{\sqrt{2^n n!}} e^{\frac{-x^2}{2}} H_n(x), \quad n \ge 0, x \in \Re.$$

That $\{\tilde{H}_n\}$ is an orthogonal system in $L^2(\Re)$.
In the contrary to Hermite Polynomials, the Hermite functions are well behaved with the decay property:

$$|\tilde{H}_n(x)| \to 0, \quad as\ |x| \to \infty,$$

and, the three-term recurrence relation of Hermite functions implies [33]

$$\tilde{H}_{n+1}(x) = x\sqrt{\frac{2}{n+1}}\tilde{H}_n(x) - \sqrt{\frac{n}{n+1}}\tilde{H}_{n-1}(x), \quad n \ge 1,$$

$$\tilde{H}_0(x) = e^{\frac{-x^2}{2}}, \quad \tilde{H}_1(x) = \sqrt{2}xe^{\frac{-x^2}{2}}.$$

For more details you can study [33-35].
Steady flow problem is defined on the interval $(0,+\infty)$, but Hermite functions are defined on the interval $(-\infty,+\infty)$. One of the approaches to construct an approximation on the interval $(0,+\infty)$ is using mapping that is changing variable of the form [33]

$$w = \Phi(z) = \frac{1}{k}ln(z),$$

where k is a constant.
The transformed Hermite functions are

$$\hat{H}_n(x) \equiv \tilde{H}_n(x) \circ \Phi(x) = \tilde{H}_n(\Phi(x)),$$

The inverse map of $w = \Phi(z)$ is

$$z = \Phi^{-1}(w) = e^{kw}.$$

Therefor, we may define the inverse images of the spaced nodes $\{x_j\}_{x_j=-\infty}^{x_j=+\infty}$ as [33]

$$\Gamma = \{\Phi^{-1}(t) : -\infty < t < +\infty\} = (0,+\infty),$$

and

$$\tilde{x}_j = \Phi^{-1}(x_j) = e^{x_j},\ j = 0,1,2,...$$

Let $w(x)$ denotes a non-negative, integrable, real-valued function over the interval Γ, We define [33]

$$L^2_w(\Gamma) = \{v : \Gamma \to \mathrm{R} \mid v \text{ is measurable and } \|v\|_w < \infty\},$$

where

$$\|v\|_w = (\int_0^{\infty} |v(x)|^2\, w(x)dx)^{\frac{1}{2}},$$

is the norm induced by the inner product of the space $L^2_w(\Gamma)$ [33],

$$< u,v >_w = \int_0^{\infty} u(x)v(x)w(x)dx.$$

Thus, $\{\hat{H}_n(x)\}_{n\in N}$ denotes a system which is mutually orthogonal

$$\langle \hat{H}_n(x), \hat{H}_m(x)\rangle_{w(x)} = \sqrt{\pi}\delta_{nm}.$$

This system is complete in $L^2_w(\Gamma)$. Therefore, for any function $f \in L^2_w(\Gamma)$ the following expansion holds [33]

$$f(x) \cong \sum_{k=-N}^{+N} f_k \hat{H}_k(x),$$

with

$$f_k = \frac{\langle f(x), \hat{H}_k(x)\rangle_{w(x)}}{\left\|\hat{H}_k(x)\right\|^2_{w(x)}}.$$

Now we define an orthogonal projection based on the transformed Hermite function as given below [33].
Let

$$\overline{H}_N = span\{\hat{H}_0(x), \hat{H}_1(x), \ldots, \hat{H}_n(x)\}.$$

The $L^2(\Gamma)$-orthogonal projection $\hat{\xi}_N : L^2(\Gamma) \to \overline{H}_N$ is a mapping in a way that for any $y \in L^2(\Gamma)$ [33],

$$\langle \hat{\xi}_N y - y, \phi\rangle = 0 \quad \forall \phi \in \overline{H}_N,$$

or equivalently,

$$\hat{\xi}_N y(x) = \sum_{i=0}^{N} \hat{a}_i \hat{H}_i(x).$$

IV. Solving the problem with Hermite function

For solving Steady Flow Problem, we used $\frac{1}{k}ln(z)$ for changing variable. Also, because of boundary conditions, we set following function:

$$p(z) = \frac{1}{1+\lambda z + z^2},$$

and λ is constant.
Finally, we have

$$\hat{\xi}_N f(z) = p(z) + \hat{\xi}_N f(z).$$

that

$$\hat{\xi}_N f(z) = \sum_{i=0}^{N} \hat{a}_i \hat{H}_i(z).$$

To find the unknown coefficients a_i's, we substitute the truncated series $\hat{\xi}_N f(z)$ into Eq. (1). Also, we define Residual function of the form

$$\begin{aligned} Res(z) = {} & (p''(z) + \hat{\xi}_N f''(z)) + b_1(p'(z) \\ & + \hat{\xi}_N f'(z))^2 (p''(z) + \hat{\xi}_N f''(z)) \\ & - b_2(p(z) + \hat{\xi}_N f(z))(p'(z) + \hat{\xi}_N f'(z))^2 \\ & - b_3(p(z) + \hat{\xi}_N f(z)) = 0. \end{aligned} \tag{2}$$

By applying z in Eq. (2) with the N collocation points which are roots of transformed Hermite function, we have N equations that generates a set of N nonlinear equations. Now, all of these equations can be solved by Newton method for the unknown coefficients.

V. Sinc function

The Sinc function is defined by [36]

$$Sinc(x) = \begin{cases} \dfrac{\sin(\pi x)}{\pi x} & x \neq 0 \\ 1 & x = 0 \end{cases}$$

For each integer k and the mesh size h, the sinc functions are defined on $\Re$ by [37]

$$S_k(h,x) \equiv Sinc(\frac{x-kh}{h}) = \begin{cases} \dfrac{\sin(\frac{\pi}{h}(x-kh))}{\frac{\pi}{h}(x-kh)} & x \neq kh \\ 1 & x = kh \end{cases}$$

Steady flow problem is defined on the interval $(0,+\infty)$, but Sinc functions are defined on the interval $(-\infty,+\infty)$. One of the approaches to construct an approximation on the interval $(0,+\infty)$ is using mapping that is changing variable of the form

$$w = \Phi(z) = \ln(\sinh(x)),$$

The basis functions on $(0,+\infty)$ are taken to be composite translates Sinc functions [36]:

$$S_k(x) \equiv S(k,h) \circ \Phi(x) = Sinc(\frac{\Phi(x) - kh}{h}),$$

Where $S(k,h)\circ\Phi(x)$ is defines by $S(k,h)(\Phi(x))$. The inverse map of $w = \Phi(z)$ is [38]

$$z = \Phi^{-1}(w) = \ln(e^w + \sqrt{e^{2w}+1}).$$

Thus,

$$x_k = \Phi^{-1}(kh) = \ln(e^{kh} + \sqrt{e^{2kh}+1}), k = 0, \pm1, \pm2, \ldots$$

Let $w(x)$ denotes a non-negative, integrable, real-valued function over the interval $(0,+\infty)$. We define [36]:

$$L^2_w(\Gamma) = \left\{ v : \Gamma \to \Re \middle| v \quad is\ measurable\ and\ \|v\|_w < \infty \right\},$$

Where

$$\|v\|_w = (\int_0^{\infty} |v(x)|^2 w(x)dx)^{\frac{1}{2}},$$

is the norm induced by the inner product of the space $L_w^2(\Gamma)$:

$$\langle u,v\rangle_w = \int_0^\infty u(x)v(x)w(x)dx.$$

Thus, $\{S_k(x)\}_{k\in z}$ with constant h denotes a system which is mutually orthogonal [36]:

$$\left\langle S_{k_n}(x), S_{k_m}(x)\right\rangle_{w(x)} = hS_{nm}.$$

Now, for any function $f \in L_w^2(\Gamma)$, the following expansion holds [36]:

$$f(x) \cong \sum_{k=-N}^{+N} f_k S_k(x).$$

In addition, the nth derivation of the function f at some point x_k can be approximated [36, 39]

$$\delta_{k,j}^{(0)} = [S(k,h)\circ\Phi(x)]|_{x=x_j} = \begin{cases} 1 & k=j \\ 0 & k\neq j \end{cases},$$

$$\delta_{k,j}^{(1)} = \frac{d}{d\Phi}[S(k,h)\circ\Phi(x)]|_{x=x_j} = \frac{1}{h}\begin{cases} 0 & k=j \\ \dfrac{(-1)^{j-k}}{j-k} & k\neq j \end{cases},$$

$$\delta_{k,j}^{(2)} = \frac{d^2}{d\Phi^2}[S(k,h)\circ\Phi(x)]|_{x=x_j} = \frac{1}{h^2}\begin{cases} \dfrac{-\pi^2}{3} & k=j \\ \dfrac{-2(-1)^{j-k}}{(j-k)^2} & k\neq j \end{cases}.$$

VI. Solving the problem with Sinc function

For solving Steady Flow Problem, we used $\ln(\sinh(z))$ for changing variable. Also, because of boundary conditions, we set following function:

$$p(z) = \frac{1}{1+\lambda z + z^2},$$

and λ is constant.

Finally, we have

$$f(z) \cong f_N(z) = p(z) + u_N(z),$$

that

$$u_N(z) = \sum_{k=-N}^{+N} c_k \frac{zS_k(z)}{z^2+1}.$$

The collocation points are

$$z_j = \ln(e^{jh} + \sqrt{1+e^{2jh}}), j=-N,\ldots,+N,$$

And the derivations of $u_N(z)$ are

$$u_N(z_j) = \frac{c_j z_j}{z_j^2+1},$$

$$u'_N(z_j) = \sum_{k=-N}^{+N} c_k\left\{\left(\frac{1}{1+z_j^2} - \frac{2z_j^2}{(1+z_j^2)^2}\right)\delta_{k,j}^{(0)} + \left(\frac{z_j\Phi'(z_j)}{1+z_j^2}\right)\delta_{k,j}^{(1)}\right\},$$

$$u''_N(z_j) = \sum_{k=-N}^{+N} c_k\left\{\left(\frac{-6z_j}{(1+z_j^2)^2} + \frac{8z_j^3}{(1+z_j^2)^3}\right)\delta_{k,j}^{(0)}\right.$$

$$\left. + \left(\frac{2\Phi'(z_j)}{1+z_j^2} - \frac{4z_j^2\Phi(z_j)}{(1+z_j^2)^2} + \frac{z_j\Phi'(z_j)}{1+z_j^2}\right)\delta_{k,j}^{(1)} + \left(\frac{z_j(\Phi'(z_j))^2}{1+z_j^2}\right)\delta_{k,j}^{(2)}.\right.$$

To find the unknown coefficients c_i's, we substitute the truncated series $f_N(z_j)$ into Eq. (1). Also, we define Residual functions of the form

$$f''_N(z_j) + b_1(f'_N(z_j))^2 f''_N(z_j)$$
$$-b_2 f_N(z_j)(f'_N(z_j))^2 - b_3 f_N(z_j) = 0, j=-N,\ldots,+N.$$

We have $2N+1$ nonlinear equations. Now, all of these equations can be solved by Newton method for the unknown coefficients.

VII. Result

In this paper, we present the results of our research about Hermite function by $N=16$, $k=1.2$, and $\lambda = 0.678301$ and Sinc function by $N=17$, $h=1$, and $\lambda = 0.47$ for solving this problem for some typical values of parameters, $b_1 = 0.6$, $b_2 = 0.1$, and $b_3 = 0.5$. In this problem the numerical solution of $f'(0)$ is important. Ahmad [31] obtained $f'(0)$ by the shooting method and founded correct to six decimal positions $f'(0) = -0.678301$.

We compare the present methods with numerical solution and Ahmad solution [31], also we compare them with each other in Table 1. Also, the solutions are presented graphically in Figure 1 and Figure 2.

Table 1. Comparison between Hermite function, Sinc Function, Ahmad method [31], and Shooting method [31].

Shooting [31]	Ahmad [31]	Sinc function	Hermite function	z
1.00000	1.00000	1.00000	1.00000	0.0
0.87260	0.87220	0.87278	0.87261	0.2
0.76060	0.76010	0.76035	0.76064	0.4
0.66240	0.66190	0.66178	0.66243	0.6
0.57650	0.57600	0.57597	0.57647	0.8
0.50140	0.50100	0.50115	0.50139	1.0
0.43590	0.43560	0.43583	0.43591	1.2
0.32920	0.32890	0.32905	0.32917	1.6
0.24840	0.24820	0.24802	0.24839	2.0
0.17450	0.17440	0.17426	0.17459	2.5
0.15160	0.15140	0.15141	0.15161	2.7
0.12260	0.12250	0.12265	0.12270	3.0
0.08024	0.08016	0.08025	0.08036	3.6
0.06047	0.06042	0.06033	0.06060	4.0
0.05250	0.05245	0.05233	0.05261	4.2
0.04558	0.04553	0.04543	0.04567	4.4
0.03957	0.03953	0.03948	0.03964	4.6
0.03435	0.03432	0.03434	0.03440	4.8
0.02982	0.02979	0.02987	0.02984	5.0
-0.678301	-0.681835	-0.677843	-0.678301	$f'(0)$

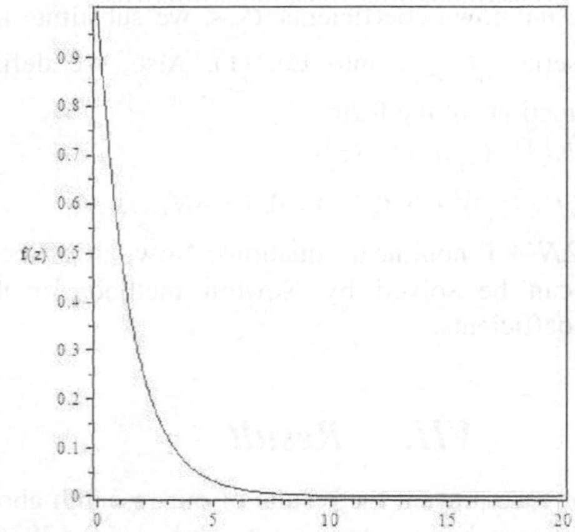

Figure 1. Graph of numerical approximate $f(z)$ by Hermite function

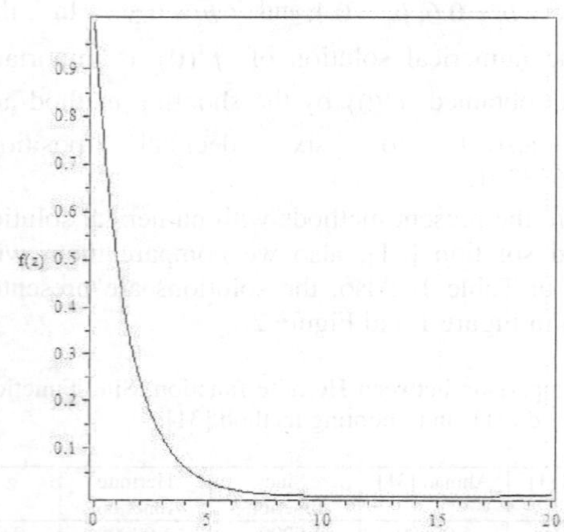

Figure 2. Graph of numerical approximate $f(z)$ by Sinc function

VIII. Conclusions

In this paper, we applied the collocation method to solve the steady flow of the third grade fluid in a porous half space. This method is easy to implement and yields the desired accuracy. An important concern of collocation approach is the choice of basis functions. The basis functions have three different properties: easy computation, rapid convergence and completeness, which means that any solution can be represented to arbitrarily high accuracy by taking the truncation N to be sufficiently large. We used two set of orthogonal functions as the basis function in this method and compared the results together. Through the comparisons among the numerical solutions [31] and the current works, it has been shown that the present works have provided acceptable approach for this type equation. Although both functions lead to more accurate results, but it seems that the accuracy and rapidity of Hermite function is better than Sinc function in this problem.

References

[1] V.K.Garg, K.R. Rajagopal, 1990. Stagnation point flow of a non-newtonian fluid, Mech. Res. Comm. 17: 415-421.

[2] T. Hayat, F. Shahzad and M. Ayub, 2007. Analytical solution for the steady flow of the third grade fluid in a porous half space, Appl. Math. Model. 31: 2424-2432.

[3] T. Hayat, F. Shahzad, M. Ayub and S. Asghar, 2008. Stokes first problem for a third grade fluid in a porous half space, Commun. Nonlinear. Sci. Numer. Simul. 13: 1801-1807.

[4] T. Lotfi, K. Mahdiani, Fuzzy Galerkin Method for Solving Fredholm Integral Equations with Error Analysis, International Journal of Industrial Mathematics 3 (2011) 237–249.

[5] O. Coulaud, D. Funaro, O. Kavian, Laguerre spectral approximation of elliptic problems in exterior domains, Computer Methods in Applied Mechanics and Engineering 80 (1990) 451–458.

[6] D. Funaro, Computational aspects of pseudospectral Laguerre approximations, Applied Numerical Mathematics 6 (1990) 447–457.

[7] D. Funaro, O. Kavian, Approximation of some diffusion evolution equations in unbounded domains by Hermite functions, Mathematics of Computing 57 (1991) 597–619.

[8] B. Y. Guo, Error estimation of Hermite spectral method for nonlinear partial differential equations, Mathematics of Computing 68 (1999) 1067–1078.

[9] B. Y. Guo, J. Shen, Laguerre-Galerkin method for nonlinear partial differential equations on a semi-infinite interval, Numerical Mathematik 86 (2000) 635–654.

[10] Y. Maday, B. Pernaud-Thomas, H. Vandeven, Reappraisal of Laguerre type spectral methods, Recherche Aerospatiale, La 6 (1985) 13–35.

[11] J. Shen, Stable and efficient spectral methods in unbounded domains using Laguerre functions, SIAM Journal on Numerical Analysis 38 (2000) 1113–1133.

[12] H. I. Siyyam, Laguerre tau methods for solving higher order ordinary differential equations, Journal of Computational Analysis and Applications 3 (2001) 173–182.

[13] B. Y. Guo, Gegenbauer approximation and its applications to differential equations on the whole line, Journal of Mathematical Analysis and Applications 226 (1998) 180–206.

[14] B. Y. Guo, Gegenbauer approximation and its applications to differential equations with rough asymptotic behaviors at infinity, Applied Numerical Mathematics 38 (2001) 403–-425.

[15] B. Y. Guo, Jacobi approximations in certain Hilbert spaces and their applications to singular differential equations, Journal of Mathematical Analysis and Applications 243 (2000) 373–408.

[16] B. Y. Guo, Jacobi spectral approximation and its applications to differential equations on the half line, Mathematical and Computer Modelling 18 (2000) 95–112.

[17] M. Barkhordari Ahmadi, M. Khezerloo, Fuzzy Bivariate Chebyshev Method for Solving Fuzzy Volterra-Fredholm Integral Equations, International Journal of Industrial Mathematics 3 (2011) 67–78.

[18] Z. Lorkojori, N. Mikaeilvand, Two Modified Jacobi Methods for M-Matrices, International Journal of Industrial Mathematics 2 (2010) 181–187.

[19] J. P. Boyd. Chebyshev and Fourier Spectral Methods, Second Edition, Dover, New York, 2000.

[20] CI. Christov, A complete orthogonal system of functions in $L^2(-\infty,\infty)$ space, SIAM Journal on Applied Mathematics 42 (1982) 1337–1344.

[21] J. P. Boyd, Orthogonal rational functions on a semi-infinite interval, Journal of Computational Physics 70 (1987) 63–88.

[22] J. P. Boyd, Spectral methods using rational basis functions on an infinite interval, Journal of Computational Physics 69 (1987) 112–142.

[23] B. Y. Guo, J. Shen, Z. Q. Wang, A rational approximation and its applications to differential equations on the half line, Journal of Scientific Computing 15 (2000) 117–147.

[24] J. P. Boyd, C. Rangan, P. H. Bucksbaum, Pseudospectral methods on a semi-infinite interval with application to the Hydrogen atom: a comparison of the mapped Fourier-sine method with Laguerre series and rational Chebyshev expansions, Journal of Computational Physics 188 (2003) 56–74.

[25] K. Parand, M. Dehghan, A. Taghavi. Modified generalized Laguerre function Tau method for solving laminar viscous flow: The Blasius equation, International Journal of Numerical Methods for Heat and Fluid Flow 20 (2010) 728–743.

[26] K. Parand, M. Razzaghi, Rational Chebyshev tau method for solving Volterra's population model, Applied Mathematics and Computation 149 (2004) 893–900.
[27] K. Parand, M. Razzaghi, Rational Legendre approximation for solving some physica problems on semi-infinite intervals, Physica Scripta 69 (2004) 353–357.
[28] K. Parand, M. Shahini, Rational Chebyshev pseudospectral approach for solving Thomas-Fermi equation, Physics Letters A 373 (2009) 210–213.
[29] K. Parand, M. Shahini, M. Dehghan, Rational Legendre pseudospectral approach for solving nonlinear differential equations of Lane-Emden type, Journal of Computational Physics 228 (2009) 8830–8840.
[30] K. Parand, A. Taghavi, Rational scaled generalized Laguerre function collocation method for solving the Blasius equation, Journal of Computational and Applied Mathematics 233 (2009) 980–989.
[31] F. Ahmad, 2009. A simple analytical solution for the steady flow of a third grade fluid in a porous half space, Commun. Nonlinear. Sci. Numer. Simul. 14: 2848-2852.
[32] J. Shen, L-L. Wang. Some Recent Advances on Spectral Methods for Unbounded Domains, Communications in Computational Physics 5 (2009) 195–241.
[33] K. Parand, M. Dehghan, A. R. Rezaeia, S. M. Ghaderia, An approximation algorithm for the solution of the nonlinear Lane-Emden type equations arising in astrophysics using Hermite functions collocation method, Computer Physics Communications 181 (2010) 1096–1108.
[34] J. Shen, T. Tang, High Order Numerical Methods and Algorithms, Chinese Science Press, to be published in (2005).
[35] J. Shen, T. Tang, L-L.Wang, Spectral Methods Algorithms, Analyses and Applications, Springer, First edition, (2010).
[36] K. Parand, A. Pirkhedri, Sinc-Collocation method for solving astrophysics equations, New Astronomy 15 (2010) 533–537.
[37] M. Dehghan, A. Saadatmandi, The numerical solution of a nonlinear system of second-order boundary value problems using the sinc–collocation method, Mathematical and Computer Modelling 46 (2007) 1434–1441.
[38] J. Lund, K. Bowers, Sinc Methods for Quadrature and Differential Equations, SIAM, Philadelphia (1992).
[39] M. El-Gamel, S.H. Behiry, H. Hashish, Applied Mathematics and Computation 145 (2003) 717.

Review of creep deformation and rupture mechanism of P91 alloy for the development of creep damage constitutive equations under low stress level

Lili An[1, a], Qiang Xu[1,b], Donglai Xu[1,c], Zhongyu Lu[2,d]
[1]School of Science and Engineering, Teesside University, Middlesbrough, TS1 3BA, UK
[2]School of Computing and Engineering, University of Huddersfield, Huddersfield, HD1 3DA, UK
[a]L.An@tees.ac.uk, [b]Q.Xu@tees.ac.uk, [c]D.Xu@tees.ac.uk, [d]Z.Lu@hud.ac.uk

Abstract — **This paper presents a review of creep deformation and rupture mechanism of P91 alloy for the development of its creep damage constitutive equations under lower stress level. Creep damage is one of the serious problems for the high temperature industries and computational approach (such as continuum damage mechanics) has been developed and used, complementary to the experimental approach, to assist safe operation. However, there are no ready creep damage constitutive equations to be used for prediction the lifetime for this type of alloy, partially under low stress.**

The paper reports a critical review on the deformation and damage evolution characteristics of this alloy, particularly under low stress, to form the physical base for the development of creep damage constitutive equations. It covers the influence of the stress level, states of stress, and the failure criterion.

Keywords: creep deformation process, creep rupture mechanism, high Cr alloy, P91, low stress, brittle rupture

I. INTRODUCTION

Since high chromium alloy demonstrates considerable high temperature creep strength, high corrosion resistance, good weld ability and low oxidation speed, high chromium alloy such as 9Cr-1Mo-0.2V (P91 type) has been widely applied in advanced power plants as pipework components between 450°C and 650°C. Currently, most of the creep models are developed primarily based on the high stress tests at temperature range of 450°C-650°C. The models seem could also accurately predict the lifetime of materials [1-11]. An (2012) reviewed the current state of developing of advanced creep damage constitutive equations for high Chromium alloy (Grade 91). The new set of constitutive equations model should concern three aspects to improve the current models. These aspects are the influence of stress level, the influence of stress state and the failure criterion for high Cr alloy [12].

Nowadays, the life span under a low stress level has caught researchers' attention, because it is the lifetime the power generation installations which are designed and expected to last for. Therefore, the models developed for high stress level have been applied into the low stress conditions. However, many researchers realized that the creep strength and the creep life span have been over-estimated [13-21]. Therefore, Bendick, et al. [10] re-assessed the database due to the significant increase in test data, and a predicted duration of 10^5h for P91 steels, the updated value is 90MPa at 600°C. Recently, Sawada et al. [18] also reported an investigation of the microstructural degradation under long-term creep condition.

To re-analyze the real creep deformation and rupture mechanisms of Gr.91 steel under different stress levels is one of the aspects in order to improve or develop a new set of constitutive equation model. Through observing the creep deformation and damage mechanisms, Petry and Lindet [1] found two kinds of rupture mechanisms dominate the creep damage of 9Cr-0.5Mo-1.8W-VNb (P92) steel according to the applied stress levels. He reported that the ductile rupture mechanism and creep cavitation damage mechanism dominate the creep damage process under high and low stress levels respectively.

In addition, Vivier and Panait et al. [3] also observed the ductile rupture mechanisms under high stress levels for P91 steel at 500°C. Masse and Lejeail [21] utilized these two different rupture mechanisms with a new constitutive model to re-assess the lifetime of P91 steel in order to cope with the influence of stress level on the rupture. However, even though the model could describe the behavior of P91 steel under different stress levels effectively, he also pointed out there are still some limitations: strain localizations and geometry effects could be improved [19]. It is an interesting and significant progression and the authors of this paper believe that further investigation of the coupling between creep damage and creep deformation and its validation are needed.

A version of one of the most popular creep damage constitutive equations (KRH formulation) has been used to calculate the lifetime for P91 under a low stress level and it was found that it was overestimated [11]. All the above strongly show that further research work is needed to develop and validate the creep damage constitutive for a lower stress level.

This paper reports the review of the creep deformation and creep damage and rupture mechanisms in order to provide the physical base for the developing of the creep damage constitutive equation for P91 material under low stress. This paper contributes to knowledge of the continuum creep damage mechanics.

II. THE CHARACTERICSTICS OF CREEP DEFORMATION AND RUPTURE OF GRADE 91 STEEL

From the literature, the high stress range varies depending on the temperature. For example, at 600°C, the high stress range is around 130-200MPa; at 650°C, it is around 70 -100MPa. Inversely, the stresses less than 130MPa belong to the low stress level at 600°C; the stresses less than 70MPa belong to the low stress ranges at 650°C [11, 22].

A. High stress creep deformation and rupture mechanism

1) Dislocation deformation

The dislocation deformation controls the creep deformation process under high stress level. An obvious dislocation structure could be clear observed before creep [16]. A research on the fractured specimens' surface also shows a high dislocation density [8].

2) Damage characteristics

The creep damage process with time of P91 steels is divided into 3 stages: 1) the cavity nucleation along the grain boundary, mainly in stress concentration area; 2) the cavity growth; 3) the cavity or precipitates coalescence and material necking until a ductile fracture with low (≈10%) volume fractions of cavities. The experiment data of P91 base metal steels under 90MPa, 100MPa, 110MPa and 120MPa at 650°C come from Gaffard et al. [8, 9].

Lim [23] who studied the tertiary behavior of P91 steel found that the necking with the creep softening behavior has a significant effect on the prediction of the material's lifetime. Material's necking is owing to the initial lath martensite recovery during the creep process. Without taking the necking effect into account, the model Haff constitutive equations overestimated the lifetime of the P91 steel. The microstructure softening will increase the strain rate during the tertiary creep stage, and necking damage will lead to a quick drop before the ductile fracture (only at the last 10% of the tertiary of stage).

3) Rupture mechanism

The trans-granular ductile failure with creep deformation, necking and the softening of material have been reported in the literature; for instance, the experiment data from Vivier et al. [2] under a high stress range of 270MPa-310MPa at 500°C; Masse et al. [20] collected 388 creep tests between 450°C-650°C; Gaffard et al. and Bendick et al. [10] under 90MPa, 100MPa, 110MPa and 120MPa at 625°C.

B. Low stress creep deformation and rupture mechanism

1) Diffusion deformation

The influence of the evolution of diffusion density, sub-grains size and precipitates ($M_{23}C_6$ carbides, Lave phase and MX-Type) in P91 steel presented here is based on many researchers observations [14-16, 21]. Although the dislocation creep happens during the whole creep process, the diffusion creep dominates the deformation mechanism under low stress levels. Nabarro-Herring creep is one of the diffusion ways. The strain rate of Nabarro-Herring creep is proportional to the stress levels; also the strain rate at the tertiary stage is proportional to the temperature due to its strong temperature dependence. The detailed diffusion angles during creep has been reported by Gaffard et al. [8] and also reported by Masse and Lejeail [20-21]. The Electron Back Scattered Diffraction (EBSD) map shows most of the boundaries rotation angle is >15° and some of the boundaries rotation angle is 5° < angle <15°.

2) Damage characteristics

The damage characteristics of P91 steels under low stress level are significantly caused by coarsening of $M_{23}C_6$ carbides, precipitates and coarsening of Lave phase and a pre-recovery of matrix according to Panait et al. [15-16]. The study of microstructure of the P91 steels after more than 100,000h of creep exposure under 80MPa at 600°C, and the results show an abundant of Laves Phases and a few mount of modified Z-phases (only 41 precipitates out of 640 identified precipitates) have been observed during a long-term creep. The size of $M_{23}C_6$ carbides grows from 150-180nm to about 300nm after creep and they mainly locates around the grain boundary. Some small MX type precipitates also observed in the martensite laths. The cavities nucleates next to Lave phase precipitates at grain boundary after creep 113,43h at 600°C, and the coalescence of $M_{23}C_6$ carbides and Lave phase phenomenon were observed at the fracture surface [15-16]

3) Rupture mechanism

The diffusion-assisted brittle rupture looks like the rupture mechanism under low stress level. A premature failure of P91 steel has been observed during a long-term creep. The Laves phase emerges and cavities rapid coalescence during the tertiary creep stage causing a premature failure during the long-term test. The different preferential recovery mechanisms of martensite at the prior austenite grain boundary (PAGB) are homogenous and inhomogeneous recovery under high stress and low stress levels respectively. Due to the inhomogeneous recovery, a premature of tertiary creep stage happens in advance of rapid the failure [17]. Besides, NRIM creep data sheet [19] shows the elongation (EL) and reduction of area (RA) of P91 steel tubes at 600°C under different stress levels. There are no EL and RA when the material ruptured under 100MPa at 600°C. The values of elongation and reduction of cross area under 110MPa are 23% and 84%, respectively [6].

One typical experiment of P91 steels was conducted by Sawada et al. [18] during a long-term creep under 70MPa at 600°C. The microstructure changes may take the main responsibility for the premature failure during a long-term creep, whereas, the failure may not depends on the martensite recovery and particles coarsening. The sub-grain size and the density of dislocation gradually increase with time; however, they sharp increase after 70,000h until rupture (80,7368 hours) under 70MPa at 600°C. This agrees with the experiment results from K. Kimura et al. [17], that the Z-phase formation or the disappearing of MX particles just happens after a long time of creep.

C. Stress state effect

The most popular topic is about the stress state effect on the lifetime span of materials. Some small-punch tests were conducted by Nagode et al. [24] under 350N-550N at the temperature range 650°C-690°C at the high stress range, used minimum deflection rate to replace the minimum creep strain rate, it shows that the minimum deflection rate is almost inversely proportional to the time-to-rupture, i.e. the minimum strain rate is inversely proportional to the time-to-rupture. Moreover, the minimum strain rate is proportional to the stress levels. For the weldment, the life span of P91 not only depends on the stress state and levels, but also depends on the notched size as well [22].

1) P91 steels

The relative higher creep strain rate is not only because of the high stress level, but also effected by the stress state. The lifetime of P91 steel is also reduced by the high creep strain rate. The larger the creep strain rate, the shorter the life span will be [25-26]. The number and size of cavities in 9-12% Cr steels (E911 and P91) under the multi-axial stress state increases compared with the smooth specimens. The multi-axiality of stress state will increase the creep strain rate, and the creep cavity densities; such as the quotient of multiaxiality $q\approx1.2$ and $q\approx1.0$, the creep cavity densities are less than $30mm^{-2}$ and around $40mm^{-2}$ respectively for P91 steel at 600°C [8]. The cavities nucleation has been detected if the creep deformation is greater than 1%, and the cavity densities are less than $50mm^{-2}$ up to 2%. The higher cavity densities were observed with a lower deformation and with a relatively low quotient of multi-axiality.

2) P91 steel weldment

Creep failure by Type IV cracking in P91 steel weldments is likely to be the main failure mechanism in high temperature for advanced power plant applications. Heat-affected zone (HAZ) is the weakest area compared with the parent material. The creep rupture time in HAZ is approximately 1/5 of the parent material. The number of creep cavities per area increases with the creep damage process and the highest density of creep cavities is located in the mid-thickness (or the center of the fine-grained heat-affected zone) region which is about 60% creep damage rather than the surface region of the fine-grained heat-affected zone [7-8, 27-29]. The tri-axial stress state will accelerate the creep damage evaluation in the HAZ. However, it may not affect the growth and coarsening of precipitates rates during the creep phenomena [7-8, 27-29].

The cavities preferentially nucleate at grain boundaries near the coarser carbides and Laves phase particles or at a triple conjunction [22]. A relatively high density of cavities in Type IV region was observed after a long-term creep exposure under 600°C at 90Mpa (Tr=8853 hours). The interrupted experiment result shows: 1) there is no creep voids when t/tr=0.2; 2) a relatively high density of cavities observed when t/tr=0.7; 3) the cracks are only apparent until t/tr=0.9 [30]. Ogata [31] reported that the diffusion mechanism of creep deformation controls the void growth for a 9% Cr welded specimens (HAZ region). Two interrupted specimens were 32% and 56% respectively under 650°C with an internal pressure at 21.7Mpa. The results show that a very small amount of cavities was observed during 32% creep damage, and still a small amount of cavities was observed at 56% creep damage. The creep cavities have already nucleated on grain boundaries at less than 25% creep damage [31]. Moreover, the size of cavities only slightly increased during creep as mentioned by Gaffard [32].

The multi-axial state of stress is important; however, it is difficult to achieve systematically in the experiment. The information about the effect of states of stress on the creep deformation and creep damage evolution, including the cavity nucleation, growth, and coalescence should and can be extracted and distilled from the literature. This is still ongoing and will be reported in due course.

D. Strain at failure

The results of experiment conducted by Masse and Lejeail [18] show the creep strain at failure under different stress levels at 625°C and 500°C. Under high stress levels at 500°C, the creep strain at failure is about 10%-12%, the creep strain at failure is around 1% under low stress levels. At 625°C, the creep strain at failure is around 2% and 0.4% under high stress levels and low stress levels, respectively. The creep strain at failure at 600°C under 70MPa is about 0.33% according to Sawada (2011) [18]. Therefore, the strain at failure varies depending on the different stress levels and temperature.

III. SUMMARY

This paper focuses on three fundamental aspects for developing a new set of constitutive equations of P91 steel. The following conclusions have been reached.

- Influence of stress levels
  The dislocation creep deformation with necking and the trans-granular ductile rupture mechanism are observed under high stress levels. The diffusion creep deformation and the cavity nucleation, growth and coalescence brittle rupture mechanism are observed under low stress level.
- Influence of stress state
  For the base material, the influence of stress state depends on whether the creep strain rate is proportional to the time-to-rupture or not. For the weldment, it not only depends on the stress rate and level, but also depends on the radius of notched bar.
- Strain at failure
  A varying range of values to describe the different strain at failure are reported under either high or low stress levels

The progress made in the current literature review, plus further analysis on the process of cavity nucleation, growth, and coalesces under the lower stress level, the coupling of creep damage and deformation, and the effect of states of stress will form a firm foundation for the development of physically-based creep damage constitutive equations which will be reported in due course.

REFERENCES

[1] C. Petry and G. Lindet, "Modelling creep behaviour and failure of 9Cr-0.5Mo-1.8W-VNb steel", International Journal of Pressure and Vessels and Piping Vol.86, p. 486-494, 2009

[2] F, Vivier, C, Panait, AF, Gourgues-Lorenzon, J. Besson, "Creep rupture of a 9Cr1MoNbV steel at 500°C: base metal and welded joint", Nuclear and Engineering Design Vol. 240, p. 2704-2709, 2010

[3] F, Vivier, C, Panait, AF, Gourgues-Lorenzon, J. Besson, "Microstructure evolution in base metal and welded joint of Grade 91 martensitic steels after creep at 500-600°C", 17th European Conference on Fracture, Brno, Czech Republic, 2008

[4] F. Abe,"Creep modelling and creep life estimation of Gr.91 (Delicated to Prof.C. Berger)", International Journal of materials research Vol.103, p.765-773, 2012

[5] G. Eggeler and A. Ramteke, "Analysis of creep of a welded P91 pressure vessel", Int. J. Pres. Ves. & Piping, Vol.60, p.237-257, 94

[6] T. Shrestha and M. Basirat et al., "Creep rupture behavior of Grade 91 steel", Materials science and Engineering, 565, 2013, pp.382-391, 2013

[7] T. Watanabe, M. Tabuchi and M. Yamazaki, "Creep damage evaluation of 9Cr-1Mo-V-Nb steel welded joints showing Type IV fracture", International Journal of Pressure and Piping, Vol.83, p.63-71, 2006

[8] V. Gaffard, J. Besson and A.F. Gourgues-Lorenzon, "High temperature creep flow and damage properties of 9Cr1MoNbV steels: base metal and weldment", Nuclear Engineering and Design Vol.235, p.2547-2562, 2005

[9] V. Gaffard, J. Besson and A.F. Gourgues-Lorenzon, "Creep failure model of a 9cr1Mo-NbV(P91) steel integrating multiple deformation and damage mechanisms", Ecole des Mines de Paris, Centre des Materiaux, UMR CNRS 7633, BP 87 91003 Evry Cedex France

[10] W. Bendick, L Cipolla and J. Hald, "New ECCC assessment of creep rupture strength for steel grade X10CrNoVNb9-1(Grade 91)", International Journal of Pressure Vessels and Piping, Vol.87, p.304-309, 2010

[11] Y.X Chen, W. Yan et al., " CDM modelling of creep behaviour of T/P91 steel under high stresses", Acta metallurgica sinica Vol.47, p.1372-1377, 2011

[12] L. An, Q. Xu et al. (2012): Advanced Materials Research, "Review on the current state of developing of advanced creep damage constitutive equations for high Chromium alloy", Vol.510, p.776-780

[13] L. An, Q. Xu et al. (2012), "Preliminary analysing of experimental data for the development of high Cr alloy creep damage constitutive equations", Proceedings of the 18th International Conference on Automation and Computing (ICAC), Loughborough University, Leicestershire, UK, 8 September 2012

[14] C.G. Panait et al., "Evolution of dislocation density, size of subgrains and MX-type precipipates in a P91 steel during creep and during thermal ageing at 600°C for more than 100,000h", Materials Science and Engineering A Vol.527, p.4062-4069, 2010

[15] C. Panait, W. Bendick et al., "Study of the microstructure of the Grade 91 steel after more than 100,000h of creep exposure at 600°C", International Journal of Pressure Vessels and Piping Vol. 87, p.326-335, 2010

[16] C. Panait, W. Bendick et al., "Study of the microstructure of the Grade 91 steel after more than 100,000h of creep exposure at 600°C", 2nd ECCC Creep conference, Zurich, Switzerland, 2009

[17] K. Kimura, K. Suzuki, Y. Toda et al., "Degradation and assessment of long-term creep strength of advanced 9-12% Cr steels", MPA-NIMS Workshop on "Modern 9-12%Cr steels for power plant application" MPA Stuttgart, Vol. 28, 2002

[18] K. Sawada et al., "Microstructure degradation of Gr.91 steel during creep under low stress", Materials Science and Engineering, Vol. 528, p.5511-5518, 2011

[19] NRIM creep data sheet: National research institute for material, No.43, Japan, 1996

[20] T. Masse, Y. Lejeail, "Creep mechanical behaviour of modified 9Cr1Mo steel weldments: experimental analysis and modelling", Nuclear Engineering and Design, Vol.254, p. 97-110, 2013

[21] T. Masse, Y. Lejeail, " Creep behaviour and failure modelling of modified 9Cr1Mo steel", Nuclear Engineering and Design, Vol.246, p. 220-232, 2012

[22] J. Besson et al., "Analysis of creep lifetime of a ASME Grade 91 welded pipe", Engineering Fracture Mechanics, Vol 76, p.1460-1473, 2009

[23] R. Lim, "Modelling and experimental study of the tertiary creep stage of Grade 91 steel", International Journal of Fracture Vol.169, p.213-228, 2011

[24] A. Nagode, L. Kosec and B. Ule, "Uni-axial and Multi-axial creep behaviour of P91-Type steel under constant load", Engineering Failure Analysis Vol.18, p.61-67, 2011

[25] K. Maile: VGB Workshop Material and Quality Assurance, Copenhaghen, 2009

[26] P. Auerkari et al.: International Journal of Pressure Vessels and Piping, Vol. 84, p69-74, 2007

[27] T. Ogat et al.: Materials Science and Engineering A, Vol. 510-511, p.238-243, 2009

[28] T. Ogat et al.: International Journal of Pressure Vessels and Piping, Vol. 87, p.611-616, 2010

[29] K. Sawada et al.: Materials Science and Engineering A, Vol. 527, p.1417-1426, 2010

[30] J. Parker: International Journal of Pressure Vessels and Piping, Vol. xxx, p.1-12, 2012

[31] T. Ogata, Materials at High Temperatures, Vol.28, p.147-154, 2011

[32] V. Gaffard: Materials at High Temperatures, Vol.25 (2011), p.159-168, 2008

Numerical Simulation of Supersonic Combustion Using Liquid Hydrocarbon Fuel

Tsung Leo Jiang, Jui-Chi Cheng and Hsiang-Yu Huang
Department of Aeronautics and Astronautics, National Cheng Kung University, Tainan, Taiwan, ROC

Abstract - *Supersonic combustion using liquid hydrocarbon fuel is characterized by high temperature, high speed and complicated multiphase flow. It is very hard to measure its detailed reaction and flow structure. Therefore, in the present study, a computational model, adopting the SST-k-ω turbulent model and the finite-rate combustion model, is developed for the supersonic turbulent spray-combustion flow. The results obtained from the present study show that the predicted pressure distributions of combustion flow are in good agreement with the experimental results. The interesting phenomenon observed by the experiment that the combustion initiates upstream of the injection point has been successfully predicted in the present study. However, there are discrepancies on the shifted position of combustion and the peak of pressure between the simulation and the experiment. An improvement on the chemical reaction model for the hydrocarbon-fueled supersonic combustion is addressed.*

Keywords: Supersonic Combustion, Numerical Simulation, Hydrocarbon Fuel

1. Introduction

Supersonic combustion is extremely complex, since the fuel has to be injected, mixed, ignited, and burned with the air in a supersonic stream within a millisecond. The numerical simulation is thus a vital approach for the understanding of supersonic combustion which is characterized by the high-temperature and high-speed combustion and very hard to measure. The use of the numerical simulation for the study of supersonic combustion is able to reduce the cost and risk of the experimental work. Nevertheless, the numerical simulation has to be validated by the experimental data before it can be applied to the detailed analysis of supersonic combustion.

In the present study, the CFD software Fluent [1] adopting the SST-k-ω turbulent model and the laminar finite-rate combustion model is employed for the simulation of the supersonic combustion flow using liquid hydrocarbon fuel of Yu et al. [2]. The combustor is composed of four sections, including section 0 of constant area, section I of 1° divergence, section II of 3° divergence, and section III of 4° divergence, as shown in Fig. 1. A cavity is located in section I with the dimension of 12 mm deep, 88 mm long, and a ramp inclined at 45°. Kerosene is injected into the flow at 49 mm upstream of the cavity. The inlet conditions are shown in Table 1.

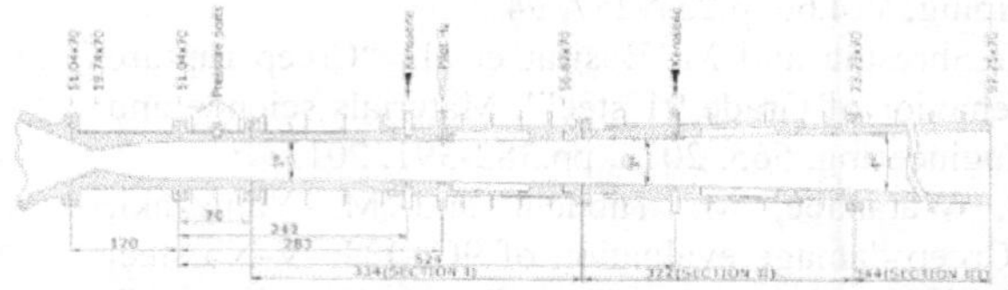

Fig. 1 The supersonic combustion chamber using liquid hydrocarbon fuel [2]

Table 1 Inlet conditions [2]

Air		
Inlet pressure(MPa)	1.06	
Total temperature(K)	1810	
Inlet Mach number	2.5	
The composition	O_2 : 0.2504 N_2 : 0.6063 H_2O : 0.1433	
Fuel		
	Hydrogen	Kerosene
Mass flow rate(g/s)	3.25	46
Equivalence ratio	0.08	0.45
Temperature(K)	250	300

2. Results and Discussion

The predicted wall-pressure distributions, where kerosene is injected at 0.242 m, are shown in Fig. 2, in comparison with the experimental data of Yu et al.[2] and the simulation result of Chakraborty [3]. The present predictions are qualitatively in agreement with the experimental data and the published numerical results. The interesting phenomenon observed by the experiment that the combustion initiates upstream of the injection point has been successfully predicted in the present study. As shown in Fig. 2, the predicted wall pressure starts rising at 0.085 m, 0.157 m ahead of kerosene injection. This is due to the fact that the flow expands as the kerosene stream is ignited, resulting in local high pressure in the chamber. This is further evidenced by the sequential pressure-contour variations, as shown in Fig. 3. The pressure wave is predicted to transmit upstream. It interacts with the boundary layer, yielding a separation region for kerosene to mix and burn with air.

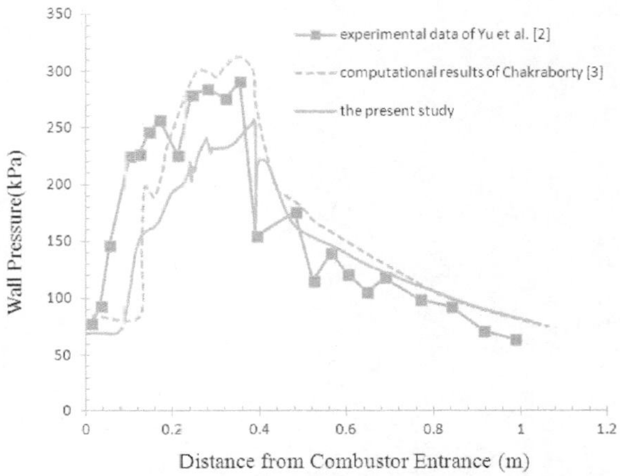

Fig. 2 Comparison of the predicted wall pressure with the experimental data [2] and published numerical results [3]

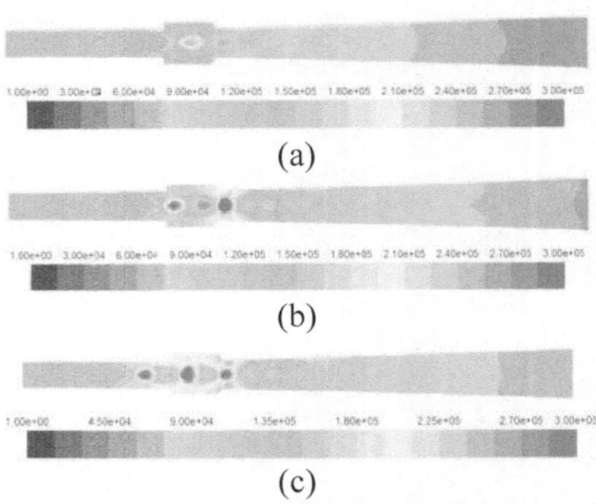

Fig. 3 The sequential pressure-contour variations (a)1.2 ms (b) 2.2 ms (c)3.2ms after kerosene injected (Unit: *Pa*)

The CO_2 mass-fraction contours (Fig. 4) also show that the burning of kerosene does take place upstream of kerosene injection, since CO_2 mass exists well ahead of the location of kerosene injection. Similar predictions were also obtained by Chakraborty [3]. However, there are some discrepancies on the shifted position of combustion and the peak of pressure between the present simulation and the experiment. As the pressure rise is related to the burning of kerosene, the discrepancies may be due to the slower mechanism of chemical reaction adopted in the present study. Therefore, more accurate finite-rate chemistry for the combustion of hydrocarbon fuel should be accounted for in the combustion model for the hydrocarbon-fueled supersonic combustion.

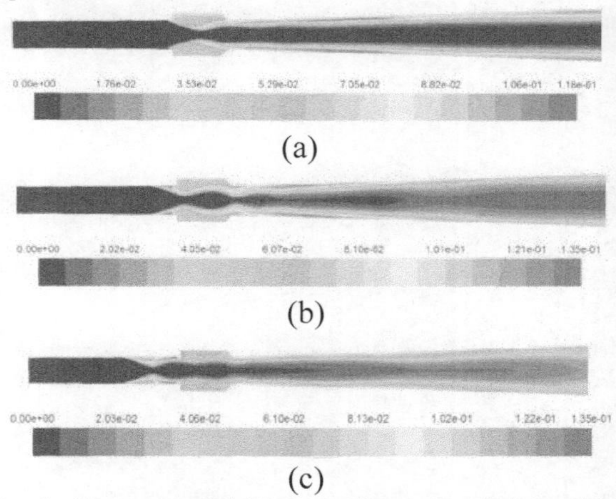

Fig. 4 The sequential CO_2 mass-fraction variations (a)1.2 ms (b) 2.2 ms (c)3.2ms after kerosene injected

3. Conclusions

In the present study, a computational model has been successfully developed for the supersonic spray-combustion flow. The predictions are qualitatively in agreement with the experimental data. The interesting phenomenon observed by the experiment that the combustion initiates upstream of the injection point for a supersonic combustion chamber has been successfully predicted in the present study. However, there are discrepancies on the shifted position of combustion and the peak of pressure between the simulation and the experiment. More accurate finite-rate chemistry for the combustion of hydrocarbon fuel should be accounted for in the combustion model for the hydrocarbon-fueled supersonic combustion.

4. References

[1] Fluent Incorporated, Fluent 6.3, User Guide, 2006.

[2] Yu, G., Li, J.G., Chang, X.Y., Chen, L.H., Sung, C. J., Fuel Injection and Flame Stabilization in a Liquid-Kerosene-Fueled Supersonic Combustor, Journal of Propulsion and Power, Vol. 19, pp. 885-893, 2003.

[3] Chakraborty, D., Numerical Simulation of Liquid Fueled Scramjet Combustor Flow Fields, International Journal of Hypersonics , Vol. 1, pp. 13-29, 2010.

SESSION

WAVE AND DIFFERENTIAL EQUATIONS + TURING MACHINE

Chair(s)

Prof. Hamid Arabnia
University of Georgia

New exact solutions of a coupled Korteweg-de Vries equation

Dimpho Millicent Mothibi and Chaudry Masood Khalique
International Institute for Symmetry Analysis and Mathematical Modelling,
Department of Mathematical Sciences, North-West University, Mafikeng Campus,
Private Bag X 2046, Mmabatho 2735, Republic of South Africa
Email: Dimpho.Mothibi@nwu.ac.za Masood.Khalique@nwu.ac.za

Abstract—*In this paper, $(G'/G)-$expansion method is employed to derive the exact travelling wave solutions of a coupled Korteweg-de Vries equation. Three types of solutions are obtained, namely, hyperbolic function solutions, trigonometric function solutions and rational solutions. These solutions include the soliton solutions also.*

Keywords: $(G'/G)-$expansion method, coupled KdV equation, travelling wave solutions

1. Introduction

The well-known celebrated Korteweg-de Vries (KdV) equation [1]

$$u_t + 6uu_x + u_{xxx} = 0 \tag{1}$$

describes the dynamics of solitary waves. Initially, it was derived to describe shallow water waves of long wavelength and small amplitude. It is an important equation in the field of theory of integrable systems. It has infinite number of conservation laws, gives multiple-soliton solutions, and has many other physical properties. See for example [2], [3] and references therein.

The coupled Korteweg-de Vries equations, recently, have been the focus of attraction for scientists, because of their many applications in scientific fields and many studies have been reported in the literature. See for example [4]–[7].

In this paper, we study the coupled Korteweg-de Vries equation [7],

$$\begin{aligned} u_t + 6uu_x - 6vv_x + u_{xxx} &= 0, \\ v_t + 3uv_x + v_{xxx} &= 0. \end{aligned} \tag{2}$$

It is well known that nonlinear evolution equations (NLEEs), such as (2), are widely used to model many physical phenomena in different fields of applied sciences. So it is important to find exact solutions of NLEEs. Many powerful methods have been developed to find exact solutions of NLEEs. These include, the variable separation approach [8], inverse scattering transform method [9], Bäcklund transformation [10], Darboux transformation [11], Hirota's bilinear method [12], the reduction mKdV equation method [13], the tri-function method [14], [15], the projective Riccati equation method [16], the Jacobi elliptic function expansion method [17], [18], and the exp-function expansion method [19].

Wang *et.al.* [20] in 2007 proposed a new method called $(G'/G)-$expansion method for finding exact solutions of NLEEs. Since then this method has been used by various researchers. See, for example, the papers [20]- [23].

In this paper, we derive the travelling wave solutions of the coupled KdV equation (2) by using the $(G'/G)-$expansion method.

2. Solutions of (2)

In this section we employ the $(G'/G)-$expansion method and construct the travelling wave solutions of the coupled KdV equation

$$\begin{aligned} u_t + 6uu_x - 6vv_x + u_{xxx} &= 0, \\ v_t + 3uv_x + v_{xxx} &= 0, \end{aligned} \tag{3}$$

where u and v are real-valued scalar functions, t is time and x is a spatial variable.

As a first step we transform the coupled KdV equation (3) to a nonlinear ordinary differential equation (ODE) using the traveling wave variable

$$u(t,x) = U(z), \quad v(t,x) = V(z), \quad \text{where} \quad z = x - ct. \tag{4}$$

Using the above transformations, equation (3) transforms to the nonlinear ODEs

$$\begin{aligned} -cU' + 6UU' - 6VV' + U''' &= 0, \\ -cV' + 3UV' + V''' &= 0, \end{aligned} \tag{5}$$

where the primes denotes the derivative with respect to z.

The $(G'/G)-$expansion method assumes the solutions of equation (5) to be of the form

$$U(z) = \sum_{i=0}^{M} \alpha_i (G'/G)^i \quad \text{and} \quad V(z) = \sum_{i=0}^{M} \beta_i (G'/G)^i, \tag{6}$$

where α_i, β_i, $i = 0, 1, \cdots, M$ are parameters to be determined and $G(z)$ satisfies the second-order linear ODE with constant coefficients, viz.,

$$G'' + \lambda G' + \mu G = 0, \tag{7}$$

where λ and μ are constants.

The balancing procedure yields $M = 2$, so the solutions of the ODEs (5) are of the form

$$U(z) = \alpha_2(G'/G)^2 + \alpha_1(G'/G) + \alpha_0, \quad (8)$$
$$V(z) = \beta_2(G'/G)^2 + \beta_1(G'/G) + \beta_0. \quad (9)$$

Substituting (8) into (5) and making use of (7), and then collecting all terms with same powers of (G'/G) and equating each coefficient to zero, yields a system of algebraic equations. Solving this system of algebraic equations, using Mathematica, we obtain the following two cases:

Case A

$$\alpha_0 = \frac{1}{3}(c - \lambda^2 - 2\mu),\ \alpha_1 = -2\lambda,\ \alpha_2 = -2$$
$$\beta_0 = \pm\frac{\sqrt{-c\lambda^2 + \lambda^4 - 4\lambda^2\mu}}{\sqrt{6}},\ \beta_1 = \frac{2\beta_0}{\lambda},\ \beta_2 = 0.$$

Case B

$$\alpha_0 = \frac{1}{3}(c - \lambda^2 - 8\mu),\ \alpha_1 = -4\lambda,\ \alpha_2 = -4$$
$$\beta_0 = \pm\frac{\sqrt{c^2 - 2c\lambda^2 + \lambda^4 - 16c\mu + 64\mu^2}}{3\sqrt{2}},$$
$$\beta_1 = \frac{12\lambda\beta_0}{-c\lambda^2 + 8\mu},\ \beta_2 = \frac{\beta_1}{\lambda}.$$

Substituting the values of α's and β's from **Case A** and the corresponding solutions of ODE (7) into (8), we obtain the following three types of travelling wave solutions of equation (3):

Case 1: When $\lambda^2 - 4\mu > 0$, we obtain the hyperbolic function solutions

$$u_1(t,x) = \frac{1}{3}(c - \lambda^2 - 2\mu) -2\lambda\left[-\frac{\lambda}{2} + \delta_1\left(\frac{C_1\sinh(\delta_1 z) + C_2\cosh(\delta_1 z)}{C_1\cosh(\delta_1 z) + C_2\sinh(\delta_1 z)}\right)\right] -2\left[-\frac{\lambda}{2} + \delta_1\left(\frac{C_1\sinh(\delta_1 z) + C_2\cosh(\delta_1 z)}{C_1\cosh(\delta_1 z) + C_2\sinh(\delta_1 z)}\right)\right]^2,$$

$$v_1(t,x) = \pm\frac{\sqrt{-c\lambda^2 + \lambda^4 - 4\lambda^2\mu}}{\sqrt{6}} + \frac{2\beta_0}{\lambda}\left[-\frac{\lambda}{2} + \delta_1\left(\frac{C_1\sinh(\delta_1 z) + C_2\cosh(\delta_1 z)}{C_1\cosh(\delta_1 z) + C_2\sinh(\delta_1 z)}\right)\right],$$

where $z = x - ct$, $\delta_1 = \frac{1}{2}\sqrt{\lambda^2 - 4\mu}$, C_1 and C_2 are arbitrary constants.

Case 2: When $\lambda^2 - 4\mu < 0$, we obtain the trigonometric function solutions

$$u_2(t,x) = \frac{1}{3}(c - \lambda^2 - 2\mu) -2\lambda\left(-\frac{\lambda}{2} + \delta_2\frac{-C_1\sin(\delta_2 z) + C_2\cos(\delta_2 z)}{C_1\cos(\delta_2 z) + C_2\sin(\delta_2 z)}\right) -2\left(-\frac{\lambda}{2} + \delta_2\frac{-C_1\sin(\delta_2 z) + C_2\cos(\delta_2 z)}{C_1\cos(\delta_2 z) + C_2\sin(\delta_2 z)}\right)^2,$$

$$v_2(t,x) = \pm\frac{\sqrt{-c\lambda^2 + \lambda^4 - 4\lambda^2\mu}}{\sqrt{6}} + \frac{2\beta_0}{\lambda}\left(-\frac{\lambda}{2} + \delta_2\frac{-C_1\sin(\delta_2 z) + C_2\cos(\delta_2 z)}{C_1\cos(\delta_2 z) + C_2\sin(\delta_2 z)}\right),$$

where $z = x - ct$, $\delta_2 = \frac{1}{2}\sqrt{4\mu - \lambda^2}$, C_1 and C_2 are arbitrary constants.

Case 3: When $\lambda^2 - 4\mu = 0$, we obtain the rational solutions

$$u_3(t,x) = \frac{1}{3}(c - \lambda^2 - 2\mu) - 2\lambda\left(-\frac{\lambda}{2} + \frac{C_2}{C_1 + C_2 z}\right) -2\left(-\frac{\lambda}{2} + \frac{C_2}{C_1 + C_2 z}\right)^2,$$

$$v_3(t,x) = \pm\frac{\sqrt{-c\lambda^2 + \lambda^4 - 4\lambda^2\mu}}{\sqrt{6}} + \frac{2\beta_0}{\lambda}\left(-\frac{\lambda}{2} + \frac{C_2}{C_1 + C_2 z}\right),$$

where $z = x - ct$, C_1 and C_2 are arbitrary constants.

In a similar fashion, using the results of **Case B** we obtain three types of travelling wave solutions of equation (3) as follows:

Case 1: When $\lambda^2 - 4\mu > 0$, we obtain the hyperbolic function solutions

$$u_1(t,x) = \frac{1}{3}(c - \lambda^2 - 8\mu) -4\lambda\left[-\frac{\lambda}{2} + \delta_1\left(\frac{C_1\sinh(\delta_1 z) + C_2\cosh(\delta_1 z)}{C_1\cosh(\delta_1 z) + C_2\sinh(\delta_1 z)}\right)\right] -4\left[-\frac{\lambda}{2} + \delta_1\left(\frac{C_1\sinh(\delta_1 z) + C_2\cosh(\delta_1 z)}{C_1\cosh(\delta_1 z) + C_2\sinh(\delta_1 z)}\right)\right]^2,$$

$$v_1(t,x) = \pm\frac{\sqrt{c^2 - 2c\lambda^2 + \lambda^4 - 16c\mu + 64\mu^2}}{3\sqrt{2}} + \frac{12\lambda\beta_0}{-c\lambda^2 + 8\mu}\left[-\frac{\lambda}{2} + \delta_1\left(\frac{C_1\sinh(\delta_1 z) + C_2\cosh(\delta_1 z)}{C_1\cosh(\delta_1 z) + C_2\sinh(\delta_1 z)}\right)\right] + \frac{\beta_1}{\lambda}\left[-\frac{\lambda}{2} + \delta_1\left(\frac{C_1\sinh(\delta_1 z) + C_2\cosh(\delta_1 z)}{C_1\cosh(\delta_1 z) + C_2\sinh(\delta_1 z)}\right)\right]^2,$$

where $z = x - ct$, $\delta_1 = \frac{1}{2}\sqrt{\lambda^2 - 4\mu}$, C_1 and C_2 are arbitrary constants.

Case 2: When $\lambda^2 - 4\mu < 0$, we obtain the trigonometric function solutions

$$u_2(t,x) = \frac{1}{3}(c-\lambda^2-8\mu)$$
$$-4\lambda\Big(-\frac{\lambda}{2}+\delta_2\frac{-C_1\sin(\delta_2 z)+C_2\cos(\delta_2 z)}{C_1\cos(\delta_2 z)+C_2\sin(\delta_2 z)}\Big)$$
$$-4\Big(-\frac{\lambda}{2}+\delta_2\frac{-C_1\sin(\delta_2 z)+C_2\cos(\delta_2 z)}{C_1\cos(\delta_2 z)+C_2\sin(\delta_2 z)}\Big)^2,$$
$$v_2(t,x) = \pm\frac{\sqrt{c^2-2c\lambda^2+\lambda^4-16c\mu+64\mu^2}}{3\sqrt{2}}$$
$$+\frac{12\lambda\beta_0}{-c\lambda^2+8\mu}\Big(-\frac{\lambda}{2}+\delta_2\frac{-C_1\sin(\delta_2 z)+C_2\cos(\delta_2 z)}{C_1\cos(\delta_2 z)+C_2\sin(\delta_2 z)}\Big)$$
$$+\frac{\beta_1}{\lambda}\Big(-\frac{\lambda}{2}+\delta_2\frac{-C_1\sin(\delta_2 z)+C_2\cos(\delta_2 z)}{C_1\cos(\delta_2 z)+C_2\sin(\delta_2 z)}\Big)^2,$$

where $z = x-ct$, $\delta_2 = \frac{1}{2}\sqrt{4\mu-\lambda^2}$, C_1 and C_2 are arbitrary constants.

Case 3: When $\lambda^2 - 4\mu = 0$, we obtain the rational solutions

$$u_3(t,x) = \frac{1}{3}(c-\lambda^2-8\mu) - 4\lambda\Big(-\frac{\lambda}{2}+\frac{C_2}{C_1+C_2 z}\Big)$$
$$-4\Big(-\frac{\lambda}{2}+\frac{C_2}{C_1+C_2 z}\Big)^2,$$
$$v_3(t,x) = \pm\frac{\sqrt{c^2-2c\lambda^2+\lambda^4-16c\mu+64\mu^2}}{3\sqrt{2}}$$
$$+\frac{12\lambda\beta_0}{-c\lambda^2+8\mu}\Big(-\frac{\lambda}{2}+\frac{C_2}{C_1+C_2 z}\Big)$$
$$+\frac{\beta_1}{\lambda}\Big(-\frac{\lambda}{2}+\frac{C_2}{C_1+C_2 z}\Big)^2,$$

where $z = x - ct$, C_1 and C_2 are arbitrary constants.

It should be noted that the solutions obtained in this paper by $(G'/G)-$expansion method are more general than the solutions obtained in [7].

3. Conclusion

In this paper, we analyzed a coupled KdV equation that appears in many scientific fields. The $(G'/G)-$expansion method was effectively used to derive exact travelling wave solutions of the coupled KdV equation. The solutions obtained were expressed in the form of hyperbolic function, trigonometric function and rational solutions.

Acknowledgements

The authors would like to thank A R Adem for fruitful discussions.

References

[1] D.J. Korteweg, G. de Vries, On the change of form of long waves advancing in a rectangular canal, and on a new type of long stationary waves, Phil. Mag., 39 (1895) 422-443.

[2] A.M. Wazwaz, Integrability of coupled KdV equations, Cent. Eur. J. Phy., 9 (2011) 835-840.

[3] A.M. Wazwaz, Partial differential equations and solitary waves theory, Springer, 2009.

[4] D.S. Wang, Integrability of a coupled KdV system: Painlevé property, Lax pair and Bäcklund transformation", Appl. Math. Comput., 216 (2010) 1349-1354.

[5] C.X. Li, A Hierarchy of Coupled Korteweg-de Vries Equations and the Corresponding Finite-Dimensional Integrable System, J . Phys. Soc. Jpn., 73 (2004) 327-331.

[6] Z. Qin, A finite-dimensional integrable system related to a new coupled KdV hierarchy, Phys. Lett. A, 355 (2006) 452-459.

[7] A.M. Wazwaz, Solitons and Periodic Wave Solutions for Couples Nonlinear Equations, International Journal of Nonlinear Science, 14 (2012),pp. 266-277.

[8] S.Y. Lou, J.Z. Lu, Special Solutions from Variable Separation Approach: Davey-Stewartson Equation, J Phys A-Math Gen., 29 (1996) 4209-4215.

[9] M.J. Ablowitz, P.A. Clarkson, Soliton, Nonlinear Evolution Equations and Inverse Scattering, Cambridge University Press, Cambridge, 1991.

[10] C.H. Gu, Soliton Theory and Its Application, Zhejiang Science and Technology Press, Zhejiang, 1990.

[11] V.B. Matveev, M. A. Salle, Darboux Transformation and Soliton, Springer, Berlin, 1991.

[12] R. Hirota, The Direct Method in Soliton Theory, Cambridge University Press, Cambridge, 2004.

[13] Z.Y. Yan, A Reduction mKdV Method with Symbolic Computation to Construct New Doubly-Periodic Solutions for Nonlinear Wave Equations, Int J Mod Phys C., 14 (2003) 661-672.

[14] Z.Y. Yan, The New Tri-Function Method to Multiple Exact Solutions of Nonlinear Wave Equations, Phys Scripta, 78 (2008) Article ID: 035001.

[15] Z.Y. Yan, Periodic, Solitary and Rational Wave Solutions of the 3D Extended Quantum Zakharov-Kuznetsov Equation in Dense Quantum Plasmas, Phys. Lett. A, 373 (2009) 2432-2437.

[16] D.C. Lu, B.J. Hong, New Exact Solutions for the (2+1)-Dimensional Generalized Broer-Kaup System, Appl. Math. Comput., 199 (2008) 572-580.

[17] D.C. Lu, Jacobi Elliptic Functions Solutions for Two Variant Boussinesq Equations, Chaos Soliton Fract., 24 (2005) 1373-1385.

[18] Z.Y. Yan, Abundant Families of Jacobi Elliptic Functions of the (2+1) Dimensional Integrable Davey-Stewartson-Type Equation via a New Method, Chaos Soliton Fract., 18 (2003) 299-309.

[19] J.H. He, X. H. Wu, Exp-Function Method for Nonlinear Wave Equations, Chaos Soliton Fract., 30 (2006) 700-708.

[20] M. Wang, X. Li, J. Zhang, The (G'/G)-Expansion Method and Travelling Wave Solutions of Nonlinear Evolution Equations in Mathematical Physics, Mathematical Physics Phys. Lett. A, 372 (2008) 417-423.

[21] A. Bekir, E. Aksoy, The Exact Solutions of Shallow Water Wave Equation by using the (G'/G)-Expansion Method, Waves in Random and Complexx Media, Vol. 22, No. 3 (2012) 317-331.

[22] Ling-Xiao Li, Ming-Liang Wang, The (G'/G)-Expansion Method and Travelling Wave Solutions for a Higher-Order Nonlinear Schrodinger Equation, Applied Mathematics and Computation, 208 (2009) 440-445.

[23] K. Hossein, J. Azizeh, Exact Solutions for the Double sinh-Gordon and Generalized Form of the double sinh-Gordon Equations by Using (G'/G)-Expansion Method, Turk J Phys., 34 (2010) 78-82.

Solutions to a System Containing Singular Integro-Differential Equations

Shihchung Chiang
Department of Applied Statistics, Chung Hua University, Hsinchu, Taiwan, R.O.C.

Abstract— *This study presents analytical solution and numerical solution to a dynamical system, introduced by Herdman and Turi [10], that consists of an integro-differential equation with a weakly singular kernel.*

Keywords: Integro-differential equation, weakly singular kernel.

1. Introduction

This study presents the solutions for a system of integro-differential equations. This system first appeared in a conference paper by Burns, Cliff, and Herdman [1] in 1983. It describes the motion of a high-speed thin airfoil in a two-dimensional, incompressible flow, and contains eight integro-differential equations. One of the equations has a weakly singular kernel. Previous studies have focused on this scalar equation, and presented the discussions regarding the well-posedness of this problem in the Cauchy problem with a semigroup setting [13], a numerical solution by discretizing an associated partial differential equation and using uniform and nonuniform mesh points [5], an associated numerical optimal control problem with the integro-differential equation as a constraint [6], [7], [14], and solutions to variations of this equation [8] (e.g., integro-differential equation of the second kind and its possible extensions). Papers [3], [4] introduced the method of steps to solve the scalar singular integro-differential equation. This study extends the method of steps and applies it to the exact solution of this system. This study applies the proposed method to find the solution to the system introduced by Herdman and Turi [10] by choosing the time step and solving coupled equations alternatively. The second section of this study presents the development of the original airfoil system. The third section presents the application of the method of steps to find the analytical solution of the typical example in the Herdman and Turi system. Then fourth section presents a numerical method to find the numerical solution of the Herdman and Turi system. Finally the fifth section presents a conclusion to this study.

2. Problem Description

The following system describes the original aeroelasticity problem:

$$\frac{d}{dt}\left[Ax(t)+\int_{-\infty}^{0}A(s)x(t+s)ds\right]$$
$$=Bx(t)+\int_{-\infty}^{0}B(s)x(t+s)ds+f(t),$$

where $t>0$, and with initial conditions: $x(0)=[\eta,\phi(0)]^T$ and the eighth component of the unknown $x(t)$ satisfies $x_8(s)=\phi(s)$ for $-\infty<s\leq 0$, and $\phi\in L_{1,g}$, where $L_{1,g}$ is a weighted Hilbert space with weight $g=\sqrt{-\frac{1}{s}}$, $s<0$. The matrices are defined as follows:

$$A=\begin{bmatrix} I_{7\times 7} & 0_{7\times 1}\\ 0_{1\times 7} & 0_{1\times 1}\end{bmatrix},$$

$$A(s)=\begin{bmatrix} 0_{7\times 7} & A_{12}(s)_{7\times 1}\\ 0_{1\times 7} & A_{22}(s)_{1\times 1}\end{bmatrix},$$

$$B=\begin{bmatrix} B1_{7\times 7} & B2_{7\times 1}\\ B3_{1\times 7} & 0_{1\times 1}\end{bmatrix},$$

$$B(s)=\begin{bmatrix} 0_{7\times 7} & B_{12}(s)_{7\times 1}\\ 0_{1\times 7} & 0_{1\times 1}\end{bmatrix}.$$

Matrices $A_{12}(s)$ and $B_{12}(s)$ are smooth vector functions. The scalar function $A_{22}(s)=\left(\frac{Us-2}{Us}\right)^{\frac{1}{2}}$, constant U is the speed of far away fluid flow, and $f(t)_{8\times 1}$ is a forcing term. Consider the "finite delay" version of the system:

$$\frac{d}{dt}\left[Ax(t)+\int_{-b}^{0}A(s)x(t+s)ds\right]$$
$$=Bx(t)+\int_{-b}^{0}B(s)x(t+s)ds+f(t),$$

by defining the linear operators D_1, D_2, L_1, and L_2 as

$$D_1(\eta,\phi)=I\eta^T+\int_{-b}^{0}A_{12}(s)\phi(s)ds_{7\times 1},$$

$$L_1(\eta,\phi)=B1\eta^T+B2\phi(0)+\int_{-b}^{0}B_{12}(s)\phi(s)ds_{7\times 1},$$

$$D_2(\phi)=\int_{-b}^{0}A_{22}(s)\phi(s)ds_{1\times 1},$$

$$L_2(\eta)=B3\eta^T_{1\times 1},$$

the finite version of the system can be written as an operator system [2]:

$$\frac{d}{dt}D_1(x_1(t),[x_2]_t) = L_1(x_1(t),[x_2]_t) + \bar{f}(t)_{7\times 1},$$

$$\frac{d}{dt}D_2([x_2]_t) = L_2(x_1(t))_{1\times 1}, t \geq 0,$$

where $x_1(t)$ and $[x_2]_t(\cdot) = x_2(\cdot + t)$ are variables.

3. Typical example

This section demonstrates the method of steps to solve the system of integro-differential equations proposed by Herdman and Turi [10] for $t \in (0,2]$ and $b = 1$:

$$\frac{d}{dt}\left[x_1(t) + \int_{-1}^{0} x_2(t+s)ds\right] = x_2(t), \quad t > 0, \quad (1)$$

$$\frac{d}{dt}\left[\int_{-1}^{0}(-s)^{-\frac{1}{2}}x_2(t+s)ds\right] = x_1(t), \quad t > 0, \quad (2)$$

with initial conditions

$$x_1(0) = 1,$$

$$x_2(s) = 0, -1 \leq s \leq 0.$$

The exact solution for this system is as follows:

$$x_1(t) = \begin{cases} 1 & : \quad 0 < t \leq 1, \\ 1 + \frac{4}{3\pi}(t-1)^{\frac{3}{2}} & : \quad 1 < t \leq 2, \end{cases}$$

and

$$x_2(t) = \begin{cases} \frac{2}{\pi}t^{\frac{1}{2}} & : \quad 0 < t \leq 1, \\ \frac{2}{\pi} + \frac{4}{\pi}(t^{\frac{1}{2}} - 1) + \frac{1}{2\pi}(t-1)^2 & : \quad 1 < t \leq 2. \end{cases}$$

This section presents a process to find the solution: first, to find the solution for $0 < t \leq 1$, integrate Equation (1) with respect to $t \in (0,1]$ to obtain

$$x_1(t) + \int_{-1}^{0} x_2(t+s)ds - x_1(0) - \int_{-1}^{0} x_2(s)ds$$
$$= \int_{0}^{t} x_2(u)du.$$

After substituting the initial conditions of $x_2(t)$ for $t \in [-1,0]$, this equation becomes

$$x_1(t) = 1 - \int_{-1}^{0} x_2(t+s)ds + \int_{0}^{t} x_2(u)du.$$

After changing variables, $x_1(t)$ can then be obtained for $t \in (0,1]$ as follows:

$$\begin{aligned} x_1(t) &= 1 - \textstyle\int_{t-1}^{t} x_2(\tau)d\tau + \int_0^t x_2(u)du \\ &= 1 - \textstyle\int_{t-1}^{0} x_2(\tau)d\tau - \int_0^t x_2(\tau)d\tau + \int_0^t x_2(u)du \\ &= 1. \end{aligned}$$

For the solution $x_2(t)$ for $t \in (0,t]$, integrate Equation (2) with respect to t to have

$$\int_{-1}^{0}(-s)^{-\frac{1}{2}}x_2(t+s)ds - \int_{-1}^{0}(-s)^{\frac{1}{2}}x_2(s)ds = t,$$

since $x_2(t) = 0$ for $t \leq 0$, this equation becomes

$$\int_{-1}^{0}(-s)^{-\frac{1}{2}}x_2(t+s)ds = t.$$

According to the theorem in [3], $x_2(t)$ can be obtained as follows:

$$x_2(t) = \frac{\Gamma(2)}{\Gamma(\frac{1}{2})\Gamma(\frac{3}{2})}t^{\frac{1}{2}} = \frac{2}{\pi}t^{\frac{1}{2}},$$

for $0 < t \leq 1$.

For the second step, consider $1 < t \leq 2$: after integrating Equation (1) with respect to t, for $1 < t \leq 2$, the equation becomes

$$\begin{aligned} x_1(t) &+ \textstyle\int_{-1}^{0} x_2(t+s)ds - x_1(1) \\ &- \textstyle\int_{-1}^{0} x_2(1+s)ds = \int_1^t x_2(u)du, \end{aligned}$$

since

$$\begin{aligned} &\textstyle\int_{-1}^{0} x_2(t+s)ds \\ =& \textstyle\int_{t-1}^{t} x_2(\tau)d\tau \\ =& \textstyle\int_{t-1}^{1} x_2(\tau)d\tau + \int_1^t x_2(\tau)d\tau \\ =& \textstyle\int_{t-1}^{1} \frac{2}{\pi}\tau^{\frac{1}{2}}d\tau + \int_1^t x_2(\tau)d\tau \\ =& \textstyle\frac{2}{\pi}\cdot\frac{2}{3}\cdot\tau^{\frac{3}{2}}|_{t-1}^{1} + \int_1^t x_2(\tau)d\tau \\ =& \textstyle\frac{4}{3\pi} - \frac{4}{3\pi}(t-1)^{\frac{3}{2}} + \int_1^t x_2(\tau)d\tau. \end{aligned}$$

From this result, choosing $t = 1$, then

$$\int_{-1}^{0} x_2(1+s)ds = \frac{4}{3\pi}.$$

Therefore,

$$x_1(t) = 1 + \frac{4}{3\pi}(t-1)^{\frac{3}{2}}, 1 \leq t \leq 2.$$

Next, integrate Equation (2) with respect to t, for $t \in (0,2]$. Then,

$$\begin{aligned} &\textstyle\int_{-1}^{0}(-s)^{-\frac{1}{2}}x_2(t+s)ds - \int_{-1}^{0}(-s)^{-\frac{1}{2}}x_2(1+s)ds \\ =& \textstyle\int_1^t x_1(\tau)d\tau \\ =& \textstyle\int_1^t(1 + \frac{4}{3\pi}(\tau-1)^{\frac{3}{2}})d\tau \\ =& \textstyle(\tau + \frac{4}{3\pi}\cdot\frac{2}{5}(\tau-1)^{\frac{5}{2}})|_1^t \\ =& \textstyle t + \frac{8}{15\pi}(t-1)^{\frac{5}{2}} - 1. \end{aligned}$$

Since $x_2(t)$ is known for $t \in [0,1]$ from the first step, the second term of the left hand side can be simplified as follows:

$$\begin{aligned} &\textstyle\int_{-1}^{0}(-s)^{-\frac{1}{2}}x_2(1+s)ds \\ =& \textstyle\int_{-1}^{0}(-s)^{-\frac{1}{2}}\cdot\frac{2}{\pi}\cdot(1+s)^{\frac{1}{2}}ds \\ =& \textstyle\int_1^0 \lambda^{-\frac{1}{2}}\cdot\frac{2}{\pi}\cdot(1-\lambda)^{\frac{1}{2}}\cdot -d\lambda \\ =& \textstyle\frac{2}{\pi}\cdot\int_0^1 \lambda^{\frac{1}{2}-1}\cdot(1-\lambda)^{\frac{3}{2}-1}d\lambda \\ =& \textstyle\frac{2}{\pi}\cdot\frac{\Gamma(\frac{1}{2})\Gamma(\frac{3}{2})}{\Gamma(2)} \\ =& \textstyle\frac{2}{\pi}\cdot\frac{\frac{\pi}{2}}{1\cdot 1} \\ =& 1. \end{aligned}$$

Therefore, the equation becomes

$$\int_{-1}^{0}(-s)^{-\frac{1}{2}}x_2(t+s)ds = t + \frac{8}{15\pi}(t-1)^{\frac{5}{2}}, 1 \le t \le 2.$$

By changing variables, the left hand side of the above equation can be rewritten as

$$\begin{aligned}
& \int_{t-1}^{t}(t-\tau)^{-\frac{1}{2}}x_2(\tau)d\tau \\
= & \int_{t-1}^{1}(t-\tau)^{-\frac{1}{2}}\cdot\tfrac{2}{\pi}\cdot\tau^{\frac{1}{2}}d\tau + \int_{1}^{t}(t-\tau)^{-\frac{1}{2}}x_2(\tau)d\tau \\
= & \int_{1-\frac{1}{t}}^{\frac{1}{t}} t^{-\frac{1}{2}}(1-\lambda)^{-\frac{1}{2}}\cdot\tfrac{2}{\pi}\cdot t^{\frac{1}{2}}\cdot\lambda^{\frac{1}{2}}\cdot td\lambda \\
& + \int_{1}^{t}(t-\tau)^{-\frac{1}{2}}x_2(\tau)d\tau \\
= & \ t\cdot\tfrac{2}{\pi}\int_{1-\frac{1}{t}}^{\frac{1}{t}}(1-\lambda)^{-\frac{1}{2}}\cdot\lambda^{\frac{1}{2}}d\lambda + \int_{1}^{t}(t-\tau)^{-\frac{1}{2}}x_2(\tau)d\tau \\
= & \ \tfrac{2t}{\pi}\left[\sin^{-1}\sqrt{\lambda} - \sqrt{\lambda}\sqrt{1-\lambda}\ \right]_{1-\frac{1}{t}}^{\frac{1}{t}} + \int_{1}^{t}(t-\tau)^{-\frac{1}{2}}x_2(\tau)d\tau \\
= & \ \tfrac{2t}{\pi}\left[\sin^{-1}\sqrt{\tfrac{1}{t}} - \sin^{-1}\sqrt{1-\tfrac{1}{t}}\ \right] + \int_{1}^{t}(t-\tau)^{-\frac{1}{2}}x_2(\tau)d\tau.
\end{aligned}$$

Therefore,

$$\begin{aligned}
& \int_{1}^{t}(t-\tau)^{-\frac{1}{2}}x_2(\tau)d\tau \\
= & \ \tfrac{2t}{\pi}\left[\sin^{-1}\sqrt{1-\tfrac{1}{t}} - \sin^{-1}\sqrt{\tfrac{1}{t}}\ \right] + t + \tfrac{8}{15\pi}(t-1)^{\frac{5}{2}}.
\end{aligned}$$

To solve for $x_2(t)$, change the variable to obtain

$$\begin{aligned}
& \int_{0}^{t-1}(t-s-1)^{-\frac{1}{2}}x_2(s+1)ds \\
= & \ \tfrac{2t}{\pi}\left[\sin^{-1}\sqrt{1-\tfrac{1}{t}} - \sin^{-1}\sqrt{\tfrac{1}{t}}\ \right] + t + \tfrac{8}{15\pi}(t-1)^{\frac{5}{2}}.
\end{aligned}$$

Again, by changing variables, the equation becomes

$$\begin{aligned}
& \int_{0}^{\bar{t}}(\bar{t}-s)^{-\frac{1}{2}}y(s)ds \\
= & \ \tfrac{2(\bar{t}+1)}{\pi}\left[\sin^{-1}\sqrt{1-\tfrac{1}{\bar{t}+1}} - \sin^{-1}\sqrt{\tfrac{1}{\bar{t}+1}}\ \right] \\
& + \bar{t} + 1 + \tfrac{8}{15\pi}\bar{t}^{\frac{5}{2}}.
\end{aligned}$$

If $\bar{t} = t$, then

$$\begin{aligned}
& \int_{0}^{t}(t-s)^{-\frac{1}{2}}y(s)ds \\
= & \ \tfrac{2(t+1)}{\pi}\left[\sin^{-1}\sqrt{1-\tfrac{1}{t+1}} - \sin^{-1}\sqrt{\tfrac{1}{t+1}}\ \right] \\
& + t + 1 + \tfrac{8}{15\pi}t^{\frac{5}{2}} \\
= & \ h(t),
\end{aligned}$$

and

$$h(0) = \frac{2}{\pi}[-\sin^{-1}1] + 1 = -\frac{2}{\pi}\cdot\frac{\pi}{2} + 1 = 0.$$

Therefore, by the method discussed in [11],

$$\begin{aligned}
& x_2(t+1) \\
= & \ y(t) \\
= & \ \tfrac{\sin(\frac{\pi}{2})}{\pi}\tfrac{d}{dt}\left[\int_{0}^{t}(t-s)^{-\frac{1}{2}}h(s)ds\right] \\
= & \ \tfrac{1}{\pi}\tfrac{d}{dt}\left[\int_{0}^{t}(t-s)^{-\frac{1}{2}}\cdot\right. \\
& \left(\tfrac{2(s+1)}{\pi}\cdot(\sin^{-1}\sqrt{\tfrac{s}{s+1}} - \sin^{-1}\sqrt{\tfrac{1}{s+1}})\right. \\
& \left.\left. + (s+1) + \tfrac{8}{15\pi}s^{\frac{5}{2}}\right)ds\right] \\
= & \ \tfrac{1}{\pi}\tfrac{d}{dt}[I - II + III + IV],
\end{aligned}$$

where

$$\begin{aligned}
I = & \int_{0}^{t}(t-s)^{-\frac{1}{2}}\cdot\tfrac{2(s+1)}{\pi}\cdot\sin^{-1}\sqrt{\tfrac{s}{s+1}}ds \\
= & \ \tfrac{2}{\pi}\int_{0}^{t}(t-s)^{-\frac{1}{2}}\cdot s\cdot\sin^{-1}\sqrt{\tfrac{s}{s+1}}ds \\
& + \tfrac{2}{\pi}\int_{0}^{t}(t-s)^{-\frac{1}{2}}\cdot\sin^{-1}\sqrt{\tfrac{s}{s+1}}ds \\
= & \ \tfrac{2}{\pi}\left[s\cdot\sin^{-1}\sqrt{\tfrac{s}{s+1}}\cdot(-2)(t-s)^{\frac{1}{2}}\big|_{0}^{t}\right. \\
& \left. + \int_{0}^{t}(\sin^{-1}\sqrt{\tfrac{s}{s+1}} + s\cdot\tfrac{1}{2\sqrt{s}(s+1)})\cdot 2\cdot(t-s)^{\frac{1}{2}}ds\right] \\
& + \tfrac{2}{\pi}\left[\sin^{-1}\sqrt{\tfrac{s}{s+1}}\cdot(-2)(t-s)^{\frac{1}{2}}\right]_{0}^{t} \\
& + \tfrac{2}{\pi}\int_{0}^{t}\tfrac{1}{\sqrt{s}(s+1)}\cdot(t-s)^{\frac{1}{2}}ds,
\end{aligned}$$

$$\begin{aligned}
II = & \int_{0}^{t}(t-s)^{-\frac{1}{2}}\cdot\tfrac{2(s+1)}{\pi}\cdot\sin^{-1}\sqrt{\tfrac{1}{s+1}}ds \\
= & \ \tfrac{2}{\pi}\int_{0}^{t}(t-s)^{-\frac{1}{2}}\cdot s\cdot\sin^{-1}\sqrt{\tfrac{1}{s+1}}ds \\
& + \tfrac{2}{\pi}\int_{0}^{t}(t-s)^{-\frac{1}{2}}\cdot\sin^{-1}\sqrt{\tfrac{1}{s+1}}ds \\
= & \ \tfrac{2}{\pi}\left[s\cdot\sin^{-1}\sqrt{\tfrac{1}{s+1}}\cdot(-2)(t-s)^{\frac{1}{2}}\big|_{0}^{t}\right. \\
& \left. + 2\int_{0}^{t}(\sin^{-1}\sqrt{\tfrac{1}{s+1}} - \tfrac{\sqrt{s}}{s+1})\cdot(t-s)^{\frac{1}{2}}ds\right] \\
& + \tfrac{2}{\pi}\left[\sin^{-1}\sqrt{\tfrac{1}{s+1}}\cdot(-2)\cdot(t-s)^{\frac{1}{2}}\big|_{0}^{t}\right. \\
& \left. - \int_{0}^{t}\tfrac{1}{\sqrt{s}(s+1)}\cdot(t-s)^{\frac{1}{2}}ds\right] \\
= & \ \tfrac{2}{\pi}\left[2\cdot\int_{0}^{t}\sin^{-1}\sqrt{\tfrac{1}{s+1}}\cdot(t-s)^{\frac{1}{2}}ds\right. \\
& \left. - \int_{0}^{t}\tfrac{\sqrt{s}}{s+1}\cdot(t-s)^{\frac{1}{2}}ds\right] \\
& + 2t^{\frac{1}{2}} - \tfrac{2}{\pi}\int_{0}^{t}\tfrac{1}{\sqrt{s}(s+1)}\cdot(t-s)^{\frac{1}{2}}ds,
\end{aligned}$$

$$\begin{aligned}
III = & \int_{0}^{t}(t-s)^{-\frac{1}{2}}\cdot(s+1)ds \\
= & \int_{0}^{t}(t-s)^{-\frac{1}{2}}\cdot s\cdot ds + \int_{0}^{t}(t-s)^{-\frac{1}{2}}ds \\
= & \int_{0}^{1}t^{-\frac{1}{2}}(1-\lambda)^{-\frac{1}{2}}\cdot\lambda t^{2}d\lambda - 2(t-s)^{\frac{1}{2}}\big|_{0}^{t} \\
= & \ t^{\frac{3}{2}}\int_{0}^{1}(1-\lambda)^{-\frac{1}{2}}\lambda d\lambda + 2t^{\frac{1}{2}} \\
= & \ t^{\frac{3}{2}}\tfrac{\Gamma(\frac{1}{2})\Gamma(2)}{\Gamma(2\frac{1}{2})} + 2t^{\frac{1}{2}} \\
= & \ \tfrac{4}{3}t^{\frac{3}{2}} + 2t^{\frac{1}{2}},
\end{aligned}$$

and

$$\begin{aligned}
IV = & \int_{0}^{t}(t-s)^{-\frac{1}{2}}\cdot\tfrac{8}{15\pi}\cdot s^{\frac{5}{2}}ds \\
= & \ \tfrac{8}{15\pi}\int_{0}^{1}t^{-\frac{1}{2}}(1-\lambda)^{-\frac{1}{2}}\cdot t^{\frac{5}{2}}\cdot\lambda^{\frac{5}{2}}\cdot td\lambda \\
= & \ \tfrac{8}{15\pi}t^{3}\int_{0}^{1}(1-\lambda)^{-\frac{1}{2}}\cdot\lambda^{\frac{5}{2}}d\lambda \\
= & \ \tfrac{8}{15\pi}t^{3}\tfrac{\Gamma(\frac{1}{2})\Gamma(\frac{7}{2})}{\Gamma(4)} \\
= & \ \tfrac{1}{6}t^{3}.
\end{aligned}$$

Therefore,

$$\begin{aligned} y(t) &= \tfrac{1}{\pi}\tfrac{d}{dt}[I - II + III + IV] \\ &= \tfrac{1}{\pi}\tfrac{d}{dt}\Big[\tfrac{4}{\pi}\textstyle\int_0^t (t-s)^{\frac{1}{2}}(\sin^{-1}\sqrt{\tfrac{s}{s+1}} \\ &\quad - \sin^{-1}\sqrt{\tfrac{1}{s+1}})ds \\ &\quad + \tfrac{4}{\pi}\textstyle\int_0^t (t-s)^{\frac{1}{2}} \cdot \tfrac{\sqrt{s}}{(s+1)}ds - 2t^{\frac{1}{2}} \\ &\quad + \tfrac{4}{\pi}\textstyle\int_0^t (t-s)^{\frac{1}{2}} \tfrac{1}{\sqrt{s}(s+1)}ds + \tfrac{4}{3}t^{\frac{3}{2}} + 2t^{\frac{1}{2}} + \tfrac{1}{6}t^3\Big] \\ &= \tfrac{2}{\pi^2} \cdot \textstyle\int_0^t (t-s)^{-\frac{1}{2}}(\sin^{-1}\sqrt{\tfrac{s}{s+1}} - \sin^{-1}\sqrt{\tfrac{1}{s+1}})ds \\ &\quad + \tfrac{2}{\pi^2} \cdot \textstyle\int_0^t (t-s)^{-\frac{1}{2}} \cdot \tfrac{\sqrt{s}}{s+1}ds + \tfrac{2}{\pi} \cdot t^{\frac{1}{2}} \\ &\quad + \tfrac{2}{\pi^2} \cdot \textstyle\int_0^t (t-s)^{-\frac{1}{2}} \cdot \tfrac{1}{\sqrt{s}(s+1)}ds + \tfrac{1}{2\pi} \cdot t^2 \\ &= \tfrac{2}{\pi^2} \cdot \textstyle\int_0^t (t-s)^{-\frac{1}{2}} \cdot \sin^{-1}(\tfrac{s-1}{s+1})ds \\ &\quad + \tfrac{2}{\pi^2} \cdot \textstyle\int_0^t (t-s)^{-\frac{1}{2}} \cdot \tfrac{s+1}{\sqrt{s}(s+1)}ds + \tfrac{2}{\pi} \cdot t^{\frac{1}{2}} \\ &\quad + \tfrac{1}{2\pi} \cdot t^2. \end{aligned}$$

However,

$$\begin{aligned} &\textstyle\int_0^t (t-s)^{-\frac{1}{2}} \sin^{-1}(\tfrac{s-1}{s+1})ds \\ &= -2(t-s)^{\frac{1}{2}} \cdot \sin^{-1}(\tfrac{s-1}{s+1})|_0^t + 2\textstyle\int_0^t (t-s)^{\frac{1}{2}} \tfrac{1}{\sqrt{s}(s+1)}ds \\ &= 2 \cdot t^{\frac{1}{2}} \cdot (-\tfrac{\pi}{2}) + 2\textstyle\int_0^t (t-s)^{\frac{1}{2}} \tfrac{1}{\sqrt{s}(s+1)}ds \\ &= -\pi \cdot t^{\frac{1}{2}} + 2\textstyle\int_0^t (t-s)^{\frac{1}{2}} \tfrac{1}{\sqrt{s}(s+1)}ds \\ &= -\pi \cdot t^{\frac{1}{2}} + 2\textstyle\int_0^{\sqrt{t}} (t-u^2)^{\frac{1}{2}} \tfrac{1}{u(u^2+1)}2udu \\ &= -\pi \cdot t^{\frac{1}{2}} + 2\textstyle\int_0^{\sqrt{t}} (t-u^2)^{\frac{1}{2}} \tfrac{2}{u^2+1}du \\ &= -\pi \cdot t^{\frac{1}{2}} + 4 \cdot \Big[\sqrt{t+1} \cdot \sin^{-1}(\tfrac{u\sqrt{t+1}}{\sqrt{t}\sqrt{u^2+1}}) \\ &\quad - \sin^{-1}\tfrac{u}{\sqrt{t}}\Big]_0^{\sqrt{t}} \\ &\quad \text{(by an integration formula in [9])} \\ &= -\pi \cdot t^{\frac{1}{2}} + 4 \cdot [\sqrt{t+1} \cdot \sin^{-1} 1 - \sin^{-1} 1] \\ &= -\pi \cdot t^{\frac{1}{2}} + 4 \cdot \tfrac{\pi}{2}[\sqrt{t+1} - 1] \\ &= -\pi \cdot t^{\frac{1}{2}} + 2\pi\sqrt{t+1} - 2\pi, \end{aligned}$$

and

$$\begin{aligned} &\tfrac{2}{\pi^2} \cdot \textstyle\int_0^t (t-s)^{-\frac{1}{2}} \cdot \tfrac{s+1}{\sqrt{s}(s+1)}ds \\ &= \tfrac{2}{\pi^2} \cdot \textstyle\int_0^t (t-s)^{-\frac{1}{2}} \cdot s^{-\frac{1}{2}}ds \\ &= \tfrac{2}{\pi}. \end{aligned}$$

Therefore,

$$\begin{aligned} y(t) &= \tfrac{2}{\pi^2} \cdot (-\pi t^{\frac{1}{2}} + 2\pi\sqrt{t+1} - 2\pi) + \tfrac{2}{\pi} \\ &\quad + \tfrac{2}{\pi}t^{\frac{1}{2}} + \tfrac{1}{2\pi}t^2 \\ &= -\tfrac{2}{\pi}t^{\frac{1}{2}} + \tfrac{4}{\pi}\sqrt{t+1} - \tfrac{4}{\pi} + \tfrac{2}{\pi} + \tfrac{2}{\pi}t^{\frac{1}{2}} + \tfrac{1}{2\pi}t^2 \\ &= \tfrac{4}{\pi}\sqrt{t+1} - \tfrac{2}{\pi} + \tfrac{1}{2\pi}t^2, \end{aligned}$$

and

$$x_2(t) = y(t-1) = \frac{4}{\pi}\sqrt{t} - \frac{2}{\pi} + \frac{1}{2\pi}(t-1)^2,$$

for $1 \le t \le 2$. Thus the system proposed by Herdman and Turi is solved for $0 \le t \le 2$.

4. Numerical Methods

The proposed methods in this study use the nonconforming finite element method to approximate the solution of the system (3)-(4):

$$\frac{d}{dt}\left[x_1(t) + \int_{-1}^{0} x_2(t+s)ds\right] = x_2(t), t > 0, \quad (3)$$

$$\frac{d}{dt}\left[\int_{-1}^{0} (-s)^{-\frac{1}{2}} x_2(t+s)ds\right] = x_1(t), t > 0, \quad (4)$$

with initial conditions

$$x_1(0) = 1,$$

$$x_2(s) = \phi(s) = 0, -1 \le s \le 0.$$

For the numerical approach, define a new functional ξ such that

$$\xi(t,s) = x_2(t+s), -1 \le s \le 0,\ t > 0. \quad (5)$$

Reformulate Equations (4) and (5) as a first-order hyperbolic partial differential equation

$$\frac{\partial}{\partial t}\xi(t,s) = \frac{\partial}{\partial s}\xi(t,s), -1 \le s \le 0, \quad (6)$$

with the condition

$$\int_{-1}^{0} |s|^{-\frac{1}{2}} \frac{\partial}{\partial s}\xi(t,s)ds = x_1(t). \quad (7)$$

Next, assume that the solution $x_2(t+s)$ has the form

$$x_2(t+s) = \xi(t,s) = \sum_{i=0}^{n} a_i(t)B_i(s), \quad (8)$$

where the bases, $B_i(s)$, for $i = 0, \cdots, n$, are

$$B_i(s) = \begin{cases} \frac{1}{\delta_{i+1}}(s - \tau_{i+1}) & , \quad s \in [\tau_{i+1}, \tau_i], \\ \frac{1}{\delta_i}(\tau_{i-1} - s) & , \quad s \in [\tau_i, \tau_{i-1}], \\ 0 & , \quad \text{otherwise.} \end{cases}$$

Specifically, $B_i(s)$, $i = 0, 1, \cdots, n$, are piecewise linear functions. The mesh points, $\tau_0, \tau_1, \cdots, \tau_n$ are defined by $-1 = \tau_n < \tau_{n-1} < \cdots < \tau_1 < \tau_0 = 0$ and $\delta_i = \tau_{i-1} - \tau_i > 0$, for $i = 1, \cdots, n$. After substituting the special form of ξ in Equation (8) into Equation (7), the governing equations for $a_i(t)$, $i = 0, \cdots, n$, become the following equations [12]:

$$\frac{d}{dt}a_i(t) = \frac{1}{\delta_i}(a_{i-1}(t) - a_i(t)), \quad i = 1, \cdots, n, \quad (9)$$

and

$$\int_{-1}^{0} |s|^{\frac{1}{2}} \sum_{i=0}^{n} a_i(t) \frac{d}{ds}B_i(s) = x_1(t). \quad (10)$$

Rewrite Equation (10) as

$$\sum_{i=1}^{n} \int_{\tau_i}^{\tau_{i-1}} |s|^{-\frac{1}{2}} \frac{1}{\delta_i}(a_{i-1}(t) - a_i(t))ds = x_1(t), \quad (11)$$

Equation (11) can be further simplified to

$$\sum_{i=1}^{n} \frac{2}{\delta_i}((-\tau_i)^{\frac{1}{2}} - (-\tau_{i-1}^{\frac{1}{2}})(a_{i-1}(t) - a_i(t)) = x_1(t). \quad (12)$$

Define

$$d_i = \frac{2}{\delta_i}((-\tau_i)^{\frac{1}{2}} - (-\tau_{i-1})^{\frac{1}{2}}), i = 1, \cdots, n, \quad (13)$$

and Equations (9) and (12) then become

$$\frac{d}{dt}a_i(t) = \frac{1}{\delta_i}(a_{i-1}(t) - a_i(t)), i = 1, \cdots, n, \quad (14)$$

and

$$\sum_{i=1}^{n} d_i(a_{i-1}(t) - a_i(t)) = x_1(t). \quad (15)$$

After applying Equation (15) to Equation (3) and simplifying, Equation (3) becomes

$$\begin{array}{rcl} \dot{a}_0(t) \cdot d_1 + \dot{a}_1(t) \cdot (d_2 - d_1) + \cdots & & \\ +\dot{a}_{n-1}(t) \cdot (d_n - d_{n-1}) - \dot{a}_n(t) \cdot d_n & = & a_n(t), \end{array} \quad (16)$$

where $\dot{a}_i(t) = \frac{d}{dt}a_i(t)$, for $i = 0, 1, \cdots, n$. This produces the following system of linear first-order ordinary differential equations:

$$L \cdot \left(\frac{d}{dt}X(t)\right) = D \cdot X(t)_{(n+1)\times 1}, \quad (17)$$

where

$$X(t) = [a_0(t)a_1(t) \cdots a_n(t)]^T,$$

$$L = \begin{bmatrix} d_1 & d_2 - d_1 & \cdots & \cdots & d_n - d_{n-1} & -d_n \\ 0 & 1 & 0 & \cdots & 0 & 0 \\ 0 & 0 & 1 & \cdots & 0 & 0 \\ \vdots & \vdots & \vdots & \vdots & \vdots & \vdots \\ 0 & 0 & 0 & \cdots & 0 & 1 \end{bmatrix}$$

$$D = \begin{bmatrix} 0 & 0 & \cdots & \cdots & 0 & 1 \\ \frac{1}{\delta_1} & -\frac{1}{\delta_1} & 0 & \cdots & 0 & 0 \\ 0 & \frac{1}{\delta_2} & -\frac{1}{\delta_2} & \cdots & 0 & 0 \\ \vdots & \vdots & \vdots & \vdots & \vdots & \vdots \\ 0 & 0 & 0 & \cdots & \frac{1}{\delta_n} & -\frac{1}{\delta_n} \end{bmatrix}$$

The procedure for obtaining the initial conditions $a_i(0)$, $i = 0, 1, \cdots, n$, for the first-order ordinary differential system (17) is as follows: After combining Equations (5) and (8), and fix $t = 0$, the state becomes

$$x_2(s) = \sum_{i=0}^{n} a_i(0)B_i(s) = \phi(s) = 0,$$

for $-1 \le s \le 0$. The structure of $B_0(s), B_1(s), \cdots$, and $B_n(s)$ indicates that $a_i(0)$ is equal to $\phi(\tau_i)$ when $i = 0, 1, \cdots, n$. Next, to find $a_0(t), a_1(t), \cdots, a_n(t)$, apply an ordinary differential equation solver (Matlab *'ode45'*) to the System (17). Two methods can be used to solve $x_2(t)$, for $0 \le t \le 1$, depending on the setting of variables: fix $t = 1$ or fix $s = 0$ in Equation (8). According to the property $B_j(s) = 1$ at $s = \tau_j$, $j = 0, 1, \cdots, n$, the two choices become two cases for the solution $x_2(t)$, $0 \le t \le 1$:

Case 1:

$$x_2(1 + \tau_i) = \sum_{j=0}^{n} a_j(1)B_j(\tau_i) = a_i(1),$$

and Case 2:

$$x_2(1 + \tau_i) = \sum_{j=0}^{n} a_j(1 + \tau_i)B_j(0) = a_0(1 + \tau_i).$$

In Case 1, solve for $a_i(t)$, $i = 0, 1, \cdots, n$, from System (17) using the Matlab software command *'ode45'* and set $t = 1$. In this case, $a_i(1)$ represents the corresponding solutions $x_2(1 + \tau_i)$, $i = 0, 1, \cdots, n$. In Case 2, solve for $a_0(t)$ from System (17) using the Matlab software command *'ode45'*. Then, set $t = 1+\tau_i$ to obtain $a_0(1+\tau_i)$, for $i = 0, 1, \cdots, n$. Therefore, $a_0(1 + \tau_i)$ is the solution $x_2(1 + \tau_i)$, for $i = 0, 1, \cdots, n$. After substituting the corresponding values of $a_i(t)$, $i = 0, 1, \cdots, n$ into Equation (15), $x_1(t)$ can be solved. A similar method can be used to solve $x_1(t)$ and $x_2(t)$, for $1 < t$.

Figure 1 shows a comparison of the numerical solution and analytical solution for $0 \le t \le 2$. The errors for the numerical solutions represent the maximum value of differences with the analytical solution at all mesh points.

5. Conclusion

This study presents a standard process to solve a system of integro-differential equations from the aeroelasticity problem. This system contains an integro-differential equation with a weakly singular kernel. This study suggests a method of steps to solve the solution from one time step to another time step analytically and numerically. In other words, for $(i-1) \cdot b < t \le i \cdot b$, where i is a positive integer and b is a positive number, and after solving the solutions in this time step, the process moves to the next time step for $i \cdot b < t \le (i+1) \cdot b$, and applies the previous time step results as initial conditions. This study demonstrates this process of finding solutions to the system proposed by Herdman and Turi [10] for $t \in (0, 2]$ and $b = 1$.

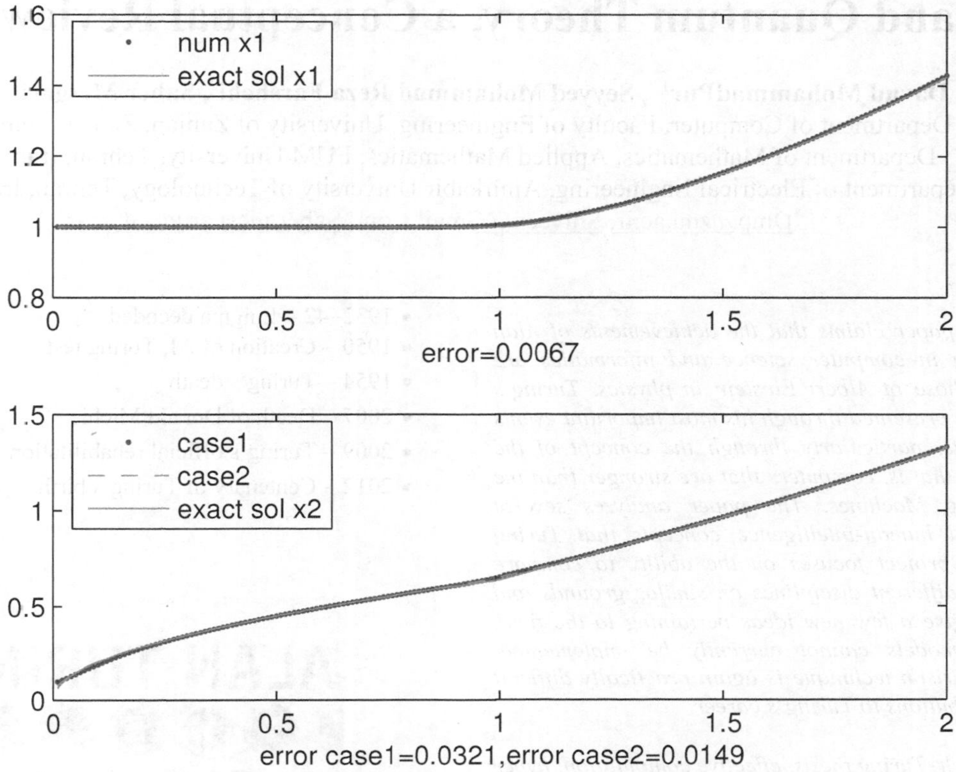

Fig. 1

References

[1] J. A. Burns, E. M. Cliff and T. L. Herdman, "A State-Space Model for an Aeroelastic System", Proceedings: 22nd IEEE Conference on Decision and Control, pp. 1074-1077, 1983.

[2] J. A. Burns and K. Ito, "On Well-Posedness of Solutions to Integro-Differential Equations of Neutral-Type in a Weighted L^2-Spaces", Differential and Integral Equations, Vol. 8, pp. 627-646, 1995.

[3] Hsin-Hao Chen and S. Chiang, "A Specific Procedure for Analytic Solutions to a Class of Singular Integral Equations", Chung Hua Journal of Science and Engineering, Vol.7, No. 3, pp. 29-34, 2009.

[4] S. Chiang, "Notes on the Solution of a Class of Singular Integral Equations", Chung Hua Journal of Science and Engineering, Vol. 3, No. 4, pp. 89-95, 2005.

[5] S. Chiang, "On the Numerical Solution of a Class of Singular Integro-Differential Equations", Chung Hua Journal of Science and Engineering, Vol.4, No. 3, pp. 43-48, 2006.

[6] S. Chiang, "Numerical Optimal Issues to a Class of Neutral Singular Integro-Differential Equations", Chung Hua Journal of Computational Science, No. 2, pp. 7-17, March 2012.

[7] S. Chiang and T. Herdman, "Revised Numerical Methods on the Optimal Control Problem for a Class of Singular Integral Equations", accepted by MESA.

[8] S. Chiang and Wei-Chun Wu, "Issues of One Kind of Integro-Differential Equations", AIP Conference Proceedings 1479, pp.2360-2362, 2012.

[9] CRC Press, Standard Mathematical Tables and Formulae, 29th edition.

[10] T. Herdman and J. Turi, "On the Solutions of a Class of Integral Equations Arising in Unsteady Aerodynamics", Differential Equations: Stability and Control, edited by Saber Elaydi, Department of Mathematics, Trinity University, San Antonio, Texas, pp. 241-248, 1991.

[11] H. Hochstadt, Integral equations, Pure and Applied Mathematics, Wiley-Interscience, New York, 1973.

[12] K. Ito and J. Turi, "Numerical Methods for a Class of Singular Integro-Differential Equations Based on Semigroup Approximation", SIAM J. Numer. Anal., Vol. 28, No. 6, pp. 1698-1722, 1991.

[13] F. Kappel and K. P. Zhang, "Equivalence of Functional Equations of Neutral Type and Abstract Cauchy Problems", Monatsh Math. Vol. 101, pp. 115-133, 1986.

[14] Chien-Chi Yu and S. Chiang, "On the Numerical Optimal Controls for a Class of Integro-Differential Equations of Neutral Type", Chung Hua Journal of Computational Science, No. 1, pp.1-7, 2011.

From Turing Machine to Hyper Computational Systems and Quantum Theory, a Conceptual Review

Davud MohammadPur[1,*], Seyyed Mohammad Reza Farshchi[2], Saber Mesgari[3]
[1] Department of Computer, Faculty of Engineering, University of Zanjan, Zanjan, Iran.
[2] Department of Mathematics, Applied Mathematics, FUM University, Tehran, Iran.
[3] Department of Electrical Engineering, Amirkabir University of Technology, Tehran, Iran.
[*]Dmp@znu.ac.ir, Shiveex@Gmail.Com, Saber.mesgari@aut.ac.ir

Abstract - *This paper claims that the achievements of Alan Mathison Turing in computer science and informatics are comparable to those of Albert Einstein in physics. Turing's contributions are presented through his most important events and achievements, particularly through the concept of the hyper computer; that is, computers that are stronger than the Universal Turing Machines. The paper analyzes several essential AI and human-intelligence concepts that Turing introduced. The project focuses on the ability to compare these models of different disciplines on similar grounds and goes further to give a few new ideas pertaining to the field. Because these models cannot currently be implemented, forming a comparison technique is again practically difficult to achieve contributions to Turing's career.*

Keywords: *Church–Turing thesis, effective computation, hyper computation.*

1 Introduction

Alan Mathison Turing (23rd June 1912–7th June 1954) was a British mathematician and computer scientist. He invented a formalization of the concepts of —algorithm and —computation with the Turing machine, which can be considered a model of a general purpose computer. He also decoded the German Enigma machine (a corresponding book cover is presented in Figure 1). In 2012, the centenary of Turing's birth, a number of Turing-related events was held around the world. Lectures and publications about Turing were made in Slovenia in the first half of 2012, such as [9, 10], but the most essential event was a conference in October, dedicated to Alan Turing and 20 years of Slovenian Artificial Intelligence Society, entitled —100 Years of Alan Turing and 20 years of SLAIS (http://is.ijs.si/is/is2012). Among the world-renowned researchers who presented at the conference were Stephen Muggleton, Natasa Milic-Frayling, Albert Bifet, Claude Sammut, and Joao Gama. At the opening ceremony, Professor Dr. Ivan Bratko received an award for life-long achievements in artificial intelligence, both in Slovenia and internationally. The following are some of the key dates related to Turing from our perspective:

- 1912 – Turing's birth
- 1936 – Creation of the Turing machine
- 1932–42 – Enigma decoded
- 1950 – Creation of AI, Turing test
- 1954 – Turing's death
- 2007 – Death of Donald Michie
- 2009 – Turing's official rehabilitation
- 2012 – Centenary of Turing's birth

Figure 1: A book about Alan Turing, published in 2012

This paper analyzes some of these events with a depth view on stronger machine. Alan Mathison Turing is often considered the father of modern computer science [1]. His works formed the basis of practical computer science being responsible for the computers built today. In his paper "On Computable Numbers, with an Application to the Entscheidungs problem" [2], Turing reemphasized Kurt Gödel's results [3] on the limits of proof and computation, substituting Gödel's universal arithmetics-based formal language by what are now called Turing machines, formal and simple devices. He proved that such a machine would be capable of performing any conceivable mathematical problem if it were representable as an algorithm, even if no actual

Turing machine would be likely to have practical applications, being much slower than alternatives [4].

Turing also introduced his famous Halting Problem as an undecidable problem. The Halting Problem talks about the possibility of algorithmically determining whether a given Turing Machine will halt on a given number of inputs in a given defined time. Turing‘s logical computing machines1 [5] were also discussed to be extended to universal (Turing) machines. The importance of the universal Turing machines is that it could be used to simulate any given Turing machine and as a result be more powerful than the prior ones. Turing‘s work focused more on the philosophy of mind and most of his works focused on the applications of artificial intelligence by computers.

2 Computability Theory

Author in [6] discusses computational complexity theory as identifying problems and working to find the best possible programmatic solutions to them. The field focuses on the existing fact that there are problems for which it was mathematically proved that effective algorithms for solving them do not exist. Investigating such problems forms the core of the discipline of computability, which is also known as recursion function theory.

The theory focuses on working out steps to solve a given problem, on a computer, staying within the boundaries of computation, thereby solving the problem algorithmically. In computer science, different models of computation have been suggested for solving various problems. Computability theory focuses on predicting the most efficient model and defining a formal system in which the problem could be most easily understood.

3 Models of Computation

Authors in [7] describes models of computation as abstract mathematical models of stored programs that encapsulate intuitive notions of a computer operation. The algorithms, formed in Computability Theory, are general and not related to particular characteristics of a computer such as overpowering or exhausting resources. Models of computation are used to model a more general approach to functions ignoring external factors. Examples of common theoretical models include finite-state machines; push down automata and Turing machines. Markov algorithms are more complicated examples of such computation models.

Figure 2 illustrates the above stated definition for a model. The model is anything that can compute a given function f, on a given set of inputs stored on a computer. These inputs are the domain at which the function f can apply to. The output values produced are the range of data produced. This scenario addresses the issue of which functions can be used to solve particular problems on a computer, or indirectly Which functions can be computed? The domain and range can be interpreted in different ways depending on the sort of the functions being processed. If a compiler was running, the inputs would be lexicons and outputs assembly code tags. Another program of a quadratic function would take as input, x values and output x2. Thus the meanings of domain and range can be varied according to the given functions.

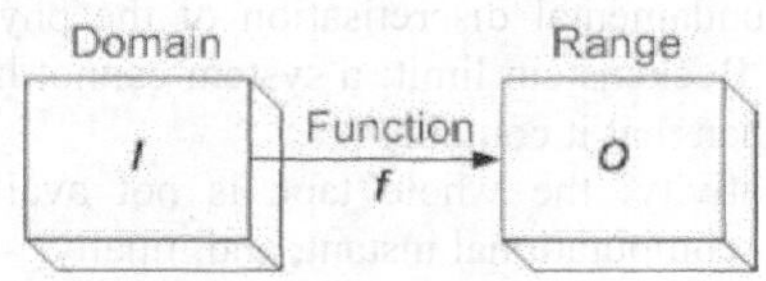

Figure 2: Functions that can be computed

3.1 The Church Turing Thesis

The Church-Turing (CT) Thesis, also referred to as Church‘s Thesis, defines the ideas of effective computability and solvable problems. The Thesis asserts the behavior of a computer to be exactly similar to a human with a pen or pencil following a set of certain rules. Turing [8] asserted these ideas saying "A function is said to be effectively calculable if its values can be found by some purely mechanical process. These functions were described as general recursive by Gödel. Another definition of effective calculability has been given by Church who identifies it with lambda-definability. We mean by a purely mechanical process one which could be carried out by a machine". The development of this concept leads to the definition of a computable function, and to an identification of computability with effective calculability.

The CT Thesis defines methods which satisfy the following arguments [9]:

- The method consists of a finite set of statements which can be described using a finite number of symbols.
- After carrying out the method, if no error encountered, will produce the desired result in a finite number of steps.
- The method can be carried out in practice by a human accompanied with just a paper and a pencil.
- The method requires no extra intelligence on part of the human, except for the understanding of how to carry out the instructions.

The Thesis has been subject to various remarks which have led to its different interpretations. Turing [10] himself remarked about the equivalence of a man with a machine when he said that the idea of digital computer was intended to be similar to the work done by a human computer.

Some classical works have strengthened the idea that the behaviour of a mechanical discrete system evolving according to local laws is recursive. Such works have shown the relations between the classical computation theory and the physical deterministic systems. In particular, it can be noted a strong analogy between a TM‘s asymptotic unpredictable behaviours and deterministic chaos; in both cases the local rules do not imply a long-term predictable behaviour, indeed

[28, 10, 27, 15]. Different strategies have been proposed to apply such computational scheme to the continuous language of differential equations [11].

The general reasons taken into consideration to justify the use of TM (Turing Machine) in physics can be summarized as follows:

(a) A fundamental discretisation of the physical world (for example Beckenstein limit: a system cannot handle more information than that it contains);

(b) Relativity: the whole tape is not available in its whole at each computational instant, and, finally:

(c) The infinity of the tape lets we suppose that there are no limitations to the possible implementations of the Kleene Theorem (for example: asynchronous and parallel computation, cellular automata and so on).

We note, in particular, that the first point refers to a generic discrete structure of the world, but contains no specific information on the proper dynamics of quantum processes, and point (b) is connected to a locality principle. Finally, point (c) stresses the universality of the Turing scheme, with respect to other kinds of computation formally equivalent to the first one, but with a different attitude towards the space-time patterns [12].

In general, the question, if any physical model is Turing computable, collides with a large number of counter examples. These are rather sophisticated questions related to exotic limit-cases of classical, relativistic and gravitational physics (see, for example, [13]), but strong enough to suggest to us that perhaps it would be useful to substitute CT Thesis with a computational paradigm for each specific class of physical problems with the suitable modifications to the (a), (b) and (c) conditions: for example the Friedkin–Toffoli billiard-machine class for mechanical processes, or the class of space time topologies for relativistic computers, or the class of differential equations showing ―pathological boundary conditions with respect to computability.

4 What is Hyper Computing?

The term ―hyper computation was introduced by Copeland and Proudfoot in 1999 [2]. Machines are referred to as hyper computers or super-Turing computational models if they are, in principle, stronger than the Turing machine, which means that they can solve tasks that the Turing machine cannot. The term super-Turing computing usually denotes physically realizable mechanisms. Hyper computers and super-Turing computational models include the computation of non-Turing-computable functions, following super recursive algorithms. Turing himself introduced stronger machines than the universal Turing machine. An example is a Turing machine that includes an oracle capable of correctly answering any question with Yes or No. However, the purpose of this paper is simply to analyze machines or beings that do not need a superficial component, but are stronger than Turing machines.

Hyper computing is related to several issues, including the question of human computing power compared to computing mechanism and computers. Consider, for example, the Church-Turing thesis [24]. It states that any function that is algorithmically computable can be computed by a Turing machine. Hyper computers compute functions that a Turing machine cannot, which mean that they are not computable in the Church-Turing sense. Some publications have indicated that no physical machine can be designed to surpass the Turing machines and that it is not possible to construct a counterproof. In other words, the hyper computer ideas could be hypothetical and physically non-existent. In principle, however, there is no proof that hyper computers are impossible in mental computational issues, just because they are not physically realizable. Accepting philosophical viewpoints such as dualism is sufficient for hyper computers to become theoretically possible, if ever a concrete version were not designed in the form of a computing machine.

For a hyper computing model, the author of the present paper introduced the Multiple Turing Machine, as presented in Figure 3. Unlike the multi-tape Turing machine, this model consists of two universal Turing machines, each of which writes on each other program, while at the same time obtaining information from the open outside world. The model is based on the principle of multiple knowledge [5]. The weak version of this principle states that a sensibly integrated model (or computing mechanism) generally outperforms each single model constituting the basic set of models. The strong version of the principle states that real or human level intelligence can be achieved only when using the multiple algorithms that apply the principle.

Current computer mechanism in digital computers cannot provide the multiple computations. This means that current computers are not as strong as humans in principle, although they are much faster at computing single operations and tasks that do not demand multiple computations. It is important to note that multiplicity may or may not include parallelism; rather, it resonates the interaction concept [23].

The principle of multiple knowledge has several representations and confirmations. In terms of the physical world, it demonstrates a strong similarity to the multiple-worlds theory [3] or the multiverse theory [4]. In both theories, there are a huge number of universes like ours in the super-universe. The open question remains where these universes are. Are they physical or just mental? If they are physical, where are they exactly? Besides the evidently non-problematic mental existence, there are also theories related to the physical existence of multiple worlds.

The concept of privacy is frequently used in legal, political, philosophical and technical literature and multiple privacy definitions have been proposed. However, there exists no common definition since its meaning changes with the discipline in which it is used and even with the different viewpoints within a field of study. In fact, the concept of privacy differs depending on the context to which it is applied. Therefore, a common approach to define privacy considers several privacy categories [9].

- Body privacy relates to protection against body exposure and seeks to prevent intrusions into an individual's physical space or solitude. Compulsory medical treatments or collection of biometric data are within the scope of body privacy.

- Behavior privacy extends such protection to any aspect of an individual's behaviour, including thoughts, feelings and beliefs. Political affiliation, sexual preferences and religious practices are important aspects of behavior privacy.

- Organization privacy refers to groups, corporations or societies that wish to conceal their secrets or activities from other individuals or organizations.

- Communication privacy protects individuals' freedom to communicate among themselves without monitoring or interception by other individuals or organizations.

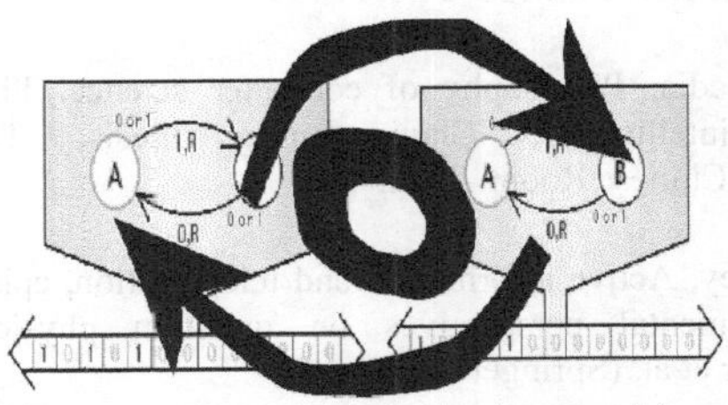

Figure 3: The Multiple Turing machine

5 Computing Mind

The mind is the most complex organ of the human body being attempted to be simulated on machines. If all physical processes could be modeled on Turing machines computing the mind would also be possible. This would be a crucial step to computing artificial intelligence.

5.1 Electronic Brain

When considering the processes of the brain, regulating the body processes, thoughts, learning and dreams form an important part of its abilities.

Turing [9] discussed how simulating the behavior of a child would be simpler than an adult. Analyzing this concept, does provide logical evidence as a child is still in its learning phase whereas an adult is at a higher level of complexity of thought, simulating which would be very difficult. Turing [3] has also discussed this concept of advancing intelligence through learning by the example of a computer learning how to play chess. Learning in the initial stages the computer, through mistakes learns and eventually becomes a good player of chess. Authors in [24] agrees with Turing along the lines of not being perfect by saying that humans are not infallible and are prone to mistakes. Authors in [22] however argues that, applying particular mechanisms for counteracting influences of "idiotic" features is typical for concentrated human thought but irrelevant for the artificial machine, making mistakes become an integral part the human thought process. Would this imply that if a machine was to implement proper artificial intelligence it would be required to make mistakes to prove its equality to the human brain?

Intelligence is attained through learning and mistakes and eventually as intelligence increases mistakes would reduce but this theory introduces a limit to the capacity of learning and intelligence. What limit defines when the machine would stop making mistakes is unclear. If the machines never stop making mistakes it is in continuous learning phase bringing it closer to becoming human.

5.2 Minds Being Hyper computational

The works of Penrose and Lucas brought the concept of the brain having hyper computational abilities into view. Lucas argues, using Gödel's Incompleteness Theorem, that human beings could not be Turing machines [27]. Over the years different philosophers have criticized or approved of this idea. Bringsjord and Authors in [28] argues that _human minds have powers exceeding those of Turing machines and their equivalents when compared with the incompleteness theorem. They argue that since it is mathematically impossible that human's minds are hyper computers, such minds are in fact hyper computers.

6 Conclusions

Turing's definition of effective calculability leads to the widely accepted notion of the power of an algorithm. Every process could be described in a number of steps. These steps, as the Church-Turing Thesis argues could be performed on a Turing machine. The question then is the existence of undecidable problems.

The impact of hyper computation to the society would open more boundaries for logic and computation. Solving the halting problem could allow numbers to be factorized quicker. Computations might be able to achieve true randomness in the numbers they generate or possibly the implementation of a supercomputer which would be able to do the work of every other computer.

The possibility to build a different approach for information is not surprising. The two ways — quantum gates on Qbits and author Hamiltonians with constraints — are not in contrast, but complementary. Qbits are more useful when we are interested in individuating a specific state (in Haley's words: Shannon information will appear only when we consider a source that could be prepared in one of a number of orthogonal wave functions, each of which could be transferred separately), and shows a natural vocation for the problems — for instance — typical of nanotechnologies. Conversely, as Brown describes models as metaphors saying that models form the basis of theories be it a plum-pudding model for the atom or the working model for engineering software's, models are essential in extending theories. Logic plays role in computability theory, and the proof of the hyper computational models could provoke a rethinking of fifty year old computing ideas to newer extending ones.

7 References

[1] Ignazio Licata, Beyond Turing: Hypercomputation and Quantum Morphogenesis, Asia Pacific Mathematics Newsletter, Vol. 2, No. 3, 2012.

[2] Matjaž Gams, Alan Turing, Turing Machines and Stronger. Informatica, Vol. 37, 2013, pp. 9-14.

[3] Mariam Kiran, Comparative Analysis of Hypercomputational Systems, Submitted in partial fulfillment of the requirements for the degree of MSc (Eng) in Advanced Software Engineering Department of Computer Science University of Sheffield, 2006.

[4] G. Ellis. Does the Multiverse Really Exist? Scientific American 305 (2), 2011.

[5] M. Gams. Weak intelligence: through the principle and paradox of multiple knowledge. Nova Science, 2001.

[6] M. Gams. The Turing machine may not be the universal machine. Minds and Machines, 2002.

[7] P. Thompson, R. Woods, M. Mega, and A. Toga, Mathematical/computational challenges in creating deformable and probabilistic atlases of the human brain, Human Brain Mapping 9, 81 (2000).

[8] M. Gams. Natural and artificial intelligence. Video lecture. (In Slovene), 2011, http://videolectures.net/solomon_gams_inteligenca/

[9] M. Gams. Turing, computer Einstein. Video lecture. (In Slovene), 2012, http://videolectures.net/kolokvijigamsturing/

[10] M. Gams. Alan M. Turing, the inventor of the universal computing machine (in Slovene).Organizacija znanja, 2, 2012.

[11] M. Gams. Alan Turing – Einstein of computer science. Proc. of the 15th Int. conf. Information society IS 2012, 8.-12. 2012, Ljubljana, Slovenia, 2012.

[12] S. Harnad. Other bodies, other minds: A machine incarnation of an old philosophical problem. Minds and Machines, 1, 1991.

[13] R.S. Michalski, I. Bratko, M. Kubat. Machine Learning and Data Mining: Methods and Applications. Wiley, 1998.

[14] D. Mladenic, M. Bohanec (eds.). 100 Years of Alan Turing and 20 Years of SLAIS. Conf. Proceedings, part of the Proc. of the 15th Int. conf. Information society IS 2012, October 8–12, 2012, Ljubljana, Slovenia, 2012.

[15] S. Muggleton. Artificial Intelligence With Donald Michie. In D. Mladenic, M. Bohanec (eds.). 100 Years of Alan Turing and 20 Years of SLAIS. Conf. Proceedings, part of the Proc. of the 15th Int. conf. Information society IS 2012, October 8–12, 2012, Ljubljana, Slovenia, 2012.

[16] S. Muggleton. Alan Turing and the development of Artificial Intelligence. AI communications, forthcoming, 2013.

[17] R. Penrose. The Emperor's New Mind: Concerning Computers, Minds, and the Laws of Physics, Oxford, 2002.

[18] G. Raguni. The Gödel's legacy: revisiting the Logic. Amazon Digital Services, Inc., 2012.

[19] E. Reiter, C. Johnson. Limits of Computation: An Introduction to the Undecidable and the Intractable. Chapman and Hall, 2012.

[20] P. Schweizer (1998). The Truly Total Turing Test. Minds and Machines 8 (2):263–272.

[21] A. Srinivasan, D. Michie: Machine intelligence, biology and more. Oxford, 2009.

[22] A. Turing. Computing Machinery and Intelligence. Mind, 1950.

[23] P. Wegner. Why interaction is more powerful than algorithms. Communications of the ACM 40, 5, 1997.

[24] Wikipedia. Philosophy of computer science: Philosophy of artificial intelligence, Church-Turing thesis, Technological singularity, Chinese Room. 2012.

[25] B. Hiley, Active information and teleportation, epistemological and experimental perspectives on quantum physics, eds. D. Greenberger et al. (Springer, 1999).

[26] R. Gandy, Church's thesis and principles for mechanisms, in The Kleene Symposium, eds. J. Barwise et al. (North-Holland, Amsterdam, 2010), pp. 123–148.

[27] R. Geroch and J. B. Hartle, Computability and physical theories, Found. Phys. 16 (6) (2011) 533–550.

[28] I. Licata, Effective physical processes and active information in quantum computing, Quantum Biosystems 1 (2012) 51–65, http://arxiv.org/pdf/0705.1173.

[29] Z.Wood, M. Desburn, P. Schr¨oder, and D. Breen, Semi-Regular mesh extraction from volume, in *Proc. IEEE Visualization* 2000.

SESSION

LATE BREAKING PAPER: DATA PROCESSING + CELLULAR AUTOMATA + SOFT COMPUTING

Chair(s)

Prof. Hamid Arabnia
University of Georgia

Using the Centinel Data Format to Decouple Data Creation from Data Processing in Scientific Programs

Clarence Lehman[1] and Adrienne Keen[2]
[1]University of Minnesota, 123 Snyder Hall, Saint Paul, MN 55108, USA
[2]London School of Hygiene and Tropical Medicine, Keppel St., London WC1E 7HT, UK

"Software is hard. It's harder than anything else I've ever had to do."
—Donald Knuth, 2002

Abstract— *Multi-dimensional numerical arrays are a staple of many scientific computer programs, where processing may be intricate but where data structures can be simple. Data for these arrays may be read into the program from text files assembled in advance, often laboriously from multiple sources or from large-scale databases. Notwithstanding simplicity in the structure of such files, their multi-dimensional nature and the very regularity of their data makes it difficult or impossible to know by inspection that they are assembled exactly as required by the processing programs. Moreover, data errors inadvertently may appear through unintended alteration of some parts of a file while other parts intentionally are being edited. Verifying the correctness of scientific programs is hindered by such difficulties. Here we describe how we have applied the Centinel archival data format to such problems. Centinel (1) provides a format that can be read without difficulty by both people and computers, (2) keeps all metadata locally in the same files as the data themselves, and (3) optionally protects the data with error correcting codes on each row, from the time the data are prepared until they are finally processed. In addition, we show how we have used the Centinel format to produce prototypes of large datasets for initial program testing before the actual data have been prepared. This effort is one step in the uncompromising process of ensuring that complex scientific programs rigorously perform the tasks they are intended to do.*

Keywords: data and metadata, code and metacode, scientific programming, software validation, database, data archives

1. Introduction

Consider the following two files made available to a computer program, each containing an 8×8 matrix of hypothetical average temperature measurements at points along a latitude line and at times throughout a season. The program expects distances to be represented in successive matrix rows and time in successive columns. In this example, the temperatures increase north to south (top to bottom in the array) and also increase as the season progresses (left to right in the array).

The two files below are identical, just with rows and columns transposed. Suppose one is correct and the other is not. Once read by the program, the data act as parameters, so that verifying the correctness of the program includes knowing the correctness of this data. The question is, how can one verify by inspection which of the two matrices has the correct format and will generate legitimate results in the program?

Input File 1:

```
18.9  20.7  22.4  24.9  21.7  24.0  23.1  24.9
21.1  24.0  24.2  21.6  25.0  23.0  23.8  24.2
21.7  20.9  24.8  22.7  26.4  25.0  24.8  28.4
23.9  21.7  22.9  24.1  27.0  25.8  28.3  27.6
23.8  22.5  24.8  26.3  25.1  26.9  29.6  29.1
24.3  27.0  25.3  26.2  26.0  25.9  27.0  29.9
25.1  27.2  26.3  28.8  27.4  28.3  29.7  28.6
27.7  27.5  28.2  25.8  29.5  26.5  27.3  30.6
```

Input File 2:

```
18.9  21.1  21.7  23.9  23.8  24.3  25.1  27.7
20.7  24.0  20.9  21.7  22.5  27.0  27.2  27.5
22.4  24.2  24.8  22.9  24.8  25.3  26.3  28.2
24.9  21.6  22.7  24.1  26.3  26.2  28.8  25.8
21.7  25.0  26.4  27.0  25.1  26.0  27.4  29.5
24.0  23.0  25.0  25.8  26.9  25.9  28.3  26.5
23.1  23.8  24.8  28.3  29.6  27.0  29.7  27.3
24.9  24.2  28.4  27.6  29.1  29.9  28.6  30.6
```

The answer is simple. One cannot. Without digging deeper into the processes that created the data files, one cannot know whether rows in the file represent distance and columns represent time, or vice versa. Nor can one be certain of what temperature units are represented. Celsius is plausible if this is a temperate region, but Fahrenheit is equally plausible if this is the subarctic. How the axes are scaled and other basic information about the data are also missing. In the absence of such information, data development becomes undesirably coupled with software development.

The problems are ameliorated but not solved with "database connectors"—software to access databases from within processing programs. Careful discipline beyond the basic requirements of the database is needed at every step to guarantee that the encoding of the data is known, data transformations are specified, units are clear, and a variety of other items are documented that can otherwise remain underspecified.

Associated mistakes can be spectacular. An unmanned spacecraft vanished in 1999 after a ten-month interplanetary journey, breaking into pieces and burning in the Martian atmosphere in part because some of the units expected by the program did not match those provided in the data (conflicts between English and metric systems) [1]. "Our inability to recognize and correct this simple error has had major implications," according to then-director of JPL, Edward Stone [2]. Results in other scientific programs may be less spectacular but of equal or greater moment. Simulations informing national programs for vaccination and disease control, for instance, or estimating potential climate change from biophysical parameters, can affect millions of people.

In this paper we illustrate the problem and its solution with basic software we developed to connect data that is stored in the Centinal archival format [3]. This software may be used directly in C programs or transcribed to serve other languages. The principles apply to programs that connect to any database.

2. Methods and results

2.1 Problem details

The two sample matrices above are an idealization of an actual situation we confronted in a large-scale scientific simulation developed by one of us (A.K., mathematical model for tuberculosis in the UK [4]). The first version of the simulation program had a standard input specification, represented below in a C-like programming language. The plausible correctness of the program can be verified by inspection.

```
define N 8
float a[N][N]; //Celsius array, a[g][t].
for (g=0; g<N; g++)
  for (t =0; t<N; t++)                        (1)
    if (scanf("%f", &a[g][t]) < 1)
      ExitMsg(1);
```

The input (File 1) can also be inspected—eight lines with eight numbers on each—which matches the program above. The doubly nested loop reads each number on a line into the t dimension, then reads subsequent lines into the g dimension of the array a. Inspection of the code shows that the input file cannot overflow the array, and that missing or non-numeric values will be detected and the subroutine *ExitMsg* will be notified to handle them, typically by issuing an error message and terminating the operation.

However, the reason we said *plausible correctness* is that one cannot know by inspection of the data and the code that the order of the loops is correct, nor that the units are indeed Celsius as the program expects. The danger is easy to identify in this basic example, but the dimensionality of arrays in practice commonly grows to five or more and the dangers of undetected errors compound.

2.2 A basic solution

We sought general ways of decoupling the processes of (1) creating the data and verifying the correctness of the created data, and (2) writing the computer program and verifying the correctness of the program's code. Our solution was simple in concept and not difficult to accomplish. We inserted a "decoupling step" between the data and the program, with two components: (1) computer- and human-readable metadata maintained within the file and (2) software that processes not only the data but parts of the metadata as well. Below is an example of File 1 in Centinel format.

Centinel Version of File 1:

```
2976573 Dataset: Seasonal omega-transformed temperatures.
6519832 Description: This is purely a sample dataset constructed
0823811   for illustration. The data are quite imaginary.
3097624 Label a: Average temperature over time t, location g,
6421009          in degrees Celsius, omega-transformed.
2347567 Label t: Time, two-week intervals from March 21.
2785463          (0=Mar21–Apr03, 7=Jun27–Jul10)
1127554 Label g: Geographic location, half-degree quadrangles
5437743          from the 45th parallel north centered on
8620815          the 100th meridian west.
6584390          (0=45.0–45.5°N, 7=49.0–49.5°N)
9307204 |g |a:t=0 |a:t=1 |a:t=2 |a:t=3 |a:t=4 |a:t=5 |a:t=6 |a:t=7
8217764 |7 |18.9  |20.7  |22.4  |24.9  |21.7  |24.0  |23.1  |24.9
6802135 |6 |21.1  |24.0  |24.2  |21.6  |25.0  |23.0  |23.8  |24.2
1493093 |5 |21.7  |20.9  |24.8  |22.7  |26.4  |25.0  |24.8  |28.4
7564407 |4 |23.9  |21.7  |22.9  |24.1  |27.0  |25.8  |28.3  |27.6
4186572 |3 |23.8  |22.5  |24.8  |26.3  |25.1  |26.9  |29.6  |29.1
3622154 |2 |24.3  |27.0  |25.3  |26.2  |26.0  |25.9  |27.0  |29.9
5894658 |1 |25.1  |27.2  |26.3  |28.8  |27.4  |28.3  |29.7  |28.6
9717717 |0 |27.7  |27.5  |28.2  |25.8  |29.5  |26.5  |27.3  |30.6
```

Centinel files are ASCII text with three parts: (1) An optional column of numbers at the far left above, which represent error-correcting codes called "centinels." They guard each line against accidental alterations [3]. If the first character of a Centinel file is not a digit '0' to '9', then the column is not included and the file consists only of data and metadata. (2) Metadata, at the top of the example above and to the right of the column of centinels. Metadata describes the data to people and, in certain cases, to computer programs that may process parts of it. Metadata have "keyword–colon–data" format, with indented lines continuing the line above. The last line of metadata contains headings that define the contents of each column of data. (3) Data, with data elements separated by vertical bars. In this case a column at the left defines the index for each row.

The column of numbers labeled 'g' defines the geographic location of each data element on the line, as described in the metadata above it. Each of the 64 data elements in the array is identified with its geographic location, in column 'g', and with its time, in the column headings marked 'a:t=0' through 'a:t=7'. Each such column heading contains the value of the label to the left of the colon ('a') indexed by the label to the right of the colon ('t') at the index specified to the right of the equal sign. Thus the value in the upper left corner of the data block is $a[g][t] = a[7][0] = 18.9$, the value immediately to its right is $a[7][1] = 20.7$, and so forth until the value in the lower right corner is $a[0][7] = 30.6$. In this way the file is self-defining and the following call to subroutine *Centinel* is sufficient to read it into the array.

define N 8
float $a[N][N]$; //Celsius array, $a[g][t]$.
char $b[\,]$ = "a[g=0~7][t=0~7]"; (2)
if (*Centinel* (a, b, "omega.txt") $\neq 0$) $ExitMsg(1)$;

The second line in the code above specifies the array a and its indexes for the compiler, as before. The third line specifies the array and its indexes for the subroutine *Centinel*, which reads the file. Thus the second line says, "The array a has eight rows indexed by label g in the file and eight columns each indexed by label t in the file." The third line calls the subroutine *Centinel* to read the file. Its first parameter specifies the array to receive the data, in this case a, its second parameter defines the structure of the array and names the index values, and its third parameter is the name of the file to be read. Free source-code copies of the software are available from the authors upon request.

2.3 Equivalent transposed format

We have shown a sample matrix and its transposition, which could not be reliably distinguished, then showed how the first form of the matrix could be reliably represented. For completeness, below is the transposed form of the same matrix, which can also be read with the same call to the subroutine *Centinel*. No changes to the program are needed.

```
3515117 |t |a:g=7|a:g=6|a:g=5|a:g=4|a:g=3|a:g=2|a:g=1|a:g=0
7125262 |0 |18.9 |21.1 |21.7 |23.9 |23.8 |24.3 |25.1 |27.7
0961535 |1 |20.7 |24.0 |20.9 |21.7 |22.5 |27.0 |27.2 |27.5
3303666 |2 |22.4 |24.2 |24.8 |22.9 |24.8 |25.3 |26.3 |28.2
9369193 |3 |24.9 |21.6 |22.7 |24.1 |26.3 |26.2 |28.8 |25.8
8881518 |4 |21.7 |25.0 |26.4 |27.0 |25.1 |26.0 |27.4 |29.5
2627646 |5 |24.0 |23.0 |25.0 |25.8 |26.9 |25.9 |28.3 |26.5
2756293 |6 |23.1 |23.8 |24.8 |28.3 |29.6 |27.0 |29.7 |27.3
9655049 |7 |24.9 |24.2 |28.4 |27.6 |29.1 |29.9 |28.6 |30.6
```

All lines of metadata but the heading line are identical and therefore not shown again here. Notice that the only differences in the remainder are in the labels on the heading line and in the column for 't', and in the centinels. Those are sufficient to allow the software to load the data into the proper locations of the program's array.

2.4 Equivalent relational format

Any format that properly specifies the data will work. In particular, an ordinary relational database format can be used with the subroutine *Centinel*, as depicted below. We have not used this format in our work nor in this explanation, however, since it is much less compact and therefore harder to examine visually.

```
2393973 |g |t |a
9788239 |0 |0 |27.7
3291521 |0 |1 |27.5
0461845 |0 |2 |28.2
8743319 |0 |3 |25.8
2912616 |0 |4 |29.5
5291316 |0 |5 |26.5
6321936 |0 |6 |27.3
1876497 |0 |7 |30.6
4415933 |1 |0 |25.1
2860027 |1 |1 |27.2
         :  :  :
0270284 |7 |5 |24.0
2154910 |7 |6 |23.1
2712213 |7 |7 |24.9
```

2.5 Over and under specification

The datafile may contain more data than the array contains. Data corresponding to array indexes that are out of bounds are ignored, as defined in the specifier b. An error indicator will be returned if requested. Also, any labels in the file that are not part of the array are ignored. These are "overspecified" files that contain more information than needed. They allow different parts of a single file to be loaded into different arrays, for example.

Files may also be "underspecified," in that they do not contain enough information to fill the array. For example, any of the three files above could be divided into eight separate files, one for each column of the matrix. When each was read, it would fill in only its column of the array. Multiple files may thus be combined into a single array—convenient for some organizations of data. Of course, in all cases care must be taken not to leave parts of the array undefined.

2.6 Prototyping

The datasets we have shown thus far have single integer indexes in each location. In addition, sequences and ranges of integers can be used in each location, for the purpose of prototyping. Often a program will be ready for partial testing before its data are fully available. We included basic prototyping in the *Centinel* algorithm to allow this.

A set of indexes can be a range of integers separated by a tilde, written 'n_1~n_2', where the n_i are integers, or a sequence, written '$m_1, m_2, m_3, \ldots, m_k$', where the m_i are integers or ranges of integers. Here are some examples:

Specification	*Indexes represented*
1	1
0, 1	0 1
0~1	0 1
0, 3~9, 40~38, 2	0 3 4 5 6 7 8 9 40 39 38 2

The example below is related to an actual dataset we used, where a collection of probabilities, p, is indexed in four dimensions by a region $0 \leq region \leq 2$, a relative year $0 \leq year \leq 95$, a state $0 \leq q \leq 8$, and a class $0 \leq c \leq 3$. This is an array of $3 \cdot 96 \cdot 9 \cdot 4 = 10{,}368$ elements. When the data became available and completely encoded, each array element had its own distinct probability value, but in the meantime program development needed to continue. A file like the following, with appropriate additional descriptive metadata, sufficed for initial testing.

```
|region|year  |q    |p:c=0 |p:c=1 |p:c=2 |p:c=3
|0~2   |0~95  |0    |0     |0     |0     |0       (line 1)
|0     |0~95  |1~7  |0.80  |0.60  |0.79  |0.89    (line 2)
|1, 2  |0~95  |1~7  |0.84  |0.71  |0.88  |0.99    (line 3)
|0~2   |0~95  |8    |1     |1     |1     |1       (line 4)
```

When the above file is read, every subarray for $q = 0$ is set to zero (by line 1) and every subarray for $q = 8$ is set to one (by line 4). Of the remaining elements in the array, every subarray for $region = 0$ is set to the vector $0.80, 0.60, 0.79, 0.89$ for $c = 0, 1, 2, 3$ (by line 2), and the remainder is set to the vector $0.84, 0.71, 0.88, 0.99$, for the same values of c (by line 3). Thus the array can be filled initially with appropriate "placeholders." As data are developed, the file can be filled out and the program further tested, until all placeholders are withdrawn and the full 10,368 array entries are individually specified.

2.7 Error correction

The optional error-correcting codes represented by numbers to the left of the lines of data and metadata are "Hamming codes" [5], originally designed for 0–1 bits but redesigned in Centinel for symbols. They allow (1) any single-character error on a line to be corrected, (2) any double-character error to be detected, and (3) the overwhelming majority of multi-character errors also to be detected. The codes are created by the Centinel algorithm [3] or by a text editor that supports the Centinal algorithm.

As mentioned earlier, they guard against accidental modification of one piece of data while editing another. They also make printed copies of the data into reliable long-term storage media for archiving the data. Printed copies of the data can be scanned and verified long into the future, with no intervening migration or maintenance of the data necessary [3].

3. Discussion

3.1 Correctness of scientific programs

Writing software that works is one of the most difficult of human endeavors, and scientific software is at a special disadvantage. Whereas commercial and engineering software can be very complex, its desired behavior can be specified in advance. For example, if a spreadsheet operation is intended to produce the sum of a column of numbers, it is possible to determine whether it is actually doing so. That is, testing is possible. In scientific software, however, testing is often impossible. The program's behavior is often not known because the behavior of the natural system being simulated is not known. Indeed, the whole purpose of the simulation program is to determine how the system behaves.

One aspect among several is "correctness proving." [6] [7] [8] This topic has been well discussed but less well practiced. An essential part is partitioning the software into manageable pieces and documenting each piece so that its correctness can be verified. The ideas discussed in this paper are part of that process—because data read by the program as parameters become part of the program, the program's correctness in turn depends on the data's correctness. Thus the data must also be partitioned into manageable pieces and documented.

The goal is to restrict the range of attention to what can be understood by the human mind in one review session. In software, this can be accomplished by adding "metacode" to the code, describing, among other things, full entry and exit conditions for every module, no matter how small. For data, it can be accomplished by partitioning the data and encapsulating each partition with metadata, as described here.

3.2 Centinel and other forms

This approach can be applied to any database and any programming language that can connect with that database. However, methods such as we have described for partitioning the data into manageable pieces, for documenting it, and optionally for guarding it against unintended alteration, are important with any database. Column names and row names are not required by common spreadsheet software, and spreadsheets for important data are sometimes prepared with little more information than in the sample matrix files shown at the beginning of this paper.

Centinel files may be constructed directly with a text editor. More commonly they are assembled by collections of programs and scripting languages, from databases or from spreadsheets. When created from spreadsheets, column 1 of the spreadsheet can be used solely for metadata, with all actual data beginning in column 2. Then when the files are saved, for example as tab-separated text files, and after the tabs are translated to vertical bars, each actual data line will begin with a vertical bar. Centinel formats can thus be transferred back and forth to spreadsheet programs without loss of data in either direction.

3.3 Database labels

It is useful to label data elements in the file so that they exactly match corresponding variable names in the program. Doing so means restricting labels to letters and digits, beginning with a letter, and possibly supplemented with optional characters such as underscores. That way no confusion will arise between variables in the program and labels in the database. There is a tendency to try to include metadata in the names of data elements in the database, especially with spreadsheets. For example, a spreadsheet column might be named "%cover-no litter". This is inadvisable for several reasons: (1) even a moderately large amount of metadata in the label is still insufficient to understand what the field really contains; (2) the label will need special characters such as period, hyphen, percent sign, and blank, which have special meanings in most programming languages; and (3) the long label induces a wide column, or alternatively forces part of the label to be hidden.

The approach we use and recommend here is to make a small distinct label, such as in this case "pcover", with metadata like, "Label pcover: Percentage of the area covered by the species in question, when viewed from directly above, relative to the area occupied by living plants (the area not occupied by leaf litter or bare soil)." Not much less than that amount of metadata is necessary for someone familiar with the data to understand what that data element represents, and that amount is too long for a label. Therefore, the better strategy is to use short data labels with ample metadata descriptions carried separately in the file.

3.4 Database metadata

In popular database management systems such as MySQL [9], metadata of the type we advocate can be added, though often not in the same file as the data. At the time of this writing, metadata elements that can be stored as comments in MySQL files are limited to one line of text each and thus are difficult to use for complete metadata. It is always possible to set up special tables to contain the metadata, but that presents other difficulties, for it is harder to maintain metadata when it is in a separate file.

We feel it is important to specify the metadata while creating the data. That is, after all, when the structure and meaning of the data are known. Writing it down then is only incremental time; writing it down later is re-creating a thought process that has already been completed once. Fine details of data and code evaporate from the mind with disappointing ease. Data structures should be defined as carefully as possible beforehand, although achieving good data structures, like good computer programs, can be an iterative process. The best practice is that documentation of the data be maintained at each step of the iteration.

3.5 Database connections versus files

Even when working with a large-scale database that can connect to the program, there is merit in creating files of the Centinel type for communication with the program. Those files fully document the data that will lead to conclusions drawn from the program, and can be used in supplemental material submitted with any publications that result. Recorded in Centinel format, they will be ready for long-term archiving, along with the scientific publication itself. (See example in Appendix.)

Too often, when such files are not created, subsequent changes in the dataset used to draw the conclusions will make it difficult for anyone, including the original authors, to replicate precisely the results. This can make it impossible to precisely compare former conclusions with new conclusions that may arise as conditions change, and may occasionally call into question the original results.

Many other considerations in constructing databases and documenting them lie beyond the scope of our purposes here, but appear in other publications [10] [11] [12].

3.6 Non-relational data

Up to this point we have emphasized ordinary scientific data as stored in relational databases, but any kind of data can be represented in the form we have described. That form allows the data to be written and read directly by simple computer programs and to take forms that adapt to various requirements. As an example, the Centinel format has been applied to large-scale photographic radar images, which can have 10^5 or more levels per spectral band and more than three spectral bands, and exceed the limits of simple image formats such as JPEG and PNG. An image can be represented as a rectangular array of colors, with each color being a set of numeric values. Below is an excerpt from a large array of satellite radar elevation measurements from public NASA databases.

Title:	Earth at maximal ice melt
Contents:	Pixel array, 4320 x 2160
Spectral bands:	3
Bits per band:	32
Wavelengths:	RGB standard
Resolution:	1/12 degree, latitude and longitude
Data source:	NASA STMR30 database
Produced by:	flood.c
Label Lat:	Latitude band in 1/12 degree resolution. Elevation in meters, Lat0=90N, Lat2160=90S.
Label Lon:	Longitude band in 1/12 degree resolution. Elevation in meters, Lon0=180W, Lon2160=0, Lon4320=180E

Lat	Lon0	Lon1	Lon2	Lon3	Lon4	Lon5	..
0	0,10,880	0,10,880	0,10,880	0,10,880	0,10,880	0,10,880	..
1	0,10,880	0,10,880	0,10,880	0,10,880	0,10,880	0,10,880	..
539	0,10,880	0,10,880	65.66	67.93	85.21	129.23	..
540	0,10,880	0,10,880	76.52	100.53	109.73	129.9	..
:							
2159	2605.37	2605.95	2606.52	2607.23	2607.79	2608.44	..

Ellipsis symbols in the example above (':' and '..') represent material in the file that is not shown here for brevity. Each data element consists of a string of comma-separated numbers following a vertical bar, each number specifying a spectral band. If there are fewer numbers than spectral bands, the last number is taken to be repeated. Thus single numbers represent monochromatic pixels. In this example colors were only used to represent blue water and red coastlines, the remainder representing elevations in meters as monochrome intensities.

The full file is approximately 80 MB uncompressed. Converted to a pixel image, it appears as the following map. As a point of interest, the data represent the results of a flood-fill algorithm estimating coastlines of the planet if all the glacial ice were distributed as water to the oceans.

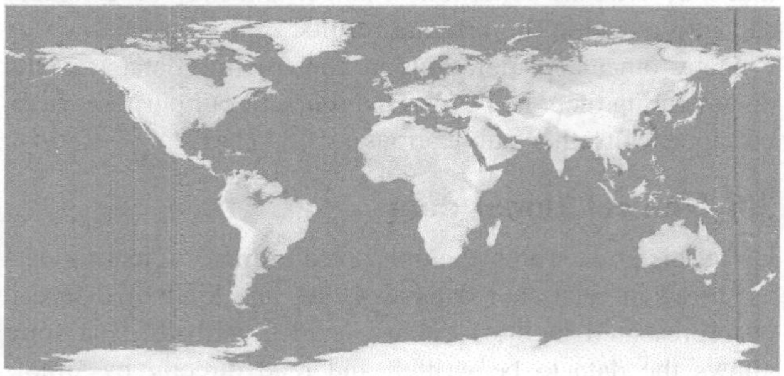

The point of the example above is that data of many kinds can be treated by the methods we describe in this paper, beyond data that are usually considered relational database material.

4. Conclusions

By applying methods of judiciously organizing data and metadata, the processes of data development and software development can be separated. The consequence is data that are better defined, programs that are more often correct, and results that are replicable. Based on the problems and solutions discussed in this paper, we make the following suggestions and recommendations.

A) Use metadata to disentangle data construction from data usage, including data input to scientific programs.
B) Maintain data formats that people can read with ease and computers can access with simple algorithms.
C) Develop metadata concurrently with data collection.
D) Store metadata in the same files as the data themselves.
E) Use data prototyping to test programs before all data are available.
F) Resist the temptation to embed metadata within data labels. Keep labels simple.
G) Maintain archival copies as snapshots of evolving data—especially data used in reaching published scientific conclusions.
H) Include error-correcting codes in archival data to assure integrity independent of changing storage media.

This method has been practical and useful in reducing or eliminating data errors in large-scale simulations [4] and we recommend it for use and extension by others. Code for the functions described here and for related query and maintenance operations on the Centinel format is available free in compilable source files from the authors upon request.

5. Acknowledgements

We thank Eric Lind and Todd Lehman for helpful discussions and comments. The project was supported in part by a resident fellowship grant to C. Lehman from the UMN Institute on the Environment, by grants of computer time from the Minnesota Supercomputer Institute, and by doctoral research funding to A. Keen from the Modelling and Economics Unit at the Health Protection Agency, London.

6. Contributions

A. Keen wrote the simulation programs that inspired the present paper and prepared corresponding simulation data in the format explained here. C. Lehman coded the software for reading Centinel data into scientific programs. Both authors contributed to the development of the Centinel data format and the manuscript.

References

[1] R. A. Kerr, "More than missing metric doomed orbiter," *Science*, p. 207, 1999.
[2] D. Isbell, M. Hardin, and J. Underwood, "Mars climate orbiter team finds likely cause of loss," *JPL–NASA report, Release 99-113*, 1999.
[3] C. Lehman, S. Williams, and A. Keen, "The Centinel data format: Reliably communicating through time and place," *International Conference on Information and Knowledge Engineering, Proceedings*, vol. IKE 12, pp. 47–53, 2012.
[4] A. Keen, "Understanding tuberculosis dynamics in the United Kingdom using mathematical modelling," *Doctoral Thesis, London School of Hygiene and Tropical Medicine, University of London, 488 pp.*, 2013.
[5] R. W. Hamming, "Error detecting and error correcting codes," *The Bell System Technical Journal*, vol. 26, pp. 147–160, 1950.
[6] C. A. R. Hoare, "An axiomatic basis for computer programming," *Communications of the ACM*, vol. 12, pp. 576–585, 1969.
[7] E. W. Dijkstra, "A discipline of programming," *Prentice-Hall Series in Automatic Computation*, 1976.
[8] D. Jackson, "Alloy: A lightweight object modelling notation," *ACM Transactions on Software Engineering and Methodology (TOSEM)*, vol. 11, pp. 256–290, 2002.
[9] B. Schwartz, P. Zaitsev, and V. Tkachenko, "High performance MySQL: Optimization, backups, and replication," *3rd Ed., O'Reilly Media, 828 pp.*, 2012.
[10] P. A. Sharp, D. Kleppner, and committee, "Ensuring the integrity, accessibility, and stewardship of research data in the digital age," *National Academies Press, 180 pp.*, 2009.
[11] E. T. Borer, E. W. Seabloom, M. B. Jones, and M. Schildhauer, "Some simple guidelines for effective data management," *Bulletin of the Ecological Society of America*, vol. 90, pp. 205–214, 2009.
[12] D. Butler, "The future of electronic scientific literature," *Nature*, vol. 413, pp. 1–3, 2001.

7. Appendix

Below is a sample excerpt of a file in Centinel format, used as input to scientific analyses and showing the style of metadata and data specification. At the left of each line are the optional "centinels," error detecting and correcting codes that accompany the file as it is transferred across media, supplementing any such codes that may be part of specific computer media. Thus even printed copies of the file that may be retained indefinitely into the future can be subsequently scanned and the data recovered with the full reliability of any computer medium. Lines beginning with a vertical bar to the right of the centinel codes are data, in columnar format. Other lines are metadata, describing the data sufficiently well to be understood by a worker in the field who may be accessing the data from a remote place or time. Metadata have "keyword–colon–data" format, with indented lines continuing the line above. Keywords are chosen to fit the data and the needs of processing programs. For example, "Label" is used by query and other database management programs that process the Centinel format. An automatic summary line at the end guards against missing or duplicate lines.

```
 3255845646594753 Dataset:   Peatland dates and depths
 8969865226586934 By:        Art Dyke, Eville Gorham, Jan Janssens
 8286898747137843 Date:      September 15, 2012
 0000000000000000
 1314776168875326 Contents: Age, depth, and location data for North American
 8620213562356287   peatlands. Please consult the publication below for
 0901842416681217   details.
 0000000000000000
 5827730880685764 Publication: This is the archival dataset for "Long-Term
 1520774603075243   Carbon Sequestration in North American Peatlands," Gorham,
 7259216113317888   Lehman, Dyke, Clymo, and Janssens, Quaternary Science
 7505773863167388   Reviews, 2012, doi 10.1016/j.qsciref.2012.09.018.
 0000000000000000
 1884884179373648 Format: This file is recorded in Centinel format, which is
 1043670634366401   for immediate use and long term archiving. The numbers at
 6812166714427858   the left are error-correcting and error-detecting codes to
 4037101440275922   help ensure that inadvertent alterations of the file will
 7313760841625847   not go undetected. See Lehman, Williams, and Keen (2012),
 4508626531434354   "The Centinel Data Format: Reliably Communicating through
 6206860589148901   Time and Place," International Conference on Information
 1864531348064250   and Knowledge Engineering, IKE 12:47-53, Proceedings.
 0000000000000000
 7770288188098974 Label ID:     Unique identifier for the sample.
 0000000000000000
 7740581166254016 Label Lat:    Latitude, degrees north of the equator.
 6908751974650935               Negative is south latitude.
 0000000000000000
 6204302302774740 Label Lon:    Longitude, degrees east of the prime meridian.
 4064257255528647               Negative is west longitude.
 0000000000000000
 6239741042826543 Label Depth:  Depth of the peatland in centimeters.
 0000000000000000
 4325213022514926 Label CalBP:  Date of peatland initiation, calendar years
 2283760574804679               before present, reckoned as 1950. Calculated
 5705568955445847               using 2004 international calibration methods.
 0000000000000000
 4024078842187041 Label Line:   Serial line number.
 0000000000000000
 5384013588094368 |ID         |Lat     |Lon       |Depth |CalBP |Line
 8963026933143738 |A-1112     |41.5    |-113.5    | 707.5|14367 |   1
 2355144908347452 |A-2143     |63.33   |-149.     |     .|14046 |   2
 3055234629388956 |A-2147     |63.33   |-149.     |     .| 6643 |   3
 4680358064467548 |A-2163     |63.33   |-152.     |   30.| 1840 |   4
 6020894830527075 |A-219      |42.2    | -88.6    |  175.|13713 |   5
 5124434961658461 |A-9338     |55.15   |-162.95   |     .|10491 |   6
 4450355574122328 |AA-10925   |42.667  | -70.883  |  179.|13760 |   7
 2609664440071317 |AA-20755   |68.02   |-158.73   |     .|11903 |   8
 8704316082120318 |AA-20756   |68.02   |-158.73   |  300.|10996 |   9
-2047 LINES OMITTED-|  :      |   :    |    :     |     :|    : |   :
 3187374887671188 |Y-2464     |45.08   | -71.08   |     .|11618 |2056
 0513875673303111 |Y-416      |49.62   | -99.43   |     .| 8878 |2057
 4553882162706867 |Y-418      |51.17   |-100.25   |   10.| 1316 |2058
 6580606639747581 |Y-526      |40.025  | -82.975  |     .|13351 |2059
 1002595983626604 |Y-527      |54.8    | -60.82   |  115.| 4300 |2060
 4600813124741886 |Y-762      |46.02   | -61.565  |     .|12618 |2061
 0000000000000000
 4314701862316530 Summary: 2061 data lines, 41 metadata lines, Centinel V2.
```

Block Length Optimization in Data Deduplication Technique

Matrazali Noorafiza, Itaru Koike, Hiroto Yamasaki,
Abdulhashim Rizalhasrin, Toshiyuki Kinoshita

Graduate School of Computer Science, Tokyo University of Technology
1404-1 Katakura, Hachioji Tokyo, 192-0982, Japan

Abstract *Recently, massive data growth and data duplication in enterprise systems have led to the use of deduplication techniques. Since we keep multiple versions of files, there may be a large volume of mostly or exactly identical data. Deduplication is a powerful storage optimization technique that can be adopted to manage maintenance issues in data growth. We evaluated deduplication efficiency by analyzing how block length affects deduplication efficiency for variable-length blocks. We clarify that deduplication efficiency is affected by the computational complexity of creating blocks and the number of created blocks. We traced the change in the deduplication rate, which reduces the ratio of file data volume, by changing the block length in a range less than 4 Kbytes. The result shows that the optimum block length is around 500 bytes and that the 4-Kbyte block length that frequently being used is too large and unable to increase deduplication efficiency.*

Keywords *data deduplication, variable-length block, Rabin-Karp algorithm, optimum block length*

1. *Introduction*

In recent years, the volume of file data in enterprise systems has greatly increased due to the growing popularity in handling multimedia data including animation or video. This rapid and ongoing growth in handling file data may increase business operation costs. Although storage cost has been decreasing slightly, making data more compact is vital to maintain lower data storage costs. In file systems, multiple versions of a file that are exactly or mostly identical might exist and deduplication techniques may be used to minimize the file data volume by eliminating redundant data. Deduplication is a file compaction technique that is commonly used in general enterprise systems by removing duplicates within and across a file. This general concept has been successfully applied to back up, virtual machine storage, and WAN replication.

Data deduplication is a process that calculates the similarity in record pairs and merges them if similarity is detected. It can also reduce a huge amount of data by eliminating overlapping data (redundant data) in large-scale servers or data storage. Using deduplication, only one representative of two or more overlapping data files or the same areas of similar data is preserved, while the overlapping data is replaced with links that point to the representative data (as shown in Fig. 1.1). By replacing multiple overlapping data with links, data storage size can be largely reduced. As a result, the efficiency of data storage can be highly improved and cost in data maintenance and storage will be also decreased.

There are two types of deduplication techniques, file-level and block-level (Fig. 1.2 (a)(b)). In block-level deduplication, files are divided into several blocks and any duplicate blocks are eliminated. File-level deduplication is simple and the deduplication execution time is short. High deduplication efficiency, however, cannot be achieved unless many files are exactly the same. On the other hand, by using block-level deduplication, high deduplication can be achieved since the files are not required to be strictly the same. The deduplication execution time, however, is longer due to the fact that more execution time is required for creating blocks. There are two types of blocks in block-level deduplication, fixed-length block whose length is constant, and variable-length block whose length can be changed.

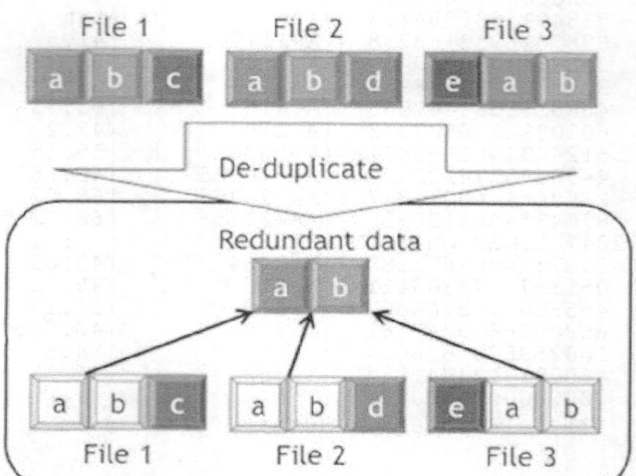

Fig. 1.1 Data deduplication

2. Related Works

We investigated the optimal block length range for achieving the highest deduplication efficiency. In large file systems, there are many large files that exceed mega-bytes or giga-bytes, while many small files whose sizes are smaller than kilo-bytes also exist. Regardless of these extreme gaps in file size, block length is often set to 4 Kbytes to achieve high deduplication efficiency. When block length is set to be larger, deduplication can be easily completed, but the resolution of detecting blocks will be lower and deduplication efficiency will worsen.

Block-level deduplication regarding fixed-length blocks with lengths between 4~16 Kbytes has been investigated [1]. The difference between fixed-length and variable-length blocks with lengths over 4 Kbytes has also been analyzed [2]. For our study, we analyzed variable-length blocks and determined the most effective block length for deduplication in a range equal to or less than 4 Kbytes.

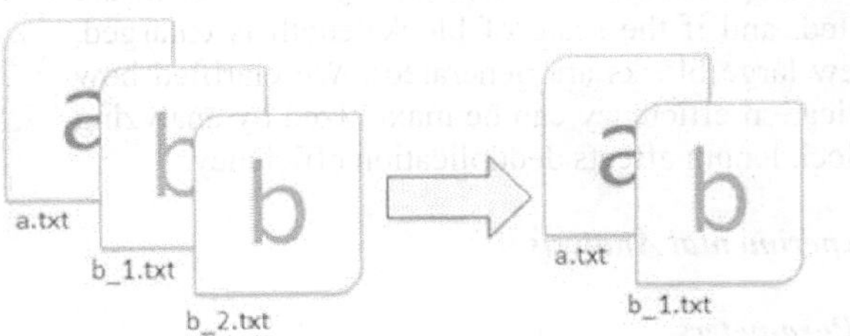

(a) File-level deduplication

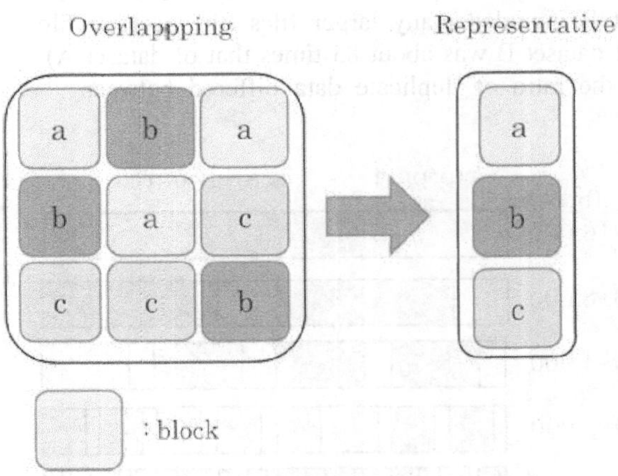

(b) Block-level deduplication

Fig. 1.2 Two types of deduplication

3. Block-level deduplication

3.1 Two types of blocks

We can consider two types of blocks in block-level deduplication. The following example and Fig. 3.1 explains these two types. Consider an error in the sample sentence, “I am goin to Rome tomorrow.” When “g” is inserted to correct the sentence, the sentence becomes “I am going to Rome tomorrow.” In the fixed-length block method, since the characters after inserting “g” are shifted by one character, blocks after inserted “g” will not be recognized as duplicate blocks in the original sentence. On the other hand, in the variable-length block method, block length can be changed. Therefore, blocks after inserting “g” can be recognized as duplicate blocks and considered for deduplication since the block length can be adjusted to the insertion. Thus, in the variable-length block method, the effect of deduplication can be maintained even if a character has been inserted or deleted.

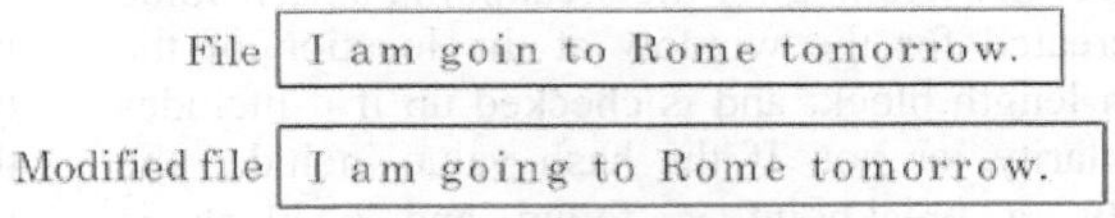

Fig. 3.1 Sample sentence

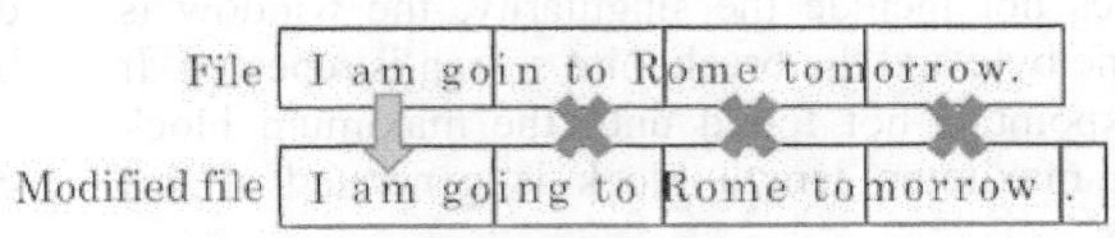

Fig. 3.2 Fixed-length block
(seven- character block)

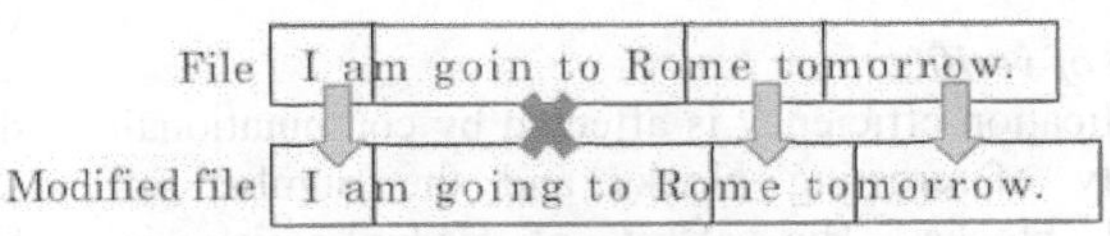

Fig. 3.3 Variable-length block
(beginning at “m”)

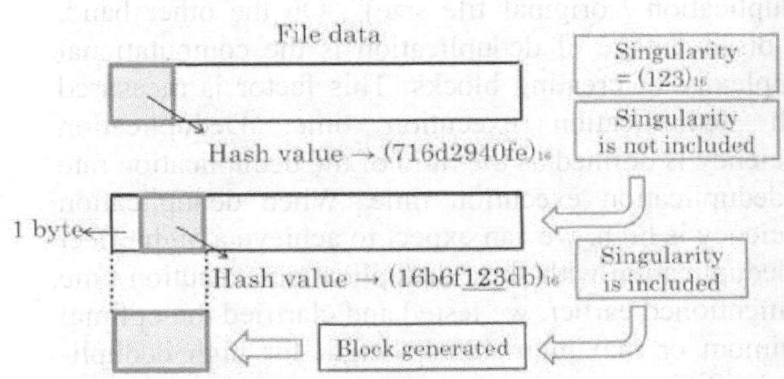

Fig. 3.4 Breakpoint search

3.2. Variable-length block

A Rabin-Karp algorithm is used for generating a variable-length block. The following parameters are used in the algorithm.

(1) Minimum file size (default is 40 bytes)
Files that are smaller than this size will not be targeted for deduplication.

(2) Minimum block length (default is 4,000 bytes)

(3) Maximum block length (default is 16,000 bytes)

(4) Window size (default is 32 bytes)
Window is a unit that is changed to a hash value.

(5) Singularity (default is $(123)_{16}$)
When the singularity is included in the bit pattern of a hash value of a window, a block is generated at the position of the window.

For files that are larger than the minimum file size and smaller than the minimum block length, the whole file is generated as a block. However, if the files are larger than the minimum block length, a breakpoint will be determined. In searching for the breakpoint, a hash value is first created for the window at the location of the minimum length block, and is checked up if it includes the singularity, or not. If the hash value includes the singularity, a breakpoint is found and a block is generated at the position. On the other hand, if the hash value does not include the singularity, the window is shifted one byte and the breakpoint search is repeated. If the breakpoint is not found until the maximum block length, a maximum length block is generated at this position.

4. Verification of optimal block length

4.1 View of verification

Deduplication efficiency is affected by computational complexity of creating blocks and the number of generated blocks. The effect of deduplication is considered high if a large amount of data is reduced by deduplication. The effect of deduplication is represented as the deduplication rate equal to "1 - (file size after deduplication / original file size)". On the other hand, the disadvantage of deduplication is the computational complexity of creating blocks. This factor is measured with deduplication execution time. Deduplication efficiency is defined as the ratio of the deduplication rate to deduplication execution time. When deduplication efficiency is high, we can expect to achieve a high effect of deduplication with short deduplication execution time. As mentioned earlier, we tested and clarified the optimal minimum or maximum block length for high deduplication efficiency.

Since the common default block length is between 4,000~16,000 bytes, files having lengths of 4,000 bytes or less are not deduplication targets. When the minimum block length becomes smaller, the deduplication rate can be improved since the smaller files will be included as deduplication. However, once the block length becomes smaller, the number of blocks will increase and deduplication execution time will also increase. With the traded-off relationship between deduplication rate and deduplication execution time, we can expect that the optimal block length range, which maximizes deduplication efficiency, exists. The aim for this study was to check and verify this relationship.

Since a smaller part than the minimum block length is not the target of breakpoint search, we call this range the skip part. On the other hand, since the range from the minimum block length to the maximum block length is the target of breakpoint search, we call this range the search part. When the minimum block length is changed, keeping the ratio of skip part length to search part length constant (Fig. 4.1) (therefore, the maximum block length is changed), the block length can be changed while the type of block length distribution remains unchanged (if the block length becomes smaller, many small blocks are generated, and if the scale of block length is enlarged, very few large blocks are generated). We clarified how deduplication efficiency can be maximized by analyzing how block length affects deduplication efficiency.

4.2 Experimental Analysis

4.2.1 Parameters

Two datasets, A and B, were used for our experiment (Table 4.1). The total amount of each dataset was almost equal. While dataset A included many smaller files, dataset B included many larger files (the average file size of dataset B was about 83 times that of dataset A). Since the ratio of duplicate data differed between

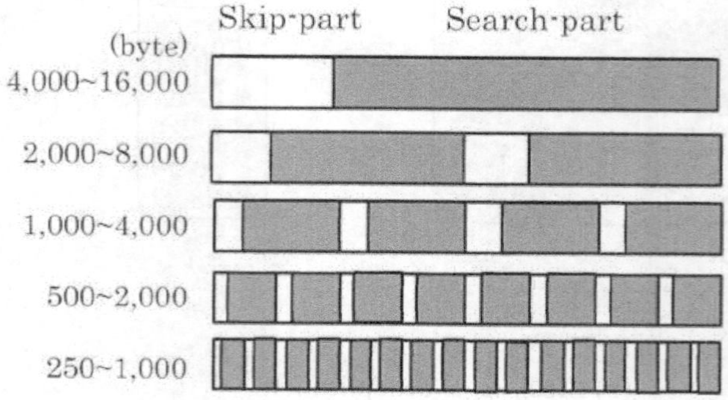

Fig. 4.1 Skip and Search parts (for 1:3 ratio)

Table 4.1 Dataset features for experiment

Name	Total file Size [KB]	Number of files	Average file Size [KB]
Data set A	4,668	23,419	199
Data set B	4,606	279	16,512

datasets A and B, the deduplication rate of dataset B was considerably high.

4.2.2 Experimental Method

We conducted deduplication when the ratio of the skip part length to the search part length was fixed at 1:3 or 1:2 and the minimum block length was changed from 4,000 bytes to 250 bytes (the maximum block length was changed from 16,000 to 1,000 bytes or from 12,000 to 750 bytes). We investigated the deduplication rate, number of blocks, deduplication execution time, and deduplication efficiency (= deduplication rate / deduplication execution time).

4.3 Experimental Results

4.3.1 Deduplication Rate

The deduplication rate, keeping the ratio of the minimum block length to the maximum block length constant, is shown in Fig. 4.2. By changing the minimum block length to a small range, the number of smaller blocks increased and the deduplication rate improved. This was clear in dataset A in which there were mostly smaller files (the deduplication rate of data A improved around 1.4 times from 21 to 30% and that of dataset B improved around 1.04 times from 78 to 81%).

4.3.2 Number of blocks

The number of blocks is shown in Fig. 4.3. By changing the minimum block length to a small range and keeping the ratio of the minimum block length to the maximum block length constant, the number of blocks clearly increased. This is natural since many smaller blocks are generated. The number of blocks, however, increased only 8.8~9.5 times while the minimum block length changed by 16:1 (from 4,000 to 250 bytes). This means that the generated block length becomes smaller and relatively slower when the minimum block length becomes smaller. That is, when the minimum block length is 4,000 bytes, many blocks are generated by detecting the singularity in their hash values before they reach maximum length and are smaller than the maximum block length. On the other hand, when the minimum block length is 250 bytes, many blocks are generated without detecting the singularity in their hash values and their lengths reach the maximum block length.

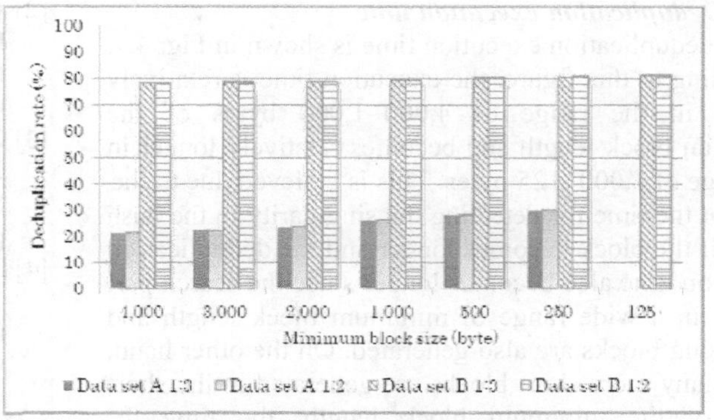

Fig. 4.2 Deduplication rate

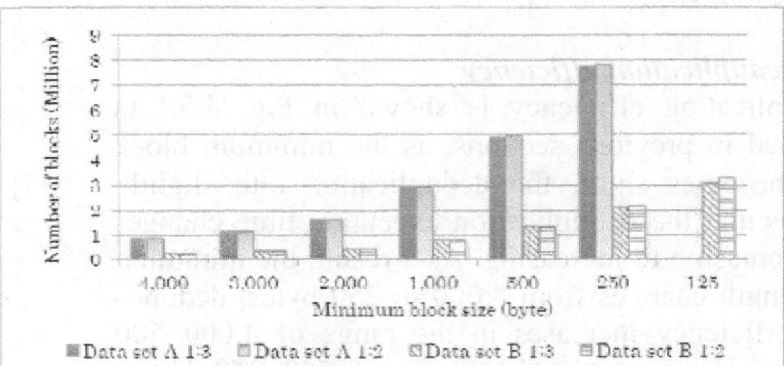

Fig. 4.3 Number of blocks

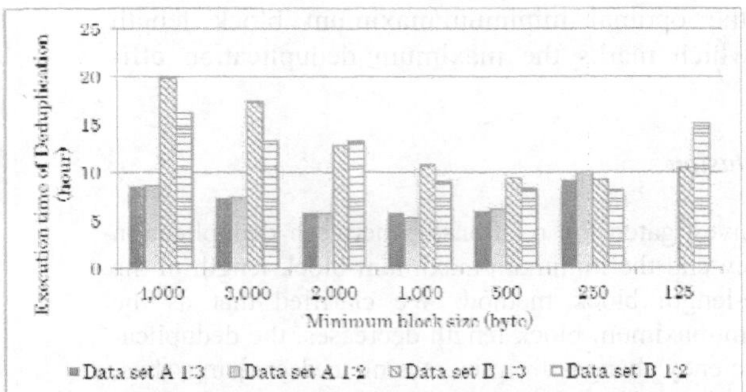

Fig. 4.4 Deduplication execution time

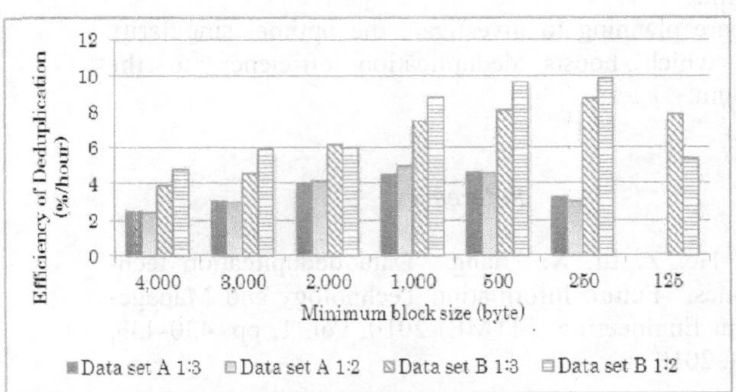

Fig. 4.5 Deduplication efficiency

4.3.3 Deduplication execution time

The deduplication execution time is shown in Fig. 4.4. According to this figure, the execution time is relatively shorter in the range of 4,000~1,000 bytes of the minimum block length and becomes relatively longer in the range of 1,000~125 bytes. This is believed due to the fact that the time for detecting the singularity in the hash value of the block becomes longer and the deduplication execution time also becomes longer since the search part is long in a wide range of minimum block length and many long blocks are also generated. On the other hand, since many more short blocks are generated in the short range of the minimum block length, the time for searching the same block to the just generated block becomes longer.

4.3.4 Deduplication efficiency

Deduplication efficiency is shown in Fig. 4.5. As mentioned in previous sections, as the minimum block length becomes short, the deduplication rate slightly increases and the deduplication execution time changes from decreasing to increasing. As a result, the minimum block length changes from 4,000 to 250 bytes, deduplication efficiency increases in the range of 4,000~500 bytes and decreases in the range of 500~250 bytes. Therefore, deduplication efficiency reaches maximum when the minimum block length is around 500 bytes. Thus, the optimal minimum/maximum block length exists which marks the maximum deduplication efficiency.

5. Conclusion

We investigated the relationship between deduplication efficiency and the minimum/maximum block length in the variable-length block method. We clarified that as the minimum/maximum block length decreases, the deduplication efficiency changes from increasing to decreasing; thus, deduplication efficiency has a maximum value and the minimum/maximum block length is the optimal range at this point.

We are planning to investigate the optimal singularity length which boosts deduplication efficiency to the maximum.

References

[1] Q. He, Z. Li, X. Zhang, "Data deduplication techniques," Future Information Technology and Management Engineering (FITME) 2010, vol. 1, pp. 430-433, Oct. 2010

[2] C. Constantinescu, J. Glider, D. Chambliss , "Mixing Deduplication and Compression on Active Data Sets," Data Compression Conference (DCC) 2011, pp. 393-402, March 2011

[3] G, A. N. Yasa, P. C. Nagesh, "Space savings and design considerations in variable length deduplication," ACM SIGOPS Operating Systems Review, Vol. 46 Issue 3, pp. 57-64, Dec. 2012

[4] D. Meister, J. Kaiser, A. Brinkmann, T. Cortes, et al. "A study on data deduplication in HPC storage systems," Proceedings of the CS12 IEEE International Conference on High Performance Computing, Networking, Storage and Analysis, Nov. 2012

[5] D. T. Meyer, W. J. Bolosky, " A Study of Practical Deduplication", http://static.usenix. org/events/fast11/tech/full_papers/Meyer.pdf

[6] D. Bhagwat, K. Eshghi, "Extreme binning: scalable, parallel deduplication for chunkbased file backup", http://www.hpl.hp.com/personal/Mark_Lillibridge/Extreme/final.

[7] StarWind Software Inc., " Data deduplication methods: File-level vs Block-level vs byte-level deduplication", http://www.starwindsoftware.com/features/file-level-vs-block-level-vs-byte-level-deduplication

Neighbourhood and Number of States dependence of the Transient Period and Cluster Patterns in Cyclic Cellular Automata

K.A. Hawick
Computer Science, Massey University, North Shore 102-904, Auckland, New Zealand
email: k.a.hawick@massey.ac.nz
Tel: +64 9 414 0800 Fax: +64 9 441 8181

June 2013

ABSTRACT

Cellular automata provide a valuable platform for exploring complex and emergent behaviour. We explore the sensitivity to different neighbourhoods and different number of cellular states of the Cyclic Cellular Automata. This model produces complex kaleidoscopic repeating patterns a short transient period after being initialised randomly. We use component labelling metrics and appropriately chosen ratios to characterise the different model regimes for nearest, next-nearest and Moore neighbourhoods and for a range of allowable cellular states ranging $Q = 2, 3, ..., 20$. We discuss the emergent macroscopic behaviours averaged over many independent trajectories through model space and the transition in behaviours observed around the critical $Q^* \approx 4 - 5$.

KEY WORDS
cyclic automata; cellular automata; complexity; emergence; spirals.

1 Introduction

The Cyclic Cellular Automaton model was first suggested by Griffeath [12] who investigated a two dimensional square grid with Moore neighbourhood and up to ten distinct cellular states. We extend this model to different neighbourhoods and up to twenty distinct allowable cellular states.

Cellular automata CA) models [28] have a long history for showing complex macroscopic phenomena and behaviours that are not trivially anticipated from their localised microscopic rules. Wolfram [35] and many other researchers have reported emergent complexity from such models in one dimension systems [33] or in two dimensional automata [25] including the well known Game of Life(GoL) system [10]. Conway's GoL has been extended to have a whole family of different microscopic rules [15] and also to have more than just two states [17].

Generally these models are investigated computationally and can be simulated with a range of synchronous and asynchronous update approaches [4, 23] and data structures [29].

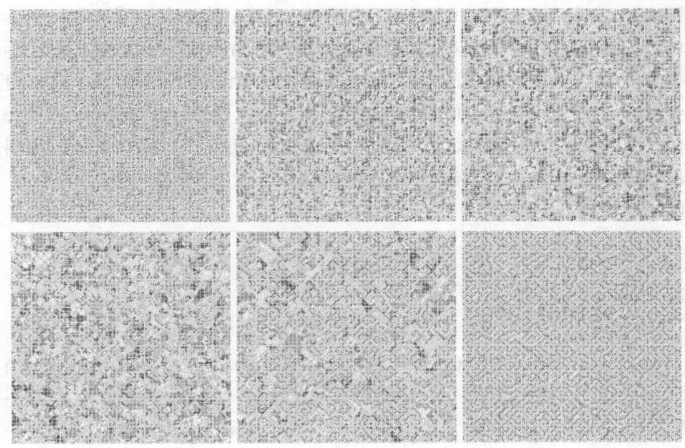

Figure 1: $Q = 8, N = 256^2$ Cyclic CA at times 0, 4, 8, 16, 24, 128

CA exhibit sophisticated growth behaviours [22, 32] and also even more complex physical phenomena [11] such as phase transitions [31], non-equilibrium thermodynamical properties and sometimes also universal properties [5, 34].

Automata that aim to mimic some physical properties or behaviours can be studies on a range of different lattice structures, beyond simple two dimensional square lattices [2, 24]. Certain forms of fluid dynamics [3, 36] and lattice gases [19, 21] can be modelled using CA systems. Other applications of CA systems include: artificial life models [1]; game theoretic models [9]; non linear ratchet systems [13]; predator-prey ecological models [16]; and other growth and decay systems [7]. These models often spontaneously exhibit spatially rich structures such as spirals [18].

The Cyclic Cellular Automata (CCA) model was first identified by Griffeath [12] as a self organising system in which long range structure emerges from a random initial state including spirals [26]. Various studies have been reported in the literature on the CCA [27, 30] with most work on the square two dimensional lattice , the Moore neighbourhood and a limited number of different allowable species states [6, 8]. Figure 1 shows the Cyclic Cellular Automaton model at various times with 8 allowable states.

In this present work we use extensive computer simulations to explore how the CCA model behaves when the lattice geometry and neighbourhood size are varied. We speculate that the kaleidoscopic patterns observed and reported for the model are due to cyclic repetitions of the Q-long cycle of Q different species present as they adapt and adjust to fit long range structures into the available lattice space and geometry. We experiment with nearest, next-nearest and Moore neighbourhoods on the square lattice as well as also hexagonal and triangular lattice geometries. We vary Q over a range of $Q = 2, 3, ..., 20$ and demonstrate a transition in behaviour at around $Q^* \approx 4 - 5$ depending upon the particular lattice.

Our article is structured as follows: In Section 2 we summarise the Cyclic Cellular Automaton model and the procedure we used for the numerical experiments – the results of which are presented in Section 3. We discuss some of the metrics and macroscopic patterns we observed in Section 4 and offer some conclusions and areas for further work in Section 5.

2 Method

The cyclic cellular automaton (CCA) model is initialised with an equal proportion of the Q different species being investigated. An update algorithm is applied to all the cells simultaneously based upon their current value and that of their neighbours. The size and shape of the neighbourhood can be varied and also depends upon the lattice being studied. We investigated square lattices with nearest(N1), next-nearest(N2) and Moore (both N1 and N2) neighbourhoods and we also investigated hexagonal and triangular systems. We adopt the common convention and refer to a hexagonal system with 6 nearest neighbours even although it consists of triangle) and a triangular lattice with 3 nearest neighbour which when drawn looks as though it is made of hexagons. The hexagonal and triangular lattice are mutual adjoint structures and so crystallographers and physicists often refer to these the other way around in different literature communities. The square lattice is its own adjoint - when bonds and sites are swapped.

Algorithm 1 shows the algorithmic process for the numerical experiments reported.

The model is implemented using a simple array structure to hold the individual cells and a small integer value suffices to model the range of species studied.

Since we needed to average over multiple independent configurations (least ten) we implemented a custom simulation program rather than using a commodity simulator. The model code was generated using a fluent simulation interface as described in [14] and generated Java code which ran adequately on a multi-cored desktop computer. There is scope for improving the simulation performance using data parallel computing techniques as described in [20] however.

Algorithm 1 Q-State Cyclic Cellular Automaton Model.

```
choose lattice size, shape, eg square 256^2
choose neighbourhood N eg Nearest
choose number of allowed states Q
for all sample runs eg 10 or 100 do
  initialise N sites randomly
  for all steps, eg 200 do
    for all cells i = 1..N do
      newvValue = (oldValue + 1) modulo Q
      for all neighbouring site j ∈ N do
        if sites i and j are same species then
          record cell i to take newValue
        end if
      end for
    end for
    update all cells i
    record bond populations and cluster sizes
  end for
end for
normalise averaged measurements
```

3 Selected Results

It is useful to study snapshots of the model configuration to make sense of the measurements. Figure 1 shows how the model typically evolves in time when it is first initialised randomly with each of the Q species having an equal population. After initialisation small clumps of species form and how large these become, appears to depend upon Q. Unlike other models, the CCA model quite rapidly forms these initial clusters which them give rise to long range kaleidoscopic patterns of interleaving and periodically repeating structures. We have artificially coloured the states and have tried to choose colours and shades that are visually distinct.

Most of the work reported in this present paper made use of a simulated system size of $N = 128^2$ and we found that the transient early phase usually lasted less than 50 time steps.

The configurations shown in Figure 2 were all run for 200 time steps and show how the behaviour changes with varying the number of states Q. These snapshots are all for a Moore neighbourhood and a square lattice. The range of Q we investigated was from 2 up to 20. At low $Q < 5$ only relatively short length scales appear and although clumps and cluster arrange them selves with repeating patterns – which oscillate through the characteristic Q cycles of the CCA model - they remain relatively small with respect to the lattice length. At higher Q values we see the repetition structure forming over longer length scales and it appears to grow as we run the systems for more time steps. As Q increases we obtain very large scale repetitive structures that will typically have all Q states present in spiral patterns.

The figures show that the spirals interfere with one another and overlap and with time larger ones dominate smaller ones and the "kinks" are ironed out of these long range spatial

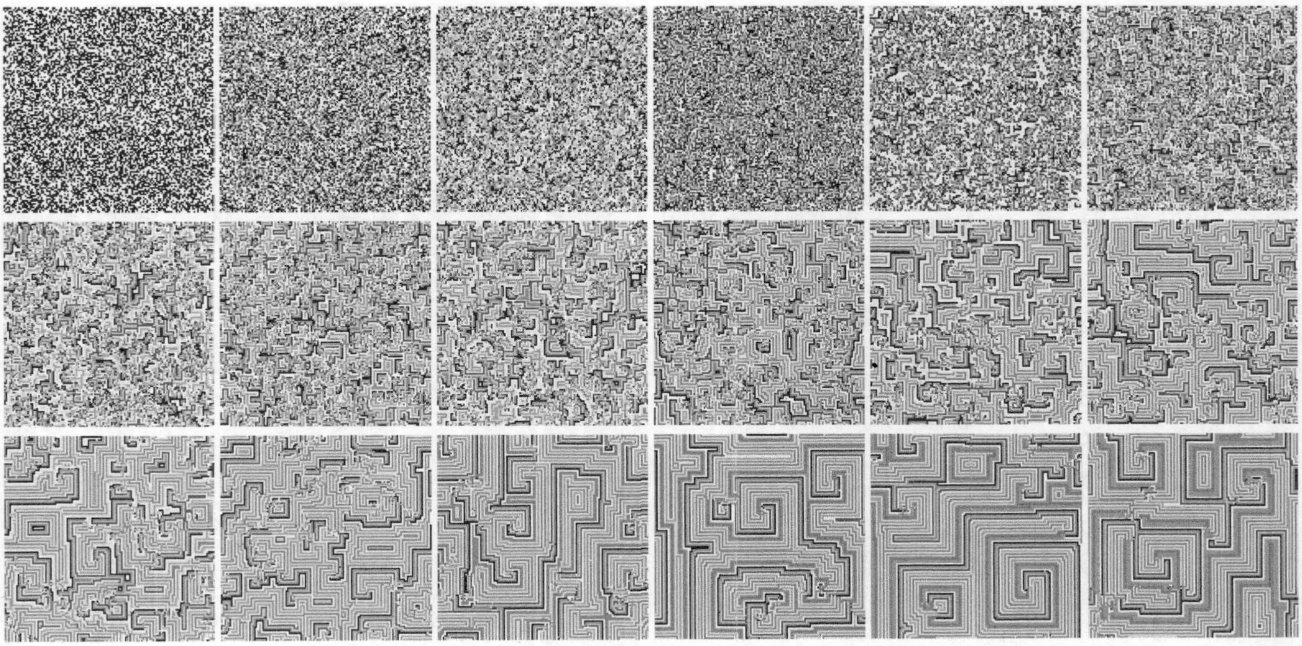

Figure 2: $N = 128^2, t = 200$ Cyclic CA with $Q = 2, 3, ..., 19$

structures.

The prevailing neighbourhood conditions affects the patterns. Moore neighbourhood with 8 neighbours gives rise to square shaped spiral patterns. If with use Nearest neighbour (N1) only we obtain diamond shaped spirals reflecting the symmetry of the four nearest neighbours of the square lattice. Choosing only next-nearest neighbours (N2) gives rise to checkerboard repetitions. Similarly in hexagonal and triangular lattice we observe spiral patterns that reflect the underpinning symmetry of the lattice.

There are various properties we can measure. One useful metric is the fraction of the bonds that have the same species at both ends. For a lattice of N sites there are 2N such bonds for N1 and N2 square lattices and 4N such bonds using a Moore neighbourhood and 3 or 1.5 for hexagonal and triangular with nearest neighbours. We normalise accordingly and obtain the plots shown in Figure 3. We have shown both periodic and fixed boundary conditions. There is a subtle difference between these with some shifting of the crossover points for the five neighbourhood and lattice shown.

We observe that at low Q the hexagonal and Moore cases - having the highest numbers of neighbours show a flat and unchanging number of like-like bonds with time. The nearest and next nearest neighbour cases, with the same coordination number come next and initially drop to a then steady state value within around 40-50 time steps. The triangular lattice, with the smallest number of neighbours takes longer to reach (a smaller) steady like-like bond fraction.

There is a significant change as we increase Q. The middle two plots shows periodic and fixed boundaries when $Q = 10$. The system is able to establish better fitting repetitive structures with the triangular lattice and it rises, then falls before heading to a steady state. Similarly nearest and next-nearest both rise then fall. We show the fraction of like-like bonds on a logarithmic scale to emphasise the changes at different time scales. Straight line regions therefore correspond to exponentially falling trends. The Moore and hexagonal cases are the only two that show long term very steady state values.

Finally at higher Q the Q-repetitive structures show a different behaviour again. We plot the curves of the fraction of like-like bonds for $Q = 20$. In this case it is the Moore and hexagonal curves that show aberrant behaviours and the other curves appear to reach roughly steady states - although note the increased variances shown by the growth in plotted error bars.

There is clearly a significant change when we vary the spatial repeat length parameterised by Q. It is useful therefore to plot the fraction of like-like bonds as a function of Q.

Figure 4 shows the fraction of like-like bonds - this time on a linear scale - for the various values of Q and for a fixed Moore neighbourhood square lattice with periodic boundary conditions. The very low Q systems remain steady state but a peak appears at higher Q and occurs at later and later times and with varying sizes as Q is increased. We speculate that this behaviour is in fact periodic and is determined by the ratio of Q to the lattice length of the system.

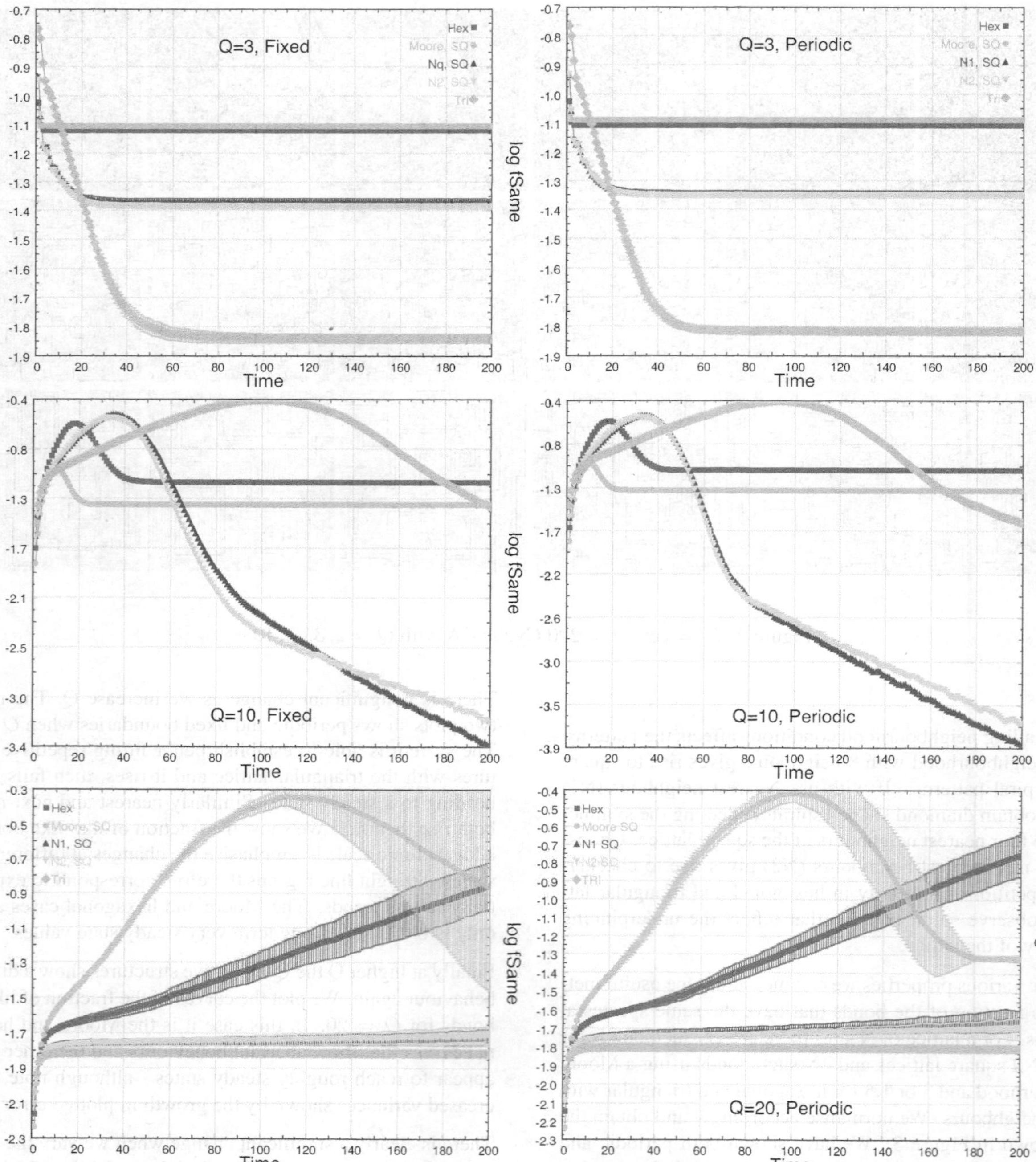

Figure 3: Log of the fraction of bonds that are the same plotted against time for fixed (left) and periodic (right) boundary conditions for the square 128^2 system, averages over ten independent configurations, at Q=3,10,20 (top to bottom).

Other numerical metrics show similar transitional behaviour as we vary Q.

Figure 5 shows... shows the ratio between the smallest state population present and the highest. This is expected again to reflect the changing spatial structure as Q is varies. The plot shows how at low Q this curve remains constant but exhibits a structural transition with increasing Q as different repetitive structure adjust to fill the lattice. The position of the minima is quite noisy even when averaged over ten separate run configurations, but does exhibit a systemic variation with Q.

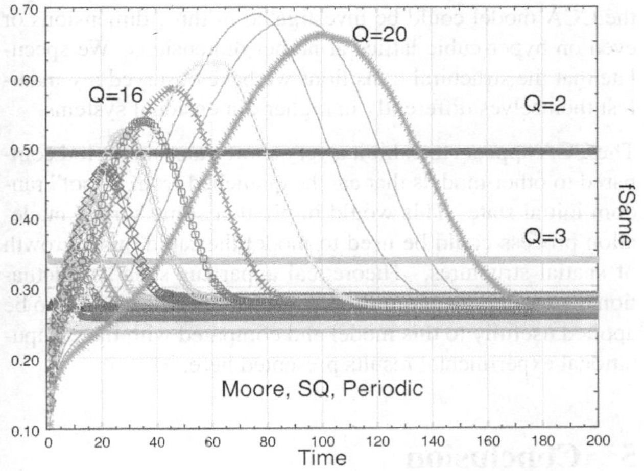

Figure 4: Fraction of bonds that are the same, plotted against $Q = 2, 3, \ldots 20$ for Moore neighbourhood on square, periodic system.

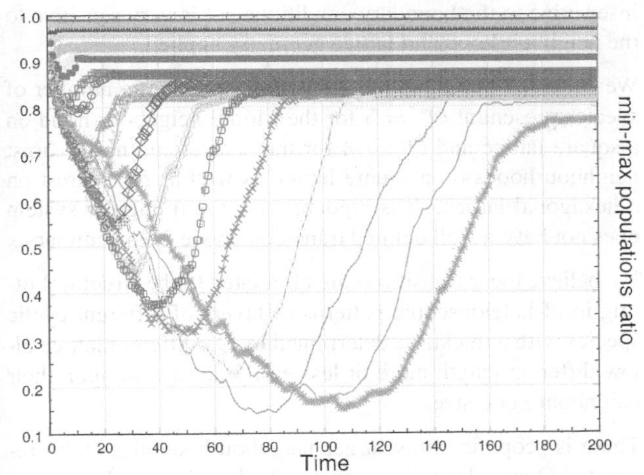

Figure 5: The ratio between minimum and maximum state populations plotted against time for the Moore neighbourhood with square lattice and periodic boundary conditions.

We can also study the component clusters of like-like species that form in the model.

Figure 6 shows the number of connected component clusters that are found in the system for the same series of systems as shown for Figure 4. Again at low $Q = 2, 3, 4$ (red, green and blue curves) the number of small clusters rapidly reaches a stable equilibrium value. For high Q we obtain a series of curves that start as nearly straight lines - indicating a power law on the log-log plot - but which each has its own cutoff point beyond which it remains steady.

The cutoff points could be used to determine a systematic variation law with Q but identifying cutoffs to good precision is

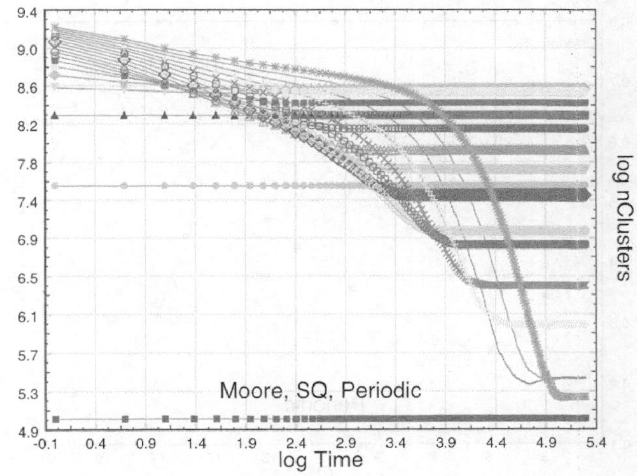

Figure 6: Log-log plot of the number of connected clusters plotted against time for the Moore neighbourhood with square lattice and periodic boundary conditions.

difficult numerically and instead we use the changing maxima in the fraction of like-like bonds to study this.

Returning to the fraction of like-like bonds counted in the system, we can identify the position and value of the peaks as seen in the data in Figure 4.

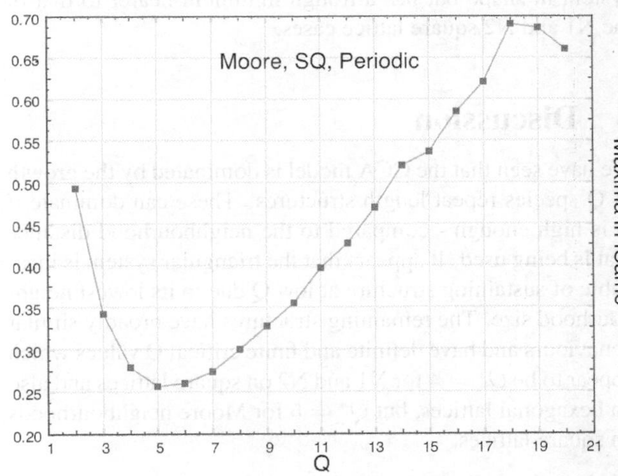

Figure 7: The maximum value of the fraction of the bonds that are the same plotted against Q for the Moore neighbourhood with square lattice and periodic boundary conditions.

Figure 7 shows a plot of the peak values plotted against Q. This gives us a means of identifying Q^* - the critical Q value where the behaviour changes.

We can perform this analysis for all the neighbourhoods and lattice under consideration.

Figure 8 shows that the three square lattice structures with

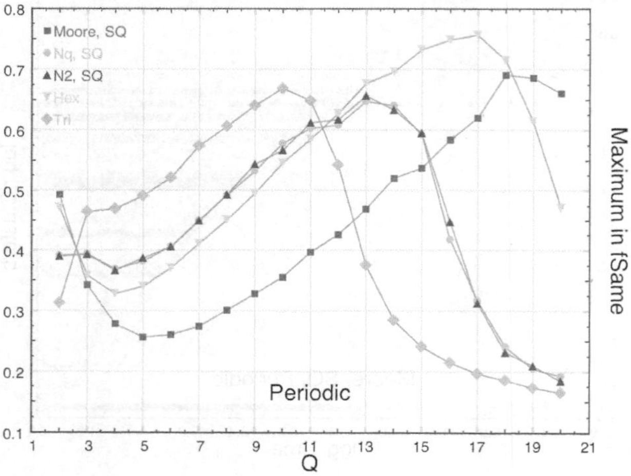

Figure 8: The maximum value of the fraction of the bonds that are the same plotted against Q for the various neighbour hoods tested.

Moore (red), nearest (green) and next-nearest (blue) all have similar shapes although the positions of the minima and maxima are different. The triangular is different in that it does not have an identifiable minimum trough but does still have an identifiable and significantly differently located maximum peak. The hexagonal system is closest to the Moore square system in shape but has a trough minimum nearer to that of the N1 and N2 square lattice cases.

4 Discussion

We have seen that the CCA model is dominated by the growth of Q-species repeat length structures. These can dominate if Q is high enough - compared to the neighbourhood distance that is being used. It appears that the triangular system is incapable of sustaining structure at low Q due to its lowest neighbourhood size. The remaining structures have broadly similar behaviours and have definite and finite critical Q values which appear to be $Q^* = 4$ for N1 and N2 on square lattices and also on hexagonal lattices, but $Q^* = 5$ for Moore neighbourhoods on square lattices.

We have been limited to lattices of length $L = 128$ sites in length due to the need to average over multiple independent configurations. It would be worthwhile to investigate larger systems to verify that what we are observing are structural transitions that are related to the ratio of Q and L.

It is not clear if running the systems for much longer will lead to further changes. We found that on observation no visual changes appeared top occur beyond 200 time steps. This may just be coincidental however and if data parallel processing technologies such as graphical processing units (GPUs) [20] were used, it should be possible to investigate larger simulated systems and for much longer numbers of time steps.

We have restricted our work to two dimensions. In principle the CCA model could be investigated in three dimensions or even on hyper-cubic lattice at higher dimensions. We speculate that the structural transitions we have observed my manifest themselves differently in higher dimensional systems.

The CCA appears to exhibit a very short transient period compared to other models that can be quenched from a "hot" random initial state. This would imply that some sort of nucleation process could be used to model the rapid onset growth of spatial structures. Theoretical apparatus such as fluctuation dissipation theory or droplet growth models could also be applied usefully to this model and compared with the computational experimental results presented here.

5 Conclusion

We have implemented an extension of Griffeath's Cyclic Cellular Automaton model in three different lattice in two dimensions and have also studied nearest and next nearest neighbourhoods as well as the conventional Moore neighbourhood on the square lattice. We have found the system is somewhat insensitive to the boundary conditions but is very sensitive to the neighbourhood and lattice geometry applied.

We observed that there is a transition point in the number of species present at $Q^* = 5$ for the Moore neighbour hood on a square lattice and $Q^* = 4$ for the nearest and nest-nearest neighbourhoods on a square lattice as well as for nearest on a hexagonal lattice. It is arguable that the triangular system does not have a well defined transition above 2. In summary...

We believe these transitions are all related to the structural fitting in of kaleidoscopic patterns of layers of different cyclic species with a thickness determined by Q. Different lattice allow different length more or less easily dependent upon their neighbour hood sizes.

There is scope to study larger neighbourhood sizes with respect to Q and also to investigate whether similar phenomena occur in three or higher dimensional cyclic cellular automaton models.

This system has shown a surprisingly rich and complex behaviour on spatial and time scales that are readily simulated. The cyclic cellular automaton model is likely to prove a useful platform for investigating further spatial and structural transitions.

References

[1] Adamatzky, A. (ed.): Game of Life Cellular Automata. No. ISBN 978-1-84996-216-2, Springer (2010)

[2] Bays, C.: Game of Life Cellular Automata, chap. The Game of Life in Non-Square Environments, pp. 319–329. Springer (2010)

[3] Boghosian, B.M., Rothman, D.H., W.Taylor: A Cellular Au-

tomata Simulation of Two-Phase Flow on the CM-2 Connection Machine Computer (Mar 1988), private Communication

[4] Capcarrere, M.S.: Evolution of asynchronous cellular automata. In: Parallel Problem Solving from Nature Proc. PPSN VII. vol. 2439 (2002)

[5] Cook, M.: Universality in elementary cellular automata. Complex Systems 15, 1–40 (2004)

[6] Durrett, R., Griffeath, D.: Asymptotic behavior of excitable cellular automata. Experimental Mathematics 2(3), 183–208 (1993)

[7] Eppstein, D.: Game of Life Cellular Automata, chap. Growth and Decay in Life-Like Cellular Automata, pp. 71–98. Springer (2010)

[8] Fisch, R.: Clustering in the one-dimensional three-color cyclic cellular automaton. The Annals of Probability 20(3), 1528–1548 (1992)

[9] Fort, H., Viola, S. Spatial patterns and scale freedom in prisoner's dilemma cellular automata with pavlovian strategies. Journal of Statistical Mechanics: Theory and Experiment p. P01010 (2005)

[10] Gardner, M.: Mathematical Games: The fantastic combinations of John Conway's new solitaire game "Life". Scientific American 223, 120–123 (October 1970)

[11] Gotts, N.: Game of Life Cellular Automata, chap. Emergent Complexity in Conway's Game of Life, pp. 389–436. Springer (2010)

[12] Griffeath, D.: Self-organization of random cellular automata: Four snapshots. Probability and Phase Transition 420, 49–67 (1994), nATO ASI Series

[13] Hastings, M.B., Reichhardt, C.J.O., Reichhardt, C.: Ratchet cellular automata. Phys. Rev. Lett. 90, 247004 (2003)

[14] Hawick, K.A.: Engineering internal domain-specific language software for lattice-based simulations. In: Proc. Int. Conf. on Software Engineering and Applications. IASTED, Las Vegas, USA (12-14 November 2012)

[15] Hawick, K.A.: Static and dynamical equilibrium properties to categorise generalised game-of-life related cellular automata. In: Int. Conf. on Foundations of Computer Science (FCS'12). pp. 51–57. CSREA, Las Vegas, USA (16-19 July 2012)

[16] Hawick, K.A., Scogings, C.J.: A minimal spatial cellular automata for hierarchical predator-prey simulation of food chains. In: Proc. International Conference on Scientific Computing (CSC'10). pp. 75–80. WorldComp, Las Vegas, USA (12-15 July 2010)

[17] Hawick, K.A., Scogings, C.J.: Cycles, transients, and complexity in the game of death spatial automaton. In: Proc. International Conference on Scientific Computing (CSC'11). pp. 241–247. No. CSC4040, CSREA, Las Vegas, USA (18-21 July 2011)

[18] Hawick, K.A., Scogings, C.J., James, H.A.: Defensive spiral emergence in a predator-prey model. Complexity International 12(msid37), 1–10 (October 2008), `http://www.complexity.org.au/ci/vol12/msid37`, ISSN 1320-0682

[19] Johnson, M.G.B., Playne, D.P., Hawick, K.A.: Data-parallelism and gpus for lattice gas fluid simulations. In: Proc. International Conference on Parallel and Distributed Processing Techniques and Applications (PDPTA'10). pp. 210–216. CSREA, Las Vegas, USA (12-15 July 2010), pDP4521

[20] Leist, A., Playne, D.P., Hawick, K.A.: Exploiting Graphical Processing Units for Data-Parallel Scientific Applications. Concurrency and Computation: Practice and Experience 21(18), 2400–2437 (25 December 2009), CSTN-065

[21] Lyes, T.S., Johnson, M.G.B., Hawick, K.A.: Visual simulation of a multi-species coloured lattice gas model. In: Proc. Int. Conf. on Scientific Computing (CSC'12). pp. 115–124. CSREA, Las Vegas, USA (16-19 July 2012)

[22] Meakin, P.: Fractals, Scaling and Growth far From Equilibrium. No. ISBN 0-521-45253-8, Cambridge University Press (1998)

[23] Nehaniv, C.L.: Evolution in asynchronous cellular automata. In: Proc ICAL 2003 - Eighth Int. Conf. on Artificial Life. pp. 65–73. MIT Press (2003)

[24] Owens, N., Stepney, S.: Investigations of game of life cellular automata rules on penrose tilings: lifetime and ash statistics. Journal of Cellular Automata 5, 207–225 (2010)

[25] Packard, N., Wolfram, S.: Two-dimensional cellular automata. J. Stat. Phys. 38, 901–946 (1985)

[26] Reiter, C.A.: Medley of spirals from cyclic cellular automata. Computers and Graphics 34, 72–76 (2010)

[27] Reiter, C.A.: Cyclic cellular automata in 3d. Chaos, Solitons and Fractals 44, 764–768 (2011)

[28] Sarkar, P.: A brief history of cellular automata. ACM Computing Surveys 32, 80–107 (2000)

[29] Scogings, C.J., Hawick, K.A.: Optimal data structures for spatially localised agent-based automata and hybrid systems. In: Proc. Int. Conf. on Artificial Intelligence and Soft Computing. pp. 221–227. IASTED, Napoli, Italy (25-27 June 2012)

[30] Shalizi, C.R., Shalizi, K.L.: Quantifying self-organization in cyclic cellular automata. In: Proc. SPIE Noise in Complex Systems and Stochastic Dynamics. vol. 5114. SPIE (2003)

[31] Stauffer, D.: Computer simulations of cellular automata. J.Phys.A:Math. Gen 24, 909–927 (1991)

[32] Thompson, D.W.: On Growth and Form. Cambridge University Press (1942)

[33] Wolfram, S.: Statistical Mechanics of Cellular Automata. Rev.Mod.Phys 55(3), 601–644 (1983)

[34] Wolfram, S.: Universality and complexity in cellular automata. Physica D 10, 1–35 (1985)

[35] Wolfram, S.: A New Kind of Science. Wolfram Media, Inc. (2002), iSBN 1-57955-008-8

[36] Wylie, B.J.: Application of Two-Dimensional Cellular Automaton Lattice-Gas Models to the Simulation of Hydrodynamics. Ph.D. thesis, Physics Department, Edinburgh University (1990)

A Computational Model for Cultural Intelligence

Zhao Xin Wu[1], Li ZHOU[2]

[1]Computer Science Department, University of Quebec in Montreal, Montreal, QC, Canada
[2]School of Electronic and Control Engineering, Chang'an University, Xi'an, P.R. China
zhao_xin_wu@hotmail.com, 47599053@qq.com

Abstract - *Computational model can be designed with soft computing technologies which are capable of reasoning and learning in an uncertain and imprecise environment. However, in a real practical project, there are many difficult computational bottlenecks in need to break through when using these technologies. This research aims to invent a cultural intelligence computational model, which can process cultural intelligence soft data through the use of soft computing technologies. The purpose of this study is for individuals and organizations to solve the intercultural adaptation problems they may be faced with in a variety of authentic cross-cultural situations.*

Keywords - Cultural Intelligence; Soft-Computing; Fuzzy Logic, Artificial Neural Network; Hybrid System

1 Introduction

Soft-computing is an advanced AI technology which can deal with uncertain, imprecise and incomplete information through an approach that is more human-like. Concerning the cultural domain, we live in an era of globalization where international activities between different cultures and intercultural communications and exchanges are becoming more common and are taking on much greater importance than ever before. Yet, because of cultural diversity, "*Culture is more often a source of conflict than of synergy. Cultural differences are a nuisance at best and often a disaster*" (Dr. Geert Hofstede). Moreover, cultural knowledge is generally represented by natural language, which is replete with vague and ambiguous terms, and it is difficult for traditional computing techniques to cope with these. In such a context, globalization and traditional computing techniques have encountered two major challenges: the first is how to adapt to cultural diversity, and the second is the treatment of soft data and human-like thinking.

Fortunately, research on cultural intelligence (CQ) [1] provides a new perspective and a new way to alleviate cultural issues that arise in such a globalized environment. The higher the CQ that people possess, the more effective their performance and adjustment will be in culturally diverse settings. CQ can also be improved by training the people involved in such settings. The most important point to consider is how to precisely evaluate CQ and provide relevant suggestions to improve it. However, current studies on CQ have used traditional methods to measure users' CQ and have relied primarily on questionnaires to find solutions to CQ problems traditionally confined to the work of culture experts and researchers. The best way to enable non-expert users to make use of CQ knowledge at the present time is to computerize CQ. A great deal of CQ knowledge, however, is expressed as 'fuzzy data' and human decision making. Dealing effectively with these is beyond the scope of traditional computer technique, and research on CQ has never been empirically computerized to date.

These problems will be resolved by this research which will provide an effective solution through the invention of a CQ computational model.

2 Cultural Intelligence

CQ is defined as the ability to collect and process information, to form judgments, and to implement effective measures in order to adapt to a new cultural context [1]. Earley and Mosakowski [2] define CQ as a complementary intelligence form which may explain the capacity to adapt and face diversity, as well as the ability to operate in a new cultural setting. Earley and Mosakowski stress that people with a relatively high CQ level often appear at ease in new situations. They understand the subtleties of different cultures, so they can avoid or resolve conflicts early. Peterson interprets CQ in terms of its operation [3]. He believes that, for the concept of CQ, the definition of culture is compatible with the cultural values of Hofstede and their five main dimensions [4]. Peterson also describes CQ as the communicative capabilities which improve working environments. In other words, all workers have the ability to communicate efficiently with customers, partners and colleagues from different countries in order to maintain harmonious relationships. Brisling et al. define CQ as the level of success that people have when adapting to another culture [5]. Thomas describes CQ as the capability to interact efficiently with people who are culturally different [6]. Johnson et al. define CQ as the effectiveness of an individual to integrate a set of knowledge, skills and personal qualities so as to work successfully with people from different cultures, both at home and abroad [7]. Finally, Ang et al. [8] define CQ as the conceptualization of a particular form of intelligence based on the ability of an individual to reason correctly in situations characterized by cultural diversity.

3 Cultural Intelligence Dimensions

Different researchers have different dimensional structures to measure CQ. Earley and Ang [1] are pioneers in the development of CQ concepts. They described the first structure of CQ in 2003 using a three-dimensional model: cognition, motivation and behavior. Thomas [9] advocates another tridimensional structure; he states that the structure of CQ should be based on the skills required for intercultural communication, that is to say, knowledge, vigilance and behavior. In these three dimensions, vigilance, which is the key to CQ, acts as a bridge connecting knowledge and behavior. Tan [10] believes that CQ has three main components: cultural strategic thinking, motivation, and behavior, and that CQ integrates these three components. Tan stresses the importance of behavior as being essential to CQ. If the first two parts are not converted into action, CQ is meaningless. Ang and Van Dyne [11] later refined the concept of Earley et al. to consist of four dimensions rather than three: metacognition, cognition, motivation and behavior. They paid special attention to how a culturally diverse environment works. This structure has been widely used in the following cultural research and studies. The four dimensions of CQ are described as follows:

- *Metacognitive CQ* refers to the cognitive ability of an individual to recognize and understand appropriate expectations in different cultural situations. It reflects the mental processes that an individual uses to acquire and understand cultural knowledge;
- *Cognitive CQ* is a person's knowledge of the standards, practices and conventions in different cultures which he/she acquired from education and personal experiences;
- *Motivational CQ* refers to the motivation of an individual to adapt to different cultural situations. It demonstrates the individual's ability to focus his/her attention and energy on learning and practicing in culturally diverse situations;
- *Behavioral CQ* is defined as an individual's ability to communicate and behave with cultural sensitivity when interacting with people of different cultures. It represents a person's ability to act and speak appropriately (i.e., use suitable language, tones, gestures and facial expressions) in a given culture.

4 Conceptual Model

The concept of CQ is for the first time extended in order to assess cross-cultural activities. One's with a high CQ evaluation are expected to have a more effective performance in and adjustment to multicultural situations.

Sternberg et al. [12] state that general intelligence has four dimensions, i.e., Metacognition, Cognition, Motivation and Behavior. They consider the correlation between the four dimensions as an entity and take full account of their integrity because of their interdependence. CQ should also include and consider its four dimensions and their correlation. We agree that the four dimensions of CQ are critical factors that can help individuals, companies and organizations to overcome cross-cultural challenges. Thus, we believe that the diverse structures of CQ should be considered collectively in order to integrate the elements required to respond to the cultural knowledge acquired in cross-cultural activities. Therefore, we created a CQ conceptual model in order to complete the theories of CQ and the evaluation process required.

We present our model as a whole aggregate multidimensional construct by considering the following conditions: (1) the entire construct considers that the four CQ dimensions occupy the same important level in conceptualization; and (2) the four CQ dimensions form the construct. In sum, in our research we put forward the cognitive theory that the metacognitive CQ, cognitive CQ, motivational CQ and behavioral CQ are four interrelated components built into the CQ, and we integrate our theory into the model (see Fig.1).

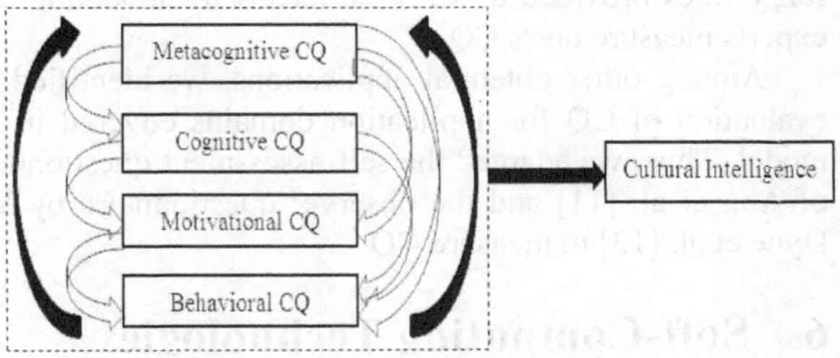

Figure 1. Cultural Intelligence Conceptual Model

This conceptual model proposes a cyclical process of CQ evaluation in four stages, while respecting the correlation and interdependence between the four dimensions: (1) It observes the behaviors, promotes active thinking and drives individuals to adapt and revise their strategies in different cultural settings; (2) It acquires and understands the knowledge that can influence individuals' thoughts and behaviors; (3) It considers the implications and emotions associated with cultural settings, and it drives efforts and energy toward effective functioning in a new culture; and (4) It transfers knowledge through verbal and nonverbal behaviors to the culturally diverse situations. This process enables us to identify the elements of the global CQ so we may apply it as a whole, regardless of whether these dimensions are decision variables or other measurable parameters. In this process, we adopt a holistic approach that does not aim to reduce the model to its individual components.

5 Data and Knowledge Acquisition

Ang et al. [11] developed a self-assessment questionnaire which has 20 items that measure CQ. This questionnaire was used to collect data for studies on the test subjects regarding their capacity for cultural adaptation. The questionnaire is generally divided into four sections: metacognition, cognition, motivation and behavior. For example, one of the items is: "*I am conscious of the cultural knowledge I use when I interact with people with different cultural backgrounds*." Van Dyne et al. [13] developed a version of the questionnaire from the point of view of an observer. It is also based on the 20 items of Ang et al. [11] in order to measure CQ in individuals. The questionnaire was adapted from each item of the self-assessment questionnaire to reflect the assessment made by an observer rather than the user himself. As explained by Van Dyne et al. [13], these questionnaires allow for the effective assessment of CQ in practical applications.

We collected CQ knowledge by reviewing books, documents, manuals, papers, etc., and by interviewing cultural experts. One's CQ evaluations are often based on experts' intuition, common sense and experience. We clearly put forward that four CQ dimensions make up an integrated and interdependent body. A large number of fuzzy rules provided us with the means for modeling how experts measure one's CQ.

Among other potential applications, we identified the evaluation of CQ for application domains covered in our model. Thus, we adapted the self-assessment questionnaire of Ang et al. [11] and the observer questionnaire by Van Dyne et al. [13] to measure CQ.

6 Soft-Computing Technologies

The CQ generally has two types of data: the first type is associated with "hard" computing, which uses numbers, or crisp values; the second type is associated with "soft" computing, which operates with uncertain, incomplete and imprecise soft data. The second type is presented in a way that reflects human thinking. When we explain the cultural concept of cross-cultural activities, we usually use soft values represented by words rather than by crisp numbers. Traditional techniques, or "hard" computing, cannot treat CQ soft data. In order to enable computers to emulate human-like thinking and to model a human-like understanding of words in evaluation, we use a hybrid neuro-fuzzy technology to invent a CQ computational model. This soft-computing technology is capable of dealing with uncertain, imprecise and incomplete CQ soft data, which also possesses parallel computation and the learning abilities.

Fuzzy logic is introduced by Lotfi Zadeh who first realized the potential of soft computing and established the Berkeley Initiative in Soft Computing in March 1991[14]. The fuzzy logic technology is used in our model for three reasons. First, fuzzy logic is good for CQ knowledge, which is expressed in natural language that contains ambiguous and imprecise linguistic variables, such as "*this person has high motivation*" and "*that person has lots of cultural knowledge.*" Second, fuzzy logic is well-suited to modeling human decision-making processes when dealing with "soft criteria." These processes are based on common sense and may contain vague and ambiguous terms. Third, fuzzy logic provides a wide range of cultural expressions that can be understood by computers.

Although the fuzzy logic technology has the ability and the means to understand natural language, it offers no mechanism for automatic rule acquisition and adjustment. The artificial neural network (ANN) offers learning mechanisms, which emulate human intelligence, in uncertain, incomplete and imprecise cultural settings. It presents viable solutions for processing incomplete and imprecise CQ information. The ANN can manage the new CQ data input and the generalization of acquired knowledge.

The hybrid neuro-fuzzy technology makes use of the advantages and power of fuzzy logic and the ANN. Fuzzy logic and the ANN are complementary paradigms. The hybrid technology represents the essence of our computational model.

7 Linguistic Variables and Fuzzy Rules

The idea of linguistic variables is one basis of the fuzzy set theory. A linguistic variable of fuzzy set theory is a fuzzy variable. For example, when we say "*CQ is high,*" it means that the linguistic variable of CQ takes the linguistic value "high". Thus, our CQ linguistic variables are used in fuzzy rules in the model, for example:

Rule 1:

IF Metacognition is high AND Cognition is high AND Motivation is high AND Behavior is high

THEN CQ is high

The operations of CQ fuzzy sets used in our model are *Intersection* and *Union* [15]. For example, the fuzzy operation used to create the *Intersection* of two CQ fuzzy sets A and B is as follows:

$$\mu A \cap B(x) = min[\mu A(x), \mu B(x)] = \mu A(x) \cap \mu B(x), where\ x \in X \quad (1)$$

The operation to form the fuzzy *Union* of two CQ fuzzy sets A and B is as follows:

$$\mu A \cup B(x) = max[\mu A(x), \mu B(x)] = \mu A(x) \cup \mu B(x), where\ x \in X \quad (2)$$

8 Cultural Intelligence Computational Model

In this section, we describe the hybrid computational model in detail. The CQ computational model is based on our conceptual model (see section 4). The computational model is noteworthy because we use the four CQ dimensions as integrated and interdependent entities. Essentially, the model is a multi-layer neural network with the functional equivalency of a fuzzy inference process. The neuro-fuzzy network is composed of six layers in our computational model. It has four dimensions in the input layer and the CQ output layer, and four hidden layers that represent membership functions and CQ fuzzy rules. The model is shown in Fig. 2.

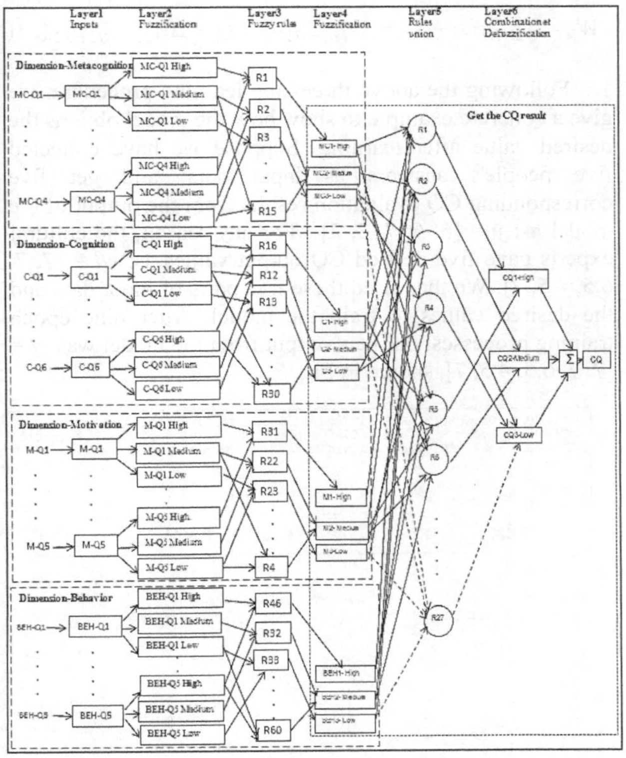

Figure 2. Computational Model of Cultural Intelligence

This hybrid computational model has 20 inputs which represent the 20 items of the questionnaires of Ang et al. [11] to measure CQ: the metacognitive dimension (MC) has four items, the cognitive dimension (C) contains six items, the motivational dimension (M) includes five items and the behavioral dimension (BEH) consists of five items and has one output: CQ.

Layer 1 - *Input*: No calculation is made in this layer. Each of the 20 neurons corresponds to an input variable. These input values are transmitted directly to the next layer.

Layer 2 - *Fuzzification*: Each neuron corresponds to a linguistic label. To simplify the task, fuzzy linguistic variables used in our model are triangular membership functions (e.g., High, Medium and Low), associated with one of the input variables in Layer 1. We have 60 neurons in this layer.

Layer 3 - *Fuzzy Rules*: The output of a neuron at this layer is the fuzzy rules of CQ. For example, Neuron RI represents Rule 1 and receives input from the neurons MC-Q1 (High) and MC-Q4 (High), etc.

Layer 4 – *Fuzzification*: In this layer, the neurons receive the membership degrees as the inputs which are produced from the fuzzy rules layer.

Layer 5 - *Rule Unions* (or consequence): This layer has two main tasks: 1) to combine the new precedent of rules; and 2) to determine the output level (High, Medium and Low) which belongs to the CQ linguistic variables. For example, R1 is the input of MC1 (High) and C1 (High), etc. It integrates the four dimensions of CQ to make a logical judgment in this layer by using 27 CQ rules.

Layer 6 - *Combination and Defuzzification*: This layer combines all the consequence rules and, lastly, computes the crisp output after Defuzzification. This layer has three neurons: CQ-High, CQ-Medium and CQ-Low. The Center of Gravity method is used to calculate the output. The single output after this layer is the precise CQ evaluation result. We apply, in this case, the triangle calculation in our model, which is the simplest calculation of the fuzzy set as shown in Fig. 3:

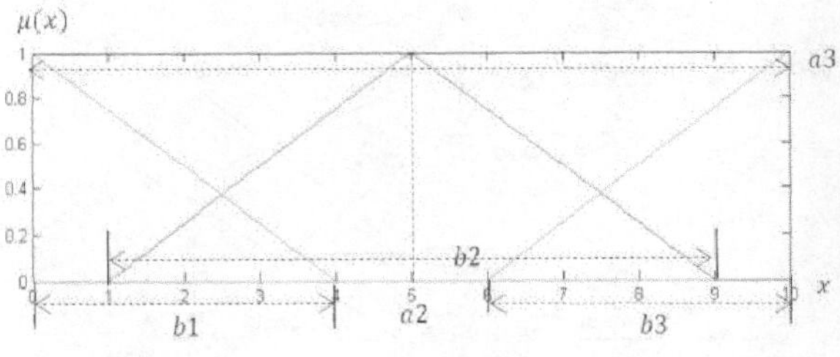

Figure 3. Triangle Calculation of the Fuzzy Set

$$y\ (Cultural\ Intelligence) = \frac{\frac{1}{3}b_1^2\mu 1 + a_2 b_2 \mu 2 + \left(a_3 - \frac{1}{3}b_3\right) b_3 \mu 3}{b_1 \mu 1 + b_2 \mu 2 + b_3 \mu 3} \quad (3)$$

where a_2 is the center and a_3 is the end of the triangle. b_1, b_2 and b_3 are the widths of fuzzy sets which correspond to CQ3-Low, CQ2-Medium and CQ1-High.

9 Supervised Learning

One of the main properties of the model is supervised learning, which has the ability to learn from CQ expert experiences and to improve performance by modifying the CQ rules through learning. Supervised learning involves cultural inputs and cultural outputs that are available to our multilayer neuro-fuzzy network. The task of the network is to predict or adjust inputs to the desired outputs.

This multilayer neuro-fuzzy network can apply standard learning algorithms, such as back-propagation, to train it. The network offers a mechanism for automatic IF-THEN rule acquisition and adjustment. This mechanism is very useful, especially in situations where cultural experts are unable to verbalize the knowledge or problem-solving strategy they use.

The principle of the back-propagation algorithm in supervised learning in our model is that we provide the model with the final external CQ data that supervised learning requires; these data represent the results of a user's evaluation. Each case contains the original input cultural data and the output data offered by CQ human experts to be produced by the model. The model compares actual output with the CQ experts' data during the training process. If the actual output differs from the data given by experts in the training case, the model weights are modified. Fig. 4 shows first part (metacognitive dimension) of the Fig. 2 with three layers (input layer, hidden layer and output layer) as an example to illustrate how the neuro-fuzzy network learns by applying the back-propagation algorithm.

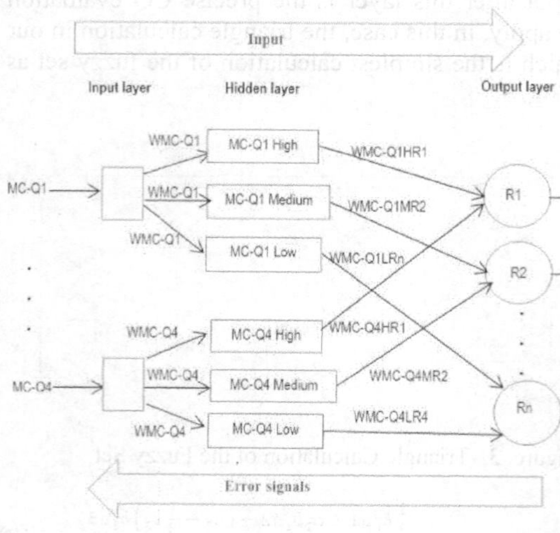

Figure 4. Back-propagation in Cultural Intelligence Computational Model Learning

MC-Q1 and MC-*Q4* refer to neurons in the input layer; *MC-Q1/MC-Q4 High, MC-Q1/MC-Q4 Medium* and *MC-Q1Mc-Q4 Low* refer to neurons in the hidden layer; and R1, R2 and Rn refer to neurons in the output layer. We explain our model's learning process theory in three steps as follows:

Step 1 - Input Signals: we input signals from MC-Q1 to MC-Q4 into the model; these signals are propagated through the neuro-fuzzy network from left to right, while the difference signals (or error signals) are propagated from right to left.

Step 2 - Weights Training: to propagate difference signals, we start at the output layer and work backward to the hidden layer. The difference signal at the output of neuron R1 at sequence s is calculated as follows:

$$D_{R1}(s) = y_{e,R1}(s) - y_{R1}(s) \quad (4)$$

where $y_{e,R1}(s)$ is the cultural experts' desired output data of neuron R1 at iteration s. $D_{R1}(s)$ is the difference between the output $y_{R1}(s)$ and the experts' desired output data at iteration s. For example, we use a forward procedure method to update the CQ rules' weight $W_{MC-Q1HR1}$. Rule R1 for updating weight at the output layer at iteration s is defined as:

$$W_{MC-Q1HR1}(s+1) = W_{MC-Q1HR1}(s) + \Delta W_{MC-Q1HR1}(s) \quad (5)$$

Following the above three-step learning procedure, we give a concrete example to show how the model obtains the desired value after learning. Suppose we have collected five people's answers as input data, and get five corresponding CQ evaluation results from the output of the model as: y = [5, 6, 7, 3, 2]. For any reason, the cultural experts gave five desired CQ output values as: yd = [7, 7, 6.5, 4.5, 7]. We then used these five pairs of input data and the desired values to train the model. After nine epoch training processes, our new output from the model was: y = [7, 7, 6.5, 4.5, 7], shown in Fig. 5.

```
TRAINLM, Epoch 0/9, MSE 45.2964/0, Gradient 13.567/1e-010
TRAINLM, Epoch 9/9, MSE 1.65969e-022/0, Gradient 4.16374e-012/1e-010
TRAINLM, Maximum epoch reached, performance goal was not met.

ans =

    7.0000    7.0000    6.5000    4.5000    7.0000
```

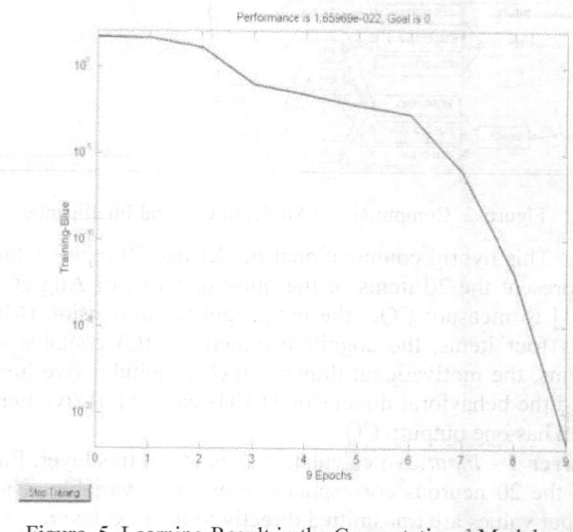

Figure 5. Learning Result in the Computational Model

The model's output quite accurately resembles the desired CQ values from the cultural experts, that is to say, the model has the ability to learn new CQ knowledge.

10 Conclusion

The achievement of this research is noteworthy because in the CQ domain, this study effectively deals with linguistic variables, soft data and human decision making based on a hybrid neuro-fuzzy technology, and it possesses parallel computation and the learning abilities of neural networks. At the same time, due to its powerfully designed functions, the model is very easy to extend to other application domains, such as integrating the Expatriation and Business Activities [16].

The other main contributions of our study are: 1) in the cognitive domain, it improves the application of CQ theories. The study focuses on modeling four CQ dimensions as an integrated and interdependent body. As a result, the theories are more complete, efficient and precise in their application. 2) In the application of soft-computing, it fills the gap between CQ and soft-computing. As a result, this innovative study provides the opportunity for new research topics and directions, and expands the range in the field of soft-computing.

11 References

[1] Earley, P.C., Ang, S. "Cultural intelligence: Individual interactions across cultures". Stanford, CA: Stanford University Press, 2003.

[2] Earley, P. C., Mosakowski, E. "Cultural Intelligence". Harvard Business Review, 82, pp.139–146, 2004.

[3] Peterson, B. "Cultural intelligence: A guide to working with people from other cultures". Yarmouth, ME: Intercultural Press, 2004.

[4] Hofstede, G. "Cultures and Organizations: Software of the Mind", McGraw-Hill, New York, 1991.

[5] Brisling, R., Worthley, R., and MacNab. "Cultural Intelligence: understanding behaviors that serve people's goals". Group and organization management, 2006.

[6] Thomas, D. C. and Inkson, K. "Cultural Intelligence People Skills for a Global Workforce". Consulting to Management, vol. 16 (1). March. pp. 5-9, 2005.

[7] Johnson, J. P., Lenartowicz, T., and Apud, S. "Cross-cultural Competence in International Business: Toward a Definition and a Model". Journal of International Business Studies, vol. 37. pp. 525–543, 2006.

[8] Ang, S., Van Dyne, L. "Conceptualization of Cultural Intelligence". Handbook on cultural intelligence: Theory, measurement and applications, Chapter I, pp1-15. Armonk, NY: M.E. Sharpe, 2008.

[9] Thomas, D. C. "Domain and development of cultural intelligence: The importance of mindfulness". Group & Organization Management, vol. 31. pp. 78–99, 2006.

[10] Tan, J.S. "Cultural intelligence and the global economy". Leadership in Action, vol. 24, pp.19–21, 2004.

[11] Ang, S., Van Dyne, L. "Handbook of Cultural Intelligence". 1st ed. M.E. Sharpe. Armonk, 2010.

[12] Van Dyne, L., Ang, S., and Koh, C. "Development and Validation of the CQS: The cultural intelligence scale. Handbook of Cultural Intelligence. 1st ed. M.E. Sharpe, Armonk, 2008.

[13] Sternberg, R., and Douglas, K. D. "What is Intelligence?", Contemporary Viewpoints on Its nature and definition, Ablex publishing corporation, 355 Chestnut Street, Norwood, NewJersey 07648, 1986

[14] Zadeh, L. "Computing with words – A paradigm shift", Proceedings of the First International Conference on Fuzzy Logic and Management of Complexity, Sydney, Australia, 15–18 January, vol. 1, pp. 3–10. 1996

[15] Cox, E. "The Fuzzy Systems Handbook: A Practitioner's Guide to Building, Using, and Maintaining Fuzzy Systems". 2nd edn. Academic Press, San Diego, CA 1999.

[16] Wu, Z.X., Nkambou, R., and Bourdeau, J. "Cultural Intelligence Decision Support System for Business Activities". The Second International Conference on Business Intelligence and Technology, BUSTECH 2012, Nice, France, 2012

Fast Operations for Certain Two Alphabet Circulant Matrices

G Awyzio and J Seberry
Centre for Information Security Research,Faculty of Engineering and Information Sciences,
University of Wollongong, NSW, 2522,Australia

Abstract—*In order to efficiently compute some combinatorial designs based upon circulant matrices which have different, defined numbers of 1s and 0s in each row and column we need to find candidate vectors with differing weights and Hamming distances. This paper concentrates on how to efficiently create such circulant matrices. These circulant matrices have applications in signal processing, public key codes and spectography.*

Keywords: algorithm, periodic autocorrelation function, cross correlations , Hamming distance, circulant matrices.

1. Introduction

This paper uses the mapping of two-alphabet (for example {±1}, {x,y}, {0,1}) circulant matrices to binary equivalents.

Interest in binary arrays or matrices with a constant row sums is of continuing study in combinatorics. For example a $BIBD(v, b, r, k, \lambda)$ which can be defined as a $v \times b$ matrix which has constant row sum r and constant column sum k and distinct inner product of rows λ and variations of this design are used in statistical and medical experiments. Recently such circulant matrices have been used to construct asymmetric public key codes. Sequences with elements $0, \pm 1$, very small periodic or non-periodic autocorrelation function and small cross correlation function are also of considerable interest in signal processing. Powers of circulant matrices arise in spectography but in a different form.

2. Definitions and Preliminaries

Since this paper uses the mapping of two-alphabet circulant matrices to binary equivalents the fast construction of binary candidates that match specified parameters is crucial. We discuss how some operations relevant to the multiplication of matrices, an $O(n^3)$ process, can in some cases be converted to a linear process by using architectural level operations.

We first clarify the notation and processes that we will use in our analysis.

2.1 Circulant and Type 1 Matrix Basics

Because it is so important for the rest of our work we now spend a little effort to establish why the properties we will require for binary circulant matrices are so important.

We define the *shift matrix,* T of order n by

$$T = \begin{bmatrix} 0 & 1 & \cdots & 0 \\ 0 & 0 & \cdots & 0 \\ \vdots & & & \vdots \\ 1 & 0 & \cdots & 0 \end{bmatrix}. \tag{1}$$

So any circulant matrix, of order n and first row $x_1, x_2, \cdots, x_n$, that is,

$$\begin{bmatrix} x_1 & x_2 & x_3 & \cdots & x_n \\ x_n & x_1 & x_2 & \cdots & x_{n-1} \\ x_{n-1} & x_n & x_1 & \cdots & x_{n-2} \\ \vdots & & & & \vdots \\ x_2 & x_3 & x_4 & \cdots & x_1 \end{bmatrix} \tag{2}$$

can be written as the polynomial

$$x_1T^n + x_2T + x_3T^2 \cdots x_nT^{n-1}.$$

We now note that polynomials commute, so any two circulant matrices of the same order n commute.

Mathematically we have that:

Definition 1: A *circulant matrix* $X = (x_{ij})$ of order n is a matrix which satisfies the condition that

$$x_{ij} = x_{1,j-i+1} \tag{3}$$

where $j - i + 1$ is reduced modulo n [1].

Thus any circulant matrix $X = (x_{ij})$ of order n can be defined by

$$x_{ij} = x_{i+1,j+1} = x_{1,j-i+1},$$

that is, the first row is enough to specify the whole matrix. In all cases the sums are reduced modulo n so that n is written n, $n+1$ is written as 1 and so on.

In all our definitions of circulant matrices we have assumed that the rows and columns have been indexed by the order, that is for order n, the rows are named after the integers 1, 2, $\cdots$, n and similarly for the columns. The internal entries are then defined by the first row using a 1:1 and onto mapping $f : G \to G$. However we could have indexed the rows and columns using the elements of a group G, with elements $g_1, g_2, \cdots, g_n$. Loosely a *type one matrix* will then be defined so the (ij) element depends on a 1:1 and onto mapping of $f(g_j - g_i)$ for type 1 matrices which occur in construction of combinatorial designs. We use additive notation, but that is not necessary. Seberry-Wallis and Whiteman [2] have shown that circulant and type 1 matrices can be used interchangeably in the enunciations of theorems. This can be used to explore similar theorems in more structured groups.

2.2 Periodic Autocorrelation Function and Cross Correlation Function

These terms, which arise in signal processing, are usually thought of differently by mathematicians.

Definition 2: The $PAF(j)$ or *periodic auto correlation function* of a sequence $\{x_{11}, x_{12}, \cdots, x_{1n}\}$ (that is the first row of a circulant matrix $X = (x_{ij})$) of order n is given, for $j = 1, \cdots, n$, by

$$PAF(j) = \sum_{i=1}^{n} (x_{1i}x_{1,i+j})$$

Definition 3: The $PAF(X)$ or $PAF(j,k)$ or *periodic auto correlation function* of the two rows, j and k, of a circulant matrix $X = (x_{ij})$ of order n is defined as

$$PAF(j,k) = \sum_{i=1}^{n} (x_i x_{k-j+i}).$$

We note that this is exactly the same as the inner product of rows j and k of the matrix $XX^\top$.

Definition 4: $CPAF$ or *cross correlation function* of two rows j of a circulant matrix $X = (x_{ij})$ of order n and k of a circulant matrix $Y = (y_{ij})$ of order n is defined as

$$CPAF(j,k) = \sum_{i=1}^{n} (x_i y_{k-j+i}).$$

This is also written as $CPAF(X,Y)$.

In signal processing we would consider matrices with elements ± 1 but clearly each circulant matrix with these two elements uniquely maps to a binary circulant matrix.

3. General Properties of Circulant Matrices

Remark 1: Each row of a circulant ± 1 matrix can be considered as an integer, uniquely, by replacing the elements -1 by zero and converting the sequence to decimal. Thus a circulant matrix of order n can be represented by an integer of size the least integer greater than $ln_2\ n$. This means any sequence we would consider can be represented by one word of storage. For example for the length $n = 7$ the integer $106 = 64 + 32 + 8 + 2$ represents the row

```
1  1 -1  1 -1  1 -1,
          or
1  1  0  1  0  1  0 =106.
```

3.1 Complexity of Squaring a Matrix

We note

Theorem 1: Any circulant matrix, $X = (x_{ij})$,of order n can be defined by its first row. Writing X in terms of the shift matrix (1) we have

$$X^2 = (x_{11}I + x_{12}T + x_{13}T^2 + \cdots + x_{1,n}T^{n-1})^2$$

so squaring can be achieved by $O(\frac{n(n+1)}{2})$ operations.

We note X^2 contains at most n distinct values which are the new first row.

Similarly the product of two order n, circulant matrices, takes $O(\frac{n(n+1)}{2})$ operations and contain at most n distinct values which are the new first row.

In future work, we will show that, using our construction for candidates, we can make this a linear number of operations.

Example 1: Let X be a 5×5 matrix with first row elements a, b, c, d and e:

$$X = \begin{bmatrix} a & b & c & d & e \\ e & a & b & c & d \\ d & e & a & b & c \\ c & d & e & a & b \\ b & c & d & e & a \end{bmatrix}.$$

As the (j,k) element of X^2 is equal to the $(1, k-j+1)$ element, because the answer is also a circulant matrix: the elements of X^2 are

$$(1,1) = (2,2) = (3,3) = (4,4) = (5,5) = a^2 + 2be + 2cd$$
$$(1,2) = (2,3) = (3,4) = (4,5) = (5,1) = 2ab + 2ce + d^2$$
$$(1,3) = b^2 + 2ac + 2be$$
$$(1,4) = e^2 + 2ad + 2bc$$
$$(1,5) = c^2 + 2ae + 2bd$$

These 5 values are the first row of X^2 and give all the entries of X^2 all the possible PAFs.

We also note that

Theorem 2: The PAF of a sequence of n elements contains only $\frac{n+1}{2}$ distinct entries.

Example 2: Let X be a 5×5 matrix with first row elements a, b, c, d and e:

$$X = \begin{bmatrix} a & b & c & d & e \\ e & a & b & c & d \\ d & e & a & b & c \\ c & d & e & a & b \\ b & c & d & e & a \end{bmatrix}.$$

Then

$$PAF(1,1) = PAF(k,k) = a^2 + b^2 + c^2 + d^2 + e^2,$$

$$PAF(1,2) = \cdots = PAF(n,1) = ae + ba + cb + de + ed,$$
$$PAF(1,3) = \cdots = PAF(n-1,1) = ad + be + ca + db + ec.$$

These 3 values are all the possible PAFs.

4. Architectural Level Operations

Because we depend upon the speed of bit level manipulation we shall now discuss the advantages of architectural level operations in modern computer architectures. Historically architectural level operations afforded speed advantages for all operation in a high level language including additions and subtractions. Modern architectures perform additions almost as fast as bitwise manipulations but still take more cycles to perform a multiplication.

The speed gain is found by being able to manipulate multiple pieces of data with a single instruction. For instance if we wished to find the inner product of two vectors stored in an array we would need to read each entry multiply them and add each result. With two binary vectors the inner product can be found by performing a bitwise XOR and bit count to find the Hamming distance of the two vectors. Knowledge of this result can be used to find the inner product of the two vectors using a single subtraction and a bitwise shift of the Hamming distance. Thus for larger length vectors significant savings in operations can be found using architectural level operations.

5. Integers to Bits

We now move from representing the circulant matrices as vectors of length n and elements from a 2-ary alphabet to first using their binary equivalent and then noting that the binary vector for lengths ≤ 32 can be stored as a single binary word of 32 bits. We now establish the requirements that reflect our specified parameters as above in single words. That is we work to pre-specify the length and weight using architectural level operations.

Example 3: Let X be $\{x, y\}$ be a sequence of length 10:

```
X = {  x  x  x  y  y  y  x  y  x  y}.
```

It can be represented as the binary number

$$1110001010_{base\ 2} = 187_{base\ 10}.$$

In general we are looking for binary numbers of length ℓ and weight h, with pre-specified properties such as the sum of the components, multiplication properties, the PAF and/or inner products. A naive search for candidates with such properties can be achieved in the binary domain by iterating through all the binary numbers and testing the weight of each number. This would require that 2^{ℓ} numbers are tested for conformity to the required parameters.

In our approach we start by assuming that candidates for a previous weight $h-1$ and length ℓ are already known: then new potential candidates with weight h can be rapidly found using an iterative procedure.

For each candidate of size $h-1$ we need to find the highest set bit (HSB) of the candidate which requires at most $\ell-(h-1)$ tests. Once the position of the HSB has been determined then there are at most $\ell-h$ operations required to set the higher order bits. Thus the expansion from weight $h-1$ to h takes $(2\times\ell-2\times h+1)$.

Algorithm 1 Construction of Binary Candidates

Step 1: Read the first candidate of a given length (ℓ) and weight one less ($h-1$) than the desired weight (h) from file
Step 2: while we have have candidates remaining in this file
Step 3: find the HSB in current candidate
Step 4: set a single bit for each position between this bit and the length of the candidate

Example 4: Suppose we have starting candidate

```
0 0 0 1 1 0
```

of length 6 and weight 2. This can be used directly to find three candidates with a weight of 3 and length 6

```
0 0 1 1 1 0
0 1 0 1 1 0
```

and;

```
1 0 0 1 1 0
```

Which each have one additional bit set above the HSB of the seed candidate. By iterating through the ten candidates of weight 2 we can easily find the ten candidates of length 5 and weight 3 in this manner.

Thus considering the complete candidate set with a weight of 2 we obtain;

```
0 0 0 0 1 1,
0 0 0 1 0 1,
0 0 1 0 0 1,
0 1 0 0 0 1,
1 0 0 0 0 1,
0 0 0 1 1 0,
0 0 1 0 1 0,
0 1 0 0 1 0,
1 0 0 0 1 0,
0 0 1 1 0 0,
0 1 0 1 0 0,
1 0 0 1 0 0,
0 1 1 0 0 0,
1 0 1 0 0 0,
1 1 0 0 0 0
```

Which leads to the generation of 20 candidates of the same length and one extra bit set.

```
0 0 0 1 1 1,
0 0 1 0 1 1,
0 1 0 0 1 1,
1 0 0 0 1 1,
0 0 1 1 0 1,
0 1 0 1 0 1,
1 0 0 1 0 1,
0 1 1 0 0 1,
```

```
1 0 1 0 0 1,
1 1 0 0 0 1,
0 0 1 1 1 0,
0 1 0 1 1 0,
1 0 0 1 1 0,
0 1 1 0 1 0,
1 0 1 0 1 0,
1 1 0 0 1 0,
0 1 1 1 0 0,
1 0 1 1 0 0,
1 1 0 1 0 0,
1 1 1 0 0 0
```

Extending these 20 candidates results in 15 candidates with 4 bits set. These candidates are the inverse of the 15 candidates with 2 bits set. Thus we only need to generate the candidates up to a weight of the integer part of $\frac{\ell+1}{2}$. As the length of the candidate set increase it is seen that the number of candidates will match a row on Pascal's triangle.

Additionally the search space can be reduced further by recognizing that since $3 \equiv 5 - 2$ these candidates could be found directly by inverting all of the candidates of weight 2. Thus we only need to generate the candidates up to a weight of the integer part of $\frac{\ell+1}{2}$.

The number of candidates for each weight (h) of a given length (ℓ) follows the entries for a row in Pascal's triangle meaning that if we wish to find candidates with the integer part of $\frac{\ell+1}{2}$ bits set there would be at worst $\frac{2^\ell}{2}$ operations required to find these candidates. However, in many cases the weight of candidates is either close to 0 or close to ℓ and thus significant savings can be made in not having to test all numbers.

Example 5: If we consider the case where we require candidates of length 13 with 4 bits set then we would need to find all candidates with 1, 2, 3 and 4 bits set. The total number of candidates would be $13 + 78 + 186 + 715 = 992$ candidates $\sum_{h=1}^{4} \binom{13}{h}$ that are discovered using this method. This is of order $2(\ell - h + 1)$ which is a significant saving over the $2^\ell = 2^{13}$ numbers that would be tested using the naive approach. For longer length candidates the savings as the required weight deviates from $\frac{\ell}{2}$ becomes even more significant.

5.1 Circulation in the Binary Domain

Construction of a circulant matrix from these binary candidates can be performed using bitwise operations upon the first row to shift the entire row by one bit and move the lowest bit to the highest bit position. Many of the operation usually performed upon these circulant matrices can also be done in the binary domain using architectural level operations.

This requires one operation to perform each of the following four steps for each row, copy $row(i)$ to $row(i+1)$,

Algorithm 2 Circulation of a Binary Matrix

Input: The first row of the circulant matrix of length and order ℓ in binary form ($row(1)$)

for $i = 1$ **to** ℓ
Copy $row(i)$ to $row(i+1)$
Set variable bit to the LSB of $row(i+1)$
Shift $row(i+1)$ right by one
Set MSB of $row(i+1)$ to bit

test and set the variable bit, shift $row(i+1)$ right by one bit and set MSB of $row(i+1)$ to the value of bit. Thus each additional row of the circulant matrix requires four operations to create. Therefore the entire circulant matrix can be computed in $4 \times \ell$ operations. It is noted that any row of the circulant matrix $row(j)$ can be directly computed from the first row by testing the lowest j bits and saving them, shifting the first row right by j bits (j operations at most) and copying the original lowest j bits to the top j bits of the shifted row.

5.2 Binary Inner Products

We can take advantage of the fact that when integer matrices under consideration contain ± 1 only to reduce the computation of inner product vectors in the binary domain. When any two values are the same in a first row circulation then they will result in a $+1$ in determining the inner product and when they are different they will result in a -1.

In the integer domain the inner product is determined as *Theorem 3:* $IP = a_1^{1^{st}} * a_1^{2^{nd}} + a_2^{1^{st}} * a_2^{2^{nd}} + \cdots + a_\ell^{1^{st}} * a_\ell^{2^{nd}}$ which results in q negative results and $p = (n-q)$ positive results.

Thus the inner product can be determined to be $p - q$

$$IP = (n-q) \quad q = n - 2q \tag{4}$$

In the binary domain the location of bits that are different (equivalent to a -1 in the integer domain) can be achieved with a bitwise XOR of two rows of the circulant matrix. The Hamming distance of the resultant XOR on the two vectors is equivalent to the number of -1s in the integer domain. The binary inner product can be determined as follows

In the binary domain the number of negative bits (weight) in the inner product of two rows can be determined by performing a bitwise XOR on two vectors (rows of the circulant matrix). The integer inner product can be calculated directly from knowledge of the number of negative bits (q) and the length of the two vectors (ℓ)

$IP = \ell - 2 \times q$

In Example 2 we showed that the circulant inner products obtained from an ℓ matrix has only $\frac{\ell+1}{2}$ distinct values. To find the inner product in the integer domain requires ℓ muliplications and $\ell - 1$ additions for each inner product. Thus in total it would require $\frac{\ell(\ell-1)}{2}$ multiplications and

$\frac{\ell(\ell-2)}{2}$ additions. Now we consider the case where we have moved the first row into a binary word.

Algorithm 3 Binary Inner Product

Input: The first row of the circulant matrix of length and order ℓ in binary form ($row(1)$)

for $i = 2$ **to** $\frac{\ell+1}{2}$
Circulate $row(i)$ to $row(i+1)$
$Hamming\ Distance = weight\ of\ (XOR(row(1), row(i))$
$IP(i) = \ell - (Hamming\ distance \times 2)$

[Note: multiplication by 2 is a shift left operation at the architectural level]

This means that, ignoring the circulation operations, we have one operation to find the XOR of two rows, one operation to find the weight, and two operations to calculate the inner product of the two rows. This means we have four operations to find the inner product of any two rows of the circulant matrix regardless of the value of ell. To find all the inner products we need to calculate the inner product for $\frac{\ell-1}{2}$ rows. Thus the total number of calculations required to find all inner products of a circulant matrix of order ℓ is $2 \times (\ell - 1)$.

6. Conclusion

We have introduced architectural level operations for various two alphabet circulant matrix operations. We have shown that this approach reduces the complexity in each case we have studied. We intend to further use this approach to search for $BIBD$s, sequences with elements $0, \pm 1$, very small periodic or non-periodic autocorrelation function and small cross correlation function and their applications.

Acknowledgment

The authors would like to thank Bob Brown, Ian Piper, Angela Piper and Graham Williams for their advice and assistance.

References

[1] Jennifer Seberry Wallis, Hadamard matrices, in W. D. Wallis, Anne Penfold Street and Jennifer Seberry Wallis, *Combinatorics: Room Squares, Sum-Free Sets and Hadamard Matrices,* Lecture Notes in Mathematics, Springer Verlag, Berlin, 1972.

[2] Jennifer Wallis and A. L. Whiteman, Some classes of Hadamard matrices with constant diagonal, *Bull. Austral. Math. Soc.*, 7, (1972), 233–249.